Growing and Becoming

Growing and

Development from

Marylin O. Karmel
Guilford College

Louis J. Karmel
University of North Carolina at Greensboro

Becoming

Conception Through Adolescence

Macmillan Publishing Company
New York
Collier Macmillan Publishers
London

The quote appearing on the following page is reprinted by permission of the Avatar Meher Baba Perpetual Public Charitable Trust, Ahmednagar, India from DISCOURSES by Meher Baba.

Macmillan Publishing Company
866 Third Avenue, New York, New York 10022

Collier Macmillan Canada, Inc.

Library of Congress Cataloging in Publication Data

Karmel, Marylin O.
  Growing and becoming.

  Includes index.
  1. Child development.   I. Karmel, Louis J.
II. Title.   [DNLM: 1. Growth.   2. Child development.
3. Personality development.   WS 105 K185g]
RJ131.K37 1984   612'.65   83-5400
ISBN 0-02-361970-8

Printing: 2 3 4 5 6 7 8   Year: 4 5 6 7 8 9 0 1

ISBN   0-02-361970-8

To penetrate into the essence of all being and significance and to release the fragrance of that inner attainment for the guidance and benefit of others, by expressing, in the world of forms, truth, love, purity and beauty—this is the sole game which has any intrinsic and absolute worth. All other, happenings, incidents and attainments can, in themselves, have no lasting importance.

Meher Baba

—to whom this book is dedicated

Preface

This book is written primarily for individuals who will be creating environments for children and guiding their development in schools, day care centers, hospitals, counseling centers, and at home. Students and instructors who are interested in the academic study of child psychology will also find the book useful. The book is a comprehensive chronological description of child development. Much of the research and theory on which the book is based approaches development as a succession of stages. We caution against interpreting such stages as achievements to be made within a rigid time frame; we have emphasized the overlapping relationship between stages as well as individual variation in progressing through them. Development, thus, is presented as a process and we have consistently translated it into an experience in which individuals engage. We encourage students to apply the information in this book in a flexible manner when they are working with children and parents. To emphasize the continuity of development we have written separate chapters that focus on the third year and the preadolescent period as transitional stages from infancy to childhood and from childhood to adolescence.

Two developmental processes are a part of this book: children in the process of developing and the emergence of child development as a social science. We recognize that the study of children is a relatively new science in which the data are incomplete but rapidly growing. We have attempted to give students a framework within which to build as new data and new interpretations of data inevitably accumulate. In this age of scientific research neither personnel in programs for children nor informed parents can afford to ignore the impact of research studies on the management of children. Thus, it is imperative that those who will be responsible for creating environments for children acquire a base of knowledge from which to make decisions and for structuring their own future growth in understanding development.

Organization

The organization of the book lends itself to flexible use by students and instructors. Chapters can be used sequentially or selected for topical study. The book is written in six parts. Part I describes the newborn, genetics, prenatal development, and birth. Parts II, III, IV, and V describe development in infancy, early childhood, middle childhood, and adolescence. Within these parts chapters are devoted to the physical, mental, and social and emotional aspects of development. Special attention is given to birth and its importance as a sociological and psychological event that affects the creation of the environment in which the child grows. Other topics that are given special attention are the development of gender and sex-role identity, sexuality, and current topics such as video games. Part VI describes methods of conducting research with children and theories.

Emphasis

The book's emphasis on children in actual situations rests solidly on scientific research and theory. The study of child development is necessarily multidisciplinary. We have drawn studies from many different disciplines including psychology, sociology, biology, medicine, education, and public health. In selecting topics for inclusion, our emphasis has been on the mental, social, and emotional development of children because these are of primary contemporary concern. The theoretical emphasis is on Erikson and Piaget; however, social-learning theory is also presented because of its considerable contribution to understanding behavior. We have not attempted to reconcile the differences among these theoretical approaches. Instead, we have highlighted their differences by presenting the approach of each to explaining identical behaviors. It is the student's responsibility to judge the value of the theories. Such judgments contribute immeasurably to the critical faculty that the student must exercise after completing formal study.

Research and Theory

The research methods and theories that were described throughout the book are explained more completely in Part VI. We encourage the instructor who wants to emphasize research methodology and/or theories to intersperse those chapters in the descriptive study of development. We suggest that Chapter 18, "The Scientific Study of Children," be studied after Part I and that Chapter 19, "Theories," be studied after Part II. In this way, students can study research methods after being introduced to the scientific study of the newborn and will acquire tools to evaluate the studies cited in the following chapters. A closer look at theories will be most beneficial after the student has been introduced to them within the context of the development of infants. Chapters 18 and 19 can be omitted in courses that do not stress research methodology and theories. Whether in a course that emphasizes or de-emphasizes these topics, students will find in those chapters valuable resource material. Understanding research methodology will help students both in writing term papers and in phrasing questions using the scientific method.

Aids for Learning

This book has been written to engage students. The first chapter, "The Newborn," immediately introduces students to real children. The newborn is approached both as a subject of scientific investigation and as an interacting member of a family. The chapter sets the tone of the book by asking students to hold simultaneously the views of objective science and of humanistic concern for the management of children. Students will be further engaged by the opening queries in each chapter: "Have you ever wondered . . .?" They are a guide to the concepts that appear in a chapter and can be used as topics for papers or class discussion. A list of words and phrases pertinent to each chapter, along with chapter summaries, will help the student to check his or her understanding of a chapter.

Supplements

A study guide and an instructor's manual accompany the text. The study guide can be used by students to gain competence with the material. The instructor's manual provides suggestions for organizing the course, a selection of items for examinations, suggestions for lectures and class activities, and a list of films that are related to the subject matter.

Acknowledgments

We gratefully acknowledge the assistance of many people in the writing and preparation of this book. First, we would like to thank Lloyd Chilton, executive editor at Macmillan, without whose foresight the book would never have been imagined. Throughout the long struggle to see it realized he never lost sight of its purpose. We would like to express our appreciation for the extremely helpful comments and suggestions from Thomas Bennett, Bowling Green State University; Tom Day, Weber State College; Mary Ellen Durrett, University of Texas at Austin; and Robert McLaren, California State University, Fullerton.

We are indebted to Dr. Helen Canaday, Administrative Director of the Preschool Centers, Department of Child Development and Family Relations, School of Home Economics, University of North Carolina at Greensboro; Dr. James P. Hendrix, Jr., Headmaster, Greensboro Day School; and Charles Benton, Principal, Mount Zion Elementary School for assistance with photographs. We are especially indebted to William Amidon and Robert Cavin who contributed not only as photographers but also offered us access to the photographic files of Greensboro Day School and the University of North Carolina at Greensboro. The illustrations are infinitely more interesting because of these resources. Appreciation is extended to Vicki Desmond, Joan Hall, Dr. A. Kelly Maness, Jr., and Dr. Donald D. Smith, who assisted in obtaining permission to photograph. Finally, we would like to thank all the parents, children, and young people who graciously consented to having their photographs used in this book.

Finally, thanks are due to our daughters, Elizabeth, Catherine, and Mary Pat, who were always encouraging and who often sacrificed their own plans and desires when writing schedules created absentee parents.

Marylin O. Karmel
Louis J. Karmel

Brief Contents

PART VI Research and Theory

Detailed Contents

**PART III Early Childhood:
The Years from Two to Six**

PART IV Middle Childhood: The Years from Six to Twelve

CHAPTER 12 Physical Development in Middle Childhood 321

13 Mental Development in Middle Childhood 337

PART V   **Adolescence:**
The Years from Twelve to Twenty

The Child Is Born

Every minute a child is born somewhere in the world. Each birth event is unique. Never have two humans had exactly the same appearance or potential. Contrary to their helpless appearance, a newborn is a remarkably competent human being. Newborns immediately engage their environment through well-developed senses and a nervous system that receives and processes information. The newborn is not actually so new but already has a notable history. In the nine months of development before birth, one cell has differentiated into many structures and systems that, at birth, number in the trillions. That one-cell beginning contained all the information for the complete individual in the form of genes, which, if written in words would resemble the *Encyclopedia Britannica*. Genes, handed from one generation to the next, are a continuation of a chain that extends from each newborn backward in time to the very beginning of life on earth. We are each a link in that chain. The newborn also enters, and immediately begins to influence, a unique social situation. Adults respond to the great charm and innate social skills of the newborn and, reciprocally, the newborn responds to ministrations of caregivers. Parents are drawn into this relationship and a life-long bond of tremendous strength begins to grow. They embark together on the long journey of growing and the adventure of becoming to fulfill the newborn's genetic potential and the hopes and values of the parents and the culture.

CHAPTER 1

The Newborn

Have you ever wondered

> if a newborn baby can see?
>
> how scientists study infants, when they can't answer questions or follow directions?
>
> if newborns have personality?
>
> if newborns really respond to people?
>
> whether there is a "maternal instinct"?
>
> if fathers feel love for their infants?

The newborn is not the chubby infant of magazine ads. In fact, many new parents are surprised at the appearance of their baby. The skin may be red and wrinkled and, until oxygen reaches the cells, it may even have a bluish hue. There is a waxy covering on the skin that served as protection during the months it remained in the amniotic fluid. As this waxy covering, called *vernix caseosa*, begins to wear off, the newborn may appear to be shedding skin. The head seems out of proportion to the underdeveloped body because it comprises about one fourth of its length. The expression may be a grimace or a wide-open stare. The process of birth may have distorted the shape of the skull, whose soft bones allow it to be molded when it passes through the pelvis. As a result of a difficult birth or of forceps having been used, there may be bruises on the head and face. Often the newborn is described as looking like a wizened little old man. Taken altogether, the unimpressive appearance of the newborn belies the significance of the great adventure of growing and becoming that lies ahead of it.

The average full-term baby weighs 7½ pounds (3,400 grams) at birth and is 20 inches (51 centimeters) long. Weight differs, on the average, for blacks and Caucasians and for boys and girls. Girls weigh about a half pound less than boys at birth. The average birth weight for full-term babies is somewhat less for blacks than for Caucasians.

New parents often marvel at the delicate beauty of their baby's miniature

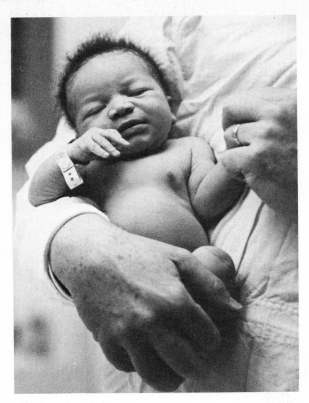

The average newborn weighs a little over seven pounds and can easily be held in two hands.

hands and feet, complete with tiny, tiny fingernails and fingerprints. When such a small hand closes over the finger of the mother, a lifelong love affair usually ensues.

Physiological Adjustment to Birth

Birth is a process during which great changes take place. The child emerges rather quickly from the body of the mother, and we can give, to the minute, the time of this event. In that short time the infant changes status from dependence on the mother's physiological processes to reliance on the functioning of his or her own small body. The physiological systems that were developing throughout the prenatal period must function immediately. The processes involved in this change are the circulatory, respiratory, digestive-excretory, and hormonal systems; organs such as the liver must function fully, and homeostasis, or the balance of all these systems, must be maintained.

The heart has been beating and pumping blood from the fourth week of prenatal life and the fetus has been producing the blood cells dictated by the individual's genetic code. In normal pregnancies, conditions before birth are relatively unstressful for the baby; however, labor and delivery may constitute great stress on the circulatory system. For that reason, in most hospitals the fetal heartbeat is monitored for the duration of labor. Because one of the first indications of fetal and

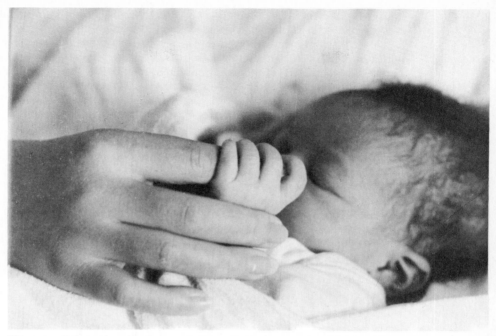

New parents marvel at the delicate beauty of the miniature hands and feet. When this small hand closes over the finger of the mother, a life-long attachment begins.

neonatal stress is indicated by abnormal heartbeat, the heart rate continues to be monitored in the neonatal period.

The immediate response to birth for the newborn is breathing. The fetus may take in and expel amniotic fluid from its lungs prior to birth, but the functioning of the respiratory system cannot be actually assured until birth. Attendants at birth watch the respiration of the newborn very carefully. As soon as the head appears, the mucus and amniotic fluids are removed to clear the nose and mouth for breathing. The newborn may be placed with its head slightly lower than its body so that mucus can drain, or a small suction syringe is used to extract mucus. Lack of oxygen can cause serious problems. If breathing does not begin in a short time after birth, brain cells may begin to die and the child may suffer irreversible brain damage. Rate of respiration, however, continues to be irregular for some months after birth, and infants sometimes stop breathing altogether for short periods of time.

Immediate survival does not depend on the functioning of the digestive-excretory system; however, eventual survival does. Whereas breathing must be accomplished within a few minutes of birth, a few days or weeks may be needed to evaluate the digestive-excretory system. The major problems with this system may be structural abnormalities or an inability to tolerate various foods. Neonatal surgery can correct many structural defects that are not apparent until birth, and careful control of diet may control other problems. Many children did not survive before new medical techniques were perfected because of problems in this system.

The functioning of many organs and systems often cannot be determined until the child is born and its physiological system is functioning independently. Many advances have been made in correcting genetic or congenital defects. When surgical procedures are necessary, preliminary surgery may be done soon after birth, with follow-up surgery when the abnormal system is more mature. Recently techniques have been developed that enable surgery to be done prenatally.

Finally, the small body of the newborn must maintain all systems in a balance, rather as a juggler keeps many balls in the air simultaneously. One of the most important homeostatic functions for the newborn is the regulation of body temperature. The human must maintain a constant body temperature within a relatively short range. The average body temperature is 98.6 degrees. An eight- or ten-degree variation above or below this is life threatening. On the other hand, humans, even when they are still babies, can survive in external temperatures over a much wider range. The fetus has lived at a constant temperature inside the body of the mother, and on being thrust into the outside world in which an average room is around 70 degrees the newborn must maintain his or her own body temperature. The premature infant has great difficulty with this function, and therefore the external temperature maintained in incubators for premature infants more nearly approximates the necessary internal temperature. The full-term infant, on the other hand, can usually maintain temperature even in a cool room; however, this aspect must be carefully watched.

The body must maintain many other homeostatic conditions, such as that between insulin and blood sugar and other hormonal and endocrine balances. Imbalance in any of the body's many systems may cause severe problems. If these are identified early, irreversible damage may be avoided. The first month after birth, the *neonatal* period, is a crucial time for the newborn, or *neonate*. Once the crucial neonatal period has passed, the young human is considered an infant. Physical adjustment has been made to independent life, and the social bond between the infant and its mother is well on its way to permanent attachment.

A New View of the Newborn

A revolution has taken place in our view of the newborn over the last two decades. This revolution has been brought about by research that has probed the behavior of the newborn. Young humans have been tested over a wide range of conditions in an attempt to discover their perceptual and behavioral abilities. The limits of those abilities have yet to be fully described. Other research has explored with equal intensity the social responses and initiatives with which the human begins to establish relationships, interactions, and attachments with other people.

Knowledge has been accumulated through hundreds of studies, by thousands of scientists, with tens of thousands of infants, mothers, fathers, and caregivers. The effect of this growing knowledge has been to change our perception and understanding of the human newborn and, by extension, of children of all ages. The evidence has exploded the myth of the infant as an unaware, unresponsive, helpless organism buffeted by random stimuli. The new view of the newborn, supported by irrefutable evidence, is that the infant, at birth, is a *competent human being*. The newborn demonstrates human competence both by responding to the environment and by changing it. The newborn has ready-made behaviors for dealing with the objects, people, and events in its environment. In dealing with the inanimate

The newborn is a competent human being who immediately begins to engage the environment and to contribute to that environment.

world, the newborn is capable of processing information received from the environment and has highly developed capacities for organizing responses to this information, including the ability to make "decisions" on preferred visual and auditory stimuli. The young infant selects attractive stimuli that hold his attention for long periods of time (Als, 1975) and defends him- or herself against sights and sounds that are obtrusive and noxious (Brazelton & Robey, 1965).

In the social area, the newborn actively solicits responses from caregivers from the first moments of birth, thus initiating a social dialogue characterized by intricate interaction. Rather than being a passive recipient of whatever care happens to be given, the infant, from birth, begins to influence his or her caregivers (Als, Tronick, Lester, & Brazelton, 1979; Yarrow, 1979). This is a nonverbal dialogue in which the very appearance and initial behaviors of the newborn attract adults, who then behave in ways that satisfy the infant by providing food and warmth, a reassuring voice, and the comfort of touch. The infant responds to these behaviors in ways that are, in turn, rewarding to adults; thus, an intricate and subtle communication system is begun. These maternal and infant behaviors complement each other and initiate a process that bonds the mother and the infant in a reciprocal rhythm (Kennel, Voos, & Klaus, 1979).

Scientific Study of the Newborn

Newborns, or neonates, are in many ways ideal human subjects. Healthy, full-term neonates possess the neurological and biological systems characteristic of all humans; yet, because their experience in the world is limited, it is possible to obtain an estimate of functioning relatively uninfluenced by experience in the environment. We cannot, of course, state that the newborn has had no experience with the world, for the fetus experiences many environmental stimuli prenatally. Certainly the fetus experiences sound and probably dim light, and the physical environment is filled with both tactile and chemical stimulation. The fetus experiences his or her own movement, and perhaps, even experiences experiencing. In addition, by studying the very earliest behaviors, scientists can often isolate an emerging behavioral system and gain a better understanding of the variables that control or mediate that behavior.

The absence of language in the newborn has made the scientific study of psychological processes difficult. Newborns can neither respond to verbal directions nor report perceptions or feelings, as can older subjects who have language. Researchers, therefore, have been forced to be ingenious in devising ways of ascertaining the experience of the newborn. The discovery that there were physiological correlates to psychological experience opened the way to measure such experience. We are aware that, when we see or hear something that signifies impending danger, our heart rate increases, our breathing may become shallow or our palms damp. In a similar fashion, if we are, for example, looking for a street sign, we may feel that our attention is especially sharply focused. At such times of sharp focus there are also changes in heart rate and blood pressure of which we may not be aware. Similarly, we may have had the experience of focusing for a long time on a puzzle or a problem. After a time, we find ourselves unable to make any further progress on the problem. It is as though we were literally turned off and our brain stopped functioning. When small electrodes are attached to the skull, changes in brain functioning can be recorded as brain-wave patterns. Changes also occur in electrical activity of the skin, heart rate, and respiration. Those physiological changes are reactions in our bodies that occur in relation to processing information.

Neonates have those same physiological reactions to processing information. Because physiological changes are directly correlated with the psychological experiences of attention, information processing, and ceasing to attend to stimuli, researchers use them as measures of the corresponding psychological processes. Using such indices, we have obtained a vast amount of information about how newborns interact with their world. We will look at some of this information here.

Early in this century the noted psychologist William James stated that to the newborn the world is a "booming, buzzing, confusion." This was the view held of the perception of the newborn for many years: total confusion. It was assumed that sounds and lights overwhelmed the infant and only after a period of several months did it learn to respond selectively to them. The implication was that the infant was too immature to make discriminations and for several months was essentially anesthetized to all but the most gross sensations.

Current knowledge of the newborn indicates a different picture in the area of perception. While the research on neurological maturity is inconclusive, behavioral research indicates that the newborn perceives and responds to the environment in a multitude of ways. In addition, it has been discovered that immediately after birth the newborn is in a state of heightened awareness in which it perceives sights and sounds and perhaps smells and touch even more acutely than an older infant. This state of heightened awareness characteristic of the newborn continues from one to four hours after birth (Desmond & Rudolph, 1966). Thus, the time immediately after birth may be a very good one for introducing the neonate to the world and for sensory stimulation.

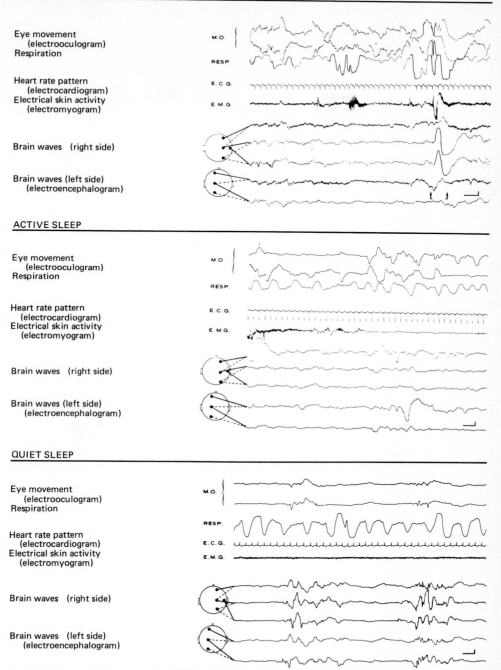

ACTIVE SLEEP

QUIET SLEEP

Polygraph records of a full-term newborn in states of wakefulness, active sleep, and quiet sleep. Since newborns cannot report their experiences, these physiological measures are correlated with many activities and states of consciousness. [From "Organization of Sleep in Prematures: Implications for Caregiving," in *The Effect of the Infant on Its Caregiver*, edited by Michael Lewis and Leonard A. Rosenblum. Copyright © by John Wiley & Sons, Inc. Reproduced by permission.]

Sensory Perception in the Newborn

All information about the world is obtained through sensory modes—that is, through sight, sound, smell, touch, or taste. For humans, vision is the most important source of information about the world. In addition to information about color, texture, and shape of objects, vision is a source of information about the emotional state of other people. Facial expressions are cues to emotional feelings. Newborns respond to these cues. Sensory perception is extremely important in the development of the child because all that he or she perceives of the world must travel through the senses. We are interested in the sensory modes in infants, for if we know these functions we can begin to construct a model of how infants gain an understanding of the world.

Visual Perception

Earlier estimates of the visual perception of the newborn concluded that the eyes were not sufficiently developed to discriminate between similar, and not so similar, stimuli. It was believed that the infant experienced a fuzzy blur for the first several weeks after birth. Anatomical studies of the neonatal visual system have been inconclusive (Cohen, DeLoache, & Strauss, 1979). Some studies have found differences in the maturity of the retina, the optic nerve, and the visual cortex in the brain between the newborn and the adult (Duke-Elder & Cook, 1963; Mann, 1964; Peiper, 1963).

Subsequent studies of the brain indicated that brain development is essentially complete by the eighth prenatal month. There are, however, such changes in the neurons as myelination (Yakovlex & Le Cours, 1967), the size of cell bodies, length of axons, dendritic branches and differentiation (Conel, 1959).

More recent studies have criticized the early findings on the grounds that the infants studied were available because of neonatal death and that they were, in fact, defective, or developmentally retarded (Haith, 1976). Recently developed research technology has enabled more sensitive measures of functioning and brain waves that have been found in the newborn. At present, the anatomical development of the visual system at birth is an open question. In addition, the exact relationship between anatomical changes in infancy and the emerging visual and cognitive behaviors is unknown and will have to wait for future research (Cohen, DeLoache, & Strauss, 1979). Many behavioral scientists have chosen to bypass the question of anatomy and have concentrated on exploring the actual visual competence of infants.

Central and peripheral vision function in a complementary manner. In mature visual processing, central vision is used to fixate on an object in order to abstract information from it. It is peripheral vision that guides eye movements by providing preliminary information about objects that should be centrally fixated to obtain greater detail. When peripheral vision is lost, the result is tunnel vision, and the organism is deprived of information about the environment. The conclusion of research in these two aspects of vision is that, although the newborn's visual system is underdeveloped, the newborn can both focus on objects centrally and detect objects peripherally.

The keenness of visual perception of newborns is less than that of older infants and adults. Researchers have attempted to estimate this acuity through many techniques. The classic method to test the peripheral vision of newborns is to present a central visual stimulus that the infant fixates. Then a stimulus that has previously been found to attract the infant's visual gaze is moved in an arc into the line of vision. The point at which the infant turns its eyes from the central plane toward the peripheral stimulus indicates the arc of peripheral vision. Research has indicated that neonates can see lights that are displaced by as much as 25 to 30 degrees from the central plane (MacFarlane, Harris, & Barnes, 1976; Harris & MacFarlane, 1974).

What this means is that, even in the first days of life, an infant who is held can visually fixate on the face of the person holding him or her. In addition, this infant is able to perceive with peripheral vision another person who enters the room and is able to break a gaze on the caregiver's face and turn to look at the second person. Very quickly the neonate recognizes the human that is most often the caregiver, and this person becomes, indeed, a beautiful sight to behold.

Form Perception

The study of the perception of newborns has revealed that they are selective in the features of the environment that they visually explore. In studying the visual perception of newborns, the technique most often used is to present two different visual stimuli and then to observe the infant looking. The eyes of the infant are watched through an apparatus, and the infant is assumed to be looking at one stimulus as long as the image of that stimulus is reflected on the pupil. Of course this is not conclusive because infants lock in on a stimulus and continue to look at it even though processing has discontinued. Therefore, the physiological measures of blood pressure and heart rate are used as measures that perceptual processing is occurring. What then attracts the visual attention of newborns?

The form that infants prefer above all others is a normal human face. In an early study of visual preference of infants, Fantz showed infants many different forms. Note in this chart that the preference for human faces is present in very young infants and reaches a peak between two and three months. Such a preference predisposes the infant to explore visually the face of the caregiver and thereby provides a medium of interchange between caregiver and infant. [From "The Origin of Form Perception" by Robert L. Fantz. Copyright © 1961 by Scientific American, Inc. All rights reserved.]

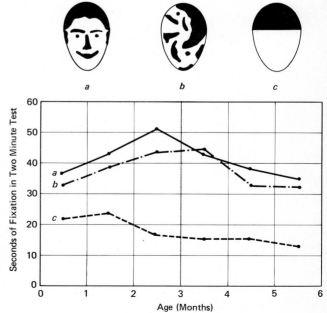

In looking at objects newborns typically scan the outer edges and angles of forms, especially when those edges and angles have high contrast (Cohen, DeLoache, & Strauss, 1979). When given a choice between curved and straight lines, newborns prefer to look at curved lines, provided that those lines formed the outer contour of the form (Fantz & Miranda, 1975).

The human infant prefers to look at human faces. When presented with line drawings of a face, newborns typically look at the outermost contour (Bergman, Haith, & Mann, 1971; Maurer & Salapatek, 1976). Fantz (1961) showed infants several visual representations of human faces: some with regular features, some with only a contour and blank inside, and some with all the elements of faces but with scrambled features. In the scrambled faces, eyes, mouths, and noses were randomly arranged in a face shape. By two weeks of age infants preferred looking at human faces and this preference increased until infants were three months old. In a similar study, Goren (1975) found that when similar representations were slowly moved in an arc around the newborn, the face with regular features was more likely to be visually followed. In addition, this study found that newborns visually followed a real face more than a drawing of a face. Goren concluded that, "The infant enters the world predisposed to respond to a face, any face" (p. 6). Other writers support this conclusion with the theoretical position that the preference for looking at human faces is a survival mechanism that is part of the hereditary package (Bowlby, 1958).

Sound Perception

When new parents say to visitors, "Shhh, the baby is sleeping," they are expressing the experience of generations of parents that the newborn does, indeed, perceive sound. This folk experience is borne out in scientific studies of infants. The sense of hearing is more acute in the newborn than that of sight, but it is somewhat less acute in newborns than in adults.

The newborn turns its head in the direction of a sound and exhibits a generalized startled reaction in response to a sudden loud noise. When newborns perceive sounds, their brainwaves and heart rates change; the measurement of which indicates sound perception. It is also true that, while the eyes cannot perceive while sleeping, the ears continue to perceive sound during sleep. By measuring the physiological response to sounds of various intensities during sleep, it has been found that neonates only two to four days old have hearing perception only slightly less than the average adult (Barnet & Goodwin, 1965). Immediately after birth, the perception of sound may be less, but sensitivity to sound increases rapidly in the first few days of life (Berg & Berg, 1979).

Sound is a sensory mode that is used prior to birth. Many sounds reach the fetus in the amniotic fluid and are even amplified by it. Throughout prenatal life the heartbeat of the mother is a constant sound engulfing the fetus. Researchers conclude that the unborn child pays attention to this sound and apparently it becomes a source of comfort. It has been found that when the sound of a heartbeat is reproduced in a newborn nursery the babies sleep more and cry less.

The newborn responds more easily to those sounds that are within the range of the normal human voice (Eisenberg, 1976). And, in fact, the fetus may even learn to recognize mother by her voice. Certainly speech resonates through the bones and tissues of the body, and the sound of the mother's voice floods the fetus *in utero*

A one-week-old baby watches his mother's face as she talks to him. Note his response to her speaking. Through such attention and response newborns encourage parents to increase care-giving behavior.

(in the uterus), as does the heartbeat. Every voice is unique in its timbre and pitch, (we recognize voices on the telephone with no other clues). Such a discrimination at birth indicates very accurate functioning of the sense of sound and the perceptual process in the brain.

Taste, Smell, and Touch

The newborn has highly discriminating senses of smell and taste. It can differentiate between human milk and a cow's milk formula carefully designed to duplicate the contents of human milk, and it will turn its head toward the smell of milk above that of water or sugar water (Brazelton, 1976). Such information about young infants substantiates the view that they are competent human beings functioning efficiently and refutes earlier estimates that they could only distinguish pungent odors such as ammonia. In earlier studies when newborns were offered substances for taste there was little differentiating behavior beyond preference of sweet to bitter. The ability to distinguish human milk and the preference for it serves the survival of the infant. Such a preference assures that the healthy newborn will be eager to nurse and in so doing receive the nourishment necessary for the rapid growth of infancy.

The response to pain has been used as an indication of the developmental level of the sense of touch. It has long been assumed that the newborn is relatively insensitive to pain, and circumcisions are performed without anesthesia soon after birth. A newborn may respond to this procedure, or to having its foot pricked for a blood sample, with a cry of protest or it may fall asleep. Both of these behaviors are defenses against stimuli that overwhelm the newborn's capacity to handle them. The defense of sleeping may have been interpreted erroneously as insensitivity to pain. The new view of the newborn is that the five senses are functioning efficiently at birth in ways that increase the probability of interaction with parents and care-givers, that help the newborn in securing food, and that enable it to select from the environment those stimuli necessary for further development.

Importance of Senses in Development

These senses are the means for all experiences in life. It is through the five senses that humans receive information and stimulation from the world, and it is again through the senses that humans send information about themselves back into the external world. From the information received through the senses the infant and child build a threefold structure. First, a mental conception of the objective world of reality is built; second, an emotional feeling of people, things, and events is con-structed; and third, from his or her own inner resources the infant, child, and adult respond to information and stimulation received in ways that build a social net-work of relationships. Let us use an analogy of the computer to illustrate the func-tion of the senses. We may think of the senses as the hardware that the infant (child and adult) uses to grow and develop mentally, emotionally, and socially. The soft-ware consists of the experiences that are fed into the five senses by parents, others, and the natural environment as growth is accomplished in many areas.

Personality in the Newborn

Does a newborn have a personality? Is personality formed by experiences, or is it some quality of being that is innate and unique to each individual? Or, is it some combination of the two? Whatever the origin of personality, the term denotes a quality in the person that is consistent and that characterizes responses over a wide range of situations: for example, the tendencies to react quickly or slowly. Perhaps young infants cannot be said to have distinctive personalities, but it is clear that they differ greatly in their reactions to similar stimuli, a difference that is consistent in the same infant over a wide variety of stimuli. In the face of environmental changes, some infants become easily upset and others remain calm. Researchers have termed this quality *temperament* and have postulated that this temperament lays the foundation for what is later termed personality.

Temperament

Temperament is a broad term that has little scientific validity. Although it lacks exactness, it does convey the concept of a consistent quality of being, under which many behavioral characteristics may be grouped. There is mounting evidence that infants exhibit different and individual styles of behavior at birth. Newborn infants vary in such physical dimensions as muscle tone, motor ability, and vigor of suck-ing response. They also differ in social responses such as frequency of smiling and in psychological dimensions such as duration of attention and the stability of sleep-ing and waking cycles (Wolff, 1971).

The physical characteristics of the infant such as muscle tone and characteristic posture affect the mother's way of handling her infant. Some infants instantly mold their bodies to that of the mother when placed with the head on the shoulder. These babies are innately cuddlers. Other babies tense and arch their backs when placed in the head-on-shoulder position and seem to be noncuddlers (Schaffer & Emerson, 1964). Whether an infant is a cuddler or noncuddler affects the mother's feeling about herself and the infant. She may feel rejected, loved, needed, competent, or incompetent in handling her baby (Wolff, 1971). In a study of mothers and infants, the behavior of mothers was viewed in terms of whether the infants were cuddlers or noncuddlers. It was found that the mothers of noncuddlers were less likely to hold their infant. Some mothers actually avoid physical contact with difficult babies and may resort to feeding their infants with a bottle propped on a pillow.

The temperament of infants goes far beyond muscle tone and cuddling. Thomas and Chess (1977) extensively investigated the temperamental styles of infants and have described three different types identifiable in early infancy. Parents or others with extensive experience with infants will recognize these temperaments as the *easy child,* the *difficult child,* and the *slow-to-warm-up child.*

Most children are in the easy-child category. They adapt easily to new situations, are generally positive in mood, and seldom reach intense levels of emotional expression. They are easy for parents to handle, as they quickly develop regular patterns of eating and sleeping. Parents respond to these children positively and feel pleased with themselves for their "good" children and their excellent parenting skills.

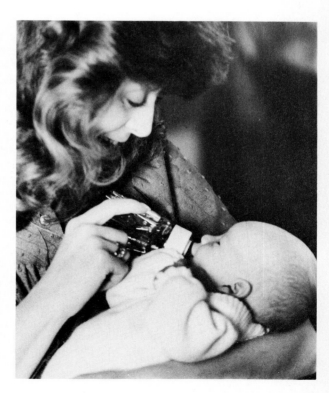

Early interaction is a reciprocal relationship. Mothers are pleased when the infant responds to their care and voice. This mother is talking to her new son and he is responding with facial expression and body motions. Feeding offers both an opportunity for interaction with exactly the correct distance for eye-contact.

The difficult child is, quite simply, difficult. Fortunately, there are fewer difficult than easy children. These children do not adapt readily to change and exhibit great distress when placed in new situations and with new people. They become easily frustrated and as a result often cry or have temper tantrums. Routines are more difficult to establish, as they eat and sleep irregularly. Parents often respond to these children with equal bad humor and in negative ways; however, they may feel guilty or worry that they are the cause of the child's difficult behavior. As a result, their self-esteem as parents is considerably lowered, and parenting is not the pleasure that they had anticipated it would be.

Children who are slow to warm up also have difficulty in adjusting to new situations and new people; however, rather than protest, these children withdraw and show their distress through passive-resistance: they cling or hide their faces. Given a new food that they find distasteful, they will let it dribble from their mouths rather than spit it out, as would the difficult child. Parents of these children also tend to blame themselves for the behaviors of their children and experience disappointment in parenthood.

Evidence indicates that the temperaments of each of these types of children have little relationship to parenting skills and styles. The parent with an easy child, may, indeed, be a good parent, but this parenting is apparently not the cause of the easy temperamental style of the child. Similarly, the parents of difficult and slow-to-warm-up children assume guilt unnecessarily for their child's temperament. These children require more patience and care in arranging routines and environments, and parents often are not prepared for the difficult adjustment required.

New parents are distressed if their newborn is limp, has poor muscle tone, is difficult to arouse, and/or is sluggish in response to nursing or other stimulation. Parents may be equally distressed with an infant that is hypersensitive to stimulation and is startled or cries in response to minor disturbances. Some newborns wake easily and cry angrily at the slightest discomfort, whereas others tolerate endless visitors, interrupted naps, delayed feeding, and soiled diapers with good humor. These individual differences among infants contribute much to the mother-infant relationship. Some mothers delight in a very active baby who is "into everything." Such a mother may feel that something is wrong with a baby who is placid and seems never to react strongly. On the other hand, some mothers feel their sense of worth as a mother rests on the apparent pleasure of the infant. These mothers may feel a sense of failure with a baby who reacts strongly and with anger at minor stimulation. Thus, the innate temperament of the infant interacts with the expectations and temperament of the mother and affects their subsequent relationship.

Most infant differences are within the range of normalcy and increase the richness of human interaction; however, those infants whose differences are beyond the range of normalcy pose difficult problems for parents. Infants who were later judged to be psychotic children were noted to have demonstrated early aversion to eye contact and to have been unresponsive or actually to have withdrawn from interpersonal relationships (Hutt & Ounsted, 1966). Abused children are often found to have characteristics and behaviors that are abrasive to their parents (Gil, 1970). Infants who spend a great deal of time sleeping or in agitated crying and little time being quietly attentive are frustrating for parents (Brazelton, 1961). Parents often need help in understanding the unusual characteristics of infants. If mothers can be sensitized to respond to these characteristics, the risk of deviant development is lessened (Brazelton, Koslowski, & Main, 1971). The characteristic that reassures parents is the ability of the infant to spend some time in quiet, alert attention. Conversely, the characteristic that distresses parents is the absence of this organization and a baby that greets stimuli with howling rage or sleepy inattention. Thus, sleep and wakefulness become a preoccupation with new parents and have also been studied by scientists.

Sleep and Wakefulness: States of Consciousness in the Newborn

The human organism is not a machine that chugs along at a continuous, unvarying rate. Rather, living organisms are a part of nature and as such are subject to the ebb and flow of their biological rhythms. A biological rhythm is a regular pattern of changes in biological functioning that is related to time. The basic biological rhythm regulating the action of humans is a diurnal (night-day) pattern of sleep and wakefulness. For most people sleep occurs at night and wakefulness during the day. This rhythm is not stabilized in newborns, so that periods of sleep and wakefulness tend to be randomly distributed over the 24-hour cycle and are easily disrupted. Much to the chagrin of parents, newborns may have their most alert period of wakefulness at 3 A.M. It is not until about six months of age that infants establish a stable pattern. This is when parents, with a sigh of relief, find that their baby sleeps throughout the night.

Sleep-wakefulness patterns emerge late in prenatal life, and very young premature infants do not have these stable patterns. The fetus neither sleeps nor wakes but exists in a continuous in-between state. The states of sleep and wakefulness are controlled by brain function. The emergence of these patterns late in prenatal life and the instability of these patterns indicate the emerging control of these functions by the developing brain.

These two states of sleep and wakefulness are characterized by different biological functioning. Chief among them is brain-wave patterns. Electrodes attached to the skull can detect electrical impulses, which can be recorded by an electroencephalograph (EEG). In addition to sleeping and waking patterns, the EEG can detect different patterns of brain function within the two states. For example, in sleep, different patterns are evident when the infant is dreaming and when he or she is in quiet sleep (see page 9). Similarly, there are gradations in the waking state that indicate intense or diminished attention. Other biological changes indicating differing states are measurable for heart rate, respiration, and electrical conduction of the skin.

These states are important in understanding the development of human behavior because they indicate organization in behavior that enables the organism to receive and to respond to environmental stimuli. For example, let us consider the waking state. As we indicated, all information about the environment is received through the senses; however, the organism must ready itself to receive those various stimuli. We are all familiar with the child (or adult) who is "turned off." Such people may be engulfed by words and sights, yet apparently never hear or see anything. In order to receive the information, the sensory pathways must be open. In this openness, physiological and psychological behavior are organized to receive stimuli. In a state of rapt attention to visual or auditory stimuli, breathing becomes deeper and slower; heart rate decreases; blood vessels in the head dilate, carrying

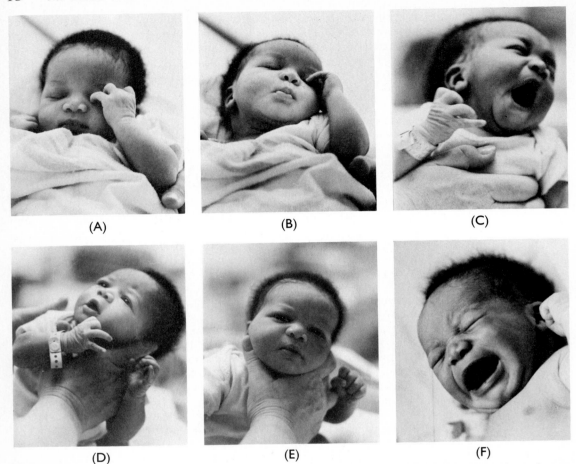

(A)   (B)   (C)

(D)   (E)   (F)

The state of consciousness in the newborn determines the "availability" to receive environmental stimulation. In state one (A) the infant is in deep sleep with regular breathing, eyes closed, no eye movement, and no spontaneous activity except startles and jerks. External stimuli may produce startles with some delay but are not likely to produce a change of state. In state two (B) the infant is in light sleep with eyes closed, irregular breathing, and eye movements under closed lids. There is a low activity level with random movements and startles; sucking movements occur irregularly. External stimuli may startle and change state, that is, awaken. In state three (C) the infant is drowsy or semi-dozing. Eyes may be open or closed and eyelids may flutter. Activity level varies and often exhibits a delayed reaction to sensory stimulation. Movements are smooth and coordinated. External stimuli usually produce a change in state. In state four (D) the infant is alert with a bright look and seems to focus attention on the source of the stimulation. The face brightens and eyebrows lift. Motor activity is minimal. In state five (E) the eyes are open and attention is accompanied by motor activity as generalized excitement characterized by spontaneous movements of the arms and legs. Excitement may escalate to fussiness. State six (F) is characterized by intense crying. Crying is a disorganized state in which attention is not directed toward outside stimuli and it is difficult to break through with external stimulation. Crying, like sleeping, is a way newborns defend against stimuli that are overwhelming. In the state of alert attention (D) the newborn is most open to environmental stimulation and is most responsive and satisfying to parents. This infant is less than 24-hours old. The photographs were taken during a routine physical examination, a diaper change, and a visit with his mother.

more blood to the brain, while those in the limbs constrict; and active physical activity ceases. A practical application of this is used by parents and caregivers in attempting to quiet a baby who seems agitated by showing him or her a novel toy or perhaps singing an attractive song. The parents cause the agitated physical activity to cease by gaining the infant's attention. Intense attention to stimuli is accompanied by physiologically based psychological changes. In this reaction, pupils dilate, letting in more light, brain waves change toward increased arousal, and the auditory and visual thresholds are lowered, resulting in response to less stimuli than is usually needed (Zimbardo & Ruch, 1976).

Through this mechanism newborns are able to focus on sounds and sights that are attractive to them and thereby immediately begin incorporating what is interesting in the environment. Newborns, of course, cannot consciously organize their behavior to receive environmental stimulation; however, the quality of their organization of behavior in the face of stimulation is a good indication of their ability to adapt and function. Some infants can direct sustained attention to interesting stimuli, others quickly reach their point of endurance and behavior disorganizes into angry crying.

Brazelton (1973) has noted that the infant has a mechanism for defending against stimulation that becomes too intense, or is in some way negative, or assaults his or her inner organization. In interaction with mothers, infants return a gaze and react to social stimulation; however, with increased stimulation they may avert their gaze, thus signaling that their capacity for stimulation has been reached. If stimulation continues, the infant may resort to crying, or the central sensory pathways may cease transmitting such stimulation and the infant may fall asleep. Needless to say, an infant in this state cannot receive or respond to sensory stimuli. In the newborn who quickly falls into disorganized behavior in the face of environmental stimuli we see the precursor of the hyperactive child who becomes overstimulated easily and cannot sustain attention.

A more immediate risk for the infant, however, is the difficulty that a mother or caregiver may have in handling behavior that is quickly disorganized into violent crying. Such an infant conveys a sense of failure to the mother who, as a result, is likely *not* to provide the quiet loving care with which an infant thrives. In fact, such an infant may solicit abusive behavior from its parents. T. B. Brazelton, a pediatrician, has constructed a procedure to evaluate this quality of state organization in the newborn.

The Brazelton Neonatal Behavioral Assessment Scale

Brazelton (1973) developed the Brazelton Neonatal Behavioral Assessment Scale to assess the behavioral capacities of the newborn in relation to states of consciousness. The instrument is a clinical procedure that attempts to lead the infant through experiences that will be typical of future interaction. It focuses on the newborn's capacity to organize behavior under the stress of recent labor and delivery and exposure to the new extrauterine environment. The administration of this instrument is such that the examiner attempts to elicit the best performance (or organization of behavior) of which the infant is capable. The order of presentation is not rigid, and the examiner handles the infant in a way that might represent the responses of a caring mother or father. The procedure assesses the capacity for interaction of the individual infant. Examiners trained to use the procedure are cautioned to make efforts to influence the infant to an optimal state for the desired response and to vary maneuvers until the best response available from the infant is produced. Thus, a poor response may result because the newborn cannot produce a better one, or it may be that the examiner's maneuvers were not effective enough. The examiner must always be sensitive to the infant's particular state of consciousness and must learn the necessary procedural maneuvers to elicit optimal responses in a baby (Als, Tronick, Lester, & Brazelton, 1979).

This assessment requires approximately a half-hour; in that time the infant is brought up from a state of light sleep to an alert state, then into a more active state, to crying, and down to an alert inactive state again. In the course of this procedure the infant is led to exhibit motor, cognitive, social, and temperamental responses through the organizations of behavior available to him or her. The examiner must be careful that the intrusiveness of the stimuli and maneuvers are graded, in order not to overwhelm the infant too early in the exam. To accomplish this, the examiner must pay careful attention to states. One important objective of the assessment is to observe the newborn as he or she reacts in all states of consciousness. In addition, the pattern of the states the infant moves through—the speed and gradation of change from one state to another—is an important characteristic. This pattern is thought to reflect the capacity of the infant to modulate his or her states of consciousness in order to be available for social and cognitive stimulation (Als et al., 1979).

The underlying model on which this instrument is based is that of an infant who responds to social stimulation by changing internal organization, such as focusing attention, opening sensory modes for reception of stimuli, and quieting autonomic activity that might be detracting. When the state of the infant changes to violent crying, reception of sensory and social stimulation ceases. The infant is, at least in part, responsible for maintaining organization in the face of external stimulation. Each infant has a different range for the optimum perception of environmental stimuli. In a continuum of infant's states from deep sleep to violent crying, it is obvious that the infant is not processing social and cognitive stimuli in either extreme. If we move in on each end of this continuum, we reach light sleep or drowsiness on one end and fussy agitation on the other. The state of unconsciousness (sleep) or physical discomfort precludes processing all but the most extreme of external stimulation. It is in the active or quiet awake states that information from the external environment can be processed by the infant. External stimulation can arouse an infant from sleep. Continued stimulation engages the infant in an interchange, but at some point stimulation reaches an intensity that overwhelms the infant and creates disorganization: crying, agitated physical activity, and inattention to environmental stimuli.

Optimal levels and preferred style of stimulation vary in different infants. The most satisfactory interaction between infants and mothers, fathers, and caregivers is that characterized by sensitivity to the intensity and styles of stimulation preferred by the infant, as well as sensitivity to the current state and changes in state.

Brazelton has stressed the educational use of his instrument in sensitizing parents to the individual patterns of their new son or daughter. When this instrument is used to counsel parents in the individual characteristics of their infants and to teach them the most effective style of relating to them, more effective parent-child bonds can be fostered. The education of parents in the optimum style of relating to their infants is especially important for infants who are "at risk" for behavioral difficulties, and through improved parent techniques, difficulties can often be avoided.

The Social Life of the Newborn

The studies cited here and the hundreds not reviewed here are overwhelming evidence that the neonate is a competent information-processing human being. We marvel at the precise and competent way that perceptual processes function in the

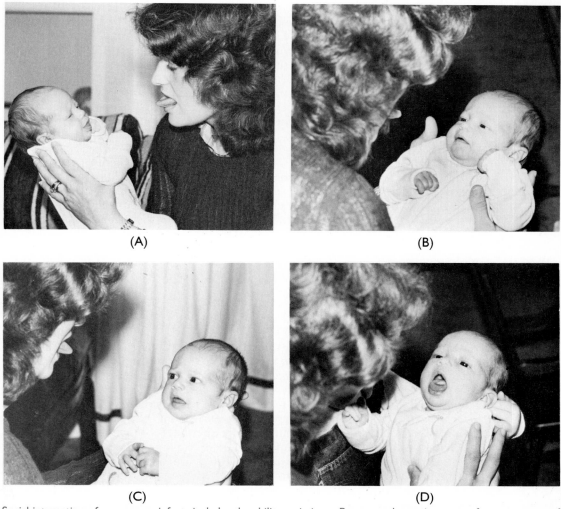

(A)   (B)

(C)   (D)

Social interaction of very young infants includes the ability to imitate. Parents and caregivers are often not aware of this subtle exchange but it serves to bond the two into a social relationship. In the photos above a three-week-old infant imitates her mother protruding her tongue. This is a complex achievement, for the infant must realize that what she sees protruding from her mother's face is the same thing that she has in her mouth (A). She must then execute the muscular actions required to protrude her tongue. Note in these pictures the look of concentration as the infant studies the actions of the mother (B), the beginning muscular reaction (C), and full opening of the mouth and protrusion of the tongue (D). A very complex maneuver indeed!

neonate; however, such accomplishments pale when compared to the extraordinarily sophisticated and subtle patterns of social interaction that the newborn exhibits. Through eye contact and body language the neonate entices the mother, the father, and other caregivers to respond, to smile, to talk in loving tones, and to make a place in their social circle for the newcomer. The social relationship is not one way. The neonate responds to overtures in ways that reward the adults and increase their desire to prolong the interchange.

Brazelton (1976) describes this early social interaction between mother and neonate as a "mating dance." It is a reciprocal relationship in which the infant signals through sighs, crying, eye contact, or other behaviors his or her status and needs. The mother perceives the cues given by the infant and responds, either appropriately or inappropriately. If the response is appropriate, the infant is satisfied by it and signals pleasure; the mother, receiving the pleasure signal of the infant, experiences feelings of self-confidence and encouragement for her maternal behavior. From the initial exchanges, mother and infant interactions become increasingly synchronized in a mutually satisfying dynamic equilibrium. The sensitivity of the mother in interpreting the signals of her infant and the appropriateness of her responses are the foundation of the child's social, cognitive, and emotional development.

It must be stressed that the infant is not a passive recipient of the mother's ministrations. Instead, the relationship is one of interaction, because the infant exerts considerable influence on the mother's behavior. Many characteristics of infants affect the mother-infant relationship. The innate characteristics of the infant—sex, temperament, and responsiveness to tactile, visual, and auditory stimuli—influence the way in which the mother responds. Transitory factors such as the state of arousal of the infant (drowsiness, alertness, or agitation) also affect the mother's response. In addition, sociological factors, such as whether the infant is first or later born, affect maternal responsiveness (Osofsky & Connors, 1979).

Bonding

Researchers and workers in child development have long known that the very survival of a child is dependent on the attachment that the child has with a specific person. This person is the *significant other* in a reciprocal relationship. This relationship becomes a social mirror in which both lover and beloved (infant-mother/father; mother/father-infant) see reflections of their personhood. Research is quite clear as to the positive effect of such a relationship and the negative effect of the lack of this relationship in older infants. The question for newborns is: When does this relationship begin and how important are those first few weeks in establishing this relationship? Following the thread of attachment through the labyrinth of environmental variables has led to the first interactions between the newborn and his or her mother; more recently attention has been directed to the father-infant interaction in the first days after birth.

As researchers have looked at the very earliest interactions between infants and mothers and fathers they have labeled these early social experiences bonding, to differentiate them from the more slowly developed, long-lasting relationship of attachment. Bonding is the first link in a chain of events that leads to a permanent attachment.

Mother-Infant Bonding

Is there a maternal instinct? Do mothers "naturally" love their infants? Researchers and others concerned with child welfare have long been perplexed by those cases in which mothers reject and even harm their infants. Such behavior indicates that maternal behavior and "mother love" is not instinctive but rather must result from some environmental events. Researchers have been interested in exactly what constitutes the most advantageous environment to facilitate the formation of an emotional bond between mother and infant. When such a bond is formed, mothers are more likely to provide the care that the infant requires for optimum development.

Studies with both human and animal infants indicate that the infant serves as a stimulus that calls forth maternal behaviors. In addition, there appears to be a sensitive time in which these behaviors are most likely to organize, and that time is the period immediately after birth. The infant's early responsiveness to the environment and the ability to interact with parents makes this period optimal for the formation of affectional bonds.

During this early sensitive period, a series of reciprocal interactions begins between the mother and infant that binds them and insures the further development of attachment. The infant elicits behaviors from the mother that satisfy her or him, and the mother elicits behaviors from the infant that are rewarding to her. These interactions occur on many behavioral and psychological levels. When the infant cries, the mother usually approaches to pick up the baby. The baby often quiets, looks at the mother and follows her with his or her eyes. During a feeding the mother may initiate the interaction. She may gently stroke the infant's cheek, eliciting the rooting reflex that brings the mouth of the baby in contact with the mother's nipple. Nursing is pleasurable to both the mother and the infant. Because maternal and infant behaviors complement each other, the probability of interaction continuing is increased. These behaviors seem to be specific and programmed to initiate the process that bonds mother and infant in a sustained reciprocal rhythm (Kennel, Voos, & Klaus, 1979).

Suspicion that the earliest minutes and hours after birth are important in establishing affectional bonds has led to great changes in the management of childbirth and the neonatal period. Many women are seeking training in childbirth in order to participate and be more fully aware during the event. They also are insisting on time with their infant in the first days following birth by keeping the infant in the hospital room, delivering at home, or leaving the hospital within a few hours. Many women seek to breast feed their infants to maximize physical and emotional contact. Fathers, too, are included in the adventure of establishing bonds with the new family member. Husbands attend prenatal classes, remain present for the birth of their child, and hold and care for the newborn.

Father-Infant Bonding

Many contemporary fathers want to acknowledge their fatherhood in concrete ways of involvement with their infants and find the experience very rewarding. Fathers have been found to develop a bond with their newborns in the first three days of life, and many express a feeling of preoccupation, absorption, and interest in their newborn (Greenberg & Morris, 1974). Greenberg and Morris (1974) found that 97 per cent of a group of fathers of newborn infants rated themselves as average to very high on paternal feelings. Most of those fathers experienced feelings of happiness immediately after the birth and were pleased with the sex of the child.

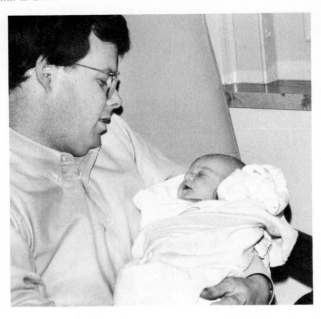

This father is engrossed in his new son who is only hours old.

Ninety per cent of the fathers thought that they could recognize their own infants in the nursery. The researchers concluded that fathers begin to develop a bond with their newborn by the first three days after birth. This bonding was labeled *engrossment*, which was characterized by a feeling of preoccupation and interest in the newborn.

Parke, O'Leary, and West's (1972) observations of mothers, fathers and infants in the first three days after delivery revealed that fathers were as involved as mothers; in fact, the fathers tended to hold the infants and rock them in their arms more than mothers. Half of the fathers had attended Lamaze childbirth classes and all but one had been present at the birth. Does this pattern of paternal involvement also hold for other fathers? In an attempt to answer this question, Parke and O'Leary (1976) studied lower-class fathers who had neither participated in childbirth classes nor been present at the birth. The fathers were observed alone with their infants and with the infant and mother. The study revealed that these fathers touched, looked at, vocalized, and kissed their offspring as often as the mothers. The researchers concluded that the fathers were as nurturant as the mothers. The fathers exhibited more nurturant behavior than the mother when mother, infant, and father were all present, and the same amount of nurturant behavior as mothers when alone with the baby, except for smiling. Mothers smiled more at the infant. The conclusion is that fathers as well as mothers engage in bonding with their infant within the first few days after birth. The word *parents* is plural, and the social bonding that takes place in the newborn period is to father as well as to mother.

Adoptive Parents

The research and management of the newborn period already cited here does not mean that bonds of parenthood can only be forged in the newborn period. We have stressed that the newborn period is a very opportune time to establish bonds of affection for natural parents. However, natural parenting is not the only path to parenthood. Parental behavior and affect are motivated by a very complex mixture of environmental and internal variables. The results of animal research studies reveals that some animals "adopt" infants not their natural offspring, with successful parenthood as the result. Preparation for parenthood is extremely important in both natural and adoptive parenting. Bonds of affection arise seemingly spontaneously in a birth situation; however, adoptive parents can increase the likelihood of forming such bonds by preparing for them. The period of pregnancy affords the natural parent time to prepare for the event of parenthood. How can the adoptive parent prepare for such an event? First, there is environmental preparation. A room is prepared, clothes, linen, and other objects are gathered that the infant (or child) will need. Then, there is mental preparation. Many decisions about management are made *before* a child enters a family. Will the baby be fed on schedule or demand? What forms of discipline are favored? Will babysitters be used? Will mother continue to work? If so, who will care for baby? What changes can be expected in the family routine? The answers to these and other questions may change once a baby has arrived, but thinking about them establishes the awareness that major changes will occur in life-style and organization. Attending group classes, reading books and articles, and discussing feelings and problems with others are ways in which parents can prepare for the baby, whether it is natural or adopted. There is also a psychological preparation for parenthood in which a couple may fantasize about their dreams and desires for the child. What kind of schools are desired for the child? Should she or he study music, or perhaps art? Should the child have a pet? A prospective mother may imagine holding and rocking the baby. In these rehearsals, the groundwork is laid for successful parenthood. If adoption involves an older child, similar preparation can be even more important. An older child brings previous experience with a caregiver and routine. The relationship with the adoptive parent and the child must be within the context of that previous experience. Whether natural or adoptive, successful parenting requires work. Parenting is "natural" only in a biological sense. Other aspects can be enhanced or made more difficult by the events surrounding parenthood.

On these bonds between mother, infant, and father rests much of the emotional, social, and intellectual development of the child. It is trust in the endurance of these bonds that forms a foundation for those things that the individual invests with value and meaning. At the risk of extending our knowledge beyond its legitimate application, we state that it is through these bonds of love, extended to other people and things in the world, that each individual finds meaning in life.

A New View of Development

The conception of the infant as a competent, decision-making goal-oriented human being interacting both with people and things from the moment of birth has fundamentally affected our view of how children develop. Essentially it has elaborated the position that development is the result of a complex interaction between the child and its physical, social, and psychological environments. In the process of such an interactive conception, both the environment and the child are changed. A child is not born into an unchanging, inanimate world. The very fact that the infant is now a part of the world changes that world. The infant immediately begins incorporating the material environment into him- or herself through breathing and eating. It has taken more sophisticated research to reveal that the infant also actively incorporates visual, auditory, and social elements that become the building blocks of internal structures as surely as oxygen and proteins become the building blocks of cells. In the interactionist's view, the infant is not merely a consumer of the environment, but also is a contributor to that environment.

Main Points

The Newborn

1. The birth process produces a red and wrinkled, possibly distorted and unattractive, infant that on the average weighs 7½ pounds and measures 20 inches.

Physiological Adjustment to Birth

2. Physiological adjustments necessitated by birth include maintaining the circulatory system under the stress of labor and delivery; establishing respiration to provide the cells with oxygen; starting up the digestive-excretory system; maintaining the function of other organs and systems; and achieving homeostasis, including maintaining body temperature.

A New View of the Newborn

3. Knowledge accumulated through scientific research supports a new view of the newborn as a competent human being.

4. The neonate is able to respond, initiate actions, establish relationships, interact, and participate in the bonding process.

Scientific Study of the Newborn

5. Researchers use physiological changes, such as brain-wave patterns, heart rate, and blood pressure to measure psychological processes in infants.

Visual Perception in the Newborn

6. Anatomical development of the visual system at birth is an open question.

7. Brain-wave measures indicate the functioning of vision in the newborn.

8. Although the newborn's visual system is underdeveloped, infants can focus on objects centrally and detect objects peripherally.

Form Perception

9. Newborns like to look at the outer edges and angles of forms and high-contrast areas; they prefer curves to straight lines.

10. Research has supported the theoretical position that infants are predisposed to look at human faces as a survival mechanism that is part of the hereditary package.

Sound Perception

11. The sense of sound was used prior to birth; it has been found that two- to four-day-old infants have hearing perception only slightly less acute than the average adult.

12. Newborns respond to the sound of a heartbeat and the human voice, and they recognize their mother's voice after birth.

Touch, Taste, and Smell

13. The newborn is sensitive to pain but in the first few days of life may respond by falling asleep.

14. The sense of smell is developed at birth and newborns soon learn the particular scent associated with their mother and her milk.

15. Newborns have been found to differentiate between human and cow's milk.

Personality

16. Personality in the newborn is not yet distinctive, and psychologists are divided as to whether experiences or heredity contribute most to its formation.

Temperament

17. There is mounting evidence that the different and individual styles of behavior exhibited by infants at birth contribute much to the mother-infant relationship.

States of Consciousness in the Newborn: Sleep and Wakefulness

18. An infant's patterns of sleep and wakefulness are not stabilized until about six months of age.

19. States of consciousness are indicated, studied, and measured by biological changes recorded in the EEG, heart rate, respiration, and electrical conduction of the skin.

20. States of consciousness indicate the organization of the newborn to receive and to respond to environmental stimuli.

The Brazelton Neonatal Behavioral Assessment Scale

21. The Brazelton Neonatal Behavioral Assessment Scale evaluates the newborn's capacity for organizing, behaving, or interacting and responding.

22. Behavioral assessment instruments can be used to counsel parents in the individual characteristics of their infants and to teach them the most effective style of relating to their offspring.

The Social Life of the Newborn

23. The mother-infant relationship consists of mutual interaction, including signaling by the child, interpreting by the mother, and responding by both.

Bonding

24. Within a critical period immediately after birth, the infant serves as a stimulus for maternal behavior, and through a series of reciprocal interactions the formation of affectional ties begins.

25. Social bonding takes place between infant and father also.

Adoptive Parents

26. The physical, mental, and psychological preparation of adoptive parents for parenthood increases the likelihood that affective bonds will form with the adoptive child.

A New View of Development

27. In the interactionists' view, the infant is a competent, decision-making, goal-oriented human being, and development is the result of a complex interaction between the child and its physical, social, and psychological environments.

Words to Know

acuity	peripheral
bonding	personality
innate	temperament
neonate	perception

Terms to Define

central vision
neonatal period
peripheral vision
sensory perception
states of consciousness

Concept to Discuss

interaction in development

CHAPTER 2

Genetics

Have you ever wondered

> what is inherited?
>
> how heredity controls characteristics?
>
> if your parents could have had another child exactly like you?
>
> if all the available genetic information is used?
>
> how the genetic code works?
>
> how traits are inherited?
>
> if genetic defects can be corrected?
>
> what the biological revolution and recombinant DNA are?

In looking at the collection of chemicals that comprises the human body, we do not find anything unusual or exotic. The basic chemicals of living organisms are carbon and hydrogen, with occasional additions of other elements. The net worth of the chemical composition of the human body has been estimated at only a few dollars. If the uniqueness of life does not lie in its materials, then it must lie in the arrangement of these materials.

The general theory of the beginning of life on this planet reasons that life first occurred in the great oceans that covered the earth in Precambrian times. The atmosphere at that time is believed to have consisted primarily of ammonia (NH_3: nitrogen and hydrogen) and methane gas (CH_4: carbon and hydrogen). All of the chemical elements necessary for life floated within the great seas and bumped against each other. Obeying the laws of chemistry, elements joined by chance and created molecules of various kinds. Scientists hypothesize that, at the beginning of life, a great electrical storm raged across the ancient oceans, and bolt after bolt of powerful lightning struck the silent seas. Finally, by some chance occurrence, the force of the electrical charges brought those molecules into a special arrangement, creating organic molecules from inorganic ones. As in Mary Shelley's *Frankenstein*, then, life was instigated by a surge of electricity. Thus, our journey began billions of years ago, in that first movement in the Precambrian seas. An unbroken chain extends from that beginning down to the present with you and me.

Slowly, through the process of trial and error, the first living molecules evolved a blueprint for duplicating themselves, ensuring the continuation of their kind after individual disintegration. The significance of life beginning in that Precambrian era is that *all* living organisms, whether plant, human, or bacteria, contain the same basic molecule that is the blueprint of hereditary information. More importantly, this blueprint, in the form of chemical molecules, is passed intact from parent to child. It is the unbroken chain of which we are all a part. The molecule varies in structure from species to species, but it is always deoxyribonucleic acid, or *DNA*.

Mendel and the First Studies of Heredity

Gregor Mendel conducted the first studies of genetics in the mid-nineteenth century. He was the son of a farmer in Austria, and as a young man joined a religious order because it was the only way he could obtain an education. Upon completing his education he was assigned to an obscure monastery in Moravia. During his stay there he conducted plant experiments in the monastery garden. Mendel wanted to know how characteristics of parents were passed to their offspring. He selected the

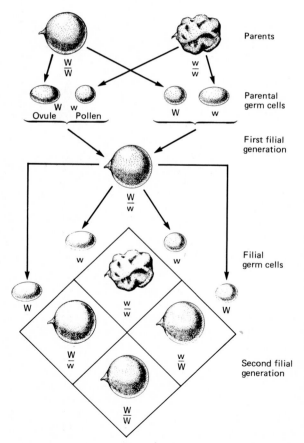

Mendel's genetic experiment with smooth and wrinkled peas. Beginning with pure strains of wrinkled and smooth peas, Mendel cross-pollinated them. *All* of the offspring of this cross were smooth peas; however, *all* of these carried a gene for wrinkled skin. When these peas were self-pollinated, some of the offspring had wrinkled skin, although all the parents had smooth skin. Through this experiment Mendel demonstrated the principle of dominant and recessive "hereditary factors." [From *Molecular Genetics: An Introductory Narrative*, 2nd edition, by Gunther S. Stent and Richard Calendar. Copyright © 1971, 1978 by W. H. Freeman and Company. All rights reserved.]

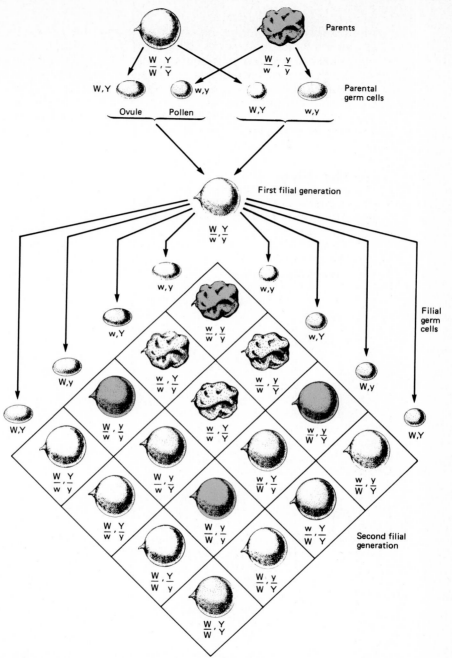

Mendel's experiment with smooth, yellow and wrinkled, green peas. This experiment began with pure strains of smooth, yellow and wrinkled, green peas. The offspring of these peas were all smooth-yellow but carried genes for wrinkled skin and green color. When these peas were self-pollinated new forms of peas appeared that were different from either parents or grandparents. For example, wrinkled-yellow peas and smooth-green peas. Through this experiment Mendel demonstrated that genetic components segregate and recombine in random order. [From *Molecular Genetics: An Introductory Narrative,* 2nd edition, by Gunther S. Stent and Richard Calendar. Copyright © 1971, 1978 by W. H. Freeman and Company. All rights reserved.]

common garden pea for his experiments. This pea has several varieties with different characteristics. In some the color varies, in others the skin of the seed is smooth or wrinkled. The theory of inheritance most widely believed in Mendel's day was that characteristics of children were a result of a mixture of parental characteristics. Thus, if a red and a white pea were crossed, the expected result would be pink. That is not what happened, however, when Mendel crossed the peas. Mendel did not find a blending of characteristics from both parents, but rather that some of the characteristics disappeared altogether in the first generation only to reappear, intact, in successive generations. Given the state of scientific knowledge in the 1850s, to Gregor Mendel this was a peculiar but provocative occurrence. He set about to discover the laws governing inheritance.

Mendel reached several conclusions about heredity. His basic conclusion was that *hereditary factors* were passed from parent to child and that those factors were responsible for transmitting traits. The word *gene* was not yet coined. It appeared in 1909 in the work of a biologist named Wilhelm Johannsen. Hereditary factors, according to Mendel, occurred in pairs, with each parent contributing one member of each pair. In addition, the factors were passed along unchanged from one generation to another. Mendel also discovered that when parents possessed different characteristics (such as yellow and green color) the characteristics appeared in offspring in a regular mathematical ratio, consistently 3 : 1. To explain this occurrence, Mendel theorized that the hereditary trait that appeared three times out of four was *dominant* and the trait that appeared once in four was *recessive*.

Mendel presented his findings to a scientific meeting in 1865 and the following year published them in a paper entitled ''Experiments on Plant Hybrids.'' Although his findings were quite new and, as we now see, had great implications, little note was taken of them at that time. It was not until 1900 that several scientists independently rediscovered Mendel's research, published some thirty-five years previously. In the years since 1900, tremendous advances have been made in our understanding of heredity. This understanding is built on Mendel's work with simple peas (Stent & Calendar, 1978).

Genes and Chromosomes

Genes, as we now call Mendel's hereditary factors, are the smallest discrete units of heredity. Thousands of these genes are grouped in long strands like beads on a string. These strings of genes are called *chromosomes*. It has been estimated that there are between 10,000 and 40,000 genes on each chromosome. Human beings possess 23 pairs (46 single) of chromosomes and between a quarter of a million and a million genes. These chromosomes are repositories of vast amounts of information. This genetic information contains directions for every detail of our physical appearance, such as hair and eye color; every detail of our chemical functioning, such as the production of hormones and enzymes as well as metabolic processes; and many psychological and behavioral characteristics, such as perception, mental ability, and perhaps to some extent personality. This genetic information has a built-in time clock and regulates development and growth according to the passage of time. It has been estimated that if all the genetic information contained in the chromosomes were to be written in words, there would be enough information to fill volumes equal in number to the *Encyclopedia Britannica* (Munsinger, 1975). However, the genetic code is so compact that it is contained within the nucleus of each cell of the body.

Every cell in the body contains *all* of the genetic blueprint for the development of the individual. Of course much of this information is ignored by particular cells. For example, cells in the eye select information that directs making blue or brown eyes and constructing "eye" cells and ignore instructions for constructing hair or toes. Cells in the toe "turn on" to genetic information that instructs how to make toes. One of the unanswered questions in genetics is how specific cells select the correct genetic information and ignore the vast amount of irrelevant information. Another unanswered question is how cells are "time coded"—that is, how they ignore information for years and, at a genetically determined time, turn on to information. Huntington's Chorea is an example of a genetic disorder that occurs at midlife. Female cycles of menstruation and menopause are other examples of time-dependent genetically controlled functions.

The chromosomes in each pair are not identical, as a pair of shoes might be. Each of the chromosomes in a pair contains information *about* the same thing, but the *content* itself may be different. For example, an individual has two sets of directions for eyes. One set of directions may order blue eyes and the other may order brown eyes. The reason that the two sets of information may differ is that one member of each pair is contributed by the father (who may have passed information for blue eyes) and one is contributed by the mother (who may have passed information for brown eyes). Genetic information is passed, as Mendel found, intact in the discrete units of genes from parents to offspring. Note that the intact transmission is of genes and not of whole chromosomes. In the formation of sperm and ovum (sex cells) each of the 10,000 to 40,000 genes on a chromosome assumes an independent position and has an equal chance of being passed to an offspring. There is such a vast amount of genetic information that the particular combination that makes up an individual is, indeed, astronomical. Truly, we have cause to celebrate the biological uniqueness of each of us.

There is one case, however, in which two individuals receive identical genetic material. In the case of identical twins, conception begins with a single egg fertilized by a single sperm, but early in the process of cell division the cell divides to become two separate individuals with identical heredity.

Karyotype

Chromosomes can actually be seen in the microscopic examination of any cell of the body. In addition, they can be photographed. Pictures reveal the chromosomes packed in random order in the nucleus of a cell. Each pair is attached in the center and resembles a starfish with four "arms." These representations of the chromosomes can be sorted and arranged by size. They are then assigned a number from one to 23. A picture of these size-graded chromosomes is called a *karyotype*. An examination of them can reveal damage or an abnormal arrangement of genetic material. We do not have full knowledge of the mapping of these chromosomes but we do know, for example, that sex is controlled by chromosome 23 and that Down's Syndrome is controlled by chromosome 21. Because a karyotype can be extracted by examining any cell, a karyotype of a fetus can be constructed early in pregnancy. The fluid surrounding the fetus contains cells it has sloughed off. Each of those cells contains full genetic information for the developing fetus, and from any one of them a karyotype can be prepared. Through a karyotype parents can know the sex of the fetus, whether the child will be subject to many genetic disorders, and other valuable genetic information. Our knowledge of gene mapping is increasing rapidly, and an examination of the physical arrangement of the chromosomes can tell us much.

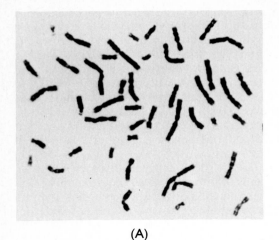

(A)

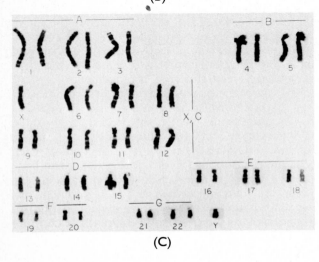

(B)

(C)

An actual photograph of the chromosomes in a human cell (A). These chromosomes were photographed through a powerful microscope. Note that they are different sizes and configurations and that each chromosome pair has a constriction near the middle that results in four "arms." These chromosomes came from a female and every cell in her body contains the identical 46 chromosomes, except egg cells. In (B), the same chromosomes have been cut apart and arranged in groups by similarity of size. Note that there are two X chromosomes, which dictate female development. The photograph at (C) is a karyotype from a normal male. Note that there is only one X and one Y. The Y is the smallest of the chromosomes. Both of these individuals are genetically normal. If one of them had Down's Syndrome, there would have been three number 21 chromosomes. [Photographs courtesy Cytogenetics Laboratory, Department of Pathology, Moses Cone Hospital, Greensboro, North Carolina; Joan Hall, M. A., Cytogenetic Specialist.]

Single-Gene and Polygene Control

Students of human development are interested in characteristics and behaviors of the child and in discovering their cause and control. Let us look further at the role of genes in the determination of traits. Geneticists are making rapid progress in identifying the exact genetic material that exerts control over characteristics, while social scientists are attempting to determine the extent of the control of genes over characteristics. This mapping is complicated by the fact that some characteristics are determined by one gene and some by many. We know, for example, that sex designation is determined by chromosome 23, and we understand fairly well how the mechanism works. We can examine the chromosomes of any person and determine his or her genetic sex. The determination of biological sex is under total genetic control. Other aspects of development, however, such as mental ability, are not under total genetic control. In addition, the genetic influence that is exerted is from a combination of many different genes (polygene) and not a single one. The amount of genetic control exerted on a trait is the *heritability* of that trait. In traits such as sex determination, the heritability estimate is easy: heritability is 100 per cent. In other areas, such as mental ability, however, estimating heritability becomes quite difficult. The heritability estimate of mental ability has varied among researchers from a high of 80 per cent to a low of 20 per cent. The remaining percentages, of course, are accounted for by environmental influences. Many traits are the results of a combination of environment and heredity. Such traits are more diverse in the general population, as the environment can serve either to suppress or be a fertile ground for the full development of genetic potential. In general, traits controlled by single genes are less susceptible to environmental modification than those traits that are under the control of many different genes. Traits such as physical structure are species specific. That is, all members of the species have the same characteristics: for example, two arms, legs, and eyes and one nose. Other traits, such as personality and intelligence, are highly variable. Species-specific characteristics are least susceptible to modification by environmental factors and more rigidly under genetic control; those traits that are highly individual are most susceptible to environmental modification. Thus, we find that different characteristics have different regulatory mechanisms.

Phenotype and Genotype

Not all genetic information received by an individual from both parents is used. The entire genetic information that an individual carries is known as the *genotype*. This is the gene pool from which future generations of individuals are drawn. Genetic information is actual material in the form of DNA present in the first fertilized cell. This actual material is transmitted unchanged from parent to child. It is the combination that changes from generation to generation, not the actual material. In rare mutations it is possible for the actual material to change. The genetic information that finds expression in the physical makeup and functioning of the individual is known as the *phenotype*.

Thus, each individual carries two sets of genetic information for each characteristic under hereditary control. One set of instructions comes from the father and one set comes from the mother. This information may be the same or it may be different. If the genes are the same, then the individual is said to be *homozygous* (*homo* means "same") for that trait. If the genes are different, the individual is *heterozygous* for that trait (*hetero* means "different").

Let us look more closely at these interrelated concepts of genotype/phenotype and homozygous/heterozygous. To keep things simple, consider eye color. Eye color is a trait determined by heredity. The phenotype is the actual color of an individual's eyes, or the genes that are expressed. The genotype comprises the total genes that a person has for eye color, both expressed and carried. Because each individual has two genes for each characteristic, to simply say that he or she has brown or blue eyes does not tell the full genetic story. To know the true genetic potential of the individual, we must know not only the expressed genes, but also those unexpressed genes, or the genotype. In genetic counseling the identification of these genes becomes very important, as they may carry genetic defects of which the individual is unaware.

DNA: Deoxyribonucleic Acid and the Genetic Code

One of the most important contributions to genetic research in this century was the discovery by James Watson and Francis Crick of the physical structure of genetic material. It led to the ability to break the genetic code. What does breaking the genetic code mean?

Scientists had long been perplexed about how information is transmitted to individual cells to make red hair, blue eyes, black skin, or—in a negative sense—diabetes or a defective brain. There had to be some intelligible language that was "read" by the individual cells of the body and executed according to directions. The search for the key to this language was spurred by the obvious implication that if this language could be understood new messages could be written.

The search for the key to this biological language was similar to the effort that archaeologists made in the early part of the century for the key to understanding ancient Egyptian hieroglyphic writing. The key to deciphering this strange language was the Rosetta Stone, which contained a proclamation in three languages, one of which was hieroglyphics. It took many scholars many years to interpret their key, which ultimately revealed the culture of the ancient Egyptian pyramid builders. Suddenly a whole period of ancient history, of which we had had only a glimpse, was open to us. With equal fervor our scientists sought to break the genetic code in order to read and interpret the basic message of life.

The early twentieth century was a time of great optimism, of discoveries, and of belief in the solution to all human problems through science. It was also a time in which an interest in genetics was reawakened. The first task in solving the puzzle of the genetic code was to determine exactly what in the cell constituted the genetic material. There were several theories. Finally, evidence settled on that mass in the nucleus of each cell known as deoxyribonucleic acid (DNA). Genetic research was at a stalemate in understanding exactly how the genetic code worked until Watson and Crick put together many isolated pieces of information and saw the structure of DNA and the mechanism of transmission.* The design of this molecule is very simple and very elegant. It is known as the double helix.

Because a helix is a spiral form, the double helix can be envisioned as a spiral staircase. The sides consist of alternating molecules of sugar and phosphate. The steps of the staircase are composed of molecules of four nitrogenous bases. These bases are called adenine (A), thymine (T), guanine (G) and cytosine (C). Each step

---

* For an exciting account of this discovery, see J. D. Watson, *The Double Helix: A Personal Account of The Discovery of The Structure of DNA*, Gunther S. Stent (Ed.). New York: W. W. Norton, 1980.

has two of these bases. Chemically, adenine (A) will only combine with thymine (T). Guanine (G) will only combine with cytosine (C). This simple rule dictates the mechanism for the genetic code. The sugar-phosphate chain forms the backbone of the DNA molecule. In the process of cell duplication, the double helix breaks apart where the two bases join. Essentially it is similar to a zipper unzipping. When the two sides become separated, the bases remain attached to different sides of the sugar-phosphate backbone, as the two sets of teeth on the sides of a separated zipper. These attached bases of adenine, thymine, guanine, and cytosine then join

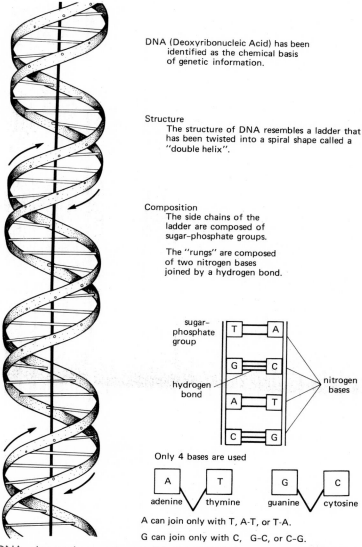

DNA (Deoxyribonucleic Acid) has been identified as the chemical basis of genetic information.

Structure

The structure of DNA resembles a ladder that has been twisted into a spiral shape called a "double helix".

Composition

The side chains of the ladder are composed of sugar–phosphate groups.

The "rungs" are composed of two nitrogen bases joined by a hydrogen bond.

sugar–phosphate group

hydrogen bond

nitrogen bases

Only 4 bases are used

A adenine   T thymine   G guanine   C cytosine

A can join only with T, A-T, or T-A.

G can join only with C, G-C, or C-G.

DNA—key to the genetic code. [Model of DNA from *Molecular Genetics: An Introductory Narrative*, 2nd edition, by Gunther S. Stent and Richard Calendar. Copyright © 1971, 1978 by W. H. Freeman and Company. All rights reserved.]

with molecules of free bases floating in the cell fluid according to the rule of combination described here. Because each base can only combine with one other base, each helix rebuilds the missing side and becomes two double helices, identical to the one before the unzipping. Thus, the genetic code that was created at conception is duplicated in each cell division throughout the lifetime of the individual. This ability to unzip is also the mechanism for transmitting instructions to the cell.

Long strands of DNA are chromosomes. These are extremely long molecules consisting of double strands twisted around each other in a very compact manner. What we designate as genes are segments of this strand. Genes, as stated, are discrete units of heredity. This genetic information is coded as sequences of nitrogenous bases (adenine, thymine, guanine, and cytosine) on the DNA molecule. A single gene, or discrete genetic message, may consist of a few hundred or thousands of these bases in a given sequence.

Mechanisms of Heredity

Geneticists have identified three ways in which inheritance functions. These are dominant, recessive and sex-linked inheritance. Each of these has a different pattern and different probability of expression in the phenotype. Let us look at these patterns.

Dominant and Recessive Genes

One of the interesting facts about genes and genetic information is that all genes do not have an equal chance of expression. Mendel discovered that some characteristics appeared three times as often as others. This ratio of 3 : 1 was consistent. He concluded that some genes were *dominant* and some *recessive*. Obviously, if the genetic blueprint for a new individual consisted of conflicting information from the two parents, there must be some way for one information package to take precedence. For example, we have already established that genetic endowment is not a blend from two parents. What then happens when a new individual receives directions to grow "tall" from the mother and information to grow "short" from the father?

There must be a consistent method for the cell to use one piece of information and to ignore the other. The method is a set of rules for dominant and recessive inheritance. We do not know exactly how this mechanism works, but we do know some of the rules. Inheritance is governed by mathematical probability. Probability theory has been worked out in great detail by modern mathematicians. According to probability theory, either of the two events has an equal chance of occurring in any given trial. The prototype of this principle can be seen in the toss of a coin. A coin has two sides, a head and a tail. On any given toss of a coin, the chance is 50–50 that either the head or the tail will be visible. Any event that is completely controlled by chance factors cannot be biased by the will of the person instigating the event. (This is the reasoning behind lotteries and games of chance.)

Let us apply this principle to the inheritance of characteristics. Imagine that any given gene may occur as a head or as a tail. The head is dominant over the tail and thus will be expressed in the phenotype. (We will indicate this by using a capital H.) In every toss, Head or tail has an equal chance of occurring. Now imagine that two coins are tossed at the same time. If each coin has an equal chance of being Head or tail, there are four possibilities for their occurrence. The possibilities are that both coins can be Heads; the first coin can be Heads and the second tails;

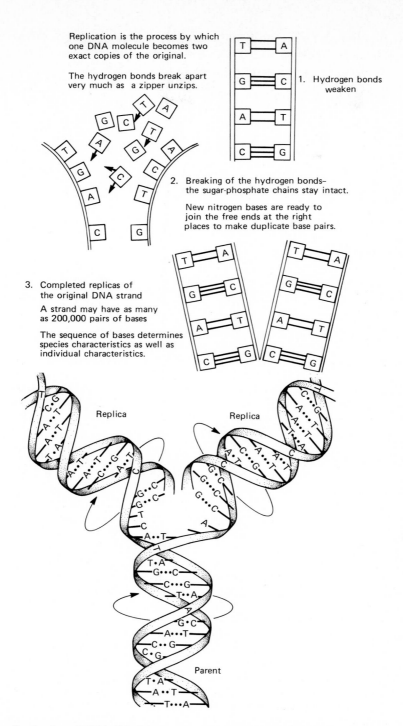

Replication is the process by which one DNA molecule becomes two exact copies of the original.

The hydrogen bonds break apart very much as a zipper unzips.

1. Hydrogen bonds weaken

2. Breaking of the hydrogen bonds–the sugar-phosphate chains stay intact.

New nitrogen bases are ready to join the free ends at the right places to make duplicate base pairs.

3. Completed replicas of the original DNA strand

A strand may have as many as 200,000 pairs of bases

The sequence of bases determines species characteristics as well as individual characteristics.

Replica   Replica

Parent

Replication of DNA. [Model of DNA replicating from G. S. Stent, *Molecular Biology of Bacterial Virus*, W. H. Freeman and Company, © 1963.]

the first tails and the second Heads; or both can be tails. This distribution is represented by the following.

HH Ht tH tt

Let us superimpose the idea of dominant and recessive genes on this chance distribution. Assume that these coins represent inherited characteristics, with Heads dominant over tails. For a dominant trait (Heads) to be expressed, it need only occur once (heterozygous), but for the recessive trait (tails) to be expressed, it must occur twice (homozygous). Thus, out of four tosses, we will have the characteristic represented by Heads expressed in the individual in three cases (one homozygous and two heterozygous), while the characteristic of tails will be expressed in only one case, even though three of the cases carry the gene for this trait.

Dominant Inheritance

A hereditary trait that is dominant will be expressed in the phenotype of the individual with only one gene for that trait. Remember, an individual carries two genes for each trait; thus, a child has an equal chance of receiving any two of the four genes carried by the parents. In the process of forming sex cells, there is an equal chance that either of the parents' genes will enter into any given sex cell. When the 23 chromosomes in the sex cells unite as egg and sperm, the result is an entirely new combination of 46 chromosomes.

In dominant inheritance if an individual has one dominant gene for a trait, that trait is expressed. The trait appears in each successive generation or is lost. Each child has a 50 per cent chance of receiving the dominant gene, and the odds are the same with *each* conception. As in playing cards, the odds are against drawing all four aces, but it does happen. It could happen that every child in a family receives the dominant gene and the trait. For a dominant trait to be expressed, it is only necessary for the individual to possess that single gene. The individual may be either homozygous or heterozygous for that trait.

Recessive Inheritance

The second pattern of inheritance is recessive inheritance. In this pattern the individual must receive *two* genes for a trait, one from each parent. The trait is not necessarily expressed in either parent. Thus, recessive inheritance is susceptible to being a hidden trait (one that a parent does not know that he or she carries) and is only expressed when the mate also carries the hidden (recessive) gene.

The chances of any child expressing the trait is 25 per cent, or one in four; the chances of being a carrier but not expressing the trait are 50 per cent, or two in four; and the chances of neither carrying nor expressing the trait are 25 per cent, or one in four. Thus, seventy-five per cent of offspring can be expected not to show the trait, while twenty-five per cent will show it. This ratio of 3 : 1 is the same that Mendel found for his garden peas.

Recessive inheritance is especially troublesome in the case of genetic defects, for parents are often shocked to discover that their child is afflicted when they are both normal. This is especially true in cases where the defect causes early death. Children may have died in previous generations and the cause forgotten. Genetic counseling seeks to help parents plot their genetic potential.

An example of dominant and recessive inheritance can be illustrated through eye color. This becomes more than an academic question for some people. Imagine that you write an advice column and receive the following letter:

Dear Advisor,

My brother and his wife have just had their first baby. Both my brother and his wife have brown eyes, but the baby has beautiful light-blue eyes. My brother is convinced that this baby could not possibly be his and is making life miserable for his wife. He insists that she tell him who is the father. His wife insists that it is possible for them to have a blue-eyed baby. Please settle this argument.

What is the answer to this letter? We know that brown eye color is dominant over blue. We know that the phenotype of both parents is for brown eyes. What we do not know is the genotype of these parents. The answer to the question, "Is it possible for two brown-eyed parents to have a blue-eyed child?" is, "It depends."

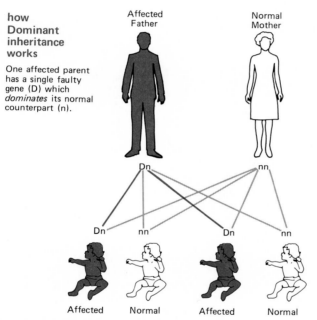

how Dominant inheritance works

One affected parent has a single faulty gene (D) which *dominates* its normal counterpart (n).

Affected Father

Normal Mother

Dn   nn

Dn   nn   Dn   nn

Affected   Normal   Affected   Normal

Each child's chances of inheriting either the D or the n from the affected parent are 50%.

a common mistake

When risks are stated in percentages or fractions, parents unfamiliar with genetic mechanisms often interpret them incorrectly.

For example, those with one child affected by a disorder due to recessive inheritance may think that a 25 per cent-or one-in-four-risk means that the next three offspring are not endangered. *This is not true.*

The risk of genetic disease is the same for every child of the same mother and father.

How dominant inheritance works. [From *Genetic Counseling*. Copyright © 1980 by March of Dimes Birth Defects Foundation, White Plains, New York. Reprinted by permission.]

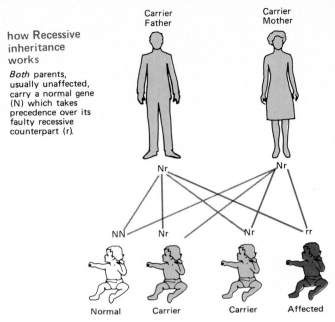

how Recessive
inheritance
works

Both parents,
usually unaffected,
carry a normal gene
(N) which takes
precedence over its
faulty recessive
counterpart (r).

Carrier
Father

Carrier
Mother

Nr   Nr

NN   Nr   Nr   rr

Normal   Carrier   Carrier   Affected

The odds for each child are:
1. a 25% risk of inheriting a "double dose" of r genes
   which may cause a serious birth defect
2. a 25% chance of inheriting two Ns, thus being unaffected
3. a 50% chance of being a carrier as both parents are

How recessive inheritance works. [From *Genetic Counseling.* Copyright © 1980 by March of Dimes Birth Defects Foundation, White Plains, New York. Reprinted by permission.]

It depends on the genotype; that is, on the unseen genes of the parents: those genes that are carried but not necessarily expressed. Let us use our knowledge of Mendelian inheritance to work out this problem. Let us begin with the grandparents. Assume that we have two parents who are homozygous, one for brown eyes and one for blue eyes. In mating, each of their children would receive one gene from each parent, resulting in each child receiving the heterozygous condition of Br bl. We can diagram this as follows:

BrBr   blbl
Brbl   Brbl   blBr   blBr

In this case each child would have brown eyes but would carry a recessive gene for blue eyes. There is no other possibility for the genotype of the offspring. Because each parent has two identical genes and one must go to any offspring, one parent can only give a brown gene and the other only a blue one. Each child of these parents would have brown eyes but would carry a recessive gene for blue eyes. We know that our distraught letter is referring to a couple who both have brown eyes. In addition, let us assume that all the siblings of both the husband and wife have brown eyes. Thus, we might find two entire families of brown-eyed people but with a parent or grandparent with blue eyes.

Each individual has }
two genetic aspects }

1. Phenotype: the characteristics the individual
   displays or possesses (blue eyes, curly hair)

2. Genotype: the genetic potential of the individual
   which is inherited from parents and part of
   which will be passed on unchanged to children

Genes May Be

DOMINANT   RECESSIVE

An individual has a gene or genes
giving information from each parent.
If these directions conflict, one bit of
information may have dominance over another.

A trait may pass through several
generations and not be evident in a
phenotype (blue eyes). It will become
evident when two recessive genes for
blue eyes occur in an individual.

PATTERN of DOMINANCE IN EYE COLOR

The laws of heredity state dominance patterns

Brown eyes: Dominant

Blue eyes: Recessive

phenotype (characteristics of
    individual)
genotype (genetic potential
    individual carries)

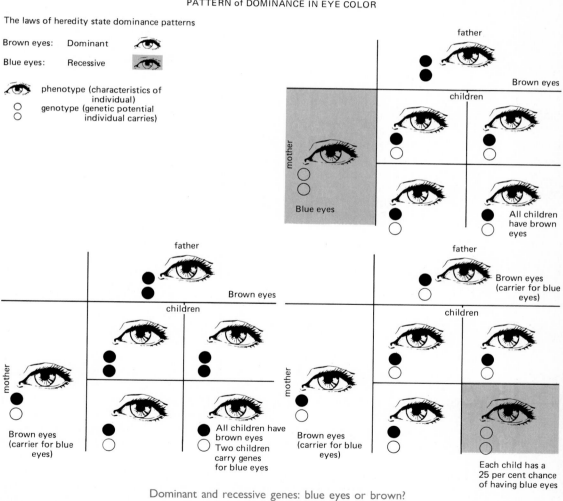

Dominant and recessive genes: blue eyes or brown?

Each of the parents, however, is heterozygous for eye color. That is, each carries a dominant gene for brown eyes and a recessive gene for blue eyes. What happens when they have children? The following diagram illustrates the expected color of their children's eyes:

	Brbl			Brbl	
BrBr	Brbl		blBr	blbl	
brown	brown		brown	blue	

As you see, out of four children, probability theory suggests that one will have blue eyes, even though neither of the parents nor any of the aunts and uncles has blue eyes. However, there must have been an ancestor with blue eyes on *both* sides for the trait to appear. Most likely it would have been a grandparent, but it could have been a great grandparent. Although we state that the chances are that one in four children will have blue eyes, this does not mean that in every four children one will have blue eyes. What it does mean is that each child will have a one-in-four chance of showing blue eyes or, stated differently, the probability of brown eyes is 3 : 1. In a large number of cases, three fourths of the offspring will have brown eyes and one fourth will have blue eyes. These ratios may vary in individual families, but in an entire population they hold. We can, then, reply to the letter that it is indeed possible for brown-eyed parents to have a blue-eyed child. If both parents can find a blue-eyed ancestor, they may happily accept the child as true progeny.

Sex-Linked Inheritance
A third pattern of inheritance involves those traits that are located on chromosome number 23. This is the chromosome that determines the sex of the individual. In the determination of a male, the twenty-third chromosome pair consists of two different chromosomes, an X from the mother and a Y from the father. These chromosomes are not identical. The Y is much smaller than the X and carries less information. We can think of sex-linked inheritance as a special case of recessive inheritance. The female carries two X chromosomes—let us think of one as dominant and one as recessive. She, then, will not express the recessive trait. Each of her children has a 50 per cent chance of receiving either the dominant X or the recessive X.

In the case of her male children, the 50 per cent who receive the dominant X will not express the trait. In normal recessive inheritance, it requires two genes for a trait to be expressed, but we postulate a different mechanism in sex-linked characteristics. Remember, in the male, sex is determined by the XY combination. Because, apparently, the Y contains less information, it has no counterinformation for the recessive gene from the X chromosome; thus, the recessive gene from the mother is expressed in the son. In the case of female children, again 50 per cent receive the dominant X and 50 per cent the recessive X. Each of these is combined with another X from the father. If he does not express the trait, the daughter receives a dominant (normal) gene from the father. Thus, females usually receive two dominant X chromosomes or one dominant and one recessive chromosome. In the first event she could not possibly express the recessive trait, as it is not in her genotype. In the second event she expresses the dominant trait and carries the recessive one. In the next generation half the sons of a daughter who carries the defective gene may possess the trait and half of her daughters may pass the trait to half of their sons.

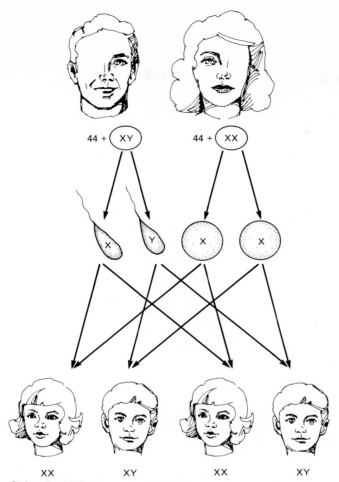

Girl or Boy? Whether an individual is male or female is determined at conception. Females carry two XX chromosomes and males carry one X and one Y. All children receive one X from the mother and have an equal chance of receiving either an X or a Y chromosome from the father. Thus, each individual has a 50–50 chance of being female or male and this is determined by the father. In actual fact, however, more males are conceived than females. The reason for this is not entirely clear.

Genetic Defects

The genetic information carried by an individual usually contains instructions for a perfectly normal, functioning person. However, in about 7 per cent of births, some defect is present. Not all these defects are the result of faulty genes. Defects may be inherited or they may be the result of environmental factors during prenatal development. Let us concentrate on those defects resulting from genetic information.

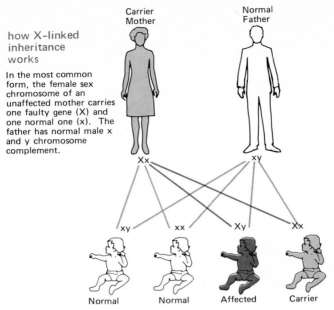

how X-linked
inheritance
works

In the most common
form, the female sex
chromosome of an
unaffected mother carries
one faulty gene (X) and
one normal one (x). The
father has normal male x
and y chromosome
complement.

The odds for each male child are 50/50:
1. 50% risk of inheriting the faulty X and the disorder
2. 50% chance of inheriting the normal x and y chromosomes
For each female child, the odds are:
1. 50% risk of inheriting one faulty X, to be a carrier like mother
2. 50% chance of inheriting no faulty gene

How X-linked inheritance works. [From *Genetic Counseling.* Copyright © 1980 by March of Dimes Birth Defects Foundation, White Plains, New York. Reprinted by permission.]

Some of them, although present at birth, do not become apparent until months or years later.

At present there are 2,811 cataloged inherited disorders. (National March of Dimes Birth Defects Foundation, 1980). Of these, 1,489 are dominantly inherited disorders, 1,117 are recessively inherited disorders, and 205 are sex linked. In addition, there is an unknown number of disorders that are multifactorial—that is, caused by many factors. Genetic defects may be minor, such as attached earlobes, or serious, such as Tay-Sachs disease, which causes death in the preschool years. Genetic defects may result also from chromosomal abnormalities such as extra chromosomes, translocation of genetic material from one chromosome to another, and mistakes in cell division.

Genetic defects resulting from dominant genes include

1. Achondroplasia: a form of dwarfism.
2. Chronic simple glaucoma (some forms): a major cause of blindness if untreated.
3. Huntington's Chorea: progressive degeneration of the nervous system.
4. Hypercholesterolemia: high blood-cholesterol levels, propensity to heart disease.
5. Polydactyly: extra fingers or toes.

Genetic defects resulting from recessive genes include

1. Cystic fibrosis: disorder affecting the function of mucus and sweat glands.
2. Galactosemia: inability to metabolize milk sugar.
3. Phenylketonuria (PKU): essential liver-enzyme deficiency resulting in inability to metabolize protein (milk).
4. Sickle cell anemia: blood disorder primarily affecting blacks.
5. Thalassemia: blood disorder primarily affecting persons of Mediterranean ancestry.
6. Tay-Sachs disease: fatal brain damage primarily affecting infants of East European Jewish ancestry.

Sex-linked genetic defects include

1. Gammaglobulinemia: lack of immunity to infections.
2. Color blindness: inability to distinguish certain colors.
3. Hemophilia: defects in blood-clotting mechanisms.
4. Muscular dystrophy (some forms): progressive wasting of muscles.
5. Spinal ataxia (some forms): spinal cord degeneration.

In addition to dominant, recessive, and sex-linked patterns of inheritance, there is a sizable number of defects that result from the interaction of many genes with other genes or with environmental factors. The probability of this type of inheritance is lower than for the other three types. With one affected child in the family, the chances of another having the same defect are 5 per cent or less, whereas with the other patterns of inheritance the chances do not change with subsequent children. The number of defects from multifactorial inheritance has not been catalogued, but some defects that are thought to be multifactorial are

1. Cleft lip and/or palate.
2. Clubfoot.
3. Congenital dislocation of the hip.
4. Spina bifida: open spine.
5. Hydrocephalus (with spina bifida): water on the brain.
6. Pyloric stenosis: narrowed or obstructed opening from the stomach into the small intestine.

Down's Syndrome

Down's Syndrome is a condition that occurs approximately once in every 700 births (Apgar & Beck, 1973). The cause is an overabundance of chromosome 21 and the effects are predictable and recognizable. Children with Down's Syndrome have similar physical characteristics, regardless of their familial inheritance. They have short limbs and fingers, an enlarged, protruding tongue, and slanted eyes. (This is the reason that the disorder is erroneously referred to as mongolism.) Their facial features and the back of the head are flattened. At birth, their muscle tone is weak and their muscles are soft. Moderate to severe mental retardation usually accompanies the disorder. Some children, however, can be taught to an eighth-grade level or higher. For that reason careful evaluation of a child with Down's Syndrome is important.

Many children with this defect have congenital heart defects, and leukemia is twenty times more frequent than in normal children (March of Dimes, 1980). Down's Syndrome is much more likely to occur in the children of older mothers. The risk of delivering a child with Down's Syndrome is 1 in 2,000 for twenty-five-year-old mothers, 1 in 100 for forty-year-old mothers, and 1 in 40 for forty-five-year-old mothers.

There are three possible conditions that can cause this disorder. In the first, chromosome 21 fails to separate during the formation of the sperm or egg. Thus, an egg or sperm may contain 22 single chromosomes and a pair of number 21 chromosomes. When this sex cell is fertilized, the total number of chromosomes is 47, with three number 21 chromosomes. This condition is known as Trisomy 21 and is the most common cause of Down's Syndrome.

A second condition may result in the usual number of 46 chromosomes, but chromosome number 15 may be unusually large because of translocation of material from chromosome 21. This condition can be carried genetically and transmitted from either parent, although this type of familial disorder is rare. In translocation of material, the chromosome count is normal, 46, but the content is an added amount of 21 material, which causes the same effect as Trisomy 21.

A third type of Down's Syndrome is called mosaicism. It is the result of an error in division of an early embryonic cell. Each developing cell duplicates the genetic material and then divides into two cells. In mosaicism the first cell division is normal. The genetic material duplicates and the cell separates normally. In the second division, however, one cell divides normally but the other, after duplicating all the chromosomes, divides chromosome 21 into one and three. In this case, three chromosomes go into one cell and one goes into the other. Therefore, in this generation there are four cells: two contain 46 chromosomes, one contains 47 chromosomes, and one contains 45 chromosomes. The cell with the 45 chromosomes dies, but the one with 47 is viable and continues to divide. Thus, the individual has two populations of cells in his or her body. One population of cells contains 46 chromosomes and another population contains 47 chromosomes. These cells are interspersed in a mosaic pattern—thus the name. In this condition the symptoms of Down's Syndrome are present but less severe. Apparently the normal cells ameliorate the effects of the trisomy.

Chromosome 23

Several genetic defects have been associated with sex chromosomes. In males there may be extra Y or X chromosomes. In females there may be extra X chromosomes, or only one X.

Klinefelter's Syndrome (XXY)

Klinefelter's Syndrome is a condition in which the male has three number-23 chromosomes. These are designated XXY. Thus, he has an extra X chromosome. The result of this is a feminized male. Characteristics typically include development of female secondary sex characteristics at puberty, including breast enlargement and diminished male secondary sex characteristics, such as small testes. In addition, such behavioral characteristics as effeminacy, homosexuality, transvestism, and transsexualism may be present (Money & Pollett, 1964). The presence of these behaviors does not necessarily mean that they were caused by the extra chromosome, but it is possible that the feminized body predisposes the male to feminine behaviors. Males afflicted with this chromosomal abnormality have been treated with the male sex hormone *testosterone*. The addition of this hormone stimulates more masculine growth in the adolescent body and seems to stimulate more masculine behavior, such as assertiveness and increased sexual drive (Johnson, Myhre, Ruvalcaba, Thuline & Kelley, 1970).

XYY Syndrome

In the XYY Syndrome the individual is male and has an extra Y chromosome. These males are taller and more muscular than the average male. In addition, they exhibit growth early in adolescence that often is accompanied by severe acne. This syndrome is also associated with lowered intelligence. It has been discovered that men in prison are more likely to possess the abnormal XYY genetic makeup. Men with this abnormality are seven times more prevalent in prisons than in the general population (Telfer, Baker, Clark, & Richardson, 1968). This has led to speculation that the XYY Syndrome predisposes men to criminal activity. We must, however, consider an alternate hypothesis. It may be that these men are considered both by themselves and by others to be unattractive at adolescence and therefore become social isolates and drift into antisocial situations, including criminal activity. Their lowered intelligence perhaps compounds the difficulty of finding other means of solving problems and might also encourage exploitation by others. Certainly not all males with XYY chromosome counts engage in criminal activity. Nevertheless, the relationship between genes and behavior remains a topic of intense research interest.

Turner's Syndrome (XO)

Turner's Syndrome is a condition in which females have only one chromosome number 23. In this condition the chromosome count is 45, with only a single X present for the twenty-third chromosome. These individuals are short in stature and mentally retarded, with webbing in the neck. Their sexual characteristics are underdeveloped and their ovaries are almost completely nonfunctional. As with Klinefelter's Syndrome, therapy at puberty with the female hormone *estrogen* encourages more normal development but does not alleviate the condition.

XXX Syndrome

In the XXX Syndrome the female possesses an additional X chromosome. The results of this abnormality are, again, poorly developed sexual characteristics and lowered mental ability.

Genetic Counseling

John and Mary Robinson's first child seemed normal at birth but later he proved to be the victim of a serious birth defect. He became physically damaged and mentally retarded. The Robinsons did their best for him, but they yearned for a normal, healthy child. What to do? Did they dare risk another pregnancy that might have the same heartbreaking outcome? [National March of Dimes, 1980]

Each year about 250,000 parents find themselves with a child born with physical or mental defects. These birth defects are heartbreaking for parents. At present we do not have the knowledge to reprogram genes and change the genetic information that causes defects in infants. Genetic counseling, however, is a medical specialty that attempts to identify parents at risk of having a genetically defective child and to help them in decision making. These parents most often have already had the misfortune of a child born with a defect; increasingly they are couples who want to have a child but have relatives with genetic defects. In genetic counseling, a genetic history is compiled to find the incidence of defects in relatives and ancestors. The couple is then given the odds of producing a normal or a defective child. They then must decide whether to take the risk. No one can tell a couple that they should not take the risk, or that they should. The responsibility for such a decision is theirs alone. Genetic counseling is not limited to defects transmitted by genes. It is concerned with *all* factors that cause birth defects. Many defects are environmentally caused and others are the result of the interaction of heredity and environment.

The New Biology

We stated previously that we do not *as yet* have the ability to reprogram genetic information. One of the predictions for our "science fiction future" is that we will have the information necessary to change and reprogram defective genes. The first step, of course, is mapping the genes. That is, finding out exactly where on the chromosome a certain gene is located. Research in this field is proceeding rapidly in both human genes and those of other animals and organisms. Gene mapping is easier in simple organisms that have few chromosomes. One of the most important discoveries of the biological revolution has been the development of techniques for combining DNA from two different species to make a new form of life. This technology is called recombinant DNA. With recombinant DNA scientists are now able to create forms of life in their laboratories that the forces of nature may never have tried in combination. This, of course, presents the spectre of creating hideous new forms of malevolent life. It was the fear of the creation of just such "andromeda strains" that prompted Congress to enact laws that limit experimentation with life forms. Ethical laboratories all over the world adhere to these restrictions.

In 1980 the Supreme Court of the United States ruled that companies could patent new forms of life that were invented in their laboratories. It is the position of these writers that decisions about science cannot be left to professional scientists. Decisions concerning the use of technology, whether it is atomic energy or recombinant DNA, *must* be made by intelligent, informed lay people in concert with scientists. We have no choice but to educate the public about science so that they can make such decisions. Although we fear their destructive possibilities, let us look at the positive results of breaking the genetic code, of genetic engineering, and of applications of recombinant DNA.

Theoretically, once genes are mapped and it is known exactly where a genetic defect is located, any one of an infant's 2,811 defective genes could be replaced with a normal gene, and the child would not be afflicted. In addition, if we perfect gene splicing and genetic surgery the child might pass a normal gene on to its offspring, rather than a defective one. Scientists are already using this new technology to combat some genetic diseases. One of them is diabetes, a genetic disease in which the body does not have the genetic information to produce insulin. Insulin is necessary in the metabolism of sugar and starch. Synthetic insulin is difficult and expensive to produce, and using insulin from animals presents problems for human consumption. Using bacteria that have very few chromosomes, scientists have been able to splice a human gene containing the information for insulin production on to a bacteria strain. The bacteria have no use for the insulin and simply keep produc-

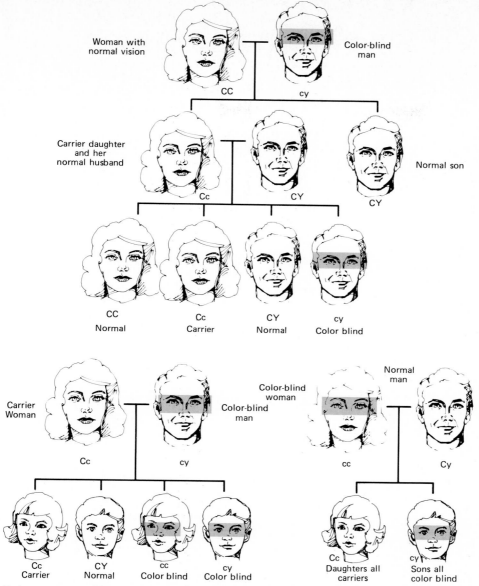

Woman with normal vision — CC
Color-blind man — cy

Carrier daughter and her normal husband — Cc
CY
Normal son — CY

CC Normal
Cc Carrier
CY Normal
cy Color blind

Carrier Woman — Cc
Color-blind man — cy

Color-blind woman — cc
Normal man — Cy

Cc Carrier
CY Normal
cc Color blind
cy Color blind

Cc Daughters all carriers
cy Sons all color blind

If the genotype of both parents is known, the probability of inheritance of a trait can be determined. Genetic counseling consists, in part, in establishing the probable heritability of traits. Through the history of genetic diseases in a family a genetic counselor can establish a probable genotype and predict the chances of affected children. This chart presents three possible patterns of inheritance of color blindness which is carried as a recessive trait on the X chromosome (sex-linked inheritance). The genotype notations are, C for normal vision; c for color blindness (both on the X chromosome) and y indicating the male chromosome with no gene for the trait. Pattern A: a color blind man and a normal woman. The grandsons of this couple have a 50 per cent probability of being color blind. The trait has been carried through daughters. Color blind men cannot pass the trait to their sons because they do not give their X chromosome to their sons. All the daughters of a color-blind man, however, will be carriers as they must receive his X chromosome. Pattern B: a carrier woman and a color-blind man. Half the daughters of this couple will be color-blind and half will be carriers: half the sons will be color-blind and half will be normal with no trait. Pattern C: a color-blind woman and a normal man. All the daughters will be carriers and all the sons will be color-blind. [From *Understanding Genetics* by Norman V. Rothwell. Copyright © 1976 by The Williams & Wilkins Company. Reprinted by permission of Oxford University Press, Inc.]

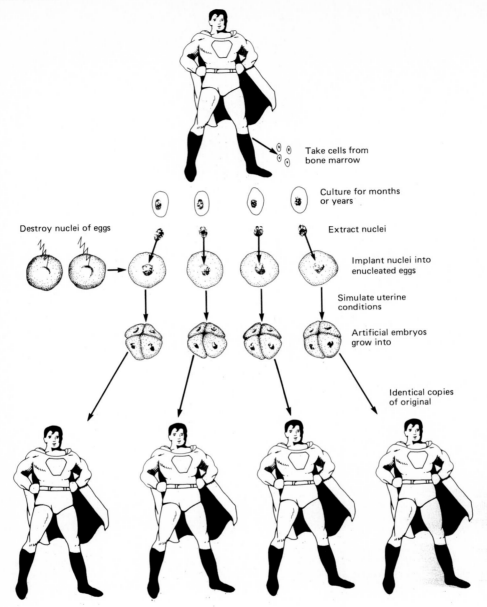

Take cells from
bone marrow

Culture for months
or years

Destroy nuclei of eggs

Extract nuclei

Implant nuclei into
enucleated eggs

Simulate uterine
conditions

Artificial embryos
grow into

Identical copies
of original

Hypothetical scheme for cloning in a human being. Since each cell contains complete information
for an individual, theoretically, an exact replica of the individual could be created with this information. Technology such as this and recombinant DNA have caused a controversy and an ethical
crisis. Who should control such information and how should it be used? [From *Understanding
Genetics* by Norman V. Rothwell. Copyright © 1976 by The Williams & Wilkins Company.
Reprinted by permission of Oxford University Press, Inc.]

ing and reproducing. In effect they are organic factories for producing insulin. The insulin is pure and can be harvested and used for treating diabetes. Scientists are now working on splicing this information onto a virus that then could be injected into a diabetic. The diabetic would have a "viral infection," the effect of which would be the production of insulin, and the diabetic would, in effect, be cured. As long as he or she had the viral infection, the needed insulin would be produced in his or her own body.

Let us look at another example. For many years, scientists have been searching for the cure to cancer. One promising lead in treating this disease is a substance called interferon, which is produced in minute quantities in the human body. The substance is so valuable that one gram of synthetic interferon costs $10 *trillion* dollars to produce. Scientists have now been able to create a new organism that produces interferon. This was accomplished by combining the genetic information for the production of interferon with bacteria that are very easy to grow. It is estimated that in time a regular harvest of interferon will be available from these biological factories at a reasonable cost.

The biological revolution may have more far-reaching effects than the development of the atomic bomb, and the effects of the explosion will be no less severe. It may not, perhaps, be as dramatic, but it will create great changes in our life times. We will have to give careful consideration to our conceptions of the value of life when it is so easily constructed and reconstructed in laboratories. Part of our awe in the face of life has, perhaps, been its very mystery. Can our reverence toward life withstand the scrutiny of the scientist's microscope?

Main Points

Mendel and the First Studies of Heredity

1. Gregor Mendel, in the nineteenth century, discovered that hereditary factors pass intact from parent to child.

Genes and Chromosomes

2. Genes are the smallest discrete units of heredity; chromosomes are thousands of genes grouped together in long strands like beads on a string.

3. Every cell in the body has 23 pairs of chromosomes that contain the genetic blueprint for every detail of an individual's physical appearance, chemical functioning, and growth.

4. Each parent contributes one member of each pair of chromosomes.

5. Except for identical twins, who begin with identical heredity, the genetic code is unique for each individual because each of the hundreds of thousands of genes of both parents has an equal chance of being included in any new individual; thus, the chance of two individuals with the same heredity is one in billions.

Karyotype

6. A karyotype is a photograph of the chromosomes arranged by size; an examination of a karyotype reveals chromosomal abnormality and the sex of an individual.

Single-Gene and Polygene Control

7. In general, traits controlled by single genes are less susceptible to environmental modification than those traits that are under the control of many different genes.

Phenotype and Genotype

8. To know the true genetic potential of an individual, the phenotype and the genotype must be known.

DNA: Deoxyribonucleic Acid and the Genetic Code

9. James Watson and Francis Crick discovered that DNA has the form of a double helix composed of a sugar-phosphate backbone and two pairs of nitrogenous bases (adenine and thymine; guanine and cytocine).

10. In cell duplication the double helix unzips and each side builds a new second side from material in the cell fluid.

Dominant and Recessive Genes

11. In dominant inheritance the individual may have a dominant gene contributed by each parent (homozygous) or a dominant gene contributed by one parent paired with a recessive gene from the other parent (heterozygous).

12. In recessive inheritance two genes are necessary for the trait to be expressed. One gene is contributed by each parent.

Sex-linked Inheritance

13. If parents are heterozygous for the same trait, each child will have a seventy-five per cent (3 : 1) probability of expressing the dominant trait and a twenty-five per cent probability of expressing the recessive trait.

14. Characteristics carried by the twenty-third chromosome are a special case of recessive inheritance: the Y chromosome received by males from the father cannot overcome traits carried by the X chromosome from the mother because the Y chromosome carries less information.

Genetic Defects

15. Genetic defects can be inherited through dominant, recessive, or sex-linked inheritance patterns.

16. Genetic defects also result from chromosomal abnormalities or the interaction of genes with other genes or environmental factors.

Down's Syndrome

17. Down's Syndrome is caused by Trisomy 21 (three number 21 chromosomes), translocation (material from the twenty-first chromosome is found on the fifteenth chromosome), and mosaicism (some body cells have trisomy while others are normal).

18. Children with Down's Syndrome have short limbs and fingers, enlarged and protruding tongues, slanted eyes, flattened facial features, and, usually, moderate to severe mental retardation.

Chromosome 23

19. Several disorders are associated with the sex chromosome. These can affect males and females and usually involve additional or missing chromosomes. Some of these disorders are Klinefelter's Syndrome (XXY), XYY Syndrome, Turner's Syndrome (XO), and XXX Syndrome.

Genetic Counseling

20. In genetic counseling, a genetic history is compiled to find the incidence of defects in relatives and ancestors; the couple is then given the odds of producing a normal or a defective child.

The New Biology

21. With recombinant DNA, a technique for combining DNA from two different species, scientists are able to create new life forms.

22. When scientists are able to locate specific genes on a chromosome, replacement of defective genes by gene splicing or genetic surgery may be possible.

Words to Know

chromosomes
deoxyribonucleic acid (DNA)
genes
genotype

hereditary
heredity
heritability
heterozygous

homozygous
inheritance
karyotype
phenotype

Terms to Define

dominant inheritance
genetic code
genetic defects
single-gene and polygene control
recessive inheritance
sex-linked inheritance

CHAPTER 3

Conception and Prenatal Development

Have you ever wondered

when a life begins?

how the developing fetus obtains food and discharges wastes?

how much interchange there is between the fetus and the mother?

when the basic human form is complete?

how rapid prenatal development is?

when a baby could survive if born prematurely?

what principles guide prenatal development?

what factors of the mother affect the development of the fetus?

if diseases that the mother has affect development?

if drugs that the mother takes affect the fetus?

if smoking and alcohol affect the fetus?

if the fetus is safe from radiation and chemicals in the environment?

what women experience in pregnancy?

Birth is not the beginning of life. For every newborn life actually began several months previously. Birth is the dramatic event, one easy to celebrate and remember by marking age. But the actual beginning of individual life is an inconspicuous event involving two microscopic cells that passes generally unnoticed. This event, of course, is conception. The Chinese calculate age from conception rather than from birth. This is more accurate and highlights the crucial importance of the period before birth known as the prenatal period. In this chapter we will describe conception and prenatal development. Reproduction depends on the sexual maturity and cycle of the male and female.

Female Sexual Cycle

When young women reach sexual maturity they begin a rhythmic sexual cycle. This cycle is completed approximately every four weeks (28 days) and because of this the cycle of woman has been associated with the phases of the moon. This cycle consists of alternating periods of *ovulation* and *menstruation*. It can be interrupted with an alternative process, that of *pregnancy* and *childbirth*. Conception can only occur within a few days of ovulation. Thus, there are only a few days within each 28-day cycle that the conditions are right for a conception to take place.

Ovulation

The female sexual organs are primarily internal. These consist of the ovaries, the uterus, and the fallopian tubes. The external genitalia are connected to the uterus by the vagina. The female infant has in her ovaries all of the ova that she will produce in her lifetime. These are immature but are essentially formed. When she reaches puberty, the ova begin to ripen, usually one at a time.

Once each month a mature egg cell is released from an ovary. This cell is the largest in the human body, measuring about $1/175$ of an inch in diameter, and appears to the naked eye to be about the size of a pin point. The release of this egg is known as ovulation and theoretically occurs at the midpoint between two menstrual periods. Organic systems such as the human body, however, exhibit great variation in function, and ovulation can actually occur at any time in a menstrual cycle. Ovulation is not an event that is noticeable to the average woman. Careful recording of basal temperature (temperature measured in the morning before beginning any activity), will reveal a slight elevation at ovulation.

An ovum is released first from one ovary and then the other in monthly cycles. Sometimes more than one ovum is released. If these are fertilized they become fraternal twins, or triplets, quadruplets, quintuplets, and so on. At ovulation, these ova break the surface of the ovary and are released into the abdominal cavity. In close proximity to the ovary is the open end of the fallopian tube, which contains small hairlike projections (*villi*) that are in constant motion. These villi move the ovum along the length of the fallopian tube toward the uterus. Several things may happen to an ovum as it travels this short journey. The first is that nothing happens. The egg has only half the potential for a new individual; it needs the other half in order to develop. In the event that the second half is not supplied, the ovum simply disintegrates and is expelled from the body with the next *menses* (menstrual period). Let us review the process, before turning to the second possibility, conception and pregnancy.

Menstruation

It is the ripening and release of the ovum and the hormones associated with this event that stimulates *menstruation*. In the time since the last menstrual period, the uterus has prepared for the reception of a fertilized ovum. This preparation entails a thickening of the walls of the uterus and a concentration of blood in its lining to nourish an egg.

If a fertilized ovum does not reach the prepared uterus, the thickened walls and extra blood break down and leave the body in the form of a discharge (menstruation). If a fertilized ovum reaches the uterus, then a state of pregnancy ensues and even more changes occur in the body.

Pregnancy is an interruption in the cycle of ovulation and menstruation. The cycle resumes after childbirth. It may resume immediately, or may take as long as two years to resume.

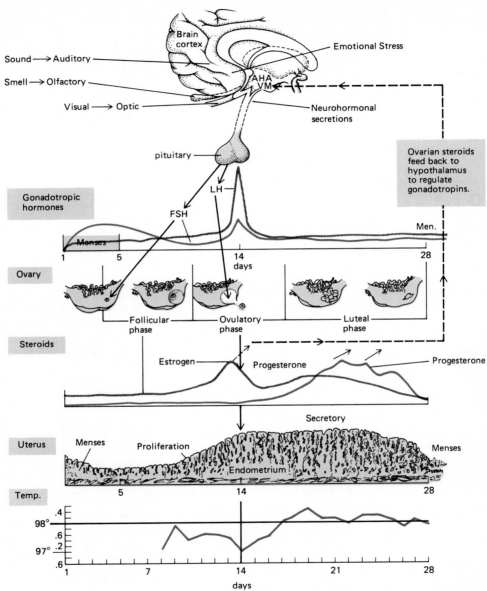

The Menstrual Cycle. This figure illustrates the fluctuation in hormones, ovarian function, steroids, uterus, and temperature as related to menstruation in a 28-day cycle. It also illustrates the feedback system between brain and hormone levels. The menstrual cycle is a complicated relationship among all of these. [From Schlossberg and Zuidema, *The Johns Hopkins Atlas of Human Functional Anatomy*, 2nd ed. Revised and expanded. Copyright © 1977, 1980 by the Johns Hopkins University Press.]

Male Sexual Function

The major function of the male in reproduction is the contribution of sperm, one of which will fertilize the ovum of the female. The male sexual function is a relatively uncomplicated process and does not have a cycle, as does the female sexual function. The production of sperm is a constant process, and a healthy male produces millions of them each day.

The sexual organs of the male are mainly external and consist primarily of the *penis* and the *testes*. Sperm are produced in the testes, as are hormones. These sperm cells are only $\frac{1}{90,000}$ as large as the ovum. Of course they cannot be seen except under a microscope. Whereas a woman usually produces only one mature ovum each month, a male may deposit as many as 200 million sperm through sexual intercourse. Sperm consist of one cell containing 23 single chromosomes with a long tail, which is used for locomotion. Sperm are essentially a bundle of DNA with a tail and have no nutrients to sustain life, as does the ovum. With the aid of the tail, sperm propel themselves at the rate of approximately three inches an hour.

Conception

During sexual intercourse sperm are deposited in the vagina of the woman. With the aid of the thrashing tail, some of the sperm find their way through the small opening in the cervix into the uterus. Some of them find their way through the

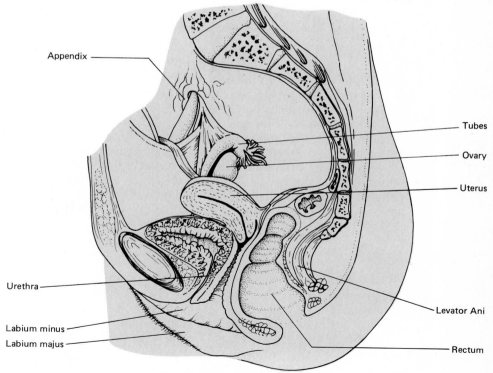

The female reproductive system.

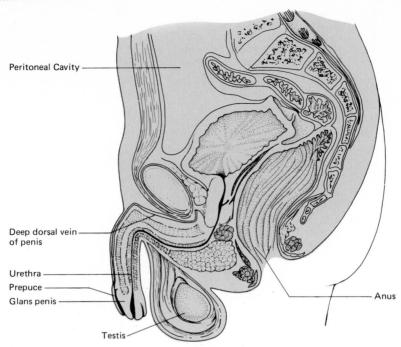

Peritoneal Cavity

Deep dorsal vein
of penis

Urethra
Prepuce
Glans penis

Anus

Testis

The male reproductive system.

uterus into the fallopian tubes. If intercourse occurs at the time of ovulation, or soon afterward, the sperm may find an ovum in progress toward the uterus in the fallopian tube. At some point along the tube, the solitary egg encounters sperm.

The movement of sperm is usually in a random pattern, however, in the presence of an egg, they move toward it in a seemingly purposeful way. We do not know the basis for this attraction. Many sperm may touch the surface of the ovum, but only one penetrates the cell wall. As soon as one accomplishes this, a barrier is set up against entrance by other sperm. The 23 single chromosomes immediately pair and a new individual begins. At the moment of conception, all of a person's genetic potential is present.

Prenatal Periods

Germinal Period (Conception to Two Weeks)

The first two weeks after conception is known as the germinal period, during which the fertilized egg is called a zygote. This period extends from the moment of fertilization to implantation in the uterus and is usually about 10 to 14 days. The egg, you remember, is a very large cell and contains, in addition to its chromosomes, all the nutrients needed to sustain life for this period.

After fertilization in the fallopian tube, the zygote is propelled by villi toward the uterus. This journey into the uterus requires about six or seven days. During this time the zygote continues to divide into two, then into four, eight, and sixteen cells, and so forth. Seventy-two hours after fertilization the zygote has divided into 32 cells. Division continues as the zygote moves the length of the fallopian tube into the uterine cavity. This division is accomplished by duplicating the DNA to furnish each new cell with a complete copy of the genetic blueprint described in Chapter 2. As the *conceptus* (product of conception) continues to divide, the process of differentiation begins. All of the first few cells were identical. Later, however, some cells begin to move to the outer surface of the mass and other cells gather in the interior. The outer cells will develop into the *placenta, chorion,* and *umbilical cord* in order to support the life of the organism; the inner mass will develop into the embryo.

How do certain cells "know" to develop into support system and others into skin, eye, or heart, when all cells contain the same genetic information? Our best guess is that contained somewhere within the genetic information is a system that switches information on and off. This system switches on the information to develop into heart for heart cells and switches off all the information about how to develop into any of the billions of other cells. It is amazing that through this process the arms, legs, eyes, fingers, and so forth end up in approximately the same place in each human. We do not find a few heart end cells scattered indiscriminately around the body. Rather, they are all gathered into the organ that is heart. Even more amazing is that face, body build, and fingerprints are constructed in exact accordance with the genetic plan, to make the individual person's family resemblance.

The uterus has been preparing for a zygote since the last menstrual period. On about the seventh day from conception, the zygote arrives in the uterine cavity and begins to burrow into the spongy surface of the uterine wall. This signals the uterus to retain its extra supply of blood and it stops the process of menstruation. The next seven days consist primarily of implanting the zygote mass firmly into the wall of the uterus. During implantation, rapid growth and development will take place in the support systems. As astronauts require extensive life-support systems in their journeys in outer space, our new earth traveler needs equally extensive support systems in order to survive. These support systems consist of the *placenta,* the *umbilical cord,* and *amniotic sac.*

The placenta is a flat, disc-shaped organ that is attached to the wall of the uterus. The side that faces the uterus contains many small capillaries that burrow into the walls of the uterus. These small capillaries join larger vessels that, in turn, join to form the umbilical cord. This cord extends from the placenta to the belly of the developing fetus. The umbilical cord contains one vein and two arteries. The vein carries oxygenated blood to the fetus and the arteries carry blood and waste products from the fetus to the placenta. The developing embryo/fetus is encased in a thick membrane that resembles a balloon and is called the amnionic sac. This tough membrane is filled with fluid in which the embryo/fetus floats. The umbilical cord passes through the amnionic sac to the fetus.

It is important to note that there is no direct interchange of blood from the mother to the fetus. All substances are screened through the placenta. This screening is known as the placental barrier. Many substances pass the placental barrier and reach the fetus. Substances actually pass through the cell walls in both directions (the process is similar to that of digestion, in which the food we eat passes through the walls of the intestines into the blood stream). The discriminating factor seems to be the size of the molecules. Blood cells themselves are too large to pass the barrier. The mother and fetus can have different, and incompatible, blood types,

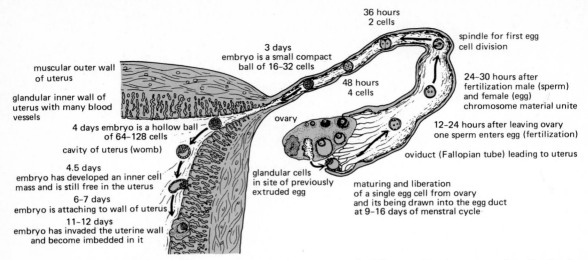

The Germinal Period. This diagram illustrates ovulation, conception in the fallopian tube, the passage of the fertilized ovum to the uterus, implantation in the uterine wall. During this time, the zygote remains approximately the size of the unfertilized egg but the number of cells has grown rapidly and differentiation begins. [*From Conception to Birth: The Drama of Life's Beginnings* by Roberts Rugh, Ph. D. and Landrum B. Shettles, Ph. D., M. D. Copyright © 1971 by Roberts Rugh and Landrum B. Shettles. Reproduced by permission of Harper and Row, publishers.]

but many substances that the blood cells transport do cross this barrier. The thinking now is that any substance that the mother ingests has the potential to reach the fetus, and many of these substances, especially drugs, alcohol, and nicotine can be damaging to the developing fetus.

The amniotic sac is filled with fluid, in which the fetus floats. This fluid cushions and protects the developing organism. The fetus has freedom of movement in this environment, is maintained at constant body temperature, and is protected from pressures from the mother's internal organs as well as pressures and blows from outside.

The end of the germinal period is marked by firm implantation in the uterus and the construction of a support system.

Embryonic Period (Two Weeks to Two Months)

The embryonic period lasts from two weeks to about two months after conception. When implantation is completed, the organism is called an embryo (the word means "a swelling"). The connotation of the word is something that is not yet formed but that has potential. That exactly describes the embryonic period of development. In the six to eight weeks comprising this period, development is rapid. All the body systems are developed during this time. The embryo continues to divide and to differentiate cells according to the function they will serve in the body. At the beginning of the embryonic period, three layers of cells are distinguishable. The *ectoderm,* the *mesoderm,* and the *endoderm.* These words designate the outer, middle, and inner cells. Within these layers the cells appear quite similar; however, further differentiation will take place. The ectoderm contains cells that will develop into the outer layer of skin: nails, hair, and some teeth, the nervous system, including the brain and spinal cord, and sensory organs. The mesoderm, or middle layer, will

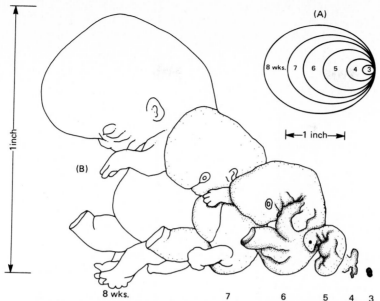

The embryonic period. The embryo begins as a pin-point of barely differentiated cells and six weeks later has all the basic form and structure of a human.
When all structures are laid down and bone cells begin to replace softer
cartilage the period of the fetus begins.

develop into the circulatory and excretory systems, the skeleton, and the muscles
attached to it. The endoderm, or inner layer of cells, will develop into the internal
organs, such as the gastrointestinal tract, liver, lungs, and various glands.

The embryo begins spontaneous movement at about six weeks, but this movement is not perceived by the mother. The perceived first movements of the fetus, in
lay terms, are referred to as quickening and occur at about 12 weeks. The term
quickening reflects an older belief that this was the time when the fetus became
alive. We know now that the fetus has always been alive and that perceived movement by the mother is simply that, perceived movement.

Fetal Period (Two Months to Birth)

At about two months after conception the developing human is referred to as a
fetus. We say ''about'' because these are descriptive terms and not exact scientific
ones. The embryo becomes a fetus when the first true bone cells form and all
physical structures have been differentiated. These are not quite in the form that
they will have at birth, but they are recognizable, nevertheless.

The fetal period is characterized by continued growth of those parts, organs,
and systems differentiated in the embryonic period. At the beginning of the fetal
period the fetus is approximately one inch long and weighs only a fraction of one
ounce. Seven months later, the normal time for birth, the newborn baby will weigh
approximately 7½ pounds and measure about 20 inches. At the beginning of the
fetal period the small organism bears little resemblance to a baby. Changes in
appearance will continue to take place rapidly, although no new systems will de-

velop. In addition to change in size and appearance during this period, many behaviors emerge: head turning, thumb sucking, arm and leg movements, hiccoughing, and so forth. These behaviors do not appear suddenly after birth but have been
rehearsed in the fetal period.

Abortion: Spontaneous and Induced

Not every conception culminates in the birth of a baby. Many conceptions slip
quietly and spontaneously from the woman's body and are called miscarriages.
When the laws and customs of society allow it, pregnancies can be interrupted
through intentional intervention. Knowledge of how to terminate a pregnancy was
known and practiced by the ancient Romans. Perhaps every woman who has been
told that she was pregnant has had at least the fleeting thought, "Must I go through
with this?"

Miscarriage, or spontaneous abortion, is most likely to occur in the first 12
weeks of a pregnancy. Garn (1966) has estimated that 30 to 40 per cent of all
pregnancies end in this manner. However, three out of four of these are in the first
three months (*first trimester*), and often the woman is unaware either that she is
pregnant or that a miscarriage has taken place. Her perception may be only a
delayed menstrual period.

Usually these spontaneous abortions are the result of gross abnormalities. The
March of Dimes (1979) estimates that four out of five conceptions with abnormalities that would result in Down's Syndrome are spontaneously aborted. Most other
chromosomal abnormalities result in fetuses that are nonviable and thus are
aborted. Other causes are a defective support system (placenta, umbilical cord) or
implantation in a location in the uterus that hinders development.

Contrary to popular belief, very little in the way of physical activity will cause a
miscarriage. Guttmacher (1973) has aptly described this state with his cryptic observation that a good human egg is as difficult to shake loose as is a good unripe
apple from an apple tree. Women have carried normal pregnancies through severe
automobile accidents and falls from several stories of a building and down flights of
stairs. Some women, however, do seem prone to repeated miscarriage. In this case,
medical assistance can be sought.

A spontaneous abortion is an act of nature, but induced abortion is the act of
a person or persons making a *choice*. The culture and values and emotions of the
woman form the matrix within which the decision is made.

A very large number of conceptions, however, end neither in spontaneous nor
induced abortion. In the 266 days from conception to birth, a great many things
happen. Let us turn to this very exciting period of growing and becoming a human
baby.

Prenatal Development

First Week (days one to seven). During the first week after fertilization the ovum
divides many times, although its total size remains approximately the same. The
zygote completes the passage through the fallopian tube into the uterus.

Second Week (days 8 to 14). The second week after conception the zygote begins
implantation into the wall of the uterus. Cell mass begins to differentiate into those

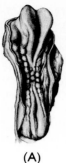

(A)

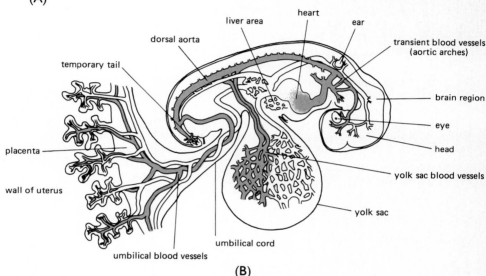

(B)

At three weeks (A), the human embryo has a strange appearance and is the size of a pinhead. By four weeks (B), the embryo's size is one quarter of an inch and the organization of the circulatory system is quite advanced, as shown in this diagram. [(A) from *Environment and Birth Defects* by James G. Wilson. Copyright © 1973 by Academic Press, Inc. All rights reserved. Diagram of circulatory system (B) from *From Conception to Birth: The Drama of Life's Beginnings* by Roberts Rugh, Ph. D. and Landrum B. Shettles, Ph. D., M. D. Copyright © 1971 by Roberts Rugh and Landrum B. Shettles. Reproduced by permission of Harper and Row, publishers.]

parts that form placenta, chorion, and umbilical cord and those that will form the embryo/fetus. Small capillaries begin to spread through the uterine wall to carry blood to the zygote.

Third Week (days 15 to 21), length: 2 millimeters. At the beginning of the third week, the embryo is the size of a pin head; however, it has already begun to affect the hormonal balance of the mother. It is firmly anchored in the uterus and the placenta is developing rapidly. With this efficient supply of nutrients, the thin two-layered disc becomes a rounded body with head, trunk, and umbilical cord.

Fourth Week (days 22 to 28), length: 5 to 6 millimeters. The development of the brain and spinal cord is pronounced. A large head projects forward over a mouth cavity. The spinal cord has exceeded the length of the embryo and gives the effect of a tail. Even though the size of the embryo is small, development is so rapid that changes are almost hourly. Growth is faster in the fore end, slower in the back, and slowest on either side. Early in the fourth week a rudimentary heart begins to beat. Between the primitive mouth and the heart, a face and throat begin to form. The embryo appears to have gills, but this cleft will become ears, while another cleft will become the lower jaw. By the end of this week the forehead, eye, mandible, mouth and pharynx, neck, aorta, heart, trachea, esophagus, future spine, liver, veins, bladder and rectum are identifiable. The embryo is now 10,000 times the size of the zygote. If a person continued to grow at this rate, an adult would weigh two million times the weight of the *earth!*

Fifth Week (days 29 to 35), length: 8 millimeters (1/3-inch). In the fifth week the embryo reaches the length of one third of an inch and weighs 1/100 of an ounce. The head and brain continue to lead in development. The eye appears as a dark spot on the head and the three primary parts of the brain are present. Blood is being produced in the yolk sac, and the heart, although incomplete, is pumping blood cells rhythmically through the embryo's blood vessels into the placenta and umbilical cord. In this week the following organs form: the alimentary canal, gall bladder, thyroid gland, stomach, intestines, pancreas, and lungs. Arm and leg buds appear and muscles form in the pelvic region. By the end of this week the beginning of germ cells are present in beginning ovaries or testes.

Sixth Week (days 36 to 42), length: 13 millimeters (1/2-inch). At the beginning of the sixth week the head is far more developed than the trunk, and the arms are more developed than the legs. The human embryo is not yet distinguishable from that of a mouse or a pig. In the sixth week, however, great changes occur in form. Cells move unhesitatingly to designated places and begin building the human form. Arms and legs lengthen and cartilage appears that later becomes bone as muscles fill out. Hands and feet differentiate from buds. This period of rapid form development is the critical time for congenital abnormalities in the arms, legs, and internal organs because the organs and limbs have not yet completely differentiated. In this week spontaneous movement may occur, although it is not discernible by the mother. These movements are the earliest reflexes. Such genetic characteristics as attached or unattached ear lobes and the shape of nose, fingers, and toes are discernible at the end of this week.

Seventh Week (days 43 to 49), length: 20 millimeters (4/5-inch). In the seventh week the head continues to lead in development. The brain hemispheres are discernible and fill the forward part of the head. Nerve cells of the eye, palate, and parts of the ear that maintain balance are forming. The face rounds out and begins to look human. All evidence of vestigial gills disappear and become fused into the jaw parts and ear. The back straightens and the tail begins to regress. All fingers are present but are not fully formed. The stomach is a miniature version of that in the newborn and all muscles are organizing. The urinary, genital, and rectal passages are becoming differentiated and separated. The sex of the embryo is discernible under microscopic examination and the anus is forming. Exposure to drugs or other traumatic events may cause abnormalities in the urological systems during this week. Note

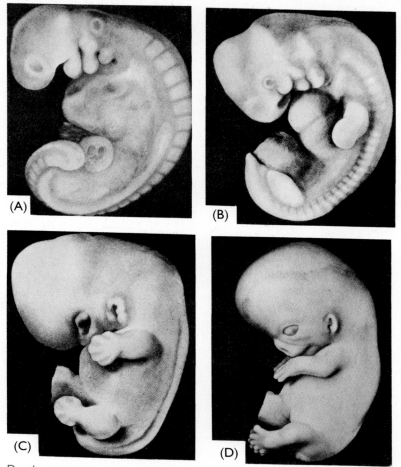

Development proceeds rapidly in the embryonic period although size remains less than one inch. The photographs above show weekly changes in embryos that are four weeks old (A), five weeks old (B), six weeks old (C), and seven weeks old (D). By the eighth week the embryo assumes human form and is called a fetus. [From *Environment and Birth Defects* by James G. Wilson. Copyright © 1973 by Academic Press, Inc. All rights reserved.]

that the mother will have just missed her second menstrual period and only now will be aware that she is pregnant.

Eighth Week (days 50 to 56), length: 30 millimeters (1¼ inches). The eighth week marks the change from embryo to fetus. The fetus now has a definite human appearance, but even so, it only weighs one gram or about 1/13 of an ounce. The face is clearly recognizable and teeth buds are present. The palate normally closes at this time, but when it does not, the result is a cleft palate. The head is one half the length of the entire body and eyes and ears are developing rapidly. At the end of this week all body parts have been laid down but require further development. Hands, fingers, and thumbs have formed on the arms and knees, ankles, and toes also have formed. A first thin skin has formed over the body. The heart beat is steady, the stomach produces digestive juices, the liver produces blood cells, the kidney removes uric acid from the blood, and cartilage is being converted to bone cells (*ossification*). Some neurological reflexes are functioning and the embryo will react to tactile stimulation.

Ninth Week (days 57 to 63), length: 1½ inches. In the ninth week the head of the fetus no longer bends over the body. The back is straighter. Fingernails, toenails, and hair follicles are forming. The skin becomes thicker and less transparent. Eyelids form over the eyes and the diaphragm of the iris is present. Both the eye and hand respond to touch by closing, which indicates that nerves are functioning. The ear is still low on the throat, but it will move up. Now the fetal heartbeat can be heard through a stethoscope. The male fetus is discernible from external genitalia and the female begins to form a rudimentary uterus and a vagina. The sex organs of both male and female form from the same tissues. The basic form of the human is female; however, in the presence of testosterone the tissues are modified into male morphology. The tissues that form the penis in the male form the clitoris in the female. The same tissues that develop into testes in the male, form ovaries in the female. The modification in development is stimulated by the beginning production of male hormones by the male embryo. Thus, interestingly, we see the organism itself to be the cause of its own development. At an earlier time a visual examination of the embryo will not reveal the sex; however, sex can be determined by a chromosome examination (karyotype).

Tenth Week (days 64 to 70), length: 2⅛ inches, head to buttocks. A ten-week-old fetus weighs only a quarter of an ounce. Head and body come more into proportion because now the body is growing more rapidly than the head. The brain has essentially finished developing and, except for refinement, is as it will be at birth. Responses increase, and if the forehead is touched the fetus will turn its head away. Reaction to touch may be found on many areas, except sides, back, and top of the head. The face is particularly sensitive. The gall bladder is secreting bile and the lungs are complete but not functioning. Blood, which first was produced in the yolk and then in the liver, is now produced in bone marrow and the blood vessels are formed.

Eleventh Week (days 71 to 77), length: 2½ inches. The fetus now exhibits many behaviors that it will perform after birth. It swallows, inhales, exhales, and may have hiccoughs. It may even "breathe" the amniotic fluid. This is not a source of oxygen but is a rehearsal of extrauterine breathing behavior. Oxygen is attained through the placenta from the mother. Twenty teeth begin to form in the jaw and sockets for them are reserved in the ossifying jawbone. The vocal cords form, as well as the thyroid and thymus glands. The liver begins to produce bile and continues to help the bone marrow produce blood cells. The blood of the fetus begins to transport nutrients, protect against disease, and scavenge debris, but it continues to depend on the mother's system to do these chores efficiently.

Twelfth Week (days 77 to 84), length: 3 inches; weight: ½ ounce. The twelfth week marks the end of the third month and of the first trimester. The thumb can now be opposed to the forefinger, which will later allow the child to pick up objects, hold a pencil or paintbrush, and ultimately use tools. The behavioral repertoire of the fetus

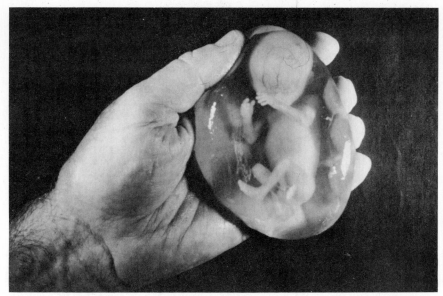

A twelve-week-old fetus held in a human hand. [From *From Conception to Birth: The Drama of Life's Beginnings* by Roberts Rugh, Ph. D. and Landrum B. Shettles, Ph. D., M. D. Copyright © 1971 by Roberts Rugh and Landrum B. Shettles. Reproduced by permission of Harper and Row, publishers.]

increases greatly by the end of the third month. The fetus can turn its head, squint, frown, bend its arms at the elbows and wrists, make a fist, move its hips, kick, and curl and fan its toes, yet it is still so small that the mother may not be aware of its presence. Fetuses of this age begin to show some individual variation in behavioral patterns. These may be particularly evident in facial expressions and probably are caused by patterns inherited from parents.

Fourth Month (16 weeks), length: 6 inches; weight: 4 ounces.   The first three months were a time of rapid development; the second three months are a period of rapid growth. The fetus begins to fill the volume of the amniotic sac and reaches one third of its birth length in the fourth month, even though it weighs less than one pound. The proportion between body and head changes; elongation of the body and legs accounts for most of the growth. The head, which was half the body length, now is only one third of the total body. Posture becomes more erect as muscles develop in the neck and back. The female sexual organs are completed now, somewhat behind the development of the male. The germ cells that will be future ova are developed, as are the fallopian tubes and uterus. The heart is circulating about 25 quarts of blood a day and beats 120 to 160 times per minute, twice the speed of the mother's heart. Reflex activities are stronger and better coordinated. Hands and feet are well formed and fingers may grasp. An electrical stimulation in the brain may cause a movement in arms or legs.

Fifth Month (20 weeks), length: 8 inches; weight: 8 ounces.   In the fifth month the mother may perceive the movement of the fetus. The five-month fetus is so well developed it looks as though it could sustain life, but it is too immature because the lungs are unable to sustain breathing. The fetus retains some features it shares with other species, such as a very large number of taste buds. There are more taste buds than will be present at birth; they are on the tongue, roof and walls of the mouth, and even in the throat. The fetus discards these vestigial characteristics and development moves unrelentingly toward human development. The process of breaking down old cells and replacing them with new ones begins; it will continue throughout life. Sweat glands, which will help to maintain body temperature, form but are not active. The fetus may develop sleeping and waking patterns and may suck its thumb. By the end of the fifth month, the fingernails have reached the tips of the fingers.

Sixth Month (24 weeks), length: 10 to 12 inches; weight: 1½ pounds.   Soft hair (*lanugo*) covers the body and a waxy covering (*vernix caseosa*) forms to protect the skin from its immersion in the amniotic fluid. The skin is reddish and wrinkled, with little or no fatty deposits underneath. A fetus born at six months has little chance of survival but may attempt to breathe. It cannot, however, regulate temperature or breathing. The hair is growing and may have to be cut at birth. In the male the testes approach the scrotum but do not descend into it yet. The intestines are filled with a pasty mass of dead cells and bile known as meconium and may remain there until birth. The fetus is cushioned in about a quart of amniotic fluid. This fluid is continuously replaced by water from the maternal plasma. It is estimated that the entire fluid is exchanged every three hours, which keeps it from becoming stagnant.

Seventh Month (28 weeks), length: 12 inches, crown to buttocks: 16 inches full length; weight: 2 to 3 pounds.   The fetus, if born in the seventh month, has a fair chance of survival, with specialized care. The fetus continues to grow larger and to deposit fat beneath the skin. This fat will serve to maintain body temperature in the newborn; it changes the red, wrinkled appearance to a soft, cuddly one. The greatest development in this month is in brain differentiation. The forepart enlarges and the surface area increases in fissures, which increases the surface area of cortical nerves. Until this time the brain was largely unwrinkled. If this stage does not develop properly, the result is reduced intellectual potential in memory, imagination, and reasoning power. The brain at maturity contains ten billion neurons, and each neuron may connect with as many as one thousand other neurons. This gives a human potential of ten *trillion* neural connections in the brain. We are just beginning to see exciting research on how all this works. These neuron connections continue to be formed even after birth and are probably affected by experience in the newborn.

Eighth Month (32 weeks), length: 13 inches, crown to buttocks: 18 inches full length; weight: 4½ to 5 pounds.   The eight-month fetus has an excellent chance of survival if born prematurely. Fat continues to accumulate and both biological and behavioral systems gain in precision. The head bones are soft and flexible. This will be an asset in the passage through the mother's pelvis during the birth process. The fetus now is beginning to be cramped in the space of the uterus. The fetus is sensitive to sound whether from an orchestra, a piano, a voice, or its mother's heartbeat.

Ninth Month (36 weeks), length: 19 to 20 inches; weight: 6 to 8 pounds.   In the ninth month the fetus is ready for independent biological life. It completely fills the uterine space, so its movement is curtailed. During this month the fetus usually assumes an upside-down position with the head engaged in the pelvis and the face

Table 3–1. Summary of Prenatal Development

1st week	Zygote reaches the uterus.
2nd week	Implantation in the uterine wall.
3rd week	Embryo affects hormonal balance of mother.
4th week	Developmental changes hourly; heart begins to beat.
5th week	Digestive system develops.
6th week	Individual genetic characteristics discernible.
7th week	Urinary and genital systems differentiated; sex is discernible.
8th week	Embryo becomes fetus with definite human appearance; weighs one gram; all forms are laid down and systems function.
9th week	Fetus responds to stimuli; heartbeat can be heard through stethoscope.
10th week	Brain development essentially complete; blood begins to be produced in bone marrow.
11th week	Behaviors emerge; fetus may swallow, inhale, exhale, hiccough, and "breathe."
12th week	Individual variation in behavioral patterns discernible; fetus may turn head, squint, frown, make fist, move lips, kick, curl and fan toes; thumb opposes forefinger.
4th month	Rapid growth; reflex activity strong and coordinated; one third birth size.
5th month	Movements may be perceived by mother; process of replacing old cells with new ones begins.
6th month	Soft hair (lanugo) and waxy covering (*vernix caseosa*) form; hair grows; testes approach scrotum.
7th month	If born may survive with specialized care.
8th month	Excellent chance of survival if born; fat accumulates and biological and behavioral systems increase in precision.
9th month	Acquires antibodies against disease; gestation complete.

toward the mother's backbone. The activity of the fetus slows down. During this month it acquires antibodies from the mother that give immunity to diseases such as measles, German measles, mumps, whooping cough, scarlet fever, colds, and flu. In addition, the fetus' own immune system begins functioning. Gestation is calculated at 266 days from conception. This is 38 weeks, nine calendar months, or nine and one-half lunar months (four weeks each). During the last two weeks preparation is made for birth: the uterus descends into the pelvic basin. This is known as lightening because breathing becomes easier for the mother. Growth slows in the fetus because of regression in the placenta. The placenta shows all the signs of "old age." Labor and birth become imminent.

Principles of Prenatal Development

Three principles of development appear in the prenatal period that are also applicable to the years after birth; however, they are more pertinent in embryonic development. The principles are *cephalocaudal development, proximodistal development,* and *critical periods.*

Cephalocaudal Development

The principle of cephalocaudal development states that the direction of development proceeds from the head to the lower extremities. In accordance with this principle the head is the most advanced part of the embryo and fetus and the brain is the leading organ in development. In comparison the lower extremities are quite underdeveloped at birth. The infant and child continue to develop in accordance with this principle. That is, the head continues to lead development.

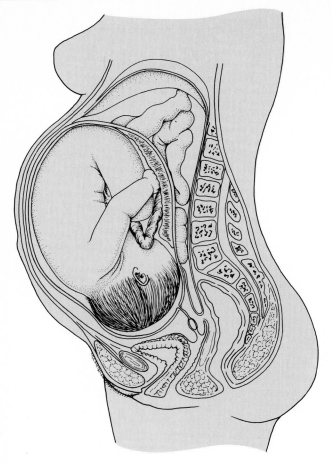

A nine-month-old fetus. Development is complete and birth is imminent.

Proximodistal Development

The principle of proximodistal development is that development proceeds from the center of the organism outward. Thus, in prenatal development we see development of the spinal cord before the outer extremities. In addition, arms develop before hands and hands develop before fingers. This principle continues to guide development, as the infant gains control of the large muscles of the arms before the small muscles of the fingers.

Critical Periods

The principle of critical periods states that an aspect of development is most susceptible to environmental influences at the time of most rapid growth. This principle can be seen most clearly in the area of physical development in the prenatal period and is most dramatically illustrated in negative development. For example, in prenatal life the system that is growing most rapidly is most susceptible to damage from some agent that adversely affects prenatal development. If a pregnant woman contracts rubella, the system damaged in the embryo will be the system that is developing; it may be hearing, sight, or organ damage. Rubella will not have as devastating an effect on a fetus after the first three months, when its systems are already formed.

Research has not been as successful in identifying the principle of critical periods as clearly in the area of psychological development. There is, however, some evidence that such periods exist. Konrad Lorenz (1957) has found a critical period in the establishment of the mother-infant bond in ducks. This research has found that newly hatched ducklings form an attachment bond with a "mother." Lorenz has had ducklings imprint attachment to himself, to a moving light bulb, and to other objects.

Because of ethical considerations we cannot deprive children of social and learning opportunities to gain knowledge, and in retrospective studies it is extremely difficult to separate congenital mental deficiency from environmental deprivation. A neglected child was found in California, with development that suggests a critical period in speech development. The California child, named Genie, was isolated and not spoken to from twenty months of age until she was thirteen and a half years old (Pines, 1981). When discovered, Genie was unable to speak. Nine years later, after years of intensive training by psycholinguists and others at the University of California at Los Angeles, she was able to put three words together occasionally, but she never spoke in a fully developed or normal way. In studies such as that of Genie it is impossible to determine how such children would have developed in another environment.

Educators debate whether there is a critical period for learning to read or perform mathematics. Terms such as *reading readiness* and the *teachable moment* reflect the assumption that timing is a crucial factor in teaching and learning. On the other hand, we have evidence for some compensation in developmental timetables. Children who have been restrained from attempting to walk—because of broken legs or some other medical impairment—at the age that most children are walking later progress through the stages of locomotion quite rapidly and catch up with their age mates.

Another interesting example of critical periods involves newborn cats, who are born blind. When these kittens are kept in total darkness during the time in which most cats normally open their eyes and sight is developed they never gain the ability to see. The interpretation here is that, in cats, there is a critical time in the development of sight when the stimulation of light is necessary for full development. Similarly, we have some indication that, in the development of human intelligence, interaction between the environment and the organism is necessary. In experimental animals, those animals that are exposed to a stimulating environment develop larger brains and a different chemical composition than those who do not receive environmental stimulation. Although we have evidence for critical periods in some areas, we need much more research to explain fully the stimuli necessary and the interaction of environment and organism in development.

Environmental Influences on Prenatal Development

In the nineteenth century it was believed that the experiences of a pregnant woman affected the development of the fetus. If a child was born with a discoloration on the skin that resembled a strawberry or a bear it was thought that his or her mother craved strawberries or was perhaps frightened by a bear during pregnancy. Victorian mothers were instructed to listen to music or to read "uplifting" literature to influence their unborn children with the aesthetic life.

Twentieth-century scientists waged a fierce battle against these superstitions and by midcentury the scientific stance was that the pregnant woman and the fetus were separate organisms and that there was very little influence from one to the other. The developing fetus needed the protection of the uterus in which to grow and "took what it needed" from the biological offering of the mother. It was also believed that the placenta acted as a barrier against most foreign agents and protected the fetus from toxic insult. The pregnant woman, in this view, could do very little to affect the course of development of the fetus.

At the present time, scientists take a more moderate view of the interchange between fetus and mother. Of course, an experience such as being frightened by a bear does not manifest itself in a blemish on the skin of the child; however, the effects of the maternal environment on the child are more pervasive than was thought at midcentury. We now know that the placental barrier is not an effective screen for many toxic elements. The body of the pregnant woman constitutes the environment of the fetus and the fetus is profoundly affected not only by the food that she eats but also by the drugs she takes, her illnesses, and even her emotions. We will consider three aspects of the environment that she provides. First are those factors that constitute her biological status, such as her age, her state of health, and her psychological or emotional state. Second are those factors that are the result of her behavior, such as the food she eats, drugs she may take, smoking, alcohol consumption, and exposure to X-ray. Third are factors beyond her control, such as toxic chemicals and radiation from the environment.

Maternal Factors

Age

The age of the woman at the time that her body is in the process of pregnancy is an important factor in the development of the child. The years between twenty and thirty-five seem to be the optimum time for pregnancy. The very young mother is more likely to have complications of pregnancy and birth. After the age of thirty-five, the incidence of birth defects increases rapidly. In addition, mothers in this age group may experience more difficulty in childbirth, especially with firstborns. They are also more likely to have miscarriages, stillborns, or underweight babies. This is not to imply that women between twenty and thirty-five do not have these problems, but the incidence is significantly lower. We also find that babies born to girls under twenty are two times more likely to die in the first years than babies whose mothers are over the age of twenty (*Teenage Pregnancy: The Problem That Hasn't Gone Away*, 1981). In addition, teenage women are more likely to die as a result of complications of pregnancy or birth.

Disease

The health of the woman is an extremely important factor in the development of the embryo and fetus. Chronic diseases such as diabetes can adversely affect the unborn child. Children whose mothers have diabetes are more likely to be born prematurely than those whose mothers are free of such disorders. Any chronic disease should be carefully controlled in a woman who is pregnant. Infectious disease contracted by a pregnant woman often constitutes a threat to the unborn.

Medical science is still in the process of cataloguing the diseases that might cause prenatal damage. At present our research is scanty and largely consists of trying to piece together the evidence through retrospective studies after the damage has been done. One of the major threats to the unborn child is rubella.

Rubella.   Rubella, or German measles, is a viral infection with little effect on adults but that carries a high risk for the embryo/fetus if a woman has the disease in the first three months of pregnancy. The possible effects of the disease are heart malfunctions, deafness, blindness, and mental retardation. The particular effect depends on the system that is developing at the time the disease entity invades the organism. The risk of permanent damage is about 50 per cent for babies whose mothers have German measles in the first month; 22 per cent in the second month; and 6 per cent in the third month. After that time, the risk of damage is minimal. Even the vaccine for rubella can cause damage in a developing embryo; the vaccine contains the live virus, which crosses the placental barrier and affects the embryo. Health educators recommend that a woman be sure that she has either had the disease or a vaccination before undertaking a pregnancy. For this reason physicians are reluctant to give the vaccine to any young woman of childbearing age, in case she may be pregnant. Other viruses, hepatitis, and chicken pox can also cause damage to the unborn.

Syphilis.   If a pregnant woman has syphilis, the spirochetes (bacteria) from the disease can cross the placental barrier and enter the fetus. This does not happen in the first months of pregnancy because the placental barrier does not allow their passage until after the fourth or fifth month. If a woman is under adequate medical supervision, the disease will be discovered, and treated, before this time and the fetus saved. Of course, in some cases, she may contract the disease during pregnancy. If the child is affected, the result may be miscarriage or, in the case of a viable birth, the child may be deformed or mentally retarded. Because of the insidious nature of the disease, the child may not manifest syphilitic symptoms for several years.

Types of defects and frequencies in children of women who were infected with rubella (German measles) early in pregnancy. Note that the greatest effect was at four weeks gestation and no effects recorded after 24 weeks. [From "Critical periods of prenatal toxic insults" by Allen S. Goldman. In R. H. Schwarz and S. J. Yaffe (Eds.), *Drug and Chemical Risks to the Fetus and Newborn.* Copyright © 1980 by Alan R. Liss, Inc. By permission.]

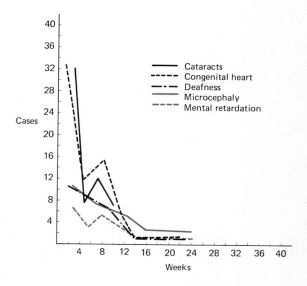

Toxemia.   A disease associated with pregnancy itself is toxemia (pre-eclampsia). Approximately 5 per cent of women are subject to the disorder. The symptoms in the woman are swelling, from retention of fluid in the tissues, rapid and excessive weight gain, and high blood pressure. The disease can lead to convulsions, coma, and even death. In severe toxemia, approximately half of the pregnancies terminate in the death of the fetus, whereas one in eight (severe cases) results in the death of the woman. Should the pregnancy go to full term, the resulting child has a higher risk of lowered intelligence. One of the benefits of careful prenatal care is that the woman can be carefully monitored for toxemia and treated immediately.

Rh Factor

Rh factor is not a disease but a genetically determined blood factor. Rh is a factor that is present in the blood of 85 per cent of the population. Thus, approximately 15 per cent of the population do *not* have the Rh factor in their blood. The possession of this factor, or lack of it, is, of course, genetically determined. A potential problem arises when a woman is Rh negative and a man is Rh positive. In the event that the child from such parents does not inherit the Rh factor (i.e., Rh negative) there is no problem. However, if the Rh negative woman conceives an Rh positive child, then some of the Rh factor may cross the placental barrier into the body of the mother. The Rh factor in her body triggers her immune system to manufacture antibodies to destroy the factor, because it is "read" as an invading body. In general, these antibodies are so few in the first child that they cause no problem. If a second child is conceived with Rh positive factor, some of the mother's antibodies may cross the placental barrier into the bloodstream of the fetus, where they begin to destroy blood cells. The effects of this destruction on the child can vary from mild anemia to cerebral palsy, deafness, mental retardation, and sometimes death.

The management of this factor has been one of the success stories of modern medical science. When the factor was first discovered, the treatment was a total transfusion soon after birth. Now the condition can be diagnosed and treated before birth. When a woman is Rh negative and it is suspected that the fetus may be Rh positive, a sample of the fetus' blood can be drawn and a definite diagnosis made. Advances in surgical technique allows the insertion of a thin needle through the walls of the uterus and amniotic sac into the fetus to find a small blood vessel. If antibodies from the mother are passing into the bloodstream of the fetus a full blood transfusion can be given to the fetus before birth. Even more recently a vaccine has been developed that can be administered to an Rh negative woman who delivers an Rh positive baby which prevents the formation of antibodies. If this vaccine is administered within a few hours after birth, she does not develop Rh antibodies. It is believed that the major transfer of the factor occurs when the placenta is dislodged from the uterus.

Emotions

At the beginning of this section we referred to the previously held belief that a birthmark was the result of a traumatic experience of the mother. We have passed the era of smugness in which we held that the emotional experiences of the woman exert no influence on the developing fetus. Scientific research has now indicated that the emotional state of the pregnant woman can, indeed, affect the unborn child. But if the mother's emotional state does not cause birthmarks that look like bears or strawberries, what can be the effect on the child? Let us look at the scientific evidence. First, consider what happens in the body of the pregnant woman or in any of us in an emotional reaction. We experience certain emotions that we call fear, anger, or anxiety. From a physiological perspective, the organism is aroused, with the result that certain chemicals are poured into the bloodstream. It is these chemicals that are responsible for the feelings we experience. Chemicals such as acetylcholine and epinephrine stimulate the production of hormones such as adrenaline. Cell metabolism is also changed. These chemicals cross the placental barrier and the fetus "experiences" anger, fear, or anxiety. Actually, we do not know that the fetus experiences these emotions; however, careful monitoring of the fetus during periods of emotional stress for the mother has revealed such measurable effects as faster heart rate and increased activity.

Infants that are affected by maternal stress prenatally show measurable differences in behavior from those infants who experienced a less stressful prenatal environment. Women who experience a high degree of stress during pregnancy are more likely to have infants who have low birth weight, are irritable, and have digestive disturbances and feeding problems. They are also prone to classification "hyperactive." Anxiety in pregnancy has also been associated with high percentages of miscarriage and prematurity, as well as extended labor and complications following birth (Ferreira, 1965).

Professional ethics does not allow scientists to subject a pregnant woman to stress to test the effect on her infant; however, laboratory animals have been the subject of such experiments. In an experiment with pregnant rats, an experimental group was subjected to stressful situations, while a control group lived in the identical environment without the stress. Stress for rats constitutes having to cross an electric grid to obtain food. The rat infants are then measured for degree of "emotionality." The infants of rats who had been subjected to the stress of electric shock were more easily aroused than those infants whose mothers experienced a less stressful pregnancy. This difference in arousal potential disappeared in time if the rat infants subsequently received the same unstressful environmental conditions.

In summary, research and logic indicate that the chemical state of the mother is also the chemical state of the fetus, and that this environment has a measurable effect on the fetus. Perhaps we will not return to prescribing soothing music for pregnant mothers, but we might want to consider the effects, for example, of the stress of a dysfunctional family, of economic concerns, and of the fears and anxieties of a teenage mother facing motherhood alone, with few skills and fewer resources.

Life-Style Factors

In many ways the pregnant woman chooses the environment for the fetus. These choices include the food she eats, the drugs she takes, whether she smokes, and whether and how much alcohol she consumes. All of these become factors in the chemical environment for the developing fetus. Therefore, the pregnant woman needs to be aware of the consequences of her choices.

Nutrition

The most important single factor in the prenatal development of a child is nutrition. The developing embryo/fetus must have a constant supply of nutrients. The chemicals that comprise the human body are rather commonplace; however, the organic molecules constructed of these chemicals are both complex and vital. While the chemical interaction in the human body is extremely complex, our scientific knowledge of this great chemical factory is embarrassingly limited. There are two aspects to nutrition: the *quantitative* and the *qualitative*. Obviously, a certain level of nutritional intake is necessary to sustain life (quantity of food). Another quantity is necessary for the individual to experience a feeling of satisfaction. Reaching the desired *quality* of nutrition, however, becomes another dimension. Qualitative hunger results in malnutrition caused by deficient supplies of the vitamins necessary for normal growth. We do not generally, in America, have people dying from inadequate amounts of food; however, we may have people who do not reach their developmental potential because of inadequate quality of food. Our research is scanty in this area, but what we have indicates the extreme importance of nutrition in prenatal life (Hurley, 1980).

Malnutrition can cause diseases such as rickets, generally poor health, and susceptibility to disease. Malnutrition is a contributing cause of miscarriage and stillbirths. There is increasing evidence that deprivation of essential protein prenatally and in early infancy results in permanent mental retardation. In many emerging countries, the protein available for mothers and infants is extremely low. Researchers have found significantly fewer brain cells in infants who suffer this deprivation than in infants of similar genetic background who have sufficient protein. Health officials are concerned about "hidden hunger" in America, the land of plenty. Perhaps the poor nutritional habits of teenagers contribute to the incidence of prematurity and defective children in this group of mothers. Can a healthy baby be made from parents who exist on fast-food hamburgers, french fries, and cola? The critical period for nutritional deprivation is in the first trimester of pregnancy. Inadequate resources to develop heart, nervous system, lungs, or eyes result in poorly constructed organs and systems. In the later months of pregnancy, the result of inadequate nutrition is a baby with a low birth weight. Medical practice at midcentury advised pregnant women to keep their weight gain to a minimum, in the belief that women who gained only a little weight were less susceptible to toxemia and had fewer complications of birth. An unexpected side effect of restricted nutritional intake, however, was babies with a low birth weight. Current standard medical advice encourages good nutrition and is much less concerned about the total weight gain.

Any pregnant woman should have a planned diet and not leave food intake simply to impulsive desires. This is, of course, true of all people, but when irreversible damage can be inflicted on an unborn child, the stakes are higher.

Drugs

Drugs have become an integral part of the American way of life. TV commercials ask: Have a headache? Take a pill. Acid indigestion? Take a pill. Can't sleep? Take a pill. Americans consume vast quantities of over-the-counter drugs each year. Equally large quantities of even more powerful prescription drugs are used. The American dream has been packaged and marketed and is now available as a small white pill.

In popular consciousness we tend to associate the word *drug* with the illegal variety (marijuana, heroin, cocaine, etc.), but for our purposes in looking at prenatal development, we will consider the effects of all drugs. The placenta does not have the badge of a narcotics agent to check to see if drugs are legal or illegal. In pregnancy *all* drugs constitute a potential hazard to the embryo/fetus and should be taken with caution. This caution encompasses over-the-counter drugs such as aspirin, prescription drugs such as sleeping pills, appetite depressants, and illegal drugs such as marijuana and LSD. Illegal drugs simply carry the additional possible hazards of completing a pregnancy in prison or paying a heavy fine. We have not yet catalogued all the drugs that may cause prenatal damage. Therefore, standard scientific advice, at this time, is *avoid all drugs and chemicals.* The effects of many drugs have only been discovered through the tragic births of deformed, defective children.

By the middle of this century standard obstetric practice was smug and self-satisfied. Techniques had been advanced that had virtually conquered the risk of maternal death in childbirth. It was a time of optimism, and women were freed from severe Victorian restrictions of confinement during pregnancy and advised to continue with normal activities. Physicians used all medical means to keep mothers comfortable in pregnancy and childbirth. Drugs to prevent nausea, sleep irregularities, difficult pregnancies, and other general discomforts were freely given in the belief that the placenta acted as a barrier, or that if a drug did not harm the mother, it would not harm the child. Then the great thalidomide tragedy struck.

The drug thalidomide was responsible for many deformed babies; it sensitized the scientific community to the danger of drugs. Thalidomide was developed as a tranquilizer but it also relieved the discomforts of nausea and insomnia in pregnant women. It had been tested with pregnant rats and found to cause no damage. It has been estimated that approximately eight thousand babies were born in Western Europe and the United States with defects caused by this drug (Schardein, 1976). The defect varied, according to the time in the pregnancy that the fetus was exposed to the teratogen. It has been found that taking thalidomide between the thirty-fourth and thirty-eighth day after conception results in a baby born without ears; taking it between the thirty-eighth and forty-sixth days results in the baby's arms being deformed or failing to form at all. Ingesting the drug between the fortieth and forty-sixth days results in the baby's legs being either missing or deformed. After the fiftieth day the critical period for damage from thalidomide was over and those women who took the drug suffered no damage to their children (Saxon & Rapola, 1969).

In the 1950s the steroid diethylstilbestrol was given to women who had suffered repeated miscarriages. It kept them from aborting the fetus. The children of these women appeared normal and healthy. It has been found, however, that this drug administered prenatally rendered the daughters of these women more susceptible to cancer of the cervix and in some cases caused sterilization (Herbst, Kurman, Scully, & Poskanzer, 1972). The drug is also implicated in testical cancer in the sons. As a result of the tragic events caused by these two drugs, physicians are extremely cautious about prescribing drugs to women who are or might be pregnant. Nevertheless, studies have shown that pregnant women continue to take drugs during pregnancy (Heinonen, Slone, & Shapiro, 1976). Hill (1973) found that, in a survey of 156 pregnant women, the average number of drugs taken was ten. This included diuretics, antihistamines, sedatives, and hormones; not included were social drugs such as alcohol and nicotine.

Prescriptive Drugs.   Drugs that can only be obtained by order of a physician are called prescriptive drugs. These are powerful chemicals that combat many diseases and organic disorders, but they also have many undesirable side effects. The physician must judge if the good that the drug does is worth those undesirable side effects. Many prescriptive drugs are now suspected of causing defects in unborn children. Among them are steroids and hormones, anticoagulants, standard drugs such as antibiotics and quinine, and narcotics. In addition, excessive doses of vitamins A and D have been implicated in birth defects. The thousands of drugs in production will need to be tested one by one on experimental animals, but even such testing may not indicate the effect on human embryos. The list of drugs known to cause prenatal damage is large and growing and is drawn from a large number of categories.

Nonprescriptive Drugs. Drugs that are less potent and that may have fewer side effects than prescriptive drugs are available over the counter in pharmacies. We tend to consider those drugs harmless, and as a result the American public consumes huge quantities of them. The care with which prescriptive drugs are recommended for pregnant women has now been extended to include nonprescriptive drugs. Recent evidence indicates that such "harmless" compounds as aspirin may cause undesirable side effects. Aspirin has been found to cause internal bleeding and is suspected of causing prenatal damage, although the exact effects are not known. The general advice to pregnant women is to avoid all medicinal compounds.

Alcohol. The argument has been advanced that the effects of marijuana are no worse than those of alcohol. That argument is not very sound, because alcohol is far from a harmless drug. Alcoholism is now considered a major health problem, and recent evidence indicates that even moderate daily consumption of alcohol by a pregnant woman can cause damage in the developing child (Smith, 1980). In the

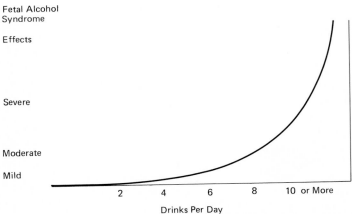

How many drinks a day are harmful to the fetus? With a nonspecific syndrome such as Fetal Alcohol Syndrome it is difficult to identify the exact amount of alcohol that will affect a fetus. Evidence indicates that two drinks a day by a pregnant woman will cause effects in the fetus. In general, a "drink" means one beer, a medium glass of wine, or one cocktail. Thus, a woman who consumes as much as two medium glasses of wine or two beers a day is endangering the unborn child. Toxic effects to the fetus escalate rapidly as alcohol consumption increases. Women who are alcoholic pose a great hazard to their unborn children. [Adapted from "Alcohol Effects on the Fetus" by David W. Smith, MD. In R. H. Schwarz and S. J. Yaffe (Eds.), *Drug and Chemical Risks to the Fetus and Newborn.* New York: Alan R. Liss, Inc., 1980. Copyright © by Alan R. Liss, Inc. By permission.]

Table 3–2. Drugs That Have Been Found to Produce Toxic Effects in Human Fetuses, the Number of Cases Reported, and the Effect That the Drug Produced*

Drug	Number of Cases	Effect
Thalidomide	8,000	Thalidomide embryopathy
		Limbs, ears, eyes, internal organs
Hormones		
Androgens	37	Females—fusion of labia
		Clitoral hypertrophy (virilization)
Progestins	>600	Females—virilization
	9	Males—hypospadias (feminization)
Estrogens		
Diethylstilbestrol	4	Females—virilization
	>90%	Females—vaginal adenosis, cervical ridges
	>200	Females—postpubertal cervical clear cell carcinoma
	28	Males—hypospadias or meatal stenosis, deficient sperm
Progestins and estrogens	28	Males—behavior and personality
Folic acid antagonists		
Aminopterin	17	Cranial dysostosis, craniofacial anomalies, cleft palate, talipes
Amethopterin	1	
Alcohol	>60	Fetal alcohol syndrome—retardation, palpebral fissure shortening, craniofacial, limb
Anticonvulsants		
Phenytoin	51	Fetal hydantoin syndrome—craniofacial, limb, hypoplasia of phalanges and nails, growth defect
Tridione	>16	Fetal tridione syndrome—craniofacial, cleft palate
Aminoglutethimide	3/5	Females—virilization
Anticoagulants		
Warfarin	14	Nasal hypoplasia—chondrodysplasia punctata: Conradi-Hünermann syndrome
Alkylating agents		
Chlorambucil	1/3	Agenesis, kidney and ureter
Busulfan	2/27	Cleft palate, eye, genitalia
Cyclophosphamide	2/5	Ectrodactyly, digit defects
Nitrogen mustard	2/7	Digital and renal defects
Iodides	39	Goiter, hypo- and hyperthyroidism
Propylthiouracil	18	Exophthalmos, goiter
Methimazole	2	Neonatal deaths
^{131}I	12	Thyroid ablation
Miscellaneous	32	Goiter

From "Critical Periods of Prenatal Toxic Insults" by Allen S. Goldman. In *Drug and Chemical Risks to the Fetus and Newborn*, edited by Richard H. Schwarz and Somner J. Yaffe. Copyright © 1980 by Alan R. Liss, Inc., New York. Reprinted by permission.

*This list is not exhaustive, nor is the number of cases complete.

early 1970s a condition known as the fetal alcohol syndrome was identified. The symptoms vary (according to the principle of critical periods) but include general slowed prenatal growth, which often results in premature birth. Specific physical effects may be microcephaly and deformities affecting the heart, eyes, ears, fingers and toes, and head. In addition, postnatal behavioral effects may occur, such as disturbed sleep patterns. The syndrome has been isolated through careful retrospective research. This research estimates that as little as two to four ounces of 86 proof alcohol per day consumed by a pregnant woman constitutes a 10 per cent risk to the infant. Risk increases with increased consumption of alcohol. It is estimated that in the United States as many as six thousand infants a year are born with this syndrome, a larger group than children born with Down's Syndrome.

Nicotine.   Nicotine is the principal chemical absorbed in the body through the lungs when cigarettes are smoked. Recent figures on the smoking population indicate that teenage girls are the fastest growing market for cigarettes. These are, or soon will be, our childbearing young women. The medical evidence indicates that smoking mothers are more apt to have premature births, and that even their full-term babies have a lower birth weight (Witter & King, 1980). The research evidence is not yet complete as to exactly how nicotine affects the fetus. One hypothesis is that the blood can carry only so much "baggage," and when it is loaded with nicotine and other products of smoking, there is no room for life-giving oxygen and the fetus then suffers from oxygen starvation.

Illegal Drugs.   That group of drugs that is forbidden for sale by law in this country is deemed illegal. This includes both psychoactive and narcotic drugs: marijuana, LSD, angel dust, narcotics, heroin, and cocaine.

There is evidence that both marijuana and LSD are responsible for chromosome breakage, which can result in abnormal development. Addictive drugs such as heroin cross the placental barrier and cause a physiological addiction in the fetus. Withdrawal from such addiction can cause death in the newborn. In all probability, a woman who is addicted to heroin has probably also neglected nutrition and other prenatal care. The infants of addicts are born addicted and are sent home with a mother who is addicted. In hospitals where there is an awareness of the problem, the infants are withdrawn from the addiction under medical management.

Environmental Hazards

A generation ago a woman of childbearing age who wanted to give her child the best start in life checked her diet, regulated her activities to get rest and exercise, and conducted the pregnancy in the secure knowledge that she was providing the best environment possible for the fetus. Today environmentally sensitive young women cannot be so secure in providing safety for the fetus. Increasingly the by-products of our complex industrial society constitute a hazard for humans in general and the vulnerable fetus in particular. There is a growing fear that industrial chemicals and radiation may cause birth defects and permanent genetic damage in future generations.

Radiation

The developing zygote, or embryo, is susceptible to physical damage from radiation. Radiation comes from X-rays used in dental and medical examinations and in the treatment of cancer, from industrial and atomic energy sources, as fallout from nuclear testing (or warfare), and from the sun. X-rays are a component of light, but they can pass through skin and bone. It is this property that enables us to obtain an image of bones and internal organs for medical diagnosis when X-rays are concentrated and passed through the body. X-rays that emanate from the sun or industrial sources are constantly passing through our bodies. When those rays pass through the body they sometimes destroy cells. Occasionally they hit the genetic material and destroy it. If an X-ray strikes a sex cell that is later fertilized, the result may be a mutation, or abnormal development. If it strikes an ovum that is newly fertilized, the developmental path may be altered. The effects of radiation damage are not fully documented, but evidence indicates that the potential danger includes malformation, brain damage, predisposition to cancer, and prenatal death. Long-range effects may be a shortened life span and genetic mutation that does not manifest itself until the genes have been passed to the children or grandchildren of the irradiated fetus.

Radiation damage to the zygote may render it nonviable, whereas damage in the stage of the embryo is thought to cause deformities. Radiation early in the fetal stage may also cause damage. After the atomic blast at Hiroshima, Japan, in 1946, there was an increase in the number of deformed children born that was attributed to the atomic fallout. Environmentalists have been concerned with the peaceful use of atomic energy and the hazard such use constitutes for the populace. We cannot avoid all radiation, for our sun's rays emit it and we are all subjected to some every day. Again, as with other agents, the advice to pregnant women is *avoid unnecessary X-rays.*

Chemical Pollution

Increasingly young men and women are becoming concerned about the effect of chemical pollutants on their offspring. Powerful chemicals can affect the chromosomal structure in adults and cause birth defects in children years later. For exam-

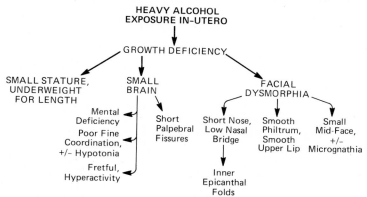

Most common features of Fetal Alcohol Syndrome. Is drinking "safe" at any level for a pregnant woman? The answer is probably "no." When any drug has been identified as a teratogen, it is difficult to specify a "safe dose." The effects depend on the individual genetic characteristics of the mother and the fetus, the timing of the exposure, and other environmental factors. [From "Alcohol Effects on the Fetus" by David W. Smith, MD. In R. H. Schwarz and S. J. Yaffe (Eds.), *Drug and Chemical Risks to the Fetus and Newborn.* New York: Alan R. Liss, Inc., 1980. Copyright © by Alan R. Liss, Inc. By permission.]

ple, Vietnam veterans who were exposed to powerful herbicides during the Vietnam War are fearful that the effects of those chemicals are manifesting themselves in increased birth defects in children being born now. Another chemical that has been implicated in causing birth defects is mercury. This relationship was confirmed when physicians in Japan noticed a sharp rise in birth defects and retardation. This rise was restricted to the population around Minamata Bay. After seven years the cause was identified as mercury; it had been dumped into the bay at the site of an industrial plant. The mercury had concentrated in the fish in the bay and found its way into the systems of the pregnant women (Milunsky, 1977).

It was recently discovered in America that a housing development had been built over an industrial chemical dump. Again, an increase in birth defects was noted in the population. An investigation revealed that the chemicals that had been buried years before were seeping to the surface. Residents were evacuated and there was great concern about the possible effects of these chemicals on children and pregnant women.

Another concern of men and women of childbearing age is the chemicals in foods and cosmetics. Thousands of chemicals are added to foods for color and to extend shelf life. Most of them have not been tested for safety (Ames, 1979). Many of them have been implicated in causing cancer; the effect is unknown on the human fetus. Our technological-industrial society is rapidly developing new chemicals and new products whose possible toxicity would take years to test. No one knows what shape our future society will take, but we can hope that it will not be one with large numbers of people with birth defects caused by the thoughtless consequences of our technology.

The Subjective Experience of Pregnancy: Three Case Studies

We have reviewed the facts of conception, prenatal development, and the terminology used to describe stages. Let us now turn our attention to the experience of the woman in this process. Each woman will have a different perception of her pregnancy, different psychological attitudes and emotions connected with it, and different social environments. These differences will have far-reaching effects on the development of their children. Consider the following three women.

Aileen and Phillip have been married for three years. Aileen is a nurse with the welfare department in the city where they live. Phillip works for a textile manufacturing firm and is being considered for a promotion in the planning and development office. Eight months ago Aileen and Phillip decided that they were ready to begin a family. They have anxiously been awaiting the report that "they" are pregnant. Aileen's mother, who lives in the same state, but in another town, has been buying little things that Aileen will need when the baby is born. Phillip's mother is a bit more cautious about the prospect, but she cannot resist telling her bridge club some of her plans for her grandson. When Aileen returns from the obstetrician on a Thursday afternoon she calls Phillip as soon as she gets into the house to tell him he is really going to be "Daddy." In the next weeks and months Aileen and Phillip talk late into the night about plans for their baby: whether it will be a boy or girl, what they will name her or him, the toys they will buy, the kinds of schools they want, the sports and activities the child will engage in. They both have a warm feeling for the family they are a part of and extending.

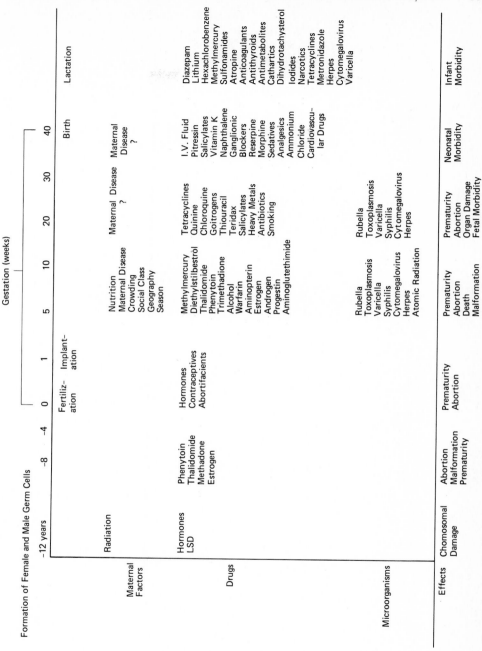

Maternal factors, drugs, and microorganisms that may have a toxic effect on the embryo or fetus with a time line of critical period of most likely effect. [Adapted from "Critical Periods of Prenatal Toxic Insults" by Allen S. Goldman. In *Drug and Chemical Risks to the Fetus and Newborn,* edited by Richard H. Schwarz and Sumner J. Yaffe. Copyright © 1980 by Alan R. Liss, Inc., New York. By permission.]

Lisa is a junior in high school. She is an average student and has many friends. Lisa is an attractive young woman from a working-class family. Her parents were recently divorced. Although she did not have everything she wanted as a child, the family lived a comfortable, if modest, life. Lisa is the second of four children. Her older sister graduated from high school last year and now has a job in an insurance office. Lisa has been dating Tom for the past six months. Tom is on the football team and many girls envy Lisa for having such a good-looking, popular boyfriend. When Lisa returns from the obstetrician on a Thursday afternoon, she throws herself on her bed and sobs. She is confused, lonely, and terrified at knowing that she will have to tell her mother and Tom that she is going to have a baby. She has put off going to the doctor as long as possible and soon, she knows, her condition will be obvious. The thought obsessively goes through her mind: "What can I do?" In the next few weeks and months, Lisa lives as though in a dream. She cannot concentrate on school. She pushes the thought of the baby out of her mind and avoids the diet and other instructions that the doctor prescribed. She feels as though she has been sentenced to prison and faces the future with dread.

Alice and Walter have been married for 22 years. They have two children who are in college. Alice did not work outside the home until her last child entered college. Then she opened a needlecraft shop. She had always done a lot of needlework and finally was able to fulfill her dream of the shop. She enjoys the days at work, talking to people about their projects, recommending one material over another, and traveling to New York on buying trips. Also, for the first time she has money that she has earned, enabling her to do some special things without asking Walter. She and Walter have had a good, if not exciting, marriage. She has been satisfied with her children, and in general, with her life. When Alice returns from the obstetrician on a Thursday afternoon she goes into the den and pours herself a drink. As she drinks it she thinks of the years of diapers, nursery schools, PTA meetings, birthday parties, little league games, class plays, and graduations. She thinks of the good times and of the bad ones. She remembers the long years of carpools and seemingly forever being "on call." She thinks about her present situation. She has money and free time and finally is beginning to find her own stride. A wave of resentment floods her for the child she knows is growing. She has not even mentioned to Walter that she suspected a "menopause pregnancy." She wonders if she can really go through raising another child at her age. And then she thinks about the increased risk of a defective child. Alice watches the birds in her manicured garden and knows she must make some hard choices.

Trimesters

In general, unless a woman avidly reads a developmental timetable, she is not aware of the development of her child. The periods of the zygote, embryo, and fetus have little meaning for her. The timetable given to mothers is more often in terms of trimesters. In referring to trimesters, the nine months are broken into three even parts. Thus, we refer to the first trimester as encompassing the first three months; the second trimester, the fourth through the sixth month; and the third trimester, the seventh through the ninth month. Let us look at the trimesters in terms of the woman's experience.

First Trimester

The first three months of pregnancy include the period of the embryo and a month into the period of the fetus. This is the time in which the body of the woman adjusts to the great physiological changes involved in pregnancy. The change is governed by hormones. When the embryo is implanted in the uterus, the production of hormones shifts and signals the body to make changes. The woman may begin to experience nausea even before pregnancy is confirmed. She may also begin to experience a fullness and tenderness in the breasts. It is extremely important for a woman who suspects that she is pregnant to seek the advice of a physician and to establish a plan of prenatal care. She is advised of diet, exercise, activities, and any special problems. Chronic diseases of the mother, such as diabetes, constitute a risk for the child and require special medical management. In addition, a pregnant woman is advised to be extremely cautious about taking any drugs, including aspirin. The first trimester, you remember, is the time of the child's greatest vulnerability to environmental damage. It is also the time of the threat of spontaneous abortion in case of genetic abnormalities. The realization that a third person is entering the family can sometimes put an additional strain on the marriage. When a new component, a child, enters the family system, the relationships *must* be altered. This alteration is first of all affected by the cultural expectations that the two people have of their new roles. Our culture has certain expectations for pregnant women and other expectations for expectant fathers. In addition, there are individual differences in how those cultural expectations are internalized and expressed. By the end of the first trimester the adjustment to pregnancy is completed and the discomfort is usually gone.

Second Trimester

Most women experience the second trimester as a time of satisfaction and a sense of well-being. In the second trimester the fetus grows very rapidly, and pregnancy becomes a reality for the mother. Instead of the abstract knowledge that she is pregnant, she feels the movement of the child and sees her abdomen expand. Sometimes an arm or a leg can be felt through the walls of the uterus and abdomen. The mother has adjusted biologically to the state of pregnancy. Her friends and family have usually adjusted to her new state and she has come to terms with any psychological ambivalence with which she might have greeted the initial news. This is the time in which psychological acceptance of the child is accomplished. The mother begins to collect clothes and other articles that she will need for the child and plans for the space that will be necessary. She fantasizes about whether the child will be a boy or girl and may carry these fantasies out in great detail. She begins to make choices as to whether to breast or bottle feed, whether she will continue work if she is then working, and about child rearing. She begins to review her own childhood and talks to her mother or other women for some guidance in her new role. Research has indicated that this preparation is important in subsequent acceptance of the child (Rubin, 1967a, 1967b). Women who do not make physical preparation for their child are more likely to abuse their infants.

The woman's physical activities are not sharply curtailed at this point, and the relationship between husband and wife is usually good. Aileen and Phillip will pick out a name for both a boy and a girl and make elaborate plans for their child. Lisa, who is unmarried, must come to terms with her situation. If she seeks an abortion, it must be before 24 weeks and would be preferable in the first trimester. If she decides to have the baby, then the decision will be made whether she and Tom should marry, or if she should have the baby and raise it with her parents. If she is living with her mother, by the second trimester, any recriminations should have subsided and she and her mother should be making plans for crib, clothes, and the routines of caring for the baby. Even in this situation, which is not socially sanctioned, there is joy and an air of anticipation for the coming baby.

Alice, too, has come to terms with her pregnancy. Walter was not pleased with her pregnancy, for he too was enjoying the increased freedom from family responsibilities. Alice's grown children were embarrassed. This was a problem that their friends at college might face, not their mother! Alice considered her well-ordered life and how easy an abortion would be. In the end, however, she decided that she could not accept the guilt of abortion and decided to keep her shop with the help of a hired assistant. The new baby would simply have to fit into her life structure. Because it was her shop, she would arrange a place for it there and take it with her. As she made plans she became excited about this new adventure and felt the new child would be great company for her when Walter was busy with business.

Third Trimester

In the third trimester pregnancy begins to seem an interminable state for many women. The overfull uterus creates discomfort with posture, in pressure on the bladder, and simply in weariness from carrying an extra 20 to 30 pounds. Often the mother has trouble sleeping and she begins to be concerned about the birth experience. She has heard so many different and conflicting stories. How will her labor go and, most importantly, will the baby be all right? Unless the husband, and others, are prepared for these anxieties and discomforts, relationships can become strained and add to the already stressful situation. The mother is torn between the wish for a premature birth to end the pregnancy and a longer pregnancy for the safety of the baby. One thing is certain, however, and that is that she is not in control of events, for no one can predict the onset of labor. She has had a suitcase packed to take to the hospital for several weeks and emergency plans have been worked out.

Aileen, Lisa, and Alice will each approach the birth of her child with different hopes and fears and with different risks. Aileen and Phillip have probably attended classes in preparation for childbirth. Phillip has, no doubt, been interested and now is as knowledgeable as Aileen about the process. They have been very careful to follow the advice of their physician and have practiced behaviors for childbirth. They will remain together and share in the event of the birth of their child. The risk of any adverse events for either Aileen or her child are slim. She is of the ideal age, has had excellent prenatal care and training for childbirth, and she has excellent social supports.

The risk for both Lisa and Alice is considerably greater. Both the teenage mother and the woman over forty have a much greater risk of a complicated delivery and birth defects. Both Lisa and Alice know this, and therefore approach childbirth with more apprehension. Lisa did not attend classes for childbirth because she was embarrassed both to be pregnant and because she did not have a husband to attend with her. Alice did not attend because she had had two children and, after all, should know how it is done. Walter, Alice's husband, was very busy in his business and left Alice to handle the details of the preparation for a new child. The third trimester ends with the advent of labor and the birth of the child.

Main Points

Female Sexual Cycle

1. Ovulation is the release of a mature egg from the ovary and occurs in a sexually mature woman approximately every 28 days.

2. Menstruation is the discharge of cells and blood that have engorged the uterine walls in preparation for a fertilized egg. When the egg passes through the uterus unfertilized, menstruation occurs.

Male Sexual Function

3. Sperm (the male sex cells) are produced in the testes and discharged through the penis into the female's vagina during sexual intercourse.

Conception

4. Conception occurs when a mature ovum encounters sperm, usually in one of the fallopian tubes.

Prenatal Periods

5. The first two weeks after conception are known as the germinal period. The zygote (fertilized egg) develops a placenta, umbilical cord, and amniotic sac and becomes firmly implanted in the uterus.

6. The embryonic period lasts from two weeks to approximately two months after conception. All body systems develop during this period from three layers of cells: ectoderm, mesoderm, and endoderm.

7. The fetal period begins at about two months when all physical structures have been differentiated and the first bone cells form. It is characterized by continued growth of the parts, organs, and systems formed in the embryonic period.

Abortion: Spontaneous and Induced

8. The interruption of a pregnancy before the fetus can live independently is termed abortion.

9. A spontaneous abortion is the result of natural causes and often is accompanied by gross abnormalities in the fetus; an induced abortion is an act based on choice.

Prenatal Development

10. In the first weeks after conception rapid changes occur; a definite human appearance is evident by eight weeks. The heart begins beating at four weeks but cannot be detected through a stethoscope until nine weeks. The sex of the fetus is discernible at seven weeks. The brain is essentially complete by ten.

11. In the third month the fetus completes development of all its major systems but is unable to survive outside the body of the mother. The fetus continues to grow larger and behavioral systems develop in the fourth, fifth and sixth months.

12. Each of the last three months before birth increases the fetus' chances of survival. Birth usually occurs 266 days after conception.

Principles of Prenatal Development

13. Development proceeds from the head to the lower extremities, in accordance with the cephalocaudal principle of development.

14. The proximodistal principle is that development proceeds from the center of the organism outward.

15. The principle of critical periods states that an aspect of development is most susceptible to environmental influences at its time of most rapid growth.

Environmental Influences on Prenatal Development

16. The maternal factors of age, disease, blood type, and emotional reactions can affect the developing fetus.

17. The most important single environmental factor in the prenatal development of a child is nutrition.

18. During pregnancy *all* drugs, including nicotine and alcohol, constitute a potential hazard to the embryo/fetus and should be used cautiously.

19. The developing zygote, embryo, and fetus are susceptible to physical damage from radiation and chemical pollutants.

The Subjective Experience of Pregnancy

20. Each woman has a different perception of, psychological attitude to, and social environment for her pregnancy.

Trimesters

21. During the first trimester (three months) of pregnancy the mother experiences physiological changes governed by hormones.

22. The second trimester is a time of preparation, planning, and psychological acceptance by the mother, her family, and friends.

23. The third trimester ends with childbirth, which each woman approaches with different hopes, fears, and risks, depending on her prenatal care, training for childbirth, age, and social supports.

Words to Know

abortion	fetus	ovulation	sperm
conception	menstruation	penis	testes
conceptus	mesoderm	placenta	toxemia
ectoderm	miscarriage	pregnancy	uterus
embryo	ova (ovum)	prenatal	zygote
endoderm			

Terms to Define

amniotic sac
cephalocaudal development
critical periods
embryonic period
fallopian tube

fetal period
germinal period
placental barrier
proximodistal development

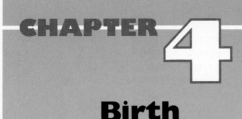

CHAPTER 4

Birth

Have you ever wondered

> how the birth process takes place?
> what causes babies to be born prematurely?
> what the effects of prematurity are?
> what causes birth defects?
> if drugs used in childbirth affect the infant?
> what "natural" childbirth is?
> what "education" for childbirth is?
> if there are alternatives to birth in hospitals?

The birth of a child is an event that can be viewed from many perspectives. Each event is somewhat different and each is an inextricable intersection of a physical, a psychological, and a sociological event. Birth has deep cultural and psychological meanings and is a theme in the sacred stories of various religions and ancient folk tales. It is a miraculous event in the human drama. It is a beginning that carries with it all the hope and possibilities of beginnings. The mystery of birth has both awed and frightened humans from the beginning of human awareness to the present.

If the genetic material of which we are composed extends in an unbroken chain from the beginning of life, so too does the process of forging this chain. The cycle of birth and death has remained unchanged from the first human to the present. Conception occurs in the same way, gestation requires the same length of time, and birth happens in the same way. It is important to understand this point before we look at our modern scientific understanding of this eternal process.

Science has supplied us with many "miracles" in the twentieth century. However, the basic physiological processes are the limits that we must accept as our guidelines. With our new knowledge through science, we have simply come to understand an eternal process; we have not invented it, at least not yet.

One more factor is important in understanding the complexity of birth before dissecting the event: because the bearer of the child is always a woman, birth is also intimately related to our understanding of and attitudes toward women. The factors of sex, femininity, women's rights, and male–female relations all have a bearing on the management of birth, the emotions associated with birth, and the acceptance of a child into his or her community.

Within this framework, we will attempt to disentangle the strands of the event of birth. First, we will look at the physical process of birth and complications that may accompany it. Second, we will look at birth as a cultural and psychological event—including alternative methods of childbirth—for the mother, father, and, child.

The Process of Birth

At the time of birth the fetus has existed for 266 days totally dependent on the biological systems of the mother. The birth process entails the biological separation of the two. The transition from dependent to independent life is a hazardous one for the infant, but one for which great preparation has been made.

When a woman is in the process of giving birth to her child, she is said to be in *labor*. This process consists of the involuntary contraction of the uterus, the opening of the mouth of the uterus known as the *cervix*, the expulsion of the fetus

A baby at full term. The baby is well developed and in the usual birth position with the head down and lying on the left side. Note the relationship of the baby to the spine of the mother. Labor has not begun, as the cervix is long and thick; but when the fetus reaches this stage of development, birth is imminent. This is not a photograph of an actual baby but a sculpture created to illustrate the process of birth. [Reproduced with permission from the *Birth Atlas*, Sixth edition, 1979, Maternity Center Association, New York.]

from the body of the mother, and the expulsion of the *placenta,* known as the afterbirth. In medical terms, this process is divided into three stages.

First Stage of Labor

The first stage of labor consists of the dilatation of the cervix. In a woman who is not pregnant, the opening of the cervix is less than one centimeter. This opening must enlarge to approximately 10 centimeters, or be large enough to accommodate the head of the fetus. This is the longest stage of labor and may last from an average of 14 to 15 hours for first children, to only a few hours for subsequent children. It is often difficult to determine the actual advent of labor for, during the last months of pregnancy, there are periodic contractions of the uterus that resemble labor; however, these contractions diminish rather than build, as they do when leading to birth. They are known as Braxton-Hicks contractions and are presumed to assist in the process by softening the cervix. During the later months of pregnancy, the cervix has thinned increasingly and becomes pliable for this stretching process.

True labor is identified by the rhythmic quality of the uterine contractions. These contractions may begin at twenty-minute intervals and last for 30 to 60 seconds. The time between contractions decreases, until they occur approximately at five-minute intervals and last from one to two minutes. When contractions occur at three-minute intervals and the intensity increases, the birth of the baby is imminent.

The last part of the first stage of labor is known as the transition phase. This occurs when the cervix is fully dilated and the head moves through the cervix into the birth canal. Many women experience transition, rather than the moment of

The first stage of labor. In the first stage of labor the cervix thins and opens and the baby descends into the pelvis. [Reproduced with permission from the *Birth Atlas,* Sixth edition, 1979, Maternity Center Association, New York.]

birth, as the most intense part of the birth process. At this time there is often an almost uncontrollable urge to push the baby out.

In the management of birth, it is important that the woman *not* push prior to this time because if the baby is forced out of the uterus before the cervix is fully dilated, it could result in a tear that heals with difficulty. Note that we are describing a normal birth in which the fetus is positioned with the head down, facing the mother's backbone. Other positions of the fetus entail complications of birth and often require different delivery procedures. When the fetus is positioned in the birth canal, the first stage of labor is over.

Second Stage of Labor

The second stage of labor is the actual birth of the baby. This stage lasts from perhaps twenty minutes to an hour and a half and encompasses the passage of the fetus through the several inches of the birth canal (the vagina), through the opening of the pelvis, and its emergence from the body of the mother. During this stage the woman can help the most in the process by continuing to push or bear down. During the long months of pregnancy, the body has been preparing for this event. In addition to the thinning of the cervix, the tissues of the vagina and vulva have obtained a stretchiness that will enable them to accommodate the head of the child. The connective tissue of the pelvis has become more flexible, to allow for enlargement. The soft pliable head bones of the fetus also allow for some accommodation.

In a normally positioned birth, the back of the head of the fetus is first visible in the vaginal opening. This is called crowning. In physician-assisted births, the physician may determine that the vaginal opening is not large enough for the head of the fetus to pass through, in which case a small incision known as an episiotomy may be made. This incision heals much more easily than a tear and recovery may thus be faster.

The head is the largest part of the fetus, and so it presents the most difficulty during the passage. As the head is born, the fetus is rotated and the nose and mouth are freed for breathing. The body continues to rotate and the shoulders are easily born, with the remainder of the body quickly following.

Given a normal birth, the crucial factor is the child's breathing. The attending person must make sure that obstructions are removed from the nose and mouth, including the amniotic fluid. The fetus has been dependent on the physiological processes of the mother, but at birth, and within a very few minutes, all of the physiological processes the mother's body performed must be taken over by the infant. The crucial component in this change is a constant supply of oxygen-rich blood. The umbilical cord is the source of food and oxygen supply for the fetus. When the fetus is born, the umbilical cord is still attached to the placenta and still functioning. This cord will continue to pulsate for several minutes after the birth of the child. While it is pulsating it is pumping oxygenated blood from the placenta into the newborn. The umbilical cord is not usually cut until the pulsation ceases. In the meantime, in uncomplicated births, the baby will have begun to breathe spontaneously. With the birth of the baby, the second stage of labor is completed.

Third Stage of Labor

The third stage of labor consists of the delivery of the placenta, the amniotic sac, and the remainder of the umbilical cord. This stage lasts approximately twenty minutes and carries little discomfort for the mother. The attending person examines

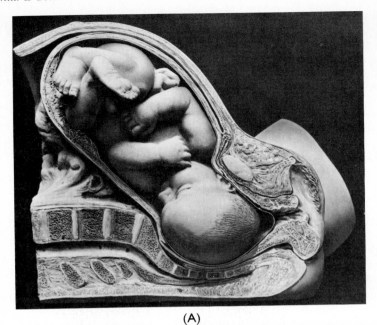

(A)

(B)

The second stage of labor. In the second stage of labor the head of the baby moves through the cervix, out of the uterus, through the birth canal, and emerges from the body of the mother. In diagram (A) the baby has turned toward the mother's spine and the head is fully engaged in the pelvis. The head and membranes are beginning to emerge from the uterus. In diagram (B) the baby's head is "crowning" as the crown of the head is the first to emerge from the vagina. Note the baby almost fully faces the mother's spine as the head leads. In this way, the delicate face is protected.

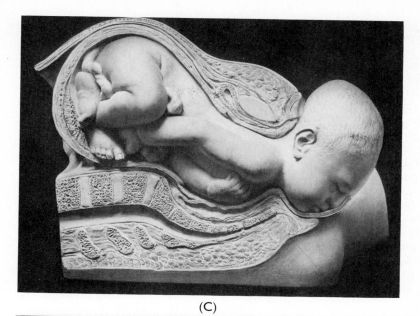

(C)

(D)

The second stage of labor (continued). In (C) the baby's head emerges and turns upwards. The head may be molded into a misshapen form from the pressure of passing through the pelvis. In a few days or weeks the baby's head will reform into the usual shape. When the head is fully born (D) birth has essentially occurred. The head and body turns as the baby is being born and the shoulders rotate. After the head emerges the remainder of the body slips easily from the mother's body. [Reproduced with permission from the *Birth Atlas*, Sixth edition, 1979, Maternity Center Association, New York.]

these membranes for any abnormalities and checks that all the afterbirth is expelled from the uterus. Then procedures are instituted to make sure that the uterus contracts and cuts off all the small capillaries that have fed the placenta. If this is not done, the woman might hemorrhage.

The Apgar Scale

The care of the child at the time of birth is of crucial importance. Many children have suffered needless damage in the past because of neglect in the first few minutes after birth. It has been said that the most dangerous journey that a person ever makes is the few inches from the uterus to the outside world. It is necessary that assistance be given if needed and that it be immediate. A physician-anesthesiologist observed that many infants did not receive the help that they needed because the danger signs were not recognized. This physician's name was Virginia Apgar. In 1953 she developed a very simple scale with which the infant's physiological functioning could be evaluated so that measures could be taken if needed. This simple scale rates five easily observed processes: pulse, breathing, muscle tone, reflex response, and color. Each of these dimensions can be rated as 0, 1, or 2. Thus, a total score can range from 0 to 10. This evaluation of the infant is made one minute after birth and again five minutes after birth. A score of 7 or above denotes a normally functioning infant. A score between 4 and 7 is a "caution" light indicating that some difficulties are present. In that case the child is watched for further problems. A score below 4 indicates "red" alert conditions in which the child is in danger and needs immediate attention. The scale is a gross measure of functioning, so a more detailed examination is done if necessary. It does not diagnose the cause of the problem, but it does serve as a quick screening device to identify those children who need special attention in the first few minutes of life. Sometimes conditions exist that need correction through surgery or other medical means that will not be taken for several weeks, but emergency measures to assist heart and breathing problems have saved many children from permanent damage or even death.

Complications of Birth

The short process of birth carries its own dangers. Those dangers are different from those that were the result of genetic damage or the prenatal environment. A great many of the handicaps that children have are preventable, with proper management: genetic counseling, prenatal care, and management of birth.

Prematurity

One of the crucial factors in the growth and development of the child is timing. So it is with the birth of the child. When a child is born before the normal gestation period is completed, it is termed premature. The normal length of gestation is 38 weeks. The infant that is born at 28 weeks has a fairly good chance of survival in a hospital with a special intensive care unit for premature infants. At 28 weeks the fetus weighs between two and three pounds and is 14 to 16 inches in length. New techniques are being developed constantly that provide specialized care for ever younger premature infants. At present we are able to save infants that would have unquestionably died in earlier times. Fetuses born at 24 weeks have attempted to breathe and at 26 weeks of gestation have an increasing chance of survival with the special care available.

It is extremely difficult to determine accurately length of gestation, and prema-

Table 4–1. Apgar Scoring Chart

Sign	0	1	2
Heart rate	Absent	Slow (below 100)	Over 100
Respiratory effort	Absent	Weak cry, hypoventilation	Good strong cry
Muscle tone	Limp	Some flexion of extremities	Well flexed
Reflex response 1. Response to catheter in nostril (tested after oropharynx is clear)	No response	Grimace	Cough or sneeze
2. Tangential foot slap	No response	Grimace	Cry and withdrawal of foot
Color	Blue, pale	Body pink Extremities blue	Completely pink

Note: The newborn is rated at one minute and five minutes on heart rate, respiration, muscle tone, reflex response, and color. This quick rating gives a composite score that indicates the newborn's general condition and level of functioning.

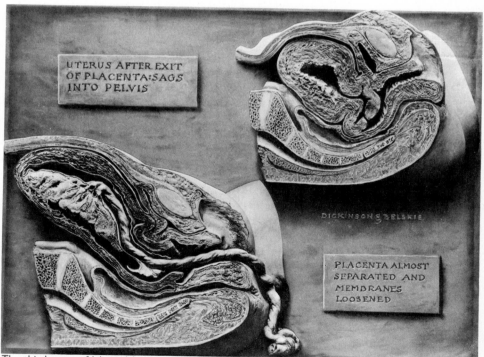

UTERUS AFTER EXIT OF PLACENTA: SAGS INTO PELVIS

DICKINSON & BELSKIE

PLACENTA ALMOST SEPARATED AND MEMBRANES LOOSENED

The third stage of labor. After the birth of the baby the placenta is separated from the walls of the uterus and expelled. In the crucial minutes after birth the placenta continues to provide oxygen-rich blood to the newborn through the umbilical cord. When the placenta is expelled, the uterus continues to contract which stops the flow of blood from the site of the placental implantation and begins the process of returning the uterus to its prepregnant state. [Reproduced with permission from the *Birth Atlas*, Sixth edition, 1979 Maternity Center Association, New York.]

turity is more often defined by birth weight rather than by length of gestation. In general, any child who weighs less than 5½ pounds at birth is considered premature and is recommended for special handling (Reed & Stanley, 1977).

The incidence of prematurity in the United States is approximately 7 per cent of all births. This percentage is higher than for many other industrialized nations and reflects a higher mortality rate for infants than in nations of comparable technical development.

The causes of prematurity are not known and, in fact, are probably multiple. Much research has been focused on describing the mothers and children who are subject to prematurity. Although we cannot pinpoint the cause, we can identify factors that are *associated* with prematurity. Some of those factors seem amenable to social intervention; some, perhaps, are not.

A first major factor associated with prematurity is multiple birth. Twins are much more likely to be born prematurely than a single infant. Whether this is because of crowding in the uterus or other factors is as yet unknown. Because prematurity is often associated with multiple births, it is especially important for a woman expecting twins to maintain careful prenatal attention to nutrition and general care. Even when gestation is the usual 38 weeks, twins tend to be low in birth weight and often need the special care of an incubator. Births of more than two infants almost always entail prematurity.

Other factors associated with prematurity are

1. Diseases of the mother, such as diabetes.
2. Drugs ingested by the mother.
3. Social conditions.
4. Low socioeconomic level.
5. Extreme youth of the mother.

Over half of the babies that are born prematurely in the United States are born to nonwhite mothers (Behrman, 1973). Mothers of thirteen, fourteen, and fifteen years of age are at high risk of prematurity. Increasingly, girls of eleven and twelve are becoming mothers, and even cases as young as eight have been reported.

We have stated that race, age, and socioeconomic status are *associated* with premature births. This means that there is a high correlation between these factors and incidents of prematurity. Correlation does not establish a cause-and-effect relationship. When such factors as race, age, and socioeconomic level are correlated with prematurity we cannot ignore the possibility that another unknown factor is the *cause*. For example, race and age may not in themselves cause prematurity. In general, young women who have few social supports, poor nutrition, inadequate medical care, and inferior education, compared to young women of similar age in different social and economic circumstances, have a greater incidence of premature infants. Therefore, we can speculate that nutritional deficiencies, toxemia, and other neglected conditions cause a higher percentage of prematurity for those young women. Thus, the typical picture of the mother at risk for a premature infant is a very young mother of low socioeconomic background. This mother may be white or nonwhite, but she is more than twice as likely to be nonwhite. Even so, it must be stated that prematurity does not respect socioeconomic level, age, or race, and any pregnancy, for reasons unknown, is subject to premature birth. In the use of scientific studies to understand the phenomenon of human growth, care must be taken not to generalize the "average" to mean the "always."

Effects of Prematurity

The effects of prematurity on the infant are diverse, and our knowledge of them is of a correlational nature. There are many factors associated with the incidence of prematurity that are without a clear cause-and-effect relationship. First, the immediate effects of prematurity will be considered and then the long-range effects. Birth is a transition from physiological dependence on the mother to reliance on the infant's own physiological mechanisms. In premature births the fetus may not have developed sufficiently to maintain its physiological independence. Two major problems arise in this connection. The first is that of breathing. The very immature infant may not have the strength to expand its lungs, or the lungs themselves may not be developed enough to sustain life. The second problem that may arise is maintaining body temperature. The body has several mechanisms to maintain its temperature within the general area of 98.6 degrees. One adaptation that the full-term infant has is a layer of fat under the skin to insulate the body and retain body heat. The premature infant lacks this fat and thus has a difficult time with temperature control. In addition to these two major problems, the general strength of the infant may be so low as to preclude its sucking either from a bottle or the breast and nourishing itself.

The premature infant also lacks the immunity to common infections that full-term babies acquire in the last two months of prenatal life. Therefore, he or she is more susceptible to disease. Other complications may be present, such as the poor development and functioning of other organs. In physiological terms, the stress of independent life may be more than the organism can meet. This stress in itself may precipitate new problems.

To overcome these physiological deficits the premature infant needs help immediately and often for several weeks or months after birth. Premature infants are placed in an incubator that maintains constant temperature and humidity. A mixture of oxygen with other gases is maintained for the easiest possible breathing with the highest oxygen content. These infants were once administered pure oxygen; it was subsequently discovered that that concentration of oxygen damaged their eyes. Infants are often fed, medicated, and cleaned in the incubator, to avoid infection and exhaustion. They are watched carefully for signs of illness or poor functioning. Given this special care, they grow rapidly and, by approximately one year of age, are the size of their age mates. They catch up with their age mates in motor development in a similar amount of time.

A secondary effect of prematurity may result from the solution to the physiological problems and manifest itself in psychological aspects. The physiological effects of prematurity can often be overcome without any long-term carryover. There are, however, behavioral and psychological problems associated with prematurity that remain evident for many years: learning disabilities, mental retardation, hyperactivity, irritability, stuttering, and general psychological disturbances. It must be noted both that children who are not premature can suffer from these behavioral disorders and that not all premature infants are subject to them. Statistically, however, a higher percentage of premature infants have these problems, which means that they are at greater risk for behavioral problems than full-term infants.

It may be that all of these factors are side effects of the handling of the premature child, rather than a direct effect of early birth. On the other hand, there has been speculation that these symptoms are the result of minimal brain damage. That is, damage that is so slight as to be undetectable by our instruments, yet great enough to cause behavioral abnormalities. For reasons that are not at all understood, boys are more susceptible to prematurity than are girls. And given a male and female child of similar premature birth, the male child is more likely to develop learning or behavioral problems in childhood.

An association between low birth weight and child abuse has also been found (Fontana, 1971; Klein & Stern, 1971; Elmer & Gregg, 1967). It is speculated that abuse occurs because the premature child violates many parental expectations, places greater demands upon the parents for physical care, financial support, and nurture. In addition, the premature infant is likely to continue to disappoint the parents with slow motor, social, and cognitive development during the first two years. Finally, the hospital care of the premature infant during the early weeks frequently interferes with establishing bonding and the subsequent attachment between parents and child.

One principle in child welfare is that prevention is better than cure and, in pursuit of this principle, much research has been undertaken in an attempt to prevent the side effects of prematurity. The quest has been made for the conditions that allow for the optimum development of those special children. Medical personnel are often primarily concerned with the physical dimensions of the developing child, but our level of medical expertise is constantly rising, and as we master the physical elements, we can afford to be increasingly concerned with the optimum psychological and sociological development of the child. As some nurseries for premature infants have looked at the psychological needs of the child, they have relaxed their strict rules about a sterile environment for the low-birth-weight baby and allowed mother and nurses to hold and rock the child as they would a normal infant. In some cases breast feeding has been encouraged, with effects that aid both the physical and emotional development of the infant.

Unfavorable Birth Position

Approximately 95 per cent of births are normal, spontaneous deliveries; however, in 5 per cent of births some assistance is needed from medical personnel. This does not include premature births, which may be routine except for the age and size of the infant. A major complication is that the fetus may not be in the usual birth position. When the fetus is either transverse in the uterus or positioned with the buttocks facing the opening of the cervix (*breech*), special procedures may be necessary. The conditions and procedures of medical intervention may constitute additional risk for the infant. But the simple use of forceps, or other instruments, can often aid the delivery of a healthy child.

Sometimes, however, the condition of fetus or mother indicates that prolonged labor would constitute a danger greater than surgical procedure, and the baby may be born by means of a surgical procedure known as a *Caesarian section*. It is said that Julius Caesar was born by such a procedure, and thus the name. Shakespeare writes that Caesar was "untimely ripped" from his mother's womb. Women sometimes request a Caesarian procedure to escape the anticipated pain from the birth of their child. A reputable obstetrician will *not* perform such an operation unless there is a medical reason for the procedure. A Caesarian birth is a major operation and recovery from the procedure is much more difficult than from the normal process of birth.

Birth Defects

The most serious child-health problem in the United States is birth defects, according to the National Foundation/March of Dimes (1981). A birth defect is defined as

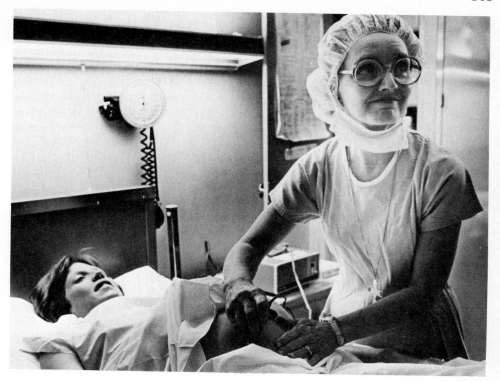

An obstetric nurse monitors the vital signs of the fetus during labor. With such careful monitoring, medical personnel follow the process of labor and if the mother or fetus begins to experience difficulty medical intervention can be instituted. [Courtesy Chuck Liddy.]

a condition present at birth (*congenital*) and is characterized by abnormality in one of three areas: structure, function, or body chemistry.

The cause of birth defects may be genetic (*inherited*), environmental factors in prenatal life, a combination of genes and prenatal environment, or an accident at birth. Any condition present at birth is termed congenital. Often the cause as genetic or environmental cannot be determined. The reason for this is that a child with a certain genetic combination may be more susceptible to environmental insult. The developing child is a continuing mix of genetic control and environmental influences.

Genetic Defects

Structural genetic defects affect the body's physical shape or size: a body part may be missing, misshapen, or duplicated. Such disorders as spina bifida (open spine), hydrocephalus (water on the brain), clubfoot, cleft lip or palate, extra fingers or toes, and dwarfism are examples of structural defects.

Functional genetic defects involve one or several parts of the body in which a structure appears normal but does not function properly. Examples of this type of defect are color blindness, glaucoma, muscular dystrophy, Huntington's Chorea, and some mental defects.

In some cases the body chemistry does not function normally. This is usually traceable to an error in the genetic code. In the case of errors in metabolism, the body is not able to convert certain chemicals into others. Galactosemia and PKU (phenylketonuria) are examples of this type of disorder. In the case of the former, the child is unable to produce the enzyme needed to break down the milk sugar, galactose. Unless the baby is immediately taken off milk, mental retardation and cataracts can result. In PKU the body does not produce the enzyme necessary for the metabolism of a certain amino acid. As a byproduct of this faulty metabolism, *phenylalanine* collects in the bloodstream and is converted to an acid. When the concentration of this acid reaches a critical level, it begins to destroy brain cells, and the result is mental retardation. Both of these inborn metabolic errors are controllable by diet. They are not, as yet, correctable. The child must continue careful control of diet for an entire lifetime.

Other errors in body chemistry have to do with blood diseases. Errors in this category may be the result of a blood component that is missing or functions poorly. In hemophilia the component responsible for clotting is missing, whereas in sickle-cell anemia the deformed cells cannot carry as much oxygen as normal cells.

Structural defects are detectable at birth, but functional defects and errors in body chemistry may not appear immediately. Diabetes is an example of an error in metabolism that may not show up for years.

Birth Accidents

Although the vast majority of births are uneventful, there are dangers associated with birth. When birth defects are not genetic and are not caused by conditions arising in prenatal life but are due to conditions during the birth process they are termed birth accidents. The National March of Dimes has an ongoing campaign for education and research into the causes and prevention of birth accidents. Those that give us the most concern cause permanent, irreparable damage. The greatest cause of this type of damage is *anoxia,* or oxygen deprivation, the major effect of which is permanent brain damage.

There are many events in the birth process that can threaten an adequate supply of oxygenated blood to the infant. Those events may take place in the birth process or after birth in delayed breathing by the infant. In either case, if the infant is deprived of oxygen for even a relatively short period of time, brain cells begin to die, and they are not replaceable. In general, those cells in the brain stem seem most susceptible to deprivation damage. One result of this type of birth accident is *cerebral palsy.* This condition is not always caused by birth accidents, but approximately 30 per cent of cases are so caused. Often the damage is confined to motor and speech areas. Prolonged oxygen deprivation can cause more severe brain damage, which results in mental retardation. Some of the causes of anoxia are prolonged labor, separation of the placenta before birth, drugs given to the mother that depress the physiological response of the infant, physical obstruction of breathing, and immaturity of the infant's respiratory organs. Actual damage to the infant's skull may occur that results in fractures and/or bleeding into the brain. These accidents can be caused by forceps or prolonged labor, in which the head of the infant is subjected to intense pressure. Unfortunately, at this point, there is nothing that can reverse damage inflicted to infants in this way.

In many instances in the past, a choice had to be made between the life of the mother and the life of the unborn child. Medical science has made great strides in the safety of both mother and child, but for many people the safety record has not been adequate.

Drugs in Childbirth

Bearing children has been both a joy to woman and her curse to bear. When society rested more heavily on the Judeo-Christian tradition, it was taken as God's ordination that "in pain [woman] should bear children" as punishment for disobedience in the Garden of Eden. For several hundred years science grappled with the hold that religion had on the human mind. One of the discoveries made in the late nineteenth century was that certain drugs such as chloroform and morphine were very effective in relieving pain. Physicians soon applied them to relieve women in childbirth. Certain moralists opposed the use of medical science for such purposes, on the grounds that it obstructed God's plan that women should suffer! Science, however, was on the ascendency and modern obstetrics embraced the use of pain-relieving drugs. Women, who had been told the horrors of childbirth by their mothers, aunts, and grandmothers, quickly embraced this modern miracle and asked to be "knocked out" for the birth of their children. Many women reported that they "didn't feel a thing." The use of these drugs proliferated in the years after the discovery of chloroform and morphine. In modern obstetrics there are many synthetic drugs that are available and variously used to control the discomfort associated with childbirth. Although they are quite effective in relieving the mother's discomfort, almost every drug administered crosses the placental barrier and enters the system of the fetus. It is only in recent years that researchers have been interested in the effects of drugs on the fetus and the newborn.

It has been found that barbiturates taken by the mother during labor are detectable in the system of the infant as long as two weeks after birth. The effect of most of these drugs is to depress physiological functioning. Babies born to mothers to whom pain-relieving drugs were administered are reported to show a more sluggish sucking response, less muscle tone, and to require more arousal in feeding (Brazelton 1970). Generally the effects of medication given to the mother during childbirth are detectable in the infant for the first weeks of life. One study (Conway & Brackbill, 1970) compared infants on the basis of the amount of drugs the mother had received in childbirth and found differences in rate of maturation, psychomotor responses, muscle tension, and vision as long as thirty days after birth. VanderMaelen, Strauss, and Starr (1975) found a direct relationship between the amount of medication administered to the mother in childbirth and the length of time required for habituation to sound in newborns. The infants who took longer to habituate had mothers who had received larger doses of drugs in childbirth.

In general the medication given to mothers in labor seems to have no lasting effect on the baby; however, the difference may be in the occasional marginal infant who has difficulty in adjustment at birth. This infant needs all the physiological responsiveness possible; sometimes the difference between an alert response and a sluggish one may be crucial.

The effect of medication on most infants seems slight and is generally restricted to responsiveness. The first days and weeks of life, however, are the time in which the initial bonding is taking place between mother and infant. When an infant is sluggish and not responsive to the ministrations of the mother, psychologists are concerned that the initial relationship does not begin as well as it would if the infant were more responsive. As an alternative, many psychologists and obstetricians recommend education for childbirth so that women can handle birth with less medication.

Education for Childbirth

A survey of cross-cultural practices in childbirth quickly reveals that there is no universal procedure for assisting women in childbirth. We find a wide range of practices, from applying extreme pressure to the woman's abdomen to administering to the husband rather than the laboring woman (*couvade*). Our culture has long assumed that childbirth is a natural occurrence and as such women "naturally" know how to give birth. The actual physiological process of birth, of course, does not vary from culture to culture, but the procedures used to assist childbirth do vary widely. Women themselves approach childbirth with a variety of attitudes, feelings, ideas, fears, and behaviors that substantiate the observation that behavior in childbirth is not innate but learned. Increasingly in the twentieth century medical personnel have been concerned with childbirth behavior and increasingly programs to affect this behavior by education have been designed.

Natural Childbirth (The Read Method)

In the 1930s Dr. Grantley Dick-Read, a British physician, noticed that there was wide variation in how women reacted to childbirth. Occasionally he found that women breezed through childbirth with no pain, without anesthesia, and experienced an almost ecstatic state of joy. Other women expressed great fear and experienced intense pain and had an unhappy experience. He reasoned that because

Many couples today know that both the process of birth and their personal experience of it is enhanced by training. These couples are attending a class in childbirth education instructed by a nurse. They will learn techniques for assisting the birth process as well as general information about the process. In most childbirth education programs, the husband is a vital part. The husband is coaching his wife as she practices breathing that she will use during labor.

childbirth was not always a painful terror, nature did not intend it to be so. He theorized that the natural condition of childbirth was intended to occur in rhythm with the body. Civilization, according to Read, had perverted the natural act of childbirth by teaching young girls to fear the event. This fear came from the horror stories that well-meaning mothers and friends told them. When, as young women, they came to childbearing, their fear caused them apprehension and great tension. Thus, Dr. Dick-Read theorized that pain was the result of a fear-tension-pain cycle and if the cycle could be broken, the pain of childbirth would automatically disappear. With fear and pain gone a woman would be free to experience the natural joy of childbirth. Dr. Read designed a program of education to counteract ignorance and fear and a program of physical exercises to teach control of the body for relaxation during childbirth. The method was called Natural Childbirth and was brought from England to the United States in the 1940s and 1950s. The method advocates abstinence from pain-relieving drugs, not for the safety of the baby or mother, but so that the woman can be fully conscious of her experience.

The Read Method of Natural Childbirth was widely advocated by the medical profession and the popular press. Many women did report joyful childbirth, but others were filled with self-doubt when difficult births failed to bring the expected joy. The final evaluation of Read's Natural Childbirth was that childbirth was not totally "natural" but could be enhanced greatly by programs of education. In the wake of this pioneer effort, many new programs were designed to educate women about childbirth. Today almost all pregnant women in the United States have at least the opportunity to attend classes about preparing for childbirth.

The Lamaze Method (Psychoprophylaxis)

Another approach to childbirth education is the Lamaze Method, or psychoprophylaxis. This is *not* natural childbirth; it does not see behavior in childbirth as natural but, on the contrary, as a learned response to the stimulus of uterine contractions. It was first developed in Russia and introduced to France by a Dr. Lamaze. The method was given his name and transported to America. In order to counteract pain in childbirth the response of "pain" to uterine contractions must be unlearned and a new conditioned response must replace it. The response that is substituted for the "pain" response is "breathing." Several types of breathing patterns become the conditioned response to uterine contractions, replacing the former response of pain. The method also involves education to remove ignorance and anticipatory fear, because fear is a distracting emotion and interferes with conditioning a new response to the uterine contractions. The Lamaze Method does not have as a cardinal principle abstinence from pain-relieving drugs. All the medical technology needed for a safe delivery is utilized. However, the effect of the method is to greatly reduce the need for drugs in childbirth so that the woman may be conscious and in control of her own body during labor and delivery. Drugs are used if they are needed to help the woman gain control and if necessitated by the best medical practice, such as an emergency Caesarean. The Lamaze Method is widely used today; similar methods are taught under the names of Prepared Childbirth and Educated Childbirth. These should not be confused with Natural Childbirth because, as previously stated, the assumptions are quite different, although the methods may be similar.

The Lamaze Method as developed in Russia was modified in France by use of a labor coach to keep the woman's concentration on the breathing exercises and to

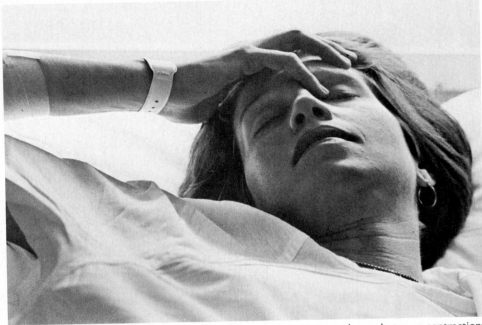

A woman trained in the Lamaze method of childbirth concentrates and rests between contractions during labor. The Lamaze method teaches women to be comfortable with their bodies, to work with the process of labor, and to maintain mental control in the process of giving birth. [Courtesy Chuck Liddy.]

help her to remain in control during labor and delivery. An additional interesting modification of the technique developed when it moved to America: the husband became the labor coach. Let us look at this method and some of its ramifications.

Husband-Coached Childbirth

It is the prevailing pattern in medically-managed childbirth that the husband and wife are separated at this most crucial time in the creation of their new family. The husband/father is excluded from the birth of his child. This was not the case when the country was more rural. In earlier times when most children were born in the home, the husband/father often assisted the doctor or midwife in the birth of the child. Husband-coached childbirth attempts to involve the father in the birth of his child and to give the mother the support she needs from the person she most needs it from—her husband.

The presence of the husband in the labor-delivery room, assisting and directing his wife, brings together several diverse strands. First, the method utilizes Lamaze techniques, sometimes modified, in which breathing and progress in labor are monitored, requiring the constant attention of a second person. America did not have trained labor coaches (in other countries usually physical therapists were used and husbands were plentiful and notoriously in the way). Second, the appearance of husbands in labor and delivery rooms coincides with an increased interest that fathers have shown in their infants. We cannot say whether fathers' interest in their

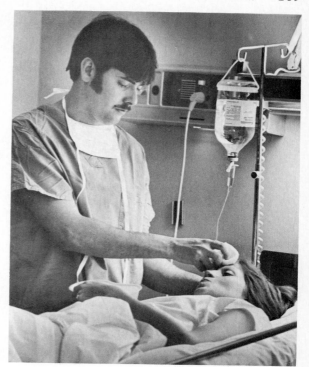

This husband is sponging the fore-head of his laboring wife in an attempt to make her as comfortable as possible. Some methods of childbirth include the husband as a vital member of the delivery team. [Courtesy Chuck Liddy.]

infants has led to husband-coached childbirth, or whether the experience of birth has led them to an increased interest in their infants. A third element that makes this approach appealing is the apparent decline of the American family and loosening of familial bonds. Proponents of the method feel that sharing this important event will weld stronger familial bonds and thereby strengthen the family structure perceived as faltering.

In both Lamaze and husband-coached childbirth the couple attends a series of classes during the last two months of pregnancy. In the Lamaze method the husband is encouraged to be with his wife in labor and delivery, if the hospital permits it; however, she is equipped to deal with her labor and delivery alone, if necessary. In husband-coached childbirth the husband is a trained member of the delivery team and his presence at labor and delivery is not optional but an integral part of the management of childbirth.

The preceding approaches to childbirth entail some education about breast feeding and are supportive of this feeding method. Indeed, breast feeding seems a logical extension of all three methods because they seek to harmonize modern technology, consciousness, and natural body rhythms.

Alternative Methods of Childbirth

Alternative methods of childbirth have developed both within the medical establishment and outside of it. Modern medical science has done a great service in increasing the safety of both mother and child in childbirth. In America at the turn of the twentieth century most babies were born at home. Even though the connec-

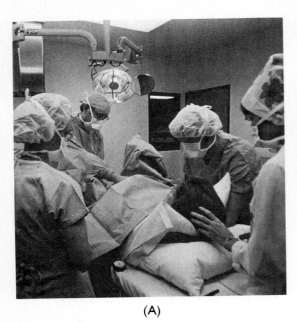

(A)

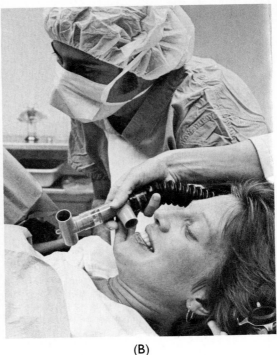

(B)

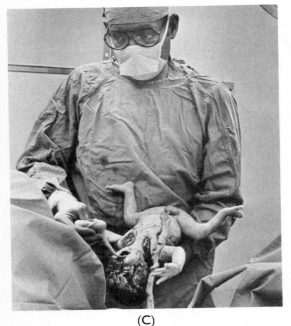

(C)

A Lamaze birth in a hospital. As the birth of the baby nears, doctor, nurses, and parents are prepared for the event. In (A) the second figure from the right is the woman's husband who continues to lend physical and psychological support. This woman has been offered anaesthesia (B) but rejects it as she and her husband are engrossed in the birth experience. Many couples report feelings of elation and joy during the birth of a child. And this experience is a healthy, robust son (C). The child, with umbilical cord attached and still pulsating, is being assisted in breathing by having mucus suctioned from nasal passages. Birth, itself does not entail blood. The blood on this baby is from the incision made in the vagina to enable the head to pass through easier.

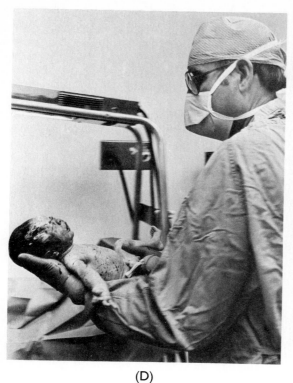

(D)

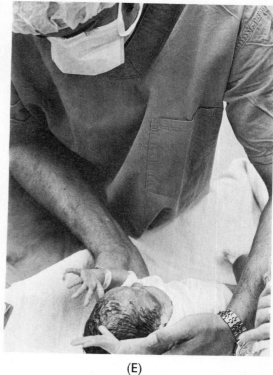

(E)

A Lamaze birth in a hospital (continued). Minutes old, the baby now breathing reliably, rests on the hand of the physician. (D) Note the prolapsed umbilical cord. The father (E) dresses his son for the first time. The birth passage safely completed, the baby rests as he is caressed for the first time (F). The waxy covering which has protected him while in the amniotic fluid is not scrubbed off but will be allowed to wear off gradually in the following days. [Courtesy Chuck Liddy.]

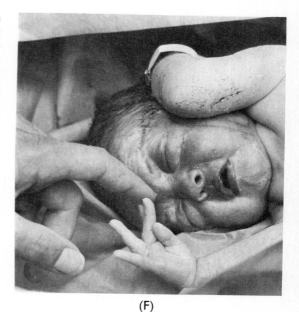

(F)

tion between sanitation and infection had been established, it was difficult to maintain sanitary conditions and, of course, special birth complications could not be satisfactorily resolved at home. The antibiotic "miracle drugs" such as penicillin were not discovered until the middle of the twentieth century. Thus, a bacterial infection contracted before that time was opposed primarily by the natural defenses of the body. Infection in childbirth remained a problem until sanitary procedures were perfected and antibiotics were discovered. This rise in technology meant that the preferred site of birth changed from the home to the hospital. In addition the discomfort of childbirth was alleviated by pain-relieving drugs more easily in a hospital.

When those technological advances could be taken for granted, psychologists, physicians, and lay people began to question whether some human value was missing from the medically managed hospital birth. The first human needs are, of course, for physiological functioning and safety, but once those had been adequately met and secured, attention could be turned to the higher needs of love and belongingness (Maslow, 1968). Medical science had secured the relative safety of mother and child in modern hospitals; the time then arose to attempt to meet other basic human needs.

Birth at Home

In America by the mid-twentieth century almost all babies were born in hospitals. One of the value shifts that occurred as a result of placing medical priorities first was that childbirth came to be viewed as a disease. This was a logical attitudinal development because the prevailing method of childbirth was hospital delivery with a physician in attendance. If we examine the assumption that childbirth is a disease, we find the following corollary attitudes deduced from that assumption:

1. Since pregnancy is an illness, the pregnant woman must be treated as though she were ill.
2. The "disease" requires the intervention of a physician for a "cure."
3. Childbirth is not a joyful event but something to be dreaded, as are all diseases.

To counteract the idea that pregnancy is an illness, a generation of young women was exposed to literature that cultivated the idea that pregnancy and childbirth were normal processes. The logical extension of the idea that birth is a natural process is that people should choose to follow natural processes and deliver their babies at home, among friends, in an atmosphere of celebration. As part of the movement to "demedicalize" childbirth, interest in midwifery was revived and is currently a growing profession.

A generation of young people came to distrust the hospital as a place for giving birth. They saw technology-oriented hospitals as impersonal, unresponsive to their human needs, and costly. They opted out of the system in favor of do-it-yourself home delivery. The majority of home births are uneventful and without problems if the woman has received good prenatal care and a careful evaluation of the development of the fetus. However, home birth does add risk to that small number of births in which complications present themselves. If transfer to a hospital becomes necessary, precious minutes may be lost that can make a difference in the safety of mother and/or baby. Many people are unwilling to take that risk, for there is no way to be absolutely certain that complications will not arise.

The Childbearing Center

Professionals sensitive to the psychological as well as the physical safety needs in childbirth sought a compromise between the hospital and the home as a place for birth. They found that compromise in the Childbearing Center. The concept of such a center was developed by the Maternity Center Association in New York City. The first center opened there in 1975 in a former residence. The aim of the Childbearing Center is to be a "maxi-home" rather than a "mini-hospital." It offers a homelike atmosphere with reliable birthing techniques.

Women are screened before being accepted for delivery at the Center; only those for whom no complications are expected are accepted. Women who are at risk for complications are transferred to other facilities. Enrollment for delivery at the Center must be begun before the twenty-second week of pregnancy. Most of the care is given by nurse-midwives, who also attend at the birth and in the immediate postpartum period; however, each woman is seen by an obstetrician on the first visit and at 36 weeks of gestation (Bennetts & Lubic, 1982). The emphasis at the Center is on normal births that do not require the technology and accompanying expense of hospitals and physicians. Couples are required to attend prenatal classes whose emphasis is on building confidence in bearing and rearing a child. The mother designates those persons that she would like to attend the birth. Husbands are welcome to attend, as are older children if the woman so desires. Mothers leave the Center approximately 12 hours after the birth and are visited by a nurse for follow-up on the first day at home and several days later as needed. Lubic (1977, 1979), one of the creators of the Center idea, states that the maxi-home invites families to remain together through the labor and delivery experience, to bring their own clean clothes to wear and their own food to eat, allows families to move freely about the unit, and most of all includes families in decision making. Lubic states, "In our opinion, it is the surrendering of all autonomy to potentially hostile strangers that is the most unpalatable part of traditional in-hospital care. We try to select our staff carefully to ensure a similarity in the philosophy of care" (1977, p. 19).

The Childbearing Center is an idea whose time had come. Six years after the first Center opened in New York there were approximately 150 centers in 27 states (Bennetts & Lubic, 1982). The record of these centers is good, the prenatal care technologically sound, and the savings in medical cost significant. But more important, the overwhelmingly positive aspect of these free-standing birth centers is the feeling of family solidarity that they foster by allowing families to come into being under safe but noninterventionist conditions.

The Leboyer Method: A Gentle Hospital Alternative

In the struggle to reform the medical management of birth to meet the psychological needs of mothers and fathers, few people thought to ask about the psychological needs of the baby. One person who did consider those needs was an obstetrician in France, Federick Leboyer. Leboyer rested his argument on the psychological theory of Otto Rank, a disciple and student of Freud, who held that birth is a trauma and that somewhere buried in our consciousness is the unarticulated memory of this primal traumatic experience. It followed that the circumstances of each individual's birth leave an indelible impression on the personality and become the model for meeting difficult situations. Some psychologists and psychiatrists had reported that their patients remembered the birth experience and could re-experience it through hypnosis or regression techniques. Some people reported memories of even earlier experiences in the womb. Dr. Leboyer himself remembered and re-experienced his own birth under psychoanalysis. He then began to question whether a brightly lighted operating room, with its loudspeaker blaring and steel implements clanging, was necessary for a medically safe birth. He concluded that it was not and began to construct procedures within the safety of the hospital that would lessen the trauma of birth for the baby. He instituted such procedures in the deliveries he managed and published his findings in France in 1974 and in the United States in 1975 under the title, *Birth Without Violence*.

Dr. Leboyer reasoned that all humans are psychologically most comfortable when physical conditions are familiar and changes in stimuli are gradual. Humans are calmed and assured by gentle movements and stroking and are distressed by slaps, jerks, stinging chemicals in their eyes, cold surfaces, and glaring lights. Because all humans cry when they are in pain, he reasoned that the crying of newborns is not simply a reflexive response to breathing, but a human response to a terrifying and painful experience. If birth is painful for the mother, he asked, why should we assume that it is not painful for the baby? The baby must experience the repeated pressure of uterine contractions, having its head pounding against the cervical muscle, and the pressure of the pelvis, which is severe enough to mold the skull. Birth is painful and difficult. Why then increase its trauma by greeting a new human being who has completed the critical passage with stimuli that increase trauma? We handle the new individual in ways that would elicit fear in anyone. We quickly pull the newborn from a warm environment, dangle it by its feet, perhaps slap it on the back, place it on a cold scale to weigh it, and put stinging chemicals in its eyes. Of course the infant cries—justifiably.

In Dr. Leboyer's technique, when the baby's head begins to crown, the lights in the operating room are lowered so that the baby can emerge from its mother's dark interior into a dimly lit room. Eyes that have never seen unfiltered light gradually become accustomed to this new stimulus. Medical personnel speak in whispers to simulate the muffled voices the baby heard in the womb; they keep their conversation to a minimum, however, so that the baby can hear the voices of its mother and father, which it can recognize because it heard them during the long months of gestation. The mother may assist the baby in the last moments of its passage through the birth canal. The baby is then gently raised and placed on her exposed abdomen in such a position that the draining of mucus from the baby's nose and mouth is facilitated. The umbilical cord remains uncut. The baby is warmed by the mother's body and reassured by the familiar sound of her heartbeat and her touch. The mother strokes the baby and they are both covered with a blanket to prevent heat loss. The baby remains in this position until the umbilical cord ceases to pulsate, usually five to ten minutes. Only when this pulsation ceases and the cord is no longer a source of oxygen is it severed. In this time, the mucus has cleared and breathing has become reliable. Then the mother and perhaps the father gently lower the baby into a tub of warm water. The warm liquid is familiar to the baby, as it simulates the womb. In this familiar environment the baby relaxes, opens its eyes and visually explores its new environment. These babies not only explore the world visually, but, liberated from the tight confines of the womb, they are able for the first time to explore their own bodies. Dr. Leboyer describes this:

The head turns—to the right, to the left—slowly, twisting around as far as the neck will allow.

The face is in perfect profile.

A hand stirs—opens, closes—and emerges from the water. The arm follows, rising. The hand caresses the sky, feels the space around it, falls again.

The other hand rises in its turn, traces an arabesque, and then, in its turn, descends.

Now they play together, meet, embrace, separate.

One moves away, the other darts after it.

One pauses, dreams, opens and closes with the slowness of the sea. The other falls under the same spell. The two dreams mirror each other: hands like flowers about to blossom. Sea anemones, they breathe with the slow cradling rhythm of the world beneath the ocean, moved by its invisible currents. . . .

The child is playing! [1975, pp. 84, 87, 90]

Both Dr. Leboyer and other physicians in the United States who have used the technique have found that with a lowered level of stimulation newborns are more alert and responsive to their environment (Berezin, 1980). Only seconds after birth the baby may lift its head and make eye contact with its mother. Gentle-birth babies do not cry; they communicate with a series of sighs, grunts, moans, and other sounds. These babies are in a state of alert attention and able to process the environment and to respond to it. Brazelton (1973) has stated that when the newborn is overwhelmed with environmental stimuli, it closes itself to further stimulation either by sleeping or crying. Leboyer has shown us that the newborn need not cry but can immediately begin to handle its new environment, provided we offer it slowly.

Rooming-in

Another aspect of the cultural pattern of childbirth in modern hospitals that concerned the people who analyzed the psychological ramifications of such management was (and is) the practice of separating mother and child at birth. In modern hospitals newborn babies are all kept together in a special nursery. In the interest of good medical management and efficient organization, hospitals evolved many rules about who could see the child, how long the child could be held, whether the child could be undressed and bathed, how and what he or she should be fed, and other arbitrary rules. The net effect of these procedures for many new parents was to prevent them from feeling that the child belonged to them. It seemed that the child belonged to the hospital and that the parents were intruding. Rooming-in is an attempt to deal with this aspect of parenting. In rooming-in, the child unequivocally belongs to the parents, and the institution of the hospital is there to facilitate the relationship, to teach the mother and father techniques for caring for the baby and to increase their skill in such techniques.

In rooming-in the baby is kept in the mother's room or, if the hospital was built with rooming-in in mind, in a small nursery that serves a few adjoining rooms. The mother assumes as much or as little care for the baby as she is able or desires and has access to her child at all times. She may bathe the baby and care for all its needs; if help is needed she can call the nurse. If she is breast feeding, she may need these few days with assistance to establish a routine. In addition, the father usually has unlimited visiting privileges and is encouraged to assume an active part in the routines and roles being established in the new triadic family.

Rooming-in has not yet been fully incorporated into hospital planning and management. Its innovators based their reasoning primarily on an intuitive grasp of human needs and scanty research from animal studies. However, recent research projects have attempted to focus on mother-infant bonding and we now have more scientific data related to the effect of this critical period and this all-important relationship. Hopefully, the result will be increased opportunities for interaction between parents and their newborns.

One of the major objections to the total medical management of pregnancy and childbirth is that medical considerations do little to enhance the growth of family and, in fact, may inhibit growth of feelings of sharing and closeness and thus interfere with the natural development of early attachment among mother, child, and father. The separation of mother, father, and baby for the first several days after birth is felt to be disruptive by many psychologists as well as the families experiencing this separation.

Main Points

The Process of Birth

1. The birth process is the biological separation of the mother and the fetus.

2. The first stage of labor consists of dilation of the cervix and averages 14 to 15 hours for first children but may only last a few hours for subsequent children.

3. During the transition phase of the first stage of labor the head moves through the fully dilated cervix into the birth canal.

4. During the second stage of labor, which lasts from 20 to 90 minutes, the fetus passes through the vagina and emerges from the body of the mother.

5. The third stage of labor, which lasts about 20 minutes, consists of the delivery of the placenta, the amniotic sac, and the remainder of the umbilical cord.

The Apgar Scale

6. Observations at one minute and at 5 minutes after birth of pulse, breathing, muscle tone, reflex response, and color are rated 0, 1, or 2 on the Apgar Scale. Seven or above denotes a normally functioning infant; a score between 4 and 7 indicates that the child needs to be watched for problems; a score below 4 alerts examiners that the child is in danger and needs immediate attention.

Complications of Birth

7. One of the complications of birth is prematurity. There is a higher incidence of prematurity in the United States than in other industralized countries.

8. Factors associated with prematurity are multiple birth, diseases of the mother, drugs, race, age, and socioeconomic status.

9. The effects of prematurity may include immediate difficulties with breathing, sucking, maintenance of body temperature, and general physiological functioning, whereas long-term effects may include lowered resistance to infection, behavior disorders, learning problems, and child abuse.

10. Another complication of birth, the position of the fetus, may necessitate the use of instruments or surgical intervention.

11. Birth defects are the most serious threat to the newborn. Congenital defects may be structural, functional, or chemical. They may be caused by genetic, environmental, or accidental factors.

Drugs in Childbirth

12. Drugs to relieve the discomforts of childbirth cross the placental barrier and enter the system of the fetus. The effect on the fetus is depressed physiological functioning. For babies with difficulties, depressed functioning may be crucial.

Education for Childbirth

13. The behavior of women in childbirth is not innate but learned. Because behavior can be taught, a number of childbirth-education programs have been developed.

14. The Read method of natural childbirth was a program of education to counteract ignorance and fear and a program of physical exercises to teach control of the body and relaxation during childbirth.

15. The Lamaze method (psychoprophylaxis) of childbirth education replaces pain with breathing as a response to uterine contractions.

16. Husband-coached childbirth educates women for childbirth and teaches the husband to monitor the progress of the birth and assist his wife, as a trained member of the delivery team.

Alternative Methods of Childbirth

17. Alternatives to hospital delivery developed in the latter part of the twentieth century to meet psychological needs and human values.

18. Birth at home has become an alternative to hospital delivery for uncomplicated births, when delivery is aided by trained personnel.

19. Birthing centers are places within a hospital or clinic that replicate a homelike atmosphere for delivery.

Rooming-in

20. In rooming-in the baby is kept in the mother's room, and she may assume as much or as little care for the baby as she is able or desires; the mother has access to her child at all times.

Words to Know

anoxia
Caesarean
cerebral palsy
cervix
congenital

placenta
premature
prematurity
psychoprophylaxis

Terms to Define

Apgar scale
genetic defects
Lamaze method
natural childbirth
process of labor
rooming-in

PART II

Infancy:
The First Two Years

The first two years after birth is the period of infancy. During this time the infant continues the process of rapid development begun in the prenatal period. Physical growth slows down somewhat while cognitive and emotional growth rapidly proceeds. In the two years that comprise infancy the small neonate, unable to speak or turn over, becomes a running, climbing, speaking, singing, loving, and sometimes angry, toddler. In these two years the infant grows bigger, grasps the world with thought, and becomes attached to another person. These changes are dramatic and often joyful experiences especially when the child has a good environment in which to grow. It is also a time in which the child is vulnerable to the effects of a deprived environment, and the poor development of too many of our children sadly attests to the promise of growth and potential not fully realized.

5

Physical Development in Infancy

Have you ever wondered

how rapidly babies grow?

if all parts of a baby's body grows at the same rate?

if there is a difference in the growth of boys and girls?

how nutrition affects growth?

what actions of babies are reflexes?

how babies develop control of their bodies and walk?

if day care or homes are better environments for babies?

Physical Growth

Weight and Height

During the first two years of its life the infant quadruples in weight and reaches approximately half of his or her adult height. Great changes in body proportions take place and dramatic motor abilities emerge.

Most infants double their birth weight by four months, triple it by 12 months and are four times their birth weight at their second birthday. The average two-year-old is between 32 and 36 inches (81 to 91 centimeters) in height. Although boys are slightly taller and heavier than girls, the differences are not significant until adolescence. There are great differences between individual children that are the result of their individual heredity patterns of development and/or their differing environments.

The growth that occurs in the prenatal and infant periods cannot be described as merely growing larger as in enlarging a picture. Different parts of the body grow at different rates, which results in changing proportions. Changes in proportions are most evident in the ratio of head size to total body length. In adulthood the head is one eighth the total body length, whereas at birth the head is one fourth the total length.

The infant also has a different relationship of weight to surface area than adults. Surface area refers to total skin surface. The relationship between total weight and surface area reflects the potential for loss of heat and water. The infant has a larger surface area in relation to total size than adults. The weight of a two-week-old, as compared to that of the average adult, is approximately 5 per cent, whereas the body surface of the same two-week-old is 15 per cent of adult body surface. This means greater potential for heat loss, more calories to maintain basic metabolism, and a greater risk of dehydration (Eichorn, 1979). In addition, the composition of the infant body is different from the adult body. The infant has more water, less protein, and, its chubby appearance notwithstanding, less fat than the average adult. The following chart indicates the comparative body composition of adults and infants.

	Water (in %)	Fat (in %)	Protein (in %)
Newborn	75	11	11
Adult (male)	62	14	33
Adult (female)	52	31	16

Changes also take place in bone structure during infancy. The process of hardening of the bones continues (*ossification*) and legs and arms become longer and stronger. The newborn's legs are bowed and do not have the strength to support the top-heavy torso and head. In the first year they strengthen and straighten, so that early in the second year the average infant can walk alone.

Head and Brain

No new brain cells will appear after birth, although the brain will continue to grow in size. At birth the brain is 25 per cent of adult brain weight. In the next two years the brain will reach 75 per cent of adult weight. Measurement of the circumference of the head is an important indication of physical growth and maturation. When gestational age is unknown at birth, the ratio of head circumference to chest circumference is accurate within two weeks (Eichorn, 1979).

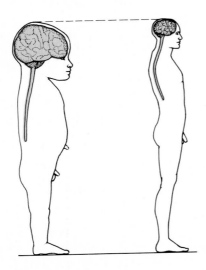

Because the brain leads in development, the head of a newborn infant is much larger in proportion to its body than in an adult. This illustration shows the relative proportions if an infant was as large as an adult. [Adapted from *Developmental Anatomy*, Revised Seventh Edition by Leslie Brainerd Arey. Copyright © 1974 by W. B. Saunders Co. By permission.]

Research in brain function has identified parts of the brain that control various functions. Infant capabilities parallel the development of these brain areas. The areas of the brain that control the senses and simple motor abilities are those that increase most rapidly in the first few months. At six months those areas that control coordination of two senses of sight and sound and more complicated motor skills, such as picking up small objects, have shown increase in size and development.

Measuring Physical Growth

Contemporary parents are at home with the growth charts pediatricians use to evaluate the physical growth of infants. In the nineteenth century, however, mothers did not have such comparisons for their children. The charts are the results of normative studies that have attempted to describe normal development. This research describes a range of development that can be used as a reference point to compare children of the same age. Systematic data from such research are called *norms*.

The data are compiled into charts used to compare the growth of children. Many charts have been gathered on samples with restricted racial and ethnic representation. For example, one widely used collection of data is that gathered by the Fels Research Institute in a longitudinal study of growth. Data were gathered over a forty five-year span. The subjects were selected from a small section of the country, were largely white and middle class, and many of the children were related to each other. The data overestimated the growth of children in the entire country when they were first gathered but, interestingly, at present they seem to match national growth trends because children are growing faster now and adults are taller at maturity than half a century ago. In 1976 the National Center for Health Statistics released growth charts for boys and girls. The charts were compiled from several national studies and are based on representative samples of children taken from the entire population. These are the first charts of growth based on a national sample.

Heredity and Environment

Physical growth is largely regulated by heredity. This regulation follows a predictable timetable, with some leeway for individual differences. This heredity schedule sets the sequence and timing of development. That is, one event occurs after another in a predictable sequence, such as the ability to sit, stand, walk, and run. In addition to regulating the sequence, genes regulate the timing of events. Thus, the average child sits at six months, stands at nine months, and walks at around one year, again with individual differences. These physical skills are species-specific, or phylogenetic. That is, all humans develop these physical skills and the timing is relatively unaffected by learning.

There are group differences in physical growth that are also largely controlled by genes. Members of a particular group may have a pattern of development that differs from that of another group. For example, black babies are slightly smaller at birth than are Caucasian babies, but black infants soon surpass their Caucasian counterparts and throughtout childhood are slightly taller and heavier than infants and children from other racial groups. Black children mature earlier, as evidenced by earlier hardening of bones and earlier sexual maturity (Eichorn, 1979).

Finally, within phylogenetic limits and group variations, each individual has genes that regulate individual patterns of development. An individual may be an early or late developer or may have characteristics of temperament and central nervous function that make acquisition of specific skills easy or difficult.

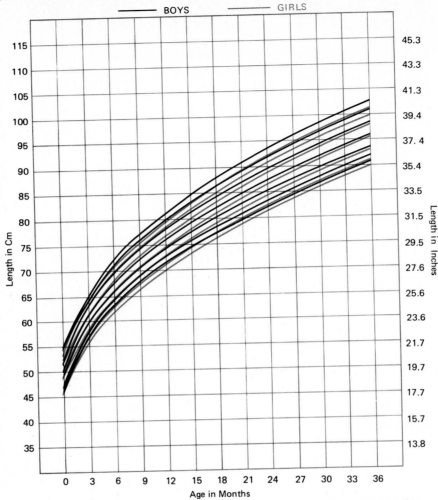

Length and weight standards for boys and girls in the United States from birth to thirty-six months. Note that the rate of growth is the same for boys and girls and that boys on the average are only slightly taller and heavier than girls. [Data from National Center for Health Statistics, 1976.]

Although the laws of heredity must be obeyed, environmental factors such as nutrition, physical conditions, social relations, and health can mold the genetic potential in many ways. If the child has sufficient nutrition and no health barriers, he or she will achieve a height approaching this genetic potential. Even though we have national and regional norms, it is important to consider the genetic potential of the individual child in evaluating growth. For example, assume that a child's height is compared to national norms and ranks at the tenth percentile. Tenth percentile is low, but not necessarily a cause for worry. On closer inspection, however, we might find that the child comes from a family of extremely tall people. The child may rank at the first percentile, or below percentile range for those persons

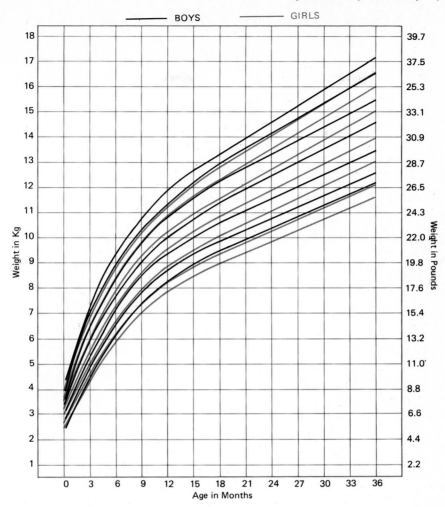

whose parents are extremely tall. In this case, a careful medical evaluation would need to be instituted and might reveal developmental problems. Without considering genetic potential, developmental problems may be overlooked (Eichorn, 1979).

Children from lower socioeconomic groups are slightly smaller than middle- and upper-class children. This may be because of poorer nutrition and health care rather than genetic differences. The United States consists of a mixture of many races and ethnic types, therefore any truly representative national sample of necessity includes all of them. Norms gathered on such a wide variety of children are useful for general growth, but more careful analysis needs to compare the child to his or her own reference group.

Nutrition

The rapid physical growth of the infant necessitates that preoccupation with feeding and nutrition characterize its care. In 1967 Congress conducted hearings on the nutritional state of the nation and subsequently authorized a nutritional survey of

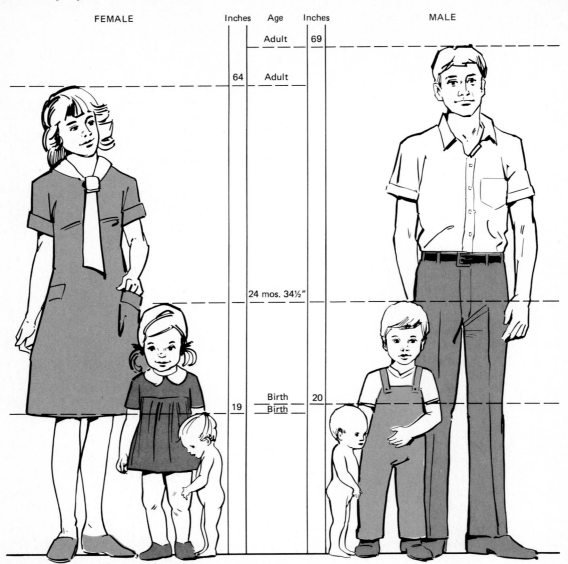

FEMALE	Inches	Age	Inches	MALE
		Adult	69	
	64	Adult		
		24 mos. 34½"		
	19	Birth / Birth	20	

Growth proportions from birth to adulthood. At two years of age, the end of infancy, the average boy and girl have attained half of their adult height. Boys and girls remain approximately the same height until boys surge ahead in adolescence, eventually reaching a height of approximately five inches more than girls.

the nation's children. Several studies were undertaken to gather the information. Two of them, the Ten-State Nutritional Survey and the Preschool Nutrition Survey, were completed by 1970. The findings revealed few severe nutritional deficiencies such as those prevalent in underdeveloped countries; however, secondary malnutrition was found in many American infants. The most common dietary lack among infants was found to be iron. The incidence of iron deficiency anemia was ranged from 8 to 40 per cent. Groups differed in the amount of this deficiency, with the average incidence for blacks at 34 per cent, whites at 13 per cent, and Hispanic Americans at 10 per cent.

Infants are fed great quantities of milk, which lacks iron, and unless iron-rich foods are added to diets iron deficiency is a likely result. Deficiencies were also found in vitamins A, C, and riboflavin. Deficiencies were found to be greater in rural than in urban areas and greater in low than in higher socioeconomic groups.

The nutritional status of infants is a risk when it is associated with the close spacing of children, unwanted pregnancy, and parental separation in pregnancy (Chase, 1975). In addition, very young mothers who are still growing themselves are at a severe disadvantage in providing adequate nutrition for the fetus. These young mothers are also less likely to have an adequate diet during pregnancy or to provide an adequate diet for the infant.

The management of feeding by mothers dictates the kind and quality of food consumed by infants. Lower-class mothers are more apt to allow the child to choose what and when to eat, whereas mothers in a higher social class are more likely to control their infant's food intake. Lower-class mothers are also more likely to use food as rewards and to withhold food as punishment than are higher class mothers (Eichorn, 1979).

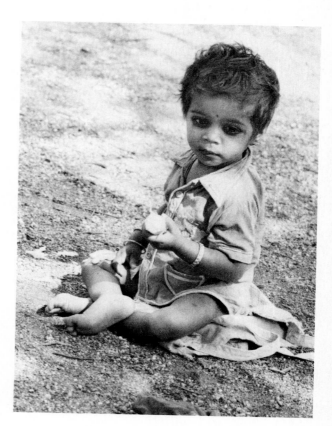

Nutrition is extremely important for the rapidly growing bodies of children. For many children in underdeveloped countries adequate nutrition is not available.

Motor Development

By the age of two, infants show great physical changes in structure and size, but even more remarkable are the uses that are made of the body at that age. In the period of infancy the child gains control of and precision in the muscular functions of the body. *Motor* is the term that is applied to *muscular movement.* Movement of the muscles is caused by nerve impulses that travel from the central nervous system to the muscles through nerve pathways. When people become paralyzed and unable to move muscles it is not usually because of damage to the muscles, but rather damage in the nerve pathways leading to the muscles. The nerve pathways originate in the brain and are connected to muscles after passing through the spinal cord. Nerves branch out from the spinal cord along its length. Severing of these nerves will result in lack of feeling and/or control of various parts of the body. At birth this system of nerve pathways is laid out but not fully developed. Development continues to take place both in the brain and in the nerve pathways leading from the brain.

Muscular movement is divided into two distinct classes of movement: voluntary and nonvoluntary (*reflex*). The newborn has a full complement of reflexive movements; more than older children or adults. Some reflexes disappear as the physical body matures. In nonreflexive movements, however, the newborn has only rudimentary, generalized movements. In nonreflexive movement the impulse to move the muscle originates in the brain and is considered *voluntary.* The newborn has little voluntary control of muscular movement. The two-year-old, however, has voluntary control of the large muscles that enable toddlers to walk, run, climb, and perform other functions. Additionally there is increasing voluntary control of small muscles, which enable the child to string beads on a cord, hold a crayon, and pick up pins from the floor. Control of voluntary movements increases rapidly in infancy, but all physical movement begins with reflexes.

Reflexes

A reflex is a specific behavior that occurs in response to a specific stimuli; the patella knee-jerk reflex is a familiar example. In this reflex the leg responds with a jerk to the stimulus of a sharp blow to the middle of the knee. This is a routine part of a physical examination. Even when the individual is aware that the stimulus is going to be applied and consciously attempts to prevent the reaction, the leg jerks in response to the blow of the hammer to the knee. The infant has many reflexes. Some of them have obvious survival value and some may be residual reflexes from our evolutionary past.

The *sucking* and *rooting* reflexes have obvious survival value. When any object touches its lips, the infant responds with sucking motions. This reflex enables the infant to suck and thereby obtain food. Accompanying the sucking reflex is the *rooting* reflex. The infant responds to having its cheek touched by turning its head toward the touch. When an infant is held in a crooked arm, the head is level with the adult breast. As the cheek of the neonate touches the breast the head turns, the lips touch the nipple, and the infant begins sucking. When food can be obtained, the chance of survival is greatly increased.

The neonate brings other less specific reflexes to independent life. Among them are coughing, sneezing, hiccoughing, gagging, yawning, and crying. These reflex behaviors may serve the purpose of defense, survival, or protection and are

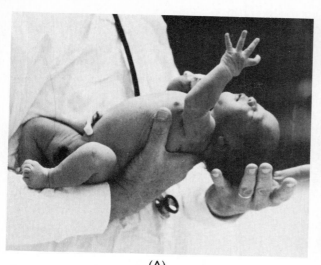

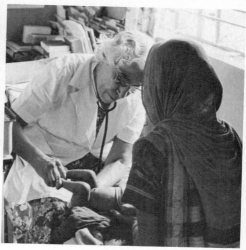

(A)   (B)

All healthy human babies exhibit the same reflexes and similar physical abilities regardless of culture. (A) A newborn baby exhibits the Moro reflex during an examination by a physician in a hospital in the United States. (B) The Indian baby is being given a routine physical examination by a physician in a clinic in rural India.

responses to rather generalized stimuli. For example, a number of different stimuli may cause the infant to sneeze.

The *grasp reflex* occurs when the palm of the hand is pressed with an object and the fingers close tightly over the object. This is not a prehensile grasp because the thumb is not involved. When an object such as a finger or a rod is placed in the hand, even a very young infant grasps so tightly that he or she may support the entire body weight. This reflex lessens with time and by twelve months of age has disappeared. It has been suggested that this reflex may be part of the hereditary package from our primate past. Newborn primates cling to their mother rather than being held. Thus, they hang on and go wherever she goes.

The *swimming reflex* is another reflex that seems to have little immediate use to the infant and may be a vestige from our even more remote evolutionary past.* Surprisingly, when a very young infant (under six months) is placed in water, it reacts with a smooth swimming motion, with its head down. The child does not drown. Swimming as a reflex action is lost at about twelve months of age. The child must then be taught to swim and may display a fear of water, especially fear of putting its head under water.

The swimming reflex can be elicited from young infants even out of water. When the infant is placed in a prone position (on its stomach), various stimuli will elicit a rhythmic kicking of the feet and simultaneous movement of the arms. The infant resembles an underwater swimmer practicing strokes!

The *Babinski reflex* is indicated by a spreading and fanning of the toes and is in response to stimulation on the sole of the foot. This reflex disappears at about four months; its presence after that time indicates a problem in the maturation of the

* Carl Sagan, in his book *The Dragons of Eden* (1977), explores the thesis that our brains have evolved as have our bodies. Thus, we carry parts and layers of brain that retain the functions from our evolutionary past. He explores our deepest brain from our earliest reptilian past. The swimming reflex may be from such a level.

central nervous system. Thus, it is used as an indication of maturation and as a diagnostic tool in identifying developmental problems.

The *Moro,* or *startle reflex* involves a reaction of the entire body. In this response the arms extend suddenly outward as the back arches and the body becomes rigid. In a symmetrical movement the arms are brought forward in a hugging motion as the legs draw up. This reaction is in response to a sudden loud noise or a sudden loss of support.

Reflexes are an important part of the heredity of the infant. Reflexive behavior is essential to survival. It enables the infant to obtain nutrients, to breathe, and to avoid suffocation and strangulation. Early reflexive behaviors are the sensory motor basis on which cognitive growth is based.

Reflexes are useful diagnostic indicators in evaluating the developmental stage and functioning of the nervous system. The nervous system continues to mature after birth. One feature of this maturation is that the nerve fibers are covered with a myelin sheath. When this takes place, the babinski reflex is inhibited—that is, prevented from occurring. Thus, the presence of the babinski reflex in an eight-month-old infant may indicate delayed or distorted development in the central nervous system. Reflexes continue to be a valuable diagnostic tool in adulthood, especially in determining neurological damage or deterioration. When there is a problem with physical functions, reflexive action can differentiate between malfunction from organic damage and malfunction without an organic base.

Motor Sequences

When you began reading this assignment, you probably walked to where your book was, picked it up, turned to the desired page, and began reading. To move from place to place *(locomote)* and to manipulate objects with the hands are extremely important physical capabilities and ones on which most physical activities depend. Neither of these capabilities is present at birth, but both are acquired during the first two years of life. They do not appear suddenly but build slowly and steadily on previous levels of abilities. Increasing control of these functions constitutes a major physical development in infancy.

Locomotion

The development of physical control of the body is dependent on brain development, increase in muscular strength, and the opportunity to practice. The sequence of abilities leading to independent walking occurs on a general timetable and leads to full, and sometimes amazing, ability to move, climb, and balance. This development follows the pattern of cephalocaudal development evidenced in the prenatal period. Control of the head and trunk occurs first, with control of the legs following. An outline of this sequence follows here.

Head and Trunk Control. When lying on its stomach the newborn can lift his or her head from a surface and move the head from side to side while visually tracking an object. The newborn is also able to hold its head upright for a short time by using the muscles of the trunk for support. In the first few months the infant can lift its head and chest clear of a flat surface, by supporting itself on its arms.

Rolling Over. Many parents are surprised to find their babies have fallen on the floor when left alone on a bed or changing table. An infant of four or five months can turn from its stomach to its back and soon can roll from its back to its stomach. This

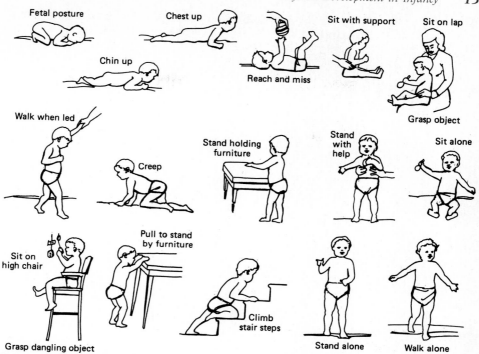

Sequence of motor development from simple reflex to independent walking. The sequence of development is the same for all children although the timing varies. Some children may walk alone at nine months and some at fifteen months. [Adapted from Mary M. Shirley, *The First Two Years*, Volume II (Intellectual Development), University of Minnesota Press, Minneapolis. Copyright © 1933 by the University of Minnesota.]

ability reflects increasing control over the legs and strength in the torso. The infant accomplishes this feat by twisting its torso and using a leg for leverage to push its body over.

Sitting. The infant gradually gains strength in its back and neck muscles and can support his or her own weight when supported on a lap. By four to six months an infant can sit alone in a high chair. By six to seven months the infant can pull itself to a sitting position from a supine one and lower itself to a sitting position from a standing position while holding on for support.

Crawling. Soon after the infant can roll onto its stomach, moving from place to place becomes possible by crawling. Crawling is characterized by wriggling on the stomach and pulling forward with the arms. The legs may also be used to push, but the arms are most likely to be used. This form of locomotion resembles out-of-water swimming.

Hitching. Another method of moving is hitching, or scooting. This maneuver is executed from a sitting position. The body is propelled by arms and legs and the buttocks slide across the floor. An infant who can sit alone soon learns to scoot across a floor.

This six-month-old infant is sitting alone. She can hold her back straight but cannot stand yet.

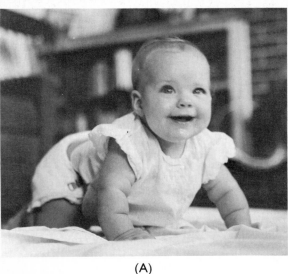

(A)

(B)

When a baby is able to support the weight of her body on hands and knees, a new sense of independence evolves as she is able to move about the home by crawling (A). Crawling soon gives way to creeping (B) as a more efficient means of locomotion. In creeping the baby moves on hands and feet instead of hands and knees.

Creeping. As muscular strength increases in the legs, the infant can raise its entire body from a flat surface using its arms and legs. The creeping baby of nine or ten months of age becomes adept at rapidly moving from place to place with its hands and feet touching the ground. This gait resembles a bear walking, although at times the infant may drop to its knees. At this stage of motor development the compact body is quite agile in changing from lying to sitting to scooting to creeping.

Pulling Up. The infant usually has a purpose in moving from place to place. Its motivation is often the desire to reach and to handle an object that appears interesting or attractive. Such objects are often on a surface that requires the infant to reach above eye level. To attain such objects, the infant must crawl to a piece of furniture, and by holding on for support, pull his or her body into a standing position. Many mothers have been dismayed to find a prized object dashed to the floor by an infant whom they did not think could reach a table or bookshelf. These locomotor activities are fired by increasing intellectual curiosity about the environment.

Standing with Help. Following closely behind the ability to sit alone is the ability to stand with help. At this stage the legs are sufficiently developed to support the weight of the body. Balance, however, has not developed to the point that the infant can remain in a standing position. Sometimes an infant may stand for a few seconds before plopping down on its buttocks.

Standing Holding onto Furniture. Soon after he or she stands with help, the infant can stand while holding onto furniture. An infant of this age is often so eager to explore the world that mother may have to change his or her diaper while the infant is standing.

Standing Alone. Soon after the infant can pull to a standing position, he or she releases the furniture and stands alone, with both feet firmly planted on the ground. If one foot is shifted, balance is usually lost and the infant topples, only to creep to another piece of furniture and repeat the process.

Walking with Help. Several months before actually walking alone, infants can shift their balance from foot to foot and walk while holding the hand of an older person.

Walking Alone. A milestone in the development of the infant occurs when the first step is taken. Families cheer and may mark the day in the baby's diary so that the exact time will be remembered. That first step may literally be one step, or the infant may cross the room. Sometimes the excitement of the adults in response to the occasion so frightens the infant that it may be quite some time before he or she attempts the venture again. Most infants delight in their newly found freedom and their mobility increases rapidly.

The timing of this developmental sequence varies considerably from infant to infant. Most infants can sit alone by six months of age, can walk with help by nine months, and walk alone by twelve months (Frankenberg & Dodds, 1967). Some infants, however, walk as early as nine months or as late as fifteen months. Both extremes are within the normal range, and it is only extremely delayed development that is a cause for alarm. Parents often suffer unfounded anxiety when they compare their infants to those of friends or to the monthly developmental guides in infant care books. When norms are given they represent the average child or fiftieth percentile of a statistical norm. Exactly half of all infants develop earlier than the fiftieth percentile and half later.

Grasping

A second motor sequence that develops in infancy is prehensile ability, or grasping. It is a cliché that the opposing thumb and forefinger of the human hand is the greatest tool ever invented. It is a tool for using tools and enables humans to hold and to manipulate large and small objects. This ability combined with a large brain and language is the physical foundation on which thousands of years of cultural achievements are based. The infant does not possess this ability at birth but develops it in the first year of life. The mother who found that her infant had rolled off the bed may be equally surprised a few months later to find her infant sitting on the counter in the bathroom with a bottle of medicine open, pills scattered on the counter, and an unknown number in his or her stomach.

There are two components of the grasping sequence. One is the ability to grasp and the second is the coordination of this grasp with visual perception. The sequence exemplifies the principle of proximodistal development: the infant can control the large sweep of the arm before he or she can control the more distant function of the fingers. Development proceeds from the center of the body outward to the extremities. The sequence of the development of grasping is outlined here.

Reflex.   The grasp reflex in the newborn is not a true grasp because only the fingers are involved. The four fingers curl around a rod, but the thumb does not oppose the fingers and lock. The grasp reflex in the infant gradually weakens and disappears.

Reaching.   Infants in the first few weeks after birth sometimes extend their arms toward an object, but are not able to coordinate reach and sight. By three months infants reach for objects they see, including faces and glasses. There is lack of precise control, however, and the movement is often a generalized sweep of the arm that may hit the object or not. Infants will hold a rattle when the handle is placed in the hand.

Palm Grasping.   As infants gain control of their arm movements and coordinate visual information with them, they reach for and touch objects. They grasp with the palm of the hand. In this motion the object is in the palm and the entire hand closes over it. Infants of four months of age hold crackers or small toys in this manner.

Finger Grasping.   In the next stage the infant grasps small objects such as blocks with the fingers. The object is braced between the fingers and the heel of the hand. Infants often bang the object on the tray of a highchair or on the floor. This stage of grasping correlates with the ability to sit alone at approximately six months.

Grasping.   The final stage of grasping occurs when the thumb is used in opposition to the forefinger. Infant hands are small, and as this motor sequence is perfected, they pick up even the smallest objects, which they usually immediately place in their mouths.

The older infant with the ability to walk and grasp is able to perform many activities. Infants learn very quickly to open cabinets, remove tops from containers, and manipulate the environment in many ways. Active locomotion and manipulation of objects are the mediators of intellectual development.

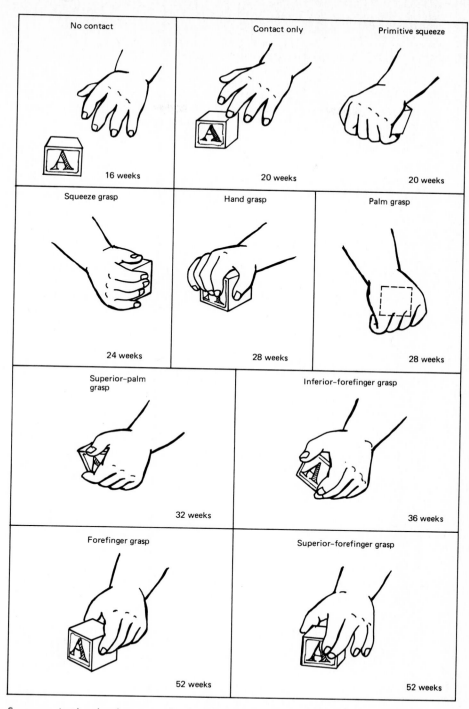

Sequence in the development of grasping. [Adapted from "An Experimental Study of Prehension in Infants by Means of Systematic Cinema Records" by H. M. Halverson, *Genetic Psychology Monographs*, 1931, *10*, 107–286. Copyright © 1931 by The Journal Press.]

Environments for Children: Home or Day Care ─────────

In the last two decades research has steadily indicated the importance of environmental stimulation in development. As this research evidence has mounted, so has the controversy over what constitutes the best environment for infants and young children. Some contend that the biological mother can provide the best of all possible environments for her infant and that this environment should be the home. Others contend that mother and child isolated at home inevitably constitute a disadvantaged environment and that young children need the skilled care of trained personnel and the stimulation of other children. These people often proclaim day care as a right of every mother and the salvation of every child.

The Home Environment ──────────

We are sure about the importance of the early environment on a child's later development; however we are not quite sure about what constitutes the optimal environment for infants and toddlers, and we are even less sure about how to measure it. Homes with young children in them are very difficult to study, and so researchers study subjects that are available. From a research perspective, the newborn leaves the hospital with his or her mother and disappears for two or three years. When the child is ready for nursery school or a toddler play group, mother and child may reappear for a few hours a week; however, for the most part, what happens in the privacy of the home is known only to members of the family. Whatever it is that happens at home has been blamed for Johnny not reading, juvenile delinquency, deterioration of morals, and a host of other things. Retrospective and correlational research has implicated many features of the home environment in subsequent behavior outcomes, both positive and negative. Few researchers have actually attempted to enter the home and evaluate the environment it provides for children. Bettye M. Caldwell, a long-time researcher in the field of child development, conducted an extensive investigation into the home environment and designed an instrument called Home Observation for the Measurement of the Environment (HOME) (Bradley & Caldwell, 1976; Bradley, Caldwell & Elardo, 1979). Caldwell and her associates began by searching other research studies to gather information about the optimal home environment for infants and toddlers. This research information was then tested in the real world. Through working back and forth between theoretical research data and the applied field, the final version of the HOME instrument identified forty-five items divided into six categories. Using these items, an observer can rate a home and the interaction between infant or toddler and caregiver and arrive at an evaluative index of the home environment. Listed here are subscales of the Home Observation for Measurement of the Environment.

1. Emotional and verbal responsiveness of mother.
2. Avoidance of restriction and punishment.
3. Organization of the physical environment.
4. Provision of appropriate play materials.
5. Maternal involvement with the child.
6. Opportunities for variety in daily stimulation.

This instrument does not focus only on the mother. Care given by siblings, father, and other caregivers is rated in the total environment. In fact, a home

**Neonatal and Infant Mortality Rates,
U.S.A., 1958–1981**

(Deaths under 28 days and under one year per 1,000 live births)

Since 1958, infant mortality in the United States has declined by more than 55 percent, at an annual rate of 2.5 percent. Since 1970, fully 90 percent of this reduction has occurred among neonates (under 28 days of age). Much of this improvement may be due to regionalized perinatal services including the introduction of Neonatal Intensive Care. [From *Facts 1983*, March of Dimes Birth Defects Foundation, White Plains, New York, 1983.]

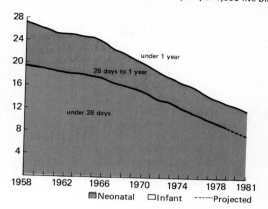

Table 5–1. International Comparison of Infant Death Rates Per 1,000 Live Births

Country	1980 Rate	Decrease Over 10 Years
Sweden	6.7	39%
Japan	7.4	44%
Finland	7.6	39%
Iceland	7.7	42%
Norway	8.1	41%
Netherlands	8.1	36%
Denmark	8.4	41%
Switzerland	8.5*	45%
France	10.0	34%
Canada	10.9*	44%
Australia	11.0	39%
Spain	11.1	60%
Belgium	11.2*	48%
Luxembourg	11.5	53%
New Zealand	11.7†	29%
United Kingdom	11.8	36%
United States	12.6	36%
Federal Republic of Germany	12.6	47%
German Democratic Republic	12.6	33%
Austria	13.9	46%

Note: Despite large reductions in infant mortality in the United States in recent years, 16 other countries still have lower rates. About 70 percent of infant deaths in the United States occur during the 28 days following birth. Nearly half of all infant deaths occur in low-birthweight newborns.

Source: United Nations Statistical Office. From *Facts/1983*, March of Dimes Birth Defects Foundation.

*1979 rate.

†1981 rate.

receives a higher rating if the father provides some caregiving and if the child eats at least one meal with the father and mother. Scores on the HOME instrument have been found to be a better predictor of later cognitive development than the results from testing infants.

Day Care

The majority of infants are cared for by their own mothers in their own homes. However, a large and growing number of women with children under six years of age work outside the home. Most of these women do not work to provide luxury items, but out of economic necessity. The question of whether a mother *should* work outside the home is not an option for them: they have no choice. Women contribute greatly to the work force and the productive capacity of our country, but the question is ever present: "Who is minding the baby?" Most of these children are cared for by fathers or other relatives. About one third of them are cared for in another person's home. The vast majority of the caregivers are friends of the family and are likely to be young mothers themselves who care for one or two children in addition to their own on a daily basis. Thus, they help a friend and augment their income.

For all the hue and cry over day-care centers, fewer than 10 percent of the children who are left each day by their mothers spend that time in homes or centers licensed for day care. The result of this conglomeration of situations is that the *quality* of care given to infants and children varies enormously. Some children receive care equal to that in an excellent home, but the care that others receive borders on neglect and abuse. Currently the laws regarding licensing and standards for day care vary widely among the states. Certainly licensing and standards will not solve all the problems of day care, but to require that homes or centers that engage in the care of children meet standards will eliminate the worst situations. There are now three distinct types of day care available: custodial, developmental, and comprehensive.

Custodial care provides for the physical needs of the child and little else. The providers of custodial care are usually untrained and may be limited in education. Few, if any, educational toys are available for the children. The number of children per adult may be greater than recommended and play space is often limited. The caregiver is custodian for the body and provides little for the mind and spirit.

Developmental day care is modeled after good nursery schools; it provides basic physical care plus experiences for social and educational development. The child-adult ratio is usually low and personnel are trained in the management and development of young children. Developmental day-care centers attempt to provide the stimulation for development that a good home provides. Often an attempt is made for individual children to have the same caregiver every day, so that attachment to one person may be formed. The child's physical needs are met through carefully planned nutritional meals, designed play space, manipulative toys, and regular health checks. Intellectual and social needs are met through appropriate materials and careful planning of "lessons" and experiences by the caregivers. The total environment in a developmental day-care center is carefully planned, the personnel are trained, and the general atmosphere is warm and nurturing.

Comprehensive child-development programs are large-scale programs designed to meet the many service needs of entire families. While care for children is at the heart of such a program, other services include health examinations and

Table 5–2. How to Choose Day Care

The Physical Facility Checklist	*The Emotional Climate Checklist*
1. Does the space seem safe? (Are lights and sockets covered or out of reach?) 2. Is there enough space, and is it well planned so there is no crowding? 3. Is the equipment inside and out varied, sturdy, and easy for a child to use? 4. Is the place attractive and comfortable? (Are there plants, pets, and special areas for activities?) 5. Can the children get inside and outside safely and without difficulty? 6. Are the materials ample, in good condition, and easily available? (Can children reach the variety of books, toys, art supplies?) 7. Are the bathroom facilities clean and easy for a child to use? (Easy-to-reach faucets, toilets, toothbrushes and toothpaste, paper towels, etc.?) 8. Are meals nutritious and well balanced. And is the food prepared and served attractively? 9. Do the children have a comfortable and quiet place for naps? 10. Does the place have provisions for an ill child?	1. Do the children show they really like and trust the adults a lot? (Do they receive respect, attention, and support?) 2. Do the children appear happy, comfortable, and relaxed? 3. Does the staff communicate easily with each child? 4. Does the discipline reflect my philosophy? 5. Are the children allowed to pursue their own interests according to their abilities? 6. Are the children's emotional needs given first priority? 7. Would my child receive the attention he or she needs and be treated fairly here? 8. Are problems handled with little upset? 9. Does the director or teacher answer my questions openly? 10. Do I feel comfortable with the staff and the place?
The Learning Climate Checklist	*The Social Climate Checklist*
1. Is the place arranged easily for learning and growing? 2. Does the program seem well planned? 3. Does the program provide many different opportunities for the individual child? 4. Can children move around and find materials easily? 5. Are the learning opportunities suitable for the different ages? 6. Are the children's questions answered easily? 7. Do the children receive enough of the kind of individual attention and assistance they need? 8. Do the children enjoy the activities available? 9. Are special events and trips usual activities? 10. Are the children's works such as drawings and child-crafted things both displayed and discussed with parents and available for the parents to take home?	1. Do I like how the children behave and relate to each other? 2. Are conflicts handled sensitively? 3. Would my child fit in with the present group? 4. Would my child have a good time here? 5. Are the language and culture of each child respected? 6. Do the children respond easily and happily to each other? 7. Do the children play without a lot of conflicts? 8. Do the staff encourage children to express themselves and participate? 9. Are the children learning balanced social roles? 10. Are parents made to feel welcome and encouraged to know each other?

Note: Day care facilities should be examined for the care they provide in the physical, emotional, learning, and emotional areas. Parents looking for day care have the right to ask questions and day care providers have a responsibility to answer them.

Source: *Choosing Child Care: A Guide for Parents* by Stevanne Auerbach and Linda Freedman. Parents and Child Care Resources, San Francisco, 1976.

needs, nutritional information, and parent education and counseling. These programs are designed to help disadvantaged families learn to care for their children in ways that will lead to the children's optimal development. Of course, while the children are in the day-care program, they have the advantage of developmental programs. Middle-class families usually do not need the counseling and information provided in these programs, but disadvantaged families often benefit from them.

There are those who advocate that day care should be available to all families who need and want it and that this should be a free government service (Greenblatt, 1977). The major question is "What is the effect of day care on the children who grow up under these group conditions?" Much research has been conducted in an attempt to answer this question. Research for the most part is conducted by university professors and most often in demonstration day-care centers at universities. The centers are of very high quality. University research may not be valid for day care of less quality and certainly is not valid for custodial care because custodial care does not offer the intellectual and social stimulation of developmental day care.

One of the pressing questions about day care in recent years has been its effect on cognitive development. When a great number of studies are reviewed (Bronfenbrenner, Belsky, & Steinberg, 1976) the conclusion is that, for middle-class children, there is little difference between those in day care and those reared at home. Disadvantaged children who have had early educational experience in high-quality day care are less likely to show declines in IQ in the early school years.

Home care or day care? The best home care remains the standard by which good day care programs are measured. Parents and professionals are concerned about whether infants and children receive care and stimulation necessary for optimum development. Most professionals agree that day care meets these needs when the caregivers have time to relate to the children, play games with them, teach social interaction, and establish a warm, happy atmosphere. In this photo, two children and a nurturing caregiver engage in a pleasant game. In such a warm environment, infants grow and thrive regardless of where they are.

Cognitive development is not a persuasive argument either for universal day care or for mother raising young children at home. Many studies have sought to examine the effects of day care on emotional development.

Opponents of day care are convinced that to break the bond between mother and child is to break the foundation of society. Surprisingly, research indicates that whether children spend the day in day care or at home with mother, there is little difference in the attachment they have to their mothers. Children in day care appear to be more dependent on their peers, to interact more with them, and to be more aggressive toward them. The differences between home-reared and day-care children remain evident through the early years of elementary school. Those children with many years in day care appear to be less motivated in their schoolwork, are less cooperative with teachers, and are more aggressive toward other children.

The issues raised by day care are almost impossible to solve through research. Each child is different and may be differently affected by group and home care. No child can have both experiences. Larger questions involve the roles of women in society and the difference between the family structure we desire and the one that evolves through necessity. In the final analysis, whether children are in group or family settings is a value decision. Thoughtful people with good information are the only ones to design and choose the environments in which children, and society, grow and fulfill their capabilities.

Main Points

Physical Growth

1. Different parts of the body grow at different rates, resulting in a change in proportions.

Weight and Height

2. Most infants double their birth weight by four months, triple it by twelve months, and are four times their birth weight at their second birthday. The average two-year-old is between 32 and 36 inches in height.

Head and Brain

3. The measurement of the circumference of the head is an important indication of physical growth and maturation.

4. Although the brain continues to grow in size after birth, no new brain cells appear.

Measuring Physical Growth

5. The first growth charts based on a national sample were compiled in 1976 by the National Center for Health Statistics.

Heredity and Environment

6. Physical growth is largely controlled by heredity. The timing and sequence of physical skills are regulated by the genes.

7. Group differences in physical growth are largely controlled by genes.

8. Both heredity (genetic potential) and environment (nutrition, physical conditions, social and economic status, health care) must be considered in evaluating an individual's development.

Nutrition

9. American infants have been found to be nutritionally deficient in iron, vitamins A and C, and riboflavin.

Motor Development

10. Motor development (muscular movement) is dependent on development of the central nervous system.

Reflexes

11. Reflexes are involuntary motor responses. The infant is born with sucking, rooting, coughing, sneezing, hiccoughing, gagging, yawning, crying, grasping, swimming, Babinski, and Moro reflexes.

Motor Sequences

12. Motor sequences occur on a general timetable following the cephalocaudal principle.

Locomotion

13. Locomotion occurs on a general timetable dependent on development of the brain, increase in motor strength, and the opportunity to practice.

Grasping

14. The ability to grasp and the coordination of this grasp with visual perception occur in a sequence of stages in accord with the principle of proximodistal development.

Environments for Children: Home or Day Care

15. The home environment can be evaluated by a systematic observation of the interaction with mother or other caregivers, the physical environment, and opportunities for variety in stimulation.

16. Custodial day care provides only for the physical needs of the child.

17. Developmental day care provides basic physical care plus experiences for social and educational development.

18. Comprehensive child development programs are designed to meet many of the needs of the entire family.

19. Research found no difference in attachment to mother for home-reared or day-care children.

20. Children in day care were found to be more dependent on peers, less motivated in schoolwork, less cooperative with teachers, and more aggressive toward other children.

Words to Know

locomotion   ossify
norms   phylogenetic
nutrition   reflex
ossification

Terms to Define

Babinski reflex
Moro reflex
motor development
reflex behavior
startle reflex

CHAPTER 6

Mental Development in Infancy

Have you ever wondered

    how the intelligence of infants can be studied?

    if the reflexes of infants, such as sucking and grasping, have any relationship to intelligence?

    if the play of toddlers is intelligent?

    how mothers communicate with their babies before the baby can talk?

    how babies develop speech?

    what IQ tests for infants measure?

We live in a world in which intelligence is highly valued. In spite of this valuation, there is considerable disagreement about exactly what intelligence is and even more about its origin and development. One of the basic disagreements about intelligence is whether it is mediated primarily through heredity or environment. That is, are some people just naturally smarter than others, or are they more intelligent because they have had a superior environment? More importantly, can we raise the intelligence of children by supplying them with intellectually stimulating environments? If so, how much can we raise it? Can we, as behaviorists early in this century claimed, make a doctor, lawyer, or thief of a child through environment, or are children destined by genes to be dull or bright? These are not idle questions. The last twenty years have seen much research directed toward answering questions about intelligence, accompanied by heated debates on both sides of the question.

    The measurement of intelligence began in 1905 with school-age children when Alfred Binet developed a test to measure "intelligence." Somewhat later a Swiss psychologist, Jean Piaget, noted that children use consistent strategies to solve intellectual problems. Let us look at the life and work of Piaget and how he has helped us to understand how intelligence develops in children.

Jean Piaget: His Life and Work

Jean Piaget was born on August 9, 1896 in Neuchatel, Switzerland. Neuchatel was a stimulating environment for the young Piaget as it offered a museum of natural history and a college. Piaget was intellectually gifted and inquisitive. His early interest was in biological science and he volunteered to work as laboratory assistant to the director of the natural history museum in his home town. When the director died, the young Piaget continued to publish the results of their research under his own name. He published his first scientific paper at the age of ten and at eleven was offered the position as curator of a museum of natural history in Geneva, which he declined.

Piaget chose instead to continue his studies. His attention turned to philosophy. He was especially interested in philosophical approaches to the problems of *epistemology* (the study of knowledge). Piaget was not satisfied with any of the philosophical approaches that he studied to the questions of how knowledge is acquired and its validity. During his adolescent years Piaget defined themes that were to occupy him for the remainder of his life. He expressed these themes in a philosophical novel but continued his studies in biological science. In 1918, at the age of twenty-two, he obtained the Ph.D. degree from the University of Neuchatel.

After completing his formal education Piaget remained undecided about his life's work. He had the tools and training of a natural scientist but the questions of a philosopher. He was dissatisfied with the methods that philosophy used to answer questions and equally dissatisfied with the limited questions that science asked with its powerful tools. He then turned to psychology and went to Zurich where he worked in a laboratory for experimental psychology and in a psychiatric clinic. In the clinic, he learned the technique of the clinical interview that he would later develop and use extensively in his work. Although the clinical interview is not standardized, it is systematic and consists of extensive verbal probes designed to reveal the structure of thought and personality underlying behavior. While in Zurich, he became acquainted with the writings of Freud and attended lectures by Carl Jung, a colleague of Freud. Again, he found that neither experimental psychology nor psychoanalysis satisfied his search for the answers to his philosophical questions. He then briefly returned to the study of natural science, investigating the interaction of nature and nurture in the development of molluscs.

In 1919 he began a study of psychopathology at the Sorbonne in Paris and simultaneously pursued his study of philosophy. While in Paris he met Henri Simon, who, with Binet, had designed an IQ test. (The descendent of this test is the *Stanford-Binet* which remains in wide use.) Simon offered Piaget a job standardizing some verbal reasoning items for use in mental testing. Piaget undertook the job, but soon found the interviewing of children for this work boring and uninteresting. Piaget did not know it, but he was on the brink of discovering his life's work. The objective of the IQ testing that Simon and Binet had developed was to measure how much a child knows relative to other children of similar age. Thus, the examiners were only interested in the predetermined right answers. As Piaget conducted these interviews, he noticed that the wrong answers that children gave had a logic of their own and that the same wrong answers were given by many different children. He also found that he could use the tool of the clinical interview to probe these wrong answers and gain access to the structure of the logic of these answers. Piaget began to publish the results of his investigation of children's thinking. Soon thereafter he was offered the directorship of the Institute Jean Jacques Rousseau in Geneva, a center for scientific child study and for teacher training. Piaget accepted this position at age 25. He intended to spend five or six years on the study of children's thinking, but instead remained at this Institute until his death in 1980.

At this institute Piaget undertook numerous studies of cognitive development in children, including language, various concepts such as space, time, and causality, and reasoning processes such as moral judgments. Piaget's studies were not confined to laboratory experiments, but also included a naturalistic record of thousands of observations of his own three children. These observations trace the development of intelligence in his children Jacqueline, Lucienne, and Laurent from the very first days through early childhood. Using these observations as a basis, Piaget constructed a theory of the development of intelligence as an adaptation that proceeds from the earliest reflexes of the infant to formal thinking in mature intellectual thought. Piaget's observation of his children are not only illustrative and interesting but reveal him as a careful, objective scientist and a sensitive father.

Piaget identified four different stages in cognitive development that differ in the quality of thought that the child exhibits. The first stage, infancy, is *sensorimotor* in which thought is tied to the physical and sensory manipulation of objects. In the preschool years the child is in a *preoperational* stage. This period is characterized by rapid growth of language and while the child may reach logical conclusions, these are arrived at by intuition and not be reliable logic. In the school years, the child gains all the tools for logical thinking and can perform logical operations—provided they are with concrete objects. Thus, Piaget designates this stage, *concrete operations*. In the teen years, as young people reach the stage of *formal operations*, all thought is possible.

Throughout this book we refer to Piaget's work in the study of mental development. His observations of his own children in their natural development are an invaluable source for the early years. We now turn our attention to *sensorimotor intelligence*.

Sensorimotor Intelligence

In the two years that comprise infancy the child moves from reflexive behavior to the ability to solve problems through mental means alone. The simple organizations of the neonate gradually broaden, merge with one another, differentiate, become more flexible, and eventually enable the child to *think* without reference to physical objects. Before advanced mental operations are possible, mental structures must develop. In the period of infancy mental structures are tied to physical activity and to sensory perceptions. We might say that thought in infancy is accomplished with the body. At least, problems must be worked out through the actual manipulation of physical objects. To underline the physical quality of mental functioning in this stage Piaget designated the first two years the *sensorimotor stage*. He further divided the stage into six substages. Intellectual development in infancy is a process of increasing flexibility in mental functioning. The newborn begins with reflexes that are rigid and stereotypically applied to a number of objects. The two-year-old leaves the sensorimotor stage capable of using mental structures to invent behaviors that he or she has never performed before. To trace this growth, the six sub-

Table 6–1. Characteristics of Thinking in the Sensorimotor Period in Relation to General Development, Object Concept, Space, and Understanding of Casuality

Stage	General	Object Concept	Space	Causality
1 Reflex 0–1 month	Reflex activity	No differentiation of self from other objects	Egocentric	Egocentric
2 First differentiations 1–4 months	Hand-mouth coordination; differentiation via sucking, grasping	No special behavior *re* vanished objects; no differentiation of movement of self and external objects	Changes in perspective seen as changes in objects	No differentiation of movement of self and external objects
3 Reproduction, 4–8 months	Eye-hand coordination; reproduction of interesting events	Anticipates positions of moving objects	Space externalized; no spacial relationships of objects	Self seen as cause of all events
4 Coordination of schemata, 8–12 months	Coordination of schemata; application of known means to new problems; anticipation	Object permanence; searches for vanished objects; reverses bottle to get nipple	Perceptual constancy of size and shape of objects	Elementary externalization of causality
5 Experimentation, 12–18 months	Discovery of new means through experimentation	Considers sequential displacements while searching for vanished objects	Aware of relationships between objects in space; between objects and self	Self seen as object among objects and self as object of actions
6 Representation, 18–24 months	Representation; invention of new means via internal combinations	Images of absent objects, representation of displacements	Aware of movements not perceived; representation of spatial relationships	Representative causality: causes and effects inferred

Source: *Piaget's Theory of Cognitive Development,* second edition by Barry J. Wadsworth. Copyright © 1971, 1979 by Longmans Inc. Reprinted with permission of Longmans Inc., New York.

stages can be grouped in pairs. Substages one and two are centered on the infant's own body. Stages three and four enlarge this basic repertoire to include the manipulation of objects in the environment, and stages five and six allow the infant to create new behavior to solve problems, first with actual objects and then with mental images alone.

Reflexes, Substage One: Birth to One Month

The infant is born with ready-made responses that organize behavior to deal with the environment. These responses are reflexes. Although reflexes are present at birth they must be exercised in order to become efficient. Experience with objects in the environment modifies them. For example, one of the primary behavioral organizations with which the infant adapts to the world is associated with feeding. The

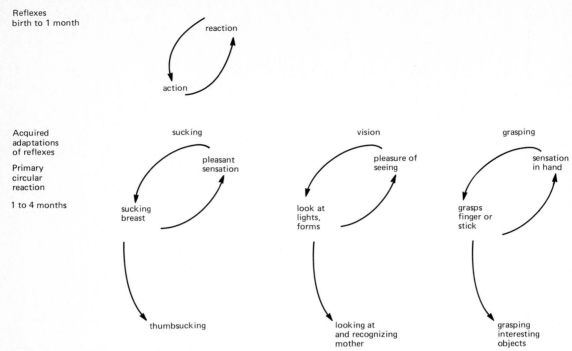

Reflexes
birth to 1 month

reaction

action

Acquired
adaptations
of reflexes

Primary
circular
reaction

1 to 4 months

sucking

pleasant
sensation

sucking
breast

thumbsucking

vision

pleasure of
seeing

look at
lights,
forms

looking at
and recognizing
mother

grasping

sensation
in hand

grasps
finger or
stick

grasping
interesting
objects

First acquired adaptations of behaviors from reflexes.

newborn applies the sucking reflex to any object that touches its lips. Piaget theorized that these reflexes were directed by mental organization, which he called a *scheme*. The result of the application of the sucking scheme to any object is that the infant has experience with many different objects. The young infant will suck fingers, blankets, bottles, breasts, or any other object. This experience with soft, hard, warm, and cool objects is assimilated into the basic reflexive sucking scheme. Piaget observed this behavior with his son Laurent.*

> *Laurent at . . . [nine days] is lying in bed and seeks to suck, moving his head to the left and to the right. Several times he rubs his lips with his hand which he immediately sucks. He knocks against a quilt and a wool coverlet; each time he sucks the object only to relinquish it after a moment and begins to cry again. When he sucks his hand he does not turn away from it as he seems to do with the woolens, but the hand itself escapes him through lack of coördination; he then immediately begins to hunt again.* [Piaget, 1952, p. 26]

First Acquired Adaptions, Substage Two: One to Four Months

For Piaget the importance of the nursing infant is that nursing requires the infant to organize behavior and that this behavior entails a directed search. Piaget (1952) states, "The precocious searching of the child in contact with the breast is a remark-

* Excerpts reprinted from *The Origins of Intelligence in Children* by Jean Piaget. (New York: W. W. Norton & Co., Inc, 1963.) Copyright © 1952 by International Universities Press, Inc. Reprinted by permission.

able thing. Such searching . . . must be conceived . . . as the first manifestation of . . . desire and satisfaction, of value and reality'' (p. 39). This directed behavior of the young infant is not governed by conscious intention, as is the goal-directed behavior of older children, rather the direction is on a purely physical level.

Infants soon begin to exhibit differential sucking: sucking when hungry and sucking for pleasure. The infant learns that sucking a blanket will not satisfy hunger, whereas sucking a breast will. This differentiation reflects a modification (an accommodation) in the sucking scheme. As the infant matures physically and gains experience in the world, the hereditary reflexes are adapted to the environment. That is, they are changed in some ways so that they are more useful in the infant's control of the environment. Because reflexes are directed by mental organization, changes are required in mental organization. These first changes are centered about the infant's own body and are called primary circular reactions.

Primary Circular Reactions

A circular reaction is one in which an action causes an effect, which in turn causes the action to be repeated, which causes an effect, and so forth. The question of which comes first, the chicken or the egg, is a circular situation. The first intellectual adaptations by the infant involve circular reactions in which reflexes are adapted to explore the range of possibilities in his or her own body. The reflexes that Piaget discusses in this context are sucking, vision, grasping, hearing, and phonation. With each of them Piaget discusses acquired habits adapted from the hereditary reflex. These reflexes are combined with increasing perceptual maturity and the coordination of two or more senses to explore the infant's own body and abilities.

Acquired Adaptation in Sucking

The sucking reflex is soon adapted to thumb sucking and to protrusion of the tongue. In the random movements of the arm, the hand sometimes comes into contact with the mouth and the sucking reflex is instituted. This action pleases the infant and over several months such an act is capable of being performed *intentionally*. Intentional behavior is quite different from random reflexive behavior. It is a hallmark of intelligence, and its first appearance is extremely important. The same sequence occurs with tongue play. The infant gradually enlarges the position of the tongue in sucking to licking lips, blowing saliva bubbles, and other mouth and tongue behavior. Both thumb sucking and putting out the tongue retain the basic structure of the reflex, but an element is added that the child has acquired by his or her own searching. The child is thus the active agent and becomes the instrument for the acquisition of new behaviors.

Acquired Adaptation in Vision

Vision in the newborn is a reflex of the sensory apparatus to the stimulation of light. This reflex carried with it a need for stimulation. The young infant looks, not to see, but to look. That is, the young infant looks at moving lights not to see the lights, but only to satisfy the inherent need to look. As stroking the cheek stimulates the sucking reflex, so a change in intensity in light (or light reflected on a form) stimulates the looking reflex. Gradually this reflexive looking is adapted to the purposes of the infant: that is, to recognition of form and coordination of vision with other senses. As visual acuity increases, the infant adapts this looking reflex to include larger and larger components. Vision thus becomes directed by intention.

 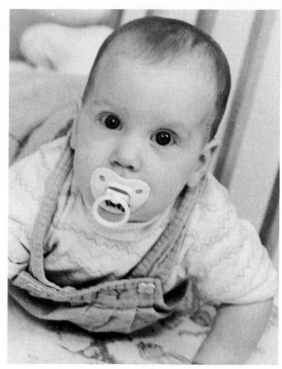

The sucking reflex which initially is used to secure food soon is adapted to sucking a thumb or pacifier.

Acquired Adaptation in Prehension (Grasping)

The hand is one of the most important instruments of intelligence. The emergence of grasping marks the third level of Piaget's sensorimotor intelligence. This substage is characterized by deliberate action and the use of secondary mechanisms. However, this ability is also based in reflexive action and must generalize from that base. The way in which the infant discovers grasping is instructive because, according to Piaget, this ability, even more than the other reflexes, illustrates "an indispensable connecting link between organic adaptation and intellectual adaptation" (1952, p. 89). Piaget has analyzed the development of grasping related to intelligence in five stages.

1. The first grasping movements are the grasp reflex and impulsive spontaneous movements of the fingers and hands.
2. The grasp reflex is slowly generalized into primary circular reactions in which objects are grasped and held simply for the pleasure of holding them. At first this holding is separate from seeing the object or attempting to move it. The generalized movements of the hands, arms, and fingers are a part of this first circular reaction. The movement itself is motivation to repeat the movement. Gradually coordinations between two modes occur, as for example, between sucking and hand movements in which fingers are carried to the mouth in order to suck them.
3. Finally, grasping is used to carry an object to the mouth in order to suck.

Here we have coordination among three schemes: grasping, vision, and sucking. The object is seen, grasped, carried to the mouth, and sucked. This level occurs in substage three and entails secondary circular reactions.

Procedures to Make Interesting Sights Last, Substage Three: Four to Eight Months

In this stage the child's activity centers on results in the external environment. The aim of actions in this stage is to maintain results that appear interesting. Means and ends begin to be separated. In the previous stage the means (sucking) and the ends (sucking) were identical. Objects were explored by sucking in order to use sucking behavior. Similarly, objects were looked at in order to look and were touched in order to use the fingers. In the third substage the means and ends become separated. Objects gradually become something to be shaken, swung, examined, rubbed, and so forth. A higher level of intellectual organization evolves in this stage, which results in a *secondary circular reaction*.

Secondary Circular Reactions

In the exercise of simple habits acquired in the previous substage, the infant may accidentally move an object in a new way. For example, in reaching for an object dangling over the crib, the infant may accidentally cause a toy to spin around in a motion that has not occurred before. The infant notices this new sight and attempts

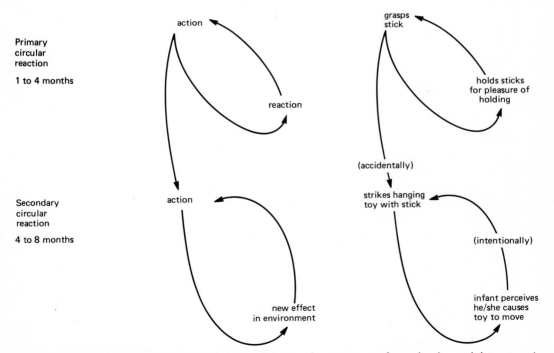

Primary and secondary circular reactions. Action and reaction become causes for each other and thus repeat in a circular pattern. Such circular behavior gradually expands through accidental occurrances and new, intentional behavior evolves.

to make it happen again; that is, he or she seeks to rediscover the action that will make the interesting sight last. Infants express their delight with such results by laughing. Contented babies will sometimes spend hours playing with objects they can reach in their cribs.

In analyzing the intellectual activities involved in such simple activities, we find three new components: memory, foresight, and self-awareness. The infant has been able to notice novel occurrences since birth. The new addition here is that the infant can remember the novel action and match an occurrence in reality with what is remembered. This substage also marks the beginning of foresight. The infant begins to know that a given action will bring with it, or cause, other events. For example, if a toy is tied above a crib and can be moved by a string, an infant of four to eight months soon learns that the toy can be made to move by pulling the string. The third new element in this stage is a rudimentary self-awareness. The infant begins to be aware that it is the action of his or her own body that causes these events to happen. Let us stress that this is not the kind of self-awareness with which adults are familiar. The infant's intellectual experience is for the most part on the sensorimotor level and so is its awareness.

> *Laurent . . . knows how to strike hanging objects intentionally with his hand. At . . . [four months, twenty-two days] he holds a stick; he does not know what to do with it and slowly passes it from hand to hand. The stick then happens to strike a toy hanging from the bassinet hood. Laurent, immediately interested by this unexpected result, keeps the stick raised in the same position, then brings it noticeably nearer to the toy. He strikes it a second time. Then he draws the stick back but moving it as little as possible as though trying to conserve the favorable position, then he brings it nearer to the toy, and so on, more and more rapidly.* [Piaget, 1952, p. 176]

The Coordination of Secondary Schemes and Their Application to New Situations, Substage Four: Eight to Twelve Months

The infant brings into this stage many behavioral strategies for handling objects, such as grasping, hitting, and carrying, as well as looking and hearing. The infant at eight or nine months of age is able to solve problems that would have been impossible before. For example, if a toy is taken from an infant of this age and hidden under or behind an obstacle (such as a pillow), the infant can remove the obstacle and grab the toy. At an earlier age if a toy disappeared from sight, the infant would simply have lost interest. When objects were no longer visible, they no longer existed. The simple act of retrieving a hidden toy requires the attainment of four complex organizations:

1. Object permanence.
2. Goal-directed behavior.
3. Understanding relationships among objects.
4. Coordination of senses.

Object Permanence
When the infant is able to retain an object as a mental image even though it is no longer visible, he or she has attained *object permanence*. If the infant can hold an image when the object is not present, then the actual object can be removed and retain reality for that infant. The infant at this stage also begins to anticipate events. This is further development of the foresight evident in the previous stage. The infant

This infant has attained object permanence. When her mother hides a favorite toy in a bag, she is able to retrieve the toy even though she cannot see it.

perceives certain sights or sounds as previsions that other events will occur and behaves accordingly. For example, seeing mother put on her coat, the infant anticipates her leaving and attempts to prevent it. When a disliked food is seen on a spoon, the infant may refuse to open his or her mouth. Hearing footsteps in the hall the infant may turn toward the door in anticipation of someone entering the room. Anticipation is the result of object permanence.

Goal-Directed Behavior

In organizing behavior to attain a goal, the infant is able to coordinate two (or more) behavior strategies into a single goal-directed sequence. Piaget states that *this kind of action represents the first actual intelligent behavior pattern of which the infant is capable* (Piaget, 1952). The infant can conceive a goal, realize that it is not directly attainable, and choose a behavior previously used in another situation to bring the goal within reach. In using several steps to reach a goal, the means and ends become separated. Previously, means and ends were all the same: sucking for the pleasure of sucking or grasping for the pleasure of grasping.

Relationships Among Objects

When the infant is able to remove an obstacle in order to attain an object, he or she has the ability to place objects in relationship to one another. At an earlier age the obstacle (a blanket, pillow, or screen) assumed primary interest for exploration; once object permanence and goal-directed behavior are attained the obstacle is only a secondary object to be removed, *before* attaining the toy. The toy retains primary importance. The relationship between cause and effect as well as the relationship between objects and events in time and space begin in these simple acts.

Coordination of Senses

The infant of eight to twelve months becomes more thoughtful in exploring new objects. Earlier, new objects were sucked, banged, or grasped first to exercise those behaviors and later to create an event. Objects are now carefully examined. The infant must incorporate objects into his or her own mental structures through the available visual, auditory, and tactile means. Let us stress that the object has no objective reality. Most people agree on the characteristics of an objective reality not because we all experience this reality directly, but because in exploring the outside world we all use similar senses that are structured in the same way. The infant must explore each object in the environment and assimilate it into his or her mental

Table 6–2. Emergence of Coordination of Senses, Goal-Directed Behavior, and Object Permanence in the Sensorimotor Period

Sensorimotor Stage	Coordination of Senses	Goal-Directed Behavior	Object Permanence

Stage 1: 0–1 month Reflexes
  sucking
  grasping
  looking			

Stage 2: 1–4 months Primary Circular Reaction Adaptation of reflexes: chance occurrences reproduced for pleasure.	Vision and grasping. Vision and touching. Grasping and sucking.		
Stage 3: 4–8 months Secondary Circular Reaction Invention of new behaviors. Actions occur accidentally and repeated intentionally.	Increased coordination. An object seen can be grasped and manipulated.	Actions performed for the results. Beginning of intentional behavior.	
Stage 4: 8–12 months Coordination of Secondary Schemes Two invented behaviors can be coordinated to solve simple problems		Actions are goal-directed. Can find a toy hidden under a blanket.	Object permanence. Toy continues to exist even if no longer seen.
Stage 5: 12–18 months Active experimentation Accidental results are varied experimentally.			While object exists when not seen, cannot conceive of movement that is not seen.

Table 6–2.   (continued)

Sensorimotor Stage	Coordination of Senses	Goal-Directed Behavior	Object Permanence
Stage 6: 18–24 months New means through mental combinations Understanding of relationships between different paths in space. Some understanding of causality.			Delayed imitation. Behavior sequence is retained mentally and performed at a later time.

structures. For example, imagine an infant with a plastic block. The infant might *see* a red cube. Perhaps there is a bell inside the cube and when it is shaken the infant will *hear* a tinkling sound. When the cube is grasped it is rigid, with smooth sides and sharp angles. The infant tries to suck the cube and finds that it does not adapt to the shape of his or her mouth and it does not have a taste. In this stage the infant systematically applies all of his or her behaviors one after another in exploring new objects. Objects are assimilated into existing schemes for seeing, grasping, and so forth. There is nothing in the redness of the cube that would give a clue to the sound it will make. Nor does the feel of the cube as it is grasped suggest the color red. The infant must bring these different sense modalities together and conclude that they all relay information about the *same* object. The infant must coordinate the eye and hand, vision and grasping. Information from several sense modalities is coordinated into one event. For example, being placed in a high chair, seeing a bowl, grasping a spoon, hearing mother's voice, all may signal "feeding" to the nine-month-old infant.

The Discovery of New Means Through Active Experimentation, Substage Five: Twelve to Eighteen Months

Substage five marks a new departure in the child's intellectual ability. Now the child actually *invents* new ways of handling objects and actively experiments in order to find new methods. In a word, the child is *creative*. He or she can now reason and solve simple problems as they arise in the manipulation of familiar objects. In manipulating objects a circular pattern of repetition of actions continues to occur, but this repetition varies a little each time and is more flexible than in previous substages. This circular pattern is referred to as *tertiary circular reactions* (third-order circular reactions). For example, infants systematically explore the action of falling objects in the environment. They may drop a small toy from a height, push it to the edge of a couch, roll it down an incline, or place it closer and closer to the edge to see when it will fall. The infant is, in effect, a little scientist. Experiments are made with food and implements from high chairs. Infants are also fascinated with playing with water and systematically explore its characteristics.

In her bath Jacqueline engages in many experiments with celluloid toys floating on the water. At . . . [thirteen months, twenty days] and the days following, for example, not only does she drop her toys from a height to see the water splash or displace them with her hand in order to make them swim, but she pushes them halfway down in order to see them rise to the surface.

At . . . [nineteen months, twenty days] she notices the drops of water which fall from the thermometer when she holds it in the air and shakes it. She then tries different combinations to splash from a distance. [Piaget, 1952, p. 273]

These circular reactions are different from previous ones in that now the child systematically seeks new results, whereas before he or she might vary movements seeking the same result. In this state it is the novelty of the events that delights the child.

The culmination of this substage comes when the child uses previous experience and the ability to experiment to solve problems it has not encountered before. For example, if a child reaches through the bars of a playpen or crib and grasps an object that is too large to pass through the opening of the bars, he or she might systematically manipulate the object until the solution is found. Consider the following example:

Jacqueline received a cardboard rooster by means of which I try the following experiment. I place it lying on the ground, outside the frame but introducing the head and tail of the cock in the direction of the child. In other words, the head passes through a space between two bars, the tail passes through the next space and the rooster's back is held back by the bar separating these two spaces. If the child wishes to pull the rooster to him he must first push it away, then tilt it up and finally bring it through head or tail first.

During this first experiment Jacqueline confines herself to merely pulling the rooster by the head or by the tail but without previously pushing it away or tilting it up; she consequently fails completely.

At . . . [fifteen months, sixteen days] on the other hand, I simplify things a little by putting the rooster back a little; it still faces a bar but, instead of being in contact with it, it is 5 cm. behind it. Here is the series of attempts:

1. Jacqueline pulls the rooster toward her and it gets caught in the bars. She pulls hard for a while, then switches hands. While she is doing this, the rooster happens to fall quite far away so that when picking it up again, she tilts it to a vertical position without difficulty. She then sees it in profile and has only to turn it full face to bring it through. [Piaget, 1952, p. 308]

In reaching this solution, the child has "thought" of a solution, but this thought is with the hands, eyes, and the object. In other words this is sensorimotor thought.

The Invention of New Means Through Mental Combinations, Substage Six: Eighteen to Twenty-four Months

This stage represents a clear break with the preceding stages. The infant moves in overlapping phases through discovering means to make interesting sights last, applying those means to new situations, systematically experimenting with objects, and discovering new means through active experimentation (substages three, four, and five). These phases, although presented as different stages, actually are a step in the process of refining means and ends. Substage six, on the other hand, is a qualitative break with the preceding stages. In this stage the infant moves from thinking with the body (sensorimotor) to representational thought. Such thought is characterized by invention and mental representation. The child at this stage actually *invents* new solutions to reach a goal. The process of this invention is carried forward through mental representation and not through slow sensorimotor groping. In order to do this, the infant must be able to form mental images of objects *and* of the relationships among them. In arriving at a practical solution to a physical problem, the infant must be able to perform mental operations on the objects and reject or select one that will solve the problem. The milestone in this stage is that the solution is not one that has been seen before and, therefore, is not an imitation. Rather, by applying the strategies for manipulating objects on a purely representational level (mental), the infant invents a behavior that is new and that solves the problem. For example, consider the following observation.

> *Jacqueline, at . . . [twenty months, nine days] arrives at a closed door—with a blade of grass in each hand. She stretches out her right hand toward the knob but sees that she cannot turn it without letting go of the grass. She puts the grass on the floor, opens the door, picks up the grass again and enters. But when she wants to leave the room things become complicated. She puts the grass on the floor and grasps the doorknob. But then she perceives that in pulling the door toward her she will simultaneously chase away the grass which she placed between the door and the threshold. She therefore picks it up in order to put it outside the door's zone of movement.* [Piaget, 1952, p. 339]

Another characteristic and milestone of this substage is the freeing of images from the perception of them. This ability to evoke mental images of objects is necessary for higher mental activity. The young infant acts as though objects do not exist once they pass from immediate perception. In substage four, the infant can anticipate when signs indicate that an event will occur. The sound of mother's voice indicates that she will appear. Through experience signs are modeled on the actual characteristics of things and so tend to form images. These signs become increasingly detached from immediate perception and finally exist as mental representations in a purely symbolic sense. When the child possesses these mental symbols, play becomes symbolic and assumes the character of "let's pretend as if" which is characteristic of older children.

This ability to hold an image of objects in mental representation is illustrated by the following observation made by Piaget of his daughter Jacqueline.

> *Jacqueline plays with a fish, a swan and a frog which she puts in a box, takes them out again, puts them back in, etc. At a given moment, she lost the frog. She places the swan and the fish in the box and then obviously looks for the frog. She lifts everything within reach (a big cover, a rug, etc.) and (long after beginning to search) begins to say inine, (inine = "grenouille = "frog"). It is not the word which set the search in motion but the opposite. There was therefore evocation of an absent object without any directly perceived stimulus. Sight of the box in which are found only two objects out of three provoked representation of the frog, and whether this representation preceded or accompanied the act is of little importance.* [Piaget, 1952, p. 356]

With the advent of symbolic images and representational thought the child is freed from sensorimotor intelligence, and with the aid of language and the guidance of parents, teachers, and peers he or she becomes increasingly capable of reflective intelligence (Piaget, 1952). Thus, intellectual infancy ends. Let us return to the young infant and trace the development of the most important aid to intellectual development—language.

Language and Communication

A baby's first words are an important milestone in its development. In retrospect mothers can often give a specific time for baby's first utterance, and baby diaries have a place to record the first words. In the scientific study of the development of language, however, it is not easy to assign a specific time or to identify first words. Language evolves slowly and is embedded in the larger question of communication.

Nonverbal Communication

Communication between infant and mother or caregiver begins from the very first days after birth and has reached a finely synchronized system long before language emerges. The earliest interchange between mother and infant is mutual gazing. Brazelton has studied the exchanges between infants and their mothers. Information is exchanged by signals involving eye contact and bodily tension, posture, and movement. These acts occur so rapidly and so subtly that it has taken the careful analysis of filmed interactions to extract the typical sequence. Brazelton (1976) sensitively describes the interaction between mother and young infant as "playing a kind of swan's mating dance." The sequence is characterized by alternating approach and withdrawal with periods of intense attention and inattention. The infant looks at the mother, then looks away, being careful to keep her in peripheral view. It is as though the infant is leading the mother into more and more involvement. Brazelton has found that mothers are very sensitive to these cycles in their

Games that mothers play with infants are often the context for learning language.

infants and withdraw when signaled to do so, so as not to overload the capacities of their infants for stimulation. Brazelton advances the opinion that the information conveyed in these exchanges is paramount,

> *I am convinced . . . that each culture's individual values and expectations are passed on and established in the infant's first few months of life by the patterns of response and the child-rearing practices to which he is exposed by his parents and other caregivers around him.* [Brazelton, 1976, p. 135]

This is, of course, opinion, but opinion based on years of research with infants and their parents and caregivers. Certainly, even if this is only partly correct, the communication in early infancy is enormous. This communication, however, like the early sensorimotor period is reflexive in nature. More advanced communication occurs when the infant performs acts of *intentional* communication. But more experience with objects and vocalizations is required first.

In the early months mutual gazing is augmented by following the gaze of another. Infants can communicate desire for an object by looking at it, and mothers read this gaze and find the object that the infant desires. Infants also follow the gaze of mothers to find an object. Soon, looking at a desired object is followed by pointing. Grunts and bodily gestures are added to gaze and pointing to express desire and intentions. Not only are intentions communicated through these means, but also the intensity of a message is communicated through facial expression and bodily position and movement.

Communication between mother and infant further develops in the social context of games and feeding. These activities become increasingly patterned into a rhythmic exchange between mother and child. The pattern is characterized by turn taking, with mother and infant playing assigned roles in a social situation.

For example, the simple game of peek-a-boo can be a delightful exchange of communication and reciprocal roles. Consider the following interplay between a mother and her infant.

Scene: Mrs. Jones has just finished bathing her eight-month-old baby, Catherine. The baby is sitting on the dressing table and Mrs. Jones places the towel over the baby's face. (This is a game they have played many times and thus it has become a ritual in which each knows her role and plays it.)

Mrs. Jones: "Where's the baby?" (A short pause, in which the baby is very still.)

Mrs. Jones: "Ah, here's the baby!! Peek-a-boo!" (Removes the towel. Catherine makes eye contact with her mother and sucks in air. Her body tenses; her eyes express anticipation and excitement.)

Mrs. Jones: (Replaces the towel over Catherine's head.) "Where's the baby?" (Baby is very still.)

Mrs. Jones: "Peek-a-boo." (Removes the towel. The baby becomes very excited, laughs out loud, and moves her arms and legs rapidly.)

This scene ends with Mrs. Jones picking up Catherine with a big hug and both of them laughing excitedly. The exchange is rich with communication on many levels. Language is involved, as is emotional pleasure, intellectual excitement, physical tension, and the stimulation of many sensory modes. An analysis of the scene's sequences such as this would, indeed, reveal much about early communication between infants and caregivers.

The infant of nine or ten months of age is able to engage in communication in which he or she *intends* to convey a purpose. Note that this is the same age at which the infant is able to construct a goal with objects and reach it (substage 4 in sensori-motor development). In some cases this communication with adults facilitates goal-directed behavior (Bates, 1979). Communication is conveyed through conventionalized signals. That is, by nine months of age the child has invented gestures or sounds that are clearly recognized by its parents or other caregivers. Those gestures and sounds constitute a private language that only the few initiates understand. The elements of the communication continue to be signals rather than true language.

Prior to this time the child has certainly signaled wants and desires and the caregiver has perceived and interpreted these signals with more or less success. At around nine months of age, however, the infant adds intention to the equation. Typical behavior includes pointing at an object, looking at an adult, looking at an object, and perhaps making agitated body movements and grunting. The infant now watches the adult to see if the message is understood. The infant clearly intends to communicate.

There are four different behaviors that infants use to communicate with adults (Bretherton, Bates, Benigni, Camaioni, & Volterra, 1979):

1. Communicative pointing. This constitutes pointing in a social context. In later development the infant looks at the adult to check whether the message is communicated.
2. Showing. The infant first shows an object already in its hand and later may pick up an object in order to show it to an adult.
3. Giving. As with showing, the infant gives an object that is already in its hand; it then picks up an object in order to give it to another; and later it may pick up an object and walk across the room to give it to an adult.
4. Ritual Requests. The infant may request an object by stretching out its hand and making a sound that has come to mean "I want," which is understood by infant and adult. Gestures such as opening and closing the hand also

Infants develop elaborate means of communication through pointing, body movement, and other signals long before language can be reliably used for communication. Parents and caregivers verbally respond to these nonverbal communications, thereby providing a bridge from experience to language.

come to be understood as requests by both adults and the infant. These rituals are usually incomprehensible to outsiders.

Let us look in on the nursery with Aileen and Matthew. Matthew has just awakened from a nap.

> *Aileen enters the room while Matthew is standing at the side of the crib. As she enters he looks at her and makes the sound ''Na-na.'' Aileen responds, ''You want your night-night?'' and she begins to look for his pacifier. Matthew points over the side of the crib to the floor and begins to bounce up and down while looking at his mother and repeating ''Na-na'' in an ever-rising tone of voice. Aileen stoops, looks on the floor, and picks up the pacifier, which she gives to Matthew. He puts it in his mouth with a smile and a sigh.*
>
> *Aileen then picks up the baby, changes his diapers, and proceeds to the kitchen. When they arrive at the kitchen, he leans forward, grunts ''Unh-unh'' and opens and closes his hand. Aileen responds, ''No, you can't have a cookie now, you must have lunch first.'' Matthew sticks out his lip and whines softly. He then leans forward again, reaches out his arms grunts ''Unnh-unnh,'' reaching with both hands toward the sink. He looks at Aileen and repeats the gestures. She responds, ''Yes, I know you are thirsty, just a minute and we will have lunch.''*

A visitor watching this exchange may feel like a stranger in a foreign land having to deal with a strange language, and wonder how Aileen ever got such complex messages from that confusion of sounds, squirms, and points.

Intentional communication in a ten-month-old infant may also include giving or showing objects to adults in order to get a reaction from the adult. In a typical sequence the infant hands an object to an adult and then alternates his or her eye contact between the object and the adult. The infant will adjust his or her behavior with various signals until the display has been acknowledged by a laugh, a nod, "That's good," or some other agreed on ritual for approval. In this sequence the infant will withdraw with obvious pride in the accomplishment and approval. Such is the complex prelanguage communication in the infant's first year of life.

Nonverbal behavior continues to be an important means of communication throughout life. When we as adults have a very important or complex message to communicate we want to convey it "eyeball-to-eyeball," meaning that words alone will not be sufficient. If we can see another person's eyes we can tell if the message is understood. Through this feedback we can modify our presentation to convey not only words, but *meanings*.

Language As Communication

Language is the use of word symbols to express thought; it rests on the child's knowledge of words, what the child desires to communicate, and his or her skill in grammatical constructions (Bates, Benigni, Bretherton, Camaioni, & Volterra, 1979). Language, then, is related to thinking in that it is a tool used to express underlying thought processes. These thought processes do not *necessarily* depend on language, although in our school system language is the predominant method of assessing both intellectual ability and achievement. Research with chimpanzees has revealed that they can communicate, use symbols to represent real objects, express emotion, reason, and solve problems (Gardner & Gardner, 1969) even though they do not possess the ability to use spoken language. Using a computer, or American sign language, primates are able to construct simple sentences and grasp the rudiments of syntax. This research has forced a reevaluation of the relationship between mental processes and language and the position that humans alone possess language.

Language, and other aspects of development, follows a sequence that is regulated by heredity, in that all healthy, normal babies follow the same pattern at approximately the same time. The timing and content of language are modified by the infant's experiences. Speech is closely related to hearing, and children who are born deaf do not develop normal speech.

Language is not simply the utterance of word sounds. It is the use of word sounds as *symbols*. The sounds that constitute a language are inextricably related to the mental symbol of an object and the emotional quality of an experience. Obviously, both words and mental symbols become more complicated with abstract concepts such as love, hunger, and time. Children often express these abstract concepts in concrete words, such as the reply of a little boy who was scolded by his mother for fighting with another child and said, "Oh, Mommie, what can I do when the fight just crawls out of me?" (Chukovsky, 1963). An outline of the sequence of language development follows.

Prelanguage Phonation

Undifferentiated Crying. The infant "cries" at birth. Its cry is essentially a reflex, but it is the basis of his or her later speech. Undifferentiated crying persists for the first several weeks after birth. To the caregiver, however, this crying constitutes a signal of the infant's condition and needs.

Differentiated Crying. In the first month after birth, the cries of the infant begin to convey different messages. Caregivers can distinguish among cries that indicate anger, pain, hunger, or fussy discomfort by the pattern, intensity, and/or pitch of the cries.

Cooing. The infant begins to explore vocal possibilities as he or she begins to explore all the aspects of the body. In the second month of life the infant makes many different sounds, generally referred to as cooing. Actually the sounds are more diverse and include grunts, gurgles, squeals, and hums. The first sounds are those we designate as vowels with perhaps the consonant *h*. The resulting sounds are aaaahh, ooooh, and so forth. Often the frequency and intensity are varied. These sounds are most often emitted when the infant is engaged in pleasing activities, such as nursing.

Babbling. The sounds of the infant gradually come to resemble human speech rather than the more biologically based squeals and grunts. In babbling the infant creates clearly recognizable vowels and consonants. The infant plays with these sounds. As in the manipulation of objects, these sounds are first for the effect on his or her own body. Babbling follows the primary circular reflex outlined in Piaget's sensorimotor period. In babbling the infant explores all vowels and many consonants. The sounds are repetitive: be-be-be, ba-ba-ba-ba-ba-, pa-pa-, ma-ma-ma-, da-da; often the repetitions employ two consonants as in ka-ga, ta-da, or mi-bi. Parents often see these as first words for "mama" and "daddy"; their reaction, of course, encourages the child to make more sounds. The child soon learns that the production of such sounds brings great rewards from the environment (mother and daddy), even though intention or symbolic use of the words cannot be assigned at this age. Nevertheless, it is good that parents and caregivers respond positively to those vocal productions. In babbling, the infant produces sounds and sequences that have never been heard from the child's caregivers. Those sounds are found in other languages but not in English, such as clicks (in the Bushman language) and front vowels such as *tu* and *bose* (in French and German) (Ervin-Tripp, 1971).

The amount of vocalization that a child engages in is related to the social class of the parents. Children whose parents are middle class vocalize more than children of lower-class parents. This is probably because middle-class mothers talk more to their infants and encourage their vocalizations more.

Imitation.   Babbling sounds gradually give way to sounds that are more specific to the language of the infant's caregivers. Between six and nine months of age the infant becomes more attentive to sounds from the environment, both those produced by others and his or her own vocalizations. The infant becomes increasingly better at this imitation and late in his or her first year can produce not only an imitation of words, but an imitation of the intonation of a sentence. We may be unaware that the rhythmic and tonal patterns of a sentence convey intentions. For example, the pattern of a command is characterized by rising pitch early in the sentence and a lower pitch at the end: i.e. "Put that glass down." The pattern for a question is that the sentence ends with a rising pitch: i.e. "Do you want a glass of water?" Thus, infants between nine and twelve months of age imitate both the words and intonation in sentence patterns. The imitation of words and intonation without concomitant meaning is known as echolalia and is apparent in older autistic children.

Understanding words precedes the ability to produce them with clear meanings. Before most children's first birthday they can understand and obey simple commands such as "Come here." "Give me the book." and "Kiss Daddy goodnight."

Holophrases (One-Word Sentences).   At around their first birthday, most babies begin to use words to communicate. This first attempt is speech in which an entire sentence is expressed in one word. A single word such as *down* may indicate a request to be put down from a high chair, or it may mean that a toy fell to the floor. Gestures accompanying such holophrases continue to assist in conveying intended meaning. In a study with American and Italian babies between nine and twelve months of age, Bates et al. (1979) found that gestures were a better predictor of language development than babbling.

What do infants say when they begin to talk? Even though all infants have been exposed to a great number of words they rather consistently begin with the same few *kinds* of words. Bloom (1973) kept a careful record of the first words of her infant daughter and found that they could be divided into two classes: words that *named objects,* such as *dog, shoe,* and *car,* and words that *expressed function,* such as *there, no, gone, away,* and *stop.* According to Bloom the earliest words of infants are heavily weighed toward the function words. Words that name are used less frequently and tend to be substituted easily for one another. Nelson (1977) studied the first fifty words produced by 18 babies. She concluded that babies learn words associated with things that act and that they themselves can act upon. Both the name and the function of the objects that the child can manipulate him- or herself are the words that are learned. Certainly that makes great common sense. We all learn words associated with the activities related to our interests. Because infants are active participants in the world, it makes sense that they too should learn the words related to their interests. Every baby hears the word *diaper* and has it changed from the first days of life, but no one has reported the word *diaper* among a baby's first words. On the other hand, *dog, kitty,* and *car* are very often among an infant's first words.

There is another factor that seems to determine what the first words will be. Nelson also reported that among her subjects individual temperament affected the kinds of words learned. Some children seemed to prefer words and phrases that were more expressive and that were used for social interaction, such as, *mommy, daddy, no, yes, want, please, stop it, go away.* Other children preferred words that referred to objects, such as *ball, shoes,* and *dog.* Using this category of word acquisition, Rosenblatt (1975) found that children who acquired expressive words spent more time in social interaction than children who acquired object words, and spent more time in solitary play.

Although the average child begins to use words at about the age of one, the development of language in the second year is not rapid. The second year is devoted to a slow acquisition of additional words. The first nouns acquired by the infant are not very exact and refer generally to a broad category. For example, a baby learns the word *kitty* for the family cat. Thereafter, all furry four-legged animals become "kitty." If, for example, the baby meets a dog it may be grouped in the category "kitty," with the unspoken logic of "I don't know quite what it is, but it's sort of a kitty." In the same way all men may be "daddy" for a long time.

Two-Word Sentences.   As the child approaches its second birthday, speech begins to involve sentences with a noun or a pronoun and a verb. Such phrases as "Me go." "Mommy bye-bye." and "John hurt." are typical. With the advent of two-word sentences the acquisition of grammar begins. The placement of words in a sentence is important in conveying meaning. Although the child uses only two words, they are usually in the correct sequence for meaning. The simple phrases "more cookie" and "me hurt" convey the correct meaning partly because of the order of the words. If the order were reversed, the meaning would be quite different.

Language is, as we stated, the use of words as symbols and must await the development of representational thought (Piaget's substage six in the sensorimotor stage), which occurs in the second half of the second year (eighteen to twenty-four months). Before this time the infant is not able to handle objects through symbolic representation but must use sensorimotor manipulation. After attaining representational thought language development is rapid.

Theories of Language Development

B. F. Skinner and Reinforcement

B. F. Skinner advanced the theory that language is learned by reinforcement and imitation. He theorized that the babbling child produces all the sounds in all the languages in the world. The specific language is molded out of this stream of sound by the adults around the infant who praise and reinforce his or her accidentally produced sounds, which resemble words in the language the adults speak. The adult then pronounces the word, providing corrected feedback to the infant and rewards him or her with a smile and approval. Thus, Skinner theorized, the infant acquires language through modeling, imitation and reinforcement. Conditioning in infancy has not been effective in establishing behaviors that are not in the usual

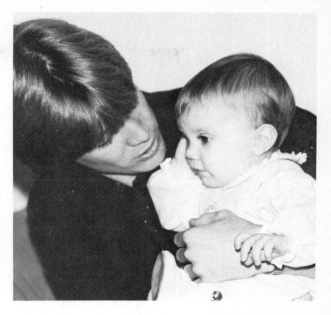

This nine-month-old girl listens intently as her father talks to her. The words that parents use with their infants are important in the development of language, although theorists disagree whether it is from modeling or from an innate ability in all humans.

range of capabilities of infants. This theory has lost adherents because infants produce words and combinations of words that are new. That is, they produce words that they have never heard modeled. They also begin to apply rules of syntax to which they have not been specifically conditioned. Noam Chomsky has advanced a theory that accounts for these factors.

Chomsky's Language Acquisition Device (LAD)

In the 1960's Noam Chomsky advanced a psycholinguistic theory of language acquisition. When linguist Chomsky with psychologist David McNeill and biologist Eric Lenneberg looked at infant speech they found that infants all over the world acquired speech in approximately the same way and at approximately the same ages. Chomsky theorized that all children have an inborn ability to learn language. Language development, according to Chomsky, is regulated and triggered by a *language acquisition device* (LAD). This innate pattern determines the listening behavior of infants in early infancy, releases babbling at six months, first words at about a year, and sentences at two years. This timing occurs in all cultures and in all races. Chomsky theorized that all children are born with knowledge of the *deep structure* of language. Deep structure refers to the commonality that all languages share and is a genetic trait inborn in all humans. Deep structure of language includes an inborn understanding of the function of communication, a grasp that differences in pronunciation are important, and an understanding of the intonation of sentences as questions, statements, or requests. Superimposed on the deep structure of language is *surface structure,* which encompasses the peculiarities of English, French, or Swahili. These must be learned, but they are learned quickly because the acquisition is guided by the underlying deep structure. Innate guidance from the LAD enables children to generalize rules of grammar from spoken language. We know that children deduce grammar because they produce words that are the result of inferred rules of grammar, but that are grammatically incorrect because of irregularities in language. For example, a young child deduces that to indicate the plural of a noun the rule is to add *s*. The child may say, "Look at the dogs." and "Look at the sheeps." Psycholinguists reason that, in order to do this, the three-year-old has already discovered the rules of grammar. The rules vary from language to language, but the search for the generalizing principles is guided by innate deep structure. Psycholinguists in the 1960s and 1970s counted words and analyzed the grammar of many children. The analysis revealed much interesting data, but the function of language seemed to be lost in the analysis. More recently researchers have concentrated on the *meaning* and the communicative function of language. (Bates et al., 1979).

Assessing Infant Intelligence

There has been increasing interest in recent years in assessing the mental ability of infants. Why would we want to test infants? Well, because there is a need to identify infants that have neurological or perceptual deficits. Parents and agencies need help in identifying infants whose development lags behind that of their age mates. Adoptive parents may want to know about the developmental level of their child and what they can expect of its future development. Research has focused on the importance of infancy in setting developmental patterns. The reason for testing infants, then, is to evaluate current developmental status, to predict future development, and to have a basis for intervention that might change detrimental patterns.

School-age children have been extensively tested since early in this century. Almost everyone at some time has taken a test that is designed to measure intellectual ability or attainment. Such a test usually depends heavily on the use of language as a written or verbal response. How then can we measure the intellectual development of infants, when their use of language is severely limited? Infant testing must of necessity draw on the responses that are available to the infant: primarily motor, perceptual, and social. The testing of infants has been characterized by the use of three distinct kinds of test instruments. Each of the three is based on a different assumption and, to some extent, uses different measures. The first kind of infant test attempts to measure intelligence by assessing the infant's maturity. The test is based on the assumption that maturation is the prime cause of development and that this development is correlated with mental ability. The second test to measure infant mental ability is the ordinal scales of cognitive development based on Piaget's theory of cognitive development. The third type of test is designed to screen infants for developmental level. The screening test evaluates present functioning and attempts to identify developmental problems. The tests assume that development is largely a function of the environment and that early identification of developmental deviations can be helped by environmental changes.

Developmental Scales

One of the first attempts made to estimate the intellectual ability of infants was by Gesell and his associates at Yale. The clinic there was among the pioneers in the systematic collection of data on the normal development of infants and children. Gesell was instrumental in standardizing growth charts for infants and children. The Yale clinic gathered data on development in a number of areas, through a series of longitudinal studies in addition to height and weight. The Gesell Developmental

Schedules were prepared from that data (Gesell and Amatruda, 1947). The schedules provide a normative standard against which a child's behavior can be compared in the areas of motor development, adaptive behavior, language, and personal-social behavior. The schedules do not "test" the infant, rather an individual infant's response to standard toys and other stimuli is observed. Information is also gathered from the primary caregiver about the infant's behavior at home. The underlying theory of the Gesell schedules is that development is largely the result of maturation. The maturational view of development holds that growth and development are largely a process of "unfolding," similar to a flower blooming, and that, provided the basic physical needs are met for food and health, the environment exerts little influence on the maturational process. Infants and children may be on schedule, ahead of schedule, or behind schedule in their development. The primary use of the developmental schedules is to find the child's place on a timetable of development. The results of the scale are reported in terms of a Developmental Quotient (DQ). The publishers of the test caution that a DQ is not equivalent to an IQ (intelligence quotient); however, the temptation has been great to equate the two in practice. There is not a high correlation between scores on infant tests and later IQ tests. The developmental schedules are most useful in identifying neurological defects and behavioral abnormalities that have an organic basis (Anastasi, 1976).

Another infant test that uses some items from the Gesell schedules, but includes many other items, is the Bayley Scales of Infant Development (Bayley, 1969). This scale is highly respected for its careful construction and the large and diverse group of children that were used in obtaining the standardization data. In order to generalize data from a study, the subjects must be representative of the entire group. Similarly, in order for a test to be valid for a large number of children, the sample of children from which the normative data are gathered must represent the entire group. The Gesell schedules have been criticized because the developmental data used to construct the scales was gathered primarily on the children of faculty at Yale. Such children are hardly representative of the entire American population. For example, when the data were gathered (the 1920s) chances are that there was not a single black child in the group. The Bayley scales, on the other hand, were standardized on a large number of children representative of the infant and child population of the United States in terms of geographic and urban-rural residence, sex ratio, white-nonwhite, and education of head of household.

Developmental scales assume that intelligence is a general factor that is consistent throughout life, that it can be identified early, and that it is relatively unaffected by environmental influences; a person either has it or doesn't. The tests of infant intelligence have not been able to identify this consistent factor. The prediction of IQ from infant tests has not been encouraging. Such prediction has been little better than chance. It appears that intelligence may not be one general factor but may, instead, be composed of many different abilities that develop at different rates and are affected differently by environmental influences. Nevertheless, these tests continue to be used and appear to be useful in evaluating the current status of the infant, if not in predicting IQ.

Ordinal Scales: Measuring Piagetian Stages

Researchers working in the context of Piaget's theory found that the infant scales in wide use were simply not relevant to a Piagetian conception of cognitive develop-

Exploring a "busy-box" is an act of intelligence, according to Piaget's theory. This infant is coordinating eye and hand in her manipulation of the toy. Note that she looks at the toy with intense concentration but her ability to grasp the knobs is not so well developed. In Piaget's conception cognitive development is inseparable from experiences in the environment. This little girl is improving her ability to explore the world by exploring it.

ment. In Piaget's framework the infant moves from one stage to another in a sequence that does not vary and between which there is a *qualitative* difference. Thus, the appearance of representational thought is a quantum jump from sensorimotor intelligence and not simply a continuous development of the intelligence factor. In addition, according to Piagetian theory, cognitive development is inseparable from experiences in the environment. Piagetian researchers were also not in accord with assigning an IQ to an infant with the expectation that it was the slot the child was destined to occupy for the remainder of his or her life.

Two scales have been developed based on Piaget's theory, the Einstein Scales of Sensorimotor Intelligence developed by Escalona and Corman at the Einstein School of Medicine (Yang, 1979) and a scale developed by Uzgiris and Hunt (1975). The Einstein scale has three subscales measuring comprehension, object permanence, and space orientation (Yang, 1979).

The Uzgiris-Hunt scale is divided into six scales. These include visual pursuit and permanence of objects, development of means for obtaining desired environmental events, development of verbal and gestural imitation, development of cause-effect relationships, object relations in three-dimensional space, and the child's use of toys. These "tests" are actually procedures in which the infant is essentially handled in a normal environment and then has its behavior noted; it is not an objective test situation. Yang (1979) notes a problem in this area because infants differ in their social responsiveness. Thus, a particularly skillful infant can seduce an examiner with smiles and winsome ways, with the result that its developmental level may be overestimated. A particularly fussy baby might do the opposite.

Screening Tests

A test that screens infants is one designed to provide a quick and simple method of differentiating normal infants from those who are at risk—that is, who have a higher probability of future problems.

We have previously discussed the Apgar screening technique with which newborns are evaluated 60 seconds after birth and possibly again at three, five, and 10 minutes after birth. This procedure quickly separates those infants who need attention from those who are able to cope with the physiological demands of birth.

The Brazelton Neonatal Behavioral Assessment Scale (see Chapter 1) is administered in the neonatal period, but after recovery from the stress of labor and delivery. Many other procedures are based on a "deficit" model of neonates and look for negative signs. The Brazelton procedure, on the other hand, attempts to elicit the infant's best response to positive and social stimuli and his or her ability to orient and to organize responses.

One major problem with the reliability of infant tests is that the state of infants varies widely; thus, the best response of which the infant is capable is not always elicited (Escalona, 1950). The Brazelton procedure takes careful account of this factor, so that each infant's optimal performance is elicited.

Another important screening test for older infants is the Denver Developmental Screening Test (Frankenburg & Dodds, 1967). This test is relatively new on the infant testing scene but has proved to be quite useful in identifying those children who need special programs and close supervision to guide their development.

The Denver Development Screening Test was developed in the 1960s and is based on data from normal children in Denver, Colorado. In screening children and infants for their level of development, the major procedure used is to ascertain the age at which motor skill is mastered. Motor items such as rolling over, sitting propped up, sitting alone, standing while holding on, standing alone, walking well, walking backward, walking up steps, and kicking a ball forward are used as items for evaluation. Using the norms provided by the screening test, an examiner can determine whether an individual infant is developing more rapidly, less rapidly, or on an average with other infants. The major use for the screening tests is to identify problems and then prescribe changes that will stimulate development. The major assumption in the screening tests is that, in healthy infants, the environment is the major cause of differences in developmental timing. The further assumption is made that, when the environment fails to provide the necessary stimulation for development, the child falls further and further behind and after some years the environmental deficits cannot be made up. Therefore, the thrust is to teach parents and caregivers to provide an optimum environment in the early formative years. We might summarize the conviction of those using this approach with the old cliché, "An ounce of prevention is worth a pound of cure."

Main Points

Sensorimotor Intelligence

1. In the sensorimotor stage of intellectual development, knowledge is obtained through the senses and through physical activity.

Reflexes, Substage One: Birth to One Month

2. In the reflexive substage development proceeds through ready-made responses present at birth.

First Acquired Adaptations, Substage Two: One to Four Months

3. The first changes in reflexive activity are called primary circular reactions.

4. The acquired adaptations in sucking are thumb sucking and tongue protrusion.

5. Reflexive looking is replaced by the acquired adaptations of recognition of form and coordination of vision with other senses.

6. The first acquired adaptation of the grasping reflex is the primary circular reaction in which objects are grasped and held simply for the pleasure of holding them.

Procedures to Make Interesting Sights Last, Substage Three: Four to Eight Months

7. In this stage the child attempts to maintain results that appear interesting.

8. Secondary circular reactions develop that involve memory, foresight, and self-awareness.

The Coordination of Secondary Schemes and Their Application to New Situations, Substage Four: Eight to Twelve Months

9. In the fourth substage, information from different sense modalities is coordinated into one event.

10. When the infant is able to retain an object as a mental image even though it is no longer visable, she or he has obtained object permanence.

11. When two or more existing behaviors are used to reach a single goal, the infant is exhibiting goal-directed behavior; this event represents the first intelligent behavior pattern.

12. The ability to place objects in relationship to one another develops in the fourth substage. This is demonstrated by the infant's ability to remove an obstacle to obtain an object.

The Discovery of New Means Through Active Experimentation, Substage Five: Twelve to Eighteen Months

13. In substage five the child actively experiments to find new ways of handling objects and applies these inventions to solving problems.

14. A circular pattern of repetition of actions continues to occur, which incorporates the new invention of behavior; it is called tertiary circular reactions.

The Invention of New Means Through Mental Combinations, Substage Six: Eighteen to Twenty-four Months

15. In substage six the infant can solve problems through purely mental means. By forming mental representations of objects and the relationships among them, various outcomes can be imagined and one chosen.

Language and Communication: Nonverbal Communication

16. Nonverbal communication between mother (or caregiver) and infant includes mutual gazing, following the gaze of the other, pointing, grunting, body gestures, facial expression, body position, and movement.

Language As Communication

17. Language is the use of word symbols to express thought and rests on the child's knowledge of words, what the child desires to communicate, and skill in grammatical constructions. It has a developmental sequence.

Prelanguage Phonation

18. Prior to language, certain phonic capacities develop: crying, cooing, babbling, imitation, holophrases, and two-word sentences.

Theories of Language Development

19. Skinner advanced the theory that language is acquired through modeling, imitation, and reinforcement.

20. Chomsky theorized that all children have an inborn ability to learn language and that language development is regulated and triggered by an innate language acquisition device (LAD).

Assessing Infant Intelligence

21. The first two years of life are important for changing detrimental developmental patterns; therefore, there has been much interest in assessing the mental ability of infants.

Developmental Scales

22. Developmental scales place a child in a timetable of development on standardized normative scales.

Ordinal Scales: Measuring Piagetian Stages

23. Two scales have been developed, based on Piagetian theory, to measure cognitive development.

Screening Tests

24. Screening tests provide a quick and simple method of differentiating normal infants from those who are at risk.

Words to Know

babbling	**prehension**
holophrase	**reinforcement**
nonverbal	**sensorimotor**
ordinal	**symbol**

Terms to Define

acquired adaptation
coordination of senses
developmental scales
Language Acquisition Device
object permanence
primary circular reaction

representational thought
screening tests
secondary circular reaction
symbolic images
tertiary circular reaction

CHAPTER 7

Emotional and Social Development in Infancy

Have you ever wondered

what emotions babies experience?

how emotions grow and change?

if emotions are related to cognitive growth?

how important it is for babies to become attached to one specific person?

what happens when a baby does not have the opportunity to become attached to a specific adult?

how a baby is affected when mothering is lacking?

what happens when babies are separated from their mothers?

if fathers are as nurturing as mothers?

how babies and toddlers relate to their peers?

The growing child is an emotional being who experiences love, joy, anger, anxiety, sorrow, and depression. It is through these and other feelings that humans are emotionally connected to the world. We have separated perception and intellectual growth and development from emotional development in this book; however, in reality they cannot be separated. Both perception and cognition are inextricably entwined with the affective (emotional) facets in humans. Development is a process of total organization. The infant learns language in the context of an affective social interchange between infant and caregiver. The language is almost incidental to the emotional exchange. The feelings that one has in a situation contribute greatly to the meaning of the transaction and, in a similar fashion, feelings provide the strongest motivation for action (Sroufe, 1979).

The child who is developing well emotionally is one who displays a zest for experiences, who expresses emotions, who enjoys people and is a source of enjoyment to them, who uses personal and environmental resources to satisfy needs and gain pleasure, and who seeks new experiences. The emotions are not merely pleasant or unpleasant byproducts of actions. They serve the function of organizing behavior in adults and children as well as in infants. Because human beings are not guided by instinct, as are many other animals, it is emotions that guide behavior (Breger, 1974). Human behavior is, thus, much more flexible and is shaped more by experiences than the behavior of animals, which are governed largely by instinct. Whether emotions are positive or negative is important, as positive affect tends to support organized behavior toward a desired goal. Negative affect may also organize behavior; toward aggressive action in the case of anger or toward flight in the case of fear. Overpowering emotions, of course, tend to disorganize behavior.

Growth of Emotion

Emotions are differentiated in the first two years of life from the state of generalized excitement of the newborn. According to our present state of knowledge the newborn is not capable of a full range of human emotions; however, by its second birthday the infant expresses most of the emotions that we consider human. Of course we can no more measure what the infant experiences and feels than we can ask what he or she sees. The physiological arousal state of general excitement is the precursor of the emotions. Sroufe (1979) has summarized the results of many research studies on emotional development in infancy into seven stages. These stages serve only as a useful description of development and should not be considered an invariant sequence. Further research may refine them. Nevertheless, these stages are useful in tracing the process of emotional development.

Stage One, Stimulus Barrier: Birth to One Month

The infant under one month of age is generally unresponsive to the subtle emotional climate in which he or she lives. The very young infant seems unaware of the joys and sorrows of its caregivers and does not indicate that such emotions are a part of his or her experience. We may speculate that such indifference is the result of a stimulus barrier that protects the newborn from overstimulation in this period of adjustment. Emotional response in the first month is generally restricted to generalized excitement and many different stimuli will arouse the same excited response. This excitement may be positive, as in alert attention, or negative, as in agitated fussiness. The emotions (positive and negative) differentiate out of this excitement (Bridges, 1932). The excitement helps to organize behavior; however, either positive or negative stimulation can escalate to the level at which the infant is overwhelmed and behavior becomes disorganized. Elsewhere we have described the role of the infant in organizing his or her own behavior and initiating or breaking off interaction with caregivers. This interaction very quickly attains an emotional component, certainly for the mother, and probably for the infant also.

Stage Two, Turning Outward: One to Three Months

In the early months generalized excitement is further differentiated into distress, indicated by agitated crying, or delight, indicated by laughing out loud. The newborn does not cry with tears or with expression. True tears appear after several weeks, as does the emotional aspect of crying. Stage two marks a qualitative differ-

Table 7–1. The Development of Some Basic Human Emotions in Infants*

Month	Pleasure–Joy	Wariness–Fear	Rage-Anger	Periods of Emotional Development
0	Endogenous smile	Startle/pain	Distress due to: covering the face, physical restraint, extreme discomfort	Absolute stimulus barrier
1	Turning toward	Obligatory attention		Turning toward
2				
3	Pleasure		Rage (disappointment)	Positive affect
4	Delight Active laughter	Wariness		
5				
6				Active participation
7	Joy		Anger	
8				
9		Fear (stranger aversion)		Attachment
10				
11				
12	Elation	Anxiety Immediate fear	Angry mood, petulance	Practicing
18	Positive valuation of self-affection	Shame	Defiance	Emergence of self
24			Intentional hurting	
36	Pride, love		Guilt	Play and fantasy

Source: "Socioemotional Development" by L. Alan Sroufe. In *Handbook of Infant Development,* edited by Joy D. Osofsky. Copyright © 1979 by John Wiley & Sons. Reprinted by permission.

*The age specified is neither the first appearance of the affect in question nor its peak occurrence; it is the age when the literature suggests that the reaction is common.

ence and a turning outward in interest and in *affect* (behavioral expression of emotion). The major event in this stage is the advent of the social smile, to which adults and children alike almost always respond positively. The roots of interest and curiosity are in this positive interaction with persons and things. Smiling begins at around six weeks of age and by three months the infant is regularly responding to human faces with smiles and laughter.

Stage Three, Reliable Social Smile: Three to Six Months

Stage three witnesses greatly increased responsiveness. The period of infant fussiness is over and parent and infant are adjusted to each other. Positive smiling and laughing continue to bond the two (or three) into a positive relationship. As the infant engages people and objects, emotions such as frustration, rage, and wariness arise. The infant can now actively avoid unpleasant situations (such as having its nose wiped) and coos and smiles at objects as well as people in the environment. A good environment for the infant maintains a preponderance of positive affect over negative emotions.

Stage Four, Active Participation: Seven to Nine Months

This stage is a period of social awakening in which the infant engages in social games such as peek-a-boo and initiates social interaction with familiar caregivers. Strangers, however, may be met with a stoical face or a scream. The infant's cau-

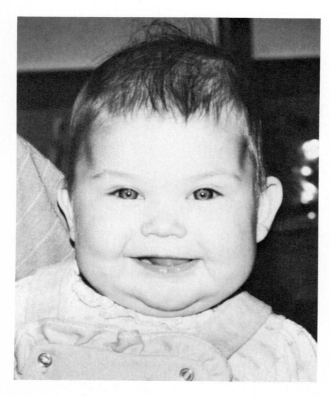

Positive emotions are conveyed through the smile of an infant, and adults respond in kind.

The understanding and feelings associated with self as a separate person are basic to the development of emotions. This infant is exploring her appearance in a mirror. (The mirror is actually a metal reflector, and the marks at the top of this picture are the result of teething.)

tion and hesitance with novel experiences carries over into other situations. For example, infants may resist taking a nap in a strange place. In this stage infants discover other infants and seek to engage them in social intercourse by vocalizing, touching, and other behaviors. The infant actively seeks environmental mastery. The emotional products of this stage are joy and surprise, fear, and anger.

Stage Five, Attachment: Nine to Twelve Months

This stage marks the strongest attachment that the infant displays toward the mother. In this stage the infant is not as expansive or as expressive as previously. Emotional tone may be subdued, and the infant may become very possessive of the mother, pushing other people away (jealously) and clinging to her. This may be accompanied by an intensification of fear of strangers. In this stage the emotional expression toward the primary caregiver becomes highly differentiated and individual. By the end of this period individual emotional patterns may be discerned in moods, subtle gradations of feelings, and clear communication of emotional states. The stage is characterized by a pulling back and regrouping before venturing out again.

Stage Six, Practicing: Twelve to Eighteen Months

Firmly attached to its loving caregiver, the infant is now free to explore the world from a secure base. The first half of the second year is a period of balance between attachment and exploration. This stage is characterized by a balance between intellectual and emotional development. Infants who are securely attached to a loving parent explore the world quite differently from those who are insecurely attached (Ainsworth, 1973). The mood of the infant is exuberant in exploring the inanimate world—in fact, it is almost cocky—and conveys a sense of confidence and well-being.

Stage Seven, Formation of Self-concept: Eighteen to Thirty-six Months

The oneness achieved in a secure attachment at one year is slowly undermined by a growing awareness of separateness in the second year. The infant is caught in a crisis between the desire to remain secure in the arms of mother and the desire to become a separate person. The increasing self-concept forces the realization of separateness from the mother. The world is not as safe and secure as mother made it seem, and this *individuation* is often accompanied by anxiety. Breger (1974) notes that young ducklings display separation distress in response to the distance that the mother is from them. Young humans display separation distress according to the anxiety that separation arouses. Some infants may display separation anxiety in close proximity to the mother, whereas others can tolerate separation at great distances and over long periods of time. This is psychological anxiety and is not necessarily prompted by a physical object, such as a strange person, as was earlier anxiety. Caught in this crisis the two-year-old swings wildly between being a dependent baby seeking comfort from its mother and being an independent, defiant child seeking to establish its newly found self in the world. The consolidation of the sense of autonomy and the resolution of this crisis constitutes the major task of toddlerhood (Erikson, 1963a).

Expression and Control of Emotions

There are strict but unwritten rules in each society concerning the appropriate way to express emotions. These rules include which emotions may be expressed by whom and in what situations. Children learn all of those subtle conventions: for example, an emotion such as anger is more appropriate for boys and men; an emotion such as love or sadness is more appropriate for girls and women. Children learn quickly through the instruction and modeling of their parents and others the rules of appropriate emotional expression. We have ritualized ways of expressing sorrow and bereavement, as well as feelings of elation and joy. The expression of inappropriate emotion is a sign of emotional illness. The long childhood of humans provides time to learn society's subtle lessons in the process of *socialization*.

In addition to appropriate expression of emotions, the child must also learn the limit of the behavior associated with emotions and how to control them. Even though society allows children to engage in aggressive play, there is a limit to the socially acceptable expression of anger and aggressive behaviors. Those behaviors must be kept under control or directed in ways that are not destructive. The child of two years often has uncontrolled attacks of rage (referred to as temper tantrums).

Sometimes adults engage in the same rage behavior. This may indicate that the person is operating on the emotional level of the two-year-old. Members of society are also expected to direct and control their affectionate feelings. This is especially true when affection develops into sexual desire.

The hyperactive child cannot control behavior. The pathological killer who writes a note to the police that says, "Catch me before I kill more," is someone who knows that he or she cannot control emotions and that emotions move to actions he or she would rather not commit. The emotionally disturbed youngster is very difficult for parents, schools, and social agencies to handle and is actually a child who either cannot control emotions, has very little emotional expression, or who expresses emotions inappropriately. The foundations of good emotional development are laid in infancy, as is the distortion of emotional life.

Cognition and Emotions

The development and expression of emotions are closely related to cognitive development. Many emotions are dependent on the emergence of related awareness. At the core of emotional development is the concept of self and the relationship of self to others. One of the characteristics of mental retardation may be blunted affect. That is, the child may be very even tempered and easy to care for, sometimes even to extreme passivity.

In tracing the development of the intellectual processes in children, we find that young children do not think as adults do. We have no reason to believe, however, that they *feel* differently from adults. Love, anger, fear, joy, and sorrow apparently are quite similar throughout the life span and in different cultures. Children experience emotions essentially in the same way adults do. Of course there are refinements that are cognitively shaped and that change with age. For example, one learns to love one's country. Young children do not love their countries, although they may have very positive feelings about their bed or home. Sroufe (1979) has stated that emotions are dependent on cognitive development and has related the development of emotions to Piaget's stages of sensorimotor development. We will consider this relationship here.

In Piaget's substage two (one to four months) the infant begins to anticipate events and to recognize familiar people. With recognition comes feelings of pleasure and disappointment. The social smile is a signal of anticipation of pleasant events and also elicits or organizes those events. In Piaget's third substage (four to eight months) the infant is first capable of intentionality and a rudimentary understanding of causality, object permanence, and meaning. With those cognitive achievements joy becomes possible (at attaining a goal) as well as anger (at failing to attain a goal). Intentions can be frustrated and anger can escalate to rage.

In Piaget's fourth substage (eight to twelve months) the infant searches for hidden objects and explores means-ends relationships. The infant develops a fear of strangers and separation anxiety when the mother leaves. Surprise and cautiousness may become evident in the exploration of the object world. In the fifth substage (12 to 18 months) new means are found through experimentation. In this stage a certain self-awareness emerges with the realization of self as the cause of events. In Piaget's sixth substage (18 to 24 months) symbolic representation becomes possible and such emotional refinements as affection, shame, defiance, and positive self-evaluation are evident. After successfully solving a problem the twenty-month-old may say with a broad smile, "Me good boy!"

Emotions and the Development of Personality: Sigmund Freud and Psychoanalytic Theory

The importance of emotional development was emphasized by Sigmund Freud in his theory of personality. Freud was born on May 6, 1856 in Freiburg, Moravia, the first son, and always the favorite, of his mother. His father, Jakob, a Jewish merchant, had been married previously and had grown sons from that marriage. When Sigmund was four years old the family moved to Vienna where he was educated and worked until he was forced lo leave by the Nazis in 1938. He emigrated to England and died there one year later.

At seventeen the young Freud began medical studies at the University of Vi-

Table 7–2. Changes in Affective and Social Areas As Related to Piaget's Sensorimotor Stage of Cognitive Development

Cognitive Development (Piaget)	Affective Development (Sroufe)	Social Development (Sander)
0–1 Use of reflexes Minimal generalization/accommodation of inborn behaviors	*0–1 Absolute Stimulus Barrier* Built-in protection	*0–3 Initial Regulation* Sleeping, feeding, quieting, arousal Beginning preferential responsiveness to caregiver
1–4 Primary Circular Reaction First acquired adaptations (centered on body) Anticipation based on visual cues Beginning coordination of schemes	*1–3 Turning Toward* Orientation to external world Relative vulnerability to stimulation Exogenous (social) smile	
4–8 Secondary Circular Reaction Behavior directed toward external world (sensorimotor "classes" and recognition) Beginning goal orientation (procedures for making interesting sights last; deferred circular reactions)	*3–6 Positive Affect* Content-mediated affect (pleasurable assimilation, failure to assimilate, disappointment, frustration) Pleasure as an excitatory process (laughter, social responsivity) Active stimulus barrier (investment and divestment of affect)	*4–6 Reciprocal Exchange* Mother and child coordinate feeding, caretaking activities Affective, vocal, and motor play
	7–9 Active Participation Joy at being a cause (mastery initiation of social games) Failure of intended acts (experience of interruption) Differentiation of emotional reactions (initial hesitancy, positive and negative social responses, and categories)	*7–9 Initiative* Early directed activity (infant initiates social exchange, preferred activities) Experience of success or interference in achieving goals

Table 7–2. (continued)

Cognitive Development (Piaget)	Affective Development (Sroufe)	Social Development (Sander)
8–12 Coordination of Secondary Schemes & Application to New Situations Objectification of the world (interest in object qualities & relations; search for hidden objects) True intentionality (means-ends differentiation, tool-using) Imitation of novel responses Beginning appreciation of causal relations (others seen as agents, anticipation of consequences)	*9–12 Attachment* Affectively toned schemes (specific affective bond, categorical reactions) Integration and coordination of emotional reactions (context-mediated responses, including evaluation and beginning coping functions)	*10–13 Focalization* Mother's availability and responsivity tested (demands focused on mother) Exploration from secure base Reciprocity dependent on contextual information
12–18 Tertiary Circular Reaction Pursuit of novelty (active experimentation to provoke new effects) Trial-and-error problem-solving (invention of new means) Physical causality spatialized & detached from child's actions	*12–18 Practicing* Mother the secure base for exploration Elation in mastery Affect as part of context (moods, stored or delayed feelings) Control of emotional expression	*14–20 Self-Assertion* Broadened initiative Success and gratification achieved apart from mother
18–24 Invention of New Means Through Mental Combination Symbolic representation (language, deferred imitation, symbolic play) Problem-solving without overt action (novel combinations of schemes)	*18–36 Emergence of Self-Concept* Sense of self as actor (active coping, positive self-evaluation, shame) Sense of separateness (affection, ambivalence, conflict of wills, defiance)	

Source: "Socioemotional Development" by L. Alan Sroufe. In *Handbook of Infant Development*, edited by Joy D. Osofsky. Copyright © 1979 by John Wiley & Sons. Reprinted by permission.

enna and he finished eight years later. In his studies at the University, Freud was especially interested in neurophysiology and decided that he wanted to be a scientist rather than a practicing physician. While he was a medical student he had the opportunity to do some original work on neurology and on graduation he continued to work in Ernst Brucke's laboratory. At twenty-five he had a reputation as a rising neurologist; however, the prospect of an academic career for a Jew was dim and he wanted to marry. He decided to practice medicine. This required an additional period in clinical training. During this time Freud spent several months studying in Paris with Jean Charcot, a world-famous neurologist. With Charcot, Freud worked with hysterics and learned that these patients had symptoms of paralysis but no physical explanation for the illness. Freud began to suspect that if there was no physical reason for their illness then the cause must lie in their minds.

He continued working with hysterics in his private practice and found that emotions and familial relationships were central to the problems that these patients developed. He abandoned traditional ways of treating neurological problems and invented a "talking cure" known as psychoanalysis, that is, analysis of the psyche.*

In treating his patients, Freud discovered several important things. First, he found that emotions have a powerful influence on physical functioning as well as on behavior. Second, he found that emotions are often attached to sexual content and meaning. Third, he found that the foundations of both emotions and sexual development are laid in childhood and that these two are closely related. Through very careful histories of his patients and his own introspection, he constructed a theory of sexual development and the relationship of this development to emotional (psychological) development. Thus, Freud described a process of development of the child termed *psychosexual.* Freud was the first to describe a psychological-sexual development in successive stages that were tied to specific ages.

In describing sexual development, Freud was not concerned with the physical development of sexual organs. He was concerned with psychological development of sexuality. Psychological aspects of sexual development, according to psychoanalytic theory, include gender identification, choice of object that will gratify the sex drive, and means of obtaining sexual pleasure with one's own body. Freud's stages of psychosexual development focus on the body parts from which the child derives pleasure at various stages. Thus, for Freud, the pleasure that the infant receives in sucking is the first step in the development of the ability to engage in and to derive pleasure and gratification from sexual intercourse in adulthood. He, therefore, assigned infancy as the *oral* stage. The toddler age, the time of toilet training, is designated as the *anal* stage. In the preschool years, children discover pleasure in the manipulation of the genitals and this stage is known as the *phallic* stage. Freud then postulated a period of latency through the remainder of childhood in which the physical body grows but psychological sexuality is in quiescence. Finally, with physical maturity sexuality reemerges in a mature form, the *genital* stage. In each of the three earlier stages, the child derives pleasure from oral, anal, and phallic activities. These three modes are all incorporated into the mature genital stage. Freud was a determinist and believed that the outcome of this process of development was greatly influenced by events surrounding feeding in infancy, toilet training in the toddler period, and sex exploration in early childhood. The circumstances and events that occur during these periods determine the shape and direction of the entire personality. The child often cannot separate real events from fantasies it invents around them. These fantasies then are incorporated into the child's interpretation of the events. Through the *feelings* associated with events and *meanings* ascribed to them by the child, personality is constructed that may be healthy or filled with neuroses.

The Oral Stage

Freud placed the mother on the hook as the major determinant of the personality of her child. Whether a person has a healthy or neurotic personality is largely determined by events in the early mother-child relationship. A mother that is loving, patient, and gives the child pleasure in the nursing situation is contributing to a

---

* The word psyche is the Greek word for soul. Bruno Bettleheim, a psychoanalyst who studied with Freud, in a recent book, *Freud and Man's Soul* (Alfred A. Knopf, 1983) maintains that Freud has been misunderstood in English translation because he used words indicating "soul" which were rendered in English as "mind." Thus, English readers of Freud understand him as an explorer of the mind whereas his actual intent was much broader.

Infants explore the world by putting everything into their mouths. Because the mouth is the primary mode of experiencing at this age, Freud termed this the *oral* stage.

personality that is generous, able to receive and to give love, and is optimistic. A mother that is devouring, hostile, and increases tension in the child is contributing to a personality that is unable to love and, generally, mistrusting of the world.

Erik Erikson and Psychosocial Development

Freud had many followers who have contributed to the development of psychoanalytic theory. For the study of child development, the most important of these is Erik Erikson. Erikson was born on June 15, 1902 in Frankfort am Main, Germany. His mother was an artist and he never knew his father because he abandoned Erik's mother before the child was born; however he carries his Danish father's heritage in the name Erik. His mother later married Theodor Homburger, a German-Jewish pediatrician. This father completely accepted the young Erik as his own son. Erik used the name Homburger for many years and began publishing his professional work under it. But finding his identity and life's work was not an easy task for him and after a long search, he adopted the name Erik Erikson (Erik, son of Erik).

Part of Erikson's search for identity stemmed from his early background. With his German and Danish heritage and his Jewish stepfather, he was at home neither in the Christian schools nor in his father's synagogue. After high school he followed his mother's profession as an artist and embarked on a sketching tour of Europe. In 1927 Peter Blos, a friend, suggested that they go to Vienna. There they both taught in a private school that had a psychoanalytic orientation. As a result, Erikson became acquainted with the Vienna Psychoanalytic Institute. Although Erikson did not have a medical background as did most of the Institute's members, he was nevertheless accepted and not only studied psychoanalysis but has also contributed to changing the content of that theory.

On coming to America, Erikson was highly influenced by the anthropologists

Table 7–3. Stages of Personality Development in the Psychoanalytic Theories of Freud and Erikson

Age	Freud's Stages of Psychosexual Development	Erikson's Crises of Psychosocial Development	Age
Infancy	Oral	Trust versus mistrust	
Toddler	Anal	Autonomy versus shame, doubt	
Preschool	Phallic	Initiative versus guilt	
School age	(Latency period)	Industry versus competence	
Adolescence	Genital	Identity versus identity confusion	
		Intimacy versus isolation	Young adulthood
		Generativity versus self-absorption	Maturity
		Ego-integrity versus despair, disgust	Old age

Margaret Mead and Ruth Benedict. He was convinced of the importance of culture on individual development and studied the Sioux and Yurok Indians in the American Southwest while working out his life-cycle theory. Erikson has held various academic positions in America including Harvard and the University of California at Berkeley although he has no academic degrees. Erikson with his wife, Joan, who is an artist, continues to hold seminars and to write and speak on refinements of his theory of human development.

Erikson recast Freud's original stages of psychosexual development into a social context and presented a theory of *psychosocial* development. He also extended Freud's stages of development into adulthood, maturity, and old age. Freud's theory of development describes an underlying strata of personality that is difficult to examine and is often inaccessible to all except psychoanalysts and clinical psychologists because the residue from Freud's stages of development permeate the personality and become embedded in unconscious wishes and hidden motives.

By presenting personality development within the social context, Erikson has made it more easily understood, as the situations that he describes are those that are familiar in everyday experiences. Freud emphasized that personality development was not a smooth maturational process but rather was a journey fraught with dangers and one in which success was not assured. Erikson presented these dangers as challenges that are presented to the developing personality at each stage of development. Erikson clearly delineates what is at stake and what is won or lost as each stage becomes a crisis in development. He presents this crisis within the context of social relationships. These relationships begin within the family and extend to peers, intimate relationships with another person, and finally to relationships with the world and its future. He also delineates tasks necessary in the social world such as mastering technology, having children, and, finally, passing wisdom on to future generations in old age.

The Crisis of Infancy: Trust vs. Mistrust

The first crisis that the personality is faced with is that between developing a sense of trust or mistrust. The infant learns that the world is a good place to be and becomes an optimistic trusting person, or, that it is not such a good world and becomes a distrusting person. As the helpless infant signals to adults its needs and these needs are met or unmet, a sense of the resolution of the crisis is left in the personality as trust or mistrust. The crux of the problem, for parents, is identifying the things that satisfy or fail to satisfy the needs of the infant. This satisfaction is not identical with hedonistic pleasure. The psychological needs of the child are not always what the child seemingly asks for. It was a misunderstanding of this difference in psychological needs and expressed desires that led to the errors of permissive parenting. The skill in good parenting is knowing when these two differ and having the sensitivity to the deeper psychological needs of their developing child. In general, infants develop a pervading sense of trust in infancy when their physical needs are met in a loving, caring, and supportive manner, when they have a social bond with one or two special people, and when these relationships bring pleasure both to the infant and to the caregivers.

Mother-Child Relationship

Nearly half a century of research and theory has focused on the relationship that develops between the mother, or mother figure, and the child. Freud stressed the importance of the mother-infant relationship in determining the course of emotional development and personality. Early research studies that attempted to verify Freud's theories in childrearing were, at best, conflicting in their results (Sears, 1943). Many of the studies focused on bottle versus breast feeding and early versus late or permissive versus harsh toilet training. Later investigators have suggested that poor methods of studying the question may have been the cause of the inconclusive findings (Ainsworth, 1973). For example, mothers were asked to remember details of their childrearing practices years after the fact. We now are aware that retrospective studies are quite unreliable. In fact, we find that mothers' verbal descriptions of their behavior with their infants often bear little relationship to the actual reality of their behavior, even when they are referring to the present. The opposing dimensions of love and hostility indicating acceptance or rejection have been found to be more important for the development of the child than the methods of feeding or toilet training (Becker, 1964; Schaefer, 1959). These dimensions have also been found to relate independently to methods of control. Love, for example, can lead to freedom or possessiveness.

Major research support for the importance of the mother-child relationship has come from research on *maternal deprivation*. This research has focused on those children who show the damaging effects of lack of mothering. We often infer the normal from the pathological. Once the devastating effects of deprivation of maternal care were described, attention turned to identifying and describing the factors that are most important in the positive development of the child. This has been researched as *attachment*. We will describe positive attachment and then examine the consequences of deprivation of this important relationship.

Attachment

When scientists study a concept, their first step is to define carefully exactly what is to be investigated. Even though there are many studies dealing with attachment, each scientist has an operational definition of the concept. One of the researchers who has done the most work in the area of attachment in infants is Mary D. Salter Ainsworth. She states,

> *An attachment is an affectional tie that one person forms to another specific person, binding them together in space and enduring over time. Attachment is discriminating and specific. One may be attached to more than one person, but one cannot be attached to many people. Attachment implies affect. Although the affects may be complex and may vary from time to time, positive affects predominate, and we usually think of attachment as implying affection or love.* [Ainsworth, 1973, p.1]

The development of love between a mother and her infant (attachment) is a process that grows and takes place over a period of time. It does not suddenly appear at birth. The result, however, is an emotional state and not a concrete object that can be examined, weighed, and measured. When the research on the importance of this relationship is reviewed, several conclusions can be drawn. The major conclusion is that interaction with a mother figure and the resulting attachment is essential for healthy development. Attachment is not limited to the one and only mother; rather, attachment can be formed to more than one person. Furthermore, fostering attachment behavior does not spoil a child, as many people think.

Attachment is dependent on timing. There is a sensitive period in which attachment is ideally attained, although under appropriate conditions an attachment

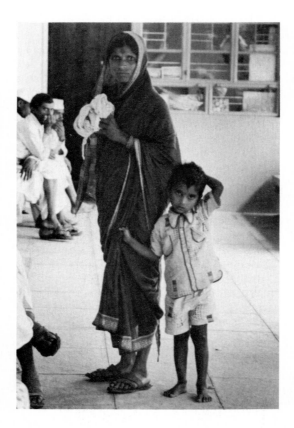

Mothers are a source of security the world over as this Indian boy demonstrates by holding onto his mother's clothing when faced with a stranger with a camera.

may develop beyond this phase. However, if an infant has no significant person in the first three years, it is almost impossible to compensate for the lack.

The characteristics of the mother or primary caregiver are important in the formation of attachment. A highly desirable maternal trait is sensitivity to an infant's signals. In addition, even though much research has been conducted on kibutzum and on other alternative environments, at present there is no known substitute for a family environment for childrearing. Once an attachment is formed, the mother becomes a source of security for the child and separations cause distress. Upon reunion after a major separation attachment behavior is likely to be heightened. Minor everyday separations may also produce effects in the infant such as increased clinging, children also exhibit fear of strangers and strange situations. Finally, exploratory behavior by the infant, a factor in intellectual development, is enhanced by a secure infant-mother attachment (Ainsworth, 1973).

These conclusions certainly are not shocking or unexpected. However, there are many questions still to be answered about attachment. How does it occur? When does it happen? What are the mediating factors? What are the consequences? Are there different qualities of attachment? What factors lead to good attachment and what factors to poor attachment? How do we design environments for infants that will offer the best chance for optimum attachment? We will review here some of the research that has attempted to answer a few of these questions.

Attachment in Animals

We cannot completely separate humans either from other animals or from our evolutionary past. Studies of maternal-infant behavior in other species have given us some clues to the emergence of attachment in humans. Lorenz (1957) found that newly hatched ducks and geese become attached very rapidly to their mother. This he called imprinting and found that the stimulus for it was a moving object. Through laboratory experiments it was discovered that newly hatched birds would imprint to a human experimenter or other moving object. The ducks apparently would consider those objects their "mother" and follow wherever it led. The stimulus the infant ducklings responded to was apparently the object's motion.

There are many species in which the infant needs the care and protection of an adult in order to survive. These newborn animals carry within their genes an unlearned response of attachment to some stimulus that elicits the attachment behavior. The behavior is programmed to remain quiescent, unless a particular stimulus occurs. The stimulus may be a visual pattern, a chemical trigger, a smell, or some other releasing mechanism.

Critical Period for Attachment

Lorenz (1957) also found that there is a critical period in which imprinting must take place. Young hatchlings imprint to the first moving object they see after hatching, but they do not imprint to an object after several weeks have passed.

Reasoning from animal studies, the question arises: Is there a critical period for the formation of attachment between a human mother and child? Research indicates that in a good environment an infant becomes attached to a specific adult during the second half of the first year of life (Ainsworth, 1979, 1973; Maccoby, 1980). A study by Rheingold and Bayley (1959) found that children who were deprived of the opportunity to become attached in early infancy developed normal attachments if they were placed in adoptive homes by the end of the first year of life. Provence and Lipton (1962) state that maternally deprived children who were placed in an adoptive home between the ages of eighteen and twenty-four months of age formed attachments only with great difficulty. Thus, research indicates that the critical period for attachment in human infants is between six and eighteen months. This does not mean that the time before six months is unimportant in forming attachments. On the contrary, indications are that the very early experiences are crucial in establishing the behavioral repertoire that leads to attachment. Let us examine this early experience in detail, paying special attention to the events that mediate attachment.

Development of Attachment

The process of attachment can be divided into four phases (Bowlby 1969), which closely follow the previously stated development of emotions. In the first three months the infant is undiscriminating and smiles at any adult who gives care and attention. From three to six months the infant recognizes familiar people, seeks to be near them, and also seeks to keep them near by crying when they leave and smiling when they are near. By six months the infant is quite skilled at keeping chosen adults close and rejecting strangers.

The third phase, from six months to one year, is characterized by more active contact seeking on the part of the infant. The fourth phase is characterized by a synchronized partnership between mother and child. This phase begins at some time after the child's first birthday and continues until he or she makes a psychological separation from the mother. In this partnership the child takes into account what the mother's plans are and they share goals. For example, the child can be told, "Wait until I finish with the telephone and then I will hold you." Between twelve and eighteen months the child grows rapidly in understanding and responds to verbal statements.

Early Attachment Behaviors

The first attraction between mother and infant is the mutually satisfying bonding interaction that begins in the neonatal period. The innate behaviors of the newborn are the foundation on which attachment is built. Inexperienced parents are often anxious about how they will relate to the new baby. The innate behaviors of the infant trigger maternal behaviors in the mother. These behaviors then become circular and increase; thus, *the infant is an active participant in establishing its relationship with its mother.* It is through these circular behaviors that the emotional tie of attachment grows. The infant has some highly organized behaviors: crying, postural adjustment, smiling, looking, and feeding.

The mechanism of *crying* to be soothed attracts adults. The penetrating crying of the newborn is innately disturbing to adults. Caretakers immediately respond to it by picking up, rocking, soothing, and touching the child. All of these behaviors tend to reduce the crying. The infant tends to listen to a high-pitched voice, and because most caretakers are women (with high-pitched voices), speaking or singing to a baby quiets him or her.

Another innate behavior of the infant that aids in attachment is that of *postural adjustment.* When a distressed infant is held in the body-to-chest position, he or she

The cry of an infant is disturbing to adults. Parents and caretakers respond by picking the child up, soothing, rocking, singing, or feeding. Both parent and child are satisfied when this strategy works and thus crying becomes a medium through which attachment grows.

tends to relax and to mold to the body of the adult. This cuddling reinforces in the adult the feeling that she or he has the ability to soothe the child, with resulting mutual satisfaction. If the infant reacts to this holding by stiffening its body and pulling away, the mother feels frustrated, inadequate, and perhaps insecure about her mothering ability.

Probably the most gratifying innate behavior of the infant is *smiling*. Most adults are totally captivated by the engaging smile of an infant. In the early months the infant is indiscriminate in smiling and almost any adult who initiates interaction can elicit it. When attachment begins to take place the infant becomes discriminating and will smile only at those few figures who are known and recognized; strangers elicit very distressed behavior.

Another behavior that is extremely important in attachment is *looking*. Eye-to-eye contact begins early and remains a way of maintaining contact with the attachment figure throughout childhood. The newborn is capable of acute vision at about eight inches, the approximate distance between it and its mother's eyes when it is held. Holding for feeding allows considerable time for mutual visual exploration. Eye contact remains an important quality of interpersonal relations throughout life. Adults feel, "You can't trust a person who won't look you in the eye," and lovers are noted for prolonged eyegazing.

Much has been written about infant feeding in the emotional life of a child. Freud considered the nature of the oral gratification that the infant receives in the

Eye contact remains a way of maintaining closeness with the attachment figure throughout childhood. [Courtesy Helen Canaday, Preschool programs, University of North Carolina, Greensboro.]

Nursing entails many sensual experiences for the infant. These experiences are all incorporated into the child's growing sense of trust or mistrust about the world.

first stage of life to be crucial for all later emotional development. Obviously when the infant is held and fed, close physical contact is important. When the infant is fed by breast, more than just nutritive substance passes between it and its mother: there is face-to-face and eye-to-eye contact, as well. In addition, there is skin contact between the child's face and the mother's breast. When the child is held close to the breast, the sound of the mother's heartbeat is no doubt a pre-eminent experience. The sound is a familiar one to the newborn because it was a part of the interuterine environment and once the aural system developed it could receive the sound. The infant learns much about contact with bodies from this early sensual experience. The learning is emotional, not cognitive.

Later Attachment Behaviors

As the child grows in its ability to manipulate the world, many behaviors emerge that serve to encourage comfort and good mothering. When one is in love one wants to be near the beloved. So, too, the infant attempts to maintain contact or close proximity to the object of its attachment. The infant between six and twelve months exhibits three different types of behaviors to keep the mother figure close: signaling, orienting, and contacting.

1. *Signaling behaviors.* Signaling behaviors indicate to the adult the emotional state of the infant; such behaviors as crying, smiling, and vocalizing are involved.
2. *Orienting behaviors.* In orienting behaviors the infant focuses on the specific adult to which it is attached; such behaviors as looking, following, and approaching are involved.
3. *Contacting behaviors.* Such active behaviors on the part of the infant as clambering up, embracing, and clinging are contacting behaviors. Through them the infant initiates and maintains continuous contact with and also seeks to avoid separation from the attachment figure. The infant uses these behaviors to remain within the range of the adult, who may be occupied with other tasks, in order to be close enough to seek protection and reassurance if frightened.

Emotional attachment is possibly the most important event of infancy. "Once formed, this attachment is amazingly persistent and is capable of enduring an extraordinary amount of absence, neglect, or abuse—although these adverse conditions are likely to affect both the quality of a child's attachment relationships and his subsequent personality development" (Ainsworth, 1973, p. 13).

Secure and Insecure Attachment

The minimum quantity of interaction that is required for the development of attachment has not yet been defined, but the quality of the interaction between mother and infant has been found to be reflected in attachment. In one study (Ainsworth & Bell, 1970; Ainsworth, 1979) the quality of attachment was discerned through the behaviors exhibited by the child in new situations. The reasoning in this study is that the infant seeks the proximity of the attached figure when in a strange or threatening situation. In this study infants were separated from their mothers and then reunited. The behavior of both the mother and infant was examined.

In these separation-reunion episodes, three different patterns of attachment were identified. One group of children were classified as being securely attached and two as insecurely attached. Ainsworth described the two broad categories of insecurely attached infants as those who exhibited avoidant behaviors and those who exhibited resistant (hostile) behaviors. She grouped them into groups A, B, and C. Let us look at Group B, the securely attached infants, and then the two deviations from this healthy development.

Group B: Securely attached. Securely attached infants do not stay particularly close to their mother when she is in the room but play easily with toys and react favorably to strangers. When separated from the mother, there is obvious distress and reduced attention to toys. When the mother returns, these children go to her immediately, seek comfort in her arms, and are quickly able to resume their play with toys. These children use their mother as a secure base from which to explore the world. They are more cooperative and less angry than either of the other two types. The mothers of these babies differed also. They were judged to be more sensitively responsive to their infant's signals than mothers of anxiously attached infants. Ainsworth (1979) ascribes this factor as crucial in the development of the child:

> *Such responsiveness, I suggest, enables an infant to form expectations, primitive at first, that moderate his or her responses to events both internal and environmental. Gradually, such an infant constructs an inner representation...[expectation] of his or her mother as generally accessible and responsive.* [p. 933]

Group A: Avoidant. Interactions between the mother and avoidant infants do not reflect comfort and accessibility. This is shown most clearly in the dimension of bodily contact. The babies behave less positively to being held and more negatively to being put down. These babies displayed more anger than those in the other two groups. Ainsworth notes that "clearly, something went awry in the physical-contact interaction Group A babies had with their mothers ... I believe it is this that makes them especially prone to anger" (Ainsworth, 1979, p. 932). These babies do not protest when separated from their mother; when they are reunited with their mother, they avoid her or oscillate between approaching and avoiding her.

How do the mothers of these babies act? Ainsworth notes that the striking finding is that they all showed a deep-seated aversion to bodily contact. They were more rejecting and more angry but less able to express any emotional feelings than the mothers of the other two groups of babies. The interaction of these babies and their mothers is explained by Ainsworth (1979):

> *acute approach-avoidance conflict experienced by these infants when their attachment behavior is activated at high intensity—a conflict stemming from painful rebuff conse-quent upon seeking close bodily contact. Avoidance is viewed as a defensive maneuver, lessening the anxiety and anger experienced in the conflict situation and enabling the baby nevertheless to remain within a tolerable range of proximity to the mother.* [p. 933]

Group C: Resistant. Interaction between resistant babies and their mother is characterized by anxiety on the part of the babies in normal interaction. In contrast to Group A babies they are intensely distressed by separation, and when reunited with the mother demonstrate ambivalent behavior. The child seeks contact, but at the same time resists contact and shows anger. For example, the child may run to the mother to be picked up but then struggle to get down. These children do not return quickly to play and keep the mother in visual contact through frequent anxious glances. This anxious behavior is demonstrated even before sepa-ration.

The question arises: To what extent is the quality of attachment attributed to how the mother treats the child and how much to the innate traits of the child? Ainsworth concludes that, "there is a strong case to be made for difference in attachment quality being attributable to maternal behavior" (p. 933). There are other studies, however (Connell, 1976), that suggest that the babies in Group C may be constitutionally difficult from birth and thus contribute to the anxious quality of the attachment. We need more research to fully explicate this process; nevertheless, we must conclude that the behavior of the mother in the first year of life has a large influence on later emotional development as well as on the exploratory behavior on which intellectual development rests.

Attachment and Exploratory Behavior

The interaction between intellectual and emotional development continues in cyclic fashion. Sroufe (1979) states:

> *Attachment has its roots in early interaction; it also lays the foundation for subsequent development. A central issue for the 12–18-month-old infant . . . is exploration and mastery of the environment. The child secure in its attachment is able to use the caregiver as a base for this exploration. . . . This psychological availability of the caregiver during exploration and later problem solving deepens the security of attachment and helps a new mode of psychological contact to evolve. The infant can be comforted by a glance across the room or by a word. . . .*
>
> *Just as the quality of attachment influences the infant's exploratory competence, these early adaptations in turn influence the quality of autonomous functioning in the toddler period. . . . The child who has developed mastery skills, the capacity for affective involvement, and a sense of confidence within the caregiver-infant relationship will be more enthusiastic, persistent and effective in facing environmental challenges on its own.* [p. 837]

Maternal Deprivation

What happens when a child does not have the opportunity to become attached to a specific adult? Research indicates that the results are disastrous. The concept of maternal deprivation focuses on deprivation of interaction with a mother figure (Ainsworth, 1973). A child may receive adequate physical care, but it is the opportunity for interaction leading to attachment that children who are maternally deprived seem to lack.

In the thirteenth century, King Frederick II inadvertently performed the first experiment in maternal deprivation. He wanted to determine the natural language of humans. Thus, he ordered the caretakers of a group of orphaned babies to speak no words to them and have as little interaction as possible in caring for them. He then reasoned that whatever language they began to speak would be the natural language of humans. Unfortunately, he never found the answer to his question, because all of the babies died. We see this experiment as ill-conceived, because we know that language is learned and not a developmental unfolding. Frederick's experiment was actually an experiment on the importance of maternal care (Ross & MacLaughlin, 1949).

Between the thirteenth to the twentieth century there are few records of the effects of maternal deprivation, although we do know that the infant mortality rate was high. It was so high, in fact, that infants and very young children were hardly considered to count (Ariès, 1962). Only if children survived the rigors of infancy were they admitted into the affection and consideration of adults. Early in the

(A)   (B)

In many countries, the traditional method of carrying a baby is on the mother's back. This is a convenient means of transport but it also provides the baby with a sense of security from the close contact with the mother's body. The woman in India (A) uses an age-old technique of tying the baby to her back with a strip of cloth; the mother in the United States (B) uses an aluminium and canvas carrier. The result is the same regardless of the method.

twentieth century pediatricians began to write clinical observations of the effect of hospitalization on young children (Yarrow, 1979). However, it was not until the mid-twentieth century that detailed clinical studies drew in bold outlines the devastating effect of separation from the all-important mother figure. These clinical studies were undergirded and interpreted by the theoretical importance of the mother figure that psychoanalysis had highlighted (Ainsworth, 1979).

In looking at the experience of mothering in the entire population we find an infinite number of variables and a continuum of experience. At one end of the continuum we find optimum mothering and infant care. This optimum is the warm, loving mother who is attentive to the needs of her infant. At the other end of the continuum is the mother who abandons her infant to be raised in an institution without the warm circle of family life and a specific caring mother or mother figure. The reality of experience for most infants lies somewhere between these two extremes. Even in the intact family we may find a mother overburdened with other responsibilities, other children, her own problems and her own pattern of childhood experiences, so that the quality of care that she gives is, in effect, depriving. We must distinguish, then, among maternal deprivation, maternal separation, multiple mothering, and distortion in maternal care. Maternal deprivation implies that the child has lacked a sufficient quantity of the touching, patting, talking, singing, holding, and rocking that normally occurs in the course of the mother-infant day. In addition, the infant is deprived of a sensitive, individualized mother figure who adapts her schedule to the infant's needs. In 1951 John Bowlby summarized the effects of such deprivation on children for the World Health Organization in a publication entitled *Maternal Care and Mental Health.* The report summarizes studies conducted in the preceding twenty years; it radically changed the practices of medical and social agencies. Bowlby found that the effects of severe maternal deprivation are a stunted personality, with the most devastating effect being the child's later inability to form deep attachments—that is, to form a love relationship with any human being. In addition, maternally deprived children are listless, show very little emotional affect (either joy or sorrow), and have a developmental quotient that is usually below the chronological age. Mental retardation is often the consequence. These children have a higher than expected mortality rate and are judged to be psychologically depressed.

Maternal Deprivation in Experimental Animals

We cannot ethically perform deprivation experiments on human infants; therefore, our most emphatic data concerning the far-reaching consequences of maternal deprivation have come from experiments with animals. The leading researcher in this field has been Dr. Harry Harlow. Harlow began his studies rearing rhesus monkeys in isolation from their mothers. A colleague suggested that what he was really doing was raising psychologically abnormal monkeys. Harlow then turned his attention to examining the mother-infant bond and the social-psychological development of his monkeys. His research revealed many surprises (Harlow, 1961, 1973).

The technique that Harlow employed was to separate mother and infant soon after birth. The infants were then raised in isolation. They were fed but were not allowed any contact with others of their species. One of the first hypotheses that was investigated was that attachment between mother and child is dependent on reinforcement with food. In other words, does the infant become attached to the figure that supplies the food? Harlow found that food was *not* the medium through which attachment was mediated. In his early experiments the infant monkeys were offered a variety of surrogate mothers. Some were constructed of wire and some were constructed of soft cloth. In some cages the wire mother held the food, and in the other cages the cloth mother held the food. Surprisingly, the infants preferred the cloth mother *regardless* of whether "she" supplied the food. Thus, the conclusion was that the comfort offered the infant by the mother was not the comfort of the breast—that is, of sucking and food—but, rather, the comfort of soft bodily contact.

The surrogate mother, however, did not meet the infant's psychological and social needs. The infant exhibited all the inviting behaviors in the infant repertoire: clinging, vocalization, and so forth. The cloth mother, however, was immobile and unresponsive. In this situation, the infant monkeys grew, but at adulthood exhibited very abnormal behavior. When they were adolescents Harlow exposed his deprived monkeys to mother-reared monkeys. The deprived monkeys were deficient in social behaviors. They either appeared quite frightened and withdrew or were unusually aggressive. At sexual maturity they did not engage in normal sexual activity and appeared not to know the pattern of reciprocal behavior. The males never learned it. A few females were mated when approached by normal experienced males, but when their infants were born, they were as inept and disinterested in maternal behavior as they had been in sexual behavior. They sat on their infants, held them upside down by one foot, pushed them away, and on occasion attacked them. With subsequent infants their behavior improved, but they never exhibited really good maternal behavior.

The young monkeys who were reared in isolation exhibited behaviors that are remarkably similar to what we see in severely disturbed human children. The young monkeys huddled in corners and engaged in rocking and in self-destructive behavior such as biting themselves, pulling their fur, and banging against the cage. These isolated monkeys were uncontrollably aggressive at maturity.

Maternal Separation

" 'Tis better to have loved and lost than never to have loved," goes a famous quote. What of the infant who forms a significant attachment to a parent and loses that parent? Bowlby (1960a, 1960b, 1961) investigated this question thoroughly and concluded that the reactions of children following such a loss are similar to the process of mourning in adults.

When children under two years of age are separated from their mothers they undergo a predictable reaction. Their first reaction is to cry and protest. When this does not bring about the desired result, the infant becomes progressively more withdrawn from the environment and from relationships with other people. Finally, a stage of resignation ensues in which the child expresses little feeling and acts as though "neither mothering nor any contact with humans has much significance for them" (Robertson & Bowlby, 1952, p. 133).

The reactions of these children are deceiving, unless adults caring for them are aware of their inner psychological reactions. When children cry and protest, adults *must* make some attempt to deal with the situation. Often when a child stops protesting adults interpret it to mean that the child has adapted to the situation and accepted the inevitability of it. Actually, the child may be withdrawing and, rather than acceptance, the feeling may be one of hopelessness and abandonment.

In 1946 Spitz and Wolf made a detailed study of young infants undergoing separation. The infants were between six and eight months of age. This is just the time when the attachment is strongest. The infants showed reactions of extreme anxiety, actively rejected adults who attempted to care for them, and finally experienced severe depression, listlessness, loss of appetite (accompanied by loss of weight), recurrent colds and eczema, and a drop in developmental quotient. In the study Spitz and Wolf noted that the physical deterioration resulted in the death of some of the infants. They sounded the warning that if such separated infants were not returned to the mother (or mother substitute) irreparable damage would occur.

Children who are returned to their mother after a separation demonstrate hostility to her, as though they were angry about the abandonment. The anger is intermingled with marked anxiety about losing her again. In addition, such children may lose bladder or bowel control, even though they were toilet trained before the separation. This is a common occurrence and is known as regression. The effect of maternal separation depends on a multitude of factors: the nature of the separation, the age of the child, the duration of the separation, the child's unique vulnerabilities and sensitivities (genetic), the quality of the relationship prior to separation, and the quality of the situation after reunion.

Unfortunately the flow of life events sometimes results in an unavoidable separation of mother and infant through death or illness. Mental illness or tuberculosis often means months of separation of the mother from the family. Broken limbs or extensive pediatric surgery may mean a long hospital stay for an infant. Mothers who work full-time are absent from their infants for extended periods each day. We are trying to evaluate the effect of this absence of the mother on the subsequent development of the child. (See Chapter 5 and the discussion of day care.)

The research on maternal separation has had a profound influence in four areas of handling children.

1. It has focused attention on the quality of care in the home situation, especially deprivation or distortions in maternal care.
2. Hospitals and other institutions have become increasingly sensitive to the psychological needs of children in their care. Mothers now may spend the night, and in fact, are encouraged to do so, whereas forty years ago a mother might have had a difficult time gaining permission to remain with her child after the hospital's visiting hours.
3. Social agencies are very careful about placing children in a succession of foster homes. An attempt is made to provide a stable mother figure for the children in their care.
4. Schools and parents, in general, are more sensitive about disrupting a child's secure attachment (Yarrow, 1979).

It is impossible to evaluate the degree of pathologic personality development that took place in previous eras. However, our awareness of the young child's psychological vulnerability increases both our responsibility and opportunity to build basically sound people capable of receiving and giving love.

Distortions in Maternal Care

The most difficult problem for people interested in child welfare to deal with is aberrant maternal care: where the mother assumes responsibility for care but the quality of that care is deviant and therefore destructive to the child's psychological or physical growth. When the deviations are so far from the social standard that they violate the level of care dictated by law, social agencies may intervene and obtain the care needed for the child. Each state has laws that define child abuse and neglect, and when those laws are broken the state can supersede the rights of the parent and intervene in the child's behalf.

There are other cases in which the care given the child is legally adequate, but nonetheless the mothering behavior is so distorted it constitutes a developmental risk for the infant. Many distortions in mothering revolve around the attachment relationship. The most devastating distortion for the infant is that in which the mother rejects the child. The infant makes the initial overtures, with the characteristic charming behaviors, but they are not reciprocated. Another distortion in the mothering process occurs when the mother is ambivalent toward the infant. That is, she sometimes feels an attraction (love) and at other times feels hostility toward the infant. This inconsistent behavior and emotion is also difficult for the child to adjust to, and it is the one that is most likely to cause personality aberrations. Childrearing extends in a chain from generation to generation. Most likely, mothers who cannot establish a stable consistent relationship with their infant were themselves victims of distortions in mothering.

Fathers and Infants

The child is the product of its two parents. Much research has been directed toward the mother and infant but very little toward the relationship between father and infant. The father has been a shadowy figure in the study of the child until recently. The rise in single-parent families has undermined the cultural ideal of the family as consisting of mother, father, and child; on the other hand, there is a trend toward more equalitarian roles for men and women in child care and in the father's involvement in childbirth.

The father has both a direct and an indirect effect on the family. The economic, emotional, and physical support that he supplies for the mother has a direct impact on the child's development (Parke, 1979). For example, if the father is supportive, the mother is more likely to breast feed; if he disapproves of this feeding method she is more likely to fail.

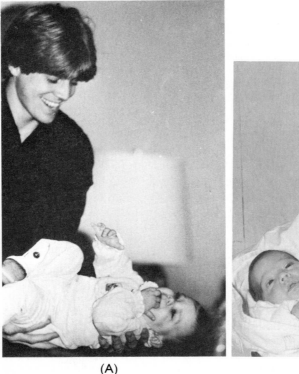

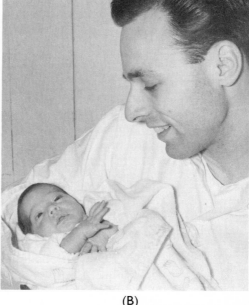

(A)   (B)

Fathers enjoy playing with their children and that play is likely to be "rough-housing" as this father (A). They also enjoy holding and talking to their infants (B).

Fathers spend less time in direct interaction with their infants than mothers. One study reported that fathers were available on an average of 26 hours a week when the baby is awake. Some fathers spent as little as 45 minutes of this with their babies and some the entire 26 hours. The average time with their babies was eight hours a week, little over an hour a day (Pendersen and Robson, 1969). During the time spent with infants fathers are more likely to engage in play than in caretaking activities. Kotelchuck (1976) found that 64 per cent of mothers were totally and solely responsible for child care and that 75 per cent of fathers assumed no responsibility for physical care. Of the 25 per cent of fathers who assumed some care for their infant, only 7.9 per cent shared physical care equally with mothers. Forty-three per cent of the fathers reported that they never changed diapers. Fathers spent 37.5 per cent of their time with their baby in play, whereas mothers spent only 25.8 per cent. Fathers were also more likely to engage in physical play, such as rough-housing, whereas mothers were more likely to engage in verbal play and to use toys as objects to stimulate the infant (Lamb, 1977).

Attachment has been researched primarily in terms of the mother-infant relationship. Does attachment also occur to fathers? The answer is yes. In a laboratory situation toddlers sought the comfort of both mother and father and protested the departure of either parent (Kotelchuck, 1976). The researcher concluded that of the eighteen-month-old infants studied 70 per cent were attached to the father.

The results of several studies suggest that fathers prefer sons and treat sons and daughters differently. When fathers are questioned before the birth they are twice as likely to state that they would prefer a son (Hoffman, 1977). Fathers are more likely to play with their infant sons and to respond to their caretaking needs. In feeding, fathers adjust the bottle more and encourage the infant to eat more when feeding a son as opposed to a daughter. Fathers, however, hold their daughters closer, more frequently, and for longer periods of time. In contrast, they look at their sons more (Parke & Swain, 1976, 1977). Early paternal involvement and nurturing are also associated with the cognitive development of sons but not of daughters (Radin, 1976). Fathers are, indeed, an integral part of the family from the very first days; we must broaden our thinking of the family from the mother-infant dyad to the father-mother-infant triad.

Infant-Infant Relations

The importance of peer influence has long been recognized in older children and adolescents. Only recently has research turned its attention to the relationship between two or more infants. Harlow (1973) found that if his maternally deprived monkeys were allowed to play daily with peers, beginning at one month of age, the interaction could compensate for the deprivation of mothering. In contrast to those deprived monkeys who had no peer interaction, the monkeys given peer interaction showed fairly normal adult social and heterosexual behavior. How soon do infants begin peer interaction and how is it characterized? Social relations follow a developmental sequence (Mueller & Vandell, 1979). Infants are attracted by the presence of other infants. When they are between two weeks and two months of age they will look at other infants. At three to four months they try to touch other infants, and by six months they smile at them regularly. As infants increase in mobility, between seven and eight months, they approach, reach for, and follow other infants.

True social interchange between infants begins at between nine and twelve

The infant on the right is teaching the younger infant to play "pat-a-cake," with obvious enjoyment by both.

months and is characterized by offering a toy and taking a toy from another infant. Infants of this age also engage in such games as peek-a-boo, run and chase, and rolling balls. In these first social encounters the exchange is not entirely reciprocal. At this stage a child may consistently offer and another child consistently take. On another occasion the roles may be reversed. The infant must practice both roles before he or she is engaging in a true social interchange (Mueller & Lucas, 1975).

Soon after the first birthday, as language begins to develop, infants engage in imitating each other's sounds. The noises back and forth resemble adult conversation. Between fourteen and twenty-four months of age, infants increase their "take" and "offer" behaviors and are able to give and receive toys in a reciprocal,

Grandfathers are an important part of the growing child's social and emotional world.

coordinated act. Not only do toddlers give and receive toys, they are often sensitively aware of the feelings and needs of other children. Meehl and Peterson (1981) cite a case in which a two-year-old girl consistently sought out a slightly older boy who was withdrawn socially and apathetic cognitively. Through her efforts at peer interaction she was effective in bringing about increased social and cognitive behaviors in this boy.

The infant is a social creature from birth. Social interactions are very important in determining who and what the child becomes. The emotional coloring of those interactions, more than any other factor, will create joy or displeasure in life. Each relationship in which the young child is valued and able to engage in a pleasant interchange adds another dimension to his or her total growth. Young children need fathers, mothers, brothers, sisters, grandparents, uncles, aunts, older friends, younger friends, and friends who are the same age. Children need to be integrated into the social fabric even as infants. In that way they sense that they are valued and truly belong. These two convictions are the foundation of social and emotional growth, and on these two pillars children grow into men and women who return the gifts in full measure to their society.

Main Points

Growth of Emotion

1. Emotions organize and guide behavior.

2. Emotions are differentiated in the first two years of life from the state of generalized excitement of the newborn.

Stage One: Stimulus Barrier (Birth to One Month)

3. The infant under one month of age is generally unresponsive to the emotional climate because of a stimulus barrier protecting him from overstimulation.

Stage Two: Turning Outward (One to Three Months)

4. Stage two marks a qualitative difference in the infant characterized by a turning outward in interest and in the behavioral expression of emotion. Smiling begins at around six weeks of age.

Stage Three: Reliable Social Smile (Three to Six Months)

5. The infant, through smiling, builds positive emotional experiences with its caregiver and avoids negative experiences.

Stage Four: Active Participation (Seven to Nine Months)

6. The infant engages in social games, initiates social interaction, and engages other infants.

Stage Five: Attachment (Nine to Twelve Months)

7. This stage marks the strongest attachment to the mother and an intensification of fear of strangers.

Stage Six: Practicing (Twelve to Eighteen Months)

8. When firmly attached to a loving caregiver, the infant is free to explore the world.

Stage Seven: Formation of Self-concept (Eighteen to Thirty-six Months)

9. The two-year-old shifts between being a dependent baby and an independent self.

Exercise and Control of Emotion

10. The child must learn society's unwritten rules concerning the appropriate ways to express emotions and also learn internal control of emotions.

Cognition and Emotions

11. The development and expression of emotions are closely related to cognitive development.

Mother-Child Relationship

12. Research on maternal deprivation has supported the importance of the mother-child relationship.

Attachment

13. Interaction with a mother figure and the resulting attachment are essential for healthy development.

Attachment: The Critical Period

14. Newly hatched ducks were found to attach (imprint) to the first moving objects they see after hatching; it was also found that imprinting was not possible after several weeks.

15. Research indicates that the critical period for attachment in human infants is between six and eighteen months.

Development of Attachment

16. Attachment develops from undiscriminating smiling to a synchronized partnership with a significant caregiver.

17. Early attachment behaviors include crying, postural adjustments, smiling, looking, and feeding.

18. Later attachment behaviors include signaling, orienting, and contacting.

Secure and Insecure Attachment

19. Securely attached infants use their mothers as a base from which to explore the world. Avoidant infants exhibit approach-avoidance conflict. Resistant babies demonstrate anxious behavior in relation to their mothers.

Maternal Deprivation

20. Maternal deprivation has a devastating effect on personality, resulting in the inability to form deep attachments.

21. Young monkeys reared in isolation—i.e., maternally deprived—exhibited behaviors similar to severely disturbed human children: withdrawal, self-destructive tendencies, uncontrollable aggression.

22. Prolonged separation from the maternal figure can have severe consequences for human infants.

23. Distortions in maternal care are likely to cause personality aberrations.

Fathers and Infants

24. Fathers are significantly involved in the care of their infants, and emotional bonds and an attachment result. Fathers treat sons and daughters differently.

Infant-Infant Relationships

25. The infant is attracted to, tries to touch, and smiles at other infants. Social interchange begins at nine to twelve months of age.

Words to Know

cognition
imprinting
individuation
self-concept
socialization
stimulus

Concepts

attachment
maternal deprivation

PART III

Early Childhood:
The Years from Two to Six

In the third year the child traverses the difficult terrain of toddlerhood, after which the world of childhood expands in unlimited vistas. It is a running, jumping, twirling, sliding, climbing world as the child conquers space and his or her physical abilities expand. It is a world of puzzles, puns, counting, and colors as the child builds mental structures and explores them as enthusiastically as playground labyrinths. It is a world peopled with giants, dragons, dwarfs, magic castles, and spaceships, as ordinary objects are transformed by imagination. It is a world of exuberance and laughter; but it can also be a dangerous world of turbulent feelings, rejection, and sometimes abuse by those whom the child loves most. It is, in fact, the world of human habitation, one that the child creates and seeks simultaneously.

Transition to Childhood:
The Third Year

Have you ever wondered

> what the "Terrible Twos" is?
>
> why children imitate adult behavior, such as shaving or using makeup?
>
> why children use objects as symbols of other objects?
>
> why two-year-olds and parents are so often in a battle of wills?
>
> how the child learns who he or she is?
>
> how problems with toddlers can best be handled?

The change from baby to child is an enormous one and, as with all great changes, it does not happen all at once. The baby-becoming-child is sometimes called a toddler. The word *toddler* is rather inexact; it generally refers to someone in the third year of life but sometimes spans the period between eighteen and thirty-six months of age (one and a half to three years). Looking at a two-year-old we are reminded of the cherubs popular with Renaissance painters. The chubby face and protruding belly and buttocks balanced by a swayed back, creased legs, and arms remains our image of Cupid, the very symbol of love. The toddler is quite lovable but also is given to strong shifts of moods. In the third year the toddler makes his or her "declaration of independence," often disrupting the entire household in so doing. This independence is fueled by an emerging sense of self as a separate person who is able to make things happen. With increasing mental and physical competence, the toddler does indeed make things happen.

Often the years from two to six are considered a single stage; however, the two-year-old is so different from the five- or six-year-old that some attention needs to be directed to this important year. Therefore, we have focused on the third year as a transition into childhood.

This is a very active time. The toddler is into everything and needs constant watching to prevent serious accidents both to self and to objects. Toddlerhood is a time of exploring limits: It is through motor activity that the limits of the physical world are learned; it is through social interaction that the limits of self and the psychological world are learned; and it is in the intellectual manipulation of symbols and language that the limits of the sensorimotor world are expanded. The major accomplishment of this period, however, is the establishment of the child as a separate and independent psychological self. This declaration of independence is often turbulent and has earned the description of this age as "the Terrible Twos." Life with a two-year-old is a difficult undertaking. Gone is the pleasant synchronism and understanding that mother and infant established in the period of infancy. Outbursts of temper and violent reactions often come unexpectedly and leave as quickly. The behavior of the three-year-old is quite different—when developing well he or she behaves much like a four- or five-year-old. The third year, then, is an important transition period between the dependent infant and the energetic preschooler exploring the world. The sense of self acquired in toddlerhood is the bridge between the two.

Physical Development

Size and Proportion

Physical growth slows in the third year. Boys and girls continue to exhibit approximately equal height and weight. The average North American child grows three inches and gains four and a half pounds in this year. This relatively slowed growth rate results in a drastic reduction in food consumption from the infant's ravenous intake. Toddlers often prefer to play with food than to eat it, much to the consternation of parents. Serious malnutrition, however, is less probable in these years than in infancy and adolescence because they are characterized by rapid growth.

In the third year, body proportions continue to change as body parts grow at different rates. At two years the head is 75 per cent of adult size, whereas height is only 50 per cent. In this year the arms and legs grow most rapidly. The typical two-year-old has short, bowed legs, but by three years of age the child's legs are more muscular, longer, and straighter. Leg growth accounts for most of the gain in height and in increasing skill in moving through the environment. The toddler's abdomen also typically protrudes, but it is not all fat; it is necessitated by the advanced growth of internal organs. To compensate for its protruding belly, the toddler is swaybacked. As the toddler's arms, legs, and torso lengthen, their proportions increasingly approach those of adults.

Motor Skills

The toddler continues to practice and gain control over muscles. There are two kinds of skills that develop, but at different rates: large-muscle skills (*gross motor*) and small-muscle skills (*fine motor*). Control of the large muscles develops first, and with it the child gains in its ability to run, climb, jump, ride a tricycle, and throw a ball. Fine motor skills enable the child to hold a pencil in order to draw and write and to manipulate small toys. Such skills lead in adulthood to the control of incredibly intricate operations, such as playing a musical instrument or performing heart surgery.

Many toys are useful in the development of large muscles for toddlers. The

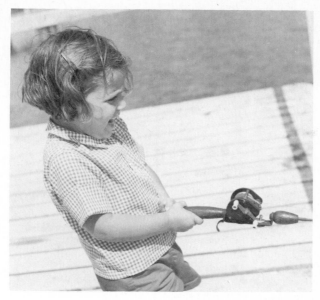

The toddler explores the limits of his or her abilities and insists on doing things alone, even when they are difficult.

Although this toddler cannot write or draw with small tools, she enjoys painting when a large brush is provided; mothers are grateful when large aprons are provided.

two-year-old enjoys pulling or pushing large objects. Wagons, baby carriages, and other riding toys are a great favorite and provide an opportunity to use the large muscles of the arms, legs, and back. The toddler, however, does not need wheels, and large objects such as boxes and chairs are often pushed and pulled to do new service.

Small-muscle development lags behind that of the large muscles. Thus, two-year-olds are neither able nor content to sit at a table and draw or use toys that

Climbing onto boxes and stairs is a challenge to toddlers. At this age, no cabinet or counter is safe from inquisitive hands.

require fine eye-hand coordination. Usually they hold a crayon in a fist grip and often enjoy painting if a large brush is provided. The product of this drawing and painting is scribbling, because they are unable to produce recognizable images. The development of fine motor skills is symmetrical—that is, the toddler shows no preference for using the left or the right hand and uses both with equal skill.

Two-year-olds are not skilled at dressing. Fine muscle control is necessary to master the skills attendant to dressing, such as using buttons and zippers and tying shoes. They are, however, skilled at undressing, especially clothes that do not have buttons or zippers. They easily untie shoes and grasp the toe of the sock to remove it. Toddlers seem constitutionally opposed to shoes and remove them often once the skill is learned. Useful at this age are educational toys or homemade ones of assembled objects that allow children to practice buttoning, zippering, and other dressing skills. Although toddlers cannot dress themselves, they are skilled at helping (or hindering) caregivers in dressing them. They can push their arms through armholes, hold out their feet for shoes, and spread their fingers for gloves. Without this cooperation dressing would be almost impossible, as many mothers and fathers who have attempted to dress a protesting toddler have found.

The most important aspect of physical development in the third year is the rapid increase in locomotor skills. When the infant begins to walk, its gait is quite unsteady and it loses balance easily. The months that follow the first step are occupied with practicing the skill, and the average two-year-old walks quite well, although there are many falls and bumps. Usually falls do not result in more than a temporary hurt or a blow to the child's pride.

Soon after their second birthday most children can ascend stairs if they hold on to a rail and place one foot on a step and then bring the second foot onto the same step. The first foot is then placed on the next step and so forth to the top of the stairs. Coming down, however, presents a different problem. The usual style is to

Climbing on a sliding board is used as a means to explore the world.

travel on the hands and knees, backward. The older toddler is quite adept at scampering down stairs backward, all the while checking over his or her shoulder for obstructions. This same technique is used to get down from chairs, sofas, tables, and beds.

As soon as the child begins to master stairs, no cabinet or dresser is safe from inquisitive hands. The child quickly learns to push a chair or stool to a counter where, using the stool as stairs, he or she manages to get to objects that were thought to be out of reach to someone only one yard tall. A toddler left alone in the kitchen may be discovered a few minutes later on the counter gleefully pouring rice, noodles, and beans onto it and the floor. In the third year the child learns to climb jungle gyms and slides. By three years of age many children enter nursery school and function quite well on climbing toys in the playground.

Mental Development

Intellectual development continues rapidly in the third year. Increasingly the child is able to use mental processes in his or her interchanges with the physical and social environment. There are many different approaches to understanding how humans use mental processes in transactions with the world, but, we will concentrate on the one developed by Jean Piaget. In Chapter 6 we discussed Piaget's development of sensorimotor intelligence. In late infancy a qualitative jump occurs in which the child can represent objects symbolically and mentally manipulate those symbols. The child then enters the preconceptual phase of Piaget's preoperational stage.

Piaget's Preoperational Stage: Preconceptual Phase

We previously stated that at the end of infancy the child reaches the ability for representational thought. Its attainment is not reached absolutely once and for all. It is an emerging ability that requires practice and environmental stimulation for full development. As the child of one year tentatively walks, often stumbles, and falls so, too, the child of two years tentatively forms mental symbols and manipulates them in endless ways. The primary mental activity in the third year is devoted to developing skill in using these mental symbols. The child of two plays with manipulating these mental symbols just as he or she plays with manipulating physical objects. Three behaviors emerge at this time that reflect the growing ability to manipulate mental symbols: deferred imitation, symbolic play, and language development.

Deferred Imitation

Imitation begins in infancy. The infant's imitations, however, are sensorimotor. That is, they are performed immediately upon being perceived by the infant. If you have ever played "Simon Says . . . " you have participated in sensorimotor imitations. These sensorimotor imitations appear as early as two weeks (Moore & Meltzoff, 1975) in such activities as sticking out the tongue, causing the lips to protrude, opening the mouth, and moving fingers. The older infant imitates sounds as well as actions, provided that the model is present when the imitative action is performed. In time, and with the attainment of representative thought (eighteen to twenty-four months of age), deferred imitation is possible.

When the child performs an action that was seen (modeled) with a time lapse between the modeling and the performance, he or she is engaging in deferred imitation. This is an important attainment for several reasons. First, it indicates that

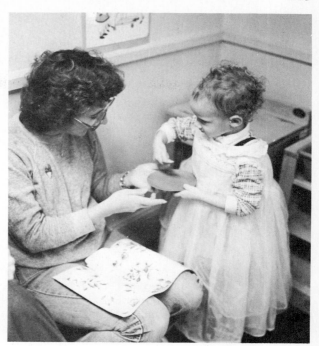

A toddler serves make-believe coffee. She probably saw her mother, dressed in a party dress, serve refreshments to guests at an earlier time and deferred the imitation of this act until an appropriate time.

a stable mental image of the action has been constructed. That is, the child can use mental images that *represent* actions and objects and thereby hold those actions and objects over time. The ability to hold the images and recall them later is the beginning of memory. In deferred imitation the child is imitating a model just as he or she imitates the model in "Simon Says"; however, the model in deferred imitation is internal and may be called forth hours, days, or even weeks after seeing the actual model.* In Piagetian terms, imitation is characterized by total accommodation on the part of the child. Thus, the child *is* a horse, a car, a plane, or a church and actually *becomes* that thing in his or her mental structure. The child can never imitate all the attributes of a person or object. In imitative activities the child extracts the essential elements of an object, which becomes the symbol of that object. For example, a child running and waving his or her arms may be a bird, an airplane, or a dancer. The symbols are usually individualistic and not readily understood by others. The second way in which the child uses representational images is through symbolic play.

Symbolic Play

The child between two and three assimilates all objects into his or her own mental constructions of the world. We see this as delightful and imaginative play and, indeed, it is both. For example, a cardboard dog becomes the mommie and a crayon becomes the child in an elaborate conversation held with the child. The child imposes his or her ideas about what mommies and a child are on the physical objects, without regard to their actual characteristics.

* Piaget (1962) states that this internal model is the beginning of conscience. Conscience is the internalized parent giving prohibitions or approval. This is essentially the same concept expressed in Freudian theory as the superego.

As delightful as symbolic play is, it is not an adequate way to adapt to the world: chairs are not automobiles, mud pies are not food, blankets are not royal robes. This imaginative (symbolic) function, however, is a precious thing; it is the essence of poetry and creative art and, in the final analysis, the essence of creative science. It must be valued for itself, for through symbolic play the child establishes the *meanings* of objects in the world. The child must not be hurried through this stage to reach more mature thought processes. Piaget does not think that acceleration of these mental stages benefits the child. The meanings that are established in this stage are often what we value as *spirit,* or individuality, in older people. Through the manipulation of representative thought by imitation and symbolic play, the child forms *preconcepts* of the world. These are not true concepts, but they are nonetheless the basis on which true concepts are later based. Both imitation and symbolic play continue in the preschool years, but with the attainment of a more stable concept of the world, rational operations gradually replace symbolic functioning.

Language Development

In the third year language facility grows rapidly. Although the average child begins to use simple words at around one year of age, the progress in the second year is slight. Most children reach their second birthday with approximately fifty words (an increase of about four words a month). We can hypothesize that the reason for this slow growth is that the acquisition of language hinges on representational thought. Thus, words learned and used before the attainment of representational thought are more apt to be imitation rather than the use of symbolic language. With the mastery of symbolic thought comes rapid language growth. After age two children may learn several new words daily. The average child entering school (age six) knows between 8,000 and 14,000 words (Carey, 1977).

According to Piaget (1962) words are signs. That is, they are assigned by the culture to represent aspects of reality. They are not symbols, in that they often have no similarity to the actual object. Each member of the culture must learn to match these signs with the object or idea that they represent. There is, of course, the influence of experience and emotional coloring that individuals superimpose on a word. Those *connotations* mark language with individual expression.

Words alone, however, do not constitute language. A simple reading of Webster's dictionary does not constitute a logical language experience. As emphasized in Chapter 6, the function of language is communication and communication is primarily meaning. Words, of course, have meaning, but in language it is not only the words themselves that convey meaning but their order (syntax).

The two-year-old rapidly learns individual words, but more important are his or her experiments with word combinations. Several investigators have carefully collected the word combinations of children. From these studies we conclude that children begin to combine words at between 20 and 24 months of age. Notable among these studies is one by Roger Brown (1973), a professor at Harvard University. He and his colleagues studied in detail the first word combinations of three children. If the children uttered one word it was one morpheme; two words or one word with a plural ending (shoe -s), two morphemes; three words were three morphemes. In studying the speech of young children, the number of utterances were divided by the number of morphemes to obtain the average morphemes. Brown found that the average two-year-old uses expressions of two morphemes.

TYPE	EXAMPLE	ILLUSTRATION
Sign A conventional symbol with no resemblance to a real object.	**Words** A word itself evokes clear mental images and meaningful mental relations with objects and events. Words serve to retrieve personal meanings to express them.	
Symbol Some resemblance to real objects, yet distinct from a real object.	**Pictures** Children who have rich experiences with objects and events can correctly interpret pictorial representations in terms of prior experience and understanding.	
	Physical models The child is able to represent a physical object by a model made from clay or a flat drawing, evoking an image of the real object.	
	Make-believe play Children use objects to represent other objects (symbolic play).	
	Imitation The child can represent the object by using his body to represent the sound and movement of the object. Children also represent common situations in their lives by acting them out (dramatic play).	
Index Part of the actual object represents the whole object.	**Part of the object** The child is able to mentally construct the missing part and recognize the object: He produces a mental image of the object by seeing some tracks or trace caused by the object.	

Signs and symbols that the child uses as representations of objects and actions. [Reproduced by permission of Constance Kamii.]

Table 8–1. Language Development in Infancy and Toddlerhood

Age	Vocabulary	Understanding
0–1 yr.	Imitates words: "dada," "mamma"; consonants more often than vowels	Follows simple instructions: "bye-bye," "no-no"; knows own name
1–2 yrs.	2 to 25 words; speaks in short sentences; can name familiar objects and common pictures	Understands names of familiar objects; can point to parts of the body such as hair, mouth, eyes, ears, hands.
2 yrs.	3-word sentences; uses pronouns; mine, me, you, I; names simple parts of the body; asks for food, water, toilet; calls own name	Follows 2 or 3 directions: "Pick up the toy and put it on the table."
2 yrs., 6 mos.	Uses past tense and plurals formed by adding "s"; identifies 3 words by use; asks, "Show me the one we cook on"; answers, "What do we do with it?"	Understands use of common objects; understands action associated with verbs
2–3 yrs.	Uses 50 words; can name one color; can ask for "another"; names common pictures	Understands action in pictures; understands social interaction such as "We must take turns."
3 yrs.	Uses sentences of 4 words; can repeat sentences of 6 or 7 syllables; uses articles "a" and "the"; expresses past and future; uses negative verbal statements; tells simple action in pictures; knows own sex	Understands prepositions "on," "in," "in back of," "in front of," "under"; answers may be personal, irrelevant, and associational

The two-word sentences of young children consist of such expressions as "Mommy here," "All gone," "Car bye," "More juice."

Some investigations have noted that a few words appear over and over in the language of children. These words may differ from child to child, but consistent with any specific child are a few words that are invested with many different meanings. These have been labeled pivot words by Braine (1963). For example, a child, Andrew, used the word *more* with eleven nouns or verbs, (i.e., *car, cereal, cookie, fish, high, hot, juice, read, sing, toast, walk*). Other pivotal words were *all, no, other, byebye, there,* and *off.* From these pivotal words the child experiments with acquiring more words and with word order. Sometimes the pivotal word is placed first, as "More cookie," "All clean," "No bed," "Other shoe" and sometimes last, as "Light off," or "Milk (in) there." Braine (1963) postulates that the child only exhibits a groping pattern in the use of this word order and does not display an innate knowledge of syntax. Through groping and trial and error, the child arrives at knowledge of positional order. This may be positional order that he or she produces (positional productive pattern), or it may be an order imitated from a model (positional associative pattern). Braine has stressed that in the early acquisition of language, the child is struggling to express *meaning.* The child gropes with language in a search for the forms that will express his or her intentional meaning. Brown (1973), on the other hand, postulates that syntax is innate and evolves developmentally. Meaning is ascribed because of the structure of the language. Actor and action are an innate function of language rather than experience seeking expression.

For Piaget the growth of conceptual representation is inseparable from lan-

Looking at picture books with adults and talking with them about the illustrations facilitates the rapid language development that takes place in the third year.

guage because "conceptual schemas are related to the system of organised verbal signs" (1962, p. 221). The language of the preconceptual child proceeds from the first immediate, action-oriented words to the construction of verbal representations involving recognition and judgments. In recognizing and judging, language is used to reconstruct past action (memory). In so doing it serves as a sign that can then evoke the action. When this happens language is detached from the earlier sensorimotor scheme and begins to approach concepts. Language as signs understood by others can convey general concepts that can be communicated, as opposed to the primitive images and individual symbols of the egocentric sensorimotor stage. The egocentric private language of the two-year-old serves as a bridge between the self-contained sensorimotor images and true concepts of the older child.

Emotional and Social Development

Autonomy: A Declaration of Independence

In the third year of life the child establishes his or her own separateness, the ability to move in the world and to adapt the world to his or her own ends. That is, the child establishes a sense of *autonomy*. In a psychological sense this is a deep-seated emotional feeling that will undergird later attempts at mastering skills. Freud has placed toilet training as the focal point around which personality develops at this stage. Erikson enlarged the context to include many areas in which the wills of the child and parent can come into conflict. Let us review the emotional behavior of the

The sense of autonomy that develops in toddlerhood fosters self-reliance, self-confidence, and competence in mastering the environment.

typical two-year-old and interpret it in the light of the psychoanalytic theory of Erikson and Freud.

The child of this age has physically conquered the world: he or she can move with grace and speed. In addition, the acquisition of mental symbols and language has opened many new avenues of exploration. The child can think of new things to do and can share thought with another person through language. The child is able to set and pursue goals that often are not in accord with those of its parents. In the previous two years caregivers patiently met the child's needs and adjusted their schedules to the infant's (Ausubel, Sullivan, & Ives, 1980). Patience, however, reaches a limit and the parent for the first time asks the child to curb its internal desires, to bring its primitive impulses under control, and to put off immediate desires for long-range goals. Let us use toilet-training as an example of this. The infant is allowed and aided in satisfying any and all instinctual desires as they arise. The crying, hungry infant is fed. Because the infant wears diapers excretory functions occur whenever they are biologically motivated. Now, at two years of age, the adults in charge suddenly change their indulgent attitude and begin to tell the child to wait for lunch and that he or she must not relieve bowel discomfort *except* at a certain time and place. If this entails waiting, then the child must simply wait. The child, meanwhile, is following his or her own schedule of mental and physical investigation of the world and becomes quite annoyed at these "unreasonable" demands by adults. We can easily extend this list of conflicts in which parents demand that children curb their natural desires: touching objects on a coffee table, putting pins and fingers in electrical sockets, opening bottles of liquid, pulling the cat's tail, and so forth. Some of these curbs are for the child's safety, as when a mother prevents a two-year-old from running into a street, and some are for the parents' convenience, as when the same two-year-old is prevented from dancing on phonograph records.

Negativism

Because of the conflict of goals and desires between the child of two and its care-givers there results a battle of wills and a tendency in the toddler to respond with a resounding "No," to even positive statements. When the child responds negatively to parental demands, it responds with its entire body, not merely with words. The child may go rigid or limp, kick, bite, scratch, run away, or lie down on the floor and have a temper tantrum. Parents are often bewildered by this violent display of emotion and may even be threatened by it. To see a human being out of control and in the grips of strong emotions is a frightening sight. Angry prohibitions on the part of the parents seem only to increase the child's negative behavior and a battle of wills can easily ensue. Firm and loving but gentle control on the part of parents and caregivers seems to lessen the child's negativism.

Driven by the drive for autonomy the toddler insists on doing everything for him- or herself and assumes control of such functions as eating, going to bed, and going to the toilet. Sometimes it is necessary for parents to pull rank and use their full authority, especially when the child is doing something destructive or danger-ous. The child, however, must be allowed areas in which he or she can take respon-sibility for doing things, because the child's sense of autonomy needs to be nur-tured. It is necessary for parents to set and keep firm limits. It also seems to be in the nature of children to test limits over and over to see if they really are the limits. When the child is forced to yield to parental demands, often a little extra care may be needed in order not to undermine the child's growing feeling of self-confidence.

Ausubel et al. (1980) have suggested that this sudden demand for control on the part of the parents is an ego devaluation crisis for the child. Freud postulated that the infant has a feeling of omnipotence in which he or she is the center of the world and people exist only to serve his needs. Thus, demands from parents, "Stop that," "Don't touch," and "No," destroy the illusion of omnipotence and create internal devaluation for the child. Ausubel distinguishes between executive and volitional independence. Infants have volitional independence, that is they have enough independence to get others to do their bidding. The kingdom of the home is ruled by the infant. As the child becomes more capable, parents cease to serve the infant, and at the same time demand that the infant control his or her own urges and behavior. The infant reacts to this revolution with rage, which is manifested as negative behavior. The parent then reacts with more demands to control the in-fant's behavior and the battle is on. Eventually, this crisis resolves itself with the child establishing executive independence—that is, the ability to do some things for himself and the responsibility to control its anger and other urges. Negativism is a normal, and perhaps necessary, stage in the development of independence. With firm, loving parents the child learns self-control, how to live with others, and develops a sense of autonomy.

Transformation of Attachment

Undergirding the search for independence in the child's third year of life is the security of the initial attachment formed in infancy; however, that attachment undergoes a transformation. Maccoby (1980) states that attachment in infancy is built on two factors: (1) the instrumental function of the attachment figure in carrying out the needs and desires that the infant cannot accomplish and (2) the emotional function of providing comfort when the infant is distressed. The infant does not remain helpless and dependent and the needs of the child in both these realms change and transform the nature of attachment. The child is increasingly able to take over the processes of dressing, feeding, going to the toilet, organizing play, and moving from one place to another and thus must rely less and less on the attachment figure for these functions. The child's growing cognitive abilities enable him or her to perceive the world as more familiar and less threatening. A more familiar world allows the child to classify experiences so that they can be related to previously encountered events. The familiar world becomes less uncertain and fear provoking and the need for physical proximity to a comforting figure lessens.

Language is another factor that helps to transform the early attachment to one figure. Through language the child is increasingly able to convey his or her needs to a greater number of people and need not depend on the private signals developed with the one significant figure in infancy. Language is understood by a large number of people, and through language even a stranger and the child can share activities. The ability to share activities with another person necessitates that the child see that person as separate, with his or her own goals and intentions. Marvin (1977) has postulated three steps in the transformation of attachment.

1. **Influencing others.** At about the age of one year infants begin to attempt to influence the caregiver's behavior. They attempt to persuade caregivers to act in their behalf: they ask for cookies or a book, or they perform certain acts that consistently bring rewards.
2. **Adapting plans to others.** In the second and third years children learn to change their plans to adapt to those of the caregiver. For example, a child may be told to wait until mother has finished cooking dinner and then she will look at a book with him or her. The child of two can inhibit immediate desire and adapt his or her plans to those of the caregiver. This exchange is executed through the mutual communication system of language. The child can tell the mother what he or she wants to do and the mother can tell the child what she wants to do.
3. **Others as separate self.** Even though the child of two and three may respond to the mother's different plans, this does not mean that the mother is perceived as a separate person with different thoughts, patterns of action, and motives. As the child matures, the attachment to the primary figure is transformed. With the development of the sense of self, the child becomes able to conceive of the attachment figure as a separate person. At that point the relationship becomes a reciprocal meshing of two individual streams of behavior, in which each partner takes account of the other's needs, actions, and plans (Marvin, 1977).

The Sense of Self

The development of the sense of self is at the heart of personality development. This sense of self begins in infancy and continues throughout the life span. "Who am I?" is a question that humans have always asked and in many different ways. They have obtained a variety of answers. The ability to ask the question is, according to some, the major distinction between humans and other animals. To be able to think about self as distinct and different from others and to attempt to derive meaning from that thinking indicate both consciousness and self-consciousness: Not only can humans think about experiences, they can think about themselves thinking about such experiences. Philosophers and psychologists have speculated on the nature of the self and the meaning of human experience. More recently, psychologists have attempted to explore this psychological self and to define its components. Psychologists see the concept of self as a very elastic hypothetical construct. Once a sense of self as a separate person is established, that self can be invested in or identified with a wide range of outside entities, including other people, such as parents or heroes or causes and organizations, such as a football team, a church, or a country. The self has many components, such as self-esteem, attitudes, motives, and values that form a constellation identifying someone as unique. That constellation continues to expand throughout the life span. The full constellation of those components constitutes the individual's *self-concept.*

Many areas of self have been the subject of research studies. Some of those areas are described here.

1. Self-recognition: How children learn to know their own faces.
2. Self-definition: How children learn to use language in reference to ''I'' and ''me'' and what these mean to the child.
3. Self as separate from other people.
4. Identification: How children come to identify self with other people.
5. Ideal self: How children develop a sense of what they ought to be.
6. Taking perspective of others: How children project self and feel and see as another might feel and see.
7. Self-esteem: How children learn to value or devalue their intrinsic selves.
8. Locus of control: Whether the individual's actions are controlled from the internal self or from external factors.

In the toddler age three components of the self emerges: self-recognition, the underlying perception of the self as separate from others, and the language by

The sense of self acquired in toddlerhood is the bridge between the dependent infant and the self-sufficient child. Part of this sense of self is self-recognition: this child studies himself in a mirror.

which the child learns to identify this self. Both self-recognition and language are measurable in the child's behaviors. Underlying both these classes of behaviors is the child's perception of itself as a separate person. It has been theorized that the infant does not differentiate self from its ongoing experience with the world. The concept of self, according to Bannister and Agnew (1976), includes the self and the concept of *nonself*. The infant gradually develops a concept of self and, in parallel, a concept of the mother or caretaker as a separate person.

Self-recognition

"Look at the baby," the young mother tells her infant, as they sit in front of the mirror. We use mirrors every day to see our faces, and we have no trouble recognizing the face in the mirror as our own. The infant, however, has never seen his or her own face and does not know whom she or he is seeing. The infant can recognize its mother and greets her with a broad smile. Soon, however, the infant will have no trouble recognizing his or her own image in the mirror and will enjoy looking at, patting, and talking to that image. The child does this at about 18 months of age, as research by Lewis and Brooks (1974) and Bertenthal and Fischer (1978) indicates. In these studies, which used similar methods, the mother was asked to initiate a play session with her child. In the course of the exchanges she unobtrusively placed a mark such as a red dot on the nose of the child. The child was then exposed to a mirror. The amount of nose touching was recorded both before and after the child was seated in front of the mirror. If nose touching increased after access to the mirror it was assumed that the child perceived the mirror image as being his or her own body and explored that body to find the cause of the distortion. Note that this does not occur before about 18 months of age. The ability to recognize self rests on prior developmental steps and is a conceptual matching process. First, the infant must develop the concept of object permanence. Second, a scheme of his or her own image must be formed, and third the ability to process mirror images must be developed. In processing mirror images the child must be able to coordinate the mirror image with spatial location, rather than seek the image in the mirror.

Bertenthal and Fischer (1978) studied the sequence of these attainments, which is presented here:

six months. The child will reach out and touch the mirror image.
ten months. The child can process mirror images as ascertained by "the hat test." In this test a special vest is put on the infant. The vest has a stick attached that extends over the child's head. Attached to the stick is a hat. When the infant moves, the hat moves. By ten months of age the average infant will turn and look directly at the hat after seeing it in the mirror. The infant thus demonstrates that he or she can correctly place an object in real space when it is seen in a mirror.
fifteen months. The child can find an object in space that enters the mirror behind him or her. In this test the infant is placed facing the mirror and a toy is lowered behind him or her, out of the direct line of vision but visible in the mirror.

Gallup (1977) found that only the great apes (chimpanzees) were able to recognize their own images in a mirror using the same research design of a spot on the face. Other primates were able to process mirror images, evidenced by their attaining food with the aid of a mirror image but gave no evidence of self-recognition. This indicates that self-recognition is restricted to only the most highly evolved animals.

Self-definition

Another aspect of the developing self-concept is the language that the child uses to refer to itself. When the child learns to use the pronouns *I* and *you* correctly, it indicates that a firm sense of self and of others has been formed. This progress is especially easy to note because the mother uses *you* to refer to the child and the child must then invert this and refer to him- or herself as *I* but refer to the mother as *you*. In addition, there are several words that families may use to refer to the child, such as its proper name, the pronoun *you,* and pet names such as *baby*. Most children seem to master this multiplicity of names and the inversion of pronouns without difficulty. Generally children begin by referring to themselves by their proper name, then I or me, and finally, you. For example, a child may say, "Sandy hungry" or "Me sleepy." In referring to another person the child first uses the proper name and then later uses *you*.

The use of *I* and *you* in their shifting reference from speaker to the person spoken to is a subtle concept but one that is mastered easily. Clark (1976) suggests that children form one of several hypotheses when confronted with the puzzle of *I* sometimes referring to mother, sometimes to father, and sometimes to other people (depending on who is using it and who is being addressed). A child may hypothesize that (1) *I* means an adult who is speaking to a child, whereas *you* means the child, or (2) *I* means whoever is speaking, and *you* means whoever is spoken to. Some children begin with hypothesis one and only abandon it when it does not work. Most children early hit on the right hypothesis.

The Competent Toddler

Competence is not a word that we generally apply to infants and young children. Yet, in the view of Burton White, a professor at Harvard and director of the Harvard Preschool Study, it is the word of choice to describe some preschoolers and kindergartners, and *incompetence* is the word to describe others. White and his associates (White, Kaban, Marmor, & Shapiro, 1972; White, Kaban, & Attanucci, 1977) observed many children from three to six years of age. Observers were both teachers of the children and research personnel. The observers judged that some three-year-olds had greater skill in dealing competently with people and organizing activities than some six-year-olds. It was obvious that age alone, or maturation, is not an adequate indicator of behavioral abilities in children.

White and his associates found very little difference between competent and incompetent preschoolers in physical and perceptual abilities but found great differences in social and cognitive abilities. The trail of research is similar to trying to figure out "Who dunnit" in a mystery novel. The researcher must follow the clues provided by his or her investigation and build a logical explanation for it. White, as the researcher on the trail of a mystery, wanted to find out if such differences in children were apparent from birth, and if not, when they emerged; what in the homes of those children differed and by implication caused the differences. When White and his associates studied infants, they found no significant differences to indicate which infants would become competent in the mastery of skills, yet differences were apparent by age three. Therefore White concluded that toddlerhood was the critical time for the development of skills that led to the mastery of the environment. Thus, further research focused on the home environment of toddlers in the second year of life. The subjects of this study were the mothers and younger siblings of the "competent" and "incompetent" kindergartners. The study sought to identify the childrearing patterns of those mothers who raised competent children and those who raised incompetent ones. The competent mothers were designated "A" mothers and the incompetent ones "C." White found many differences between the A and C mothers, most of which evolved around interpersonal relations.

The A mothers seemed to enjoy their toddlers and talked to them often on a level that they seemed to understand. Those mothers organized the home environment so that it was safe and interesting to the toddler and expressed the attitude that the infant's learning and happiness were more important than good housekeeping. They allowed their toddlers to take minor risks and at the same time set reasonable limits on their behavior. The A mothers themselves were busy and seemed happy with their own lives. While they placed a high priority on their children's learning and happiness, they also found time to pursue their own interests. Neither education, nor money, nor time available for childrearing characterized the A mothers. Some A mothers worked part time; some were on welfare; some had not finished high school; some had other children to care for (one was the mother of eight). The A mothers spent less than 10 per cent of their time in caring for the toddlers, but they were nearly always available to answer a question, set up a new activity for the toddler, or give a word of encouragement.

The C mothers were less interested in providing a stimulating environment either for themselves or for their children. Many were disorganized, depressed, or listless. Others focused on housekeeping and ignored their toddlers. The orderliness of the house received a higher priority than their children's learning. Thus, the toddlers were discouraged from exploring and "making a mess." Other C mothers were overprotective and did not allow their children to take risks or to satisfy their natural curiosity and establish independence.

The second year of life is a critical time for the development of competence as the older infant explores the physical limits of the world, develops language, and increases social skills. The interpersonal style of the parent or caregiver is the most important factor in the development of a competent child.

The conclusion of the Harvard preschool study was that any mother can be an A mother. Although poverty may make it more difficult, money and the availability of resources are not the deciding factors in good childrearing skills. Neither is it necessary to have a degree in child development to have those skills. The most important factors for rearing competent children appear to be personal qualities and interpersonal style.

The interpersonal style that was identified as the most important was when the mother is a consultant to the toddler. Those children who developed competence were able to use adults as resources. Serving as a consultant meant that the adult was available when the child needed comfort, assistance, or simply wanted to share an exciting discovery. The child made the overtures for interaction (was in control) and the adult then responded. When A mothers responded to expressed needs of the child, the need was quickly identified and the child was provided with whatever he or she needed, whether it was comfort, unscrewing a bottle top, a compliment, or sharing excitement in a project. Some verbal comment usually accompanied the consulting service. In addition, the adult often used the opportunity to contribute an idea on the topic or to teach some realistic limit about the activity. These mini-sessions required 20 to 40 seconds and occurred frequently in the daily routine of the toddlers. After these short exchanges the toddler returned to explore on his or her own with little direction by the adult.

White's research has changed our views of the importance of the early years of the child's life in terms of intellectual growth. He hypothesized that, in general, American infants develop rather well in the first six months of life. Infants of this age demand little from the environment for their development, and the level of care in the United States is generally adequate to meet the demands. However, at around six months of age the infant begins to interact more with his or her environment, thereby requiring more environmental input both in sensory stimulation and in interpersonal relations.

At the same time, many abilities are emerging that constitute basic human qualities: language, social attachment to another person, sense of self, manipulation of the environment to satisfy curiosity, and using another person as a resource. With the emergence of these abilities the infant becomes more difficult to care for, and a wide variety of caretaking styles develop among caregivers.

As a consequence of these differing styles, some environments support emerging abilities and help the child to develop, whereas others are nonsupportive or actually oppose the child's emerging competence. Between the ages of six months and two years, these emerging abilities crystallize into structures that can predict the child's development. Once this crystallization has taken place, those structures resist change. The structures that White explored reflect the abilities of language, curiosity, problem-solving skills, social skills, and attachment behavior. Mastery of these skills is what White refers to as competence. The conclusion drawn from White's research is that the *critical time for the development of competence as reflected in language, curiosity, problem solving, attachment, and social relations is the second year of life.*

Management Problems with Toddlers

The toddler period is crucial in the development of a sense of self and in the development of social relationships. The patterns of relationship that are set in this period will, in all likelihood, continue. Those patterns may be positive or negative.

The problem for parents is how to continue a loving relationship while setting limits on the child's behavior. The parent must curb the child's impulses, yet allow him or her to maintain a sense of individuality, selfhood, and freedom.

Brazelton (1974) has identified several problem areas that are often conflictual for toddlers and parents. Some of the situations that are particularly troublesome are that children may be withdrawn, hyperactive, overly demanding, or jealous of a sibling. Each of these requires wisdom and patience on the part of the caretaker during the crucial toddler period.

The Withdrawn Child

The demand for independence does not always come from the child. It is a mutual decision on the part of parents and child. Mother must wean the child from baby ways and demand toilet control. Often the demands come too quickly for the toddler, and the feeling engendered is not one of growing independence but one of rejection. This situation most often arises when children in a family are spaced close together and the toddler is pushed aside to make room for a new baby. The sensitive toddler may feel replaced by the smiling baby as he or she becomes the "knee baby." Overworked mothers may feel that the demands on them are beyond their capacity to respond, and the young child is the most vulnerable for being neglected. Brazelton (1974) states,*

> One can see pathetic, depressed two-year-olds leaning against doorways, trying to hang onto the skirts of their mothers or grandmothers, attempting to climb into an empty lap. But they give up easily and withdraw, beaten, when the lap is filled with a smiling younger baby. [p. 121]

The Hyperactive Child

Some children seem from birth to react more strongly to stimuli and to be unable to regulate their behavior once they have been stimulated. These children are difficult babies and a source of frustration for their parents. As infants they seem to react intensely to any stimuli and to cry incessantly. As toddlers they are apt to become intense, demanding, clumsy, and extremely active. They create endless chaos throwing physical objects and emotional tantrums throughout the house. Most children learn self-control in the face of new and novel stimuli, but some seem never to be able to accomplish this and are continuously overwhelmed by situations. These children may be called hyperactive. The cause or treatment for such children has yet to be identified. The cycle of relationships in the family with these children is a source of concern to parents and professionals. Brazelton (1974) states,

> The difficulty with such an infant is that he provides a negative feedback system for his mother. Everything she might do naturally to mother a baby meets with a negative response from him, and she cannot help but take it personally. She soon begins to feel his behavior is her fault, due to her inadequacy as a mother. And no mother can tolerate that feeling indefinitely. In fact, the more she may care about being a good mother, the more difficult this kind of behavior may be for her. Her response will inevitably be to turn away from this continuous negative assault—to avoid responding in kind by battering the baby. It is no wonder that a distant, insensitive, even hostile relationship gets built up around such a baby. [p. 163]

* Excerpted from the book *Toddlers and Parents: A Declaration of Indepedence* by T. Berry Brazelton M.D. Copyright © 1974 by T. Berry Brazelton. Reprinted by permission of Delacorte Press/Seymour Lawrence.

The Demanding Child

The overly demanding child is created by the interaction between parent and child. For various reasons the parent is hesitant to set the limits that the toddler needs and seeks. In the toddler's search for these limits, the demands escalate and appeasement on the part of parents is greeted with more demands. This cycle continues until the toddler becomes an insatiable tyrant and a very poor social companion. Many circumstances can initiate and perpetuate this cycle. Among the more common self-destructive behaviors are the breath holding and head banging common among two-year-olds. Brazelton (1974), in commenting on the import of breath-holding spells, states:

> [the parent is] *so frightened of setting off a spell by crossing the child that the parent avoids any confrontation. Normal frustrations become something to be avoided. The parent hovers protectively over the baby in order to keep him from becoming upset. Advice to require normal limits or to punish the child when necessary falls on deaf ears.*
> *I have seen parents at the mercy of a child as a result of these spells. The child becomes jazzed up as a result. He begins to be more and more demanding, manipulating his anxious parents. To control them, he seems to learn to produce spells at will. This cycle represents the evolution of a "spoiled" child—an anxious child who knows he needs limits, desperately wanting them but unable to place them on himself, and not receiving them from the adults around him.* [p. 137]

Sibling Rivalry

Conflict between brothers and sisters—and jealousy for the attention of parents—is a theme that is as old as the biblical story of Cain and Abel. No doubt it is an element in all families that have two or more children, no matter what the age

Envy for the new baby can often be averted by including the older child in the relationship.

A safe passage through toddlerhood into childhood is assisted by loving parents and caregivers who give help when it is needed and who let the child discover independence and self-control when possible. [Courtesy Helen Canaday, Administrative Director, Preschool Programs, University of North Carolina at Greensboro.]

differences. Sibling rivalry becomes particularly difficult when children are one to two years apart. When a baby is a toddler (just walking) and an older brother or sister is two or three, the stage is set for intense conflict. The two-year-old has a very low tolerance for frustration and the toddling baby has an insatiable urge to explore. This exploration often invades the play space of the older sibling. The natural inclination of the mother is to protect "her baby"; unfortunately, the older child may already be smarting under the rejection engendered by the intrusion of the little usurper. Brazelton (1974) speaks of that situation.

> *I am convinced that sibling rivalry can be a positive learning experience for the involved siblings. It is the triangle (child, interfering parent, child) that keeps it alive as a negative experience. When the mother reinforces the rivalry, not seeing their struggle as a way of involving her and calling her from other duties, the two children will continue the pattern. When she doesn't come, the importance of perpetuating the struggle is soon lost in favor of more constructive play. A positive relationship between the children can never take place when the mother steps in to interfere. It is a difficult role for a mother to learn—and it is hard to see the value of leaving such a rivalrous situation up to unequal competitors.* [p. 51]

A Safe Passage

Primitive tribes have rituals that mark the change in status from one state to another. These are called rites of passage. The passage is a time of transition—that is, a time of becoming. We do not have rituals to mark these passages, but nevertheless we recognize these times as important and uncertain. Transitions are always times of risk. As the child makes the passage from the safety of infancy to the freedom and expansion of childhood, much is at stake. It is in many ways a terrifying time for the child. No child really enjoys the lack of control that is evident in temper tantrums. In new-found independence the child seeks the limits of that independence. A firm, loving hand is needed to guide the child to greater independence and self-control. The key to a safe passage, however, is that the guide not be afraid to impose controls when needed. Guiding a child through the Terrible-Twos is rather like changing drivers in a car while it is moving at high speed on an interstate. We are all on a high-speed interstate in the process of living, but in this transition the controls are being handed gradually from the parent to the child. The passage is crucial in determining how the child will grow and what he or she will become.

Main Points

Physical Development

1. In the third year physical growth slows, resulting in a reduction in food intake; arms and legs grow the most rapidly.

2. Gross motor development enables the toddler to run, climb, jump, ride a tricycle, and throw a ball; fine motor control proceeds slowly and is symmetrical.

3. The most important aspect of physical development in the third year is the rapid increase in locomotor skills.

Mental Development

4. At the end of infancy the child moves into the preconceptual phase of Piaget's preoperational stage.

5. With the attainment of representative thought (at eighteen to twenty-four months of age) the child is able to perform deferred imitation of actions observed at some previous time.

6. In symbolic play the child establishes the meaning of objects and forms preconcepts of the world.

7. With the mastery of symbolic thought, language facility grows rapidly.

Emotional and Social Development

8. In the third year the child establishes a sense of separateness, or autonomy.

9. Attachment is transformed in the third year from dependence to reciprocal interaction. The attachment figure is seen as a person with separate motives. The toddler realizes his or her power to influence these motives and the necessity to sometimes adapt his or her desires to those of another.

10. In the toddler age, three components of self emerge: self-recognition, perception of self as separate, and self-referent language.

11. Self-recognition rests on the development of object permanence, scheme of the self-image, and the ability to process mirror images.

The Competent Toddler

12. The critical time for the development of competence as reflected in language, curiosity, problem solving, and social relations spans the toddler period.

Management Problems with Toddlers

13. A child who is withdrawn, hyperactive, overly demanding, or jealous may cause management problems for parents.

Words to Know

autonomy
connotation
negativism
preconcept
preconceptual
syntax

Terms to Define

deferred imitation
self-concept
signs
symbolic play

Concept to Discuss

self

CHAPTER 9

Physical Development in Early Childhood

Have you ever wondered

why preschoolers seem to be moving constantly?

if age is the best indication of physical maturity?

what research has shown about child abuse?

if child abuse can be understood in the entire context of the culture and community?

Physical Appearance

The slowed but steady growth during the toddler period continues in the preschool years. Both boys and girls add about three inches in height and between four and five pounds per year. Of course there is a wide variation in the actual size and weight of children of the same age in these years. Genetic potential and nutrition continue to be the most important determinant of these differences (Meredith, 1969). In general, urban children are taller than rural children and upper-class children are taller than lower-class children. When class membership is controlled, black Americans show earlier development and are taller than white Americans of the same age. Whites are taller than Asian Americans. In addition, as our perspective of children enlarges to include children all over the world, we find that children in underdeveloped countries are on the average considerably smaller and lighter than well-nourished children in the United States and Western Europe. The fact that the growth patterns of children in the upper classes of these countries are comparable to those in the industrialized West suggests that nutrition is the cause of the retardation. Increasingly, adequate food is becoming a problem in the entire world community.

Slowly the preschool child loses its protruding belly and the toddler's sway back. Proportions continue to change in the direction of longer legs and arms. The six-year-old schoolchild assumes proportions that remain characteristic of physical

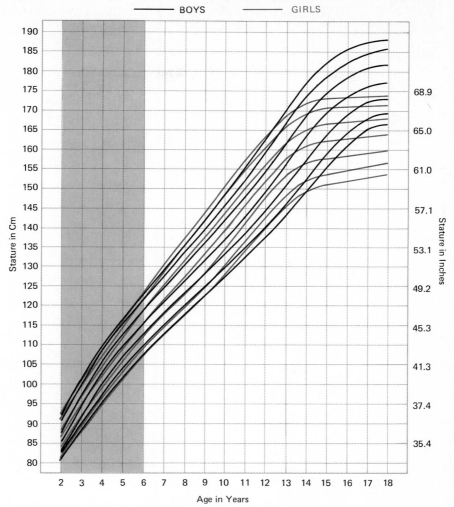

──── BOYS　　　──── GIRLS

Standards of height for boys and girls age two to eighteen with emphasis on ages two to six. [Data from National Center for Health Statistics, 1976.]

appearance in both boys and girls until puberty. Sex differences are not only slight in physical appearance but also in composition of muscle and fat in these years although boys remain slightly taller, heavier, and more muscular than girls until girls overtake them in the prepuberty growth spurt.

Facial features and proportions change in that the features and the jaw become more prominent. By three most children have a full complement of twenty primary "baby" teeth; by six they begin to lose them, but before the baby teeth are replaced by permanent teeth, many children are plagued by dental caries. It is important that these teeth be cared for, even though in a few years they will be replaced. A diet rich in sweets has been implicated in the incidence of the problem. The late-weaned child who is put to sleep with a bottle may be especially susceptible to decay in teeth. The sugar in the liquids is, of course, the cause of the decay. Dentists recommend that if a bottle must be used to lull the child to sleep, it be filled with water.

Internal Growth

Changes in physical appearance reflect the internal growth of the preschool years. Cartilage continues to harden into bone in the ossification process. Childrens' bones have less mineral content than they will have at adulthood. The brain and nervous system continue to lead in development. By the time the child is three years old, the brain has reached 75 per cent of its adult weight and by the time the child is six, 90 per cent. The entire nervous system comprises 5 per cent of total weight in a five-year-old, whereas in adults, it is only 2 per cent. The brain in-

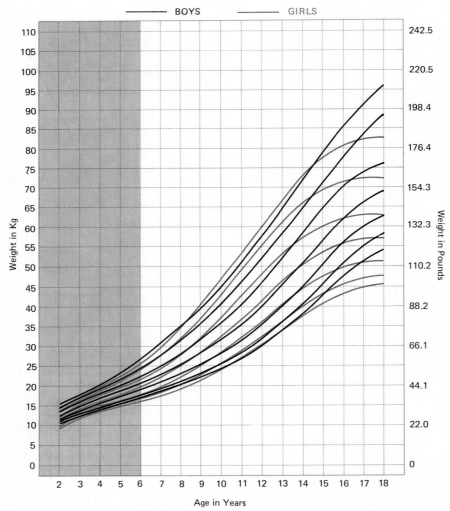

Standards of weight for boys and girls age two to eighteen with emphasis on ages two to six. [Data from National Center For Health Statistics, 1976.]

These two children are both four years old. Although boys are, on the average, slightly taller than girls in early childhood, individual children show great variation in size. The difference in the heights of these two children is probably due to genetic variations. [Courtesy Helen Canaday, Administrative Director, Preschool Programs, University of North Carolina at Greensboro.]

creases not only in volume, but also in complexity and organization. New learnings result in increases in the number, size, and complexity of connections between cells in the cortex and in different levels of the brain.

Motor Development

Large Muscles

In the years from three to six the child approaches the nearest human equivalent to a "perpetual-motion machine." Active is the best way to describe healthy preschoolers. The three-year-old has mastered running, which becomes the usual method of locomotion. The favorite activities are those that entail large-muscle activity, such as riding a tricycle, pushing a wagon, or climbing. At three the average child can walk on tiptoe, descend a long flight of stairs, stand on one foot, hop on both feet, jump from a small platform, and perform a standing broad jump of about 18 inches. The average four-year-old perfects these skills and can gallop, descend stairs with alternating feet, skip on one foot, and perform stunts on a tricycle, such as putting his or her feet on the handle bars or leaning over while cycling to pick up a small toy. The five-year-old continues to refine these skills and can skip on alternating feet, hop on one foot many times, descend ladders alternating feet, and walk a straight line or balance beam (Corbin, 1973). These activities are usually performed while another game or activity is in progress. The true development of motor skills is in the coordination of perceptual abilities and one or more motor activities. For example, the ever-popular game of "It" affords much opportunity for running, galloping, twisting, and dodging. In this game the child watches "It" and judges "Its" speed and distance to see just how far from "home" is safe. The game increases in interest and tension the closer these calculations are. When a player miscalculates and is caught by "It," he or she is getting immediate feedback to change judgments of distance and speed and/or the ability to move. In these active games preschool children are experimenting with the mastery of new skills. A typical neighborhood game of hide-and-seek or "It" will cover a range in age from about three through to perhaps nine or ten years. In such situations the older children are the teachers of the younger ones, and many aspects of physical, social, and emotional mastery are interlocked.

Fine Motor

Preschoolers continue to show progress in eye-hand coordination and fine motor control. This is expressed in such activities as working puzzles, stringing beads, working buttons and zippers on clothing, and in writing and drawing. Most American middle-class families provide their children with ample opportunity for learning to manipulate a pencil and crayons and probably give some instruction in writing their name. Children need these skills before beginning school because the early school years concentrate on experiences with paper and pencil or crayon.

Health inspections in preschool programs and day care centers help to prevent the spread of infection. [Courtesy Helen Canaday, Administrative Director, Preschool Programs, University of North Carolina at Greensboro.]

The energy of early childhood finds expression in outdoor activities. Running, jumping, riding, exploring, these children find sheer joy in bodies that are growing and experiencing the world. Bumps and falls are of no consequence and for the most part the child simply tries all over again until physical mastery is achieved. [Photograph center, top row, courtesy Robert Cavin; all others courtesy Helen Canaday, Administrative Director, Preschool Programs, University of North Carolina at Greensboro.]

Manipulation of small tools such as scissors requires practice and the development of fine muscle control.

Bone Age and Maturation

Physical growth proceeds remarkably well on a time schedule, but the age of the child is not the most accurate correlation with size. We use age because it is a statistic that is easy to gather and in a rough sense it correlates rather well with growth in size. However, when a child is obviously shorter or taller than its age mates, closer investigation than age may be in order. If age is not the most accurate correlate with size, then what can be used? The most accurate estimate of maturational age is the percentage of cartilage that has been replaced by bone. Usually an X-ray is taken of the wrist and from this the percentage of ossification can be determined and a good estimate of bone-age determined. In most children chronological age, bone age, and size correlate rather well, and each can be guessed from any of the others. However, children who are extreme in either tallness or shortness may have a problem in growth regulation. In these cases a medical determination of bone age may be necessary. For example, a child of five who is at the 99th percentile in height for chronological age may show a bone age of six or seven years. In that case, eventual height will, in all likelihood, be within normal range. On the other hand a child at the 99th percentile with a bone age of four is growing more rapidly than average. The same is true for children who are extremely short. If a very short child has a young bone age (less than its chronological age) then normal growth will most likely occur. The medical treatment for retarded growth is the administration of growth hormones, which are normally produced in the pituitary gland (Lowery, 1978). Of course, before taking such a powerful drug, the possibility of a nutritional deficiency or other debilitating disease should be ruled out.

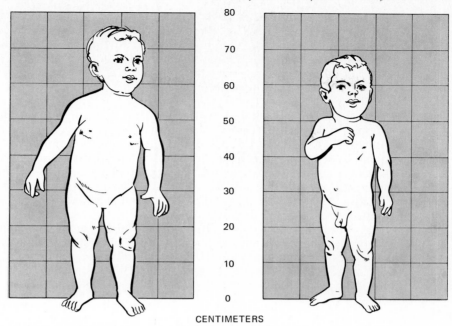

Twins, normal and dwarfed, offer evidence of the effect of emotional deprivation on infants. This drawing is based on photographs made when the children were almost 13 months old. The girl was near normal in weight and stature but her twin brother was the size of a seven-month-old. Some four months after the twins were born a period of stress began between the parents; the father then lost his job and left home. It appears that the mother's hostility toward her husband included the son but not the daughter. [From "Deprivational Dwarfism" by Lytt I. Gardner. In *Scientific American*, July 1972. Copyright © 1972 by Scientific American, Inc. All rights reserved.]

Growth retardation may also be caused by psychological stress. A child that does not receive affection and is subject to hostility from caregivers may exhibit *deprivation dwarfism*. This condition is extremely difficult to identify and to correct. The child is not necessarily physically abused, and the psychological conditions are difficult to diagnose. Frazier and Ralison (1962) report the case of a five-year-old child to whom growth hormones were administered, to which she did not respond. The physicians in charge knew of the effects of maternal deprivation on children and, suspecting that situation, recommended that the child leave the mother and spend some time with a relative. In the time spent with the relative her growth rate was twice what it had been at home. When she returned home her growth rate slowed again.

Child Abuse

A child was found in New Jersey who had spent her life in a chicken coop with no opportunity to learn how to live and love in human society; in New York a mother placed her infant in an oven to drive out evil spirits. In a large urban hospital medical personnel struggle to save the life of a very young premature infant, only to find him some months later in the emergency room dying from neglect or from injuries inflicted by his mother. Physicians and nurses are appalled at the broken, battered, blinded, burned children who finally are brought to them for treatment. People concerned with the care and welfare of children find this one of the most difficult of all problems to understand and to treat. How can a parent, entrusted with the care of a child willfully inflict harm on that child, even to the point of death?

Child abuse may include any number of transgressions against the child, ranging from physical harm, including sexual acts, to psychological abuse and neglect. Thus, while the child may be abused through the actual commission of harm, it also may be abused by needed food, clothing, shelter, or psychological comfort being withheld. There are children in this country who have been contained for years in a closet, attic, or crib and denied those human experiences that we deem necessary for healthy development. In such cases the withholding of care is as abusive as the administration of physical abuse.

It is quite difficult to obtain the statistical incidence of child abuse. Reported incidence is usually restricted to physical abuse, and estimates of this are approximately one in 100,000 children. Thus, estimates of physical abuse in the United States range from 40,000 to 160,000 (Starr, 1979). However such estimates are unreliable because:

1. Many cases are not reported. Therefore, professionals have to extrapolate from reported cases to estimate the actual incidence.
2. Reported cases are usually restricted to physical abuse because psychological abuse is very difficult to prove and sexual abuse is shrouded in cultural and familial secrecy.
3. The definition of *abuse* differs among reporting agencies.

Starr (1979) reports on a survey of professionals designed to obtain agreement over what constitutes abuse. Eighty percent of professionals agreed that "abuse occurred when the act involved either direct harm, a direct intent to injure, or intentionality without injury" (p. 872).

Even with difficulties in identifying the problem, we can say that when parents or caregivers impose harm on the child in their care, either through active commission or neglectful omission, it constitutes abuse. Who are these abusing parents and what are the factors that cause such behavior? Several decades of intensive research have revealed factors that are associated with child abuse. Some research has suggested that child abuse is the result of characteristics of the parents (Spinetta & Rigler, 1972). Other researchers have concluded that the characteristics of the child may precipitate his or her own abuse (de Lissovoy, 1979; Friedrich and Boriskin, 1976). Several studies have sought, and found, the cause of child abuse in the sociological conditions of the family unit. Burgess (1978) concluded that abuse results not from disturbed individuals but from disturbed family interaction patterns, whereas Gelles (1973, 1975, 1976) has indicted social stress on family units as a causative agent. Finally, Gil (1971) and Zigler (1978) have suggested that the cause of child abuse resides in the total context of cultural attitudes and beliefs in interaction with personal characteristics.

Interrelated Factors in Child Abuse

Belsky (1980) has proposed that child abuse must be viewed from an ecological perspective. That is, the final action of child abuse is the result of many interrelated factors that are arranged in an hierarchical manner. This hierarchy includes personal factors referred to as the microsystem, community factors known as the exo-system, and factors from the entire cultural system known as the macrosystem. Thus, child abuse is the result of interrelated factors from the microsystem, such as the personal characteristics of the parents and child and family interactions; the presence or absence of community supports, the exosystem; and such factors from the macrosystem as the cultural system of attitudes, beliefs, and practices within which the exosystem and microsystem are embedded. This is an important analysis of a difficult problem, because it has been impossible to understand child abuse in the context of one of these factors alone. Belsky states that,

> *child maltreatment is multiply determined by forces at work in the individual, in the family, and in the community and culture in which the individual and family are embedded . . . these multiple determinants are ecologically nested within one an-other.* [1980, p. 320]

Belsky has attempted to integrate a lot of research into this larger context. the ecological approach has been avidly recommended by Bronfenbrenner (1977, 1979a, 1979b) as necessary in relating research to the actual experiences of children in order to increase its understanding by professionals. Let us ascend this hierarchy of causal factors in an attempt to place child abuse in its ecological context, remembering that it is a combination of situations that finally triggers abuse, not one factor alone, and that the combination differs in each case.

Characteristics of the Abusing Parent (Microsystem). Study after study has found that one common characteristic of abusing parents is that they themselves were abused as children. However, this alone does not mean that the parent will abuse his or her child. Many adults who were abused as children do *not* abuse their children. Perhaps more important than abuse are the psychological scars that these parents bring from their childhood. Often, abusing parents indicate psychological patterns that suggest that they were maternally deprived.

Green (1976) has characterized the personality of abusing parents as consisting of a poor self-concept, with little awareness of their feelings. They have dependency needs that have not been met (deficient mothering) and project their parental expectations onto the child. This is corroborated by clinical impressions that such parents seek maternal care and love from their own children, and when the child or infant cannot provide this psychological support, their reaction is abuse. Many researchers have noted this *role reversal*. Playing the parental role, abused children often show a protective attitude toward their parents. For example, they worry about what the parent will do without them, they often express the desire to return to the parent, and offer words of comfort and encouragement to the parent.

Characteristics of the Child (Microsystem). Many studies suggest that the child may have characteristics that invite a high risk of abuse. For example, a disproportionate number of abused children are premature. Premature children are more difficult to care for and thus are less satisfying to parents. By extension, any difficult child seems more prone to being abused. Babies that are especially irritable and colicky and those who are unresponsive both seem to be at higher risk for abuse. However, let us stress that not all difficult children are abused, nor are all "good" babies excluded from abuse. Many mothers and fathers are able to submerge their own needs and meet the exceptional needs of difficult children *even* when they themselves experienced deprived, abusive childhoods.

Family Interaction (Microsystem).   The personal characteristics of the child interact to create a family environment. Burgess and Conger (1978) studied the interaction among abusive families and found both children and parents to display *more* negative behavior than children and parents from matched nonabusing families. Mothers expressed 40 per cent less affection and supportive behavior and 60 per cent *more* threats and complaints toward their children. In addition, the children in abusive families displayed 50 per cent more negative behavior than similar children from nonabusing families. In another study it was observed that toddlers who had been abused displayed more aggression toward their peers (George & Main 1979).

The second aspect of family interaction implicated in child abuse is the husband-wife relationship. In families that function well, the competence of the mother is closely related to the support she receives from her husband. Many studies have found marital conflict high in abusive households (Clarke-Stewart, 1977; Green, 1976). There may indeed be a relationship between battered wives (or husbands) and battered children. Steinmetz (1977) found that families that use aggressive tactics to resolve husband-wife disputes tend to use similar methods in disciplining children. From a psychological viewpoint, child abuse may result from displaced anger in marital conflict, or it may simply be the only behavior available to the parent.

From many research studies we can construct a composite description of abusing families. First, many of them live in poverty, although popular reports stress that abuse occurs at all social and educational levels. Research nevertheless indicates that the vast majority of *reported* cases are from poor families. In addition, a disproportionate number of families with a large number of children closely spaced in age is reported. The abusing parent is likely to be a mother (or father) who is stressed by having many children close in age (demanding much physically and psychologically) and who have few material resources. The parent may resent the child for consuming the meager resources available, may feel guilty for not being able to provide more, or may suffer frustration in the situation.

The Community (Exosystem).   Families are embedded in communities that, in the best of situations, provide support in terms of work and formal and informal relations for them. Families without these supports are under considerable stress. Gil (1971) analyzed a national sample of abused children and found that almost half of the fathers had been unemployed in the year immediately preceding the incident. In fact, unemployment of the father is associated with all forms of domestic violence (Steinmetz & Strauss, 1974).

Abusing families also appear to be isolated from both formal and informal support systems in the community. (Garbarino, 1977; Kempe, 1973). These families neither belong to formal organizations, such as church or clubs, nor have the lifeline of family or friends that could offer advice, keep the child for a while, or relieve some of the constant physical demands of too many children with too little money. It is not necessarily that these opportunities are not available in the community, but more likely that the family members do not have the social skills to become a part of them. These maladaptive social patterns may be handed from generation to generation, as one study of abused toddlers indicated. Abused toddlers, even in the "safe" environment of a day-care center, exhibited socially isolating behaviors such as rejecting friendly overtures and avoiding both peers and caregivers (George & Main, 1979).

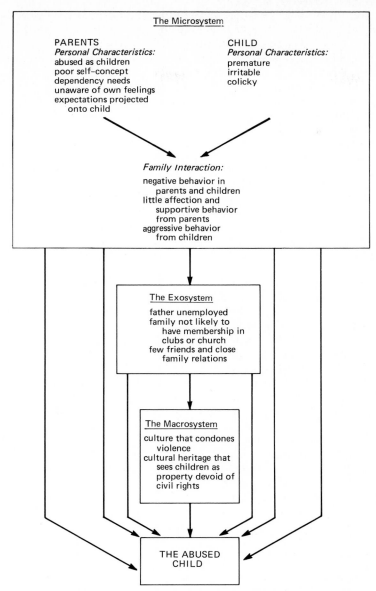

The Microsystem

PARENTS
Personal Characteristics:
abused as children
poor self-concept
dependency needs
unaware of own feelings
expectations projected
   onto child

CHILD
Personal Characteristics:
premature
irritable
colicky

Family Interaction:
negative behavior in
   parents and children
little affection and
   supportive behavior
   from parents
aggressive behavior
   from children

The Exosystem

father unemployed
family not likely to
   have membership in
   clubs or church
few friends and close
   family relations

The Macrosystem

culture that condones
   violence
cultural heritage that
   sees children as
   property devoid of
   civil rights

THE ABUSED
CHILD

Summary of interrelated factors in child abuse. [After Belsky, 1980.]

The Culture (Macrosystem).   Families are embedded in communities and communities are embedded in a larger culture. Finally, in understanding child abuse the cultural attitudes toward physical violence must be considered—more specifically, the acceptance of violence toward children. Only recently have we attempted to construct a documented picture of the historical treatment of children to replace our sentimental view of them as having been carefree and idyllic in the past. DeMause (1974) has stated that the history of childhood is a history of physical and sexual abuse and infanticide. In other words, Western culture has long accepted violence against children. We can trace this attitude to Roman law and the writings of Aristotle. Under Roman law the father in a family had the power of life and death over his children, even over the protest of their mother. Aristotle considered both children and slaves to be property: children belonging to a father and slaves to a master. In such relationships, according to Aristotle, no action constitutes an injustice because "there can be no injustice to one's own property" (Belsky, 1980, p. 329). Although today we do not allow fathers the right to life and death over their children, the principle of the privacy of the home and the (property) rights of parents continue to be rights considered in investigating suspected child abuse.

In our system of cultural values parents have not only a right, but also a responsibility, to discipline their children. However, the line between discipline as physical punishment and child abuse is one that is difficult to draw both legally and morally. Our Supreme Court, the body that expresses the finest distinctions of law, has upheld the right of schools, which act in the place of parents, to use physical punishment in disciplining children. School personnel have at times crossed the line in exercising this right and have been charged with abuse in disciplining children. Belsky reports a survey of educators, police officers, and religious leaders that found that two out of three of these community "helpers" approved of physical discipline in the form of spanking for children, whereas 10 per cent of them sanctioned the use of belts, straps, and brushes for maintaining control. Finally, faced with rising rates of violent crime, political assassinations, random violence, and the escalating portrayal of horrendous violence on television and in other media, critics of the culture conclude that we do, indeed, live in a violent society. Child abuse, then, can partially be seen as one more violent action in a violent society.

There is a cultural countercurrent arising from belief in the rights of all people, that champions the rights of children, abhors the use of physical punishment as a means of controlling them, and seeks other means of teaching them self-control. Proponents of these views attempt to institute means that are directed to the final goal: teaching children self-discipline and skills that will enable them to reach satisfaction in life without imposing harm on others. This can be accomplished by refusing to use physical punishment as a control and by substituting knowledge about child development and the variety of techniques that are appropriate in dealing with the child's developmental level.

Main Points

Physical Appearance

1. Growth during the preschool years is slower than in infancy; height increases 3 to 4 inches per year and 4 to 5 pounds of weight are gained per year. Children in underdeveloped countries are on the average smaller and lighter weight than well-nourished children in the United States.

Internal Growth

2. Internal growth is led by the brain and nervous system. The brain increases in volume and complexity and the ossification process continues.

Motor Development

3. Large-muscle activity progresses to include riding a tricycle, pushing a wagon, climbing, tiptoeing, climbing down, hopping, jumping, skipping, and walking in a straight line.

4. Preschoolers develop eye-hand coordination and fine motor control, enabling them to work puzzles, string beads, button, zip, write, and draw.

Age and Maturation

5. The most accurate estimate of maturational age is the percentage of cartilage that has been replaced by bone (bone age). Growth retardation may be caused by delayed bone age, nutritional deficiency, debilitative diseases, or psychological stress.

Child Abuse

6. When parents or caregivers impose harm on the child in their care, either through active commission or neglectful omission, child abuse has been committed.

7. Child abuse is multiply determined by forces at work in the individual and the family (microsystem), the community (exosystem), and the entire cultural system (macrosystem).

8. Abusing parents often were maternally deprived, have a poor self-concept, and seek maternal love from their own children.

9. Premature and difficult-to-care-for children are at a higher risk of abuse than others.

10. Children and parents from abusive families display less affection and support and more complaints, negative behavior, and aggression.

11. Abusive families usually lack community supports such as jobs, economic security, and family and group systems.

12. Community attitudes accepting and approving physical violence toward children contribute to the problem of child abuse.

Words to Know

exosystem
macrosystem
maturation
microsystem

Terms to Define

child abuse
deprivational dwarfism
fine motor
gross motor

CHAPTER 10

Mental Development in Early Childhood

Have you ever wondered

if the thinking of young children differs in quality or only in degree of experience from that of older children?

how young children develop an understanding of the natural world?

what a young child thinks about?

why children are so persistent in asking where babies come from?

why children speak of everything as being alive?

if mental development can be accelerated by training?

how children learn the structure of language?

if the type of language used in a family affects a child's school experience?

what compensatory education is?

if Head Start has really been a head start?

Intellectual processes are developing rapidly in the early childhood years. The mental world of the child is one in which fantasy and reality are interchangeable. This fantasy, of course, consists of mental constructions. Language, which also develops rapidly is the intellect's major tool. The way in which language is explored characterizes children's thinking in early childhood. The child begins to attend school and the formal process of education is under way. The way in which schools are structured reflects the way adults understand and respond to their understanding of children's thinking in early childhood. In this chapter we will examine the preoperational thought of young children as presented by Piaget, language development, and schools for the early childhood years that have attempted to stimulate intellectual development and compensate for disadvantaged environments.

246

Piaget's Preoperational Stage: Intuitive Phase (Four to Seven Years)

We have already discussed the preconceptual phase of Piaget's preoperational stage of cognitive development in Chapter 8. In the preconceptual phase the child is preoccupied with building mental constructions (schemes). As in many other areas of development, when a skill is emerging, the child practices it constantly. So, too, when the child of two is able to form mental representations of objects, events, and processes, he or she engages in endless variations of them. It is through these mental constructions that the child experiences the world, builds a relationship to it, and thinks about objects, events, and processes. Often the ideas and concepts formed by the young child are distorted and reasoning fails to be logical. The concepts formed are therefore termed preconcepts, because they lack the full elaboration and stability that will come when they grow into actual concepts.

The intuitive phase of the preoperational stage is marked by the child's increased success in solving problems about objects and events in the natural world. This success, however, is erratic, and correct solutions are often achieved by intuitive guesses rather than sound reasoning. The child of four or five may accurately state that a tight circle of ten pennies will buy the same amount of candy as a line of ten pennies, yet when questioned about the reason for this answer may not reason that both sets have the same number of pennies. Piaget has stressed that *correct answers are not an accurate criterion of thought*. The reasons behind answers must be explored to assess the actual level of a child's thinking.

The preoperational stage is a transitional stage and, as such, is marked by a process of change rather than the attainment of abilities. When the child enters the preoperational stage, he or she is able to form representational symbols of objects, events, and processes but is unable to transform them mentally and thereby think logically. The reason that the young child cannot perform these mental operations is that the child between the ages of two and seven has characteristic ways of thinking that serve as barriers to logical thinking. One by one these barriers are overcome and thinking becomes increasingly logical.

Characteristics of Preoperational Thought

Let us underscore that this period is a transitional stage and therefore the thinking of children in this stage is quite uneven. Because of individual differences and different experiences children enter and leave stages at different times. In addition, in any transitional stage, behavior is erratic. That is, a child may think logically

Table 10–1. Piaget's Preoperational Stage of Cognitive Development

Substage One: Preconceptual Phase (two to four years)
  Appearance of symbolic function
    deferred imitation and symbolic play
    rapid language development

Substage Two: Intuitive Phase (four to seven years)
  Inconsistent in the solution of concrete problems because both thought and language are:
    egocentric   focused on states
    centered   irreversible
    transductive

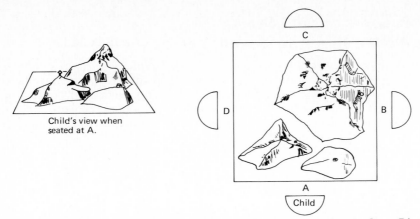

Three mountains problem. What does the doll see when seated at B, C, or D? Children's *egocentrism* prevents them from taking the view of others. They assume that others experience the world as they do. [From *The Child's Conception of Space* by Jean Piaget and Barbel Inhelder. Copyright © 1967 by Humanities Press, Inc. Reprinted by permission of Humanities Press, Inc., Atlantic Highlands, N.J.]

about a problem one day and regress the next day. With this in mind, let us look at the characteristics of preoperational thought that are barriers to concrete operations. The thought of the preoperational child is characteristically

1. Egocentric.
2. Centered.
3. Transductive.
4. Focused on states.
5. Irreversible.

Egocentric Thought*

Egocentric thought, according to Piaget, means that the child cannot mentally take the position of another. For example, in an experiment conducted by Piaget and Inhelder (1963) children from four to eleven years were shown a three-dimensional exhibit of three mountains. The mountains were placed on a table and the child sat in a chair at the table. A doll was seated in various positions around the table. Each child was then shown pictures that illustrated the view of the mountains from the four sides of the table. Each child was asked to choose the picture that showed what the doll saw. Can you guess the children's answers? Those children under six thought that the doll saw the same scene as they. Children between six and seven knew that the doll saw a different view but were not sure which one. They were in the intuitive phase, where sometimes reasoning is correct and sometimes not. Children between seven and nine more often chose correctly, but some still made errors. It was not until children were between nine and eleven that they consistently selected the correct view for the doll. To choose the correct view for the doll the child must mentally change the position of the mountains and

---

* Egocentric in this sense does not mean egotistic. Piaget himself has suggested that perhaps the choice of the term was unfortunate (Piaget, 1962, p. 285); nevertheless, it is the one used in the translation of his work from French to English.

visualize the scene. This image can then be compared with the actual photograph and the correct one selected. Actually, this is quite a complicated task. The young child has not had sufficient experience with the world nor does he or she have well enough developed mental structures to perform the transformations.

Children also demonstrate their egocentrism in everyday exchanges. Piaget (1962) reported this comment by his daughter to her mother, "You must have another little baby, then I'll have a little brother" (p. 232). In this statement, her desire for a baby brother distorted the reality that a new baby might be a girl. Young children do develop empathy for other people, however, and may offer a favorite toy or pacifier to comfort mother or father who has hurt a finger. Although the child can empathize that mother hurts, the thinking is that she will be comforted by the same things as the child, namely a pacifier.

Centration (Centered Thought)

The preoperational child centers on one aspect of an experience and cannot take into account other relevant dimensions when reasoning. This focus on a single aspect often leads to erroneous reasoning. For example, if pennies are arranged in two lines, each line containing the same number of pennies, but in one line the

DENNIS the MENACE

"WHEN I GROW UP I WANTA BE ITALIAN."

Children in the preoperational stage do not understand that people and things have an identity that is constant even when certain transformations take place. Young children believe that when they put on a cape they can actually *become* a superhero. In Piaget's terms, they have totally accommodated to their conceptions. Adults are often amused at these errors of thought, as the cartoon by Hank Ketcham illustrates. [DENNIS THE MENACE® used by permission of Hank Ketcham and © by Field Enterprises, Inc.]

distance between the pennies is greater, a preoperational child will conclude that the longer line has more pennies. In the same manner, if water in a tall thin glass is poured into a short wide one, the child will conclude that there is more water in the tall glass than in the short glass (or maybe the opposite). In this erroneous reasoning the child depends on *perceptions* rather than logic. Gradually the child begins to reason logically and dependence on perceptions is undermined.

Transductive Reasoning

"If I eat spaghetti, will I become Italian?" asks the preoperational child. The child observes that Luciano is Italian and Luciano eats spaghetti; therefore, he or she reasons that being Italian must be caused by eating spaghetti and eating spaghetti will cause him or her to become Italian. We laugh at the child who reasons in such a manner, yet transductive reasoning is rampant in popular culture: movie star X is sexually attractive; movie star X uses product Z; therefore, if I use product Z I will be sexually attractive. How many of us have bought a cosmetic, toothpaste, or other product based on such flimsy reasoning? Western rational thought is characterized by deductive and inductive thinking. The preoperational child, however, reasons neither deductively nor inductively, but transductively. Deductive reasoning is from the general to the particular: All children reason transductively. John is a child. Therefore, John reasons transductively. Inductive reasoning is from the particular to the general: John reasons transductively. John is a child. Therefore, children reason transductively. Transductive reasoning, on the other hand, reasons from particular to particular. In transductive reasoning when two events occur together in time or space, one is assumed to be the cause of the other without regard to their logical relationship. In inductive and deductive reasoning the relationship of events is from a particular event to a class or from a class to a particular event, whereas in transductive reasoning the movement is from particular event to particular event.

One reason that the preoperational child does not reason deductively and inductively is that the concepts of *class* and *class inclusion* have not been attained. The concepts of class and class inclusion are necessary before inductive and deductive reasoning is possible. For example, if an assumption is true of *all* members of a class, it *must* follow that it has to be true of any particular member of that class (deductive reasoning). In similar fashion, if a statement is true of particular members of a class, it *may* be (probably is) true of all members of the class. Deductive reasoning is infallible, provided that the first statement is true. Inductive reasoning is not infallible, but we can calculate the probability of it being true. There is always the chance that it may not be true for *all* members of the class. Children gradually outgrow transductive reasoning and begin to use systems of induction and deduction.

Focus on States

The preoperational child mentally moves from one static state to another and cannot take transformations into account. Even while they watch materials being physically changed they do not understand the process of transformation. When the physical appearance of a material is altered, young children are not sure that it is the same material. For example, if a ball of clay is transformed into an elongated shape, the preoperational child is not sure that it is the same. The preoperational child depends on perceptions and does not realize that things remain the same (retain identity) even when they change perceptually. Children may conclude that people become someone different in different clothes or places. When Piaget's daughter Jacqueline saw her sister Lucienne in a bathing suit and cap she wanted to know the baby's name, but when Lucienne was changed into a familiar dress, she remarked, "It's Lucienne again" (Piaget, 1962, p. 224).

Jacqueline also asked if she had been Lucienne when she was little. Similarily, children often refuse to believe that baby pictures of their parents actually are of their parents. This is quite logical within the framework of preoperational thought. When a little girl puts on a crown, she actually becomes a princess, and with a cape or costume the little boy becomes Superman. The preoperational child has not grasped the essential identity of objects which remains constant. While on a trip, Piaget's daughter saw the sun rise in an unaccustomed place and thought it was another sun. She had not attained the concept that the sun is the same sun when seen in different times and places. The preoperational child experiences events separately, constructing a different scheme for each experience. With increasing experience these schemes generalize and the concept of identity is achieved. When the child realizes that objects have an unchanging identity, he or she can reason that objects remain the same through physical transformations.

Irreversibility

When the child's thinking becomes reversible, different states of objects are linked one with another in such a way that movement in either direction is possible. When the child attains reversibility in thinking, she or he can mentally roll elongated clay back into a ball (reverse the process) and reason that the elongated clay is the same as the ball of clay. This movement is horizontal. Reversibility in think-

The thinking of the preoperational child is not *reversible*. Therefore a child may not understand the reciprocal relationship of both having a brother and being a brother. Because he centers on one relationship, he cannot understand that he is his brother's brother.

ing is also hierarchical as in reasoning about classes and groups. For example, boys are children. Children are people. People are mammals. Mammals are vertebrates. When reversibility is reached, one can reason up and down such a hierarchy. Reversibility, according to Piaget (1962), is "the possibility of retrieving an earlier state of the data which is not inconsistent with its present state . . . and is as real or as realisable as that present state" (p. 240). When reversibility is achieved, thought is mobile and concepts and judgements can be conserved in the face of changing situations and perceptual transformations.

What Does the Child Think About?

The preschool child uses thought in an avid exploration of objects in the world—in ideas of space, time, and causality. The thought of the preschool child proceeds in two directions simultaneously: in practical manipulations and in questions of origins.

Practical Manipulations

The preschool child continues sensorimotor experiments with solid and liquid objects in the world. These explorations enable the child to construct ideas about space, time, and objects. At the beginning these constructions are permeated with

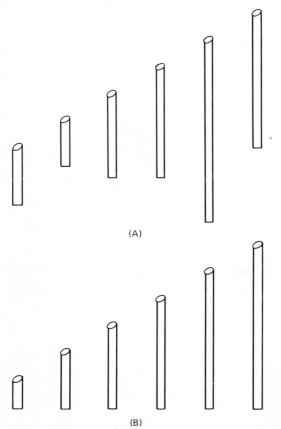

(A)

(B)

In arranging a set of sticks from shortest to longest, preoperational children are apt to focus on one level and fail to take into account the other ends of the sticks.

subjective elements such as personal perspective and his or her own muscular strength. Gradually they become more objective, and finally identity and reversibility are reached and true operations are possible. Two major tools that the child will use in dealing with objects and the relations among them are *seriation* and *classification*.

Seriation.   In constructing a logical view of reality, Western thought often uses the device of arranging objects, or even ideas in a series. Such a series has a logical basis and may range from large to small, earlier to later, lighter to darker, or any number of other dimensions. Through the elementary years the young child generally must deal with concrete objects in such tasks. We may ask a child to arrange sticks of various lengths in order from smallest to largest. The child younger than five or six may arrange the sticks with the tops ascending like stairs but overlook the irregular pattern at the bottom. This is an example of centration, in which the child centers on the top and ignores the bottom. Generally, six-year-olds are able to construct the series when they are given all the sticks at once; however, if asked to insert sticks into the series they may have difficulty.

Classification.   The ability to group objects that are alike is another basis for logical thought. There are many dimensions in which objects may be grouped, such as color, size, and shape. In preschool programs and the early elementary grades children are often given objects and told to "put things together that are alike." Young children find this task difficult. For example if children are given an assortment of different colored shapes such as circles, squares, and triangles and told to put things that are alike together, children of differing ages perform differently.

Children in the early preoperational stage (2–4) generally use these shapes to build constructions such as houses, animals, or people. They may begin to classify circles or squares but soon are distracted by the size or the color of the shapes and end up with piles of unrelated shapes which suggest the configurations. Late in the preoperational stage, between five and seven, children can consistently group objects that are alike together if there is only one dimension to consider—for example, they can group all the circles or all the triangles; all the large shapes or all the small shapes; all the blue shapes or all the red shapes. When the problem becomes more complicated as when children are asked to consider size, shape, and color in their groupings, even six-year-olds have difficulty. However, by the age of seven or eight, children can sort such shapes into large blue triangles, small red squares, and so forth.

Class Inclusion.   Even after children can consistently classify objects they have difficulty in understanding the relationship between groups at different levels in a classification system. That is, they have difficulty understanding that one class is included in another and that an object can be a member of two groups simultaneously. Piaget (1965) presented a box of wooden beads to children. All of the beads were brown with the exception of two, which were white. To test for the ability to understand class inclusion and the relationship between the whole class and a subclass, children were asked, "Are there more wooden beads or brown beads?" Children of six years, who were able to classify objects reliably on some dimension were unable to answer this question accurately. The usual answer was that there were more brown beads. When queried as to whether the brown beads were wooden, children agreed that they were made of wood. Having established that the

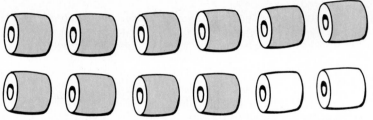

Are there more wooden beads or more white beads? This is a difficult question for a child in the preoperational stage to answer. (All these beads are wooden.)

brown beads and the white beads were wooden, and queried again whether there were more brown or wooden beads the children persisted in the answer that there were more brown beads. Piaget asked many questions to make sure that the children understood that all beads were wooden and rephrased the question in several ways, such as "if a necklace was made of the brown beads and of the wooden beads which would be longer?" In Piaget's study, children under seven or eight were unable to solve problems of class inclusion.

Questions of Origins

The preschool child is not only a scientist experimenting with the physical world, he or she is also a philosopher seeking the answers to philosophical questions. Such questions are possible because of the rapid development of language. The child seems almost driven by a constant barrage of "whys"—as anyone who has spent much time with a four- or-five-year-old knows. Children begin to form hypotheses about events and functions and seek verification from any available adult. In pursuit of the answer to origins, the child spontaneously develops many myths. These myths are partly based in intelligent investigation and partly in imaginative symbolism. The thinking of the child at this age is characterized by *artificialism* and *animism*.

Artificialism.   The preoperational child believes that everything was made by someone. In attempting to reason about nature, the child begins to experiment with cause-and-effect relationships. Piaget suggests that such inquiries begin with curiosity about birth. Consider the following statements and questions made by Jacqueline over a period of 27 months as she struggles to understand the origin of babies. Note that even when she has hit on the solution she wavers and the next day may revert to a former belief.*

Jacqueline: *"Daddy, where did you find the little baby in a cradle?"*
[3 yrs, 3 mos]   My reply was simply that mummy and daddy had given her a little sister.
[3 yrs, 7 mos]   *"How are babies made?"* and two days later: *"How are plums made?"* then *"and cherries?"* *"Where did that little baby come from* (i.e., L[ucienne]).

* Reprinted from *Play, Dreams, and Imitation in Childhood* by Jean Piaget, by permission of W. W. Norton & Company, Inc. Translated by C. Gattegno and F. M. Hodgson. Copyright 1951. All rights reserved.

Piaget: What do you think?

Jacqueline: *"I don't know. Out of the wood* (troubled). *There wasn't a little baby before."* The next day: *"She came out of the wood. A long way away in the trees. It was mummy who brought her out of the wood."*

[3 yrs, 8 mos] When we were in the wood we passed a woman with two small children: *"She's been looking for little babies."*

[3 yrs, 11 mos] *"That little baby was bought. They found her in a shop and bought her. Before that she was in the wood, and before that in a shop. I don't know all the rest."*

[4 yrs, 3 mo] *"It was daddy who went to fetch her. He found her at the edge of the water in the wood."*

[4 yrs, 10 mos] Babies came *"from the clinic. There's a mother in the clinic. All the babies in the clinic have the same mummy and then they change their mummy. This mummy gets them ready and then they grow. They have teeth and a tongue put in them."*

[5 yrs, 3 mos] J[acqueline] discovered some kittens behind the wood-pile. *"How did they come?"*

Piaget: What do you think?

Jacqueline: *"I think the mummy went to fetch them."*

[three weeks later] *"The babies were bought in a factory."* [Jacqueline had just been given guinea pigs to help her discover the true solution]; *"Where do little guinea pigs come from?"*

Piaget: What do you think?

Jacqueline: *From a factory."*

[5 yrs, 4 mos] *"What are you before you're born?"*

Piaget: Do you know?

Jacqueline: *"An ant. Lots of little ants* (laughing).*"*

[two days later] *"Are you dust before you are born? Are you nothing at all, are you air?"*

[5 yrs, 5 mos] [The guinea-pig gave birth to a litter during the night in a box in the hen-house, which was securely locked.] *"The mother guinea-pig went to fetch them."*

Piaget: How did she get out?

Jacqueline: *"Oh, the hen-house is locked. Then she made them!"*

Piaget: Yes, that's it.

Jacqueline: *"But where were they before?"*

Piaget: That's easy.

Jacqueline: *"In the mummy guinea-pig! Inside her! In her tummy!"*

[next day] *"Were the little guinea-pigs inside their mother? I think they were."* But two days later: *"They come from the factory."*

Mother: You know they don't.

Jacqueline: *"Where do babies come from?"*

Mother: What do you think?

Jacqueline: *"From inside you!"*

[5 yrs, 6 mos] *"How do babies make themselves? They're bubbles of air. They're very tiny. They get bigger and bigger and when they're big enough they come out from inside the mother's tummy."*

[next day] *"Babies are air at first, aren't they? They're so very small. So they must be air at first. But there must be something in the air that babies are made of: a tiny little bit like that* [pointing to some dust].*"* [pp. 246–47]

Each child spontaneously invents myths about the natural world. These myths are not restricted to where babies come from, but include change of seasons, weather, and other facets of nature. The child of five or six years begins to doubt his or her own conclusions but cannot quite arrive at the actual cause of events. Interaction with parents, teachers, and older children, who can lead the child to logical conclusions about these causes, are very important in taking the step to logical thinking. This is education in the best sense of the word. Without an opportunity to test hypotheses about natural events children may mentally remain in the twilight zone of mythical explanations. Mythical explanations have a great attraction for the child in us all as witnessed by the great charm that fairy tales hold. The scientific basis of Western thought encourages the child to ask questions about origins. Such questions, however, lack systematization and children are not immediately convinced that the scientific answers given by adults and older children are true. Thus, they give a logical, scientific explanation one day and a mythical one the next.

In Piagetian terms, the child assimilates natural processes to human activity, its own or another's. In the mind of the preoperational child someone made the sky, sun, moon, clouds, and wind. These things cannot happen without someone being responsible for their construction.

Animism.   Closely related to the myth that everything is made is the idea that everything has life. Thus, the preoperational child invests inanimate objects and forces with intentions and feelings. In this we see the child project internal feelings and experiences onto inert objects or physical forces. The child assimilates these objects into his or her schemes and by so doing distorts external reality. Consider the following statements by children (Piaget, 1962 p. 251):

> *"You can hear the wind singing. How does it do it?"*
> *"There aren't any boats on the lake; they're asleep."*
> *"Do they like dancing (dead leaves)?"*
> *"Why do clouds move? To hide the sun. It's funny, the sun moves. Why has it gone? To go and bathe in the lake? Why is it hiding?"*
> *"Is the grass real? It's moving."*
> *"The clouds go very slowly because they haven't any paws or legs; they stretch out like worms and caterpillars, that's why they go slowly."*
> *"Why don't stones die like insects when you put them in a box?"*

Piaget (1962) reports the decline in animism at about six years of age. In observing Jacqueline he reports,

> *At about [six years] there was little evidence of animism, except in affective reactions. For example, at [six years, five months, 21 days] she screamed with fright when the door of the hen-house, blown by the wind, hit her in the back. Then crying, she said: "The wind's horrid, it frightens us."*
> *[Piaget] But not on purpose.*
> *"Yes, on purpose. It's horrid, it said we were naughty."*
> *[Piaget] But does the wind know what it does?*
> *"It knows it blows."* (p. 251)
> *At [six years, seven months, eight days] I questioned J[acqueline] about her earlier remarks. Nothing was then alive except people and animals. Even the sun and the moon did not feel or know anything. At [six years, seven months, eighteen days] however, I told her that L[ucienne] had just said that the sun knew when it was fine:*
> *"Yes, she's right, because it's the sun that makes it fine. That's what I told you the other day."* (having said the opposite!)
> *"And does a stone know it's rolling?"*
> *"Oh, no, it's the person who throws it that knows."* (p. 251)

Children in the preconceptual stage of thought believe that everything was made by someone and that everything is alive.

Piaget reports that after that Jacqueline revealed no further trace of animism. These are preconcepts, which attempt to deal with causality. Slowly they are replaced by realistic concepts of the world *provided* the child participates in activities and language experiences with adults and older children, which lead them to more advanced concepts.

Piaget in Education

Piaget sees the child as the *active agent* in the learning process. In his view, children are constantly refining concepts of the world and of themselves through their *interaction* with objects and forces in the physical world and social exchanges with the social world. Through these interactions the child's mental constructions become increasingly organized, objective, and capable of handling abstractions. The element to stress here is that the child must be an active participant in the learning process. That means physically handling objects and manipulating them in endless ways. It means hypothesizing and trying to reason the answer, not being told the correct answer and repeating it by rote. Children can learn the words that are expected of them if they are pressured enough, but children do not believe words until they can verify them through their internal conviction. To see that this is true, you need only a few days with four- and five-year-olds. Even when they have been told facts, they "reason" around them and turn them this way and that. What they believe must be what they experience, and their mental experience of the world is different from that of adults. They, as do we all, finally believe their own experi-

(A)

(B)

(C)

(D)

(E)

In Piaget's view, children are constantly refining concepts of the world and of themselves through interaction with objects and forces in the physical world (A, B, C) and through social exchange (D, E). [Courtesy Helen Canaday, Administrative Director, Preschool Programs, University of North Carolina at Greensboro.]

ence. Education must exhibit patience and synchronize with the child's mental experience.

Can Piagetian Concepts be Accelerated?

The issue has naturally arisen whether, if the attainment of concepts is achieved through interaction with the environment, those concepts can be accelerated by intensive early training. Piaget considers this an "American question"—that is, Americans seem to consider early attainment of any skill or ability a mark of superiority. It is true that much research in America has been directed toward determining whether Piagetian concepts can be speeded up by specific learning experiences. The answer to this question is yes, and no. First, the ages that Piaget identifies for stages are actually a general average; individual children vary considerably in the ages at which they attain concepts. Research has suggested that American children may indeed reach the conservation stages somewhat earlier than the Swiss children Piaget studied. On the other hand, attempts to teach such concepts as seriation, classification, and conservation generally indicate that if the child is close to reaching the concept, teaching may accelerate the attainment; however, if the child is not close, teaching does not seem to affect the attainment. Apparently, in developing such concepts there is a time at which the child wavers in his or her conviction. It is at that time that instruction may push the concept forward. For an illustration, see Jacqueline and Piaget discussing where babies come from. Piaget considers verbally acquired responses to specific situations to be "deformed." Such responses are unstable and not permanent. The child cannot generalize this response to similar situations and will revert to former errors when confronted with the same problem in a different context. To attain true concepts the child must reach an internal equilibrium (Pulaski, 1971).

Language Development in Early Childhood

The years between three and six are a time of rapid progress with language. Words seem literally to explode from the young child. But language growth is not simply accumulating words. The young child is also a remarkable grammarian—that is, he or she uses the rules of grammar and syntax that older students (including those at college level) struggle to understand. The development of this remarkable ability has received much attention both theoretical and empirical. We will examine here the sequence of language development, and some of the factors that affect individual differences in acquiring language.

Vocabulary

As previously stated the average two-year-old knows approximately fifty words. After the attainment of representational thought this rate of acquisition skyrockets. In the third year the number of words a child learns quadruples and at three the child knows about two hundred words. In a recent study of the language use and language development of preschool children (Kayler, 1983), two-year-olds had average vocabularies of 160 to 170 words and used an average of three-and-one-half words a minute. Three-year-olds had average vocabularies of 206 to 245 words and used an average of four words a minute; while four-year-olds used 394

Table 10–2.   Language Development in Early Childhood

Age	Vocabulary	Understanding
3 yrs., 6 mos.	Uses 4 or more prepositions, on, in, under, in back of, etc; tells about a picture; names 3 objects in picture	Discriminates between big and little
3 yrs., 6 mos.– 4 yrs.	Says full name; tells experiences; recites a nursery rhyme, poem, or song; names colors	
4 yrs.	Uses 5-word sentences; uses adverbs and adjectives; much questioning; multiple responses in answer to questions	Understands compound sentences; able to follow two action directions: "Get the book in your room and bring it to me."
4 yrs., 6 mos.	Uses words to express cause and effect and simple relationships; can use words to classify by size, shape, and color, but may not understand fully the concept	Understands two simple relationships: "A bird flies, a fish _____ ."
4 yrs., 6 mos.– 5 yrs.	"Reads" pictures; draws with a pencil; prints simple words	
5 yrs.	Uses compound and complex sentences; uses pronouns correctly; defines two or more words; gives age; uses description in telling a story; retells familiar stories and personal experiences; uses words to describe location, distance, sizes, weights, weather and time	Understands abstractions; follows logic as answers are direct and pertinent; can give main theme of pictures
5 to 6 yrs.	Relates fanciful tales; names coins (penny, nickle, dime); recites numbers; asks meaning of words	
6 yrs.	Language complete in structure and form; uses interpretation in telling a story of picture; recalls main details of stories; tells original stories; recognizes verbal absurdities; sense of humor	Anticipates outcomes; draws conclusions; makes inferences; understands like and opposite; expresses gratitude; has logical sequence in story telling

to 404 different words at rates averaging nine to thirteen words a minute. In an early survey Smith (1926) estimated that the average six-year-old knows 2,500 words, but more recently Carey (1977) estimated that the vocabulary of the six-year-old is between 8,000 and 14,000 words. Both of these assessments are probably accurate. We can attribute the larger vocabulary of six-year-olds fifty years later to exposure to television and other mass media.

Preschool children are especially sensitive to new words and do not have to understand them fully to use them. Whenever they hear a new word, you can be sure that it will appear in a conversation in the near future, even if it is misused. Adults are often amused at the malapropisms of young children. They learn to use profanity quite accurately, however, which all families are sure they learned from the neighbor's children! Young children are so entranced with words that they quite readily make up their own. The results are quite creative: for example, *stocks* to indicate articles of clothing between socks and stockings. Not only do preschool children learn a lot of words, they gain phenomenal skill in reproducing the structure of language.

Plurals and Verb Tense

The toddlers' two-word sentences usually consist of a noun and a verb. These sentences name a person, a place, a thing, and an action, such as "Mama gone," "Me sleepy," "Doggie come." From three to six years children make assumptions about the structure of language and try out those assumptions. They hypothesize rules for making nouns plural and for changing the tense of verbs, and they begin to use prepositions, modifiers, articles, and other grammatical rules of language without ever having been told, "This is the rule." Children make rules that are hard and fast and they generalize the rules in all cases. In fact, they *overgeneralize* the rules. English has many irregular verb and noun forms that must be learned separately. When young children apply a rule incorrectly, we can infer from the incorrect form the rule that they are generalizing. For example, children apparently form the hypothesis that to indicate more than one of the same object, the rule is to add *s*. Thus, children may speak of *deers, sheeps,* and *mouses.* Clearly these are not words that they have heard adults use, so they are not producing language by imitation (as the social-learning theorists hold). The logical explanation for these new productions is that the child has created a rule for plurals and is applying that rule.

To find whether children had memorized words or were indeed using rules that they had generated, Jean Berko (1958) devised a test using nonsense verbs and nouns. She presented such problems as the following: The child was shown an imaginary creature and told, "This is a wug. Now there is another one. There are two of them. There are two _____." The child was asked to supply the plural of the noun *wug*. The child had to apply its self-made rule to produce the word *wugs*. We notice that children generate this rule when they begin to make plurals of such words as *sheeps*. In a similar fashion we know that they have discovered a rule for putting verbs into the past tense when they produce sentences such as:

> *I* holded *Patricia's new puppy.*
> *Grandpa* goed *with me.*
> *We* runned *all the way home.*

Children also persist with these forms. A usual conversation between a child and an adult about Patricia's new puppy might be the following,

> *"You mean you held Patricia's new puppy."*
> *"Yes, that is what I said, I* holded *it."*

This responsiveness to correction by adults indicates again that children are guided more by their own logical rules than by adults modeling language.

Sentences

The child develops the ability to communicate in meaningful ways through an identifiable sequence. In the preschool years the *holophrase* (one-word sentence) of the toddler becomes elaborated into the *telegraphic* sentence (the bare bones of verbal communication). The one-word sentence expresses an entire communication in a word, as in *eat* or *mine*. Communicating with a two-word sentence is great progress for the toddler. In the third stage the child *elaborates* this basic structure of the sentence reflecting more complex relations with a three-part sentence consisting of an agent—an action—and an object. The child constructs such sentences as "Mommy go store" and "Dog hurt me." From this skeletal sentence structure the child adds prepositions such as, *on, in,* and *of,* articles such as *a* and *the,* and case endings for plural nouns and verb tense. These are elaborations on the simple declarative sentence.

By the age of five children are able to use complex adverbial clauses as well as noun phrases and verb phrases. Language development continues throughout the elementary school years, but it is not until the child is eleven or twelve years old that language is fully developed. As already mentioned, the first sentences produced are simple declarative sentences. Other types of sentences are more difficult for the young child to understand and produce.

Negative Sentences

In the structure of the English language the negative is constructed by transforming the simple declarative sentence. Thus, the sentence, "The boy is riding the tricycle" can be made negative by adding the negative *not:* "The boy is *not* riding the tricycle." Young children typically construct negative sentences by adding the word *no* to an affirmative sentence:

> *"No bed." (I do not want to go to bed.)*
> *"No push truck." (Do not push my truck.)*
> *"Daddy no here." (I cannot find Daddy.)*

It appears that children in many different languages including Russian, Japanese, and French begin negations in the same way (McNeill & McNeill, 1968). Bloom (1973) has suggested that children first use *no* to indicate absence or nonexistence, as when a person or thing is no longer present. For example, in the preceding example, "Daddy no here" indicates that Daddy is gone. The second use of *no* is to indicate rejection. The phrase *no bed* indicates rejection of going to bed. Later the child uses *no* as denial in which *no* is a substitution for *not.* For example, if the child requests Coca-Cola and is given juice, the response might be "No co-co," meaning, "This is not Coca-Cola." Soon after mastering these negations the child can construct grammatically correct sentences using negative constructions. Menyuk (1964) related the following constructions by a child approximately three years of age:

> *You can't knock mine down.*
> *I didn't have any turns.*
> *You won't kick it down yet?*
> *It's not getting dark either.* (p. 134)

Questions

In the first stage of one-word sentences, the child phrases questions by intonation. Rising intonation indicates a question. The word *cookie* with falling intonation may express the child's attempt to name an object, whereas the word with rising inflection may mean "May I have a cookie?" or "Is that a cookie?" Thus, even the very young child indicates a basis for the use of the interrogative to acquire information about the world. One of the characteristics of the language of the preschool child is the liberal use of *why, when, where, which, what, who,* and *how.* Psycholinguists call these wh-questions. In tracing the development of questions, linguists distinguish between those requiring a simple yes–no answer and those requesting more extensive information. For example, when the child can say, "Look at Peter ride the tricycle," it requires only a simple transformation of word order to ask, "Can Peter ride the tricycle?" This is a question that requires a yes–no answer. The transformation consists of placing the word *can* in place of *Look at*. Wh-questions, however, are more complex and require further transformation on the part of the child. The question, "Where did Peter ride the tricycle?", requires a conception of *location* or *time* which is replaced by *Where* at the beginning of the sentence. This sentence requires an answer with information such as "Peter rode the tricycle to the park with his mother." When children can use the wh-question form, a world of information opens to them via questions such as

> Where does the sun go when it disappears?
> Why does the rain fall down?
> Where do babies come from?
> How does God make apples?
> When will I be all grown up?

Teachers and parents are often mentally challenged by the chain of whys that the four- and five-year-old asks.

Passive Voice

The simple declarative sentence and its transformation into a question are easily mastered by the young child. When sentences are phrased in the passive voice, however, children have difficulty understanding who is performing the action. Consider the following sentences:

> The dog chases the cat.
> The cat is chased by the dog.

In the first sentence children clearly understand that the dog does the chasing. In the second sentence the intent is not so clear. Preschool children often understand sentences of this kind to indicate that the cat does the chasing. In a similar way young children cannot understand satire, sarcasm, and jokes based on subtle word play. Parents and teachers are advised to speak in direct language and to avoid sarcasm. This does not mean talking down to the child but speaking directly, openly, and honestly. If a child needs correcting, he or she should be told what is wrong rather that be given a sarcastic, "You certainly left a clean desk," when the intent is, "You really messed up your desk, and I am unhappy about it."

Preschool children do enjoy giggling over jokes, either jokes about bathroom functions or nonsense jokes such as, "Why did the chicken cross the road?" When adults are stumped on the answer to this, children collapse in peals of laughter as they instruct, "To get to the other side."

Articulation

Articulation is another facet of language development in children that has been studied considerably. Young children typically have trouble making the sounds of language. Each language has a number of distinctive sounds characteristic of it. English has 44 such sounds (even though there are only 26 different letters in the alphabet). Some letters, particularly vowels, have several sounds and some blends (such as *ch, th*) have a distinctive sound. These sounds are called phonemes. The immature speech we call baby talk reflects the difficulty that the preschooler has in producing phonemes. In most cases the child acquires the ability to produce the

I saw the
cat chased
by a dog.

Young children may misunderstand a communication in the passive voice because to understand it they must reverse the order of action that they have learned in simple declarative sentences.

more mature sounds as he or she grows older; by seven years of age most children have mastered the sounds. Generally it is best not to call undue attention to these mispronunciations, letting time take care of them. It is best for adults to speak clearly and distinctly to children. Some typical problems in articulation are,

th for *s*   *thoup* instead of *soup*
w for *r*   *wabbits* instead of *rabbits*

When problems of articulation continue into the elementary school years, some speech therapy may be needed.

Receptive and Expressive Language

The child's understanding of language (reception) is usually advanced beyond his or her ability to produce language forms (expression). This is evident when children of a year or eighteen months of age are able to follow simple directions, yet their ability to produce language is quite limited. Similarly, a three-year-old may follow a story line quite well when read to, yet not be able to retell the story with the events in sequence. Adults are often misled about a child's competence when they take the child's production of language as an indication of his or her ability to

Children can understand many more words than they can use, and enjoy listening to stories whether they hear them read aloud or, like this girl, on recordings.

This young girl is using "inner speech" to guide her behavior as she types her name on a type-writer. [Courtesy Helen Canaday, Administrative Director, Preschool Programs, University of North Carolina at Greensboro.]

understand. A word of caution is in order, however, for children also use words they do not understand. It is easy for teachers of young children to assume that children have attained a concept when they use words easily. For example, children learn easily the number words *one, two, three,* etc. However, teachers of young children soon discover that the children do not so easily grasp the underlying concept of number that these words reflect. Similarly, children glibly use words such as *biodegradable, ultrasonic,* and *bionic,* giving the impression that they understand the words, when they may, in fact, only be repeating them. Skillful teachers and parents will question and probe to lead children to understand and explore concepts.

A concept related to receptive language is inner speech. In the early years, learning becomes increasingly controlled by language. As children play they can be observed repeating the words that direct and control their behavior. For example, a child in kindergarten playing in the housekeeping corner can be heard talking to her- or himself.

Now, put the baby to bed. Be sure to turn the light out and tuck in the covers. Now, you must cook dinner, because we have to eat at 5 o'clock.

This speech becomes more internalized as the child grows older. In the elementary school classroom you can see nine-year-olds doing arithmetic and almost hear the inner speech, "nine and three are twelve."

Group Differences in Language

Linguists have studied the structure and content of language—grammar, sound combinations, and meaning—as they make generalizations across cultures. Divisions within the field of linguistics include *psycholinguistics,* the study of the relationship between language and the characteristics of the individual language user, and *sociolinguistics,* the study of the language or dialect differences associated with ethnic, geographic, and social-class variables. We will now look at some of the differences in language acquisition.

Restricted and Elaborated Language

Linguists have found that different families have different styles of language. Two distinct styles have been identified: restricted and elaborated (Bernstein, 1970).

Restricted language consists largely of exclamations or incomplete sentences and depends largely on stereotyped repetitions of expressions that are popular in the folk culture. Communications tend to be repetitive and redundant and highly charged emotionally. Often the nonverbal emotive component of the communication carries more of the message than the words. This restricted language underscores action and supports moods but is an inefficient method of conveying precise information.

Elaborated language more nearly resembles written language. Sentences tend to be complete and grammatically correct, and there is relatively little redundancy or repetition. This formal, elaborated language tends to be accompanied by few gestures and emotions. Many families, especially middle-class families, may use restricted language in intimate groupings, but they switch to the more formal structure on special occasions, when strangers are present or when there is a need to convey more precise information. Thus, children from these families tend to speak two languages. They can communicate in the more primitive restricted language

(A)

(B)

Adults can assist children in their cognitive development through talking with them as they explore materials and concepts (A) and by careful questioning of the meaning of their verbalizations (B). Children from restricted environments need special attention in the learning process. This child (C) is blind and is receiving special instruction in coordinating touch and verbalizations. Each child brings unique experiences and abilities to the classroom. Teachers cannot assume that every child is building the same concepts from the material presented. [Courtesy Helen Canaday, Administrative Director, Preschool Programs, University of North Carolina at Greensboro; (B) and (C) also courtesy Robert Cavin.]

(C)

and they can switch to the formal language in which words convey exact meanings and stand on their own, independent of the action being carried on.

The child who comes from a home in which the only language spoken is restricted learns to disregard words and to read the emotion in a communication. Often such homes are crowded, noisy, and disorganized. The child learns to tune out words and to pay attention to the louder, more emotionally laden signals. In such an environment the child may seldom be required to deal with the abstraction of words as his or her experience has primarily been with the more primitive stimuli. This child approaches school accomplished in disregarding the unique communicative function of words as symbols that stand alone. The child who begins school with only a restricted language at his or her command begins at a considerable disadvantage when compared to the child who begins with five or six years' experience with elaborated language.

These two children also are likely to have had a different experience with the written word. In the home which uses elaborated language, the child is likely to have had books read to him or her since infancy by parents and caregivers. Perhaps in quiet moments he or she will sit contentedly turning pages and looking at books. In contrast some of the children from homes in which only restricted language is used have never owned a book. The parents themselves may be illiterate and the homes may be devoid of either magazines or newspapers. These children have never been read to, have never quietly turned the pages of a book; and, in fact, may not know the left-to-right sequence for reading or the correct way to turn the pages of a book. When the first-grade teacher gathers these children in a group and begins to read a story to them and later to discuss it, the child from the elaborated-language home will show the increased attention that has been learned in those warm, intimate experiences when he or she was read bedtime stories. The child from the restricted-language home will show decreased attention because in the emotionally charged language of home he or she learned that you do not need to listen to soft voices. In the experience of the middle-class child, language plays a unique and important role. The child is reinforced by interesting experiences for listening closely to different words. There is little temptation to tune words out and there are many rewards for giving words high priority. The classroom is simply one more place to use the elaborated, formal language with which they are already familiar.

No small amount of effort and money has been expended to compensate for the differences in school achievement of middle- and lower-social-class youngsters. However, it must be noted that not all studies have found this social-class difference. We will explore this issue later in the chapter in the section on compensatory education.

Individual Differences

Other differences exist in language development besides social class. Girls tend to acquire language facility sooner than boys and continue to perform better than boys in tests of aptitude and achievement for language until far into the school years. Somewhere in the high school years the two seem to equate. The reasons for this difference have not been identified.

The composition of families seems to be related to language development. Twins develop language more slowly than single children, and children from large families show less advanced development than children from small families. Although research has not revealed the causes of these differences, the hypotheses have been advanced that twins communicate with each other and are not motivated to develop communication with other members of the family. It has also been suggested that children from large families receive less attention from parents and, thus less language stimulation, than children from small families. If a year-old child spends most of his or her time in the company of a two-year-old whose language production is barely beginning, the language environment is not highly stimulating. Children with low intelligence do not develop language as rapidly as children who are brighter, and so their vocabulary and comprehension are limited.

Bilingualism and Dialect Differences

Many children come from homes in which standard English is not the family language. There are regional dialects, for example, in New England, the South, and in many black families. These dialects have their own rules for construction and pronunciation, which differ from standard English. In black English, for example, the verb *to be* is not conjugated as in standard English. The word *be* serves many purposes:

> *I be going home. [I am going home.]*
> *My sister be upstairs. [My sister is upstairs.]*
> *You be going to the game? [Are you going to the game?]*

Linguists have been at a loss as to whether to consider these dialects inferior nonstandard English or another language. Initially such dialects were considered inferior and educators attempted to change the language behavior of children who spoke them. Then the pendulum swung to the opposite position with the Civil Rights movement in the late 1960s and 1970s, and many educators accepted black English as correct in spoken and written work. This issue has not been fully resolved, but it seems clear that higher education, national and international business, and society functions through the medium of standard elaborated language, English or otherwise. It seems equally clear that anyone who is to achieve in education or business must master the tools of those systems.

Bilingualism is related to the question of dialects. Children in the United States who learn to speak a language other than English at home are bilingual. Our school systems have many children who come from Indian tribes and who live near French-speaking Quebec and Spanish-speaking Mexican communities. In addition, the United States continues to have a large influx of immigrants from South America and Asia and moderate numbers from Europe and Africa. The first language of these children is usually the language of their parents. The English learned in school and in the larger society becomes their second language. In the past these children have been pressured to use English in the schools and even punished for using their native language. Coleman (1966) found that children for whom English was the second language did better in school when their lessons were presented in their native language. They also performed better on IQ tests when they were written in their native language, in contrast with children who speak a dialect. Because these differences were found for bilingual children, an attempt has recently been made to offer lessons in the children's native language. Again, the evidence is not clear, and the future of bilingual education is uncertain.

Compensatory Education in the Great Society ———————

In the 1950s America entered a period of unprecedented affluence. Post-World War II productivity raised the income of millions of American families, and industrial profits soared. The country was riding high on a feeling of well-being and self-satisfaction. Various writers and social critics threw bombshells into this complacency with the charge that there was an "other America" (Harrington, 1964) characterized by hunger, poor education, joblessness, and hopelessness. Critics went on to state that these people were systematically excluded from participation in affluent America and that the major tool for this exclusion was the education the poor received. The cycle of poverty perpetuated itself in that poor education excluded those other Americans from obtaining jobs, which meant that they had little money or power to purchase the health care, food, and education that would equip their children to participate in the larger society.

In answer to this social criticism, Lyndon Johnson (1908–1973), then president of the United States, launched a plan for "The Great Society" in which all citizens would have equal access to the benefits of the society. It was known as the War on Poverty. Social scientists and child development experts joined in an alliance with government agencies to plan a strategy for conducting that war. It was fought on many fronts, including job training, legislation for civil rights, increased welfare benefits, and, most importantly for the study of child development, *compensatory education*.

Rationale for Compensatory Education ———————

Compensatory education is based on the rationale that all children do not begin the educational race at the same starting line. Children from middle-class, advantaged homes begin first grade or kindergarten with a considerable head start in the learning process because of the experiences provided at home and in society. Children from impoverished homes, however, enter first grade with little or no previous experience on which to base learning. Poor children begin school behind their middle-class counterparts in the educative process and fall further behind as the years progress. At the end of ten or twelve years of schooling the middle-class child moves on into technical training, college, and managerial, professional, and business opportunities: into participation in the affluent America. The disadvantaged child may end public school as a drop-out or, with no hope for further training, may enter the unskilled labor force with few opportunities for advancement, thereby perpetuating the other America and the poverty cycle.

Compensatory education was dedicated to breaking that cycle by *compensating* for the deficits that the disadvantaged child brings to school. The major focus of compensatory education was on the preschool child. The decision to concentrate compensatory education on the child under six was based on two very important pieces of scientific evidence: the influence of early experience on intelligence and the stabilization of this intelligence early in life. The spokesman for these two lines of reasoning were Benjamin Bloom (1964) and J. McVickers Hunt (1961). On the basis of massive research data they reinterpreted the concept of human intelligence and challenged the traditional idea that intelligence is fixed, or predetermined, by genetic forces. Instead, Hunt argued, intelligence is a network of central neural

These children from an inner city neighborhood attend a community program, Happy Club, that gives them an opportunity for outdoor experiences, organized group play, and creative activities such as puppetry, music, and arts and crafts. Such programs for children with limited economic and educational resources have a strong positive impact, particularly in areas of leadership, communication skills and self-esteem. The experience of this community effort at the Meher Spiritual Center, Inc. in Myrtle Beach, South Carolina has been that the children are the pivotal element around which services for the entire community have been established. This has been borne out in many other programs and communities. [Courtesy Micky Lawn.]

processes and information-processing strategies that is significantly affected by the kinds of experiences a child encounters in his or her environment.

Bloom (1964), on the basis of longitudinal studies and other data, concluded that intellectual development reaches its highest rate of growth during the early years of childhood and that by the time a child reaches six years of age, approximately 75 per cent of intellectual capacity has already been developed. The obvious conclusion then was that children who began school with lowered learning capacities were operating from irreparable deficits that could only widen in the years of schooling. First grade was already too late to change the path of educational progress. The schools could only work with what the homes had already developed and, perhaps if excellent techniques were used, add one-quarter growth. Clearly, some *intervention* was necessary to provide children experiences that would stimulate their intellectual development to full capacity. The first program to attempt this task was Project Head Start.

Head Start

In the summer of 1965 a program was launched that was designed to provide to large numbers of educationally disadvantaged children a preschool experience. The Head Start program was initially modeled on existing nursery schools. That is, the program was based on the belief that developmental stages are primarily determined by genetic influences. Those developmental stages are nurtured by educational environments to the extent that a good environment enables the stage to unfold easily and fully. A good environment can also guide development in constructive directions for, "as the twig is bent . . . " (Cowles, 1971). The first summer program enrolled four- and five-year-old children whose socioeconomic status predicted failure or, at best, marginal success in elementary schools. After the first summer the program enrolled children for a full academic year prior to their entering kindergarten or first grade. Within a year Head Start programs were established all over the country and hundreds of thousands of children were attending. This rapid growth necessitated an instantaneous bureaucracy with staff, teachers, aides, and administrators. Many of them were inexperienced and relatively untrained, with the result that the program was uneven in the early years.

Head Start was directed not only at relieving educational disadvantages of children, but also at seeking to involve parents by providing social and health services and offering career development for adults. The staff that worked with children were parents recruited from low-income areas. In the first six years of the program more than nine thousand people of low-income and ethnic backgrounds received a college education as a result of having participated in Head Start (Zigler, 1972). From the beginning Head Start was guided by the following principles (Grotberg, 1969):

1. Improving the child's physical health and physical abilities.
2. Helping the child's emotional and social development by encouraging self-confidence, spontaneity, curiosity, and self-discipline.
3. Improving the child's mental processes and skills, with particular attention focused on conceptual and verbal skills.
4. Establishing patterns and expectations of success for the child, which would create a climate of confidence for future learning efforts.
5. Increasing the child's capacity to relate positively to family members and others, while strengthening the family's ability to relate positively to the child and his or her problems.
6. Developing in the child and his family a responsible attitude toward society and fostering constructive opportunities for society to work with the poor in solving their problems.
7. Increasing the sense of dignity and self-worth in the child and his or her family.

The first full-scale evaluation of Head Start, the Westinghouse Study, found that children with Head Start experience maintained a below-average position on national norms for standardized tests of language development and scholastic achievement (Cicirelli, Evans & Schiller, 1969). The conclusion of specialists in the field was that Head Start was "too little, too late." Therefore, demonstration projects were designed and launched to deliver more and to deliver it earlier: highly structured behavior-modification programs, Piagetian approaches, Open Education, intensive language drill, and infant education. We will review these briefly here because they have served as models for early childhood education and will continue to do so. However, one last word about Head Start is in order. Later evaluations of Head Start were more positive as Head Start children experience fewer retention and fewer placements in special education than similar children without Head Start experience (Lazar & Darlington, 1978). Although students have never made significant and lasting IQ gains as a result of the program, many critics voiced the opinion that IQ gain was an erroneous measure of success and that the program has been worth the effort in social gains: in a rise in children's self-concept and in parental involvement in the education of their children. Many other experimental programs in preschool education were attempted at this time. These experiments have left a lasting effect on preschool education. Because language ability is a major factor in measuring intelligence and ultimately separates children in the school years, as soon as language differences were identified as the key to success in advantaged and disadvantaged youngsters, the immediate question was what and how to teach for language development. The question was answered in different ways in different programs. Many programs for compensatory education had strong language components. One major effect of this emphasis was to change the priorities of early childhood education from *socialization* to *academic competence*. Whether this is a desirable redirection of priorities remains to be proven. Programs directed to fostering language development ranged from highly structured artificial situations to an exploitation of children's natural productions. We will review some of them here.

Language Development Programs

Patterned Language Drill (Distar).   The Distar Instructional System was developed and packaged for commercial use by Science Research Associates. The program consists of carefully prepared instructional objectives and procedures arranged in increasing complexity and inclusiveness. The system has a language, arithmetic, and reading component. The recommended class size is thirty students and three or more teachers. Groups of seven or eight children meet with a teacher and engage in a patterned leader-response language exchange. These exchanges lead the children to the correct responses in the use of such language concepts as affirmative and negative statements, prepositions, class concepts, and simple deductive reasoning using if-then, if-not, and if-or forms, as well as in other basic thinking skills using language. The children do not manipulate materials in gaining these concepts but rather gain them through a fast-paced language experience such as the following (Evans, 1975):

Teacher presents a tall plastic bottle full of colored liquid: Is this bottle tall?

Children: Yes!
 Teacher: Is this bottle full?
Children: Yes!
 Teacher: Is this bottle tall and full?
Children: Yes!
 Teacher: Say the whole thing!
Children: This bottle is tall and full!

Tutorial Programs.   Another approach to stimulating language development in early childhood avoided the group-response approach characteristic of Distar and stressed individual interaction between a teacher and one student. These individual fifteen- to twenty-minute lessons are interspersed throughout the school day. Through them the child develops the language skills necessary to thinking. Instead of set-patterned responses the child is led to develop skill in questioning and probing for information and for logical connections. The use of language to structure and guide thinking is stressed rather than specific vocabulary. Through these techniques the child gradually realizes that much of the information about the world is not self-evident, but that knowledge can be derived from his or her own experiences.

The program content is built around concepts such as number, speed, direction, temperature, and emotions. The creators of the program (Blank & Solomon, 1968, 1969) designed the strategies to compensate for the deficiencies in thinking that they theorized characterize a disadvantaged child. Some of those deficiencies have to do with the child's sense of control, such as an awareness of possessing language to make changes in the world, the use of inner language to regulate his or her own behavior, and the ability to attend to some stimuli while ignoring others. Some have to do with language skills, such as the ability to categorize. Others have to do with the level of abstract thinking, such as conceptualizing future events, using models for cause-and-effect reasoning, understanding words as symbols that are separate from objects or actions, and sustaining sequential thinking.

Peabody Language Development Kit.   A third approach to language development for disadvantaged youngsters was developed by Dunn and Smith (1965). In this method language is stimulated in a gamelike atmosphere. Teaching sessions are structured as interludes from regular classroom work and utilize a large variety of materials, such as picture cards, story posters, puppets, mannequins, plastic fruits and vegetables, magnetic geometric shapes, and sound recordings. The teacher is given general suggestions for managing the learning environment and specific directions for sequencing activities in individual lessons.

Tucson Early Education Model.   The approach to language development that avoided structured approaches began with the child's own spontaneous language production, including vocabulary, syntax, and dialect. The key to it is individualized instruction and is based on the child's natural biological capacity for language learning (Hughes, Wetzel and Henderson, 1969). The developers of this system believe that this natural capacity can be developed best by an environment rich in language stimulation and opportunities for language expression. In this method such everyday activities as cooking, walking, and bus trips are organized to stimulate sensory perceptions and verbalizations. The teacher records the child's exact verbal productions and analyzes them to find cues to structure the next level of individualized instruction. The teacher responds to the child's short verbalizations with expanded sentences and leads the child to verbal recall and other language skills.

Many of these techniques and commercial materials are now widely used in eclectic programs for early childhood education. Stimulation of language development continues to be a priority in early childhood education, so the methods have made an immeasurable contribution to the field.

Behavior Analysis Program: Behavior Modification

Behavior analysis programs are based on the scientific laws of behavior advanced by B. F. Skinner. The technology that has been developed from these laws is known as *behavior modification*. As this technology is applied to early childhood education it encompasses a highly structured environment of cues and reinforcement contingencies. The teacher controls the cues and the reinforcements and, by means of them, controls both the academic and social behavior of the child. Whenever possible positive reinforcement is used, not because of concern for the child's inner emotional condition, but because positive reinforcement leads to more efficient learning. However, negative reinforcement and punishment are also used to condition the child's behavior. Teaching in a behavioral analysis system requires careful attention to schedules of reinforcements. In addition, the learning activities are very carefully sequenced in small steps and stated in observable behavioral objectives; this maximizes the probability of the child's academic progress. Educational techniques such as token economy, time out, programmed and individualized instruction, team teaching, and the teaching machine have been developed within the behavior analysis framework. (Bushell, 1973). The practical objectives of programs built on behavior analysis are to increase appropriate social and academic responses and to decrease inappropriate responses (Resnick, 1967; Risley, 1969).

Piagetian Preschools

Piaget's cognitive theory has had a strong impact on the direction of early childhood education. Yet, although Piaget wrote extensively on the cognitive development of children and conducted many experiments, he made no pronouncements on how the school experience should be organized to effect that development. Advocates of his theory have had to attempt translating it into practice with little guidance from Piaget. Piaget has offered only three suggestions for teachers: (1) provide children with actual objects to manipulate, (2) assist children in their development of question-asking skills, and (3) know why particular operations are difficult for children. Preschools based on Piagetian theory are generally loosely structured, provide many different objects for children to handle, and encourage a casual interaction among students, teachers, and materials. Child–child interactions and exploration of materials are encouraged, as are teacher–child interactions. In this atmosphere the child learns by active self-discovery and inductive reasoning. The teacher guides learning by arranging novel and challenging experiences and by asking probing questions about the child's discoveries. The curriculum in Piagetian-based preschools is usually focused on classification and seriation and exploring the physical world in terms of number, measurement, and space operations. Through these activities the child forms representations of self and the environment and is led to use them in increasingly complex thinking operations by the teachers (Lavatelli, 1970). Staff development is very important in a Piagetian school. The teachers must understand the basis for the learning experience and question each child carefully to understand the mental structures in progress. Much of the activity in these preschools may look like aimless wandering. The teacher must be able to discriminate between activity that leads to further growth and that which is simply to pass time.

Open Education

Open education as it is practiced in preschools in the United States owes much to the British Infant Schools. These schools are based on Piaget's theories and on those of the philosopher John Dewey (1859–1952). Open education has many forms but all maintain the position that children are innately motivated to learn and curious about their world; children spontaneously display activity and exploratory behavior directed toward this learning; learning is best accomplished through social exchanges; there are individual differences in rate and style of learning; and that children develop best in a permissive atmosphere (Barth, 1972). In open schools the children set the pace for learning. Teachers plan lessons on the basis of cues from the children and their readiness to learn. The key to learning in the open classroom is *interaction*—among children, teachers, and materials. The open classroom stresses play and the concept of learning as fun, or at least as enjoyable.

Compensatory education in the 1960s and 1970s was serious business, as the objective was to equip children for work in later life. Thus, open education, with its casual, child-paced structure and permissiveness, came under severe criticism. With the open classroom, however, educational practice has come full circle, for this method has much in common with the traditional nursery school, kindergarten, and play schools. Open education also is the direct descendent of Dewey's Progressive Education, which made an impact on American public education in the 1930s. It was abandoned in the 1950s when the schools were charged to produce students who could compete with the more advanced technology of the Russians. Open Education, Progressive Education, and the traditional nursery school are all dedicated to developing the whole child. In recent years facets of preschool and upper-level education have been focused on intellectual development alone. We are at a crossroads now and are again reexamining the direction that schools for our children should take. The question we must all answer still is: How do we want these children to grow, and what do we want them to become?

Education Through Television: "Sesame Street"

The creation of "Sesame Street" was a direct result of society's concern with providing disadvantaged children experiences in words and symbols that were already available to most middle-class children. "Sesame Street" began as an experiment that was underwritten by private foundations and the federal government. The initial cost was eight *million* dollars over a two-year period. Again, based on the evidence that children needed educational stimulation *before* kindergarten, "Sesame Street" attempted to capitalize on the facts that 97 per cent of homes in the United States had television sets and that preschool children had already spent more time watching television before first grade than they would spend in the classroom in the next five years. "Sesame Street" was designed as a blend of high-interest, fast-paced commercial programming and instructional objectives. The final programs selected the following instructional objectives (Evans, 1975):

1. Symbolic representation skills: letter recognition, word matching and meaning, and number labeling and counting.
2. Cognitive organization skills: perceptual discrimination, classification, and relations among objects.
3. Reasoning and problem-solving skills: making inferences and evaluating solutions.
4. Concepts of self: body parts and functions and recognizing emotions.
5. Knowledge of social roles, groups, and institutions.

"Sesame Street" did not achieve the miracles that its creators intended. First, the children who watched it tended more to be middle class rather than disadvantaged. Second, some critics held that television did not reach the deficit of the

(A)

(B)

These children are intently watching a turtle (A). Through discussion of what they see and guidance by the teacher, they learn many things. Other experiences common in preschools include a variety of materials (B), again with the guidance and assistance of a teacher. [Courtesy Helen Canaday, Administrative Director, Preschool Programs, University of North Carolina at Greensboro.]

disadvantaged child because television only offers the opportunity to listen and not the opportunity to produce language and manipulate ideas, which *is* the deficit of disadvantaged children. Nevertheless, experiments in learning via television continue, and the technology of television is a factor to be considered in any education program interested in the growth and development of young children.

Infant Education

As the War on Poverty continued, the incessant evaluation was "Too little, too late." In response to this researchers and demonstration programs focused their efforts on younger and younger children. This direction was bolstered by the finding of Burton White (1971, 1975; White, Kaban & Attanucci, 1977) that "competent" children could be distinguished from other children by three years of age. Massive data from compensatory programs indicated that as early as age three disadvantaged children, and especially blacks, scored lower than their age mates on any standardized scale of intelligence. Infant programs were instituted to give these disadvantaged children the head start that they needed as early as the neonatal period, but certainly in the first two to three years. Based on research, the focus of these programs was to intervene in the parents' teaching styles and the children's learning styles. Infant education programs have primarily been focused on providing a stimulating environment for infants; the most successful have been those that directed training to the mother (who then implemented the stimulation for the infant). The central feature of infant education programs is an emphasis on verbal abilities and manipulation of materials. Factors such as nutrition and prenatal care are also included.

Infant education, if you will excuse the pun, is in its infancy. However, given the weight of evidence of the importance of these early years for all facets of growth and development, it is a direction that will surely be pursued in the future.

The Ethics of Intervention and Social Policy

Compensatory education and intervention programs raise many questions about values, ethics, and public policy. Critics have opposed compensatory education because its basic assumption is that a group of people, largely black people, is *deficient,* and therefore inferior, when those people are merely different. Having decided that a group of people is deficient, the decision is made to intervene—that is to intrude—into their lives to tell them that they do not know how to raise their children and to show them how it should be done. The decision is made without asking them whether they *want* to change. The charge has been made that this constitutes an imposition of middle-class white values on a group that is different from that majority standard. The position was the mainstream social policy by the federal government for two decades. The questions that arise in this connection are: Who makes public policy? Whom does it serve? and What should be the ultimate goals of public policy?

Social scientists, and particularly child-development researchers and theorists, were inextricably drawn into an alliance with Washington bureaucrats and legislators in setting social policy for the War on Poverty, executing programs, evaluating programs, and doing cost-analysis accountability. In the years since compensatory education has been public policy, billions of dollars have been spent on programs designed to provide equality of educational opportunity (Zigler & Trickett, 1978). These expenditures require sound social policy and sound evaluation. What then has been the track record of compensatory education? The evidence is mixed. It depends on the criteria that are used to evaluate these efforts. If the narrow criterion used is whether lower class children have caught up with their middle-class age mates in school achievement, the answer is no. Children from lower socioeconomic families continue to perform below their middle-class counterparts. Black children, as a group, continue to perform below white children.

If the criterion used is IQ gain, the evidence is mixed. Many programs that enrolled disadvantaged children in compensatory programs cited a gain in IQ of approximately ten points for those children; however, the gain seemed to be lost in later years of schooling. On these two counts, then, perhaps the attempts at early education have not been worth the effort and expense.

If, however, the criterion for success is gauged in broader terms of social competence, the evaluation is somewhat more positive. Many child-development professionals have been uneasy with measuring IQ gain as the sole criterion for the success or failure of programs that were so broad in scope and that had such a wide range of objectives. In addition, they question IQ as a valid measure of the quality of being human and assert that the business of childrearing (and the education of the young) is the development of a large number of competencies of which IQ is only one. Zigler and Trickett (1978) have proposed a broader evaluation of programs for young children based on the concepts of *social competency* and *adaptation,* which have the following components:

1. Physical health and well-being.
2. Social competence, including a measure of cognitive ability.
3. Achievement (a measure of actual productions of the child rather than simulated tests).
4. Motivational and emotional aspects.

There are many questions yet to be answered by professionals and parents interested in children, the most important of which concerns our final expectations for children as adults: How do we design environments that will assure us of reaching our expectations? That is how do we get there from here? Only thoughtful, informed people can answer these questions.

Main Points

Piaget's Preoperational Stage: Intuitive Phase

1. In the preoperational stage the child forms concepts based on intuition rather than logic.

Characteristics of Preoperational Thought (Intuitive Phase)

2. This period is a transitional stage; children's thinking is erratic and uneven, logical one day and regressed the next.

3. The thought of the child in this stage is characteristically egocentric, centered, transductive, focused on states, and irreversible; these characteristics are barriers to concrete operations.

What Does the Preschool Child Think About?

4. The preschool child uses thought in the practical manipulation of objects through seriation, classification, and class inclusion.

5. Preschool children pursue questions of origins with thinking characterized by artificialism and animism. Artificialism is the belief that everything was made by someone and animism that everything has life.

Piaget in Education

6. The implication of Piagetian theory is that the child must be an active participant in the learning process, physically handling and manipulating objects in endless ways. Education must be given patiently and in synchronization with the child's mental experience.

Can Piagetian Concepts Be Accelerated?

7. Teaching may accelerate the attainment of Piagetian concepts if the child already is close to reaching the concept.

Language Development in Early Childhood

8. Language development is rapid between the ages of two and six.

Vocabulary

9. Children at two use about 200 words, and at six this number may be as high as 14,000.

Plurals and Verb Tense

10. Children hypothesize grammatical rules for making nouns plural, changing verb tenses, using prepositions, modifiers, and articles: then they may overgeneralize and use grammar inappropriately.

Sentences

11. The child develops the ability to use language through an identifiable sequence: holophrases (one-word sentences), telegraphic sentences, and elaborated sentences.

Negative Sentences

12. Children first use *no* to indicate absence or nonexistence; the second use of no is to indicate rejection; later the child uses no for *not,* as denial.

Questions

13. At first children phrase questions with voice intonation; then they formulate yes-no questions; later they use complex wh-questions.

Passive Voice

14. Preschool children show little understanding of the passive voice.

Articulation

15. Preschoolers frequently have difficulty producing some of the phonemes.

Receptive and Expressive Language

16. Receptive language is usually more advanced than expressive language; "inner speech" or internalized language develops in the preschool years.

Group Differences in Language

17. Some families use restricted language, which consists largely of exclamations, incomplete sentences, repetition, and emotionally charged communication; other families use elaborated language, which resembles the written form with complete, grammatical sentences that convey precise, exact meanings.

Individual Differences

18. Girls acquire language facility sooner than boys; twins develop language more slowly than single children; children from large families show less advanced language development than children from small families.

Bilingualism and Dialect Differences

19. The issues of accepting dialectal variations of English as correct in formal, educational settings and of teaching bilingual children in their native tongues have not been settled.

Compensatory Education in the Great Society

20. Compensatory education was part of the War on Poverty launched by President Lyndon Johnson.

Rationale for Compensatory Education

21. Compensatory education is based on the rationale that all children do not begin the educational race at the same starting line.

Head Start

22. Head Start was directed at relieving the educational disadvantages of children, involving parents, providing social and health services, and developing careers for low-income adults.

Language Development Programs

23. Language was identified as the key to intelligence scores and school success therefore many programs developed to promote preschool language development.

Behavior-Analysis Program: Behavior Modification

24. Educational techniques such as token economy, time out, programmed and individualized instruction, team teaching, and the teaching machine have been developed within the behavior-analysis framework.

Piagetian Preschools

25. Preschools based on Piagetian theory are generally loosely structured, provide many different objects for children to handle, and encourage a casual interaction among students, teachers, and materials.

Open Education

26. The key to learning in the open classroom is interaction among children, teachers, and materials.

Education Through Television

27. "Sesame Street," which cost $8 million initially, began as an experiment underwritten by private foundations and the federal government to provide experiences with words and symbols to disadvantaged children.

Infant Education

28. Infant education programs have primarily been focused on providing a stimulating environment for infants, especially by giving training to the mother.

The Ethics of Intervention and Social Policy

29. Some critics question the right of educators to impose white, middle-class values on groups who differ from the majority standard; they oppose the social policy of intervention.

Words

animism	classification	irreversibility
artificialism	dialect	Piagetian
bilingualism	egocentric	phonemes
centered	holophrase	seriation
centration	intervention	transductive

Terms to Define

elaborated language	restricted language
expressive language	telegraphic sentence
open education	transductive reasoning
receptive language	

Concept to Discuss

class (class inclusion)

CHAPTER 11

Emotional and Social Development in Early Childhood

Have you ever wondered

what an Oedipus complex is?

what is meant by penis envy?

how children form an identification with the parent of the same sex?

how children learn sex-role behavior and gender identity?

how parenting styles affect the development of children?

if strict or permissive parenting has the same effect on boys as girls?

if the play of young children contributes to development or is only a way of passing time?

The years between three and six are a period of expanding social horizons and emotional experiences for the child. Socially, the child's world expands beyond the family with group experiences in nursery school, kindergarten, or other group situations. Emotional development continues to build on the strengths of the previous age, and in particular the love, stability, and sense of individuality fostered by the parents and other caregivers. These strengths are the basis on which a sense of self continues to be constructed. In this stage the child who has such a basis is generally happy, expansive, full of projects, and full of imagination. The well-developing child is pleased with his or her own ability to plan and carry out projects. These projects, for the most part, are characterized by imaginative play and often are rehearsals for roles in adult life. The child in this stage endlessly explores the question of sex roles and role assignments for boys and girls, mommies and daddies, men and women, through play and argument with peers. This preoccupation with the role assignments of the society is undergirded by the phallic stage of personality development described in psychoanalytic theory.

The Phallic Stage

The phallic stage is the third stage in Freud's theory of psychosexual development. In the phallic stage the organ mode that affords the most gratification to the child changes from anal to genital. The dependent years of infancy are past, along with the associated oral stage in which primary gratification was gained from feeding and other oral means. The defiant anal period is past, in which the child assumed control of his or her own excretory functions and assumed executive independence in social areas. The phallic stage ushers in a period in which the defiant ego of the child is tempered by the superego. The child is no longer guided by what it is *possible* to do, but rather what it is *right* to do. The superego embodies the rules that society has set to determine right and wrong.

Superego

The superego is a psychological defense against the instinctual impulses of sex and aggression. The child feels impulses of *sexual attraction* toward the opposite-sexed parent and feelings of *aggression* toward the same-sexed parent. The superego is that part of the personality that internalizes parental and societal prohibitions. It is that aspect referred to as conscience. The superego also serves as the dispenser of internal approval for good behavior. The punishment that the superego metes is *guilt*, and because the superego is internal, not only deeds, but even thoughts of wrong doing warrant the punishment of guilt. All societies attempt to curb the primitive drives toward sex and aggression. Played out in the safe situation of the family, the child learns to sublimate its impulses toward sex (incest) and murder (aggression) and to use the energy in ways that are constructive for society. The preschool child is often distressed by these violent feelings and needs a stable, loving environment in which to learn self-control. The mechanism for the acquisition of the superego, according to psychoanalytic theory is the *Oedipus complex*.

Oedipus Complex

The development of the superego and the fulcrum on which the entire personality turns, for Freud, is the resolution of the *Oedipus complex*. Freud considered this to be one of his greatest discoveries. It is one for which he has been criticized. In ancient Greek legend, Oedipus, a king of Thebes, killed his father and married his mother. Freud took the name of the mythical Theban king for his psychological complex because the young child fantasizes marriage (or at least love relations) with the parent of the opposite sex and hostility or death for the parent of the same sex. The young child chooses the opposite-sexed parent as the love object that will satisfy his or her instinctual sexual needs. Freud termed this choice of object for instinctual gratification catharsis. Although Oedipus the king was male, in psychoanalytic terms the Oedipus complex is applied to both boys and girls.

The boy develops strong feelings of possession toward his mother and wants to remove his father, while the girl directs those feelings of possession to the father and wishes to depose the mother. This Oedipal *fantasy* takes place on the unconscious level but manifests itself in jealousy of the same-sex parent and the development of a loving, close relationship with the opposite-sexed parent. Any family with preschool children is familiar with this love triangle. Hank Ketcham has cap-

The Oedipus myth states conflict between parent and child in the starkest of terms. In everyday life, the conflict is more commonly expressed as jealousy, as this cartoon of Dennis the Menace illustrates. [DENNIS THE MENACE® used by permission of Hank Ketcham and © by Field Enterprises, Inc.]

tured this situation with Dennis the Menace in the comic sequence shown here. Freud's critics were horrified by his insistence on the sexual interests of young children. Even today we are still uncomfortable with the idea of such emotions in a young child. The child cannot stay in this state of conflict forever, and the Oedipal situation must be resolved. It is the *resolution* of the Oedipal complex that forms the superego.

Resolution of the Oedipus Complex: Identification

How does the child resolve the psychological conflicts engendered by feelings of desire and fear? The aggressive fantasies that the young son has toward the father instill fear in him. He becomes afraid that the father can read his thoughts and will punish him for such hostile impulses. This fear is focused on the sexual organs. Freud called this castration anxiety. The boy realizes that the father is larger and stronger than he, and that he could not realistically depose the father. Therefore, on an unconscious level, he magically *becomes* the father, thereby removing the threat of retaliation. He then vicariously possesses the mother. She becomes his ideal love object and later he will seek a wife with the qualities of his mother. In psychological terms this magical becoming is known as introjection. Through introjection of the father's traits, the son forms an identification with the father (they become the same). Through this identification the son incorporates the values, actions, and personality of the father into his own. This is the foundation of the superego. Identification with the same-sexed parent grows until it reaches a peak at around eight years of age (Ausabel, Sullivan & Ives, 1980). Then it slowly erodes, but each of us carries imbedded in our personalities that identification with the like parent that is a component of our basic personality.

The Electra Complex and Penis Envy

The psychological development of girls must differ from boys both in the parent chosen for identification and the parent chosen for the love object. Although the term *Oedipus complex* technically refers to both boys and girls, this psychological conflict in girls has been referred to as the Electra complex, to differentiate female development from that of males. The word *Electra* is also taken from a Greek myth, one in which Electra killed her mother as revenge for her murdered father. For both boys and girls the original love object is the mother. The girl, however, must replace the mother with the father as the love object. Something must motivate her to do this. Freud theorized that when the young girl realizes that she does not have a penis, her reaction is invariably disappointment at what she feels is her loss and envy for those who possess the valued organ. Thus, the girl develops a feeling of *penis envy*. The girl holds her mother responsible for the loss of this valuable commodity and then turns to the father because he has it, after which the complex proceeds in the same way as the Oedipus complex. That is, the girl seeks to possess the father alone and experiences hostile feelings toward the mother. Hostility toward the mother arouses anxiety and fear that the mother will punish her for having these hostile feelings. She resolves her conflict by identifying with her mother, thereby gaining her mother's affection and vicariously possessing the father.

Even Freud's supporters have felt that although the Oedipal complex worked as a reasonable explanation of development for boys, the Electra complex leaves something to be desired in explaining the development of girls. Feminists have been especially vocal in rejecting penis envy, as have other psychoanalysts. Karen Horney (1885–1952), a follower of Freud, and an original thinker in psychoanalytic theory, especially in the area of the psychology of women, objected strongly to Freud's concept of penis envy as the determining factor in the female personality. Horney implicated an overemphasis on the love relationship between parent and child and its resulting lack of self-confidence as paramount in female psychology. Freud himself was not satisfied with his understanding of female psychology and is reputed to have said late in his life that after thirty years of work his theory of female psychology was incomplete. This is an area of active development at present.

Initiative Vs. Guilt: Erikson

Parallel with Freud's phallic stage in psychosexual development is Erikson's stage of psychosocial development in which the crisis is between the qualities of initiative and guilt. The child at this age is exuberant and energetic, forgets failures quickly and is able to direct actions to desired ends. "Initiative adds to autonomy the quality of undertaking, planning and 'attacking' a task for the sake of being active and on the move, where before self-will, more often than not, inspired acts of defiance or, at any rate, protested independence" (Erikson, 1963a, p. 255).* In the previous stage of autonomy the child experienced feelings of infantile jealousy and rivalry most often directed toward its age mates and younger siblings. In this stage, the child realizes its dethronement from a favored position with the mother and reacts with jealousy and rage. The child meets this dethronement, and its accompanying sense of failure, with resignation, guilt, anxiety, and fantasy. This is the stage in which fairy tales are most vivid and the child is preoccupied with fantasies of giants, wild animals, and magical events.

Even though Erikson stresses the social values in this period of development, he proves himself in agreement with Freud: "Infantile sexuality and incest taboo, castration complex and superego all unite here to bring about that specifically human crisis during which the child must turn from an exclusive, pregenital attachment to his parents to the slow process of becoming a parent, a carrier of tradition" (Erikson, 1963a, p. 256).

The negative aspect of this crisis is that the child will acquire an overly strict superego and a debilitating sense of excessive guilt. Erikson states,

> *the fact that human conscience remains partially infantile throughout life is the core of human tragedy. For the superego of the child can be primitive, cruel, and uncompromising, as may be observed in instances where children overcontrol and overconstrict themselves to the point of self-obliteration; where they develop an overobedience more literal than the one the parent has wished to exact; or where they develop deep regressions and lasting resentments because the parents themselves do not seem to live up to the new conscience.* [1963a, p. 257]

The resolution of this crisis, of course, is some combination of initiative and guilt. When the crisis is positively resolved, the child can undertake projects with feelings of assurance and confidence.

Criticisms of Psychoanalytic Theory

Psychoanalytic theory has been criticized as being too philosophical, too "mentalistic" and not testable as a scientific hypothesis. Most of the criticism has come from behavioral scientists who adhere to a mechanistic view. (The mechanistic view is contrasted with an organismic view in Chapters 18 and 19). The major thrust of the criticism is that psychoanalytic theory is needlessly complex. The second objection is that Freud offers explanations for human behavior that are unscientific and cannot be proven using the scientific method. Behaviorists offer alternative simpler explanations for children's behavior that they have subjected to analysis. Many child psychologists object to Freud's explanation of the Oedipal conflict and the desires of the young child. The psychoanalytic response to this objection is that the psychologists deny young children's feelings because they repress their own feelings toward their parents.

One writer has confessed to having thought that Freud was "complete nonsense" until her own daughters reached early childhood and engaged her in the following conversations.

* Excerpts reprinted from *Childhood and Society,* 2nd Edition, by Erik H. Erikson, by permission of W. W. Norton & Company, Inc. Copyright 1950, © 1963 by W. W. Norton & Company, Inc.

[**First daughter**]

Rachel: When I get married, I'm going to marry Daddy.

Me: Daddy's already married to me.

Rachel: (With the joy of having discovered a wonderful solution to this problem) Then we can have a double wedding!

[**Second daughter**]

Bethany: When I grow up, I'm going to marry Daddy.

Me: But Daddy's married to me.

Bethany: That's all right. When I grow up you'll probably be dead.

Me: (Determined to stick up for myself) Daddy's older than me, so when I'm dead, he'll probably be dead too.

Bethany: That's all right. I'll marry him when he gets born again.
(Our family's religious beliefs, incidentally, do not include reincarnation.)

At this point, I couldn't think of a good reply. Bethany must have seen my face fall and taken pity on me.

Bethany: Don't worry, Mommy. After you get born again, you can be our baby. [Berger, 1980, p. 340]

On the point of infantile sexuality Freud was, and continues to be, severely criticized. His own comment was that it was his lot in life to discover what any nursemaid knows. Theoreticians and researchers object on logical grounds, but conversations with children do lead to the conclusion that they think of these issues a great deal. Whether or not one accepts the psychoanalytic interpretation, there are several questions that need to be answered. Some of them follow here:

1. How does a child come to internalize the rules and mores of society?
2. What force makes the child obey those rules, even when there is no external regulation?
3. How does a child come to accept his or her sexual assignment?
4. How much, if any, choice does a child have in sexual assignment?
5. How does a child learn the specific behaviors associated with male and female?
6. What motivates someone to choose the opposite sex as love object?

The Biology and Culture of Sex

Biology

Biological sex is assigned at conception, according to whether the chromosome pattern of the zygote is XX (female) or XY (male). It is perhaps erroneous to think of these two conditions as opposites, as is current in our culture. In ancient Greek literature (Plato's *Symposium,* Heritage Press, 1968, pp. 77–78) an account is given of the origin of two sexes. The story relates that the two forms, male and female, were not originally separate, but were one. In the beginning the human form consisted of a creature with four legs, four arms and two heads. Through a disagreement with the gods this form was split into two and condemned forever to struggle to become reunited. As with many Greek myths, there is an essential truth to this account of sexual origins. The human form does indeed begin as a unity, but rather than the wrath of the gods decreeing two forms, it is prenatal hormones. Thus, in both science and myth male and female have inherently more similarities than differences. From a scientific perspective, male and female have 45 identical chromosomes and differ in only one: the Y chromosome of the male. The other 45 may as easily belong to a female as to a male. In the process of prenatal development two forms are differentiated from the embryonic mass. This is known as dimorphism (two forms). The sexual system is the only biological system that differentiates male and female forms. There is no difference in the digestive system or the circulatory system of males and females.

According to Money (1980) nature's first preference and biological command is to differentiate a female. This is known as the Eve principle. It is believed that the fertilized ovum utilizes hormones already present in the mother's system or that are manufactured in the placenta. In order to differentiate a male from the original embryonic mass, something must be added. This is known as the Adam principle (Money, 1980). The something that is added is androgen, or more specifically, the hormone testosterone. Incidentally, it should be noted here that, although testosterone is known as the male hormone and estrogen as the female hormone, both males and females utilize both hormones in their chemistry. The difference is in degree. This is other evidence for the sharedness rather than the oppositeness of sexuality. The chemical environment of the pregnant woman does not provide enough testosterone to differentiate a male. The fertilized zygote/embryo itself must provide that impetus. If the chromosome pattern is XY, the Y chromosome contains a substance called H-Y antigen. It is believed that this substance stimulates the differentiation of male gonads (sex organs, i.e., testes) from the basic female form. These embryonic testes in turn begin to produce the hormone testosterone at about six weeks of gestational age. The prenatal hormonal environment immediately affects the physical structure of genitalia and also the neural pathways in the brain.

The prenatal hormones act on the hypothalamus to program, in the case of the female, a cyclic pattern that in later years will result in the cycle of menstruation and ovulation (see Chapter 3). The presence of testosterone suppresses this cyclic pattern and determines a continuous hormonal pattern. These brain differences in male and female are clear; what is not clear is whether there are other brain differentiations as a result of these hormones that cause different behavior and abilities.

There is not a one-to-one correspondence between the biological sex of the child (XX or XY) and the resulting differentiation. This is because many other factors enter into the hormonal condition in the prenatal period. For example, the mother may take drugs that have androgenic properties, or have an androgen-producing tumor, with the result of a masculinized XX (female) fetus. On the other hand, the individual cells of an XY fetus may be insensitive to androgen and the result is a feminized XY (male) fetus (Money, 1980).

Gender Identity/Role (GI/R)

Gender identity and sex role include anything and everything that have to do with behavior and psychological differences between the sexes. This differentiation between biology and psychology and behavior is not meant to perpetuate a mind/body dichotomy, for in sexual development this dichotomy does not exist. This division is only for the convenience of thinking about a very complex process. Although biological gender is set at conception, the first three years are crucial for gender identity and the preschool years are crucial in gender role development.

Regardless of the biological gender assignment when the statement, ''It's a boy'' or ''It's a girl'' is made at birth, another process of gender assignment is under way, that of *gender role assignment*. Gender role assignment is that sex that society assigns to the child. Parents treat boys and girls differently: in dress, in the ways in which they are cared for, in the toys that they are given, in the esteem in which they are held, and in the expectation for them and their behavior.

Gender Identity

It seems quite obvious that boys grow up to be boys and girls grow up to be girls. However, sexual identity must be learned, and it is not necessarily concordant with biological gender. Transsexuals attest to the elusiveness of the process of identity. Transsexuals know their genetic sex, have been reared in accordance with the expectations of that sex, and yet experience a psychological conflict between their physical and psychological sex. Morris (1974) relates the experience being "entombed" in the body of a male before surgery enabled him/her to live as a female.

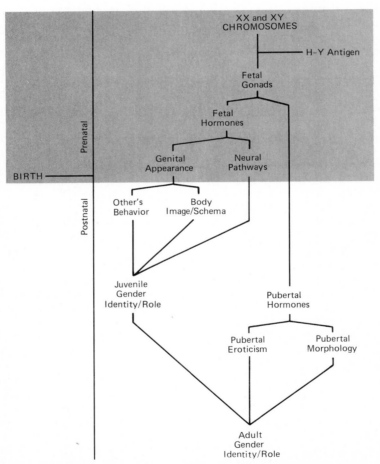

Developmental sequence and differentiation of Gender Identity/Role (GI/R). [From *Love and Love Sickness* by John Money. Copyright © 1980 by The Johns Hopkins University Press. Reprinted by permission of John Money.]

Incidentally, she had had a successful career, had been married and had fathered children when this change was accomplished. Transsexuals are actually rare, but the fact that the psychological role is so difficult for some indicates the complexity of the process. Gender identity is private and subjectively experienced.

John Money, a medical sociologist and research scientist at Johns Hopkins, has conducted considerable research into gender identity and has concluded that (1) a child will accept whatever gender identity is assigned, whether or not it is consistent with the child's genetic sex, (2) this identity is fully established by three years of age, and (3) a child's gender identity can be changed without creating great psychological trauma if it is done before the age of two and one-half (Money, Hampson, and Hampson, 1957).

Money (1975) relates the case in which a change in gender assignment was necessitated for medical reasons. The case involved a pair of identical twin boys, one of whom lost his penis during circumcision when he was seven months old. After lengthy conferences with medical personnel, the parents, psychologists, and sociologists, the decision was reached to reassign the twin as a girl. In making this reassignment, the social and biological aspects were treated differently. First, the social aspects were modified. The parents changed the child's name, hairstyle, clothing, and began to treat her as a girl. When the children were preschoolers the mother reported that the girl was "so dainty," loved to have her hair brushed and curled, and was much neater than her brother. She also related amusement when her son urinated outdoors, but expressed quite a different attitude about her daughter attempting the same thing. She insisted that the girl come inside and not engage in such behavior. The girl was described as being a "tomboy," not especially interested in dolls, and bossy (the girl had been the more dominant twin). She enjoyed helping her mother in the kitchen and taking care of her father and brother. The biological aspect of the gender change was effected through several surgical procedures combined with hormone therapy that was to begin at puberty. The rationale for this change in gender assignment was that it could be accomplished without undue psychological effect at that age and that the child could live a more nearly normal life as a sterile female than as a male without a penis. With the gender change she could expect to marry, have a normal sex life as a female, and become a mother through adoption. As a male without a penis, an adequate sex life would have been impossible. She would be told the details of her condition when she was older.

In an interview when she was in late childhood, a recent trip to the zoo was discussed. She was asked her favorite animal, to which she responded, the monkeys. The interviewer then asked her if she were a monkey would she rather be a boy or a girl monkey? She replied that she would prefer being a girl monkey, because she was already a girl. Such cases are rare but constitute a natural experiment in which the flexibility of gender identity is demonstrated.

Thompson (1975) explored the ages at which children understand gender words. Boys and girls of two, two and one-half, and three years of age were shown pictures on small projection screens. Above each screen was a bunny face that could be lighted. The children were shown two pictures and asked: "Where is the man?" "Where is the lady?" "Where is the boy?" or "Where is the mommy?" They indicated knowledge of gender words by touching or pointing to the pictures. In a similar task the children were asked to sort the pictures and paper dolls that were of a stereotypical boy and girl. The children were also asked their own sex and its similarity to that of the paper doll children. Finally, the children were shown neutral pictures, such as of apples that were labeled "for boys" and "for girls," and told that they could take one home with them. Thompson concluded that two-year-olds understand little about gender identity. They are beginning to understand the meaning of the gender words *man* and *woman* and also that certain articles are associated with each sex. For example a necktie is "for daddies" and lipstick is "for mommies." They can identify their own pictures but do not know that they share a gender category with others.

Children of two and one-half exhibited a clearer understanding of gender as a category, which is solidified by age three. Although objects and activities are identified as sex typed, the children have not internalized the sex role. That is, they do not consistently choose for themselves those things appropriate to their sex.

Emmerich, Goldman, Kirsh, & Sharabany, (1976) found a relationship between sex constancy and cognitive level. Sex constancy is an expression of Piaget's concept of identity as discussed in Chapter 10. Young children believe that sex can be changed by clothes or a haircut; however, children who have reached the concept of sex constancy realize that it is independent of the transformations of clothes and activities. Emmerich states that sex constancy is achieved as part of the transition from preoperation to concrete operations. This research found that children at a higher cognitive level achieved sex constancy earlier.

Gender Role

Once sex constancy is achieved, children show a greater interest in same-sex persons. It is as though once they discover their own sex and that a large category of other persons share this characteristic they observe such persons closely to discover the generalities about behavior, values, and attitudes of people of their own sex (Kohlberg, 1966; Slaby & Frey, 1975). Sex typing exists in all cultures. Perhaps it is less rigid in our culture at present than in most, but it nevertheless is done considerably. One cultural observer noted that in the United States even food is sex typed: steak and potatoes are for men and salads are for women. If you don't think this is so, check the menu at the Rotary and at the local Woman's Club.

The traditional blue for boys and pink for girls may be lessening in some quarters, but most parents are unsure of the consequences if girls are raised as boys and boys as girls. Preschool children not only learn in great detail the activities, artifacts, and behaviors associated with each sex, they also learn the cultural attitudes associated with sexuality. One study (Damon 1977) examined children's concept of the social expectations for male and female. Children aged four through nine were told a story about George, a little boy who liked to play with dolls. George's parents tell him that little boys shouldn't play with dolls, only girls should, and they buy him many toys designed expecially for boys. However, George still prefers to play with dolls. The children were then questioned about whether George was right or wrong. The children were asked questions about George and his behavior. The issues that were explored were the following:

1. Why do people tell George not to play with dolls? Are they right?
2. Is there a rule that boys shouldn't play with dolls? Where does it come from?
3. What should George do?
4. What will happen to George if he keeps playing with dolls? What if no one ever sees him? Does George have a right to play with dolls?
5. Is it fair for George's parents to punish him for playing with dolls?

6. What if George says that his sister Michele, gets to play with dolls all she wants, so why can't he? Is that fair to George?

7. What if George wanted to wear a dress to school? Can he do that? What's wrong with that? Does he have a right to do that?

The results indicated that at four children thought it was right for George to do whatever he wanted to do, but by age six they thought that it was wrong for George to play with dolls or dress like a girl. Some children felt that the parents were justified in punishing George if he persisted in playing with dolls. Older children became more flexible in their responses and again thought that George had the right to dress as he pleased. Children six and older relied heavily on the response of other people to George's behavior and stressed that he will be teased by the boys and rejected by the girls. Even those children who thought that George had the right to dress and play as he pleased recognized that others would disapprove.

Preschool children are quite rigid in their sex typing. Maccoby (1980) suggests that perhaps they exaggerate this sexist attitude in order to attain cognitive clarity about their own identity. After this identity is stabilized, they may become more flexible, as Damon (1977) found. Parents who attempt to raise children in an egalitarian environment are often puzzled by their children's rigid sex expectations.

Gender Preference

Children easily learn to identify their own sex (gender identity); they learn gender role equally well. But what of the behavior that they actually exhibit? In addition to the two biological forms there are two forms of behavior for male and female. The acquisition of the gender role is not the simple assignment of a role that the child adopts and carries out. Each person has his or her own personal compilation that is put together during the course of development from various social and cultural inputs (Money, 1980). No one questions that male and female in our culture exhibit different behaviors. The question paramount at this time is the cause of the two forms of behavior. Do prenatal and later hormonal differences cause such behavior, or is it the result of learning? In this context, a dichotomy should not be made between the biologically based and the environmentally learned. An uncritical assessment of these would be that biology is rigidly set and learning is easily changed. Money (1980), however, argues that this is not the case. Biological processes involving hormones are influenced by environmental events and learning is a biological process that changes neural structures and chemical neurotransmitters. Thus, learning is as solidly grounded in biology as genetically determined factors. Sexual differentiation both biologically and behaviorally is a prime illustration of the interactive relationship between genes and environment or nature and nurture.

Money has advanced the theory that gender role preference is better understood as shared sex behavior rather than opposing behaviors. In this concept both sexes are able to engage in the same behavior (share that behavior), but a particular behavior may be more easily elicited from one sex than the other. Under special circumstances either sex may engage in these behaviors. For example, research has shown that either sex will nurture young; however, females, and especially the mother, are more responsive to the stimulation of young. Males of many species will eventually engage in nurturant behavior if they are exposed to the young long enough. We can only theorize that the sight, sound, smell, and touch of those young serve as stimuli to organize nurturant behavior. Might we hypothesize that playing with dolls in the preschool years will predispose boys to be more loving and nurturant fathers, and that by forbidding them to play with dolls we predispose them to being indifferent fathers? The issue is not whether males are categorically active and energetic and females are maternal and nurturing; rather, the issue is whether different stimuli are required for eliciting behaviors from males and females. Whether these stimuli are biologic or perceptual is the focus of current sex research.

Hartup and Moore (1963) offered children an opportunity to play with materials appropriate to their own and to the opposite sex. Boys were more likely to choose toys and play activities that are "masculine"; they avoided "feminine" materials such as lipstick, mirrors, nail polish, hair ribbons, and handbags more than girls did guns, cowboy hats, shaving materials, and neckties. When the experimenter left the room, however, the boys secretly experimented with the feminine materials, whereas the presence or absence of the experimenter made no difference in the girls' exploration. This indicated that boys learned quickly that negative reactions would follow their interest in feminine objects. Boys also expresssed more fear of being a sissy than girls of being a tomboy.

Within each sex there is a wide range of gender role behavior, even though cultural standards are generally known. Some boys may adhere to the masculine ideal with sports, no sissy stuff, and strong aggressive behavior, while others are noncompetitive and enjoy such feminine activities as dancing, music, and cooking. Boys who are seriously interested in these activities may bear the brunt of much harassment in childhood even though there is general cultural admiration for dancers such as Mikhail Baryshnikov, singers such as Luciano Pavarotti, and French chefs. In similar fashion some girls adopt extremely feminine behavior and others are tomboys who compete with boys in climbing trees, playing sports, and in academic subjects such as math and science. Research will be better directed to identifying the conditions that elicit these behaviors in either sex, rather than focusing on the exclusive categories of unilateral sexual behavior.

Theories of Sex-Role Acquisition

What are the forces that push a child to assume the behavior that is designated appropriate to his or her biological sex? Sex differences are obvious, and so are their characteristic behaviors. The question arises whether such differences are the result of biological causes that are immutable or of social pressures that can, and certainly will, be changed in a changing society. At present, competing theoretical explanations attribute the primary cause to psychological, biological, social, or cognitive factors. In the previous section we discussed the psychoanalytic theory of sex-role acquisition as a psychological process of identification that involves the fantasy of the child in the Oedipus complex. Other theorists reject this explanation as unnecessarily complicated and obscure and offer a more direct explanation of sex-role acquisition and identification with same-sex parents.

Biological Theory

Freud has been rebuked for writing that "anatomy is destiny," especially by those persons who wish to see more equality between the sexes. There is evidence that biology may indeed affect behavioral destiny in specific ways. Strong evidence exists from animal studies that male and female animals exhibit quite different behaviors. Animals do not have the cognitive ability to incorporate the values of culture or parents who socialize them in sex typing. Environmentalists might ques-

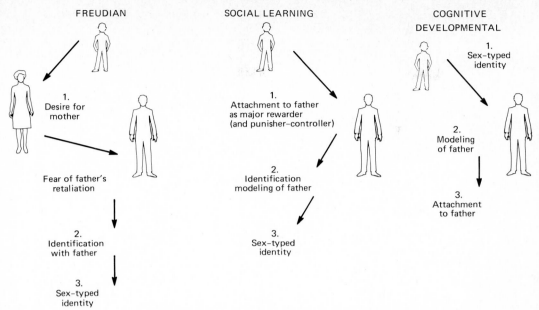

FREUDIAN   SOCIAL LEARNING   COGNITIVE
                                              DEVELOPMENTAL

Theoretical sequences in psychosexual identification. [From "A Cognitive-Developmental Analysis of Children's Sex-Role Concepts and Attitudes," by Lawrence Kohlberg. In *The Development of Sex Differences* edited by Eleanor E. Maccoby (Stanford University Press, © 1966 by the Board of Trustees of the Leland Stanford Junior University). Reproduced with the permission of the publishers.]

tion whether such research can be generalized to humans on the grounds that humans are not subject to instinct, as are lower animals. The seat of instinct, however, is hormones, and the hormones in question are the same testosterone and estrogen found in humans. Young female rats who were administered testosterone changed their behavior and exhibited typical male patterns *after* female patterns had been established (Gray, Lean, & Keynes, 1969). Female monkeys who were masculinized by testosterone prenatally acted more like males as juveniles (Phoenix, 1974).

In research on humans, Money, Ehrhardt, and Masica (1968) studied girls who had been masculinized prenatally by synthetic hormones, which have the same androgenic qualities as testosterone. They were identified as girls at birth and were reared as girls by their parents. They accepted the female identity and looked forward to being wives and mothers. When their behavior was studied, it was found that all but one of them were considered tomboys. They preferred toys such as trucks, guns, and other typical "boy toys" rather than dolls and "girl toys." They liked sports and seemed to enjoy competing with males. Our culture is relatively tolerant of tomboys and many girls are; however, it seems more than coincidental that 90 per cent of this group exhibited such behavior. Although this research is only suggestive and further studies need to be done, it raises the question about the relationship between hormones and behavior in humans.

Social-Learning Theory

Social-learning theorists ascribe a greater role to imitation and cognitive processes in the attainment of identification. The selected adult becomes a model for the child through an interrelated process of cognitive and emotional components, desire, and behavior. Kagan (1971) has described the process that establishes and strengthens identification.

1. *Cognitive.* Children are told and come to believe that they share particular physical or psychological attributes with the model. Little boys are told, "You look just like your father," and girls may be told, "You have your mother's good looks and sweet disposition." They are also very early instructed that they are girls, like mother, or boys, like daddy.

2. *Emotional.* As children watch the parent whom they are told they resemble, they experience their model's emotions. When daddy comes home and announces that he has received the office award, his son feels the same pride. When daddy is happy that his favorite football team has won the game, junior is happy also and tells his friends happily and proudly that "our" team won the game. Similarly, when mother is proud that she received a promotion at the office, daughter Mary feels a sense of pride and accomplishment, a feeling that "we" did it.

3. *Desire.* Children want to be like their adult model because they perceive that the particular qualities the model possesses enable the attainment of desirable goals. The child is positively reinforced for demonstrating attributes of the correct model and punished or not reinforced for demonstrating other attributes. Therefore, the child desires these positive social rewards and wishes to be like the model.

4. *Behavior.* Finally, the child behaves like the model. Preschool children are keenly aware of the "correct" behavior for men and women and mommies and daddies. Much of their play is playing house and acting out the roles of adults. The child uses the adult model's mannerisms, voice inflections, and words, often to the amusement of family and friends.

Cognitive-Developmental Theory

Cognitive-developmental theory suggests that cognitive development exerts a strong influence on the acquisition of sex role. According to this theory many aspects of sex-role acquisition are related to cognitive development in the preoperational stage. For example, the understanding of classification (I am a boy or a girl); the ability to conserve (sex remains constant in spite of transformations in clothing, etc); the language facility to question appropriate behavior, values, attitudes, and expectations; and finally the use of imitation to try out these concepts in preschool play. In the cognitive-developmental view, gender identity is first a cognitive acquisition. Children then model the behavior of the parent that is like them. If they are boys, they model the behavior of fathers; if they are girls, they model the behavior of mothers. Attachment then forms for the parent that the child models. The concept of an appropriate gender role changes over time. Some of this change is related to the age of the child or adult, which suggests that it is developmental, and some is related to changes in the society, which suggests that it is the result of learning and reexamination. For example, we now see women attending the Naval Academy and preparing to be astronauts. Fifty years ago it would have been unthinkable.

We are now perplexed in our society about how much of the gender role is determined by biology or by psychological processes over which we have no control and how much we can adjust by social pressures and cognitive examination.

When the social system of reinforcement is concordant with biological systems, development proceeds more easily. To accept the sharedness of gender-role behaviors by boys and girls will create a climate in which boys' nurturant behavior can be approved and girls' activity and competitiveness equally accepted and approved. In such an atmosphere parents can more easily accept a wide range of behaviors from their children and children can be more relaxed about exploring different behaviors and becoming what they potentially are, complete human beings.

Influence of Parents on Development

All of the theories that we have discussed, as well as current cultural opinion, hold that parents exert a powerful influence on the development of their children. Regardless of the differences that opposing theories have in other areas, there is agreement on the importance of the first few years of life in shaping the child. In the psychoanalytic view the years before school are paramount. Freud theorized that neuroses are acquired in the first six years of life, even though they may not be manifested for years (Hall & Lindzey, 1970). For behaviorists the parent is the prime shaper of the child. Watson (1928) states, "once a child's character has been

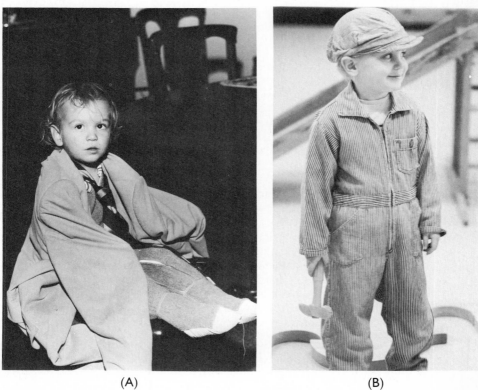

(A)   (B)

The desire to dress in the clothing of the father is an indication that identification is taking place as in this young boy who is wearing his father's much-too-large clothing (A). In his workman's suit and tools this boy (B) is playing out what he thinks grown men do in their work. [Photograph (A) courtesy William Heroy.]

spoiled by bad handling, which can be done in a few days, who can say that the damage is ever repaired?'' The importance of parental presence has been underscored by research on maternal deprivation and attachment. Bowlby (1969) states that ''mother love in infancy and childhood is as important for mental health as are vitamins and proteins for physical health.'' White (White, Kaban, Mamor, & Shapiro, 1972) has underlined the importance of the early years in cognitive development.

Many researchers have attempted to explore the intricacies of the parent-child relationship and its effect on subsequent development. Once all of those studies have been taken into consideration, two major adjustments must be made in our understanding of the role of parents in shaping the child. First, ever more careful research has forced the weight of professional opinion to shift in the direction of an interactionist approach to personality development. That is, the child influences the parent, who then influences the child, and so forth. The second adjustment concerns the flexibility of the human being and if development is consistent from one stage to another, or whether new environmental conditions can bring about change. In other words, is a child who has a poor environment in the first six years doomed? If not, how much change can be made later? The related question is whether we can predict development. We will now review some of the research and then discuss these two questions.

Parental Dimensions: Love and Control

A very large amount of research in this century has pointed to the significance of whether parents are loving or hostile to their children and how much and what kind of control they exert over them. Early research was directed toward identifying those behaviors of parents that were related to their children's characteristics. Symonds (1939), in one of the first attempts to generalize such research, identified two behavioral dimensions of parents as important. They were conceived as a continuum from most to least: acceptance-rejection and dominance-submission. They have stood the test of time. In an attempt to examine these continuums more closely, several studies rated mothers on behaviors related to child interaction. Some of the factors studied were such contrasting behaviors as fostering dependency or autonomy; positive evaluation of the child or perceiving the child as a burden; ignoring or emotional involvement; use of punishment, punitiveness, strictness; and using fear to control or equalitarianism. Other single dimensions such as irritability, concern about the child's health, anxiety, intrusiveness, excessive contact, and achievement demand were measured. Schaefer (1959) suggested a circular model of parental behavior with two independent dimensions: acceptance-rejection (love-hostility) and permissiveness-restrictiveness (autonomy-control). Many researchers have used these dimensions to study parental behavior. In general, researchers have seen these two dimensions as follows (Martin, 1975):

[Love] Acceptance-rejection (or warmth-hostility). *The nonaccepting parent is dissatisfied with the child, inclined to be critical and derogatory of many of his abilities or personality characteristics, does not seek out the child or enjoy his company, does not provide much positive reinforcement, and is likely to be insensitive to the child's needs and point of view. The accepting parent is characterized by the opposite attitudes and behaviors.*

[Control] Permissiveness-restrictiveness (or autonomy-control). *The permissive*

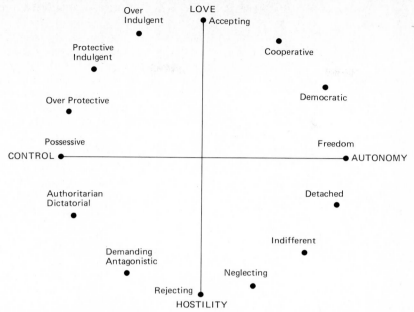

A model for maternal behavior. This model illustrates the opposing dimensions of love and hostility and how either of these can lead to control or autonomy. [From "A Circumplex Model for Maternal Behavior" by Earl S. Schaeffer. (In *Journal of Abnormal Social Psychology*, 1959, *59*, pp. 226–235. Copyright 1959 by the American Psychological Association.) Reprinted by permission of the publisher and author.]

> *parent does not clearly state the rules or the consequences for violations, does not firmly or consistently enforce rules, and is likely to give in to the child's coercive demands: The restrictive parent does the opposite.* [p. 466]

Acceptance-rejection and permissiveness-restrictiveness are conceived as independent. A parent cannot be both hostile and loving but may be loving and either permissive or strict in control. Similarly, a parent may exercise strong control either from hostility or from love. Researchers have been interested in the relationship of these parental dimensions to the child's characteristics.

Effect of Parents on Specific Behaviors of Children

Parents have been held responsible for their children's specific behaviors. Their behaviors were often seen as a direct result of general dimensions of love and control. Research has looked carefully at the correlates of parental behavior and the specific child behaviors of dependency, achievement, internalization, aggression, and withdrawal.

Baumrind (1967) examined the relationship between child and parent behaviors and found an identifiable *pattern* of relationship. She studied a group of 110 three- and four-year-old nursery school children over a period of fourteen weeks. On the basis of her observations the children were divided into three groups:

1. Competent children (Pattern I, six girls and seven boys). These children were characterized as self-reliant, interested, curious, self-controlled,

achievement oriented, cheerful, friendly in peer relations, and as having a high energy level.

2. Withdrawn children (Pattern II, seven girls and four boys). These children were characterized as passively hostile, unhappy, and vulnerable to stress. They were aggressive and hostile to peers, expressed this hostility indirectly, and found it difficult to get over unhappy moods. They seemed to have a more careful attitude toward work than the nursery school expected.

3. Immature children (Pattern III, three girls and five boys). These children were characterized as impulsive and lacking in self-discipline. They were hostile and aggressive to peers but were more cheerful and recovered from conflict more easily than the children in Group II.

To determine whether there was a relationship between the behavior of these children and parental style, Baumrind studied the parents and children interacting in a three-hour unstructured home observation, a forty-minute structured observation of mother and child, and an interview with the mother and father.

Four dimensions of parent behavior were studied for their relevance to child behavior. These were parental control, maturity demand, parent-child communication, and nurturance. The four dimensions are defined here:

1. Control. Parents rated high in control were willing to exert influence over the child, were able to resist pressure from the child, and were consistent in enforcing directives. High-control parents also attempted to modify the child's expression of dependent, aggressive, and playful behavior and to promote the child's internalization of parental standards.

2. Maturity demands. Parents rated high in maturity demands exerted pressure on their children to perform up to (or beyond) their ability in social, intellectual, and emotional areas. They also gave children the freedom to make their own decisions and insisted on their independence.

3. Parent-child communication. Parents rated high in this area used reasoning to obtain the child's cooperation, asked the child's opinion, and asked how the child felt about issues. They also allowed the child to present reasons and were influenced by sound reasoning on the child's part. Parents rated low in this area gave in to the child's whining and crying. Their style of control was also manipulative. That is, the parent attempted to get the child to comply with his or her desires by distracting the child or otherwise disguising the fact that control was intended.

4. Nurturance. Parents who were rated high in this area were able to express love and compassion to the children as well as pride and pleasure in the child's accomplishments. Through acts and attitudes they promoted the child's physical and emotional well-being.

When these data were analyzed, it was found that the parents of children assigned to the same groups did indeed exhibit similar characteristics. The parental characteristics are described here:

1. Pattern I parents (competent children). These parents were highest on all four measures: control, maturity demands, communication, and nurturance. They exercised a good deal of control over their children and demanded responsible, independent behavior from them; however, they also explained, listened, and provided emotional support.

2. Pattern II parents (withdrawn children). These parents were rated low in

nurturance and communication and moderately high in control and maturity demands. They tended to be less controlling than parents of competent children but more than parents of immature children. Similarly they demanded more maturity than parents of competent children but less than parents of immature children. They were the lowest of the three groups on nurturance and sometimes rejected their children. They were only slightly higher than parents of immature children on communication.

3. Pattern III parents (immature children). These parents were moderately warm and nurturant but markedly low in exercising control and demanding mature behavior from their children. They did not consistently enforce demands if the children opposed them and they gave in more to the children's nuisance behavior.

Baumrind (1971, 1973) extended this initial study to identify parental patterns further. She began with the behaviors of the parents rather than the children, identifying three distinctive parental styles: *authoritarian, authoritative,* and *permissive*. These styles were then correlated with the children's characteristics. The patterns are reviewed here:

1. *Authoritarian parents.* These parents attempted to shape, control, and evaluate their children's behavior and attitudes in accordance with an absolute set of standards. They tended to value obedience, respect for authority, work, tradition, and preservation of order. They discouraged verbal give-and-take and sometimes rejected their children.
   Children of authoritarian parents. The children of authoritarian parents showed little independence and accepted moderate social responsibility.
2. *Authoritative parents.* These parents attempted to direct their children in a rational, issue-oriented manner. They encouraged verbal give-and-take and explained reasons behind demands and discipline but also used power when it was necessary. They expected the child to be independent and self-directing but to conform to adult requirements. They set standards and enforced them. Those standards were somewhat flexible but were not based primarily on the child's desires.
   Children of authoritative parents. The children of these parents met their parents' expectations for independent behavior and were socially responsible.
3. *Permissive parents.* These parents used little punishment and tended to accept the child's impulses, desires, and actions. They made few demands on the child either for household responsibility or for more mature behavior. They allowed the child to regulate his or her own activities as much as possible and avoided exercising direct control. They attempted to sway the child using reason but avoided the direct use of power when in conflict with the child. They tend to give in to the child's demands.
   Children of permissive parents. These children tended to exhibit insecurity, lack social responsibility, independence and to be low achievers.

Two questions arise when interpreting research of this kind. First, do different children react differently to different styles of parenting, and second, are children's characteristics consistent over a period of years? That is, do children who are withdrawn at age three exhibit the same behavioral patterns five or fifteen years later? Baumrind found that these different styles of parenting had different outcomes for boys and girls. Boys developed less positive characteristics under both authoritarian and permissive parenting. Both these styles produced boys who were angry and defiant. Girls seemed to meet the demands from authoritarian parents, but both boys and girls developed better under authoritative parenting. Boys with those parents were more friendly and cooperative, whereas girls from authoritative families seemed more self-reliant and achievement oriented.

Are these characteristics consistent over the years? In an attempt to answer this question, Baumrind (1977) returned to the original sample of children when they were eight and nine years old, to find out how they were functioning in elementary school. All of the children were evaluated in terms of their ability to function in social and cognitive spheres. They were evaluated on their tendency to take initiative, assume control of situations, and to deal with daily problems in both areas. The social area included leadership and social interaction. The children were evaluated in terms of the leadership they displayed and whether they were anxious in peer interactions or approached and interacted easily with other children. The cognitive area included intellectual curiosity and motivation. Children were evaluated in terms of whether they were capable of independent work (setting their own standards) and of whether they enjoyed intellectual challenges and displayed originality in thought. When the patterns were correlated with the patterns identified when the children were three and four years old, it was found that those children whose parents were rated authoritative in preschool were higher both in the social and cognitive area at eight years of age. Sex differences identified earlier persisted, with boys more likely than girls to show a loss of interest in achievement and to withdraw from social interaction as a result of authoritarian parenting. We cannot, however, assume that the parental behaviors caused the children's characteristics. It is possible that happy, self-confident, achieving, self-reliant, curious, and friendly children foster an open give-and-take relationship with their parents. It is equally possible that parents become authoritarian in reaction to hostile, sullen, unhappy children. Similarly, perhaps parents resort to permissiveness with children who seem unable to acquire self-control but who recover from set-backs quickly. We must recognize that the parent-child relationship is a two-way interaction and influence flows both ways. We know from the research reviewed in Chapter 1 on neonates that children begin influencing their social world from the moment of birth. There is no reason to assume that children become less skillful in exercising influence.

Dependency/Independence

We have discussed the importance of attachment in infancy and its transformation in the toddler period. The relationship between the preschooler and its parents, especially the mother, undergoes further modification in the years between three and six. Behaviors that were appropriate for the infant and the toddler become inappropriate for the older preschooler. The mother is the prime agent of socialization and moves the child toward self-reliant, independent behavior. Preschoolers often exhibit behaviors such as attention seeking, reassurance seeking, touching and holding, wanting to be near mother, and help seeking. These behaviors are often viewed as signs of dependency and mothers and teachers are admonished to discourage dependent behaviors in children. Maccoby and Masters (1970) found that dependency responses can be increased by rewards and decreased by punishments; however, in the laboratory, it has been found that when a mother mildly punished or ignored a preschooler's bid for attention that demand increased rather than diminished (Sears, Rau, & Alpert, 1965). Theorists have suggested that the dependent relationship between mother and infant is mutually satisfying and that the mother continues to reinforce the child's dependent behaviors in an attempt to continue the interchange. In any case, giving up formerly satisfying behaviors for more mature, but anxiety producing, behaviors becomes difficult for some children, while others greet new challenges with assurance and expectation.

Sex Differences

The series of studies by Baumrind (1967, 1971, 1973, 1977) found that different parenting styles affected boys and girls differently. This sex difference is consistent and is evident in many areas of development. Observations from several studies with children of different ages in a variety of settings indicate that boys and girls interact differently with their parents (Maccoby, 1980). In general, boys appear to be more resistant to the efforts of parents to teach or train them and they make more counterdemands. In addition, boys appear to be more vulnerable to disruption in family situations (Rutter, 1970; Wolkind & Rutter, 1973).

Mothers and fathers treat boys and girls differently from birth (see Chapter 1). In the first year, differences are discernible in the ways in which boys and girls relate to their parents. Martin (1980) found in a laboratory experiment that boys were less likely to accept a mother's withdrawal of attention and to escalate their demands for attention when she was busy with a questionnaire. Girls were more likely to accept a nod, a smile, or a word from the mother and allow her to withdraw and continue working.

Several studies have confirmed the popular conception that boys are less likely to conform to parental restrictions than are girls. Maccoby (1980) reported that boys are more likely to handle forbidden objects in a waiting room situation. This behavior was confirmed in observations in homes in which boys were more likely to touch fragile or dangerous objects, climb on furniture, and pull at curtains (Minton, Kagan, & Levine, 1971; Smith & Daglish, 1977). Boys seem no more likely to respond to a father's demands than a mother's. Heatherington, Cox, and Cox (1977) found boys less likely than girls to comply with parental demands, regardless of which parent made the request. Gunnar and Donahu (1980) found in another laboratory study that girls return overtures more readily to mothers than do boys. The mothers were instructed to initiate a playful gesture with their infants. The girls were more likely to respond with a reciprocal gesture, while the boys were more likely to ignore the overture. This pattern continues with older children when the interaction between parents and boys is more likely to focus on disciplinary issues; girls and parents share more activities. Young boys attempt, even when very young, to control or dominate their mothers or to demand a service. As a result, coercive cycles of parenting and a battle of wills is more likely to develop between boys and parents.

When families are under stress, such as in divorce, boys are more likely to respond with rebellion at home, deterioration in schoolwork, and behavioral problems (Heatherington, 1979). More research is needed to explicate these relationships fully. The evidence seems clear, however, that there is no one set formula for development that cuts across age levels and sex differences.

Play

In the 1960s play for children fell into disrepute as early childhood education got down to the serious work of learning. This disparagement of play suited our puritanical heritage and the Protestant work ethic. Play has always been regarded with some suspicion in our cultural milieu. As we gain some perspective on compensatory education, researchers are again turning attention to the function of play in the development of children. Free play is a cornerstone of the traditional kindergarten and is an essential element in the organization of the Piagetian classroom. Recent thought about play suggests that it undergirds both cognitive and social development (Vandenberg, 1978). Exploration, which leads children to play with objects, is necessary for cognitive development and tool manipulation; rough-and-tumble and language play with peers are a factor in social interaction. What is play? One of the problems that has held back research in play is finding an adequate definition for it. The researcher's first problem is to define what it is that he or she wants to study. This turns out to be no small task, for the word *play*, appears to be elusive and difficult to pin onto a dissecting board. Perhaps this is because play is a process and it is difficult to stop as are all processes. One writer (Rubin, 1980), struggling with a definition of *play*, asked his five-year-old daughter to supply a definition—which she readily did. "Play," she said, is "fun stuff that kids do 'cause they like to do it" and "work is not much fun 'cause it's what kids hafta do for adults." [p. viii] Researchers phrase it a little differently, but the essence is the same. Garvey (1977) has defined play as having the following characteristics:

1. Play is pleasurable, enjoyable. Even when not actually accompanied by signs of mirth, it is still positively valued by the player. *(fun stuff)*
2. Play has no extrinsic goals. Its motivations are intrinsic and serve no other objectives. In fact, it is more an enjoyment of the means than an effort devoted to some particular end. In utilitarian terms, it is inherently unproductive. *(cause they like to)*
3. Play is spontaneous and voluntary. It is not obligatory but is freely chosen by the player. *(kids [choose to] do)*
4. Play involves some active engagement on the part of the player. *(do it)*

How Children Play

Voluntary activities that children spontaneously engage in follow patterns and are similar for most children. One of our first studies of play was conducted by Mildred B. Parten (1932). She observed two- to five-year-olds during free play in nursery school and identified six different kinds of activity that occupied the children, ranging from unoccupied activity to cooperative organized play. Descriptions of these kinds of play activities follow here.

Unoccupied Behavior.   Unoccupied behavior is not strictly play, and it occupies the least amount of time among preschoolers. Children engaged in this activity watch anything that may be of interest at the time. They may crawl under tables, get on and off chairs, follow the teacher, handle their own bodies, or sit and glance around the room without sustained attention.

Onlooker.   The child who is an onlooker concentrates on a particular activity conducted by other children but does not actively engage in it. He or she may offer suggestions, ask questions, or interact with the children in other ways, but not actually participate in the activity. This child is a kind of "sidewalk superintendent" in the activity.

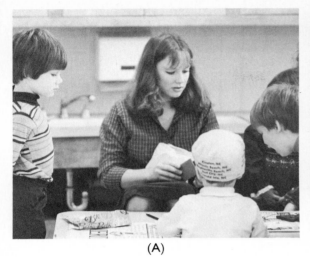

(A)

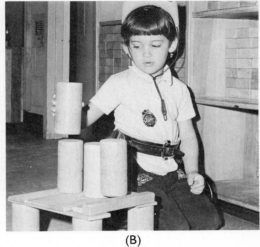

(B)

(C)

(D)

(E)

The play of children varies in amount of social involvement. Sometimes children enjoy the role of observer (A); at other times, they engage in solitary play (B). Very young children often engage in parallel play (C) while older preschoolers are apt to engage in associative play (D) and an elaborately constructed fantasy of cooperative play (E). [Courtesy Helen Canaday, Administrative Director, Preschool Programs, University of North Carolina at Greensboro.]

Solitary Play.   Children of all ages engage in solitary play. This type of play involves an activity undertaken alone, independent of other children. No effort is made to involve other children or to initiate conversation or enter into association with others, although the activity is conducted within speaking distance of others. This type of play is characteristic of children between the ages of two and three. As children progress in social skills, group play takes precedence, but solitary play may continue in more mature forms with puzzles, blocks, and arts and crafts. Immature solitary play in older children involves pouting, pointless wandering, sulking, and social withdrawal (Moore, Evertson, & Brophy, 1974).

Parallel Play.   Parallel play is the first step in group play, yet apparently the child does not have the skills to launch a truly cooperative venture. Children of two and three often choose the same type of toy, sit very close to each other, obviously are aware of each other's presence and actions, yet make no attempt to influence each other's actions. They simply play compatibly alongside others. A prime example of parallel play is a group of two-year-olds in a sandbox. Each has a shovel and container and each pursues similar activities, yet there is little interaction.

Associative Play.   Slightly older (three- or four-year-olds) or more experienced children engage in associative play. In this activity children engage in the same general activity and may borrow or lend objects, talk about the activity, or lead or follow one another. Some effort may be made to control who can and cannot play, but no attempt is made to organize the activity or to assign different tasks to different group members. Each child plays as he or she wishes and does not surrender autonomy to the group. For example, a group of nursery school children may be playing "cars." Each child may have a car or a truck and "drive" it over an imaginary countryside. Each child will contribute to the fantasy, but no one dominates or attempts to change what other children propose.

Cooperative Play.   The five-year-old kindergarten child is most likely to engage in cooperative play. In this form of play children coalesce into a group organized to make some material product, strive to attain a competitive goal, or to dramatize situations of adult and group life. There is much discussion about who can and cannot play and a consequent sense of belonging or not belonging to the group. One or two children assume leadership and direct the activity toward a goal. Reaching this goal requires division of labor and the assumption of different roles by different members of the group.

From the preceding it is clear that play becomes more complex and more socially interactive with age. One characteristic of play is its high spiritedness. Preschool children are sometimes so caught in this spirit of mirth that they literally collapse in a heap and you think they will "die laughing." Sherman (1975) has called this spontaneous eruption of screams and giggles, which is sometimes accompanied by jumping up and down and hand clapping, group glee. Sherman observed 596 directed-activity sessions over a period of two years for children three to five. In this time he observed 633 outbreaks of group glee. Almost any event in the nursery school could precipitate this behavior: intense physical activity, such as dancing; an incongruent perception, as when a child called a teddy bear a "teddy dog"; bad words or breaking rules; awkward behavior, such as tripping; and ending or beginning another activity.

What Children Play

Rough-and-Tumble: Chase and Retreat

Rough-and-tumble play is a free-wheeling, high-energy activity characterized by running, chasing, mock fighting, and high verbal exchange. The young of many species engage in this type of play, including puppies, kittens, and young monkeys. Children typically engage in it at ages four or five, but it is evident on the playgrounds of elementary schools also. Researchers have identified rough-and-tumble play as being composed of many different activities. Among them are run, hop, jump, fall over, chase, flee, wrestle, hit at, laugh, and make a face. Vocalizations may include scream, laugh, and play noises (Smith & Connolly, 1972). Typically such play occurs out-of-doors and most often erupts just after children have been released from a classroom. Such play gives the impression of a raging torrent held back by a dam that finally breaks its containment. When a school bell rings for dismissal this type of unorganized play is evident in the surging mass of children leaving the school building.

Consistent with our previous discussion of sexually dimorphic behavior, boys are found to engage in somewhat more vigorous activity than girls, with more noise and shouting and more close physical contact, such as wrestling and tumbling (Garvey, 1977). However, it should be noted that girls also engage in rough-and-tumble play; in puppies and kittens there seems to be no noticeable sex difference in vigorous activity. Although girls do engage in this type of play, they tend to restrict their play to more confined areas, nearer to adult supervisors or playground equipment, whereas boys tend to move toward the periphery of the playground area in larger, more mobile groups. Groups of girls chasing around actively tend to be smaller than groups of boys, and the groups tend to be composed of children of the same sex. Children younger than three typically watch this kind of play rather than engage in it. First-born children also are more reluctant than others to throw

Boys are more likely to engage in rough-and-tumble play than girls. [Photograph at right courtesy William Amidon and Greensboro Day School.]

themselves into a mass of tumbling children; they spend more time watching. Newcomers to the playground tend to be integrated into this fast-moving social group only after being accepted in other activities. The invitation to be a part of this moving mass signals acceptance into the preschool social group. For the preschooler the object of play seems to be movement, whereas in older children kinetic activity is integrated into games with other objectives, such as jump rope, cops and robbers, hide and seek, and, later, organized team sports such as football, basketball, and soccer.

Object Play

Almost from birth children are given objects with which to "play." Objects that are especially designated for children's play are, of course, toys. Children display an immediate and lasting fascination for objects in the environment, toys or otherwise. Objects connect the child to his or her environment in many ways. First, they serve as the means for cognitive development as the child explores, becomes familiar with, and eventually understands properties of the physical world. When this exploration is analyzed as cognitive development, it looks like work, but in truth, it is only child's play. Objects with which the child plays also provide a means by which the child can represent feelings or concerns. A major means in which psychotherapy with children is conducted is through play therapy, in which the child acts out concerns and relationships with the aid of objects. Finally, objects serve as a means of social interaction with adults or other children.

It is through play with objects that the child gradually develops the rich and varied repertoire of make believe and "Let's pretend." Children develop an understanding of objects in a predictable sequence. Marianne Lowe (1975) conducted a series of experiments with children who were from nine months to three years old and found that children played with objects in similar ways at similar ages. In these sessions, a child was seated at a table and miniature objects were placed before him or her: a cup, saucer, spoon, hairbrush, truck, trailer, and a doll. The child was then observed to see what he or she would do with the objects without receiving direction from an adult. This is the sequence of object play that infants develop:

1. **Nine months:** Children are attracted by bright colors. In a typical action a child grasps an object and brings it to his or her mouth. This is followed by random actions with the object, such as waving it, banging it on the table, inspecting it visually, or rotating it.

2. **Twelve months:** Visual inspection takes precedence over "mouthing" in exploring objects. The child may make some attempt to use the objects, such as by placing a spoon in his or her mouth or putting a cup on a saucer. Actions are interspersed with random behaviors of waving, banging, and mouthing objects.

3. **Fifteen months:** The inspection and exploration of objects are the clear priority in object relations. Objects are appropriated to conventional uses. Children at this age may attempt to drink from the cup, run the brush through their hair, roll the truck back and forth, stand the doll up, or attempt to eat from the spoon.

4. **Twenty-one months:** The child actively searches for a companion object. For example, after placing the cup on the saucer, he or she may look for the spoon, stir imaginary coffee in the cup with it and then drink the coffee. The doll or an observer may be offered a drink from the cup. The doll may be placed on a truck and taken for a ride.

(A) (B)

Through play with objects children develop their world of "make-believe" (A) and an understanding of the real world (B). [Courtesy Helen Canaday, Administrative Director, Preschool Programs, University of North Carolina at Greensboro.]

5. Twenty-four months: By two years of age the child plays realistically with the doll. The doll may be fed, put to bed for a nap after lunch, awakened, have its hair brushed, and be taken for a ride in the truck. The truck may be attached to the trailer and objects sought for loading the truck.

6. Thirty-six months: At this age the doll is made to perform actions such as eating, brushing its own hair, washing dishes, and putting them away. In the child's scheme the doll has the power to act purposefully. Play is elaborated with make-believe purposes, places, and events: for example, the doll may drive the truck to an imaginary place and back.

Over this two-year period, through acting on and interacting with things and people around him or her the child,

1. Differentiates action patterns that are appropriate to various objects (puts spoon in mouth but not doll).
2. Combines objects in functional relationships (cup and saucer).
3. Links action patterns in sequence to form larger behavior patterns (cooking, eating, washing up).
4. Applies action patterns to self, others, or replicas of others, such as a doll. Finally, action is attributed to the doll itself (doll brushes hair or dog barks while moving).
5. Invents appropriate objects that are necessary to complete action patterns (imaginary coffee in cup).

6. Transforms objects for use in actions if an appropriate one is not present (uses a toy rake to stir imaginary coffee if spoon is absent).

When the child can *invent* absent objects and transform those present into something else, it has entered the wonderful world of "Let's pretend!" Between three and six, or seven, this is where the child lives.

Language Play

Between the ages of two and six the child is fascinated with the resources of language and is sensitive to the play potential in this newly discovered skill. The child explores and exploits all aspects of language, such as phonology (rhyming) and grammar arrangement and meaning (puns) with the same high spirit characteristic of other forms of play. In this use of language children most often spontaneously create forms and do not use quoted material (Garvey, 1977). The manipulation of the sounds themselves are an obvious source of pleasurable play for children. In the prelinguistic child repetitive rhythmic sounds constitute language play. In older children noises often accompany activities, such as beep-beep (a horn blowing), ding-a-ling (telephone), pow-pow (gunshots), and varoom, varoom (motors). These noises add a realistic touch to the make-believe situation. Children also distort their voices both to be funny and to change their identity when playing at make believe.

The most characteristic play with language, however, is a kind of free association in which words and sounds tumble over each other in an interplay of sense and nonsense. Children move from a context to a rhymed word to another context. Researchers must be inconspicious in examining spontaneous productions because play is elusive and children change the character of their play when they are aware of being observed. Children cannot be taken into a laboratory and told that they must produce word play for the next five minutes so they can be observed. In such a situation anyone would freeze. One ingenious researcher placed a tape recorder in the bedroom of her two-year-old son as he was going to sleep and captured the following word play. Notice that Anthony's productions are accompanied by the researcher's comments (Weir, in Garvey, 1977, p. 65).

Anthony's speech	**Weir's Comments**
That's office. That's office.	Sound play with the pronunciation of "That's
Look Sophie.	office" and "Sophie," with substitution in the
That Sophie.	sentence frame. Breaking down a complete
Come last night.	sentence. Recall of recent event and self-con-
Good boy.	gratulations on keeping hands off forbidden
Go for glasses.	glasses. More systematic substitution in frame.
Go for them.	Rhyming phrase.
Go to the top.	
Go throw . . . , etc.	

Children also use words in social play with other children. Such interchanges are characterized by verbal banter back and forth. The banter is not to exchange information but simply to enjoy the sound and rhythm of the words. Often the banter is the "Yes, I can." "No, you can't." "Yes, I can." variety of exchange. Sometimes the conversation goes in other directions, including rhyming. Garvey (1977, pp. 68–69) cites the following exchange between two five-year-olds, a boy and a girl.

[Both children simultaneously wander and handle various objects; little direct gaze.]

Boy: And when Melanie and . . . and you will be in here you have to be grand mother grand mother. Right?

Girl: I'll have to be grand momma grand momma grand momma. [In distorted voice]

Boy: Grand mother grand mother grand mother.

Girl: Grand momma grand momma grand momma.

Boy: Grand mother grand mother grand mother.

Girl: Grand momma grand mother grand momma.

Boy: Momma.

Girl: Momma I . . . my mommy momma.
Mother humpf.

Boy: Hey.

Girl: Mother mear [Laugh] mother smear.

Boy: [Laugh]

Girl: I said mother smear mother near mother tear mother dear. [Laugh]

Boy: Peer.

Girl: Fear.

Boy: Pooper.

Girl: What?

Boy: Pooper. Now that's a . . . that's a good name.

Often the exchanges are pure nonsense, as in the following one between two four-year-old girls. (Garvey, 1977, pp. 71–72)

1st Girl: [On the car, writing letter] Dear Uncle Poop, I would like you to give me a roasted meatball, some chicken pox . . .
and some tools, Signed . . .
Mrs. Fingernail. [Smiles and looks up at partner]

2nd Girl: [Listening and drumming on the stove] Toop poop. [Laughs] Hey, are you Mrs. Fingernail?

1st Girl: Yes, I'm Mrs. Fingernail. [In a grand, dignified voice]

2nd Girl: Poop, Mrs. Fingernail. [Giggles]

Social Role Play

In the years between three and six children engage in a great deal of make-believe play. It is usually engaged in with at least one other person, but on occasion, a single child may play a sequence with an imaginary friend or an imaginary telephone caller. Make-believe play is sometimes called dramatic, or thematic, play. It is not haphazard but usually is either constructed around a story line or a role identity. The most popular roles are mother, father, baby, and child. Other roles are out of the child's social environment: fireman, doctor, nurse, patient. Less frequently, characters from fairy tales and TV, or other media sources are enacted: Big Bird, Batman, Robin, a witch, a dragon or the President. In the beginning of a sequence a child will announce what is to be played, such as "Let's play house, you be the daddy and I'll be the mommie. Johnnie can be the baby." (Johnnie is usually a younger child and will have little to contribute to the development of this play. The baby must be obedient, is often punished, and often is not permitted to talk.)

The second organizing feature of make-believe is a story line or a plan. In this case a child may propose a plan such as, "Let's go on an airplane trip." Two popular plans for dramatic play are treating-healing and averting threat (Garvey, 1977). In treating-healing one child is sick the other, who is the doctor, mother, nurse, or advisor, solves the problem in some way. In averting threat, the threat may be a monster, creatures from outer space, or hostile soldiers. Dramatic play is

These two girls are engaging in dramatic play. The girl on the left, in a pin-striped suit, is the President and has asked the First Lady, "Would you like to dance?" [Courtesy Helen Canaday, Administrative Director, Preschool Programs, University of North Carolina at Greensboro.]

carried by language similar to, "Here comes a monster." "He's going to eat us." "I'll kill him." "Call our friend the bear to help." "He ate me, I'm dead." "I got him."

Although children move quite readily into make-believe they are equally aware of the distinction between what is make-believe and what is real. They are adept at switching from themselves to the role they are playing and often do this especially to prompt others in their role or to correct another child who performs the wrong actions. Make-believe may look like unfettered fantasy, but it is governed by rules that all the players must obey, especially those with roles. Often the action is broken and punctuated with, "Daddies don't wash dishes," or some other role restriction. This is the time that children are working out gender role behavior, and the rules of make-believe demand rigid adherence to these roles. When children come to a kindergarten with different ideas of the rules, the rules must be argued out and a consensus formed. Many props in the way of costumes and other objects are used in this kind of play. However, if the needed objects are not available, another object will be transformed to fill the need, as, "Here, this box is our space ship." The play is guided by plans and ideas but not limited by reality.

Positive Benefits of Make-Believe.   In make-believe the child is able to use all of the cognitive, social, and emotional elements at his or her command. They are combined to test the child's conception of the social world. In addition, some studies have shown a relationship between rich imaginative play in the preschool years and later creative or divergent thinking (Vandenberg, 1980). Through such play, the child re-enacts situations that he or she is not immediately able to assimilate into emotional life. Through repetition of the events, such as the arrival of a new baby in the family, the child may finally come to emotional terms with those events (Walder, 1978).

It is, perhaps, a mistake to analyze play in terms of its contribution to other areas of development, because we began with the definition of *play* as "fun stuff," with no motivation for it other than the enjoyment it allows. The danger is that schools begin to "teach for play." When play becomes a sought after condition to reach another goal, it ceases to be play and becomes something else, perhaps work. One could envision a teacher or parent sternly speaking to a child with, "Now you go and play some make-believe so that you can get into Harvard and become a creative scientist." Of course, such strategies do not work. Many parents and educators fear that that is just the kind of thing that has happened with Little League ball teams, for example. When games are so highly organized it ceases to be fun stuff and moves into the serious business of life. Nevertheless, one last word is in order here on play and its positive applications.

Harlow's Monkeys Revisited

Harlow's monkeys illustrated the devastating effect of maternal deprivation (Harlow and Harlow, 1966; see Chapter 7). The Harlows, however, were not only interested in the effect of maternal attention, they were interested in identifying and describing the larger area of social development. As a consequence of this quest their research comprises the most comprehensive analysis of the role of play in social development of any species (Vandenberg, 1978). Let us take another look at that research.

Harlow attempted to examine the relative importance of maternal and peer groups for social development. Two groups of monkeys were raised. One group was raised with their real mothers but were not permitted to have contact with peers. The other group was raised with a surrogate mother and allowed to play each day with peers. The monkeys raised with their natural mothers alone did not have normal social and sexual behavior as adults, whereas the monkeys raised with the surrogate mother (which alone resulted in aberrant behavior) *and* were allowed peer relations exhibited normal social and sexual behavior as adults. This study implicates the powerful effect of peer relations for normal social development in rhesus monkeys. The question, of course, is, whether the same relationship holds for human children.

A further study was designed to determine if monkeys raised in social isolation could regain social development. Previous data had indicated that if monkeys were isolated for six months the effects were irreversible. Harlow and Suomi (1971) found that when such deprived monkeys were allowed to play with *younger* monkeys, they showed rapid social improvement and by one year of age demonstrated normal social development. In a later study Novak and Harlow (1975) found that social rehabilitation was possible through younger playmates even when there had been isolation for more than one year. The explanation for the positive effect of younger playmates versus same-age playmates is that younger monkeys provided play experiences without threat of aggression. In the normal development of monkeys a dominance hierarchy is formed by threat and aggression after a period of

Peers and play with peers are an important factor in the growth of children. [Courtesy Helen Canaday, Administrative Director, Preschool Programs, University of North Carolina at Greensboro.]

rough-and-tumble play. The deprived monkeys were *socially* the age of the younger monkeys although chronologically older. The obvious factor in this data is the potent effect of peers and even younger children as a socializing agent. Vandenberg (1978) concluded that in social play the young of the species may commit social blunders and exhibit inappropriate behaviors without fear of severe consequences. Furthermore, he speculated that such an arena of experimental free play is necessary for normal social development. It is not an inconceivable jump from peer play in rhesus monkeys to make-believe in human children. In make-believe when children play out inappropriate behaviors for mommies and daddies they are quickly corrected by their age mates, without undue fuss or pain. That is simply the rule. Perhaps the free-play advocates are right after all and the land of make-believe is not simply a pleasant interlude before the hard work of grade school but in itself constitutes a necessary element in development.

Main Points

The Phallic Stage

1. The phallic stage ushers in a period in which the defiant ego of the child is tempered by the superego.

Superego

2. The superego is that part of the personality that internalizes parental and societal prohibitions.

Oedipus Complex

3. Freud termed the young child's fantasies of marriage and love relations with the parent of the opposite sex and hostility for the parent of the same sex the Oedipus complex.

Resolution of the Oedipal Complex: Identification

4. Through identification the child incorporates the values, actions, and personality of the same-sexed parent.

The Electra Complex and Penis Envy

5. The term *Electra complex* refers to the girl's choice of the opposite sexed parent as love object and her feeling of hostility for the parent of the same sex. Freud speculated that the realization that she does not possess a penis fosters penis envy.

Initiative vs. Guilt: Erikson

6. Erikson's third stage of psychosocial development is characterized by a crisis between initiative and guilt.

Criticisms of Psychoanalytic Theory

7. Criticisms of psychoanalytic theory include objections to its complexity, lack of scientific principles, the Oedipal conflict, and infantile sexuality.

Biology and Culture of Sex: Biology

8. Biological sex is assigned at conception according to whether the chromosome pattern of the zygote is XX (female) or XY (male).

Gender Identity/Role

9. Although biological gender is set at conception, the first three years are crucial for gender identity; the preschool years are crucial in gender role development.

10. Gender identity is private and subjectively experienced as maleness or femaleness.

11. Gender role refers to social expectations of behavior, values, attitudes, and appearance specific to male and female.

12. Actual gender role behavior varies greatly within each sex, and many behaviors are shared by both sexes; however, some behaviors are more easily elicited from one sex than the other.

Theories of Sex-Role Acquisition

13. Social-learning theory holds that gender role acquisition is the result of selective reward and punishment given by parents and other adults.

14. Evidence exists that biology through hormones (testosterone and estrogen) determines gender role behavior.

15. Many aspects of gender role acquisition are related to cognitive development in the preoperational stage.

Influence of Parents on Development

16. All theories of development hold that parents exert a strong influence on the development of their children.

Parental Dimensions: Love and Control

17. An important emotional aspect of parental influences on children consist of four factors occurring along two dimensions: acceptance–rejection (love–hostility) and permissiveness–restrictiveness (autonomy–control).

Effect of Parents on Specific Behaviors of Children

18. Baumrind found that authoritarian parents have children who show little independence and accept moderate social responsibility; authoritative parents have independent, socially responsible children; permissive parents have insecure, dependent children who are low achievers and lack social responsibility.

Dependency/Independence

19. The mother is the prime agent of socialization; she molds the child toward self-reliant, independent behavior or may continue to reinforce dependent behaviors if she finds them satisfying.

Sex Differences

20. Boys appear to be more resistant to parental teaching and training, make more counterdemands, and are more vulnerable to disruption in family situations.

Play

21. Recent thought about play suggests that it undergirds both cognitive and social development.

How Children Play

22. Parten identified six kinds of play activity that become more complex and socially interactive with age; unoccupied behavior, onlooker, solitary play, parallel play, associative play, and cooperative play.

What Children Play

23. Rough-and-tumble play is a free-wheeling high-energy activity characterized by running, chasing, mock fighting, and high verbal exchange.

24. Play with objects aids cognitive development and emotional expression; it proceeds in a developmental sequence.

25. Between the ages of two and six the child is fascinated with the resources of language and is sensitive to the play potential of words.

26. In the years between three and six, children engage in a great deal of social role play. Some studies have shown a relationship between rich imaginative play in the preschool years and later creative or divergent thinking.

Harlow's Monkeys Revisited

27. Harlow's research showed the importance of peer play for normal social development and the therapeutic effects of play with younger monkeys on monkeys who had been socially isolated.

Words to Know

authoritative
authoritarian
dimorphism (dimorphic)
introjection
permissive
testosterone

Terms to Define

Adam principle   **gender-role preference**
castration anxiety   **Oedipus complex**
Electra complex   **penis envy**
Eve principle   **phallic stage**
gender identity   **sex typing**
gender role

Concept to Discuss

identification

Middle Childhood:
The Years from Six to Twelve

Middle childhood, like Tolkien's Middle Earth, is a different world and culture from that inhabited by adults. Sturdy bodies are tested to their physical limits in stretching, running, and jumping—and in sitting still in classrooms. Through schools children leave the culture of childhood and venture into the world of adulthood, where the tools of contemporary society are learned: language, mathematics, science, social studies, and the arts. Children search for the limits of their mental horizons as they manipulate the entire world—past, present, and future. Here also they are judged and found competent, or wanting. Middle childhood creates its own culture in which peers replace parents and teachers. It is a culture of jokes and jingles, and sometimes ridicule for adults. Children find their own measure of self-esteem within the closed circle of their friends. This culture is bounded by age and we can no more visit their unique age culture than they ours. They, and we, are stamped forever with the particular character of our childhood cultures. We can only try to understand theirs and to give them the tools to build a better world.

CHAPTER 12

Physical Development in Middle Childhood

Have you ever wondered

whether children today grow faster, slower, or at the same rate as children in previous generations?

if there are sex differences in physical development?

why some people are left-handed?

how physical skill and appearance affect self-esteem?

what health problems children have?

Growth Patterns

In the middle years of childhood, children settle into a slow but steady pattern of sustained growth. By the age of six, when children enter elementary school, they have lost the cherubic appearance of the preschooler and have assumed the characteristic body proportions of childhood. Their legs and arms are nearly 50 per cent longer than they were at age two. The proportions of childhood are pleasing and graceful. Growth continues at a relatively even pace, with children gaining an average of five pounds (2¼ kilograms) and 2½ inches (six centimeters) per year. The average six-year-old has attained 70 per cent of his or her adult height, by eleven years, 90 per cent. There are, of course, wide individual differences in size, shape, and weight.

Visit any elementary school and you will see a tremendous variety in the appearance of children between the ages of six and twelve. What strikes the visitor immediately is the great variation in height. Among children of average growth, there is an 18-inch spread in height from first to sixth grade. When the shortest first graders and the tallest sixth graders are compared, the variation in height in the elementary school is astounding. Even more astounding is the variation in height among age mates. In a comparison of eight-year-olds from many different countries, Meredith (1969) found a nine-inch difference. The eight-year-old children

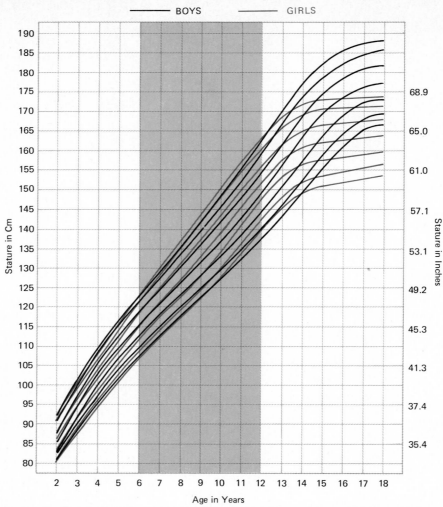

Standards of height for boys and girls ages two to eighteen with emphasis on ages six to twelve. [Data from National Center for Health Statistics, 1976.]

from underdeveloped countries tended to be smaller than children from Europe and North America. Such data implicate nutrition in the growth of schoolchildren.

The Secular Trend

Visitors to historical museums often note the small size of adult clothing and beds. It is not that our ancestors were cramped while they slept or saved cloth by wearing tight clothing. They were, in fact, considerably shorter than we. Researchers who have compiled normative tables of height have noted both an increase in size and a decrease in the age of puberty for our population. This trend toward earlier maturation is known as the secular trend. Tanner (1968) compared children of various ages in 1965 with children who were similar ages in 1905 and found differences of two, three, and four inches. A five-year-old in 1965 was two inches taller than a five-year-old in 1905, and at eleven years of age the difference was four inches in favor of the 1965 model. Similar trends have been noted in the age of menarche (first menstruation). Researchers estimate that this age has been moving downward at the rate of three months every ten years. This means that in the short space of forty years, girls are maturing an entire year earlier. The causes of this earlier maturation have not been identified. Among the hypotheses suggested are better nutrition for children and increased exposure to light, as children spend the night hours in artificial illumination. Child development professionals speculate that this trend must have a ceiling, or eventually children would reach puberty almost before reaching school age. Incidentally, a similar increase in either mental or emotional

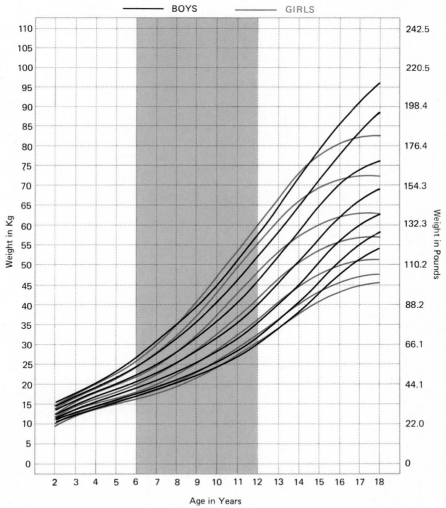

Standards of weight for boys and girls ages two to eighteen with emphasis on ages six to twelve. [Data from National Center for Health Statistics, 1976.]

maturity has not been noted, perhaps because in our increasingly complex society maturity in those areas requires more time. The trend toward earlier menstruation has, in many cases, pushed puberty from adolescence to late childhood. Most fifth and sixth grades will have a few girls who have reached menarche, and it is not rare for this to occur as early as fourth grade. Some girls may enter the prepuberty growth spurt at the age of eight. School personnel and parents need to be sensitized to the special psychological needs of these children, especially in relating to their physically immature age mates. This should not be interpreted to mean that boys are not affected by this secular trend. They also are maturing earlier; however, boys do not have a definite event such as menarche to mark puberty. Growth trends toward earlier maturation affects both boys and girls.

Skeletal and Muscular Development

In accordance with the principle of cephalocaudal development, the head, which has led development to this time, grows more slowly, and the extremities assume a faster rate of growth. Ossification of bone continues and will not be completed until the early twenties. Internal organs continue to grow. Lungs increase in capacity and the heart grows stronger and larger. These capacities, combined with increased muscle growth, are reflected in increased physical endurance in late childhood.

Most six-year-olds begin losing baby teeth and replacing them with permanent ones. This process of replacement continues throughout middle childhood. As a result the jaw elongates and the proportions of the face change. Muscles continue to increase in size, shift proportions, and make a firmer attachment to the bone. Bones, however, grow faster than muscles, which probably accounts for the ''growing pains'' that some children report. As the muscles grow and develop, they fairly demand to be used, which in part accounts for the inability of schoolchildren to remain still for long periods of time. It also constitutes a challenge to children to discover their muscle capacity.

Motor Development

In middle childhood children gain control of their bodies and test the limits of their physical abilities. They are comfortable with their bodies and confident of their abilities. Because growth is relatively slow, grace and coordination can be maintained in the skills they develop. Grace and precision are lost in the adolescent growth spurt when body proportions change rapidly. During the rapid growth of adolescence, eye-hand and eye-foot coordination must be recalculated constantly.

Large Motor

Six-year-old children generally can ride a bicycle, jump rope, and roller skate. Early in the school years children perfect running, throwing, jumping, catching, ball-hitting and ball-kicking skills, which are the basic skills for many team sports. These physical abilities in middle childhood are related to age and size. Because boys and girls are similar in size in these years, they do not differ markedly in skill development. Boys tend to be more muscular than girls, especially in the legs and shoulders, and they excel in activities that require developed leg muscles, such as broad jumping as well as in accurate distance throwing, which requires well-developed arms and shoulder muscles (Keogh, 1965). Girls excel in hopping and jumping tasks, which require precision and accuracy (Cratty, 1970). These differ-

The components of motor fitness: (1) coordination, (2) agility, (3) balance, (4) speed, and (5) power. [From *Understanding Motor Development in Children* by David L. Gallahue. (Copyright © 1982 by John Wiley & Sons, Inc., New York.) Reproduced by permission.]

ences reflect the more mature visual-motor coordination of girls and the larger muscle development of boys. Improvement in coordination and balance is related to age but not to size. Older children are, as you might guess, more coordinated and engage in more intricate physical activities. Although there is little difference in the skills of boys and girls in middle childhood, these differences increase markedly in early adolescence and continue to widen in late adolescence. Espenschade (1960) measured the skills of boys and girls from ages five through seventeen on running, jumping, and throwing skills. This study revealed that at around the age of thirteen girls' skills level off or decline, whereas boys' skills continue to improve even more rapidly between the ages of thirteen and seventeen.

Although groups of boys and girls differ, there is a wide range of individual differences; those children who are good in one area tend to excel in other areas as well (Espenschade, 1960). Apparently the all-around athlete is a reality. Keogh (1965) observed over a thousand boys and girls from kindergarten through sixth grade in terms of their relative performance in running, jumping (broad and hurdle), throwing for distance and accuracy, hopping (fifty-yard hop and stationary hop), balance (standing and walking on a beam), side stepping, cable jump (jumping over a rope held in the jumper's hand), and grip strength. Keogh found that

These sixth-grade children in a physical education class are perfecting skills of running, throwing, jumping, and catching that are the basis of many team sports. [Courtesy Mount Zion Elementary School, Greensboro, North Carolina.]

the boys excelled in running speed, distance and target throwing, and in grip strength, and that these improvements were related to age. Govatos (1959) found that boys and girls of similar size tended to perform equally well in running and jumping, but that boys excelled in throwing.

Table 12–1. Motor Fitness Components, Common Tests, Aspect of Development Measured, and Synthesis of Development

Motor Fitness Component	Common Tests	Specific Aspect Measured	Synthesis of Findings
Coordination	Cable jump	Gross body coordination	Year by year improvement with age in gross body coordination. Boys superior from age 6 on in eye-hand and eye-foot coordination.
	Hopping for accuracy	Gross body coordination	
	Skipping	Gross body coordination	
	Ball dribble	Eye-hand coordination	
	Foot dribble	Eye-hand coordination	
Balance	Beam walk	Dynamic balance	Year by year improvement with age. Girls often outperform boys, especially in dynamic balance activities until about age 8. Abilities similar thereafter.
	Stick balance	Static balance	
	One-foot stand	Static balance	
Speed	20-yd dash	Running speed	Year by year improvement with age. Boys and girls similar until age 6 or 7, at which time boys make more rapid improvements. Boys superior to girls at all ages.
	30-yd dash	Running speed	
Agility	Shuttle run	Running agility	Year by year improvement with age. Girls begin to level off after age 13. Boys continue to make improvements.
Power	Vertical jump	Leg strength and speed	Year by year improvement with age. Boys outperform girls at all age levels.
	Standing long jump	Leg strength and speed	
	Distance throw	Upper arm strength and speed	
	Velocity throw	Upper arm strength and speed	

Source: From *Understanding Motor Development in Children* by David L. Gallahue. Copyright © 1982 by John Wiley & Sons, Inc. Reprinted by permission.

Sex Differences. There is little difference in boys and girls in either height or weight at the beginning of elementary school. Girls tend to mature one to two years earlier than boys, and therefore it is not unusual in late elementary school for them to tower over their less mature brothers. Many researchers have identified sex differences in physical abilities in middle childhood, however slight they may be. But no one has determined whether the behavior or the skill comes first. Perhaps these differences are the result of sex typing of behavior. Perhaps because girls are encouraged to play jump-rope and hop-scotch their visual-motor abilities become honed. Similarly, perhaps because boys are encouraged to throw, run, kick and bat balls they become skilled in these activities. More research is needed to ascertain the cause of the drop in athletic skills for girls at puberty: Is it a natural development or another culturally prescribed sex-related behavior? When our grandmothers were girls they were forbidden to engage in physical activities. It will take some time to ascertain the natural abilities of girls. Only recently have they been allowed to form teams and to play on Little League teams. Women athletes are attracting attention in tennis, golf, and in college team sports such as basketball.

Cultural values and proscriptions notwithstanding, children in the middle

Is jumping rope a "natural" ability of girls, or is it a skill they learn because they are encouraged to do so? [Courtesy William Amidon and Greensboro Day School.]

years are a bundle of energy and they are found participating in team sports of all kinds, including swimming, football, soccer, and basketball; in individual sports such as tennis, golf, and horseback riding; and in highly skilled activities such as gymnastics and dance. In addition to organized sports, children often spend free time in rounding up a neighborhood game for sandlot ball, bicycle riding, snowball fighting, and any other activity that requires high energy and a chance to test their developing bodies.

Fine Motor

Parallel with large motor development is precision in the control and coordination of the small muscles of the hands and fingers. Many first graders have difficulty holding a pencil and often are given large ones with which to write. Their writing is shaky, and they use large sheets of lined paper to practice the skill. In the next six years these children will learn to play pianos and violins, to build intricate models of ships, buildings or planes, to draw minute detailed pictures, and to take apart and rebuild machines and electronic equipment. In other words, in these years children literally learn to take apart and put back together the technology of the culture. The skills that develop reflect control of the fine muscles and their coordination with vision and thought processes.

Left Hand or Right Hand.   Infants use both hands impartially—they are as proficient in the use of one as the other. At some time in early childhood most children develop a distinct preference for using one hand over the other to execute fine motor sequences. A few children remain forever *ambidextrous*—that is, equally skilled in using either hand. In our culture and in Eastern cultures, there is a decided preference for children to use their right hand. The cause of handedness is believed to rest in the development of the brain. The brain is composed of two symmetrical hemispheres. The two are joined by a neural connection, or pathway; the right hemisphere of the brain connects with the left side of the body and the left hemisphere with the right side. This means that the left brain controls the right hand and the right brain controls the left hand. In infancy both hemispheres exert equal control, but gradually the two hemispheres assume control of different functions (lateralization), one assuming dominance over the other. If the left hemisphere is dominant, then the child finds control of the right hand easier, and if the right hemisphere is dominant then the child finds it easier to use his or her left hand.

Many words in our language indicate a cultural bias against *left*. Words such as *sinister* and *gauche* originally meant "left" and reflect the disfavor in which left has been held. In addition, there is much folklore around left. For example, until the eighteenth century it was generally believed that whether a child was a boy or girl was determined by left and right orientation. If a fetus developed on the left side of the uterus, it was female, and if on the right side, it was male. An alternative explanation for sex determination held that if the sperm came from the left testicle

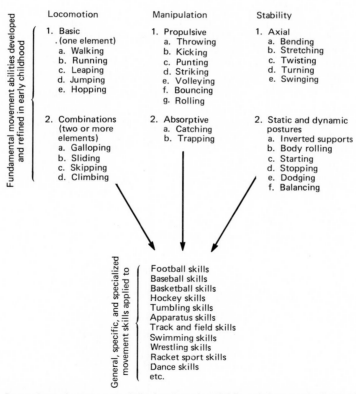

Basic physical movement skills developed in childhood that are the basis of later team and skill sports. [From *Understanding Motor Development in Children* by David L. Gallahue. (Copyright © 1982 by John Wiley & Sons. Inc., New York.) Reprinted by permission.]

Physical education in the elementary school helps children to develop basic movement skills; these children are practicing jumping. [Courtesy William Amidon and Greensboro Day School.]

the product was female and if from the right testicle it was male. (Money, 1980). This belief was proven false when a scientifically minded physician reported the case of a man with only one testicle who had fathered both girls and boys! Left, then, was associated with the female sex.

It is no wonder that with these connotations parents and schoolmasters went to great lengths to force a child to use his or her right hand. Clinical reports indicate that forced attempts to change handedness in children results in emotional disturbance, and in such behavioral abnormalities as nervousness and stuttering. The current thinking is that children should not be changed from left- to right-handedness. (It often does not work anyway.) Even so, "lefties" often feel that they must live in a world not designed for them. Many tools and implements, such as scissors and golf clubs, are designed for the right-handed, and the left-handed must either adjust to them or search for those scarce items designed for the left-handed.

Another problem arises in developing such learning skills as playing a guitar or violin because the instrument must be changed to the opposite side and comprehension adjustments must be made. However, whether with the right or the left hand, most schoolchildren make tremendous strides in fine motor coordination during these years.

Physical Abilities, Self-esteem, and Peer Evaluation

A child's physical appearance and accomplishments have a strong influence on self-esteem. The effects of peer evaluation in the middle-childhood years persist until long after the circumstances and events have faded into history: The girl who is obese in fourth grade and who cannot compete in games may forever see herself as an "ugly duckling"; the boy who is uncoordinated and the last to be chosen for the team may forever carry the perception of being unworthy and having nothing to contribute to a group effort; or even more tragically, the boy or girl who has a physical handicap and is teased by thoughtless schoolchildren has a double handicap to overcome. In our not-too-distant village past, the village idiot and the village cripple were taunted by adults and children alike. Victor Hugo in his novel *The Hunchback of Notre Dame* relates the torment that was inflicted on Quasimodo so that his only friends were the bells of the cathedral. In our modern "enlightened" view of the value of all people, we attempt to teach children to accept others as they are. This strategy is not always successful, and cruel encounters are apt to occur on school playgrounds. Unfortunately the ability to "take the view of another" is dependent both on maturation and learning. Teachers and parents must help children to develop this sensitivity.

Health Problems

We picture schoolchildren as vibrantly healthy and full of abundant energy and insatiable curiosity—smiling, rose-cheeked children busily pursuing learning and recreation. The stereotype, however, does not describe all children. For some, a more accurate picture is one of illness, listlessness, and a resulting depression of both learning and recreational skills. Middle-class children in developed nations have the highest standards of health that the world has ever seen. The United States does not lead this list of countries, even though it is probably the wealthiest developed nation. If we assume that more money can buy better health care, then the United States should be able to afford the best; yet sixteen nations report fewer

 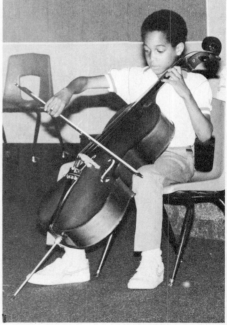

Developing control in fine motor skills enables school-age children to master such intricate feats as playing musical instruments. [Right hand photograph courtesy Anna Fesmire and Greensboro Day School.]

(A)

(B)

(C)

Physical appearance and skills affect both how children evaluate themselves and how other children evaluate them. [Photographs (A) and (B) courtesy Mount Zion Elementary School, Greensboro, North Carolina; (C) courtesy John King and Greensboro Day School.]

infant deaths per 1,000 population than the United States (March of Dimes, 1983). Nevertheless, in the view of many nations, the record of the United States is enviable. High standards for public health have been arrived at through long and arduous efforts. The health of children in the United States in the last century was wasted by parasites, malnutrition, and a high incidence of communicable diseases. Many children from homes in the low socioeconomic range continue in the 1980s to suffer from these conditions. For example, it was found that 30 per cent of the children enrolled in Head Start programs were anemic (Zigler & Trickett, 1978). Underdeveloped countries today are plagued with these same problems; unfortunately, programs that decrease the infant mortality often create greater pressures on the resources available to school-age children in these countries.

Children in affluent America are not free from health problems and illness. In 1978 children between six and sixteen lost a total of 220 million days from school because of illness, or an average of 5.4 days for each schoolchild. In addition, almost two million children between the ages of five and fifteen spent some time in hospitals. Child health has been a major concern of public health in the twentieth century.

Early in the twentieth century, children were subject to many diseases, such as measles, whooping cough, mumps, diphtheria, tetanus, and polio. Through the heroic efforts of public health workers and private physicians, most children can be spared these illnesses—and their devastating effects—if they are inoculated against them. Protection against these diseases is not automatic; *each* infant and child must receive the inoculations to gain protection. Many children are not immunized even though immunization is available from public health departments. In spite of the worldwide effort of health workers, only one disease has actually been eradicated—smallpox. The strategy for all other diseases is to hold them under control and prevent epidemics. When a large number of children has not received immunization against diseases such as polio and measles, the threat of an epidemic exists. In 1976 such an epidemic of measles threatened the United States, and a massive campaign to immunize all schoolchildren was undertaken. The real danger in a measles epidemic is not to schoolchildren but to the unborn children of the pregnant women they may infect. For various reasons parents and caretakers neglect to obtain health protection for children, leaving them at risk for serious illness. A second category of serious illnesses that affect children affects all people: tuberculo-

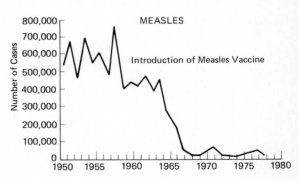

Childhood diseases such as measles and poliomyelitis are not the threat to children that they once were. These charts indicate the decline in reported cases of these diseases in the last thirty years. Note the rise in incidence of measles in the early and middle 1970s. Such epidemics can be prevented if children receive immunizations. [From "Behavioral Health's Challenge to Academic, Scientific, and Professional Psychology" by Joseph D. Matarazzo. (In *American Psychologist,* 1982, *37(1),* pp. 1–14. Copyright © 1982 by the American Psychological Association.) Reprinted by permission of the publisher and author.]

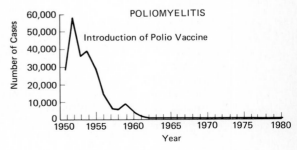

In underdeveloped countries, children and families have health standards comparable to those in the United States in the nineteenth century. These mothers and children are waiting their turn to see the doctor in a small rural dispensary in India.

sis, cancer, influenza, and increasingly, gonorrhea and syphilis. The third cause of illness in children is genetic. There are no cures for these diseases: they range from fatal diseases such as Tay-Sachs, to diseases in which strict routines must be observed to maintain health and life.

Accidents

Accidents are the leading cause of deaths for children of all ages. Accidentally ingesting poison is a leading cause of death in the very young; physical mishaps, such as being hit by an automobile, drowning, falling, or being burned, affect children of all ages. Many accidents are preventable with careful adult supervision: placing dangerous drugs and substances in locked cabinets, supervising young children near water, and paying careful attention to fire regulations. School-age children must be taught safety regulations for walking or riding bicycles in traffic. Even with the best precautions, childhood is a time of high-energy exploration and little experience—conditions that invite accidents.

Physical Handicaps

Not all children can run, jump, climb, or even hold a pencil. An accident may leave a child crippled; a genetic disorder may cause a structural defect; a birth accident may leave a child with cerebral palsy, or a drug taken in pregnancy may result in an infant with deformed hands and feet. Imprisoned in bodies that will not function adequately, these children may learn as easily as others or exhibit talent in music and art; certainly they have the same emotional and social needs as other children. It is easy to equate a physical disability with mental inferiority and emotional limitations. However, the current trend in schools toward mainstreaming creates an opportunity for all children to function in the least restricted environment possible. If we obey the spirit as well as the letter of this federal law, we will provide each child with an environment in which he or she can best grow to reach the fullest fruition of the promise of childhood.

Main Points

Growth Patterns

1. During the middle years of childhood children grow at a slow, steady, even pace, averaging 5 pounds of weight gain and 2½ inches of height increase per year; there is wide variation in height among children.

The Secular Trend

2. Researchers have found an increase in size and decrease in the age of puberty in this century.

Skeletal and Muscular Development

3. In middle childhood the head grows more slowly, the extremities grow at a fast pace, bone continues to ossify, internal organs continue to grow, and muscles increase in size.

Motor Development

4. Middle childhood is a time of bodily control, grace, and coordination.

5. Large motor development enables six to twelve-year-olds to ride bikes, jump rope, and roller skate and to perfect running, throwing, jumping, catching, hitting, and kicking skills.

6. Boys and girls do not differ markedly in skill development, but boys are more muscular and girls have more mature visual-motor coordination.

7. Fine motor development in middle childhood brings precision in control and coordination of the small muscles of the hands and fingers with vision and thought processes.

8. It is believed that handedness results from brain lateralization, which occurs during early childhood.

Physical Abilities, Self-esteem, and Peer Evaluation

9. Children's physical appearances and abilities and their peers' evaluations of those have a tremendous influence on self-esteem.

Health Problems

10. Children in affluent America are not free from health problems and illness: many children do not receive inoculations to protect them from childhood diseases, children are subject to the illnesses prevalent in society, and there are many genetic diseases that affect children.

Accidents

11. Accidents are the leading cause of death for children.

Physical Handicaps

12. Children have physical handicaps for many reasons, but each child should be provided with the environment in which he or she can best grow and develop.

Words to Know

ambidextrous
lateralization

Term to Define

secular trend

CHAPTER 13

Mental Development in Middle Childhood

Have you ever wondered

> how the thinking of children changes in the elementary school years?
>
> if the jokes children tell reflect their language and mental development?
>
> how mental development is measured?
>
> why schools use standardized tests?
>
> if there is a difference in mental ability between boys and girls?
>
> how moral development takes place?

In all cultures the years between six and twelve are those in which the child learns the tools of the culture. It does not matter whether the tools are a bow and arrow and a weaving loom or computers, mathematics, and language skills. These are the years in which children's intellectual abilities can be turned to mastering the physical and technological world. Learning becomes patterned and sequenced in schools and school personnel are challenged with measuring and evaluating this learning. Moral development rests on the child's cognitive development. In this chapter we will consider cognitive development in the school years as outlined by Piaget, development of language, the measurement of intelligence, sex differences in intellectual ability, and moral development.

Piaget's Cognitive Development in the School Years

In Piaget's theory of cognitive development the years between seven and twelve to fourteen encompass the stage of concrete operations. The child becomes capable of logical thought and of performing mental operations, provided they involve con-

337

crete objects. The ability to perform such operations with abstract ideas begins to evolve at the end of this period. The child can incorporate information from the external world into his or her own mental constructions without distorting the information and can adapt ideas to new realities without being absorbed by those experiences.

Gradually, in the years between five and seven, preoperational thought is eroded. The child becomes less egocentric and is able to take the point of view of another. In solving problems the child is able to decenter and thus to take into account all important elements in drawing conclusions. The ability to seriate and classify increases rapidly and concepts are no longer shaped by the belief that everything has life and everything was made by someone. Reasoning ceases to be transductive, and inductive and deductive methods are used more frequently. By eleven or twelve years of age the thinking of children is stabilized and no longer subject to the errors characteristic of young children. Piaget states that children of this age can consistently perform logical operations on concrete objects. He has demonstrated the attainment of concrete operations in a series of experiments he calls conservation studies.

Conservation

The child is said to be able to conserve when he or she recognizes that two equal quantities remain equal even if one is changed in some way but nothing is added or taken away. The ability to conserve rests on three previously attained concepts: *identity, reversibility,* and *compensation. Identity* is the concept that certain properties of things remain constant even when their outward appearance changes. *Reversibility* is the concept that procedures can be reversed and objects can regain their original state. In *compensation,* changes in one dimension are balanced by equal and opposite changes in another. When a ball of clay is rolled into an elongated shape, the child who has a concept of identity understands that the object remains clay. If the child can mentally reverse the process of distorting the clay ball and conceive the elongated object as the original ball of clay the concept of reversibility has been

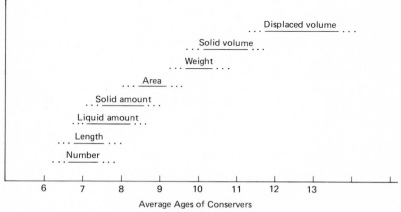

Average ages of conservers. [From *The Piaget Primer* by Ed Labinowicz. (Copyright © 1980 by Addison-Wesley Publishing Company.) Reprinted by permission.]

attained. Finally, if the child understands that the increase in length of the clay compensates for the reduction in spherical breadth the concept of compensation has been reached. In other words, in spite of changes in appearance, the object itself not only remains clay, but the same amount of clay, despite its transformation. To arrive at the conclusion of sameness (conservation) the child must be able to mentally reverse the operation performed on the object. Although the concepts of identity, reversibility, and compensation are reached at around six to eight years of age, the ability to conserve the various physical properties stretches from seven to twelve or thirteen years. Piaget also has explored the child's ability to conserve number, length, liquid amount, solid amount, area, weight, solid volume, and displaced volume.

Number

Many preschool children know how to count—that is, they repeat the words *one, two, three, four, five, six, seven, eight, nine,* and *ten,* in correct sequence. They even learn to repeat these numbers while touching objects. Sometimes, when a child is counting, there may be more objects than number words, or more number words than objects, because these children do not actually have a concept of numbers: they have only learned words. To test whether a child can conserve any material, the following procedure can be used:

1. Establish equivalency: Gain agreement with the child that two materials are equal.
2. Transform one of the materials only in a physical way. Do not add or take away any material.
3. Question the child as to whether the two forms of the material are still the same.

The procedure Piaget developed to assess conservation of number follows:

1. Establish equivalency. Show the child two sets of objects, such as red and black checkers. Arrange them in two equal lines. Discuss the number of checkers in each set with the child and count them until you both agree that the two sets contain the same number of checkers.
2. Transform *one* of the sets in some way. Typically the space between each object is increased, so that one set makes a longer line than the other.
3. Ask the child if the number of red checkers remains the same as the number of black checkers. Children respond to this simple question in a variety of ways depending on their ability to conserve number.
   a. Preconserver: These children usually say that the longer line has more checkers. They have focused on the length of the line and cannot take into consideration the distance between objects.
   b. Transitional: These children may answer correctly but, given the same concept in a different context (for example, if one set of checkers is arranged in a cluster), may not be able to conserve. In addition, when questioned, the transitional children may justify a correct answer by faulty reasoning: "It looks like more but they are just dancing, so they are the same." The transitional children are unsure of the reasoning and are in a state of disequilibrium.
   c. Conserver: Children who can conserve numbers reply that the two lines

PRECONSERVER	TRANSITIONAL	CONSERVER
The child centers on only one of the dimensions and states that the tall glass has more or less water than the short glass.	The transitional child is inconsistent in his replies to two related tasks. He may conserve liquid amount in one situation but not in the other. This inconsistency may be noted even after the child logically justifies his first conservation response.	The child judges that the amount of water is conserved regardless of the container(s) involved. One logical justification is sufficient for each variation of the task. Piaget considers a logical justification to be critical to judging a conservation response.

CONSERVATION TASKS:	ESTABLISH EQUIVALENCE	TRANSFORM OR REARRANGE	CONSERVATION QUESTION AND JUSTIFICATION
Conservation of Number Number is not changed despite rearrangement of objects	○○○○○○○○ ○○○○○○○○	Rearrange one set	Are there the same number of red & green chips or...?
Conservation of Length The length of a string is unaffected by its shape or its displacement		Change shape of one string	Will an ant have just as far to walk, or...?
Conservation of Liquid Amount The amount of liquid isn't changed by the shape of the container.		Transfer liquid	Do the glasses have the same amount of water, or...?
Conservation of Substance (Solid Amount) The amount of substance does not change by changing its shape or by subdividing it.		Roll out one clay ball	Do you still have the same amount of clay?
Conservation of Area The area covered by a given number of two-dimensional objects is unaffected by their arrangement.	Grass Is there still the same amount of "room" for planting or...? Garden	Rearrange one set of triangles	Is there still the same amount of grass to eat or...?
Conservation of Weight A clay ball weighs the same even when its shape is elongated or flattened.		Change shape of one ball	Do the balls of clay still weigh the same or...?
Conservation of Displacement Volume The volume of water that is displaced by an object is dependent on the volume of the object and independent of weight, shape or position of the immersed object.		Change shape of one ball	Will the water go up as high or...?

Judging the levels of the child's response on Piagetian conservation tasks. [From *The Piaget Primer* by Ed Labinowicz. (Copyright © 1980 by Addison-Wesley Publishing Company.) Reprinted by permission.]

contain the same number of checkers *because* "you didn't add any or take any away, you just spread them out."

Some children can conserve numbers as early as the age of five. They usually have had preschool experience and ample opportunity to manipulate objects while adults asked relevant questions. Piaget reports that children can conserve numbers between six and eight years of age. In establishing the equivalency of sets, the child must have an understanding of one-to-one correspondence; in evaluating the transformed sets, the child must also have an understanding of "more than" and "less than." Another feature of number concept is class inclusion: one is included in two, two is included in three, three is included in four and so forth.

Length
The ability to conserve length is generally reached a little later than number but between the ages of six and eight. Problems such as the following determine the child's ability to conserve length.

1. Establish equivalency. Show the child two unsharpened pencils of equal length. Place them side by side on a surface and discuss the length until the child agrees that they are the same length.
2. Transform one length. Move one of the pencils forward noticeably.
3. Question the child about whether the pencils are still the same length or if one is longer.

In an interesting variation, establish the equivalency of two strings; then change the shape of one string and ask: "Will an ant have just as far to walk from one end of the string to the other on the wiggly string as the straight one?" The responses will be similar to those for number, depending on whether the child is a preconserver, transitional, or a conserver. If the child is a conserver, the answer will be that the ant will have the same distance to walk on both strings because neither was changed.

Liquid Volume
The concept of conservation of liquids is attained between the ages of seven and nine years. This is an experiment that children enjoy. You will need two tall clear glasses and one that is short and wide.

1. Establish equivalency. Pour water into the two tall glasses until the levels are exactly equal. Discuss this with the child and adjust the water until you agree that the glasses contain the same amount. (Interest increases in this problem if the water is colored.)
2. Transform one glass of water by pouring the water into the short, wide glass.
3. Question the child. Ask if one glass contains more water or if they are the same. If the child replies that one has less or more water, the water can be returned to the original container and the child's logic questioned again. The conserver will reply that both glasses contain the same amount of water because none has been added or taken away.

Area
In the conservation of area the child is able to reason that the area covered by a given number of two-dimensional objects is unaffected by their arrangements. Children are able to conserve area between eight and ten years of age.

1. Establish equivalency. This problem can be stated as a story problem: "Farmer Brown and Farmer Jones each have a cow and a pasture with grass for the cow to eat. Reach agreement with the child that both cows have the same amount of grass to eat.

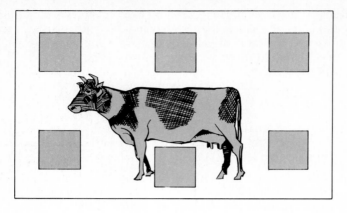

Which cow has more grass to eat?

2. Transform the area. "Both Farmer Jones and Farmer Brown decide that they need a barn in the pasture." Place a square representing a barn on each piece of paper representing the pasture. One farmer builds his barn in the middle of the pasture and one builds his barn on its perimeter. Ask if the cows have the same amount of grass to eat, or if one has less. Continue to build barns in the pastures; place one set of barns randomly in the pasture and have the others touching.

3. Question the child. Inquire after each barn building whether the cows have the same amount of grass to eat. The child who is a conserver will continue to state that the cows have the same amount of grass to eat because the same number of barns has been built on each pasture.

Solid Substance (Mass, Weight, and Displacement)

Conservation of mass (solid amount) is attained between the ages of seven and nine. Conservation of weight is attained between the ages of nine and eleven. The conservation of displacement volume by a solid mass is an advanced concept and is attained quite late—between eleven and thirteen years. Conservation of mass, weight, and displacement volume can be evaluated with two balls of clay. Each experiment begins with the clay formed into two equal spheres.

1. Establish equivalency. Reach agreement with the child that both balls of clay contain the same amount (weight) of clay. (Pinch and add to each ball until this agreement is reached.) Equal mass is ascertained by visual inspection; weight by estimating how the two balls feel in your two hands or by actually weighing them on scales; and displacement of volume by placing the balls in glasses of water and obtaining agreement that the water rises to the same level in each glass.

2. Transform the clay. In each of these experiments one of the balls of clay is elongated.

3. Question the child. Ask the child if the pieces have the same amount of clay; still weigh the same; and, in the case of displacement of volume, if the water will go up to the same level. The child who conserves will stick to the logical position that the amount, weight, and displacement of the clay remain the same because no clay has been added or taken away. In spite of changed appearances, the clay remains the same in these dimensions.

Testing for conservation ability is a way of demonstrating a *qualitative* change in thinking by children in middle childhood. Piaget has investigated how these changes affect the child's thinking about number, length, mass, area, weight, and displacement. He has also investigated the transformation in thought about time,

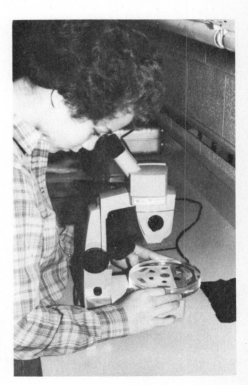

The ability to conserve underlies the ability to conduct scientific experiments and to ask and answer questions using the tools of science. [Courtesy William Amidon and Greensboro Day School.]

space, causality, and reasoning and moral judgments. Other investigators have expanded studies into other areas. It is important to note that these changes permeate all areas of the child's thinking and relations to others and are not simply isolated pieces of information that are learned.

Effect of Training Conservation

Piaget has stressed the importance of maturation in the attainment of conservation; in fact, in an interview in *Psychology Today* (Hall, 1970) he stated, "As for teaching children concepts that they have not attained in their spontaneous development, it is completely useless" (p. 30). Many American psychologists, however, hold that the major influence on development is environmental. As a result, there has been a running controversy on this question for many years, in which claims and refutations are made through research studies. We will review some of the evidence. First, we will look at naturalistic, or cross-cultural, studies in which children are not specifically trained in conservation tasks, but in whom differing life experiences have created two identifiable groups. The second kind of research that has been conducted is laboratory studies, in which children are actually trained in conservation.

Piagetian concepts have inspired hundreds of studies in numerous countries in the world. These studies generally support Piaget's general statements about age progression and sequence (Cowan, 1978). The question of rate of development, however, is not as clearly indicated by research. Kohlberg (1968) found differences in rate of development in American, Mexican, and Taiwanese children, and Bergling (1974) found differing rates of development in Swedish and Indian children.

Studies have been conducted comparing children of different socioeconomic status within single cultures. They have generally found that children from low socioeconomic families perform Piagetian tasks at lower ages (Kohlberg, 1969; Hunt, 1976; Wachs, 1976). This information tells us very little for many reasons. First, it must be noted that children at low and middle socioeconomic levels do *not* comprise two different groups on such measures as Piagetian tasks. Rather, they form two overlapping groups. This means that many high-scoring children of low socioeconomic status score higher than many low-scoring children of middle socioeconomic status. The children are not identifiable as separate groups because of their performance, but because of socioeconomic membership. The differences between the groups are between the groups' *average* and not between individuals in the groups. Second, there are many other differences between low and middle socioeconomic groups such as in use of language, in attitude toward the testing situation, in relations between children and parents, and in childrearing practices that might influence the child's performance in Piagetian tasks.

In industrialized countries most children attend schools. Researchers have wondered if school affects the attainment of conservation and thus sought to find children without any school experience. Such a naturalistic experiment became possible in Prince Edward County, Virginia, when the public schools were closed for several years because of a controversy over integration. Mermelstein and Shulman (1967) compared six- to nine-year-old black children in that county who had not attended school, with northern urban black children, who had attended school. The researchers found no differences between the children in concrete operational levels. Greenfield (1966) found another natural experiment in the Woloff children who belong to the dominant tribe in Senegal, Africa, a former French

(A)

(B)

Mental growth, according to Piaget, occurs best when children solve problems presented by materials in "hands-on" experiences (A). Peers stimulate each other to higher levels of mental organization when working together (B) and teachers set the stage for mental growth by asking stimulating questions rather than by supplying definitive answers (C). [Photograph (B) courtesy Richard Michaels and Greensboro Day School; (C) courtesy Mount Zion Elementary School, Greensboro, North Carolina.]

(C)

colony. Greenfield studied three groups of these children, all of whom had a similar genetic and cultural heritage. One group of children lived in the cosmopolitan capital of Dakar and attended French-style schools; a second group lived in the bush and did not attend school; and a third group lived in the bush but also attended a French-style school. When the three groups were compared on Piagetian conservation tasks, little difference was noted between those children who lived in Dakar and those who lived in the bush and went to school. However, differences were found between those children who attended school and those who did not, even when both groups lived in the primitive conditions of the bush. For example, virtually all the children who attended school could conserve liquid by the age of eleven or twelve (which is comparable with Western-schooled children); however, only half of the unschooled children could. The implication seems clear that schooling affects this ability. Some researchers have suggested that individuals in non-Western countries and in rural tribes may never reach the stage of formal operations (Cowan, 1978). However, the attainment of formal operations is not universal in Western culture: even some college students may not function on this level. Education seems an important adjunct for this abstract level to be obtained.

Schools generally have broad curriculums, and are not designed to teach conservation tasks directly. What if strategies were specifically designed to do this? Would they aid in teaching conservation? Various researchers have attempted such intervention techniques. Some of the techniques used have been simple feedback of information to the child (Brainerd, 1977); teaching verbal rules (Beilin, 1965); and giving training on the components of the problem (Gruen, 1965). The components varied from verbal labels such as "the same" or specific training in the results of adding and taking away. Another approach to conservation training used by Gelman (1969) was discrimination training. The child was taught to focus on relevant cues and to disregard others in judging the number of checkers or the length of sticks. Other studies have attempted to teach conservation by having adults model conservation behavior for children (Botvin & Murray, 1975; Zimmerman & Lanaro, 1974). Another strategy tried by researchers is to pair conservers and nonconservers on conservation tasks. The children are instructed to discuss and jointly decide on a response (Botvin & Murray, 1975; Murray, 1972). The expectation is that the conserver will lead the nonconserver to a higher level of thinking. The evidence from these studies indicates that laboratory training produces some significant changes in cognitive level for some children.

Barbel Inhelder, a colleague of Piaget's, looked more closely at individual children who were trained in conservation tasks in order to understand more fully the role of teaching. Inhelder and Sinclair (1969) divided a group of nonconservers into those who were "frankly preoperational" and those who were "in transition." All of these children were trained in conservation of liquid. After training, only 12.5 per cent of the frankly preoperational children showed any progress, and none of them achieved conservation; however, 75 per cent of the children in transition showed progress, and half of them achieved the level of concrete operation with liquid. In a second study (Inhelder, Sinclair, & Bovet, 1974) the children selected for training were differentiated for five levels. They were given several pretests and were then classified according to their level of thinking. All the children were then given training in conservation of liquid and clay. Three weeks after the last training session they were given a posttest, which was similar to the pretest. The results of the pretest and posttest are reviewed here.

Pretest
Level I. Preoperational level: No correct answers.
Level II. Beginning transitional: Mostly incorrect answers but a few correct ones.
Level III. Middle transition: About half correct answers and half incorrect.
Level IV. Late transition: Correct answers to clay but not to liquid.
Level V. Conservers: Consistently correct answers in conservation.

These data were analyzed for each subject (rather than for group behavior). The results revealed a strong relationship between the childs' beginning level and the effect of training.

Posttest
Level I. Thirteen of fifteen children made no change.
Level II. No children attained conservation.
Level III. Some children attained conservation.

Level IV. All children attained conservation.

Level V. No change. (These children already had attained conservation, and they served as a control group.)

In this study we see that children in transition are susceptible to the influence of teaching, and that the child solidly in a stage must await further development before teaching is effective. The implication of this for the teacher in the classroom is enormous. Such results add depth to the concept of readiness and provide a means for evaluating that readiness. It also underscores the importance of individualized instruction and the necessity of the teacher knowing and understanding the cognitive level of each child in his or her classroom. Cowan (1978) has suggested principles to be followed when designing strategies for teaching cognitive development. These principles are useful for teachers and researchers interested in children's mental growth.

1. Training sessions (learning situations) should resemble natural conditions outside the laboratory (or classroom).

2. The more active a subject is, the more successful his or her learning is likely to be, because development results from interaction with material. A word of caution is injected, however: A child can be mentally active without physically manipulating objects. Here we are seeking mental activity.

3. Problems should not be made so simple that the child does not experience any difficulty or confusion in attempting to solve them. However, learning situations should be carefully structured so that only those difficulties occurring naturally in the situation are included.

4. The errors in logic that preoperational children make are not errors to be eliminated by learning correct verbal responses. More mature schemes can only be built on existing ones. The child will integrate and coordinate existing schemes into new structures. For the preoperational child, the conclusion that quantity of liquid increases when poured into a taller glass is a legitimate inference based on the fact that liquid in the taller glass has a higher level. The best way to lead the child to new mental structures is to provide ample experiences with materials.

5. The adult should help the child use his or her present developmental schemes to recognize the need for new information or organization: this disequilibrium should lead to the attempt to resolve new problems.

6. Training (teaching) must be matched to the level of the child and proceed in the natural sequence. Teaching should be aimed at the level directly above the current level of the child. This is an *optimal mismatch*.

7. The focus of training or teaching should be on inducing disequilibrative conflict and developing cognitive operations in the child, not on conveying more facts or new and specific rules (Cowan, 1978). The teacher, following Piagetian principles, thus asks provocative questions rather than supplies definitive answers.

Language Development

The child entering first grade has a working knowledge of language, but development in this area is incomplete. Language development continues throughout the school years and the child's life. The preschooler may be quite adept at using language for self-expression but may not be as proficient when called on to use it in more formal communication. Closely aligned to growth in communication is understanding the subtle and connotative meanings of words. It is in these areas that language continues to develop between the ages of six to twelve.

Vocabulary and Meaning

The child's knowledge of words increases steadily in the middle years of childhood. As is true throughout life, receptive language, or reading and listening vocabulary, far exceeds productive language, or speaking vocabulary. Reading vocabulary may approach 50,000 words by sixth grade (McCarthy, 1954), whereas the speaking or writing vocabulary may be only a fraction of that number. Even more important than vocabulary in these early school years is the increase in precision of meaning. Language is a system of *encoding* and *decoding*. Encoding is the process of enclosing thought in words, whereas decoding is the reverse process of extracting thought and ideas from the words in which they are encapsulated. Words and language, then, are a kind of cultural code. Thoughts, feelings, and perceptions are translated into this code so that they can be sent into another person's perceptual field. No one can directly perceive our thoughts, experience our feelings, or sense our perceptions. We must enclose those experiences in discrete little packets of words and then send them to another person through the sensory mechanisms of sight, hearing, or touch (as with Braille). These word packets are similar to the pneumatic

Reading vocabulary increases rapidly in the elementary school years; by sixth grade reading vocabulary far exceeds speaking vocabulary. [Courtesy Mount Zion Elementary School, Greensboro, North Carolina.]

tubes used at drive-in banks to send business messages to the teller. To the extent that two people ascribe the same meaning to these little word packets, communication is achieved and language serves its function. Language development in the school years, in large measure, consists of honing these meanings to increased precision.

Young children often confuse concepts that are similar. For example, first-grade children often confuse concepts such as *heavy*, *big*, and *strong*. When asked to judge two objects that are identical except in weight, they often describe the heavier object as "bigger" or "stronger." Precision in meaning increases throughout the elementary school years; sixth-grade children are unlikely to confuse such concepts. As children grow older they are also increasingly able to understand abstract relationships expressed in words.

Children's understanding of language and their ability to express relationships are related to their cognitive development. In a series of experiments to test this, Sinclair-deSwart (1969) assigned children preoperational, transitional, and operational levels. The children were then tested on their ability to *describe* simple qualitative differences among physical objects. To test their *comprehension* of these differences, the experimenter asked the children questions. For example, children were shown two pencils, a short thick one and a tall thin one. To check whether the children comprehended the differences, questions such as, "Find the pencil that is shorter but thicker than this one," were asked. No difference was found in the comprehension of the three groups of children; however, there was a difference in the *language* used to describe the differences. The children in the stage of concrete operations produced language that *compared* the two, not that separated them. For example, a concrete operational child might say, "This pencil is thin, but that one is fat."

Perhaps the relationship is the other way around. That is, perhaps language changes cognitive level, rather than cognitive level changing language. In a follow-up study to test this, Sinclair-deSwart (1969) attempted to teach preoperational children the language that the concrete operational children used in describing the objects. These children had difficulties learning comparatives, and of those who learned the correct language, only 10 per cent showed any progress toward attaining the level of concrete operations. It is evidence such as this that underscores the futility of teaching children the correct *verbal* answers without giving them the opportunity to manipulate materials and to grow in cognitive operations. The young child is dependent on his or her perceptions. When adults and teachers impose answers that do not coincide with those perceptions, the child either comes to distrust his or her own experiences or to distrust answers from authority. In the first instance, the child's self-confidence is undermined; in the second, a cynical distrust of authority is fostered. Many children, and even college students, learn the "right answers" without comprehending their own verbal responses. Children should be led carefully through their own experiences and perceptions; in time they can relinquish concrete experiences for abstract thought, but they must set the pace.

Communication Skills

"Yeah, I know where you're coming from," is a statement that we often hear in casual conversation. Although it may leave something to be desired in terms of syntax and style, it performs the function of language, which is communication. If a friend uses this expression, we are reassured that our attempt to communicate has been understood. Young children are limited in their ability to communicate with others, not only because of limited vocabulary, but also because they are *egocentric* —that is, they find it difficult to put themselves in the place of the listener and adapt their language to the requirements of this audience. Piaget (1946) examined the way in which children express egocentrism in speaking to others. He told eight-year-olds a story and then asked them to repeat it to someone who had not heard it. The eight-year-olds related the story as though the listener had heard the original. In a similar investigation Flavell, Botkin, Fry, Wright, and Jarvis (1968) showed children from seven to seventeen years of age a series of seven pictures that illustrated sequences in a story. The children were then asked to relate the story. All of the children could. Then they eliminated three of the pictures and told a different story. The children again were asked to relate this story. Older children could, but younger children confused the two story lines. Children below fourth grade were less able to take into account that the listener had not heard and seen the entire sequence of seven pictures. In another experiment Flavell (1977) tested children's capacity to relate directions to a game to both a sighted and a blind (blindfolded) listener. The youngest children could not adapt their directions to the requirements of a blind listener, but the older children were increasingly able to eliminate visual cues.

Language Play: Telling Jokes

Many other animals play, but humor is indeed human. Humor, or play with words, is dependent on cognitive development. Preschool children may attempt to use the forms but lose the essence of humor—that is, the punch line. A child may ask, "Want to hear a dirty joke?" and in reply to an avid "Yes," say, with a straight face, "A white horse fell into a mud puddle." A preschooler on hearing this, may counter with the riddle, "Why did the little boy take a bath?" When the child's listeners are stumped and give up, she or he will instruct, "Because he was dirty." Understanding and producing humor requires a more subtle discrimination of meanings than young children possess. The humor in the "dirty" joke here rests on the double meaning of the word *dirty*—and on being able to perceive the two simultaneously. Young children, because they center on one meaning, cannot successfully juxtapose two meanings. The preschooler in this example centered on the meaning of *dirty* as "soiled," whereas the older children simultaneously played this meaning against the "naughty" sexual connotation of the word.

Children in middle childhood enjoy play on words and the similarity in the sounds of words such as the following joke: "Knock-knock." "Who's there?" "Banana." "Banana who?" "Knock-knock." "Who's there?" "Banana." "Banana who?" "Knock knock." "Who's there?" "Orange." "Orange who?" "Aren't you (är-ən-j) glad I didn't say banana?"

Other popular forms of children's jokes are based on their concept of reality and absurdity (Yalisove, 1978). In finding humor in reality for example, a child may ask, "What time is it when a hippopotamus sits on your fence? You don't know? Time to get a new fence." It is the realization of the absurdity of a hippopotamus sitting on a backyard fence that makes this joke funny while caught trying to figure out a rational relationship with time.

Absurdity has its own logic, and once the absurd premise of a joke is accepted, the situation can appear to be perfectly logical. For example: "What did the wild-game hunter do when a herd of elephants wearing sunglasses stampeded toward him? Don't know? Nothing, he didn't recognize them." The humor here is the juxtaposition of absurdity and reality. It is based on the cliché in our culture that one can travel incognito by donning sunglasses, which is juxtaposed on the reality of it being impossible to disguise an elephant—let alone a herd of them.

Assessing Mental Achievement and Aptitude

It is almost a cliché that every child is different, with different potential and a different rate of development. In no area are these differences harder to measure than in the area of mental potential and achievement. When a new baby is born parents dream that the child will go far. They may fantasize that the child will be a noted scientist, a physician, a concert pianist, a famous artist, a star athlete, or president of the country. They watch for signs of this potential in the child's first words, in physical development, and in the mastery of toys.

When children begin school, teachers identify individual differences with comments such as, "Susan is always in the science corner, I think she is going to be a scientist," "John is so good with people and with working out conflicts, I think he is going to be a diplomat," or "Marion seems never to be able to understand the projects that we present, I just wonder if anything is ever going to be easy for him (or her)?" Children are aware of the evaluations of parents and teachers and this information is incorporated into their self-concept. These adults are evaluating the child in relation to some standard. How accurate are their evaluations? Teachers, regardless of their years in a classroom, have, at best, experience with a few hundred children; and parents, usually, are even more restricted in their basis for making comparisons. Typically, the comparison is with other infants and children in the family. To assess potential accurately we need an objective measure of an individual child in comparison to a very large group of children. Can the teacher accurately evaluate the potential of children who do not speak English, who come from homes that differ markedly from those of the majority of children, who have a handicap that results in poor physical coordination or in a speech impediment, or who have undetected hearing and vision problems? Can teachers, or any of us, accurately separate intellectual potential from personality traits that are particularly repugnant? Can teachers evaluate the potential of children who are hyperactive and always into trouble; or who are withdrawn, unsocial, and perhaps cry at minor problems; or who are from an impoverished background and wear soiled clothes, lack social skills, and have parents who may be hostile and combative?

The behaviors that the teachers and parents see in the classroom and the home are the child's achievements. When a child writes an essay for a school paper or a contest, that is achievement. The predictions that parents and teachers make for the child's future achievements, such as his or her becoming a great writer, are estimates of the child's aptitude. Aptitude is not directly observed but most often inferred from other behaviors. Thus, although in theory achievement and aptitude are different, it is extremely difficult to separate them. Another way of looking at aptitude is how quickly and easily achievement is accomplished. Those who achieve easily are considered to have great aptitude, whereas those who achieve with difficulty have little.

If schools and other institutions are to help all children to reach their potential there has to be a way to estimate each child's potential for growth and development so that his or her environment will challenge that potential and develop it. It is exceedingly cruel to place a child with limited potential for mental growth in a classroom that demands work beyond that potential. It dooms the child to certain failure in the eyes of others and self. Conversely, it is a waste of human resources to place a child with great potential in a classroom that offers few opportunities to develop potential.

Our society is depending increasingly on technological skills. Those children who achieve in school will be the ones with access to training in those skills. However, we also need to be able to find those children who have aptitude but who may not be achieving and guide them to realize their potential. Achievement and aptitude tests are a fact of life in most modern schools. Let us look more closely at how achievement and aptitude are tested.

Achievement Tests

Teachers have always presented their students with tasks to test their understanding and mastery of the material studied. Tests devised by teachers are a measurement of *achievement*. That is, they are a measure of what the student has actually achieved. Achievement, then, is a product that can be measured. For example, a teacher may have conducted a unit study on the multiplication table. At some point it will be necessary to test the students to determine their ability to recall the multiplication facts and to use them in arithmetic problems. As our educational system grew and students moved from one school to another, some means of comparing achievement on one teacher's test with that on another teacher's in another section of the country was necessary. In order to have a national comparison of children in achievement, large testing companies have developed standard tests of achievement. The items on the tests are directly related to the material studied at various grade levels as identified by state and local school systems. In constructing these tests, the test companies work directly with actual classroom curriculums and then try the test in classroom situations. A national standardized test may go through many such trial administrations and revisions of items. When the authors of the test are satisfied that it reflects the teaching in most American schools, the test is given to a representative sample of children. Ideally the sample will include children from every section of the country, from rural and urban schools, and a representation of both boys and girls from every identifiable ethnic group. The children's test scores are analyzed and the data become the criteria against which future children taking the test will be compared. When these data are tabulated in charts for this purpose they constitute the *norms* for that test.

Teachers, school counselors, parents, and children can compare an individual child's achievement with these norms and gain an estimate of the child's standing compared to the entire country. There is no doubt that this helps many children and their parents to set realistic goals and make obtainable career choices. On the other hand, critics of standardized testing using national norms charge that this practice labels children and sets up stereotyped barriers that they will never be able to surmount. These critics are especially sensitive about children who differ from the majority of American children and are difficult to test because English is not their native language, because they have physical or emotional problems, or because of their individual pattern of development. The most vehement of these accusations have been leveled against the tests of aptitude known as intelligence tests.

Intelligence Tests

One of the most controversial topics in education today is that of measuring intelligence. IQ tests are a fact of life for any child going through the American public school system. They are also a fact of life for parents and teachers because the tests are a prime criterion for identifying mental retardation, for placing children in classes for the gifted, and as indicated earlier, for evaluating the results of compensatory education. In these and many other ways the test results are used to provide educational opportunities for children—or to exclude them. Therein lies the crux of a problem: Should important questions that determine the future course of a child's life be determined by tests? Let us clarify the issue. The tests determine nothing. People make decisions, and test results may or may not be a salient factor in helping people make those decisions. Whether to assign prime importance to intelligence test scores is a decision that must be made by people. Intelligence test scores are often used by schools to group children into classes and within a classroom; perhaps even more importantly, they are used to convey to teachers and parents a child's potential for achievement. The problem in using and reporting such scores is that often the people using them do not understand their limited application.

What Is Intelligence?

The question "What is intelligence?" may seem a strange one. Surely everyone can recognize a "brain" among his or her friends and classmates. Some people "have it" and some do not. But think for a minute, what exactly makes the "brain" different from others? What is this thing called intelligence? Psychologists have been asking this question for a long time. No one clear answer has emerged. David Wechsler (1975), the author of a number of highly respected intelligence tests, states that intelligence is having the capacity to understand the world and the resourcefulness to cope with its challenges. This definition sounds very good until we examine it further and realize that both understanding the world and coping with it vary considerably from culture to culture. For example, for the Bushmen of South Africa intelligence is understanding the movement of game and being a successful hunter. Bushman transported to an American city, however, might find the world impossible to understand and have no resources for coping. Someone may perform brilliantly as a concert pianist but be unable to cope with the practical details of life. Thus, even such a broad definition of intelligence as Wechsler's cannot be applied in all situations. Some psychologists abandon any effort at defining intelligence and accept the position that intelligence tests do indeed measure something and measure it consistently, but they give up trying to define what they measure. These psychologists are inclined to accept that intelligence is whatever it is that intelligence tests measure.

Intelligence as One or Many Factors

If we can only define intelligence as "that thing" measured by intelligence tests, what is it they measure? The two standards for intelligence testing today are the Stanford-Binet Test and the Wechsler Scales. Although both of these have different forms for children of different ages and for adults, they reduce intelligence to a numerical quantity. The implication is that intelligence is a single global measure.

Psychologists interested in understanding intelligence have attempted to break intelligence down into its component parts, much as physical scientists break compounds down to their basic atoms in order to understand the physical world. Early in this century Spearmen (1904, 1927) stated that intelligence consisted of a general factor, g, that undergirds all ability. Resting on this general factor may be specific abilities, s, in various areas. The more of the g factor that an individual possesses, the higher the achievement in all areas.

Thurstone and Thurstone (1941) identified about a dozen different factors that comprise intelligence. Among them are verbal comprehension, word fluency, number, space, associative memory, perceptual speed, and reasoning. These factors were reduced to four: verbal ability, number, perceptual speed, and spatial relations. The Primary Mental Abilities Test was developed around these factors and remains widely used with elementary children.

What Is Mental Measurement?

The vast majority of tests used for schoolchildren are based on the theory that intelligence is a quantity of something a child possesses that affects the quality of his or her mental functioning. This "something" may be one general factor or several. Let us look more closely at tests to understand the uses and limitations of them.

There are some questions that are useful in exploring intelligence testing. What exactly is mental "measurement"? How can we best use the results of mental measurement to help children to reach their potential?

Perhaps the term *measurement* is misleading if we apply it to mental ability. In the late nineteenth and early twentieth centuries, scientists in many areas were interested in measurements. The height and weight of large groups of children were carefully measured. Head circumference and bone ossification were plotted. Alfred Binet became interested in measuring reasoning and judgment. He wanted to know the ways in which "smart" and "dull" children differed. In his attempts to study those differences, he used many types of measures, including size of cranium, tactile discrimination, and digit recall. In 1904 he was appointed to a commission that was to recommend to the educational establishment in Paris a procedure for identifying pupils who were mentally incapable of profiting from normal schools. Binet was asked to produce a method to distinguish those retarded children from "normal" pupils. In collaboration with Simon, Binet published his first intelligence scale. The scale covered the various functions Binet considered components of intelligence, such as comprehension, reasoning, and judgment. Children between the ages of three and six were asked to give their names, to copy figures, to point to their right and left ear, and to obey simple commands. Older children were asked to name the month of the year, make up sentences, define abstract words, and name various coins.

Lewis M. Terman (1877–1956), an American psychologist, began to experiment with the Binet tests, and in 1916 produced the Stanford Revision of the Binet Scale (Terman 1916) in English translation. The Stanford-Binet remains the standard for intelligence tests; it was revised in 1937 and 1960 and restandardized in 1972. There is, however, no instrument or procedure that can measure mental ability directly. Binet and all intelligence-test builders after him set various tasks for children and then observed the children as their young intellect was put to work attacking the tasks (Chauncey & Dobbin, 1966). Tests then measure children's responses to questions or tasks; mental ability is inferred from those responses. The approach is similar to asking children how far they can throw a ball or how heavy a weight would have to be to balance their own weight on a seesaw and then inferring their weight and strength. As you see, there would be many possible opportunities for error.

When we measure a child's height we compare it to an absolute standard of length. The standard by which all other instruments are gauged is registered in the United States Bureau of Standards in Washington. It has taken centuries to reach some standardization on measurement of length. Originally the foot measure was exactly that, the measure of someone's foot, probably the king's. The measure fluctuated greatly according to whether his foot was large or small. It has been estimated that as late as the eighteenth century there were as many as 280 different measures of length in Europe (The New Columbia Encyclopedia, 1975). The last vestige of this confusion of measurement are the coexisting U.S. system (inches, feet, yards) and the metric system.

Intelligence testing today is similar to length measure in the eighteenth century. There is no universal standard. Each test builder must construct his or her own yardstick to infer the size of this thing called mental ability.

What Do IQ Tests Measure?

It is impossible to measure mental ability directly. Nevertheless, IQ tests are useful for guiding children because they can predict rather well the potential to achieve in school. Therefore, they are sometimes called scholastic aptitude tests. An aptitude test is one that predicts a child's *potential* to learn, whereas *achievement* tests measure what a child has already learned. Because most IQ tests consist of tasks similar to those required in school, it is not surprising that they predict school success. Success in school is a highly valued accomplishment in our society. It is the first link in a long chain that will determine the course of a person's work life.

Sex, IQ, and Mental Ability

There is no indication that there is a difference in overall IQ between boys and girls. Boys are not smarter than girls; girls are not smarter than boys. However, it must be noted here that standardized IQ tests were constructed so they would not reveal sex differences (Hoyenga & Hoyenga, 1979). In the process of constructing the tests, each item was tested on groups of children. Any item that was more often answered correctly by boys or girls was discarded.

A more careful examination of the data from specific groups reveals a slight difference in the measured IQ of boys and girls in disadvantaged populations. In overall measures of IQ girls from disadvantaged backgrounds tend to score somewhat higher than boys. The reasons for these differences are not entirely clear; however, there is evidence that lack of family harmony and disruption affects boys and girls differently. Many disadvantaged families live in crowded and poor urban environments in which the family is under great stress and its organization is often tenuous. There is evidence that family stress and disorganization have a more negative effect on boys than on girls. We might speculate that, in stressful family conditions, girls are better able to use their abilities than boys and therefore perform better on tests.

So far we have considered the performance of groups on tests. When groups are tested over time, some individuals may increase their scores, and others show a decline. When an individual's IQ score declines, that individual is more likely to be a girl, especially if the decline follows adolescence (Kagan, Sontag, Baker & Nelson 1958). Those who increase their IQ scores tend to be male. Gifted males tend to continue to increase their IQ well into adult life, whereas gifted females are not as likely to do so (Kangas & Bradway, 1971). A decline in female IQ and an increase in male IQ after adolescence can probably both be explained by the sex-role typing of intellectual expectations. That is, there are more social supports and there is

Table 13–1. Contrasts in Methods of Assessment and Conceptions of Intelligence

Psychometric Approach	Piaget's Approach
IQ intelligence is measured by standardized psychometric tests.	Intelligence is assessed by the unstandardized but still systematic clinical method.
IQ is expressed as a quantitative measure, based on the number of correct responses to items of differing content.	Intelligence is treated as a quality of understanding. The child's level of intelligence is described in terms of stages, based on logical structures presumed to underlie the specific content of responses.
The IQ number is an index of the rate of intellectual development shown by an individual in relation to his or her age peers. With an IQ of 100 usually selected as average, people with scores considerably less than 100 may be described as retarded, and those with scores considerably above 100 may be described as accelerated or gifted.	Individual differences in rate of development are not central to theory; rather interest centers on universalities and regularities in developmental sequence. Comparisons are not made with age peers. Stage levels describe the kinds of interpretations the child will tend to make, as compared with the hypothetical high point of cognitive development (the structural model underlying Formal operations).
IQ levels do not specify specific cognitive skills. (A two-year-old and a twenty-two-year-old, each with an IQ of 100, display very different intellectual abilities.)	Stage levels do specify a particular organization of cognitive skills.
The focus of IQ tests on correct answers tends to suggest a picture-copy view in which intelligence becomes more accurate with age. In IQ tests there is little explicit distinction between perceptual and cognitive tests.	The essence of intelligence is the child's symbolic representation function which constructs more complex meanings at higher stages. The emphasis in Piaget's study of intelligence is primarily on cognitive rather than perceptual development.
The IQ is a score which represents the average of abilities demonstrated by a child over many items and subtests.	In the Piagetian approach, children are categorized at the highest levels which they display during assessment.
Psychometric approaches tend to separate cognitive and motivational aspects of test performance.	Piaget's model of symbols includes emotion and motivation as intrinsic aspects of cognitive functioning. The clinical method of assessment attempts to make certain that the child's answers are related to questions in which he or she has developed some interest.
There is a pervasive assumption that IQ intelligence should remain constant over time. Four-year-olds at the middle of their age group are expected on the average to have IQ's near 100 when they are 14 and 24 years old. (This expectation has not generally been supported; the younger the children tested and the longer between test and retest, the greater the change in IQ score. While IQ is expected to remain relatively constant, mental age changes over time as a gradually increasing function of age, at least until early adulthood.	The organization of the symbolic function develops over time; development is defined as an increase in differentiation and integration of structures.
While there is now great dispute about this matter, IQ intelligence tends to be interpreted as an inner-determined trait or ability.	Intellectual functioning and development is always a result of person-environment interaction.

Source: Adapted from *Piaget: with Feeling* by Philip A. Cowan. Copyright © 1978 by Holt, Rinehart, and Winston. Reprinted by permission of Holt, Rinehart and Winston, CBS College Publishing.

greater encouragement for boys to excel in intellectual pursuits. The social climate is rapidly changing, however, and females are finding more acceptance and greater opportunities in academic and professional areas that were traditionally dominated by males.

Let us examine the question of sex differences in ability even more closely. Thus far we have considered the overall IQ score, which is a composite of scores from different abilities. When these tests are dissected and the performances of boys and girls are compared, different *patterns* of abilities are found. This analysis explodes some myths about differences in the intellectual abilities of boys and girls and confirms some real differences. Maccoby and Jacklin (1974) reviewed hundreds of studies that compared girls and boys on many different abilities. The conclusions from their exhaustive research follows.

False 1. Girls are better at rote learning and simple repetitive tasks; boys are better at tasks that require higher-level cognitive processing.

False 2. Boys are more "analytic."

False 3. Girls are more affected by heredity, boys by environment.

False 4. Girls are auditory; boys more visual.

False 5. Girls lack achievement motivation.

Research *does* bear out the following differences:

True 1. Girls have greater verbal ability than boys. Girls' verbal ability matures earlier than boys'. Girls and women consistently reveal a verbal superiority that includes verbal fluency, vocabulary, listening, speaking ability, verbal analogies, comprehension of difficult material, creative writing, and spelling. These differences continue into old age. Girls' scores have been found to be higher both on college entrance exams and the Graduate Record Examination.*

True 2. Boys have greater mathematical ability than girls. In the preschool years and during middle childhood boys and girls have equal skill in understanding mathematical concepts. In late childhood (around eleven or twelve) boys begin to surpass girls in mathematical achievement. This does not appear to be related to the number of math courses taken. These differences have been found in other countries (Wood, 1976) and are present even when the content is "feminine"—that is, when mathematical computations are done for food shopping.

True 3. Boys excel in visual-spatial ability. Spatial ability is the capacity to visualize objects in three-dimensional space. For example, the ability to visualize how a two-dimensional drawing would look if it were three-dimensional and seen from an opposite point of view. Another aspect of visual-spatial ability is field independence-dependence. This ability involves being able to keep a rod vertical to the earth's gravitational field even when it is in a tilted frame. (This ability is necessary for keeping your balance at carnivals in rooms in which the floor and walls are tilted.) Another task that uses this ability is finding figures embedded in a series of complex figures. This type of puzzle is often found in children's magazines ("Find the toys hidden in the picture"). These seem rather insignificant tasks, because we soon give up doing children's puzzles and our houses are generally level. The ability, however, is highly correlated to other tasks. Spatial ability, for example, is highly

* Hoyenga and Hoyenga (1979) report that the verbal items on the SAT have been balanced in recent years so that discrepancies between the scores of males and females have been lessened. They comment, however, that a similar balancing of scores has not been attempted in the mathematical area, where even greater discrepancies exist. The yardstick one uses in measurement is a factor in the results obtained.

correlated to performance in science and math courses, to such careers as drafting, engineering, and working with machines, and to following mechanical details in watch repairing, for example. However, it is negatively correlated with ability in languages and is not related to general school success (Peterson, 1976). This is probably because general school success rests heavily on verbal skill and abstract reasoning.

What Causes Sex Differences in Ability?

There are two candidates for the causes of sex differences in ability. Biology, through hormones, may stimulate differences in brain structure or the environment may shape learning and behavior by directing male and female toward different interests and academic subjects (sex typing). The evidence indicates that both biology and environment influence intellectual development, but they influence it differently in male and female.

Biology

There is no math gene or verbal gene. Genes are related to IQ, but there appears to be no sexual difference in IQ. As was previously discussed, prenatal hormones structure the brains of males and females differently. The issue in intellectual development is whether those hormones also predispose males and females to learn differently. Evidence from animal and human studies in which females have been masculinized with prenatal hormones indicate that hormones are implicated in patterns of learning. Moderate levels of both estrogen and testosterone are associated with an increase in brain activity, and males and females who are estimated to have moderately high levels of these hormones have been found to be high in

(A)

(B)

The results of testing many children reveal that girls (A) excel in verbal abilities and boys (B) in visual-spatial abilities. [Photograph (B) courtesy William Amidon and Greensboro Day School.]

Are the differences in intellectual achievement between boys and girls due to biology or to environment? [Photographs (A) and (C) courtesy John King and Greensboro Day School; photograph (B) courtesy Richard Michaels and Greensboro Day School.]

(A)

(B)

(C)

verbal ability (Hoyenga & Hoyenga, 1979). Testosterone is associated with high physical activity. It has been hypothized that estrogen may suppress physical activity in both male and female that then allows verbal abilities to emerge. The high physical activity level of males may act to suppress verbal abilities but allow for the emergence of visual-spatial abilities. Also, the hormones that suppress female physical activity may suppress exploration and visual-spatial abilities (Hoyenga & Hoyenga, 1979). Thus, verbal and visual-spatial abilities are sometimes—but not always—reciprocal. Some females are high in both abilities; some males are high in

As girls receive equal opportunities and encouragement in science and math oriented experiences, we may find that differences in abilities are not so great. These first-grade girls are conducting simple chemical experiments. Through early and continuous experience in a science laboratory they will be able to develop their abilities in this area—whatever those abilities are.

both abilities; some males and females are low in both. Although there seems to be a connection between hormones and these abilities, the interaction is dynamic, complex, and different for each individual at different times. Pre- and postnatal hormones affect brain structures permanently. After the maturation of the brain, the effect of hormones on learning behavior is variable, according to the level of hormones in the blood at any given time. In laboratory animals the administration of either testosterone or estrogen changes the rate and style of many different behaviors. It appears that the optimal utilization of abilities occurs with a moderately high hormonal level in both sexes.

There is some evidence that visual-spatial ability may be genetically controlled. The largest measured difference in male and female ability is consistently in visual-spatial ability. Maccoby and Jacklin (1974) suggest that this ability may be a sex-linked recessively inherited trait. The measured abilities in male and female correspond with sex-linked inheritance. Tests of spatial ability consistently reveal that 50 per cent of males reach a score obtained by only 25 per cent of females. In sex-linked inheritance 50 per cent of all males and 25 per cent of females have the trait, although another 25 per cent of females are carriers and pass the trait on to their sons. The consistency of findings on the distribution of this trait suggests genetic rather than environmental control, but the evidence is inconclusive.

Environment

When we say that the two sexes differ in verbal and visual-spatial abilities, this does not mean opposing abilities but, rather, shared ones. Certainly males are not mute and females are not at a complete loss in a three-dimensional world. It means that both sexes have both abilities, but females perform more easily and extensively in verbal areas and males perform more easily and extensively on spatial tasks. These abilities may be related to hormones but also are subject to the influence of sex typing. This may, of course, turn out to be a chicken-and-egg question. That is, these differential abilities may be related to experience and only coincidentally to hormones, or hormones may cause both sex-typed behavior and sex-typed abilities. In cross-cultural studies females have been found to perform below males on spatial abilities, except among Eskimos. The Eskimo culture is one of the few in which women are not taught to be dependent. Does the early learning of dependent behaviors depress exploratory behavior and the development of visual-spatial abilities in girls? In our culture girls are generally equal to boys in intellectual achievement until puberty. After puberty girls tend to decline in general academic achievement and in math and science in particular, which are strongly related to spatial ability and also strongly sex typed in our culture. Girls may suffer anxiety in crossing this barrier.

Main Points

1. In all cultures children between the ages of six and twelve learn the tools of the culture.

Piaget's Cognitive Development in the School Years

2. In this period the child becomes capable of logical thought and of performing mental operations with concrete objects. The child is able to reverse thought, decenter, seriate, and classify.

Conservation

3. The recognition that equal quantities remain equal when one is changed in form but nothing is added or taken away is conservation; it rests on attaining concepts of identity, reversibility, and compensation.

4. Conservation of number is established when the child is able to reason that two identical sets of objects contain the same number even when one set is transformed in some way.

5. Conservation of length is established when the child is able to reason that objects of equal length remain equal even if one is changed in some way.

6. Conservation of liquid volume is established when the child is able to reason that two equal amounts of liquid remain equal even if one is placed in a differently shaped container.

7. In the conservation of area the child is able to reason that the area covered by a given number of two-dimensional objects is unaffected by their arrangements.

8. Conservation of mass, weight, and displacement volume are attained when the child is able to reason that two equal lumps of clay remain equal when one is elongated or changed.

Effect of Training on Conservation

9. Children in a transition between the preoperational stage and the stage of concrete operations are most susceptible to the influence of teaching or training on conservation ability.

Language Development

10. Language continues to develop between the ages of six to twelve, especially in the understanding of the subtle and connotative meanings of words.

Vocabulary and Meaning

11. The child's knowledge of words increases steadily between the ages of six to twelve.

Communication Skills

12. Communication skills are limited by egocentrism, which lessens during the years six through twelve; communication skills increase with age.

Language Play: Telling Jokes

13. Humor, especially play on words, is confined to humans and is dependent on cognitive development.

Intelligence Tests

14. Intelligence tests are widely used in American education today.

15. There is controversy about the definition of *intelligence*.

16. Some psychologists believe that intelligence is one general factor that undergirds all ability; others have identified many factors that comprise intelligence.

17. Mental measurement is the indirect assessment of mental ability by inference from responses to questions and/or tasks.

18. IQ tests measure a child's scholastic aptitude or potential to achieve in school.

Sex, IQ, and Mental Ability

19. IQ scores reveal no sex differences in the general population, but girls from disadvantaged backgrounds tend to score higher than boys from the same background.

Sex Differences in Mental Ability

20. Girls have greater verbal ability than boys, and boys have greater mathematical ability and visual-spatial ability than girls. There are no differences in ability to learn by rote, perform repetitive tasks, use higher-level cognitive processes, do analytical thinking, or in auditory and visual learning or motivation.

21. Biology, through hormones, may stimulate different brain structures in males and females; some evidence exists that visual-spatial ability may be genetically controlled; the environment, through sex typing, may shape males and females toward different interests and academic abilities.

Words to Know

compensation   preconserver
conservation   reversibility
decoding   transitional
encoding

Terms to Define

achievement test
conventional morality
intelligence quotient (IQ)
intelligence test
standardized test

Concept to Discuss

intelligence

14

Emotional and Social Development in Middle Childhood

Have you ever wondered

> **how self-esteem is related to competence and independence?**
> **how the sense of self develops?**
> **how peer-groups develop in children's social structure?**
> **how relations between parents and children change in the school years?**
> **what is the effect of divorce and working mothers on children?**
> **what is the effect of television on children?**

Many adults look back on childhood as an idyllic time. The child is seen as independent, competent, and invulnerable; not needing adults and, in fact, somewhat superior to them. Peter Pan, Huckleberry Finn, Pippi Longstocking, Annie, and a host of other child heroes and heroines present the child as the possessor of secret powers and knowledge that make his or her world superior to the work-a-day world of adults. (The books in which these child protagonists appear, incidentally, were all written by adults and may reflect more their disillusionment with adult society than the reality of children's experience.) Nevertheless, children read such books avidly and apparently find a reflection of their experience and fantasy in them. Is the picture mythical, or is it real? What are the facts of childhood? Unfortunately, we have no such books written by children themselves. We assume that they do not have the technical skill and sustained discipline to recreate their experience in art form. However, all indications are that children create their own culture, complete with rules, games, and hierarchies. Some children even invent their own secret code and language.

The child who is developing well emotionally and socially is competent and
self-assured. [Courtesy Richard Michaels
and Greensboro Day School.]

The child who is developing well is competent and self-assured and creates a
culture independent of adult society. In middle childhood the child's social sphere
widens to include the school and the peer group. Through the school the child
strives to become skillful in manipulating the material world and through interaction with peers becomes skillful in social relations. From a theoretical point of view,
the years of middle childhood are stable and without intense conflict. In this chapter we will consider the theoretical underpinnings of personality growth in middle
childhood, relations with peers and family, the effects of television, and finally the
deviant child.

Psychosexual Development: The Latency Period

In the theory of psychosexual development presented by Freud, the years from six
until puberty are a quiescent period between the turbulent Oedipal stage and the
equally turbulent genital stage of adolescence. Freud termed this long interlude the
latency period. It is not, strictly speaking, a stage of psychosexual development but
rather a suspension of psychosexual conflict during which physiological processes
mature. In the latency period the psychic conflicts of the preschool years are resolved. The child who is developing well moves into identification with the parent
and psychic energy is directed to mastering the society's tools. At the end of childhood increasing cognitive maturity and contact with the wider culture undermine
the implicit faith that young children place in parental judgment. Older children
begin to see adults in a more realistic light and to question the wisdom of parents
and teachers (Ausabel, Sullivan, & Ives, 1980). Emotional life in middle childhood
is smooth and settles into a coherent pattern. This pattern is broken with the advent
of puberty and it is some years until the adolescent is able to construct from these
pieces his or her mature, individual relationship with the world and self.

Psychosocial Development: Industry vs. Inferiority

Erikson has interpreted the latency period in terms of the social tasks and values developed in it. For psychosocial development this is a very important time in the development of *competence*. In Erikson's view the years between six and twelve are socially the most decisive. In those years psychic energy is turned outward toward mastering the tools and skills needed in life. The child is ready to enter into the work of society; he or she is ready to leave the fantasy world of the young child and to grasp the impersonal laws of tools and technology (Erikson, 1963a). The child struggles to master the tasks assigned by society, and thereby evolves a sense of industry and competence or, if this fails, a sense of inferiority. Industry in this period involves working with others; children begin to perceive that different abilities and opportunities come to different children as the child seeks to win recognition by producing objects (Erikson, 1963a).

Children in all societies are involved in mastering the tools and skills that are used by adults in their society. From a psychological point of view, the ego boundaries expand to include these tool skills. Accomplishment of skills, then, becomes a source of pleasure. Accomplishment is reached by steady perseverance. In primitive societies these skills may be hunting, fishing, weaving, or caring for younger children. Children in preindustrial societies work closely with their parents and can clearly see the relationship between the work their parents perform and their own tasks. In the specialization of our technological society, the roles of mother and father in the work world are vague to the child. In a complex industrial society, the tools of work are the three Rs; literacy becomes the widest basic education that will lead to the greatest number of careers (Erikson, 1963a). As a consequence, the goals of the child's own initiative lose their immediate connection to adult roles and responsibility. The child must learn to cope with an abstract and complicated social reality.

In the preschool years the superego was the element of the personality that came to the fore. In most primitive cultures children of seven or eight years are believed to know the difference between right and wrong and are held responsible for their actions. Both the Catholic church and English common law hold the child of this age responsible for right and wrong. In middle childhood, the ego component of the personality assumes ascendency and this is tied to increasing competence both with tools and people (*independence*) and the child's self-evaluation of this competence (*status*). Let us examine how the ego component of personality secures independence and status for the individual.

Independence and Status: The Work of the Ego

The ego component of the personality comes into being to fulfill two needs: independence and status. Through an independent ego the individual is able to set and reach goals that enable him or her to function realistically in the world. Through status the individual sustains the growth of the ego with self-esteem (Ausabel, Sullivan, & Ives, 1980).

(A)

(B)

(C)

(D)

From ages six to twelve children learn the basic technological skills of their culture. In mastering these skills they learn industry or, in failing, a sense of inferiority. In preindustrial societies these skills may be tending cattle (A) or caring for younger children (B). In technological societies, the skills are more likely to be computers (C) and require more emphasis on formal schooling (D). The boy tending cattle is making a valuable contribution to the economic support of his family and village, but it will be many years before the computer-trained children can make economic contributions to their culture. [Photograph (C) courtesy Greensboro Day School.]

Primary Status

Status is gained or lost according to the judgments made by others about independent actions. Information about status is obtained by a feedback system on how realistic and effective the goals and actions of independence are. The individual uses information on his or her status in a group to build self-esteem and a self-concept. Thus, actions in the environment (independence) and status have a reciprocal relationship in which information from one affects the other. Consider the following examples:

1. John wants to act independently and decides to help the teacher wash the boards. He brings in a pan of water and spills it on the floor. The teacher scolds him and the children laugh and call him clumsy (not able to act independently). His self-esteem is lowered and his status needs are unfulfilled. He concludes that this is not an effective way to independence and will not attempt such ''help'' again.

2. Angela seeks to express her feelings about a story with an illustration. The teacher judges the illustration poorly done and humiliates her. To add salt to the wound, the other children ridicule the attempt. Her esteem is lowered and her status needs are unmet. She concludes that drawing is not the way to independent action and will probably not attempt an illustration again.

Good management skills with children enable teachers and parents to correct children and lead them to more competence *without* damaging their self-concept. Children *can* accept being wrong: they *cannot* accept being judged ''bad'' because they are wrong.

Children must protect their vulnerable ego—as we all must. Erikson's stage of industry or inferiority is the feeling of being competent or inferior rather than actual accomplishment. Of course this must be based on reality, or the person is not operating within reality. In this period the basic sense of being competent or inferior is developed. If the overriding sense is toward inferiority, the individual must forever struggle against this barrier in future accomplishments. Such barriers need not be placed before children, but many procedures that are ostensibly designed to help children have the effect of erecting barriers. For example, children who are enrolled too early in competitive sports may develop the idea that they are not able to compete. Similarly, children who are placed in slow-learner groups may perceive themselves as ''dummies'' and may in fact, be called that by other children.

Derived Status

Not all status is earned by the individual. Status may be derived from a relationship with a person or group with primary status. The individual by virtue of his or her relationship with an admired person or group gains status and raises self-esteem and self-concept. For example, in elementary school many children want to be the friend of the most popular children. They thereby gain derived status and esteem from their association with these desirable friends. Children also derive status from their families. The prototype of derived status is the identification that the child forms with parents. Children from affluent, influential families have higher status than children from poor families. The son or daughter of a president or a movie star has higher status in a school group than a child from a poor immigrant family, regardless of the children's individual abilities.

Children gain primary status through talents and accomplishments that are admired by others. [Courtesy William Amidon and Greensboro Day School.]

Status can be derived from an ever-widening circle of belonging to the "right" clubs, admiring the "right" people, rooting for the "right" teams, wearing the "right" clothes, eventually going to the "right" college, having the "right" job, living in the "right" neighborhood, and so on. Preadolescents and adolescents carry derived status to an extreme and construct rigid peer groups to uphold these "right" values.

Derived status is a normal stage in the ego development of both boys and girls. At the beginning of middle childhood boys as well as girls derive status from their parents. Variations on the old theme "My daddy can beat your daddy" abound, in which the superiority of "daddy" (and mommie) is expounded. Through identification with the parent, the child has invested his or her ego in the parent and derives self-esteem and status from parental accomplishments. The child's ego must undergo many modifications before it can sustain the tasks and decisions necessary for optimum independent functioning in adult society. We will sketch this development here. Note that this description is not restricted to development in middle childhood but covers ego development from birth to adulthood. We have placed the description in this chapter because middle childhood is the crucial time for ego development.

Development of an Independent Self (Ego)*

Ego is one of three components of personality in psychoanalytic theory and the major personality component in the development of trust, autonomy, initiative, and competence, as outlined by Erikson. Ego is present in some form in all stages.

---

* The following discussion of ego development is adapted from D. P. Ausabel, E. V. Sullivan, and S. W. Ives, *Theory and Problems of Child Development.* 3rd ed. New York: Grune and Stratton, 1980.

Differentiation of Self-concept

Even before possessing language the child develops the rudimentary concept of what is self and what is not self. This is essentially a concept of what is internal and what is external. We postulate that this concept is formed when the child exhibits object permanence—that is, the cognitive concept that objects are separate and remain in existence even when out of perceptual range. Thus, the delineation of self from non-self is a function of both emotional and cognitive development.

The Omnipotent Phase

The ultimate function of the ego is to secure for the organism needs for survival and satisfaction. This is independence. There are two aspects of independent action. First is the ability to set goals, which originate as wishes, or desires, and are volitional independence. Second is the ability to attain these goals, which is executive independence. The infant has many wishes and desires (volitional independence) but is quite helpless in attaining any of them by his or her own efforts (executive independence). The only tools at his or her command are crying, smiling, and otherwise enticing parents and caregivers to accomplish his or her ends. For example, the infant wishes food and cries; caregivers appear with food. The process continues as the infant desires objects and by looking at or touching them communicates desires and goals to its caregivers. Such communication continues in a thousand subtle ways. (See Chapter 6 on nonverbal communication.) In such a paradise, the infant perceives him- or herself as all-powerful—that is, omnipotent: to wish something is to have it. "Good" parents are indulgent with infants, and indeed, the baby will need this cushion of self-esteem and the accompanying sense of trust and intrinsic value to fall back on in the times to come.

Ego-Devaluation Crisis

The parents, weary of being the slave of the omnipotent baby, eventually cease to do his or her bidding. In fact, they demand that the child assume some responsibility for self-care, such as toilet training, dressing and feeding, and controlling impulses. The child is expected to show more *tolerance for frustration, control of infantile aggression,* and *less demand for immediate gratification.* These radical changes in parent behavior undermine the infant's self-perception as omnipotent; the effect is a devaluation of the infantile ego. The reaction of the infant is rage, referred to as the terrible twos, and the ego devaluation crisis is in full swing. The child grows rapidly between two and four in terms of language and cognitive maturity and perceives more clearly his or her actual dependence and lack of power and the parents' actual power and independence. Children of this age often have a fear of being lost or abandoned and realize that they, like Hansel and Gretel, could not find their way alone.

Satellization

The ego organization that worked so well in infancy (volitional independence and executive dependence) fails to secure either needs or satisfaction in early childhood. The resulting ego-devaluation crisis has revealed that to compete with adults will result in marginal self-esteem because young children are realistically less competent than adults. Therefore, the ego must be reorganized to meet the new conditions. Because the child cannot be omnipotent, the next best thing is to become a

The satellizing child seeks the guidance and approval of the parent and through this relationship learns to set goals for living and working in the culture.

satellite of people who are. Those people are, of course, the parents (or significant caregivers). By becoming a satellite of a parent who can both choose goals and has the means to reach them, the child can avoid the serious blow to self-esteem that would result from a realistic appraisal of his or her own ability.

As a satellite of an all-powerful adult, the child maintains self-esteem through *derived status* from that adult. In effect, the ego of the child is turned over to the other person for safekeeping. In order to do this the child must feel that he or she is truly valued for his or her own intrinsic worth. When parents reject the child or value him or her for the parents' own ego needs the child may find satellization difficult.

The satellizing child seeks the parent's approval. Through parental guidance sought by the satellizing child *ego-maturity goals* are set. These ego maturity goals appear across a variety of cultures:

1. Being able to put off immediate satisfaction in order to satisfy more important long-term aspirations. This is needed to discipline oneself for school, work, and eventual childrearing.
2. Gaining the ability to care for oneself in physical matters and in earning a living.
3. Accepting the moral standards of the culture.

The commitment to growth toward these ego-maturity goals is emotional and a function of personality development although each has a cognitive component. The satellizing child spans the preschool years and the first half of middle childhood. Obviously there are great differences between a three-year-old and an eight-year-old; yet, from the standpoint of ego development, they are in the same stage of development. After the crisis of devaluation, the three-year-old is generally accepting, loving, and obedient. He or she is more anxious to please and conform, whereas the four-year-old has been called "out of bounds." This may seem a contradiction but it actually is not. We must underscore that the child never entirely

In late childhood children are able to plan and execute projects independently of adults. The approval of the peer group becomes an important source of status and parental approval becomes less important. [Courtesy Greensboro Day School.]

abandons the infantile dream of omnipotence, but the reality of the situation at two years of age forces another path. At four, the former power and exuberance resurfaces and the child, once again confident of abilities, may insist on doing everything. Of course, many of his or her schemes are doomed to disaster, and the child is torn between drives for independence and dependence. The five-year-old is again accepting of a quieter status, and life is smoother and more conforming. At this age the parents are idealized by the child and seem more omnipotent that ever.

Entrance into school upsets this idealized view as the child begins to attain an official status independent of the home. The six-year-old may overestimate this gain in competence and again test the limits of his or her real ability. As a result, the personality of the child at this age is characterized by aggression, expansiveness, boastfulness, and resistance to direction from adults. The child in the first three grades of school increases in satellization, which reaches a peak at around eight years of age (third grade). A great change occurs in ego development at around fourth grade. Again, the ego organization of satellization ceases to ensure satisfaction or to meet the child's needs and a new crisis ensues. This is a maturation crisis, which forces a new ego organization. As a result, the child ceases being a satellite of the parent and begins to attain primary status and independence.

Ego Maturation Crisis: Desatellization

Between the ages of eight and sixteen many things happen in the ego development of the child. The eight-year-old begins to disengage his or her ego from that of the parent and by age sixteen the youth essentially has a mature, intact ego. Five factors contribute to this growth.

Late childhood is a time of emotional stability before the turbulence of adolescence. Generally, children are competent, self-confident, and pleased with themselves. (A) These children reflect such feelings as they leave school for the day carrying the tools of their competence: muscial instruments, tennis shoes, and books. (B) Positive self-regard is also reflected in the self-portraits that children in the same school have drawn. [Courtesy Mount Zion Elementary School, Greensboro, North Carolina.]

(A)

(B)

1. The child achieves competence in social interactions with age mates.
2. The peer group attains more importance as a source of status for the child.
3. The child realizes that he or she is excluded from the adult world. A resentment arises against parents, teachers, and those in authority.

4. Sexual maturation brings new sources of perceived competence and status.

5. The expectations of adults change and force new competencies on the child.

Again the solution reached at an earlier age becomes maladaptive and a new organization of personality is required. Both biological and social status change as the child grows older. The early elementary-school-aged child is indeed physically and socially dependent on parents and teachers and a deferential attitude toward parents and teachers is the best way to attain satisfaction and meet needs. (Remember, these are not thought-out responses but unconscious organizations.)

Resatellization: The Teen Peer Group

In primitive societies children move directly from the satellizing stage into responsible positions in adult society (Hallowell, 1976). In Western culture, prior to education being made mandatory until the age of sixteen, children of seven or eight were apprenticed and began to produce real goods in the real adult world. Thus, they were given access to gaining competence and status by their own production.

In our modern, complex society, several changes have taken place that prolong ego maturation. First, most children and adolescents have little real responsibility. They have little opportunity to gain primary status in the "real" world of work. In addition, the actual work that their fathers and mothers do is a vague abstraction for children, removed as it is from their day-to-day activities. Even though children of ten or twelve years of age have gained competence and the ability to function independently, our society offers them few opportunities to develop competent independent behavior. Without the necessary experiences for ego maturation such growth tends to lag.

The second way in which modern society differs from preindustrial ones is that children are segregated from adult society and confined in age-graded groups from nursery school through college. Cut off and segregated from the mainstream of society, children must rely on peers and fantasy to fulfill their status needs. Although they are in many ways quite competent, they must rely on peripheral activities such as little-league sports or individual hobbies for primary status or attain it by vicarious identification with public figures. Hallowell (1976) has suggested that this trend toward exclusion from work and toward social segregation has been going on for four hundred years, and that the rebellion seen in America in the last two decades and in Europe in the present one has been brewing all that time. We find not only that ego maturation is postponed in our society, but that there is another step in the process. Because the pubescent child cannot enter adult society, he or she is forced into another round of satellization: with the peer group and its heroes. The final step to ego maturity and desatellization then takes place when the youth can take his or her place as a productive member of society. For lower-class youth this tends to be at the end of high school and for middle-class youth at the end of college or professional school.

A third consequence of this pattern of ego maturation is that the parent loses status in the eyes of the child and a long period of estrangement must be endured between parents and youth. Often neither school nor peers know the child's parents. Parents and children share little in the way of activities and therefore little in feeling, understanding, or communication.

These problems smoulder in late childhood but may erupt in adolescent rebellion. Increasingly, children as young as ten or less are involved in crime and acts of violence. Schools, in many cases, have become armed camps and teachers are physically attacked. Thoughtful, creative educators, parents, and civic and business leaders can offer older children real opportunities for responsible participation in the society. Can we afford not to offer our youth better opportunities to develop ego strengths?

Peers and the Society of Children

The decrease in dependence on parents seen in middle childhood is accompanied by an increase in involvement with age mates. In late childhood, children create their own society, which extends into adolescence. Even infants are interested in and are attracted by age mates, but parents remain the primary focus of their social relations in early childhood. Parents, of course, continue to be important throughout life, but in middle childhood the peer group assumes ascendency and a certain animosity is directed toward adults. At first the peer group is rigidly kept to the same sex. Boys and girls form separate groups, complete with separate organizations and leaders. In seventh and eighth grades (sometimes sixth) interest in the opposite sex increases and boys and girls begin to share activities such as parties, going to the movies, or other group activities. Same-sex groups, with their separate leaders and activities, are maintained along with participation in a larger group.

In the first few years of elementary school children are concerned with the approval of the teacher, but around the fourth grade the opinion of peers becomes the primary reference point. Children who previously worked obediently when the teacher left the room now begin to engage in practical jokes in a conspiracy against adult authority. This conspiracy of childhood helps to create an entire society, which has been referred to as the last and greatest of savage tribes (Opie &

Childhood is a time of secret clubhouses, languages, and rituals as children create their own society. [Courtesy Richard Michaels and Greensboro Day School.]

Opie, 1959). The society of children is pervasive and, like the little people in the book *The Borrowers*, exists under the noses of adults, yet is almost undetected by them. Teachers go on teaching and parents go on parenting, while children are busy passing notes, whispering, composing taunting verses, struggling for dominance, and creating their society in a thousand little ways in classrooms, in the back of station wagons, and primarily in school bathrooms. This is a time of secret clubs and clubhouse meetings, some children even create their own secret language. For those who do not, there is the universal child language of pig latin, which can be used to say things that adults will not understand—unless, of course, the adult remembers the language from his or her own childhood. Usually, though, the ways of childhood, once left, seem subject to amnesia. When the line is crossed to adulthood, life in the "other society" is lost, only to be glimpsed in such fantasies as C. S. Lewis' Narnian chronicles.

There is scant research on this spontaneously erupted society, especially considering that it exists in every school and in every country. Opie and Opie (1959) conducted an extensive study of five thousand British children and described their society as an oral culture in which games and songs are handed down from child to child. It has been theorized that these songs and games are hundreds, maybe thousands, of years old; quite similar forms have been found in parts of the world quite distant from each other—in Australia, England, and the United States. Obviously many years ago these children had the same ancestors. In addition to songs and games, children have their own lore, superstitions, and their own way of ridiculing adults and authority. The culture is difficult to study because children learn the "right" answers to give to adults and are reluctant to reveal the inner workings of their tribe. However, a friendship with a ten-year-old might gain you access to this secret society, if you are found worthy. Puberty seems to disrupt the society formed in childhood, while it increases peer-group bonds. Their overwhelming preoccupation with physical attractiveness propels emerging adolescents to leave childish things behind.

Families in Middle Childhood

Even though children appear competent and self-sufficient, the fact remains that children are dependent on adults and require a protected environment in order to develop physically and psychologically. The family is the institution that society has designated to provide this protection. The family is responsible for dispensing the good things of the society to children. The provision of a certain quality of life is not simply left to the good will of the parents; they are constrained by law to provide various beneficial things for their children. Parents must see that children are educated, must not abuse or neglect them, and in some states, must provide a safety seat when transporting them in an automobile. Fathers, and sometimes mothers, must provide financial support for their children whether or not they live with them.

In previous chapters we have stressed the importance of emotional bonds between mother and child and father and child. As the child grows older, the relationship between child and parents changes. Parents of young children are occupied primarily with their physical care and spend a great deal of time with them. When children enter school, parents spend less time with them and also tend to become less protective and to show less physical affection. Means of controlling

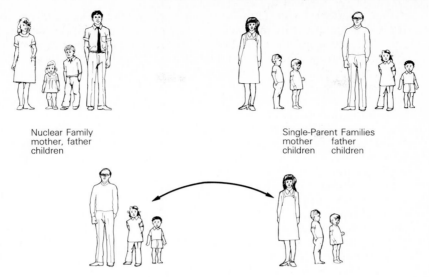

Nuclear Family
mother, father
children

Single-Parent Families
mother   father
children   children

Reconstituted Families
natural parent, step-parent
step-siblings

Children live in many different kinds of families.

the child shift from the physical to using reason and moral exhortations as the child becomes more responsive to verbal control. Although, to some extent, the authority of the family is undermined when children attend school, the family continues to exert enormous influence on their development.

The ideal form of the family in our culture is the nuclear family. The nuclear family consists of a mother, a father, and children living in the same household as a social and economic unit. The nuclear family is most likely the model used in social role-playing that kindergarten children engage in.

This model, however, is not the reality for a great number of children. With a rising divorce rate and an increase in never-married parenting an increasing number of children live in single-parent families and with step-parents. The traditional nuclear family has also been changed by an increasing number of mothers who work outside the home. We will look now at the effect of these family patterns on children.

Children and Divorce

Many divorced couples have young children, and research has indicated that those children are deeply affected by their parents' divorce. Of course, the final effect of divorce on children is largely dependent on the arrangements that the couple makes. Some of the factors that determine how the children are affected are whether the divorce was bitterly contested or amicably settled, what the custody arrangements are, and what the mother's financial status is after the divorce. Divorced mothers with children often find themselves on a path of downward social mobility. Women are largely unprepared to provide financial security for themselves and their children, and often with divorce they join the ranks of the poor. In addition, because they usually are pressed to devote time to working and/or education to upgrade any vocational skills they may have, their time with the children is limited. These pressures are compounded by the necessity of finding supervision for the children while they are working or studying. Hetherington, Cox, and Cox (1977) in an extensive study of divorce found that the behavior of both parents and children changes following divorce. In the families studied the mother retained custody of the children and the fathers had visiting privileges. Heatherington and her colleagues found that, in the first year following divorce, both parents suffered from such emotional distress as anxiety, depression, anger, and self-doubt. Both parents changed their behavior toward the children. Mothers increased their negative control with more punishments and commands. The children, however, were less likely to accede to those threats and punishments and actual control decreased, especially with sons. The father, on the other hand, assumed more permissive and indulgent behavior immediately following divorce, in an apparent effort to maintain contact and affection with the children.

Divorced parents made fewer demands on children, showed less affection, communicated less well, and were inconsistent in discipline. Divorce may be the best solution in desperate circumstances, but parents and children pay a price for it.

One consequence of a rising divorce rate is that many children do not grow up living with both parents. At any one time fully 10 per cent of American children are living in a single-parent household, and the parent is overwhelmingly likely to be the mother. Among blacks living in low-income neighborhoods, as many as half of the children may be living with only one parent. Traditionally, when parents divorced, the courts automatically gave custody of the children to the mother. This is changing, however, as courts are looking at which parent can provide the best environment for the child, rather than assuming that the better parent is automatically the mother. Between six hundred thousand and one million children now live in one-parent families headed by fathers, while between six and seven million children live with their mother. In some families with divorce children are divided between fathers and mothers.

The effect of growing up in a single-parent home is difficult to determine. The assumption is that such a family comprises a deprived environment. That is, the child is deprived either of a father or of a mother; if we assume that the influences of both are desirable for healthy psychological growth, then there must be an adverse effect in having one parent absent. Most of the research to date has been conducted on homes in which the father is absent; in general, studies indicate that children from those homes do not fare as well as children from two-parent homes. The effect of the absence of the father is greatest for boys, when the absence occurs in the preschool years. Biller (1970), in a review of many studies of father absence, concluded that boys without fathers have a more difficult time with identity and suffer the lack of a masculine identification. These boys appear to be less motivated toward careers and achieve less well in school. In addition, they are more likely to become delinquent and are characterized by lack of impulse control and inability to delay gratification. Not only is the masculine image distorted, but these boys also may have trouble establishing a relationship with a woman in later years. Not all of the studies are conclusive, however, and other studies indicate that the final evaluation is not in on father absence. It appears that the detrimental effects of the father being absent can be ameliorated when another male is present to provide a masculine image, when losing a father does not mean a drop in standard of living, and when someone provides extra attention for the child (Shinn, 1978). The effect on girls of the father being absent is somewhat different. Hetherington, Cox, and Cox

(1977) studied girls whose father was absent and found that they were more apt to be sexually promiscuous and had a more difficult time adjusting socially. Divorce seems especially disruptive when it takes place during a girl's early adolescence.

The effect of an absent mother on school-age children has received little research attention. Generally when fathers choose to rear their children, they are especially caring, loving, human beings, have adequate financial resources, and strive to maintain a rich environment for the children. Nevertheless, the question remains, can father also be mother?

Working Mothers

The role of working mothers is rather like the role of "It" in a game of hide and seek: "Here I come, ready or not." The popular press has bandied about for years the question of whether a mother should work outside the home. The fact is, that the number of women in the work force is rising. Over half of the mothers who have school-age children are employed outside the home, and fully one-third of the women who have preschool children are employed. Most women who are employed outside the home work because the family needs the additional income. A few upper-middle-class women seek employment for self-fulfillment. Most women are concentrated in low-paid factory and service jobs. In addition to their outside employment, women must still perform the work of the home, and many feel guilty if they cannot fulfill this responsibility to meet their ideal. Accusations and guilt aside, what is the effect of a mother's employment on children?

Among school-age children, it appears that the effect of a mother's employment is positive for girls but negative for boys. Girls whose mothers are employed express a positive attitude about growing up and think of women as competent, effective, and active. On the other hand, girls whose mothers are housewives see women as being restricted in physical and social roles and in economic possibility (Hoffman & Nye, 1974). Boys, on the other hand, tend to show insecurity and less self-confidence when their mothers are employed than those boys whose mothers are always at home.

Clearly when mothers are employed other family members must assist in household chores. One positive benefit for both sons and daughters is that they assume more responsibility in household tasks and must rely on themselves to solve problems. The real question is not whether mothers are employed, but the quality of supervision that the children have when mother is not present. The economic system requires that women earn income. The sole responsibility for supervision of children can no longer rest on the shoulders of the mother. Alternative plans with shared responsibility for the rearing of our children must be sought, for truly they are all our children.

Television

- Saturday morning in America children rise early so they won't miss the cartoons.
- Every weekday afternoon America's schoolchildren arrive home with, "Hi, I'm home," pause at the refrigerator to fix a snack, and hurry to the television set for their favorite afternoon show.
- Mornings in homes and day care centers across the country preschoolers are huddled around "Sesame Street," and then sometimes watch the morning movie.

- When dinner turns into the "crisis hour," mothers place their infants in front of the television set, grateful for the electronic baby-sitting.

America's children watch a lot of television, and the amount gradually increases from age three to the beginning of adolescence (Stein & Friedrich, 1975). Television watching declines more for boys than girls in adolescence (Lyle, 1972). In one survey the mothers of preschool children reported that their children watched from 5 to 88 hours per week—an average of less than one to more than twelve hours per day, seven days a week (Stein & Friedrich, 1975). It has been estimated that the average American child watches five or six hours of television per day and that the average adolescent has spent a total of twenty thousand hours watching television, which is considerably more than the number of hours spent in the classroom in twelve years of schooling (Comstock, 1975a).

Researchers have found that viewing patterns are related to social class and race. Children from homes lower in social status watch more television and more violence than those from homes with higher status. When social class is controlled, blacks watch more television and more violence than whites. Researchers and interested professionals have long been concerned about the effect on children's development of this massive exposure to the ubiquitous TV screen. The content analysis of television programming has from the very beginning revealed a high incidence of violent, antisocial behavior. That content is as high in children's programs as in adult programs, and this is especially true of cartoons. Children, however, do not confine their viewing to children's programs.

Television burst on a cultural scene in which children were carefully nurtured and books for children highly censored. Fairy tales had been rewritten because it was feared that such violent scenes as the Big Bad Wolf eating Grandma might psychologically upset children. Interestingly enough, parents seem unable to censor children's television viewing, although they continue to censor their books. Television as a means of mass communication has developed since World War II. During those years the cumulative amount of time that American children spend in this activity has increasingly concerned responsible child psychologists. Logic tells these professionals that anything that occupies so much of a child's formative years *must* have an effect. However, gathering scientific information about this process has been extremely difficult, mainly for methodological reasons.

Professionals fear that the process of socialization that has evolved over thousands of years is threatened by replacement with electric technology. It is through this time-honored socialization process that humans learn to belong to their culture. In countless ways children learn the traditional behaviors and values that give meaning and purpose to their lives. This structure is a fragile one, and we have seen ancient cultures disintegrate with industrialization and modern technology. Television is a potent component of this modern technology, and one of the areas that has most concerned researchers is the effect of television on aggressive behavior.

Does Violent Television Create Violent Children?

Almost from the beginning of television in America there were vocal critics of children's television. This criticism motivated social scientists to attempt to unravel the effect of this new medium. In the early 1970s the Congress of the United States ordered a full-scale investigation on the effect of television on children. Social scientists then were preoccupied with attempting to determine the effect of televised violence on subsequent *behavior*, especially aggressive behavior. The issue predominated in the 1960s and was summarized in the Surgeon General's 1972 report, *Television and Growing Up: The Impact of Televised Violence* (Surgeon General's Scientific Advisory Committee on Television and Social Behavior, 1972).

In the early investigation of the effect of aggression on children there were conflicting views. One view held that watching violence on television served as a *catharsis*—that is, it was a means of a vicarious emotional outlet, especially if children were frustrated and/or angry. Their pent-up emotion could be harmlessly expressed by the vicarious experience of watching someone else perform acts that the children would secretly like to perform.

The second view, supported by early research was that when children watched characters on television perform aggressive acts those characters served as models for the children's behavior. This is an easy hypothesis to investigate, and many studies have been conducted in this area. In general, studies of this kind assign children to an experimental or control group (being careful to balance for sex, socioeconomic level, race, and perhaps other factors that the researcher deems pertinent). One group, the control, is shown nonviolent television fare and the second group (experimental) is shown violent fare. Immediately after this viewing aggressive behavior is measured in some way. For example, in some studies, the children are allowed free play with toys that can be used violently and with nonviolent toys. The choices of toys are noted, as is the incidence of aggressive behavior. A favorite toy for this situation is the "Bobo" doll. When children are allowed to observe a model hitting the "Bobo" they tend to increase the frequency of similar aggressive acts. Researchers have investigated whether children are more likely to model the behavior of the same or opposite-sexed models, live or filmed models, or realistic or cartoon models. The overwhelming conclusion of this research has been that children model the aggressive behavior they see, whether it is modeled by a live model, a realistically filmed model, or a cartoon figure. They are more likely to model the behavior of a same-sexed model, but not exclusively, and preschool children are more likely to model aggressive behavior than older children. The aggressive behavior of school-age children is apparently also affected by such factors as individual personality characteristics and cognitive level. These differences are consistent with the intense interest in role modeling that preschool children exhibit, whereas school-age children begin to pull away from adults as role models and temper this with other factors. However, for those school-age children who have a predisposition to aggressive behavior, observing a model engage in aggressive behavior seems to increase aggressive behavior. If the child has good impulse control, the model seems to make little difference. Some factors that predispose children to aggressive behavior are being male, having a violent or very permissive family, and being in a low social class.

Learning Aggression from Television

Observing a model engage in aggressive acts may lead the child to express aggressive behavior through two different, but related, processes. First, the child may learn how to be aggressive. Second, the observance of aggressive behavior may disinhibit behaviors already in the individual's repertoire (Bandura 1969). In the first instance, the child may learn to hit, as he or she learned to tie shoes or to write the alphabet. Once the behavior is learned, it is practiced, especially if it results in positive reinforcement for the child. In this process the child actually acquires the aggressive behavior by watching the model; therefore it can be said that the modeling *causes* the aggressive behavior.

In a second process the effect of a model may essentially be to grant permission to engage in aggressive behavior that the child already knows how to perform. One of the goals of socialization that parents stress with young children is control of impulses. The average toddler exhibits a healthy dose of aggression, and parents insist that he or she inhibit that impulse. When an adult or an admired cartoon character engages in aggressive behavior, the effect is to *disinhibit* a behavior that the child already knows how to perform, but for whose performance there is an inhibition. When that inhibition is removed, the child may perform the behavior and act aggressively. In this case, of course, the model has not created the aggression but has only facilitated the performance of a behavior already in the child's behavioral repertoire. Each of us has many behaviors that we know how to perform but may never have actually done. For example, airlines attempt to use this capacity of humans to learn behavior but to delay actual exhibition in teaching what to do in case of emergency. The stewardess models behavior in case the cabin is depressurized. Travelers on planes do not indiscriminately grab the oxygen mask and use it; however, should the cabin become depressurized they know what behavior to institute even though they may never have performed it before.

And so it is with aggression. There are times when aggressive behavior is in self-defense and is justified. In the normal course of social relations, however, aggressive acts are inhibited, even when anger is aroused toward another person. Children are taught to inhibit the impulse to hit first and talk later and are encouraged to attempt to settle differences in peaceful ways. Adults, of course, are responsible for teaching this to children. When adults model aggressive behavior, this disinhibits or encourages the behavior.

The question of the relationship between violence on television and behavior was examined in seven congressional hearings between 1952 and 1974 (Comstock, 1972, 1975a). Comstock, the major writer of the Surgeon General's report (1972) stated that, "the most scientifically justifiable conclusion . . . is that violent television entertainment increases the probability of subsequent aggressive behavior on the part of the children and youth."

In summary, the research evidence indicates that television content can indeed arouse or stimulate behavior, probably by lowering inhibitions to aggressive behaviors. Second, children learn what they see, even without the opportunity to practice it, and third, the effect of content differs according to the internal state of the viewer and environmental factors.

Critics of society are concerned about increasing violence in an increasingly violent world. The source of aggression, in both individuals and nations, remains a perplexing problem for psychologists, philosophers, and political scientists. Students of child development are concerned about the vast number of shootings, stabbings, beatings, and other sadistic acts that twenty thousand hours of television have taught our youth. It defies logic to accept that such a vast amount of time spent watching persistent violence is only idle recreation. As Nicholas Johnson, commissioner of the FCC, has stated, "All television is educational television. The only question is, what is it teaching?" (Liebert, Neale, & Davidson, 1973).

Television and Prosocial Behavior

If television characters can serve as models for aggressive behavior what about prosocial behaviors: caring, cooperation, and sharing? Can television serve as a model and increase the acquisition of these behaviors? "Mr. Rogers' Neighborhood" was one of the first programs designed for children that attempted to effect positive behaviors in children. Friedrich and Stein (1975) found that kindergarten children were able to generalize what they had learned from a prosocial program. The concepts investigated were very complex, much more complex than aggressive actions: helping a friend, trying to understand another's feelings, knowing that wishes do not make things happen, and valuing a person for inner qualities rather than appearance.

Stein and Friedrich found that social interaction became more positive for lower-class children but did not change for middle-class children after a series of sessions with Mr. Rogers' Neighborhood. Boys were slightly more cooperative but girls showed no change. The major effect appeared to be in sharing with little change in cooperation or helping. In several studies these investigators found that boys became less aggressive after exposure to the prosocial programs but girls tended to become more aggressive (Friedrich & Stein, 1973, 1975). Other behaviors, such as self-regulation and imaginative play, have been studied, but the evidence is not clear. Friedrich and Stein (1973) found that prosocial programs increased task persistence for some children but not for others. Many programs for children use puppets to stimulate imaginative play. A study by Singer and Singer (in Stein & Friedrich, 1975) found that imaginative behavior does increase when the program encourages it, if the child watches the program with an adult.

One of the problems with television is that there is so little prosocial programming, especially for older children. In addition, it is virtually impossible to control the television that children watch outside of the classroom or experimental situation. These stored images may influence behavior long after they are viewed. Not only do children watch television intended for them, children of all ages watch adult programming, and there is very little prosocial content in it. It is difficult to assess the effect on the mind and personality of the children who sit in the semi-darkness of living rooms across America watching images on television.

The Television Medium

Almost all of the criticism of American television has been in terms of content, but what is the effect of television beyond content? Marshall McLuhan (1964) a professor who investigated the effect of technology on culture has asserted that we fail to understand each new technology and instead evaluate it in terms of the one that it replaced. Television has replaced the printed word. The cultural effect of the printed word was to create people who needed privacy (to read and reflect on it) and the effect was to end the public pattern of medieval society. Both logic and our research on the importance of experience in determining the development of children indicate that television viewing must have a profound effect on society. But what *is* the effect?

Winn (1974) and Mander (1978) suggest that television per se has a hypnotic effect and bypasses the cognitive process. Winn compares viewing television to maintaining an addiction with effects as serious as narcotics. The written word, to be understood, must be translated into meanings through cognitive processes. Visual images, on the other hand, are processed differently by the human brain, and television is visual images. Support for these differences can be found in the different functions of the right brain and the left brain. The left hemisphere processes verbal material and is the seat of analytical thinking, whereas the right hemisphere is nonverbal and processes images. Thus, the printed word and television images are processed differently in the brain. Liss and Reinhardt (1979) state that "without being taught in the strict educational sense and without their own knowledge, [children] are molded by the characters they admire on television"(p. 7).

Mander (1978), in an extremely strong statement, suggests that, by its nature, television undermines the very cornerstone of Western civilization. This cornerstone consists of those values reflected in the philosophy and literature—in the ideals and tortuous progress toward knowledge, democracy, and freedom—that are the heritage of Western thought and tradition. Let us look more closely at his assertions. Mander offers four main reasons for his denunciation of television. First, he asserts, television changes the viewer's experience and perception of reality. From the Greek philosophers to the present, Western civilization has been based on our understanding of and relationship to nature. Television does not and cannot accurately represent nature. By its inherent technology, television distorts reality, a child's subsequent view of the world, and his or her understanding of causal relationships.

Second, Mander suggests that television is a new form of colonization: colonization of the mind and spirit. This effect is especially evident in American television advertising in which need is created for unnecessary products by insistent advertising. However, the *process* of creating an artificial domination of mind and spirit is the same, regardless of whether the content is product advertising or "General Hospital." This quality of the medium makes it a perfect tool for totalitarian politics and leaders who use demagogic techniques.

Mander's third argument against television is based on his extensive review of the effects of television on humans:

1. People addicted to television report the subjective symptoms of feeling sick, crazy, and hypnotized.
2. The effects of the immense exposure to the artificial light from television sets have yet to be determined.
3. There is a tendency to bypass consciousness and critical evaluation and to store images. For increasing numbers of children, the images that previously were formed by parents and teachers are being replaced by television personalities.
4. The greatest reservoir of creativity, the human imagination, is suppressed by a constant flow of ready-made images.

Mander's final and strongest argument is that the medium itself has inherent biases that cannot be overcome. They are a real and present danger to human growth and development and to freedom. Television, by its nature, is biased toward the easy, the superficial, and the focused leader. War, conflict, desire, lust, the bizarre, and death make better television images than peace, harmony, satisfaction, and everyday life. Uncritical facts, action, and a charismatic leader are better television than process, being, and reasoned discussions. The danger, of course, is that children reared with a constant diet of such mental images will accept them as reality and demand a world in which there is one right answer and a quick gun to silence all others.

There remain many unanswered questions about television's effects on our children. We need to view the medium with something less than uncritical acceptance. We need to investigate the following areas:

1. The nature of the medium of television itself.
2. The influence of television in socializing our children—that is, its psychological and behavioral effects.

3. Means for influencing public policy toward television programming. In spite of the criticism of televised violence and its condemnation by the Surgeon General of the United States, a recent survey of programs revealed increased levels of violent content in network programming. Violent images make effective television and effective television makes high Neilson ratings.

4. The role of television on culture, politics, and on such special populations as the poor, underdeveloped nations, and women. Repeatedly critics have alleged that the televised images of affluent middle-class America adds to the alienation of lower-class children and to crime statistics.

Video Games and Computers

The most recent corrupter of youth, according to many adults, is video games. They require intense concentration and many children and youths spend a great deal of time (and money) in video arcades and with their own games at home. Parents and educators have begun to express concern about the effects of the games, concerns revolving around suspected damage to personality and about the unknown effect of hours of exposure to video light. Little research has been done in this area, but video games promise to become the point of struggle between youth and adults in the 1980s. We are, no doubt, at the beginning of a ''computer revolution.'' Our children in the future will be much more at home with the computer than with the printed page. Many children have already mastered programming and are using the tools of this technology to invent their own games and programs. Many schools have computers and use them to teach various subjects. In addition, a growing number of children have personal computers and some colleges are requiring personal computers as part of the equipment that students bring with them to college. We have yet to assess the full effect of this revolution.

The Emotionally Disturbed Child

Emotional and social development do not always proceed with beauty and grace. Contemporary American society creates many psychological stresses, and children are not immune to them. An increasing number of children who are problems to their parents and the schools have been judged to be emotionally disturbed. A large number of disorders may fall under the category of emotional disturbance. The most disruptive type of disorder is manifested by children who cannot control their emotions and behavior. They may fly into a blind rage, disrupt the classroom, and harm themselves or others—other children, teachers, or parents. These children are more likely to be boys, and as puberty approaches and physical strength increases parents may actually fear their own sons. The unmanageable child with poor impulse control is very difficult to treat, and parents may ask the court to relieve them of the responsibility. Psychotherapy and behavior modification are often used to treat these children, but the results are slow and the task difficult.

Often overlooked is the withdrawn child. This child may increasingly withdraw from people and things, but because he or she causes little trouble either at home or in the classroom, the problem may be overlooked. This emotional problem, however, is as severe as that with the explosive child. Such children need careful attention to bring them out of their own private world. The book *Dibs In*

Search of Self (Axline, 1965) is an interesting recounting of the work of a therapist with a child for whom the psychological realities of life were overwhelming. Not many such children have Dibs' innate resources or such a skillful therapist to guide them back into the world of reality.

The Hyperactive Child

"Would you please sit down. You're like a Mexican jumping bean," John's mother says in exasperation. Similar exasperation is felt by thousands of mothers and teachers every day. The hyperactive child seems unable to concentrate, is constantly jumping up for one thing or another, annoys other children, and is generally disruptive. Many theories have been advanced to explain this behavior. Prime among them is that hyperactivity is caused by a chemical imbalance or some minimal brain damage that is not medically detectable. However, no physical evidence has been found to support either of these theories. Others hold that hyperactivity is caused by emotional problems, additives in food, or allergies. Many treatments for hyperactivity have been advanced. Among them are control with drugs, diet, and behavioral techniques. Some of these do work with some children, but the problem is far from solved. Many people suspect that labeling a child hyperactive is a way of relieving adults from dealing with the problems created by a difficult child. Such labels, however, do not help the parents and teachers who live with the child daily.

The Autistic Child

Autism is a condition that ocurs in a very small number of children. It is characterized by extreme disorder in personal relationships and mental organization. Autistic children seem unable to establish contact with and to relate to others. Often they will not make eye contact. They also display disorder in speech and exhibit *echolalia*. That is, instead of carrying on a conversation, they repeat what was said to them. For example, when asked, "John, do you want a cookie?" John may reply, "John, do you want a cookie?" In addition, their speech is mechanical and lacks the expression that gives it emotional texture. Things seem to hold little meaning for them, and they tend to use their bodies for stimulation, often engaging in repetitive actions such as rapidly shaking their hand or other part of their body. It has been suggested that these children suffer from stimulus deprivation and thus attempt to stimulate themselves through such actions. Autistic children may be self-destructive; they bite themselves and bang their head against objects. The cause of autism is not clear, but many theorists are of the opinion that it is the result of chemical malfunctions. At present there is no cure, and the treatment rate is discouraging. Through constant work and careful behavior control these children can learn rudimentary self-care skills, but the progress toward relating emotionally and toward intellectual competence is small and slow. Most parents find that as these children become adolescents they simply cannot manage them and seek to institutionalize them.

The Rights of Children

A survey of the history of Western civilization will reveal concern with the extention of rights to an ever-increasing number of people. Events such as the Magna Charta, the American and French revolutions, and the civil rights movement in the

Every child is owed the best that mankind has to give to be enabled to develop physically, mentally, morally, spiritually, and socially; and is owed health, love and understanding, an education, and special protection from abuse and exploitation. The United Nations Declaration on the Rights of Children states that these are the rights of all children, not only those in advanced countries. [Courtesy Richard Michaels and Greensboro Day School.]

United States attest to this concern. In all these events and the declarations that issued from them, children, as a group, are not mentioned. Yet, the quality of life for untold numbers of children in the world is increasingly poor. The United Nations has taken such a step in a document on the declaration of the rights of the child. This document states ten principles that outline the rights of all children throughout the world. These rights state that the full development of their *potential* is a human right of all children, not a privilege of country, class, race, or religion. These principles are outlined in the following paragraphs.

Principle 1.   All children shall enjoy these rights. No child, without exception, can be excluded or discriminated from them because of race, color, sex, language, religion, political or other opinion, national or social origin, property, birth, or other status either by himself/herself or of his/her family.

Principle 2.   The child shall enjoy special protection, and shall be given opportunities and facilities to enable him/her to develop physically, mentally, morally, spiritually, and socially, in a healthy and normal manner and in conditions of freedom and dignity.

Principle 3.   The child shall be entitled to a name and a nationality from his/her birth.

Principle 4.   The child shall be entitled to grow and develop in health; to this end special care and protection shall be provided both to him/her and to his/her mother, including adequate prenatal and postnatal care. The child shall have the right to adequate nutrition, housing, recreation, and medical services.

Principle 5. The child who is physically, mentally, or socially handicapped shall be given the special treatment, education, and care required by his/her particular condition.

Principle 6. The child, for the full and harmonious development of his/her personality, needs love and understanding. He/she shall, wherever possible, grow up in the care and under the responsibility of his/her parents, and any case in an atmosphere of affection and of moral and material security. A child of tender years shall not, save in exceptional circumstances, be separated from his/her mother. Society and the public authorities shall have the duty to extend particular care to children without a family and to those without adequate means of support.

Principle 7. The child is entitled to receive education, which shall be free and compulsory, at least in the elementary stages. He/she shall be given an education which will promote his/her general culture, and enable him/her on a basis of equal opportunity to develop his/her abilities, individual judgment, and sense of moral and social responsibility, and to become a useful member of society.

The child shall have full opportunity for play and recreation, which should be directed to the same purposes as education; society and the public authorities shall endeavor to promote the enjoyment of this right.

Principle 8. The child shall in all circumstances be among the first to receive protection and relief.

Principle 9. The child shall be protected against all forms of neglect, cruelty, and exploitation. He/she shall not be the subject of traffic, in any form. The child shall not be admitted to employment before an appropriate minimum age; he/she shall in no case be caused or permitted to engage in any occupation or employment which would jeopardize his/her health or education, or interfere with his/her physical, mental, or moral development.

Principle 10. The child shall be protected from practices which may foster racial, religious, and any other form of discrimination. He/she shall be brought up in a spirit of understanding, tolerance, friendship among peoples, peace and universal brotherhood, and in full consciousness that his/her energy and talents should be devoted to the service of humankind.

Main Points

Psychosexual Development: The Latency Period

1. During the years from six to puberty there is a suspension of psychosexual conflict while physiological processes mature. The well-developing child moves into identification with the parents, and psychic energy is directed to mastering the tools of society.

Psychosocial Development: Industry vs. Inferiority

2. The child struggles to master the tasks assigned by society; if the child succeeds, a sense of industry and competence evolves but if he or she fails there is a sense of inferiority.

Independence and Status: The Work of the Ego

3. Through an independent ego the individual is able to set goals, strive to reach them, and to function realistically in the world.

4. The individual uses information on his or her status in a group to build self-esteem and a self concept.

5. Status may be primary (earned by the individual) or derived (gained from a relationship with a person or group who has primary status).

Development of an Independent Self (Ego)

6. Ego, one of three components of personality in psychoanalytic theory, develops in a series of stages.

7. In stage one of ego development, differentiation of self-concept, the child develops the rudimentary concept of self and not-self.

8. In stage two of ego development, the omnipotent phase, the infant perceives him- or herself as all-powerful, as parents and caregivers meet his every need.

9. An ego-devaluation crisis, the third stage of ego development, occurs when parents demand that the child assume some responsibility for self-care, such as toilet training, dressing and feeding, and impulse control.

10. In the fourth stage of ego development, satellization, the child becomes a satellite of a parent who chooses goals and has the means to reach them.

11. An ego maturation crisis between the ages of eight and sixteen results in desatellization.

12. Resatellization occurs for teenagers with their peer group and its heroes and heroines.

Peers and the Society of Children

13. In middle childhood peers assume importance in influence and reference points for children.

Families in Middle Childhood

14. In middle childhood the parents' behavior toward the child changes, but the family continues to exert enormous influence on the child's development.

15. The nuclear family, consisting of a mother, a father, and children living in the same household as a social and economic unit, is the ideal in our society but decreasing as the norm.

16. Children are greatly affected by their parents' divorce and following divorce the behavior of both the parents and the children changes.

17. Boys whose fathers are absent suffer problems with their own identity, are more likely to be delinquent and less likely to be motivated to school work and careers. Girls are more likely to be sexually promiscuous and have more difficult social adjustments than children from homes with fathers present.

18. Among school-age children, the effect of the mother working appears to be positive for girls and negative for boys.

Television

19. The television viewing of American children increases from age three to the beginning of adolescence.

20. The research evidence indicates that television content can arouse or stimulate aggressive behavior through learning or lowering inhibitions.

21. Cooperative and helping behaviors, sharing, and understanding others' feelings have been shown to increase when children view prosocial programs.

22. Television by its nature is biased toward the easy, the superficial, and the focused leader.

Video Games and Computers

23. There is much concern about the effect of video games on children.

The Emotionally Disturbed Child

24. Broadly grouped, a disturbed child is unmanageable, has poor impulse control, and is disruptive and harmful to himself and others; the withdrawn child is often overlooked because he or she causes little trouble.

25. The hyperactive child is unable to concentrate, constantly moving, annoying, and disruptive.

26. Autism is characterized by extreme disorder in personal relationships and mental organization.

The Rights of Children

27. In a declaration on the rights of children the United Nations has identified ten principles that assure every child the right to develop physically, mentally, morally, spiritually, and socially in freedom and dignity.

Words to Know

desatellization
disinhibit
echolalia
gratification
impulse
inhibition

omnipotent
peer
prosocial
resatellization
satellization

Terms to Define

derived status
ego-devaluation crisis
ego-maturation crisis
ego-maturation goals
executive independence

impulse control
primary status
self-concept
volitional independence

Concept to Discuss

self

15

Transition to Adolescence:
The Years from Nine to Twelve

Have you ever wondered

how children make the transition to being adolescents?

what changes accompany puberty?

why adolescents feel that everyone is watching them?

how strategies for interpersonal relationships develop?

if physical development is coordinated with social and psychological development?

There is no sharp line between childhood and adolescence, yet there is a vast difference between the two stages of development. Childhood is generally characterized by self-confidence and positive growth. Adolescence, on the other hand, is characterized as a period of self-doubt, self-consciousness and mounting social problems. The happy child does not suddenly awaken one morning as an adolescent. There is a period of transition in which many changes take place. This period is receiving increasing attention and is referred to as *preadolescence*. In this chapter we will define the period, indicate the physical changes that take place, the reorganization of personality, and the social transformations that mark the transition to adolescence.

Defining Preadolescence

In terms of chronological age, the preadolescent period includes children between nine and twelve (sometimes thirteen) years of age. In school systems that organize grades into elementary school, junior high school and senior high school, the preadolescent is found split between elementary school and junior high. The years nine to twelve usually correspond to the fourth, fifth, sixth, and seventh grades.

Neither of these school organizations is specifically designed to meet the developmental needs of the preadolescent. At a time when they need more independence and responsibility, they are constrained by the organization of the elementary school (fourth, fifth, and sixth grades). Conversely, at a time when they are literally bursting with growth and feelings of expansion and competence and need to be given opportunities to try new organizational and executive abilities (seventh grade), they are entering a junior high school, at the bottom of a hierarchical structure, with little opportunity to compete with eighth and ninth graders in clubs and athletics. Junior high schools offer the same type of organization, the same emphasis on sports, and the same clubs as high schools. They are a smaller, that is, junior, version of the high school experience.

A more recent organization of schools has attempted to meet this problem by grouping grades five through eight into a middle school. This arrangement is more in accord with the abilities and interests of the preadolescent. The evaluation of the middle school as an organization for education has not yet been completed and cannot be until we have assessed the children who have attended them.

In terms of physical development, the preadolescent is a pubescent child—that is, a child in the process of the rapid physical and sexual maturation known as puberty. Quite often the preadolescent is seen as just that, *pre*adolescent. Thorn-

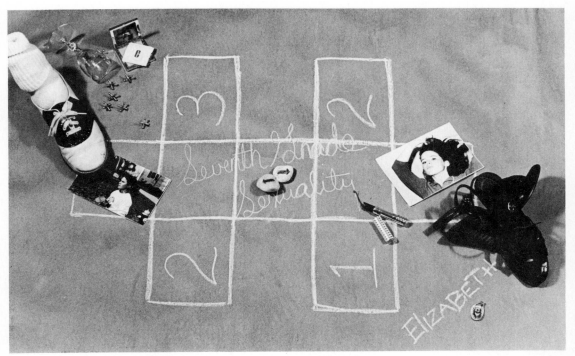

As the body matures, the preadolescent begins the quest for personal identity. Crucial to this identity is coming to terms with sexuality. This composition shows the dual experience of the maturing girl. At left are the saddle shoes and jacks of presexual childhood; at right are high-heeled sandals and lipstick, symbolizing sexual maturity or womanhood. At center are two stones side by side; the arrows point in opposite directions, showing that the presexual and sexual identities are simultaneous and mutually exclusive for the growing girl. [Courtesy Anastasia.]

burg (1974) has questioned what joy there could be in being *pre* anything? Rather than being seen as a legitimate stage of development with its own special needs, strengths, and dangers, pubescence is seen neither as childhood or adolescence. The consequence of this attitude and organization both in the larger society and in schools is that children in these years rush headlong into adolescence and adolescent activities such as dating, driving, and other allegiances in an effort to appear "cool" and "with it" before they are intellectually and psychologically ready.

Parents are also guilty of the same blindness toward the preadolescent. Girls are encouraged to wear bras and use lipstick as soon as any indication of physical maturity takes place—and often long before. Parents often encourage dances and single-couple dating for both sons and daughters at an age when the preadolescent is more comfortable with group activity and tentative relationships with the oppo-

Preadolescents are not always so anxious for involvement with the opposite sex as this letter from a preadolescent girl to her parents shows. Such prearranged social occasions often create discomfort; friendships between boys and girls flourish more easily in the natural day-to-day activities in schools and neighborhoods.

site sex. These parents are well meaning, but they offer little guidance about appropriate activities for the not-child and not-yet-adolescent.

On the other hand, the answer is not to extend childhood. A child of eleven or twelve years cannot be treated, or be expected to behave, as a child of eight or nine. We make a plea for designing programs in schools, churches, and homes appropriate to the preadolescent child's level of development. The eleven- or twelve-year-old needs protection and supports that an eighteen- or nineteen-year-old does not. Within that protection, however, children of this age need freedom to explore and—more importantly—to make mistakes without the dire consequences that are often associated with the actions of older adolescents. They need time to learn and to grow.

The most essential growth needs of this age are in the area of personal identity and social relations. The old comfortable relationships formed within the family begin to break up, and the older child is thrown into a personal quest for the answer to the question "Who am I?" and is forced into working out his or her own relationship to other people.

As girls and boys reach and pass through puberty, they are increasingly subject to cultural attitudes toward males and females as sexual beings. Every culture controls and patterns the sexual behavior of its members. This control and patterning is aside from the question of whether the culture is permissive or repressive. A society controls just as much as stimulating and goading members into sexual activity as by repressing such activity. With the advent of puberty, the moratorium of childhood is over. In primitive societies the pubescent youth undergoes a rite of passage, a ritual that marks the transition from child to adult and makes it obvious to all. In many cultures both boys and girls undergo such ceremonies. The rules of adult behavior are made explicit, as well as its rights and obligations. After such a ritual the young person takes his or her place among the adults of the culture. In our more complex society, we have no such rituals. Adults often exhibit great anxiety about children reaching sexual maturity. Perhaps a ritual, a definite event that could be pointed to as coming of age, would alleviate some of this cultural anxiety. We can point to birth, marriage, and graduation as milestones in life, but we have no such event to mark change in the status in adolescence. Adolescents themselves, perhaps, consider obtaining a driver's license as the event that marks their passage, especially since it is accompanied by independent use of the family car or sometimes by ownership of a car, but this event is long past the physical coming of age of puberty.

Physical Changes in Preadolescence

Puberty

Puberty refers to the period of rapid growth and development that results in maturation of the reproductive capacity. Petersen and Taylor (1980) underline the concept that puberty is a part of a process of sexual differentiation that begins early in prenatal life. Although it is not entirely clear what triggers the rapid development of puberty, it is evident that hormone levels direct it. What is not clear is what causes the change in hormone levels. Although boys and girls develop into quite different physical beings, there are, strictly speaking, no male and female hormones. High levels of estrogens are associated with female development and high levels of androgens are associated with male development. Let us stress again, however, that the hormone systems of males and females have both estrogens and androgens. Thus, the hormones of males and females are sex-shared rather than dichotomous.

Let us return to the idea that puberty is a continuation of a process begun in prenatal life (Petersen & Taylor, 1980). In the first few weeks after conception, the development of male and female is identical. At about six weeks after conception the male embryo begins to produce testosterone and this, in turn, stimulates the differentiation of male genitalia and neural pathways. Both male and female fetuses have high levels of sex hormones. The presence of these hormones often produce such effects as enlarged genitalia, milk in the breasts, and erections in male infants. In the prenatal period, hormonal levels in the fetus may approach those of adults. Thus, we find that the mechanism for sex hormones and their effects are quite well developed before birth. Late in the prenatal period a *negative feedback system* is established that suppresses the production of hormones and raises the threshold of sensitivity to them. This suppression holds sexual development in check, and holds the level of sex hormones low throughout infancy and early childhood. Puberty occurs when this negative feedback system is removed and the development that began in the prenatal period is continued. The sex-specific hormone system is a complicated interchange of messages among the hypothalamus, the pituitary gland, and the gonads (testes and ovaries). The ultimate control of sexual development is located in the brain, *not* in the sex organs. The hypothalamus signals the pituitary gland to produce or cease production of substances that stimulate the testes and ovaries to produce the specific hormones. The hormones in turn stimulate other activities in the body.

Beginning of Puberty

It becomes increasingly difficult to contain puberty within clear limits when we conceive of sexual development as a process begun in prenatal life. Menstruation and the production of sperm (indicated by the first ejaculation) have traditionally been cited as events that mark puberty. It is clear now, however, that such events are far from the beginning of puberty; they are rather, dramatic events that more nearly coincide with the midpoint of pubertal development. It is more accurate to consider that puberty begins with the increasing sensitivity of the hypothalamus to the sex hormones and to the consequent rising levels of those hormones in the blood stream. If we consider these rising levels of hormones to signal the beginning of puberty, we then find that such changes begin as young as seven or eight years of age (especially in girls). By ten most children demonstrate the elevated hormonal levels associated with puberty (Petersen and Taylor, 1980). Increased hormonal levels are not immediately evident in outward physical changes; however, over a period of time these hormones cause many physical changes to take place. Let us stress, then, that puberty is a gradual process of change. Children, parents, and teachers have time to adjust to it, provided they give it their attention.

The Growth Spurt

In puberty boys and girls both experience a period of rapid growth and related changes in body proportion and contour. The growth pattern for most children from infancy to late childhood has been one of smooth, continuous growth. In puberty, during their most intensive year of growth, girls may grow as much as 3½ inches and gain 20 pounds. Boys often grow as much as four inches and gain 26 pounds (Tanner, 1972). Girls enter this growth spurt about two years earlier than boys.

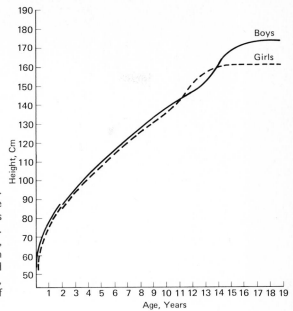

Typical growth curves for boys and girls to age eighteen. Note that girls begin the growth spurt around age twelve and surge ahead of boys. The boys' curve crosses the girls' at around fourteen and thereafter surges ahead. [From "Standards from Birth to Maturity for Height, Weight, Height Velocity and Weight Velocity: British Children, 1965" by J. M. Tanner, R. H. Whitehouse and M. Takaishi. (Published in *Archives of Disease in Childhood*, 1966, Vol. 41, pp. 454–71). Reproduced by permission of the publisher and the author.]

For girls, rapid growth begins at eleven years and for boys at thirteen (Thissen, Bock, Wainer & Roche, 1976). Thissen et al. attribute the difference in height between *adult* men and women to the fact that girls enter the growth spurt earlier than boys. These researchers found that boys were four inches taller than girls when they entered the pubertal spurt. The prepubertal growth of girls was 139 centimeters (52 inches) and the prepubertal growth of boys was 140 centimeters (56 inches). Boys gained an average of 30.80 centimeters (12 inches) in puberty and girls gained an average of 28.05 centimeters (11 inches). Thus, the average five-inch difference in adult males and females is the result of the four inches gained by males *before* puberty and the single inch gained by males over females during puberty.

Because males lag behind females by two years in physical development, girls of eleven years and boys of thirteen years are at similar stages of physical development. As a consequence of these growth patterns, girls are usually several inches taller than boys in the years between eleven and thirteen (sixth, seventh, and eighth grades). This fact, as well as changing physical dimensions, causes social and psychological upheaval. In the growth spurt the long bones of the skeleton grow rapidly. The smooth coordination that was evident in middle childhood is replaced by awkward stumbling. Arms and legs seem to lengthen overnight. Feet seem out of proportion and are a source of embarrassment. It seems to older children that suddenly their hands, feet, and legs are not where they were a few weeks before, and thus distances in relation to their body must be recalculated. At the end of this growth period the ends of the bones seal over and no further growth can take place. Again, this occurs earlier for girls than for boys. Girls reach their full potential of height, on the average, by eighteen, whereas boys do not reach their potential until twenty-one.

Sports become important to the preadolescent as bodies mature and physical skill and strength increases. [Courtesy Greensboro Day School.]

The primary manifestation of the growth spurt is physical height, but other aspects of the body are also involved. The general body contour changes. Boys' shoulders become wider and girls' hips widen. Lungs and heart increase in size and capacity and blood increases in volume. Muscles increase in both size and strength. These changes result in greatly increased physical endurance. Adolescents appear to be able to run, play, and dance endlessly. Physical endurance and prowess enable adolescents to become superb athletes; many compete in Olympic games, become tennis champions, and excel in college and high school sports.

Boys develop larger hearts and lung capacity relative to their size than girls and more red blood cells and hemoglobin. These differences predispose them to excel more than girls in sports. Tanner (1974) suggests that those physical differences may, in fact, be the result of the greater amount of physical activity engaged in by boys. Typically, when girls reach puberty they are discouraged from engaging in "masculine" activities (that is, sports). But if girls are given similar opportunities to use their bodies in athletic activities at the time that the heart and lungs are growing, the gaps in capacity may lessen. There is some evidence that adult women possess more endurance in physical activities than men. Changing social patterns and social expectations will unquestionably change our understanding and evaluation of physical differences between males and females.

Secondary Sex Characteristics

The hormones that direct pubertal development instruct rapid physical growth and sexual maturation. There can be no doubt that puberty has begun when breast development is evident in a girl. Parallel to breast development in girls is the growth in boys of the penis, testes, and scrotum. Finally, both boys and girls experience growth in body hair which is distributed in characteristic sexual patterns. The development of these systems follows an invariant sequence but it is not coordinated. For example, a girl may have underdeveloped breasts and a lot of body hair or advanced breast development and little body hair. Similarly, a boy may begin growing a beard and still have a small penis or he may have experienced considerable growth in penis size and have little body hair. Let us look at these developments.

Breast Development.   The first indication that breast development is taking place is enlargement of the nipples (papilla). In the breast bud stage the pigmented area surrounding the papilla (areola) enlarges in diameter and the entire breast is elevated as a small mound. Breast and areola continue to enlarge and to elevate. As the breast develops, the areola and papilla form a secondary mound that projects above the contour of the breast. In the mature breast the areola is recessed into the general contour of the breast and only the papilla projects. Stages of breast development are used diagnostically to determine pubertal progress. Breast development is also a rough indication of the approaching menarche and is usually nearly completed before it.

Hair Growth.   During puberty both boys and girls show a change in body hair color and texture. In addition, hair begins to grow in regions that were previously smooth. The first area in which this is evident is the pubic region. This hair first appears as sparse and slightly pigmented. Gradually it increases in area, darkens in color and becomes coarse and curly. Axillary hair also begins to grow. Facial hair increases in boys so that they may need to shave, and sometimes soft facial hair appears on girls. Late in boys' adolescent development chest hair grows; a few hairs may appear around the areola on girls' breasts.

Sexual Maturation
Puberty is most often associated with the maturation of the reproductive system. Throughout puberty internal changes take place, stimulated by hormones. In girls the uterus grows larger, the vaginal lining thickens, and the ovaries begin to produce hormones and to mature. In boys, corresponding changes take place. The internal glands and ducts increase in size, as do the external organs: penis, testes, and scrotum. As the sexual organs grow they reach near-adult size and the young person becomes capable of reproduction. It is generally believed that girls are able to bear a child (that they are fertile) at menarche, and that boys are fertile when they achieve ejaculation or when sperm appears in their urine. Actually neither of these are sure signs of fertility. Ovulation usually does not occur with the first several menstrual periods, but it is not safe to consider a pubescent girl infertile. The tragic occurrence of girls of eleven and twelve bearing children attests to this. Similarly, the ability to ejaculate does not mean that there are viable sperm present. There is wide variation in the age at which menarche is reached. It is within the normal range for this to occur in girls as young as ten or as old as sixteen (Higham, 1980). The average girl, however, reaches menarche at twelve years of age.

Early and Late Maturers
The girl who is in third grade, is five feet tall, has developed breasts, and is menstruating may encounter great psychological and social problems. The boy who towers above his classmates and has a mature penis and erections (detected by classmates when he gives reports) suffers embarrassment. Both these children can be taunted by their classmates and suffer damaged self-esteem and body image. On the other hand, boys and girls of sixteen who remain a head shorter than their classmates

and are trapped in a child's body also suffer an assault on their esteem. All of these patterns occur, and although they are extreme, they are within the range of normal development.

Precocious puberty is diagnosed when sexual maturation begins before age eight in girls or nine and one-half in boys; delayed puberty is diagnosed when the maturation *process* has not begun by age thirteen in girls and thirteen and one-half in boys (Higham, 1980). Children and their parents often seek medical advice in these cases, but the causes of early and delayed puberty remain unclear. Some of the factors are individual variation in development, familial patterns, and nutrition. It is suspected that social and psychological factors influence pubertal development, but the exact nature of this influence has yet to be explained. Delayed development may be caused by abnormal function of the brain (hypothalamus) or by failure of the testes or ovaries to produce enough hormones to stimulate development. Delayed puberty can be stimulated by hormone-replacement therapy. In this case, puberty proceeds as usual, even though it is delayed.

The major effect of both early and late maturation, however, is not in physical development, but in the lasting effect on sexual and psychological self-concept, social relations with peers, and psychosexual functioning. In general, early-maturing boys and late-maturing girls have better self-concepts than late-maturing boys and early-maturing girls. Our culture values masculine strength, and the boy who is unable to compete in athletics and strength at fifteen or sixteen develops a poor body image and a sense of inferiority. Ironically, these boys, when they do develop, tend to be tall and to have masculine bodies, whereas the boys who for so many years were the tallest of their peers often end up among the shortest. Nevertheless, the early self-image persists and late maturers have a difficult time erasing a poor self-image. Girls who develop early have poorer self-concepts than girls who develop late. Although our culture values the beautiful feminine body, the young girl who develops a woman's body is subject to many suggestive sexual remarks, teasing, and perhaps even propositions that she is not ready to handle.

It has been estimated that in colonial times the average age for girls reaching menarche was sixteen or even eighteen years. Today in North America girls reach menarche on the average at the age of twelve. The cause of this downward trend is unknown but is generally attributed to the quality of nutrition and health care children now receive. As researchers began to gather data in this century and could compare studies over a period of fifty years or more, it was noticed that first menstruation seemed to occur approximately three months earlier every ten years. This means a full year in the space of 40 years. Fortunately, this downward trend seems to be leveling off, and menarche is stabilizing at around twelve years of age.

Psychological Reorganization in the Preadolescent

In the preadolescent period the secure pattern of childhood begins to break apart and a reorganization of personality is forced. Children in the middle years have an easy and relaxed relationship with their parents and other adults. The peak of identification with parents occurs at approximately eight years of age. Soon after this, increasing cognitive maturity, combined with skill in executive independence, forces a reevaluation of the parent. The perceptive child notices cracks in the image of the perfect parent. There are areas in which knowledge is lacking, there are times when parents do not keep their word, or a parent may be caught in an outright lie. The child is then forced back on his or her own resources and must fashion a new ego organization out of old parts. Many writers see the psychological reorganization evident in adolescence as the result of the physical changes that accompany puberty. Josselson (1980) emphasizes that this reorganization is not entirely dependent on the internal push from rising pubertal hormones, but rather is a psychological and social necessity that must take place in the total context of maturation.

Developmental Tasks in Preadolescence

Thornburg (1974) describes six areas in which developmental tasks must be met in the preadolescent period. They arise out of earlier developmental stages and are an important base for the adolescent period. The areas in which tasks are evident are intellectual, body image, social sex roles, friendship with peers, independence, and moral values.

Intellectual. As mental processes move from concrete thinking into a more abstract reflective thinking style the youth is challenged to develop and organize a mental approach to solving problems for everyday functioning. This includes planning and arranging his or her own personal affairs, organizing schoolwork and activities, and other practical details of living.

(A)

(B)

Developmental tasks in preadolescence include more challenging intellectual problems (A) and friendships with peers (B). [Photograph (A) courtesy Lea Williams and Greensboro Day School; photograph (B) courtesy William Amidon and Greensboro Day School.]

Body Image.   The physical changes of puberty cause the preadolescent to be preoccupied with appearance; there is often marked anxiety about the final outcome of body changes: Will he or she be too tall, too short, have a nose too large, breasts too small, hips too large, or a penis too small? The ability to accept, use, and feel comfortable with physique is a task that must be met in these years. If this does not happen, the youth must drag, like an albatross around his or her neck, a poor body image through life.

Social Sex Roles.   The preadolescent moves toward clarifying masculine and feminine sex roles. In early childhood stereotypical roles were learned in a rigid, noncritical way. Along with physical sexual development is a parallel exploration and clarification of acceptable sex roles. In this exploration and clarification, the preadolescent is extremely sensitive to the feedback from peers and teachers. Parental influence is diminishing. It is as though the preadolescent learned all parents had to teach in earlier years and in these years is gathering other ideas from the wider culture and attempting to put together his or her own individual style. This exploration and investigation is often manifested in inconsistent behavior. For example, one day a girl may appear at school dressed very seductively and in heavy makeup (perhaps applied secretly after leaving home). She will be very aware of the reaction that her looks get from other girls, boys her own age, older boys, and teachers. The next day, she may appear in a demure outfit and again monitor the feedback. Boys also experiment with their sex role. One day a boy may attempt to be macho and chauvinistic with girls, and then another day treat them as his friends and peers. He, too, is carefully studying the effects of his actions on others—on boys as well as girls. Although we usually consider adolescence the time in which this is done, a great deal of preliminary exploration is accomplished in the years between nine and twelve. Teachers and adults who work with these children are often unaware that such intensive sex-role exploration is a taking place—or, they view it as an annoyance and inappropriate behavior rather than a valid developmental stage.

Friendships with Peers.   As the dependency on parents weakens and parents and teachers are no longer seen as infallible, the preadolescent begins to view peers as people on whom he or she can and must depend. Intense interest is seen in finding out who are one's friends and, again, in assessing the qualities of those individuals. In early childhood, play groups are formed by parents or by proximity to other children. In the preadolescent period, groups and friends are selected for their personal qualities. Friendships may form among children who cannot see each other except at school and may form across racial and economic lines. In an attempt to seek experiences beyond the family, preadolescents may seek such friends but not wish to let the family know of their exploration. In later adolescence social pressures become more controlling and friends tend to be chosen who are similar in social background. The preadolescent peer group can be quite competent in organizing clubs, governing their own behavior, and making decisions. Schools should allow and encourage such exploration.

Independence.   A major developmental task for the preadolescent is gradually learning independence. Generally in our culture adolescents have great independence from adult supervision in making a monumental number of choices. In the preadolescent period the ties to parents are gradually loosened. Such activities as spending the night away from home or going to summer camp aid the growth of independence. The task of independence includes many aspects of caring for oneself.

Moral Values. As preadolescents begin to judge individuals for their inherent qualities, so they also begin to judge situations and actions as right or wrong. Formerly the child accepted the moral strictures of parents and teachers because they were given. But preadolescents begin to question the basis of rules and often break them to see what will happen. They may begin to experience the forbidden: smoking, drugs, and sex. They may shoplift, often just to see if they can get away with it. Their growing sense of independence, involvement with peers, and self-concept no longer permit their blind acceptance of parental values. Preadolescents need sympathetic adults to help them work out their own relationship to ''good'' and ''bad.'' It seems to be a rule of developmental tasks that when they are not met at the time most appropriate, their solution becomes immeasurably more difficult. For example, when the question of right and wrong is explored only in later adolescence, it may be worked out through serious offenses that lead to delinquency.

The Imaginary Audience

Preadolescence is a time of rising self-consciousness. Elkind and Bowen (1979) attribute it, in part, to the mental creation of an imaginary audience that monitors every action and every detail of one's appearance. As mental development progresses to the stage of formal operations, the preadolescent is able to think in abstract terms and to ''think about thinking.'' This stage of development along with

Preadolescents often feel that an imaginary audience is watching everything that they do, which causes self-consciousness and characteristically ''staged'' actions.

increasing skill in taking the perspective of others enables the youth to construct an elaborate imaginary audience. The self-consciousness of the pre- and early adolescent is largely a result of reactions he or she imagines from this invisible audience. Motivated by the belief that this audience can and will examine every facet of his or her physical appearance, behavior, and interactions with peers and others, the preadolescent pays careful attention to the details of dress and public behavior.

The Personal Fable

A second mental construction that arises in the preadolescent period is the personal fable (Elkind, 1980). The personal fable is the myth that each young person comes to believe about him- or herself. It is based in part on the feeling that everyone is watching his or her performance; it involves such general notions as ''Others will grow old and die, but not me,'' and ''Others may not realize their ambitions, but I will.'' This personal fable includes dreams for accomplishment; it is the vehicle through which goals are set and tentative plans are made for structuring one's life: careers are imagined, marriage and romance are fantasized, and the details of where and how one's life will be lived are often elaborated. Construction of this belief about the self continues throughout the adolescent period and peaks in late

When I grow up, I am going to be a famous scientist and discover the cure for cancer.

A PERSONAL FABLE
Beginning in preadolescence, boys and girls construct beliefs about themselves and their future accomplishments. This construction is a personal fable and it guides expectations and often future development.

Day-dreaming about developing personal qualities and romantic relationships is a component of the personal fable. [Courtesy Greensboro Day School.]

adolescence when the search for identity reaches a crisis stage. In some form this personal fable remains a part of the self-concept throughout life. With more mature thought the belief in one's immortality gives way to an acceptance of the reality of death, but the self-concept continues to include beliefs about abilities, potentialities, and possibilities that may not have been borne out in life situations. In times of failure, crisis, and devaluation by life's events, the belief in one's possibilities and destiny is a comforting and healing tool. Thus, the personal fable, which has its origin in the preadolescent period, is an adaptive mechanism that is a permanent part of the self-concept.

Social Development in Preadolescence

The End of Innocence: Strategic Interactions

Young children are open, honest, and direct in asking questions, and giving answers, showing little awareness of whether they are hurting or shocking others. Young children are not embarrassed by bodily functions and will question and discuss such topics openly. Adults, on the other hand, are not always open, and sometimes find that honesty is not the best policy. In social, business, and political relations adults often seek to conceal and distort rather than to arrive at objective truth.

One of the complexities that develops in the preadolescent period has been identified by Goffman (1969) as strategic interactions. Strategic interactions are interpersonal encounters that have as their aim the acquisition, concealment, or revelation of information through indirect means. Adults who are skilled in interpersonal relations use such strategies almost unconsciously, both for constructive and destructive ends. Skillful interpersonal strategies are used by diplomats in negoiating for international treaties, and they are used by men and women in sexual relationships. They are used in unscrupulous business deals and in repairing ruptured family relationships. The preadolescent begins to use strategies in relating to others, often with comic results. With time and experience, however, the youth becomes skilled and is able to plan strategies for successful personal relationships. Much of preadolescent peer activity involves mastering these strategic interactions in which interpersonal relations become more subtle and motivations behind actions are increasingly concealed. Elkind (1980) has identified the following strategic interactions:

1. Friendships.
2. Phoning and being phoned.
3. Cutting and being cut.
4. Relations with the opposite sex.
5. Forbidden acts.

Strategic Friendships

The strategic importance of friendship becomes apparent in the pre- and early adolescent years. The motivation for friendship is not only the enjoyment of being with a person, but also that friends often can affect opinions of the imaginary audience. An attractive girl may choose an unattractive friend so that by comparison her own beauty and brilliance are heightened for the imaginary audience. At the same time the unattractive girl may imagine that the audience is acknowledging her innate appeal because she has such a beautiful and brilliant friend (Elkind, 1980). Because of these strategic colorations peer groups tend to become cliquish and to exclude those who cannot enhance others in some way. Two classes of actions become paramount in negotiating these strategic friendships: phoning and cutting.

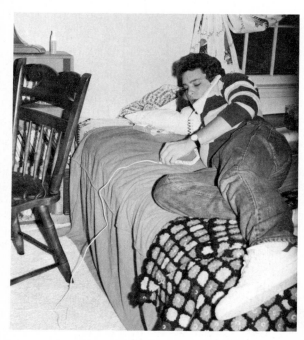

The telephone is a very important means of practicing strategies for developing friendships.

Phoning and Being Phoned

In pre- and early adolescence the telephone takes on a social value far beyond the function of giving or receiving information. Phoning and being phoned become measures of popularity and therefore possess great potential for enhancing self-esteem. Popular people receive phone calls and can feel high self-esteem, whereas unpopular people never hear the phone ring for them and may feel left out and friendless from the end of the school day until the next day. Young people experiment in manipulating this bit of technology and friends. "Call me tonight, I have something really important to tell you," a young person may urge at school. Such a strategy seldom fails to secure a phone call, as the eager friend can hardly wait to hear what the special information will be. The information is often neither news nor earth shaking, but the shared moment of conspiracy feeds the growing capacity for friendship. The important information may be of a romantic nature, what someone said about the person, or a request for advice. When all else fails, the phone can be used to call another person for clarification of a homework assignment. Often these phone conversations can be used to get the person to deliver a message to a third party on the following day, especially if the nature of interest in the party is romantic.

Cutting and Being Cut

The greatest agony for adolescents is walking into a room full of people and being ignored by a group of peers. In such a case not only the imaginary audience, but an actual audience, is witness to the humiliation. Recognition in public carries with it the power to raise or depreciate self-esteem. The ability to take the place of another and to imagine another's perception enables preadolescents to recognize the power that they have over the esteem of others and, conversely, the power that others have over their esteem. Thus, one of the strategic interactions that preadolescents develop is gaining recognition or witholding it from others. Knowledge of this power increases the self-consciousness of the young adolescent and strengthens the tendency toward cliquish friendships. Young people seek to have friends in the "in" group so that they can be assured that they can approach a group and gain recognition and avoid the humiliation of being ignored, or worse, humiliated for attempting to approach the "beautiful people."

Relationships with the Opposite Sex

The age of puberty also initiates an interest in the opposite sex, for the very reason that it is the opposite sex. In middle childhood, friendships are structured around single-sex groups. Within those groups members share secrets, spend the night with each other, and spend a lot of time with each other both in and out of school. From the secure basis of these friendship groups, individuals may venture forth and form a liaison with a person of the opposite sex. As early as fifth or sixth grade (and sometimes earlier) a few couples who are "going with" each other may form. This "going with" may not involve actually going anywhere. Often teachers and adults cannot see any outward sign of interest; however, among the peer groups it is a constant topic of conversation. There are rules that govern those relationships that include what constitutes unfaithfulness. Boys and girls seldom approach the person of their romantic interest directly; they often use an intermediary who is a trusted friend. In these dating rehearsals boys and girls learn the strategic interactions used in relating to the opposite sex. The telephone is often used in these interactions. Romantic interest is a prime excuse for a phone call or for soliciting a phone call.

Not all relations take place at a distance, and often parties, field trips, and play groups are opportunities for some form of sex play or games involving kissing. These are often "kiss-and-tell"—grist for the school and peer group's gossip mill.

Later, these approaches to the opposite sex evolve into dating patterns. In early dating the strategy for the boy is how to ask the girl for a date without suffering rejection or humiliation. The strategy for the girl is how to arrange for the boy to ask her for a date. Dating in early adolescence has as much to do with the imaginary audience as with the attraction to the person dated. Not all preadolescent behavior is so innocent and exploratory, however. In recent years society has become increasingly explicit about sexual matters and less protective about exposing preadolescents to sexual stimulation. The incidence of sexual activity among preadolescents is steadily increasing; it is no longer unusual for girls of eleven or twelve years of age to be sexually active.

Forbidden Acts

Strategic interactions are for the purpose of acquiring, concealing, and revealing information through indirect means. Through engaging in forbidden acts, the preadolescent tests his or her skill in concealment and indirect behavior. The adventure and suspense of such escapades add immeasurably to their enjoyment and challenge. One of the first acts that many preadolescents try is skipping school. Such an action requires elaborate plans and careful control of behavior so as not to arouse suspicion. First, one must plan where to spend the day. Then, one must be careful to act normally to avoid arousing suspicion that something is amiss. One must not appear too eager to go to school with parents watching, must not forget one's lunch, and must act as though it were any other day. Sometimes the day is spent at the home of someone whose parents work; in large cities, it may be spent in a section of the city far from the school. If one has older friends who drive, and the weather is warm, the day may be spent in a park or at the beach. Then, a

Smoking cigarettes often requires strategies for concealment from parents and school officials. [Courtesy Helen Brooks.]

strategy is required for behavior at home in the evening, for answering questions about the school day. Finally, a note must be taken to school. Strategies for concealing involvement in forbidden acts includes smoking cigarettes or marijuana; involvement with drugs, alcohol, or sexual activity; driving a car underage, buying beer underage, or going to an entertainment spot that requires identification and proof of age.

Strategic interactions are not negative acquisitions, even though they may involve choices about what to reveal and what to conceal. In applying for a job, for example, we learn how to reveal the best that we have to offer and to conceal our weaknesses. In social entertaining, we seek to present ourselves at our best. In professional situations we present our most assured and knowledgeable selves and conceal our doubts and confusions. Everyone, of course, needs those special people with whom nothing has to be concealed and all can be revealed. The search for that special friend is the task of late adolescence and early adulthood. By learning to conceal and to reveal, preadolescents make the transition from childhood to a more complicated world of social interaction. They need thoughtful guidance and, more than anything else, time to make the transition successfully. Schools, parents, and society need to give them this time to grow and to gain the skills necessary for the complicated world of the adolescent.

Discrepancy of Ages: Chronological, Physical, Social, and Mental

At no other time in life is there such discrepancy among the various aspects of development as in the preadolescent phase. It is very handy to use chronological age as a quick means of placing people in categories. In that way we can pull out our handy expectations for a specific age level and need not look at the individual. This guide to placing others works reasonably well with young children and reasonably well with young adults, the middle aged, and the elderly. It simply does not work with preadolescents. Five different ages comprise each unique individual.

Chronological Age. Chronological age is the actual time that has passed since birth.

Physique Age. Physique age can be determined by estimating bone age: Through X-ray examination the progress of bones toward reaching physical maturity can be determined. Physique age is not always the same as chronological age.

Psychosocial (Recreational) Age. Boys and girls with advanced physical development tend to relate to older people and to engage in activities characteristic of older persons. For example, girls of ten or eleven who are physically mature may be interested in social relations with boys and girls who are older than they.

Psychosexual Age. Interest in and response to erotic stimuli determine one's psychosexual age. With the rise in androgens at puberty, boys experience a sudden upsurge in their sexuality. One effect of this is increased interest in sexual imagery. Sex dreams (often accompanied by ejaculation) and fantasies (often accompanied by masturbation) are a playing out of visual imagery that continues in males to maturity. Both boys and girls show increased interest in the opposite sex and rehearse courting behaviors.

Academic (Mental) Age.   Mental age is the level at which a person can function intellectually. There does not seem to be a correlation between it and other ages. The stereotype of the egghead is of a physically underdeveloped, socially immature, and sexually disinterested person. It implies that advanced mental age is a compensation for lack of development in other areas; this is untrue. In general, people with higher intelligence develop earlier mentally, but undoubtedly, have experiences and opportunities that affect their rate of mental development. In extremely advanced mental development, a young person of twelve or thirteen may have mastered high school material and be able to function in college courses. If they happen to have underdeveloped physiques they are treated as though their minds were similarly underdeveloped when they may actually be quite advanced intellectually.

There is no "normal" pattern for the development of these ages. Every individual has a different rate of development, a rate that may differ for each specific area. This makes preadolescent age evaluation quite difficult and the variations almost infinite. These variations make it a difficult time for teachers and parents as well. Formulas never seem to work, and each boy, girl, and class must be treated in a creative, individual way. It is an age that many teachers dread and avoid and one that parents face with trepidation. However, for those who can approach the preadolescent openly and creatively, it is an exciting time of discovery and creativity. Every day brings a new development in which some new aspect of growth is discovered because puberty forces reorganization in psychological and social relations.

Moral Development

Freud described the superego as the repository of moral order, and the resolution of the Oedipus complex and resulting identification as the mechanism for acquiring moral rules. Social-learning theorists see moral development as the accumulative building of socially approved behaviors that are reinforced and maintained by the environment. When society agrees on the rules and reinforces adherence to them, most people in the society live by that moral order. Social-learning theorists hold that those who do not are reinforced more by breaking codes than by upholding them. Cognitive-developmental psychologists, in particular, Piaget (1948) and Kohlberg (1964, 1969), have investigated moral development as a cognitive process and have described the growth of moral judgments as they are related to the overall pattern of cognitive growth. Although moral behavior certainly has an emotional component, especially in relation to guilt, and it is true that reinforcement increases behaviors, cognitive processes play a crucial part in both the acquisition and maintenance of moral judgments. The largest body of research and theory on moral development comes from the cognitive psychologists and their investigation of moral judgment and reasoning.

What Is Moral?

Every society sets up rules for behavior and belief. These rules are a code of what is right (to do) and what is wrong (to do). Some of these rules are set in law, the violation of which elicit punishment. Other rules are set by custom, and violating them is not illegal but may engender negative social sanctions (for example, having children outside of marriage). Obviously, rules are quite different from society to society. One culture may have both laws and customs regulating food and another may ignore the question of food altogether but have intricate rules governing sexual behavior. In Islam, for example, it is forbidden to represent a human form in religious art while Christianity's cathedrals and churches are lavishly decorated with human forms. In investigating morality, we are not concerned with the content of the rules, but with the process that children undergo in understanding rules in general. Piaget first began to study moral development in children by investigating the ways in which young children understood and applied rules to the game of marbles. Can we equate the rules children follow in playing marbles with the laws that embody moral codes in adult society? Piaget believed that moral order in adult society is essentially the respect or disrespect with which individuals treat a system of rules (Piaget, 1948). If we substitute the word *laws* or *ethics,* for the word *rules,* we come close to a definition of *moral order.* Therefore, Piaget reasoned that children develop an understanding of moral order through manipulating rules applied to games and behavior in the same way that they develop an understanding of the physical world through manipulating objects. He reasoned further that moral development is a cognitive process of judgment and reasoning.

Stages of Moral Development

Piaget was the first to investigate moral development in children, but Kohlberg (1963, 1969) extended and modified the theory of stages of moral development. The infant has no conception of right and wrong. The child of three or four may begin to use rules to govern behavior, but he or she is prone to make them up to suit the situation. For example, with a child of that age, the rules may be changed in the middle of a game, especially if the child is losing! Both social conventions and game pieces are adapted to the child's own purposes. The idea that there are outside rules to which one must adhere is foreign to young children. The rules imposed by parents are simply obstacles in the way of attaining desired ends. The child of kindergarten age is aware of outside rules and often enforces them with a vengeance. Rules are sacred and cannot be broken; if they are, the result is immediate and harsh punishment. In the school years the child accommodates rules to his or her own needs and ends and adheres to them to gain approval, as a "good citizen" who gives allegiance to law and order. Finally, with careful cultivation, a balance between assimilation and accommodation is reached and rules can be judged in the light of individual motivations and intentions. Moral decisions and actions finally can become a function of principles and conscience—that is, personal judgments. An outline of Kohlberg's stages of moral development follows.*

I. Preconventional Level
At this level the child is responsive to cultural rules and labels of good and bad, right or wrong, but interprets these labels either in terms of the physical or the hedonistic consequences of action (punishment, reward, exchange of favors) or in terms of the physical power of those who enunciate the rules and labels. The level is divided into the following two stages:

   Stage 1: The punishment-and-obedience orientation. The physical consequences of action determine its goodness or badness regardless of the human meaning

* From "The Future of Liberalism As the Dominant Ideology of the West" by Lawrence Kohlberg. In *Moral Development and Politics* edited by Richard W. Wilson and Gordon J. Schochet. Copyright © 1980 by Praeger Publishers, New York. All rights reserved.

or value of these consequences. Avoidance of punishment and unquestioning deference to power are valued in their own right, not in terms of respect for an underlying moral order supported by punishment and authority (the latter being Stage 4).

Stage 2: The instrument-relativist orientation. Right action consists of that which instrumentally satisfies one's own needs and occasionally the needs of others. Human relations are viewed in terms like those of the marketplace. Elements of fairness, of reciprocity, and of equal sharing are present, but they are always interpreted in a physical, pragmatic way. Reciprocity is a matter of ''you scratch my back and I'll scratch yours,'' not of loyalty, gratitude, or justice.

2. Conventional Level

At this level, maintaining the expectations of the individual's family, group, or nation is perceived as valuable in its own right, regardless of immediate and obvious consequences. The attitude is not only one of conformity to personal expectations and social order, but of loyalty to it, of actively maintaining, supporting, and justifying the order, and of identifying with persons or groups involved in it. At this level, there are the following two stages:

Stage 3: The interpersonal concordance or "good boy—nice girl" orientation. Good behavior is that which pleases or helps others and is approved by them. There is much conformity to stereotypical images or what is majority or ''natural'' behavior. Behavior is frequently judged by intention—''he means well'' becomes important for the first time. One earns approval by being ''nice.''

Stage 4: The "law-and-order" orientation. There is orientation toward authority, fixed rules, and the maintenance of the social order. Right behavior consists of doing one's duty, showing respect for authority, and maintaining the given social order for its own sake.

3. Postconventional, Autonomous, or Principled Level

At this level, there is a clear effort to define moral values and principles that have validity and application apart from the authority of the groups or persons holding these principles and apart from the individuals' own identification with these groups. This level again has two stages:

Stage 5: The social-contract legalistic orientation, generally with utilitarian overtones. Right action tends to be defined in terms of general individual rights, and standards that have been critically examined and agreed upon by the whole society. There is a clear awareness of the relativism of personal values and opinions and a corresponding emphasis upon procedural rules for reaching consensus. Aside from what is constitutionally and democratically agreed upon, the rights are a matter of personal ''values'' and ''opinion.'' The result is an emphasis upon the ''legal point of view,'' but with an emphasis upon the possibility of changing law in terms of rational considerations of social utility (rather than freezing it in terms of Stage 4 ''law and order''). Outside the legal realm, free agreement and contract is the binding element of obligation. This is the ''official'' morality of the American government and constitution.

Stage 6: The universal-ethical principle orientation. Right is defined by the decision of conscience in accord with self-chosen ethical principles appealing to logical comprehensiveness, universality, and consistency. These principles are abstract and ethical (the Golden Rule, the categorical imperative); they are not concrete moral rules like the Ten Commandments. At heart, these are universal principles of justice, of the reciprocity and equality of human rights, and of respect for the dignity of human beings as individual persons.

Examples of Behavior at Three Moral Levels

The second level of moral development is designated conventional morality and consists of adherence to rules with little actual judgment or reasoning. In this stage rules are obeyed because they are rules and they have a life and justification of their own, which is beyond question. For example, when children of six or seven are in disagreement about play procedures, the rules are the final authority in settlement. In another situation the child may resort to "My mommy said. . . . " Rules become ritual and taboo that must be obeyed; dire consequences will ensue if they are broken. This rigid application of rules also applies in the social area, in, for example, the way kindergarten children apply rules for sex-appropriate behaviors in play. According to Piaget (1948) and Kohlberg (1963, 1964), this rigid adherence to rules comes from the child's innate mental structures and not from authoritarian parents or an overly strict superego. Some people never grow to understand laws and ethics, they obey laws as ritual and taboo or because something may be "in it" for them. For example, recently a book with the title *Pray and Grow Rich* (Ponder, 1968) was advertised. The very title describes a hedonistic bargain such as the following: If you pray (and obey God), then He will reward you by making you rich, or, to be more direct, if you scratch God's back by giving Him what He wants (prayer and obedience), he will scratch your back and give you what you want (money). This popular appeal, obviously directed to literate adults, is aimed at the *first* level of moral development. Let us take another example: People often say, "I can't believe in a God that would allow deformed children to be born." Translated, this means: "Why should I scratch God's back by believing in Him when he won't scratch my back by preventing unpleasant things from happening in the world?" Again, this is the *first* level of moral reasoning.

Most people advance to the second level of moral development. This is the level of conventional morality. It is the level of the good, law-abiding citizen. People who reason at this level about moral behavior conform to the social norms in both law and custom, without any deep conviction in the matter. The overriding concern is with fitting in with the social order and gaining the approval of others. This is accomplished by obeying the law of the land and thereby gaining a stable, orderly society. People at the level of conventional morality may feel that a law is not just or equitable (such as the claim of a natural mother to a child over the claim of a foster mother who has reared the child since birth), but they will support or uphold it because it is the law. Children, and adults, who are at the level of conventional morality are apt to go along with the crowd. A preadolescent boy may become swept along with the excitement of belonging to a group and engage in taunting and robbing an old man even though alone he would never engage in such behavior because he knows it is wrong. Such a boy may feel that he must perform according to the standards of his social group. A young woman may find herself in a group in which unkind and untrue things are said about an absent friend of hers. How many such women have kept silent, nodded assent, or even contributed a juicy bit of gossip? Each of these people is acting at the second level of conventional morality.

The third level of moral development is that of self-accepted moral principles. At this level the individual has examined those roles, social conventions, and laws that have been handed down in the society. He or she reaches a reasoned conclusion on the rightness or wrongness of the issues. This individual has evolved a set of principles that he or she can accept and live by with conviction. Those principles are based on a sense of justice, generosity, sympathy, and compassion for others. They are the principles on which a democratic society is based, in which each person has individual rights that are recognized and respected by others. Morality at this level is flexible, and this can be seen in the variable sentences that court judges hand down. In a judicial system based on flexible morality, there is room for mercy. Although there are many faults to be found in such a judicial system, it is constructed so that the *intention* of the person who committed the crime enters into the judgment. In a system based on a lower level of morality, a given crime merits a given punishment, regardless of intention. For example, in some cultures and countries the penalty for stealing is to have a hand cut off and the penalty for adultery is death. Intentions are not considered. Individuals at the third level of moral development gauge their behavior by a set of *moral* principles that they themselves have constructed. These principles are of a higher priority than social custom or secular law, and when there is a conflict between principle and social convention, the person with self-accepted moral principles obeys those principles. It was this level of morality that led Mahatma Gandhi and Martin Luther King to civil disobedience in which the "law of the land" was disobeyed, in order to appeal to a higher principle. Not many of us will attain the status of Gandhi or King; nevertheless, in countless ways each of us must choose among actions that reflect the principles of justice and equality and those that do not. Each of us is afforded the opportunity to act from compassion and generosity.

A Closer Look at Moral Development

Kohlberg began his research on moral judgment over twenty-five years ago. His original subjects were ten to sixteen-year-old boys who were presented stories that contained a dilemma. They were then asked what was right or wrong in the situation. Kohlberg used Piaget's technique of clinical interview and probed the subjects to discover their reasoning behind the judgments they made. An example of one of Kohlberg's dilemmas follows:

Heinz and the Drug Dilemma

In Europe, a woman was near death from a special kind of cancer. There was one drug that the doctors thought might save her. It was a form of radium that a druggist in the same town had recently discovered. The drug was expensive to make, but the druggist was charging ten times what the drug cost him to make. He paid $200 for radium and charged $2,000 for a small dose of the drug. The sick woman's husband, Heinz, went to everyone he knew to borrow the money, but he could only get together about $1,000, which is half of what it cost. He told the druggist that his wife was dying, and asked him to sell it cheaper or let him pay later. But the druggist said, "No, I discovered the drug and I'm going to make money from it." So Heinz got desperate and broke into the man's store to steal the drug for his wife. Should Heinz have done that? Was it wrong or right? Why? [Rest, 1979, p. 8]

Kohlberg and his associates at Harvard have continued to follow these subjects and study their moral development. Other studies have been conducted with male and female subjects both by Kohlberg and his associates and by researchers at other institutions. One of the findings of research, using Kohlberg's stages of moral development, is that women, in general, do not reason at the highest level about moral issues. Carol Gilligan (1982), a colleague of Kohlberg's at Harvard, has challenged the validity of Kohlberg's stages of moral development for women.

While conducting research on moral reasoning, Gilligan noted a similarity in the reasoning that women subjects used and that these themes were seldom used by male subjects. She then conducted studies to more clearly identify the reasoning and themes that women used in judgments on moral questions. Gilligan concluded that women are more concerned with relationships and responsibilities and reason from this perspective. Males, on the other hand, are concerned with legal rights and rules. Kohlberg's levels of moral development are structured around rules. Because the data that were used to construct Kohlberg's developmental stages were gathered only on males, Gilligan contends that they are not a valid standard by which to judge women's moral reasoning.

Gilligan continues to conduct research and to refine her understanding of female development. Many other researchers are engaged in similar extensions of our understanding of development. As students and practitioners we must be open to new data and new interpretations of previous research. In our scientific study of the child, we are both creating and applying information at the same time. Sheldon White (1979) has characterized the study of child development as "going for a voyage on a boat while you are still building it, arguing with your crewmates about whether it ought to be a motorboat or a sailboat, and simultaneously arguing with paying passengers about where your whatever-it-is is going to take them" (p. 814).

Main Points

Defining Preadolescence

1. The preadolescent is the pubescent child, generally between nine and twelve years of age. At this stage children need freedom to explore but with protection and support.

Physical Changes in Preadolescence

2. Puberty refers to the period of rapid growth and development that results in maturation of the reproductive capacity.

3. Puberty begins with increasing sensitivity of the hypothalamus to the sex hormones and the consequent rising level of hormones in the blood stream.

4. The rapid growth of puberty begins on the average at eleven for girls and at thirteen for boys.

5. Hormones stimulate development of the secondary sex characteristics.

6. Stages of breast development are used to diagnose pubertal progress and indicate approaching menarche.

7. During puberty both boys and girls develop pubic and axillary hair; facial hair develops in boys.

8. Sexual maturation occurs for boys when the penis, testes, and scrotum reach adult size, ejaculation occurs, and sperm are produced; for girls, the uterus grows, the vagina thickens, the ovaries mature, menarche occurs, and ovulation begins.

9. Precocious puberty is diagnosed when sexual maturation begins before age eight in girls or nine and one-half in boys; when the maturation *process* has not begun by age thirteen in girls and thirteen and one-half in boys, delayed puberty is diagnosed.

Psychological Reorganization in the Preadolescent

10. In the preadolescent period the secure pattern of childhood begins to break apart and a reorganization of personality is forced.

11. The preadolescent has developmental tasks in the areas of intelligence, body image, social sex roles, friendship with peers, independence, and moral values.

12. The self-consciousness of the pre- and early adolescent is largely the result of the child's imagined reaction from its mentally created "imaginary audience."

13. The personal fable (myths about the self that include dreams for marriage, romance, and career) is a second mental construction that arises in the preadolescent period and may remain a part of the self-concept throughout life.

Social Development in Preadolescence, the End of Innocence: Strategic Interactions

14. Strategic interactions are interpersonal encounters that have as their aim the acquisition, concealment, or revelation of information through indirect means.

15. Strategic interactions involve friendships, phoning and being phoned, cutting and being cut, relationships with the opposite sex, and forbidden acts.

Discrepancy of Ages: Chronological, Physical, Social, and Mental

16. During preadolescence every individual has a different rate of development; it may differ for different aspects of development and may result in discrepancies between chronological age, physique age, psychosocial age, psychosexual age, and academic age.

Moral Development

17. Although moral behavior has emotional and socially learned components, cognitive processes play a crucial part in both the acquisition and maintenance of moral judgments.

18. Piaget believed that children develop an understanding of moral order through the manipulation of the rules of games.

19. Stages of moral development have been delineated by Kohlberg.

20. The first level of moral development is preconventional morality and is governed by reward and punishment. The second level of moral development, conventional morality, is characterized by the good, law-abiding citizen who conforms to social norms, laws, and customs. The third level of moral development is that of self-accepted moral principles, in which the individual develops principles of a higher priority than social customs and secular laws.

Words to Know

areola	menstruating	puberty
ejaculation	ovulation	pubescent
fertility	papilla	pubic
menarche	preadolescent	
menstrual	pubertal	

Terms to Define

axillary hair
developmental tasks
early maturers
growth spurt
imaginary audience
late maturer

personal fable
postconventional morality
preconventional morality
secondary sex characteristics
secular trend
strategic interactions

Concept to Discuss

morality

PART V

Adolescence:
The Years from Twelve
to Twenty

Adolescence is an invention of complex industrialized societies. It is a moratorium on growing up, in which physically mature young people are assigned a new round of education and social experiences in which to learn skills for living and earning a living in modern society. The task of adolescence is the unremitting search for identity. Many choices are open and many questions must be answered. Parents' values must be examined and made their own or rejected. Relationships must be explored with friends of the same and the opposite sex. Career choices must be explored and some sense of contributing to the future and of their own place in the culture's historical process must be constructed. Ideologies and causes must be explored and commitments made to causes greater than the individual.

Adolescence is a time of hope and idealism; of false starts and creative exploration; and of experimentation in the service of the eternal quest for identity and meaning. Those who fail to accept the challenge and forge their individual identity from the elements of their culture and their intuition risk alienation and confusion about their role in society. The responsibility for the developing adolescent extends beyond the family. It is a joint venture involving the many institutions that shape young citizens into becoming society's new generation. The question that such institutions must constantly ask is: What do we want them, and our society, to be?

Physical and Mental Development in Adolescence

Have you ever wondered

> how to define adolescence?
> why we have adolescence when less advanced societies do not?
> if physical development continues in adolescence?
> what anorexia nervosa is?
> how thinking changes in adolescence?

The word *adolescence* calls forth a wide variety of attitudes and opinions from the population of Americans over twenty-one years of age. Some people see adolescence as the best period of the human condition—a time of idealism, vitality, and promise. Others perceive adolescence as evidence of the certain decline of our civilization, with its sexual promiscuity, lack of responsibility, and barbarism. Still others view adolescence as a social problem and continual threat to society because of crime and violence. Americans are unsure of this strange, volatile, and energetic group. Who are these "adolescents?" Can we, indeed, characterize them?

Defining *Adolescence*

Adolescence is the period of development between puberty and young adulthood. Its beginning is marked by the physical event of puberty. Its end is a social attainment, an unspecific event that cannot be pinpointed in a time frame.

Sexual maturity is attained at puberty. Most researchers and professionals concerned with adolescents focus on the psychological and social dimensions of the period. Adolescence roughly corresponds to the second decade of life. There is a

421

great difference in a ten-year-old, twelve-year-old, and a twenty-year-old. Therefore, adolescence is generally subdivided into early, middle, and late adolescence.

Chronological Age	Subdivision
9 to 12	Preadolescence
12 to 14	Early adolescence
14 to 17	Middle adolescence
18 to 21	Late adolescence

Adolescence As a Cultural Invention

The difficulty in defining *adolescence* partly stems from its being *cultural invention*. In our complex technological society the short period of childhood is not enough time in which to learn the intellectual skills needed for productive work or the complex social skills and psychological maturity required to construct a satisfying personal life. Thus, it was necessary to create a period in which additional mental, social, and psychological growth could take place. At least part of the tension associated with adolescence is caused by the discrepancy between having a mature body and social and psychological characteristics deemed immature by society. We have created special institutions to support the period of adolescence, which we will take a look at in Chapter 17. We will investigate how well those institutions serve adolescents and consider some alternative organizations.

Childhood as a separate stage of development is also an invention of society that took place at the end of the Middle Ages. For several hundred years the idea that childhood is separate and different from other stages in life was continuously refined. By the late nineteenth century, childhood stood apart as a separate and protected period in the life span. Following the trend to separate and define periods of life, adolescence was created early in the twentieth century. G. Stanley Hall is credited with the major role in its creation as a result of the publication of *Adolescence* in 1904. Hall was a leading American psychologist and a professor at Clark University in Massachusetts. He was instrumental in shaping American psychology, and his influence is felt to this day. It was at Hall's invitation that Sigmund Freud made his only trip to the United States, giving American psychologists the opportunity to hear Freud's psychoanalytic views firsthand.

Hall used Freud's idea of stages of development related to chronological age, understanding adolescence to be the end of quiescent childhood and the eruption of conflicts and drives suppressed from the Oedipal stage. Hall described adolescence as a time of storm and stress, a time of great potential but also of great danger. He saw the physical advent of puberty as an event that sweeps the child into a period of great upheaval, a sexual awakening he likened to unleashing a sleeping giant of sexual and aggressive drives—a giant the adolescent has a difficult job controlling. Great emotional turmoil, wild swings of mood, and erratic behavior are all consequences of that stress, which threatens to undermine character and morals.

For Hall that period of storm and stress was an internal battle for the body and soul of the adolescent. Its positive potential lay in the idealism and capacity for altruism and self-sacrifice that would enable each generation of young people to surpass the generation before it in the ever-ascending progress of the human race.

The word adolescence means many things to many people and the period has been difficult to categorize and to describe for professionals. Who are these adolescents? [Courtesy Greensboro Day School.]

The idea persists in our view of youth as the country's hope, and as tomorrow's leaders.

Hall viewed adolescence as a dichotomy in which the dangers involved equalled the potential: while the adolescent climbed the mountain of promise, dangers that threatened to corrupt the morals, dissipate the body, and decay the mind lurked on all sides. Hall believed that even normal youths often passed through phases of cruelty, laziness, and lying and even committed illegal acts such as stealing. This idea also persists today in our fear and suspicion that within every adolescent there is a juvenile delinquent.

No one can know all the adolescents in a society. Therefore, we must rely on indirect sources to help us understand the reality of the situation. Experts such as Hall are important in shaping the consciousness of the whole society about a group

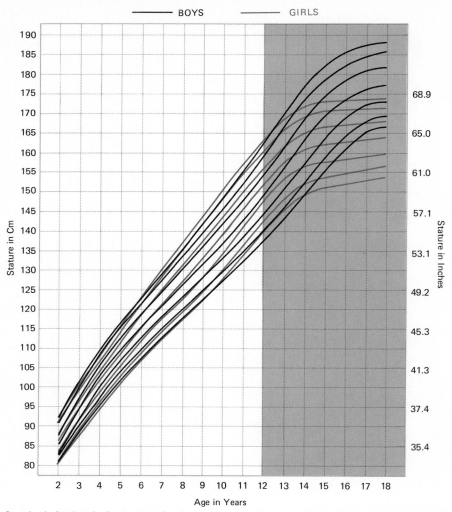

Standards for height for boys and girls age two to eighteen with emphasis on the teen years. [From National Center for Health Statistics, 1976.]

of people. This consciousness, in turn, shapes the laws that are passed and the institutions that are created to serve segments of the people. The view of adolescence as a time of turmoil and erratic behavior has had a decisive effect on the kind of institutions our society has created for adolescents. Two special ones have been developed in the twentieth century in response to our perception of adolescence: our elaborate educational system and our juvenile justice system.

Physical Development in Adolescence

The adolescent growth spurt takes place either in the preadolescent period or in early adolescence. Physical maturity is not completed with this spurt, however, because body changes continue into late adolescence. The general pattern of growth

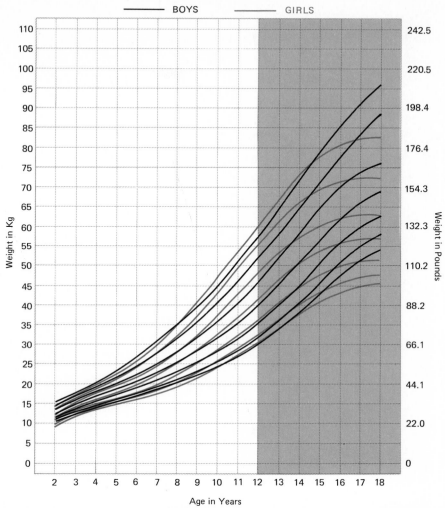

Standards for weight for boys and girls age two to eighteen with emphasis on the teen years. [From National Center for Health Statistics, 1976.]

for both boys and girls is a steady increase in height from the prenatal period to pubescence, but at an ever-decreasing rate. That is, although children steadily grow bigger, they do so more slowly.

Skeletal Development

The ultimate control of height is in bone growth. Linear growth occurs at the ends of the bones, in an area composed of soft cartilage called *epiphysis*. As growth takes place this cartilage becomes true bone and merges with the main body of the bone. The changing of cartilage to bone is *ossification*. Examination of X-rays of an individual's hands and wrists will reveal a skeletal score of the percentage of physical maturity that one has attained (Tanner, 1970). Eventually, all healthy individuals

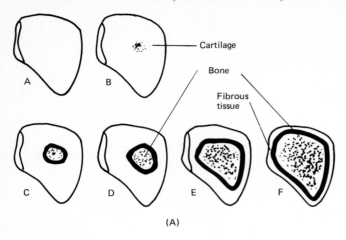

(A)

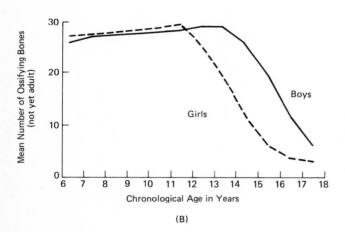

Chronological Age in Years

(B)

Skeletal maturation is a process that extends from the prenatal period to adulthood and involves the gradual replacement of cartilage with bone tissue. Figure (A) illustrates this process of ossification. The approximate age scale is as follows: *A*, prenatal (entirely cartilage); *B*, 1–3 years; *C*, 4–5 years; *D*, 6 years; *E*, 10 years; and *F*, adulthood. The graph (B) plots the mean number of bones that are in the process of ossifying (not yet adult) for boys and girls. Note that there is little difference in the sexes until approximately 12 years of age. At age 12 the line representing girls makes a precipitous drop, which corresponds with girls' earlier maturity and growth spurt. Ossification in boys continues at the same level of childhood and accelerates at ages 13–14. [From National Center for Health Statistics, Series 11, No. 160, 1976.]

Table 16–1. Locomotor, Manipulative, and Stability Skills Used in Various Sports

Sport Skill Themes	Locomotor Skills Stressed	Manipulative Skills Stressed		Stability Skills Stressed	
Basketball sport skills	Running Sliding Leaping Jumping	Passing Catching Shooting Dribbling	Tipping Blocking Rebounding	Selected axial movement skills Pivoting Dodging Guarding Picking	Blocking Cutting Faking
Combative sport skills	Stepping Sliding Hopping (karate)	Dexterity (fencing) Striking (kendo)		All axial movement skills Dodging and feinting Static balance skills Dynamic balance skills	

Table 16–1 (continued)

Sport Skill Themes	Locomotor Skills Stressed		Manipulative Skills Stressed		Stability Skills Stressed	
Dance skills	Running Leaping Jumping Stepping	Hopping Skipping Sliding	Tossing Catching		All Axial Movement skills Static balance postures Dynamic balance postures	
Disc sport skills	Stepping Running Jumping		Tossing Catching		All axial movement skills Static balance postures Dynamic balance postures	
Football sport skills	Running Sliding	Jumping Leaping	Passing Catching Carrying	Kicking Punting Centering	Blocking Tackling	Pivoting Dodging
Gymnastic skills	Running Jumping Skipping	Leaping Hopping Landing			Inverted supports Rolling landing All axial movement skills Static balance tricks Dynamic balance tricks	
Implement Striking sport skills (tennis, squash, racketball, hockey, lacrosse, golf)	Running Sliding Leaping Skating Walking		Forehand Backhand Striking Driving Putting Chipping	Lob Smash Drop Throwing Catching Trapping	Dynamic balance skills Turning Twisting Stretching Bending Dodging Pivoting	
Skiing sport skills	Stepping Walking Running Sliding		Poling		All axial movement skills Dynamic balance skills Static balance skills	
Soccer sport skills	Running Jumping Leaping Sliding		Kicking Trapping Juggling Throwing Blocking	Passing Dribbling Catching Rolling	Tackling Marking Dodging	Feinting Turning
Softball/baseball skills	Running Sliding Jumping Leaping		Throwing Catching Pitching	Batting Bunting	Selected axial movement skills Dynamic balance skills Dodging	
Target sport skills			Aiming Shooting		Static balance skills	
Track and field skills	Running Hopping Vertical Jumping	Horizontal Leaping Starting	Shot put Discus Javelin Hammer	Pole vault Baton passing Throwing	All axial movement skills Dynamic balance skills	
Volleyball sport skills	Running Sliding Rolling	Jumping Diving Sprawling	Serving Volleying Bump Dig	Spike Dink Block	Dynamic balance skills Selected axial movements	

From *Understanding Motor Development in Children* by David L. Gallahue. Copyright © 1982 by John Wiley & Sons, Inc. Reprinted by permission.

Note: Skills that culminate in sports activity begin in infancy, develop in early and middle childhood, and are perfected as bodies mature.

(A)

(B)

(C)

Because there is a great difference in physical maturity there is a corresponding difference in physical strength and endurance in early adolescence (A). As boys reach maturity (B), their larger muscles and structure gives them great strength and endurance. Girls are increasingly participating in competitive team sports (C). [Courtesy Greensboro Day School.]

reach the same point of development, which is full ossification. When the epiphyses of the long bones of the arms and legs fuse completely with the metaphyses, growth in height is complete. This stage is reached by the end of adolescence.

During adolescence, however, boys and girls differ in the timing of skeletal maturity. As with puberty, boys' development is about two years behind that of girls. The average girl has attained 70 per cent of ossification by age thirteen, whereas the average boy is fifteen before reaching 70 per cent of ossification.

Strength and Physical Endurance

At sexual maturity a divergence is noted in physical strength for boys and girls. Before puberty boys and girls who are the same size show similar strength. Under the stimulation of the hormone testosterone, which floods the bodies of boys at puberty, boys develop more muscle tissue in relation to fat than girls. In addition, the muscles that boys have are more efficient—that is, boys achieve more force per gram of muscle tissue than girls. Boys' greater muscle efficiency may be the result of their having a larger heart and lungs, with greater capacity for carrying oxygen and more experience with physical activity while growing.

Metabolism

Eating is a primary activity for adolescents. An afterschool snack for a high school student would look like a banquet to an adult. The amount of food consumed by adolescent boys is well known. It is converted into new tissue, energy, and waste products. The rate at which this conversion takes place is known as basal metabolic rate (BMR). The BMR reaches a peak in early infancy, gradually declines in childhood, and prior to puberty increases again. The prodigious appetite of adolescents is partly a function of their higher metabolic rate. Males have an even higher BMR than girls, the result of their greater muscle content.

Nutrition and Diet

Adolescents are notorious for having poor diets, even though they consume large quantities of food. In a period of rapid growth and expanding energy needs, adolescents require food to build tissue and food to provide energy. The body utilizes three categories of food: protein, fat, and carbohydrates.

Protein is the body's basic building material for tissues in muscle and in internal organs. Protein is a chain of amino acids. Some amino acids can be synthesized by the body, but nine of them must be present in the food eaten *each day*. Amino acids are found in animal muscle, such as beef, chicken, or fish. Some are found in vegetables, such as rice, beans, peanuts, and soybeans, but not all and not in the right proportion. To build new tissue, the body must have all of the amino acid building blocks or tissue cannot be built. Thus, if a diet lacks one or more of these acids, the ones that are present are not used. Some animals can synthesize essential amino acids from vegetable sources, but humans cannot. Without careful attention to the correct combination of vegetable sources people on vegetarian diets, for example, may end up seriously malnourished. In underdeveloped countries populations with little or no access to animal protein suffer protein starvation, which is a major cause of illness and abnormal development.

Fats comprise a high proportion of the diet of Americans. Fat contains more than twice the calories per gram (nine) of either protein or carbohydrates (four). Because it takes longer to convert fat to energy, the sensation of hunger takes

Fast foods are a favorite of adolescents, but not the most nutritious. [Courtesy Greensboro Day School.]

longer to recur on a high-fat diet. Adolescents consume large quantities of fat through fried foods, the animal fat in hamburgers, the vegetable oil in peanut butter, and the oil in salad dressings. Excess consumption of fat most often results in excess fat being stored in the body. Carbohydrates are the quickest and easiest source of energy. All foods that are not fats or protein fall into this category. Vegetables may contain some protein and some carbohydrate.

In early adolescence the body's caloric requirements are enormous, and adolescents develop an appetite to meet the demand. When growth ceases in late adolescence those eating habits may continue, with the result that obesity becomes a problem.

Strictly speaking *diet* simply means what a person eats. But in the parlance of the adolescent, diet means restricting what one eats to control the body's shape and size. Body image is a very important part of the psychological composite of "self." Adolescents are preoccupied with their appearance and as their bodies develop adult configurations and sexual attributes, they seek to exploit those characteristics to the maximum. Boys may engage in muscle-building activities and supplement regular meals with concoctions advertized to enhance them, such as liquid protein or mega-vitamins. Sometimes such procedures are encouraged by athletic coaches who seek bigger bodies for their teams. Girls seek to redesign their bodies so they can resemble fashion models. Very few adolescent girls are satisfied with their physical appearance and advertising plays (or preys) on this tendency. The message of all cosmetic advertising is that there is something wrong with your body as it is, and Product X can correct it. Thus, girls often restrict their diets so severely that they endanger their health. Some girls cease eating altogether.

Anorexia Nervosa

Sandra grew up in a caring, loving, middle-class family in a time of affluence. There had always been plenty of everything—toys, clothes, and food. Family gatherings and holidays were feasts. Sandra loved to cook and to urge others to eat their fill. As a child, Sandra had been considered "pudgy," but during her adolescent growth spurt Sandra's pudginess stretched out and her body assumed pleasing adult proportions. Sandra began menstruation with some misgivings and watched with disapproval as her hips became wider and fuller. She and her friends enjoyed leafing through fashion magazines. Sandra began to control her weight and became widely admired for her sleek proportions, which were those of a high-fashion model. She was determined that she would never have her mother's over-abundant figure. With extreme self-control she would not eat for days. When family pressure forced her to join in a family meal, she would go to the bathroom as soon as she was excused from the table and force herself to vomit the food she had eaten. Her weight continued to plummet and she went from looking like a fashion model to looking like a concentration camp inmate. As she became thinner and thinner her menstrual periods ceased and she became listless. The smallest exertion seemed difficult for her. Her parents could no longer see her simply as a teen-age girl attempting to lose weight. Something was definitely wrong concerning food. The family physician confirmed that Sandra had *anorexia nervosa*.

Anorexia nervosa is an eating disorder that mainly affects adolescent girls, although it is not unknown among boys. It is characterized by a prolonged refusal to eat and is often accompanied by self-induced vomiting. The origin of the disorder is psychological, although after the continual refusal of food, physical symptoms develop. Because essential nutrients are withheld from the body, symptoms of starvation become evident and in from 5 to 15 per cent of cases death follows.

The treatment of severe cases may involve hospitalization with intravenous feeding and medication to prevent vomiting. However, such measures only prevent immediate death and debilitation. The cure must come through a long counseling process. Programs treating anorexics include intensive psychotherapy to uncover the phychological roots of the disorder combined with behavioral management, such as rewards for eating.

Anorexia nervosa was hardly mentioned twenty years ago, yet now it seems epidemic among adolescent girls. The disorder seems to entail a refusal to grow up and a rejection of the mother figure. These psychological aspects coincide with the cultural ideal of feminine beauty as wispy and thin—very thin. There is so much written about and advertised for feminine beauty that it is probably difficult for any young girl to feel that her body is all right. When psychological disorder and faulty body image underlie this cultural attitude, accepting the body that she has may be difficult for an adolescent girl.

Mental Development in Adolescence

Characteristics of Adolescent Thought

Mary is on the debating team for her high school. The issue to be debated this year is capital punishment. Mary enjoys the discussions that the team has to prepare for the debate. With friends she discusses related questions of justice, freedom, and morality.

Paul has become active in a political organization. At political meetings he is in the forefront in discussing the nature of society, the role of government, and the ideal relationship between citizen and the state.

Philip and Joan are lab partners in the advanced chemistry section in their high school. They conduct advanced experiments with little supervision from the teacher and can propose hypotheses and devise experiments to test them.

All of these adolescents are involved in solving problems by using their cognitive abilities. Children, too, solve problems and discuss the state of the world. There is, however, a *qualitative* difference between the thought of adolescents and children. Of course, with more years in school and more experience in the world, there is a cumulative increase in vocabulary and in sheer information for high school students. These additions, however, do not explain the quantum jump made in thinking ability from childhood to adolescence. Keating (1980) suggests five ways in which the thinking of adolescents broadens, moving toward greater abstraction and away from concrete situations:

1. Thinking beyond the obvious reality of a situation to the consideration of all possibilities.
2. Forming and thinking through hypotheses. In this mode of thought hypothetical situations can be considered.
3. Thinking about a plan for problem solving. In this strategy, adolescents are able to outline a plan for solving a problem, anticipate the kind of information that will be required, and the general form of the solution.
4. Thinking about the processes of thinking and problem-solving themselves. With increased introspection, adolescents are conscious of their own thinking and learning processes. They are aware of their own activities and performance in processes such as memory, communication, and attention.
5. The content of adolescent thought expands to include broad topics of society and identity: existence, religion, justice, morality, love, and friendship.

Adolescents think about possibilities that are not immediately present. In late childhood children become quite comfortable and proficient with observed reality and inferring conclusions from observed evidence. In adolescence, the concrete reality becomes secondary to a wider range of possibilities and is the hallmark of formal operations outlined by Inhelder and Piaget (1958). This is not to say that adolescents live in an abstract world. It is only to say that in the face of a realistic problem, they are capable of conceiving of a wide variety of possibilities for a solution.

A second way in which adolescent thinking deviates from children's is in the generation and testing of hypotheses. Hypotheses testing is an essential part of the Western scientific tradition. Although the exploration of possibilities is tied to the realistic situation, the generation of hypotheses may extend beyond it into the negative, or the nontrue. Adolescents can logically think and agree about hypothetical situations such as utopian societies and the philosophical problems of God, existence, and death.

The third way in which adolescent thinking differs from children's is in the ability to think ahead, and the fourth way is that they are able to think about thinking. Adolescents are aware of cognitive activity and the mechanisms that can make it more or less efficient. For example, they understand how in studying they are using and exploiting their ability for memory. Concomitant with this awareness is increased introspection. Adolescents can monitor their own thinking and feeling

Adolescents are able to think about a wide range of subjects in a logical manner, including thinking about thinking. [Courtesy Greensboro Day School.]

and can compare their opinions and approaches with those of their friends. Finally, the content of adolescent thought enlarges to include any and all the problems and philosophical speculations in the human intellectual repertoire. Many discussions by adolescents on the nature of existence has lasted until the early hours of the morning. All of these changes in thought indicate a move toward formal operations.

Characteristics of Formal Operations

The main way in which formal operations differs from concrete operations is that *all* possibilities of a situation are considered. The person who is able to think in terms of formal operations is able to consider several variables and the relationships among them to reach a conclusion. Inhelder and Piaget (1958) devised several strategies to test formal operations. We will consider two of them, the pendulum problem and the chemistry problem.

The Pendulum Problem

In the pendulum problem the subject is given a string with a weight on the end. The subject is shown that the pendulum swings back and forth but may swing at different speeds. The subject is shown four variables that may be manipulated on the pendulum:

1. The weight on the end of the string can be made lighter or heavier.
2. The length of the string can be adjusted.
3. The height at which the pendulum is dropped can be varied.
4. The force with which the pendulum is pushed can be varied.

The subject is asked to determine which of the variables or which combination of variables determines the speed of the pendulum. When this problem is given to

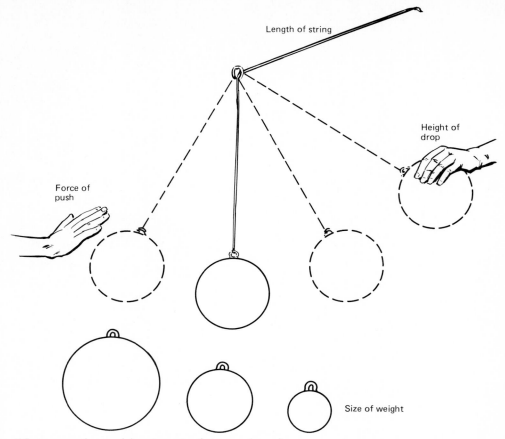

Length of string

Height of drop

Force of push

Size of weight

What causes the pendulum to swing faster or slower?

elementary-school-age children, they experiment with it and arrive at an answer. It may or may not be the right one. Children in concrete operations may hapazardly try to change the length of the string, vary the weight, push harder or less hard, or drop the weight from a greater or lesser height. They may try two of these simultaneously.

When this problem is given to a person who has attained formal operations, he or she is able to separate the four variables, hold three of them constant and vary the fourth, one at a time. In this way, each variable can be explored for its fullest contribution to the movement of the pendulum. The person who has reached formal operations has a systematic *plan* for exploring possibilities, perhaps like the one that follows:

Step one. Set a standard for the four variables. Then set the length of string, the weight on the end of the pendulum, the height of drop, and the force of push.

Step two. Holding weight, length, and height constant, vary the force when the pendulum is pushed. The result shows no change in the speed of the pendulum.

Step three. Holding weight, length, and force constant, vary the height from which the pendulum is dropped. The result shows no change in the speed of the pendulum.

Step four. Holding weight, force, and height constant, vary the length of the string. The result shows that the speed of the pendulum varies according to the length of the string. *The experiment is not over.* It is important that *all* possibilities continue to be explored. A person who has attained formal operations will immediately understand that the speed of the pendulum can be affected by more than one variable and he or she will continue to explore the other variables

Step five. Holding length, force, and height constant, vary the weight on the end of the pendulum. The result shows no change in the speed of the pendulum. Therefore, the correct answer is that the speed of the pendulum is determined by the length of the string. This principle is used both in setting clocks and setting time for music with metronomes.

The Chemical Problem

Inhelder and Piaget (1958) devised another experiment to test the attainment of formal systematic thinking in older children. In the chemical problem, subjects were presented with four identical bottles, each containing a different colorless and odorless liquid. The bottles were identified with the numbers 1, 2, 3, and 4. In addition the subjects were presented with a small flask containing a fifth odorless and colorless liquid labled g. The experimenter then produced two previously prepared bottles. The subjects were told that a yellow solution could be obtained by combining some combination of the liquids in the first four large bottles with the liquid from the small flask (g). The subjects were asked to find the solution that would produce the yellow color. The four bottles contained (1) diluted sulphuric acid, (2) water, (3) oxygenated water, and (4) thiosulphate. The small flask contained a solution of potassium iodide. (The answer to the problem is that adding potassium iodide (g) to a solution of diluted sulphuric acid and oxygenated water (1 + 3) will produce the yellow color.)

Young children usually begin with the individual bottles and add the g solution ($1 + g, 2 + g, 3 + g$, and $4 + g$). When this fails to produce a result they may begin to combine two liquids. Often, however, this step must be suggested to them. At such a suggestion, the children may begin combinations such as 1 + 2 and 3 + 4. They may still miss the correct combination. Often they then begin mixing solutions indiscriminately. They may stumble on the color but cannot state how they arrived at it.

By the ages of twelve to fourteen, adolescents can systematically plan all the possible combinations and execute them. Thus, the actual solution to the problem is not in attaining the color but in approaching the solution. In this problem there are fifteen possible combinations of the four solutions:

One at a time	1	2	3	4		
Two at a time	1 + 2	1 + 3	1 + 4	2 + 3	2 + 4	3 + 4
Three at a time	1 + 2 + 3	1 + 2 + 4	1 + 3 + 4	2 + 3 + 4		
Four at a time	1 + 2 + 3 + 4					

Cowan (1978) has illustrated the logical exploration of all possibilities in formal operations with the simple statement: *working hard leads to good grades.* Is this statement true? To examine this question all possibilities of the relationships be-

The chemical problem: What combination of liquids make a yellow color?

tween work and grades must be considered including the affirmative and negative: *work and no work; good grades and not good grades.* The least inclusive statement is that none of the statements are true concerning work or grades and the most inclusive is that all statements are true. Between these two extremes any possible combinations of the statements can be considered. All of the binary operations on the possibilities in this statement can be arranged in a lattice arrangement of truth tables from the least inclusive to the most inclusive. When this is done, there are sixteen binary operations. Some of the boxes are negations of others, some are reciprocals, some are correlates, and some are identity operations. Such a lattice of operations about logical statements exactly corresponds with algebraic operations. When adolescents reach this level of formal operations, they have reached a level of cognitive organization that is more flexible and comprehensive than concrete operations. Through this organization they can adopt a hypothetical attitude, explore all possible combinations, formulate and verify hypotheses, and conduct experiments using several strategies for isolating variables. In addition these activities in themselves stimulate the adolescent's cognitive development (Cowan, 1978).

Elkind and Weiner (1978) suggest that the same formal operation thinking is operative in a restaurant when we order from a menu with appetizers, entrees, desserts, and beverages because we have the same combinational choices. We can,

1. Order nothing.
2. Order only one thing:
   (a) An appetizer.
   (b) An entree.
   (c) A dessert.

  (d) A beverage.
3. Order two things:
  (a) An appetizer and an entree.
  (b) An appetizer and a dessert.
  (c) An appetizer and a beverage.
  (d) An entree and a dessert.
  (e) An entree and a beverage.
  (f) A dessert and a beverage.
4. Order three things:
  (a) An appetizer, an entree, and a beverage.
  (b) An appetizer, an entree, and a dessert.
  (c) An appetizer, a beverage, and a dessert.
  (d) An entree, a beverage, and a dessert.
5. Order four things:
  (a) An appetizer, an entree, a dessert, and a beverage.

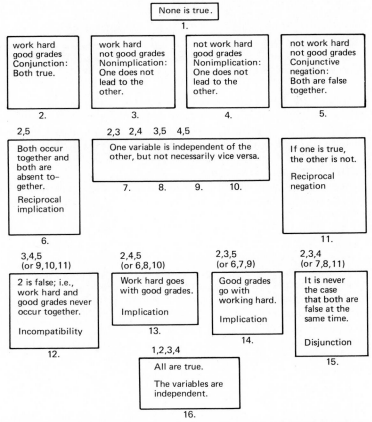

The lattice of sixteen binary operations. [From *Piaget: With Feeling* by Philip A. Cowan. Copyright © 1978 by Holt, Rinehart, and Winston. Reprinted by permission of Holt, Rinehart and Winston, CBS College Publishing.]

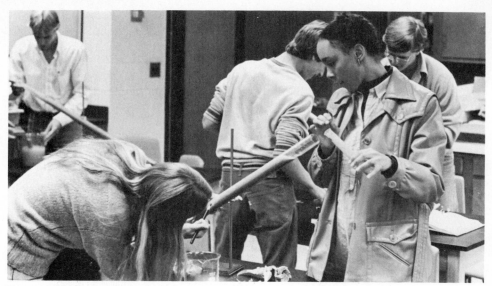

These students are conducting scientific experiments. Formal schooling assists in the attainment of formal operations and scientific method is an ideal content for this stage of cognitive development. [Courtesy Greensboro Day School.]

Of course, the possible choices are even greater as choices must be made within each category. Elkind and Weiner (1978) suggest that one of the reasons that fast-food restaurants are so popular with young children is that the level of cognitive operations required is better geared to their chronological age!

Formal Operations and Schooling

The attainment of formal operations is not a given at an appropriate chronological age. Inhelder and Piaget (1958) identified early adolescence (ages twelve to fourteen) as the time when formal operations is possible, but this is not likely to happen without the benefit of formal schooling and/or social interaction with others who practice formal logic. Even in a culture where formal schooling is required, not all adolescents or adults can follow a logical argument or demonstrate Piaget's criteria of formal operations. Neimark (1975), in a review of Piagetian studies found that many American adults cannot reason abstractly. Furthermore, in many cultures when Piagetian tests of formal operational thought are given no one in the culture reaches Piaget's standard. Flavell (1977) stresses that the difference between the thought of adults and children is that adults are aware that they use logic. In the adolescent years there is a growing awareness that some statements are logical and some are not. This awareness extends to the ability to recognize a logical flaw or to acknowledge a physical truth if it is demonstrated.

Main Points

Defining Adolescence

1. Adolescence refers to that period of development between puberty and young adulthood.

Adolescence As a Cultural Invention

2. Adolescence is a cultural invention that provides a period beyond childhood in which additional mental, social, and psychological growth can take place before admitting young people into full adult status.

Physical Development in Adolescence

3. The generalized pattern of growth for both boys and girls is a steady increase in height from the prenatal period to pubescence, but at an ever-decreasing rate.

4. Skeletal development proceeds as ossification of the soft cartilage occurs. The average girl attains 70 per cent of ossification by age thirteen; the average boy is fifteen before reaching 70 per cent of ossification.

5. Strength and physical endurance diverge in boys and girls.

6. The prodigious appetites of adolescents are partly a function of high metabolic rates; males have even higher BMRs than girls.

7. The rapid growth and energy needs of adolescents require nutritional elements that may not be met even though large quantities of food may be consumed.

8. Anorexia nervosa is a disorder of eating that mainly affects adolescent girls. It is characterized by prolonged refusal to eat and is often accompanied by self-induced vomiting.

Mental Development in Adolescence

9. There is a qualitative difference in the concrete thinking of children and the ability to think abstractly in adolescence. Adolescents can systematically explore all possibilities, generate and test hypotheses, and think about thinking and other abstract philosophical ideas.

Characteristics of Formal Operations

10. The person who is able to think in terms of formal operations is able to consider several variables and the relations among them to reach a conclusion.

11. Inhelder and Piaget tested for the attainment of formal operaions with the pendulum problem and the chemistry problem.

12. Formal operations are not likely to develop without formal schooling and/or social interaction with others who practice formal logic.

Words to Know

amino acid
epiphysis
obesity

Terms to Define

anorexia nervosa
basal metabolic rate (BMR)

Emotional and Social Development in Adolescence

Have you ever wondered

> **if historical events affect adolescent experience?**
>
> **how the search for identity develops during the teen years?**
>
> **if adolescents depend more on family or friends?**
>
> **how peer groups are structured?**
>
> **if many adolescents are delinquent?**
>
> **if mental problems are more serious during adolescence?**
>
> **if adolescents today are actually more or less sexually active than they were in previous generations?**

Content of Adolescent Experience

Adolescence is a time of transition from a secure but dependent life in the parental home to an independent life that is filled with choices and change. As adolescents move out of the closed world of their childhood into the larger society they meet with many new choices and demands. They may, for the first time, come into contact with values and behaviors that are in opposition to those learned in the home. The adolescent begins an internal quest for self and also an external search involving the following questions:

1. Who is in my primary reference group? (Friends)
2. What life-style shall I establish?
3. Where is the place of religion in my life?
4. What is my sexual identity?
5. What qualities do I want in friends?
6. What do I owe friends, family, community, and country?
7. What will I do for my life's work?

Adolescence is the time when each person must face the riddle of his or her own existence: "Who am I?" [Courtesy Anastasia.]

These and other issues are the *content* of adolescent experience. This is not to say that all adolescents resolve them once and for all. Questions of identity are continually asked over the life span. However, in this case, not to choose is to choose, as we all answer these questions in the daily choices we make. Our choices, however, cannot be approached absolutely freely, for each of us is constrained by his or her background and by the historical period in which we make our choices.

Cohort Differences

Individuals are indelibly marked by the historical period and events of their formative years. Researchers are aware of the effect of historical time and when studying changes over the life-cycle attempt to take them into consideration. For example, many people who were youths during the Great Depression of the 1930s have a pervasive sense of deprivation and vulnerability that they attribute to the experience. Those who were adolescents in the 1960s may carry with them a sense of distrust for society's institutions because of the Vietnam War. Many veterans of that war feel a sense of alienation and futility as a result of their experience, in stark contrast to the sense of moral justification and pride that veterans of World War II have.

Each decade gets its label and character largely from the actions of its youth. Thus, we refer to the "Silent Fifties," and the youth of that period belonging to the "beat generation." The 1960s was a time of activists and "flower children," and the 1970s of a narcissism that spawned the "Do your own thing" generation. The character of the 1980s is not yet set. Writers viewing the social scene suggest that this decade may be a time of new commitment. They point to a more conservative trend in sexual and community behavior and an increasing concern with world issues such as nuclear control and environmental protection. We will now attempt to describe the psychological and social aspects of adolescent passage.

The Search for Identity

Much of our understanding of the adolescent phase of personality development comes from the psychoanalytic view. This has been most insistently and elegantly stated by Erikson (1963a, 1963b). For Erikson the stage of adolescence is primarily concerned with the individual's search for an answer to the question "Who am I?" This search becomes a crisis in adolescence that provides much of the individual's drive to experiment and find a suitable life-style. The identity crisis of adolescence does not descend in a flash of lightning on the unsuspecting adolescent. Erikson has emphasized the life span concept of ego development. The search for identity begins when the infant can differentiate self from those things that are not self. Identity continues to occupy a central position in ego development until the final phase of ego integration in old age. Adolescence is a crucial time for identity because the earlier solutions involving identifications with parents are no longer workable. Like it or not, the adolescent is forced into physical and psychological independence, and that independence requires a separate identity.

Identity formation in adolescence involves at least three commitments: a sex-

Identity achievement involves discovering one's unique abilities and sharing them with another.

A commitment to identity achievement involves vocational choice. Whether to attend college and what to study are choices to be made. Going to college entails other activities, such as playing frisbee. [Courtesy Elizabeth Karmel.]

ual orientation, a commitment to an ideology, and a vocational choice. Identity is arrived at through affirmation of what one believes and negation of what one does not. Both affirmation and negation require choices on the part of the adolescent. Often the negations are easier than affirmation and require less risk. Choosing to be the first in a family to go to college, going to a distant city to work, making a commitment to save the environment or fight world hunger, and becoming involved in a love relationship all contain elements of great risk. The first young person in a family or social circle who chooses to attempt college is affirming the values of college and negating the values associated with friends and activities in the familiar home town. Talking against and rejecting the known elements of one's family, social status, school, or provincial town are not so difficult, but actually moving into the unknown is fraught with danger and risk. The danger of journeying into the unknown is a recurring theme in myths and folk tales. Although those stories recount dangers in physical terms, they are also symbolic tales of the psychological dangers of traveling into new territory. Bruno Bettleheim in *Uses of Enchantment* (1976) notes the uses of such tales to solve psychological conflict.

Identity achievement is an interplay of negation and affirmation. Marcia (1980) states that this fear of the risk in choosing an uncertain future prevents some young people from forming an identity or gives them only a partial identity. Although the achievement of identity is a crisis of adolescence, it is not accomplished dramatically in one fell swoop. As with most elements of growth, it occurs in bits and pieces, through countless decisions and experiences, which seldom are irrevocable. Adolescence is a time for trying new situations and finding the best "fit" between friends, activities, commitments, and work. A myriad of small, almost trivial decisions about who to date, whether to break up, whether to take drugs, whether to have sexual intercourse, whether to go to college or to work, what to study, what clubs and activities to join and whether to be politically active, all contribute to one's composite identity.

Identity in Early Adolescence

Early adolescence is a continuation of preadolescent concerns. The early adolescent is keenly aware that the old solutions will not work forever—that he or she cannot remain a child in the family. However, a clear sense of direction, strengths, and abilities is not yet evident. The psychological solution of identifying with one's parents becomes maladaptive; lacking a strong, independent identity, the early adolescent forms a new identification with the peer group. It is in this stage that adolescents gain the reputation of being conformists and mindless followers of the group. Group mentality leads to both positive and negative consequences. In a positive sense, early adolescents form strong and lasting allegiances. Through belonging to groups they begin to give their allegiance to a movement larger than themselves. The tendency can be distorted, however, and used for political means, as Hitler's youth movement was in Germany in the 1930s (Erikson, 1963b). In a negative sense, this group tendency can be used to build antisocial gangs. The tendency of early adolescents to form cliques and to exhibit extreme insensitivity and cruelty to "outsiders" is well known. Sexual orientation occupies prime concern in these years, and both boys and girls experiment with sex-role behaviors and relations with others as sexual beings.

Identity in Middle Adolescence

Middle adolescence corresponds roughly to the last three years of high school. By then the uncertainty of puberty is over for most people, as are the painfully awkward first steps toward exploration of the opposite sex. Boys and girls generally have easy, comfortable relationships. Middle adolescents continue to explore aspects of identity; and are generally comfortable with who they are and can risk rejecting their identification with the peer group. In middle adolescence friends are chosen more on the basis of who they are as individuals than on their acceptability to the group. Conversely, senior high students are themselves more individualistic and less fearful of appearing to be "different." In American society, graduation from high school necessitates the choice of going to work, vocational training, or to college. There are vast differences in the outcome of the choices. Generally, those who aspire to attain or to maintain middle-class status choose college. Entering the labor force from high school almost guarantees a lifetime membership in the working class. However, choosing to be the first in one's family to go to college involves many additional decisions and negations. For lower-class youth it is a bid for social mobility—that is, for moving up into the middle class.

Identity in Late Adolescence

Since Erikson introduced the concept of identity as a crisis of adolescence other psychologists have elaborated on his theory and studied it in more detail. Marcia (1980) has identified four different modes for dealing with the issues around identity. He has used those modes to evaluate the progress that an individual may be making toward identity. Marcia looked at the issues of choosing a vocation and an ideology and classified late adolescents according to whether they had experienced a decision-making period in these two areas. He found that there were four patterns for solving these issues:

1. *Identity achievement.* Individuals who have achieved an identity have experienced a decision-making period and are pursuing self-chosen occupational and ideological goals.
2. *Foreclosures.* Some individuals are committed to occupational and ideological positions, but the choices were made by their parents. They rarely indicate that there was a crisis period in which there was a struggle for the correct decision.
3. *Identity diffusions.* There are individuals who may have experienced a decision-making period, but they have no set occupational or ideological direction.
4. *Moratoriums.* Young people *in* an identity crisis are in the throes of a struggle concerning occupational or ideological issues.

Erikson presented the identity crisis as between identity achievement and identity confusion: that is, one either achieved or did not achieve an identity. Marcia (1980) has explored a wider range of styles in progress toward identity. He avoids Erikson's simple dichotomy and suggests that there are both healthy and pathological expressions of each of the statuses.

Relationships

Finding an identity and one's place in the world intimately affects one's family and friends. As adolescents move from the family orientation to the wider world in which they must make choices, changes occur in both those relationships. Let us examine these and see how they change.

Belonging to a special group may entail initiation ritual and special proof of loyalty. [Courtesy Greensboro Day School.]

In middle adolescence boys and girls generally have an easy, comfortable relationship.

Identity Status

Positive		Negative
commitment to self-selected vocational and ideological positions	Identity achievement	premature commitment that precludes further growth and exploration
steadfast, committed, cooperative	Foreclosure	rigid, dogmatic, conforming
carefree, charming, independent	Identity diffusion	careless, psychopathic, schizoid
sensitive, highly ethical, flexible	Moratorium	anxiety-ridden, self-righteous, vacillating

Family Relations Between Generations

In the 1960s there was a lot of publicity about generation gaps. The anthropologist Margaret Mead repeatedly pronounced that the year 1945 represented a chasm that could never be crossed by those born before that year or those born later. It was the year we entered the Atomic Age: the first atomic bomb exploded on the city of Hiroshima.

Certainly there were students in the 1960s who were radical and seemed in violent opposition to society's institutions. But on closer inspection, many social critics have noted that the politically active students were often the sons and daughters of parents who shared their principles. That is, while those students seemed to be in rebellion against society, they were actually in agreement with their parents. The parents themselves were also in opposition to society's institutions.

We know that as children advance through adolescence they become more involved with their peers. It has been commonly assumed that increased involvement with peers means rejecting parental values. In reviewing many studies on this question Coleman (1980) notes that this is not always the case. There are differences in style and taste between parents and children, involving clothes, music, and domestic issues (Coleman, George & Holt, 1977), but on closer analysis those differences are seen not to extend to fundamental values. In a study that looked more carefully at the areas in which young people rely on parents and on peers, it was found that there is a difference in which situation calls forth reliance on parents or peers. When questions involve "norm orientation," peers were most important. That is, when asked to indicate whose ideas were most like those of the subject on a variety of topics, peers were most likely to be indicated. However, when asked who understood them better, parents or friends, parents were more likely to be indicated. Similarly, when asked who they would most like to be like when they grew up—parents or the people they think their friends will be—again parents were more likely to be chosen (Bowerman & Kinch, 1959).

This orientation to parents has been found in later studies as well. Brittain (1963, 1969) asked girls in grades nine, ten, and eleven to solve hypothetical dilemmas that involved parent-peer conflict. The stories were so constructed that two courses of action were offered: one course by peers and one by parents. The conclusion from this study was that parents and peers are not in competition with each other for influence; rather, adolescents use peers and parents as competent guides in different areas. When decisions involve choices for the future, parents are the valued counselors; when decisions involve current status and identity peers may be more influential.

Many adolescents continue to have strong relationships with parents and through this relationship parents have an influence on their decisions, such as this young woman's decision to attend college, shown here on her first day there.

Lesser and Kandel (1969) studied the relative influence of parents and best friends on decisions involving educational plans and life goals. These researchers found that the opinions of best friends and parents tended to support the same choices but concluded that parents have a stronger influence than peers. In addition, those adolescents who agreed with their parents were more likely to agree with best friends, whereas if there was parent-adolescent disagreement, such disagreement tended also to be present with best friends.

Not unexpectedly, the stronger the relationship between adolescent and parent, the greater the influence. Larson (1972) attempted to study this question by evaluating the quality of the parent-adolescent relationship as reflected in parental interest and understanding, willingness to help, the number of family activities shared, and so forth. Those adolescents who had the highest involvement with parents were most likely to think as they did and also were less likely to see a need to differentiate between parental influence and peer influence.

Friends

One of the major elements in the search for identity is the choice of friends, for friends determine life-style, affect value orientation, and comprise a reference group. A best friend is someone on whom to test values and ideas and is a guide in the search for identity (Osterriech, 1969). Friendships have a developmental pattern in adolescence. Douvan and Adelson (1966) studied changes in friendships in early, middle, and late adolescence. In early adolescence (eleven through thirteen) friendships tend to focus on the activity that friends can perform together rather than on their interaction. In this way, friends are somewhat interchangeable, provided they can engage in a desired activity. In middle adolescence (fourteen through sixteen) friendships are sought for the security they provide. This is the time that the most anxiety is shown concerning friends. Adolescents express the desire for a friend who is loyal and trustworthy. Erikson (1963a) has stressed youths' need to find fidelity in themselves, in others, and in institutions. The other side of finding a friend is being a friend. In late adolescence, beyond the age of seventeen, friendship becomes a more relaxed, shared experience. There is greater emphasis on the friend's personality and interests and on the relationship's interpersonal quality. This developmental pattern is supported by several studies that found middle adolescents (age fifteen) to be the most insecure about friendships and to exhibit the most fear of rejection from friends (Douvan & Adelson, 1966; Coleman, 1974). In late adolescence, even though friendship is still important for sharing confidences, an increasing sense of autonomy allows the older adolescent to be less fearful of being abandoned and betrayed (Douvan & Adelson, 1966).

Boys and girls appear to seek friends for different reasons and to react to friends somewhat differently. Girls express more anxiety about their friendships than boys. This is most likely because the different socialization of girls leads them to place a higher value on intimacy and interpersonal relationships. Boys are generally encouraged to achieve autonomy and independence and to believe that they do not really need anyone else. Thus, the friendships that boys form are based more on doing things with friends.

The Peer Group

The social organization of adolescents is not restricted to best friends. Friendship patterns are arranged in larger and larger groups in a hierarchical fashion. At the base are best friends; several best-friend groups form a clique, and several cliques

(A) (B)

(C) (D)

The structure of adolescent social groups is three-tiered. At the base of this structure are best-friends. Girls tend to stress relationship in friendship (A) while boys tend to prefer friends with whom they share activities. Girls and boys can also be best friends and share interesting activities (B). Several best-friend groups that do things together comprise a clique, such as this group at a beach party (C). Such cliques form the second level of social hierarchy. Several such cliques that gather for larger events and that are all known to each other form the peer group or crowd (D). [(B) Courtesy William Amidon and Greensboro Day School; (D) Courtesy Helen Brooks.]

form a crowd. The entire crowd with which an adolescent has friendly relations is his or her peer group. A typical high school may have several large crowd groups and many small cliques.

Cliques generally have a range of from two to nine members; the average number is five (Coleman, 1980). Cliques tend to be closed to outsiders, which gives adolescents the reputation for excluding others. Cliques form in pre- or early adolescence, usually on the basis of school or recreational neighborhood activities. In early adolescence cliques almost always are exclusively single sex. In middle adolescence, they tend to include both boys and girls. One of the most complete studies of school cliques was conducted in Sydney, Australia. Dunphy (1963) discovered 44 cliques in a total population of 303 boys and girls. The subjects were predominately middle class and ranged in age from thirteen to twenty-one. The average size of the cliques was six members. In general, cliques are composed of members at the same socioeconomic level; they usually are limited to those in the same grade level. Typically the members of a clique have the same values, interests, tastes, and moral standards and express great intolerance and contempt for those who are different. It is also probably not coincidental that the average clique size is similar to that of the average family. The controlled size of the clique enables adolescents to transfer the allegiances and relationship differences they learned in the family to the clique.

Dunphy found that among his 303 subjects there were 12 identifiable crowds with a membership of from 15 to 30 people and an average membership of 20. Crowds were composed of cliques, and membership in a clique was a prerequisite for belonging to a crowd—although not all cliques were members of a crowd. Crowds and cliques serve different functions in the social life of adolescents. The large size of the crowd precludes intimate relationships; cliques serve this purpose through conversation and communication. The crowd tends to facilitate organized social activities such as parties and dances. Crowd activities are concentrated on weekends. Dunphy theorized that the crowd provides a means for adolescent social relations to move from those involving a single sex to heterosexual activities. This is accomplished under the umbrella of the crowd and clique without undue risk to the fledgling adolescent. From the safety of the single-sex clique, within the context of an organized social event (such as a dance or swimming party), an individual can move at his or her own pace toward relationships with the opposite sex. There are same-sex friends to advise and offer some strategic advice when necessary. As greater skills in dating are gained, the safety net of the clique becomes unnecessary. Thus, we see that peer groups serve different purposes at different stages in the adolescent's social development. Adolescents' seemingly endless gossiping and superficial activities are actually social-learning experiences. The peer group, too, undergoes developmental changes and will ultimately evolve into another form.

Popularity

Within cliques and crowds stand individuals. Cliques and crowds do not claim to be democratic, so leaders emerge and exclusions are made. The adolescent leadership in cliques and crowds can be best understood in terms of that elusive quality called popularity. Popularity is generally ascribed to the individuals who are most admired in the group. When a young person is admired, others seek to form friendships with him or her and he or she is then "popular." Researchers have been interested in discovering the characteristics that are judged to make a person popular. It is clear, and not surprising, that in American high schools popularity rests on athletic ability for boys and social skills for girls. In a survey of crowds in ten high schools, Coleman (1960, 1961) found that students generally identified athletic ability, personality, and good looks as necessary qualities for boys' popularity and good looks, personality, and good clothes as necessary for girls'. Cavion and Dokecki (1973) found that physical attributes determined popularity only for the most and least attractive. For the vast number of adolescents with average looks, personality factors determine attractiveness. In an earlier study Kuhlen and Lee (1943) found that the most admired personality characteristics were cheerfulness, friendliness, enthusiasm, a sense of humor, and being an initiator of games and activities. And what of academic achievement? Even though most adolescent

Popularity is most affected by personality factors such as cheerfulness, friendliness and a sense of humor. [Courtesy Greensboro Day School.]

crowds form within the schools, the evidence is that academic achievement has little relationship to group status. Where academic achievement is sometimes a factor in popularity, it seems related to social class. Youths from higher social classes tend to evaluate academic achievement more positively than adolescents from lower classes. However, those youths in whom academic achievement is combined with excellence in athletic ability are rated highest of all. They are those rare adolescents who have everything (Coleman, 1980).

Peer groups in adolescence function as severe and uncompromising socialization agents. Parents will love and accept children who are awkward, unattractive, and mentally slow. Peer groups are not so charitable. They stamp society's approval or disapproval on the individual *because* of his or her characteristics. We might speculate that such primitive evaluation is an innate feature of human social relations because the mechanism appears in adolescent social organizations in many different settings. Primitive tribes literally cast misfits and handicapped individuals out of the tribe to fend for themselves. They usually cannot do so and so do not survive. Overcoming this primitive tendency to judge requires the civilizing force of democratic principles such as equality. The principle that all individuals are of equal value is a highly evolved philosophical stance, and not, as Thomas Jefferson contended, self-evident. Adolescents need guidance from caring and civilized adults to temper the natural primitive evaluation of others with the higher ethic of individual worth.

Delinquency

In the minds of many Americans adolescence and delinquency are synonymous, yet research has found that many adolescents are rather compliant, behaving in accord with parental values and growing into responsible adults. What is the truth?

What is delinquency? And what part does delinquency play in adolescence? In general, when we speak of delinquent behavior, we are referring to the behavior of juveniles that is in willful and deliberate violation of law and that will bring them under legal judgment if the act is brought to the attention of law enforcement officers (Gold & Petronio, 1980). Let us clearly differentiate between moral law and civil law—between what is immoral and what is illegal. America is pluralistic, which means that there are many different standards of morality; but it is also a democratic society with laws, and acts that are illegal are illegal for all. For example, an adolescent may masturbate and feel guilty about such behavior, but the act is not illegal and the adolescent is not a delinquent. On the other hand, an adolescent may smoke marijuana and feel no guilt because of a belief that the act should be decriminalized (Gold & Petronio, 1980). Nevertheless, smoking marijuana is illegal and when juveniles smoke it they are performing delinquent behavior. It is interesting that only adolescents can be delinquent. When young children break the law they are not held accountable because it is presumed that they lack sufficient understanding to assume responsibility for their actions.

The concept of juvenile delinquency evolved following the cultural invention of adolescence. Traditionally when children reached the age of reason they were accountable for their actions and could be tried for their crimes. The category of juvenile delinquency protects the adolescent from the severe penalties imposed on adult criminals, while not completely forgiving the act.

What is the incidence of juvenile delinquency and how pervasive is the problem? In one study 522 boys and girls aged thirteen to sixteen were asked if they had broken any laws in the last year. Of them, 83 per cent confessed to one or more chargeable offenses. Most were minor crimes such as smoking marijuana, drinking alcohol, or having sexual intercourse with an underage girl (Gold, 1970). Very few adolescents are actually arrested and charged—about 5 per cent; however, this small percentage accounts for 30 per cent of all arrests and for 45 per cent of arrests for serious crime such as murder, assault, and robbery. These statistics refer only to those adolescents between thirteen and eighteen years of age; those between nineteen and twenty-one are treated as adult criminals and not as juvenile delinquents.

If we include older adolescents in these statistics the actual number of serious offenses by this small segment of the population is greater. Thus, it is clear that a small number of adolescents cause a great deal of trouble. Although that means that 95 per cent of adolescents *do not* become involved in serious delinquent behavior, it is a serious problem and the incidence of murder, rape, assault, and robbery apparently is increasing. In addition, more and more violent acts are being committed by younger and younger children. As social behaviors have moved down into the preadolescent age group, so have antisocial behaviors. Children of twelve, eleven, ten, and younger are now involved in serious crimes.

Causes of Delinquency

Sociologists, psychologists, criminologists, and parents have tried to understand the causes of delinquent behavior, and each offers a different explanation for it. One explanation is that delinquency is a result of individual psychopathology; another is that it is a result of deviant socialization.

One form of psychopathology responsible for delinquent behavior is a *character disorder*, in which the youth is unable to distinguish between right and wrong and feels no remorse when he or she harms others. Another form of psychopathology is *acting out*. In this instance, the youth is unable to contain or control internal conflicts and acts them out. Rape is an example of antisocial acting out. It is a violent, hostile act. When it is committed it is an expression of intense rage against women in general and of an internal conflict with a particular woman, most likely the mother. *Everyone* has unconscious, primitive feelings of rage and aggression. Most of us successfully repress and transform and never actualize them. Some people, however, cannot control these impulses and commit crimes. Society traditionally has reinforced the repression of aggressive impulses through prohibitions against them ("Thou shalt not . . ."). Many critics of our society are concerned that a constant barrage of violence on television loosens societal restraint and, in effect, gives permission to people to commit acts of violence. The effect of televised violence is most pronounced on those who have only tenuous control over their impulses. In a society less permissive about violence, they might never act violently.

This explanation for delinquent behavior is based on the psychoanalytic theory, which assumes that internal drives motivate behavior. G. Stanley Hall (1904) publicized this theory early in the century, and along with it the idea that internal drives become so insistent and difficult to control during adolescence that delinquent behavior is almost to be expected in the age group, especially among boys. Hall saw youths valiantly striving to maintain some stability against a raging torrent of new and strange emotions and drives. When that torrent was coupled with an unstable and deprived social background, Hall saw the adolescent as a victim needing the help and support of society, not its condemnation and punishment. This was the thinking that created our juvenile justice system.

Another disturbing source of delinquent behavior comes not from youths with psychological problems, but from those who are socialized to be delinquent. For them, acts of violence and theft against others are an acceptable way to live. They often come from families in which they are abused and live in a community in which violence is unremarkable. In self-protection, they join a street gang where they gain status and acceptance through antisocial acts. They are members of a society that is deviant. Whatever the cause of their delinquent behavior, the cost to the larger society is enormous, and growing.

Mental Disorders in Adolescence

As adolescents approach physical adulthood, they become susceptible to adult mental problems. Two major mental disorders are especially likely to appear in adolescence: schizophrenia and depression. Closely connected with depression is suicide, which is the leading cause of death among college students and the fourth cause of death for all adolescents.

Schizophrenia

Schizophrenia is more likely to make its appearance during adolescence and early adulthood than at any other time in life. In adolescence girls who are later diagnosed schizophrenic become less passive, but they become increasingly withdrawn, shy, and inhibited (Watt, 1978; Watt & Lubensky, 1976).

Depression

Depression and negative behavior seem to be a normal part of adolescent development; thus the question is, when does it become a mental health hazard? Depression, according to Weiner (1975), can be broadly defined as a pervasive sense of loss. It may be a social loss, a psychological loss, or an actual physical loss. In social loss a personal relationship may be disrupted by death or another separation or by a broken friendship. When the parents of children or adolescents divorce, such a sense of loss may occur. The death of a parent or especially a loved grandparent may result in a depressive loss. Psychological loss may involve loss of self-esteem and resulting guilt and a sense of failure. Failure in school, or sports, low SAT scores, or rejection from a social group may lower self-esteem and create a sense of loss. A depressive sense of loss may result from a loss of body integrity as a result of illness, physical injury, or disfigurement. The sense of loss of body integrity may ensue from such insignificant impairments as wearing glasses or teeth braces. Because adolescents are preoccupied with body image, they may become morbidly depressed over minor bodily changes. Even the normal bodily changes that occur at puberty may be perceived as a psychological loss. We have previously discussed anorexia nervosa as an obvious disturbance in body image. Depression in adolescents manifests itself in fatigue, hypochondriasis, and difficulty with concentration (Weiner, 1980). Schizophrenics have a distorted view of reality and suffer a diminished ability to establish and maintain comfortable and rewarding interpersonal relationships. They also exhibit a weakened control of impulses and an inappropriate expression of ideas, emotions, and impulses (Arieti, 1974). When schizophrenia appears in adolescence, the chances of recovery are lessened. Half of those diagnosed and admitted to a hospital for schizophrenia in adolescence make little or no progress and remain hospitalized indefinitely (Warren, 1965), whereas only one third of all patients fail to make any progress. Similarly, one third of all schizophrenic patients recover, but only one quarter of adolescents hospitalized for schizophrenia recover.

Prior to hospitalization, schizophrenic youths have few friends, see the friends they have infrequently, and share few common interests and activities with them. The friendships they establish tend to be for exploitative ends rather than for mutual benefit (Kreisman, 1970). There appear to be differences in the behavior of boys and girls in the years before the onset of schizophrenia. The preschizophrenic behavior of males becomes increasingly irritable, aggressive, negative, and defiant, whereas that of girls is emotionally immature and passive. The pattern for girls have been noted as early as elementary school in retrospective case histories.

The great danger in adolescent depression is alienation. Because the major task of late adolescence is to find a place in the world, adolescents who are depressively concerned with their adequacy may withdraw from the effort. The risk of failure prevents such young people from stating long-term goals and making a concerted effort in any direction. They may protect a vulnerable and insecure ego with a stance of not caring, cynicism, and a pervasive "What's-the-use-of-it-all?" attitude.

Sexual promiscuity and drug use are sometimes a reaction against depressive feelings. Such activity offers stimulation and excitement in a world that is perceived as colorless and stagnant. In addition those activities become a focus for companionship and sharing and bring attention and notice, even if it is negative (McGlothlin, 1975; Kantner & Zelnik, 1972). Often the final solution the adolescent chooses for depression is suicide.

Suicide

In its apparent injustice, the death of a young person from accident, illness, or homicide is difficult for friends and family to accept. Beyond such acts of fate, the mind and emotions reel and reject as completely incomprehensible the willful choice of death over life that is being made by an ever-increasing number of adolescents and children. Only a numb "Why? Why? Why?" can be flung into the void that answers with silence. What do we know about adolescents who choose death over life?

The adolescent between fifteen and nineteen who commits suicide is three times as likely to be male, although females *attempt* suicide three times more often than males. This young man is most likely to die by shooting or hanging. In late adolescence a suicide is more likely to be a college student. Among college students who are suicidal, poor academic performance appears *not* to be a factor; suicides have been found to have higher grade-point averages and more academic honors than their peers (Seiden, 1969). However, their feelings about academic performance may be a factor. Perhaps even above-average achievement is not enough to bolster their self-esteem (Cantor, 1976).

There appear to be many negative personality and social factors in the general population of young people who attempt suicide. Cumulative negative factors must make life seem unbearable to them. Rohn, Sarles, Kenny, Reynolds, and Heald (1977) conducted a counseling program for children seven to nineteen who had attempted suicide. Those children in the program were predominately black and from a low socioeconomic level. They tended to be social isolates without close friends. They had failed to gain competence in academic studies. A third had dropped out of school and of those remaining, 75 per cent were doing very poorly. Almost a third had failed one or more grades. In addition to poor performance in school, a third of them had a history of behavior problems in school. They also had disrupted home situations in which there was a high rate of divorce and alcoholism; many of them lived with someone other than their parents.

Another study (Jacobs, 1971) found that adolescents aged fourteen to eighteen who had attempted suicide were more likely to have been chronically depressed for as long as five years before their suicide attempt. As a group they were more alienated from their parents, to the point of being unable to talk to them. To compensate for this lack, they tended to become involved in an intense romantic relationship and to cut off all other friends. When the relationship failed, they lacked any inner or social resources to help them over the crisis. More than half of those adolescents were breaking up with a boy- or girlfriend when they made their suicide attempt.

Cantor (1976) found that young women who attempted suicide were impulsive and had a low tolerance for frustration and stress. Cantor also found that young women who had attempted suicide were likely to be in conflict with their parents and did not feel that they could enlist their help in solving problems. Those young women were especially estranged from their fathers and lacked the support of a male. In many cases the father was absent from the home or, if he were present, communication was lacking. Not enough research has been conducted on the importance of the father-daughter relationship as the young girl moves into womanhood. But it is known that she needs a masculine figure to verify her sexuality at that time. A loving and admiring father can do this in the safety of the family unit; otherwise she may seek verification in a succession of other masculine figures and be crushed when each relationship ends.

Suicide is a needless waste of human resources. The pursuit of happiness is one of the tenets of our Bill of Rights. If we were to practice treating each person as an individual with a unique contribution to make, we might be able to alleviate some of the pressure that adolescents feel about "making it."

Life-Style Choices

In all large high schools, many different groups exist. There are, as anyone who has been associated with an American high school recently knows, "jocks," "brutes," "druggies," "freaks," "eggheads," "weirdos," "Jesus freaks," and the "cool crowd." Each of these groups imposes a life-style on the adolescents who belong to it. The druggies do different things and think different thoughts from the Jesus freaks. As young people reach adolescence they are confronted by the variety of choices that society affords. Family background and socioeconomic level affect the choices they make. The "cool crowd" usually is composed of sons and daughters of the most influential and the highest socioeconomic levels in the school. Individuals who do not have this family background can become members if they possess special athletic skills or an unusually attractive physique or personality. They may find, however, that they cannot keep up and may exclude themselves from the group. The choices made in high school may have consequences that affect both current and future life-style. The weightiest of those choices are whether to "do drugs" and whether to become sexually active.

Drugs

With the topic of drugs we come full circle in this book. In the chapter on prenatal influences we differentiated between legal and illegal drugs. We placed the responsibility for drug ingestion on the prospective mother. Now that embryo has developed through infancy and childhood into adolescence and is faced with the problem of drugs. In the world of the adolescent we are focusing exclusively on illegal drugs—marijuana, cocaine, and heroin—and the abuse of legal drugs. Illegal drugs have become a pervasive element in the life of American schoolchildren. There was a time when drugs and their damaging effects were rather neatly confined to the ghettos of large cities. Now illegal drugs are available in virtually every high school and college in the country, and in a shockingly large number of elementary schools. Every child has the opportunity to do drugs and will have to make a choice in the matter. The use of drugs is so widespread today that some members of almost every group may be using drugs.

The drug problem is a knotty one. The parents of high school adolescents may take Valium or a stimulant prescribed by the family physician to help them get through the day. Television commercials extol the virtue of pills to solve one problem or another. It is illogical that the children of such parents who give a friend two dollars for an "upper" or a "downer" should be participating in an illegal activity while their parents are clearly operating within the law. Such situations foster a cynical attitude in youth and confirm their notion that who you know is more important than what you do.

Alcohol

Alcohol is a legal drug that is readily available in our society. Many states, however, require that individuals reach a minimum age before purchasing alcoholic beverages. Nevertheless, alcohol is available to adolescents who use false identification to

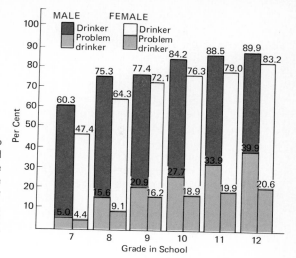

Percentages of youngsters in grades 7 through 12 who admitted being drinkers or problem drinkers—defined as drunkenness six times during the past year or trouble related to alcohol. [From "Behavioral Health's Challenge to Academic, Scientific, and Professional Psychology" by Joseph D. Matarazzo, *American Psychologist,* 1982, *37* (1), 1–14. Copyright 1982 by the American Psychological Association. Reprinted by permission of the publisher and author.]

purchase it or get it from older friends and even their parents. The leading cause of death for adolescents is accidents, the leading cause of accidents is automobiles, and the leading cause of automobile accidents is drunken drivers. When the legal age for drinking is raised to twenty-one an immediate drop in traffic fatalities occurs. There is now a national campaign to stop drunken driving and to reduce the large number of fatalities.

Another danger of drinking is the disease of alcoholism. Among people who consume alcohol, some will not be able to control it. The alcoholic is not always a skid-row bum but can as easily be a high school student. There is no way to predict who will become an alcoholic, but the result is predictable: grades plummet, behavior becomes erratic, and getting a drink becomes the most important thing in the person's life. The tasks of adolescence cannot be accomplished under these circumstances, so the result of alcoholism is an unfulfilled future. Whether to use alcohol is another choice the adolescent must make. Alcohol is a widespread and available social drug. It is the lubricant of business exchanges and smooths the edges of social occasions. Many adolescents see their parents use and serve alcohol at home, and in fact, may even tend bar when their parents give parties. Many adolescents try their first drink by sneaking it from the family liquor cabinet. The choices of whether and how much to drink are important life-style choices for adolescents.

Sexuality

One of the major tasks of adolescent identity is establishing a sexual identity. Of course, every child knows from a very young age that she is a girl, or that he is a boy. But exactly what being a boy or girl means is not so clear. The current thinking by sex educators is that sexuality (boyness and girlness) affects every aspect of experience and life. We are created male and female for the obvious purpose of biological reproduction, but the psychological and social aspects of sexuality have achieved ascendency in and been shaped by our culture.

One of the pressing tasks of the adolescent search for identity involves finding a comfortable social expression of the internal sexual aspects of self that are in agreement with the nonsexual sense of self (Miller & Simon, 1980). This is a very complicated task involving many psychological aspects. First among them is gender role. The adolescent brings from his or her family experience deep-rooted expectations for appropriate gender-role behaviors. These are gained through identification with parents. Gender-role expectations are modified by the behaviors that the larger society conveys as appropriate to male and female. In early adolescence the parent of the same sex, who was formerly the ideal of perfection, becomes the enemy. Parents suddenly appear dowdy and old-fashioned and suggestions are met with, "Mother, how *could* you . . . (wear that dress, think such a dumb thing, ask him that)?" The adolescent then turns to the peer group and experiments to find a congruence between behavior and gender-role expectations. Adolescents are given conflicting messages regarding sex and sexuality and it is no wonder that confusion reigns supreme. There are probably as many different attitudes toward sex in our culture as there are people to express them.

The immediate cultural ancestor of modern society was the Victorian period, whose hallmarks were sexual repression and the double standard. The enjoyment of sex was the prerogative of males—and "fallen women." Queen Victoria is reputed to have told her daughter, who was about to be married, that when her husband was having "his way with her" she should simply lie there and think of Britannia. One of the major achievements of twentieth-century popular thought has been to break the hold of Victorian sexual attitudes.

Within American society there remains a wide spectrum of opinions on acceptable expressions of sexuality: in religious schools, for example, boys and girls may not be permitted even to hold hands; at the other end of the spectrum there is the blatant sexuality of entertainment personalities and the provocative clothes and actions displayed by many young people. There are those who advocate unrestrained sexual expression in people of all ages, including children, and who preach and practice nudity and free and open sexual relations with adults and children. However, there remains in our society some residue of Victorianism apparent in the feeling of many that there just might be something wrong with sexual permissiveness. It is no wonder that many parents are confused about what to tell adolescents. They do not want to stifle their children's budding sexuality, but they do not want to seem to encourage promiscuous behavior. Therefore, they do nothing, and young people devise their own standards of behavior. What then, is the sexual behavior of adolescents? Ever since Kinsey asked thousands of Americans about their sexual behavior, researchers have been asking the same question. This is a particularly difficult area to research because there is no way to ascertain whether subjects are telling the truth.

There is general agreement in our society that children should not engage in sexual relations. There is also agreement that adults, and particularly married adults, should have an active and satisfying sex life. Given the fact that sexual maturity is reached between the ages of twelve and fourteen, marriage and adult status is attained in the early twenties, and males reach their sexual peak at around the age of eighteen, it is always provocative to ask, "What are the young people doing?"

Sexual Behavior in Adolescence

Adolescent sexual behavior is watched by society as a barometer for the "sexual revolution," some social critics contend that the sexual ethic is as rigid today as in previous times, but its content has been reversed. Whereas earlier it was considered

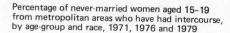

Percentage of never-married women aged 15–19
from metropolitan areas who have had intercourse,
by age-group and race, 1971, 1976 and 1979

White 15–17
White 18–19
Black 15–17
Black 18–19

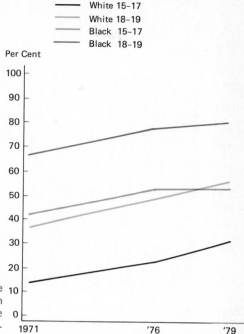

Percentage of never-married women who have
had intercourse. [Reprinted with permission from
*Teenage Pregnancy: The Problem That Hasn't Gone
Away*, published by The Alan Guttmacher Institute, New York, 1981.]

wrong or sinful to have sex, it is now considered equally wrong to close oneself off from any area of sexual expression. In some groups it may be more embarrassing and humiliating to admit virginity than to admit to being sexually active. Young people may feel that there is something wrong with them if they have not had intercourse.

Surveys taken over a period of years reveal a trend toward increased sexual activity by adolescents. In 1948 Kinsey reported that only 25 per cent of men had had intercourse by the age of eighteen. In his survey of women a few years later, only 10 per cent admitted having had intercourse by the age of eighteen (Kinsey, 1953). In 1972 Hunt found that 50 per cent of all males had had intercourse by the age of seventeen and that 20 per cent of married women and 33 per cent of single women had had intercourse before the age of eighteen. A survey conducted in 1976 (Zelnik & Kantner, 1977) found that 55 per cent of single women had had sexual intercourse. Thus we see a 30 per cent increase in sexual activity of late adolescent women between 1971 and 1976.

Those youths who have had sexual intercourse remain the exception in early adolescence. Surveys of ninth graders (or fifteen-year-olds) indicate that about 10 per cent have experienced intercourse (Jessor & Jessor, 1975). Such statistics are not static, however. It appears that the incidence of sexual activity is increasing. Vener and Steward (1974) conducted surveys on two cohorts of fifteen-year-olds in a predominately white, small-town community. The two surveys were taken three years apart. In 1970 the researchers found that 25 per cent of fifteen-year-old boys

Number of males aged 13–21, and number of females, aged 13–19, who are sexually active, by
age and marital status, United States, 1978

☐ Not sexually active

■ Sexually active, unmarried

■ Sexually active, married

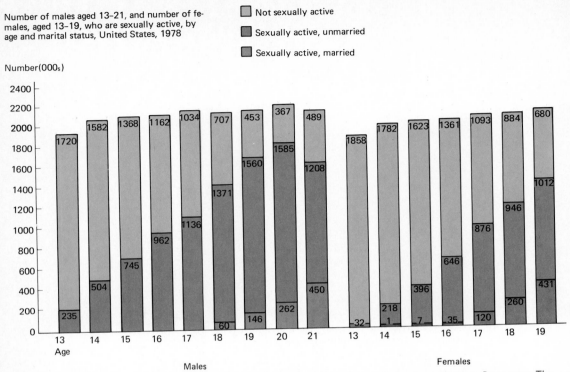

Number of males and females who are sexually active. [Reprinted with permission from *Teenage Pregnancy: The Problem That Hasn't Gone Away* published by the Alan Guttmacher Institute, New York, 1981.]

and 13 per cent of the girls had had intercourse. Three years later this percentage had risen to 38 per cent of the males and 24 per cent of the females. Chilman (1978) reviewed many studies and concluded that between 1967 and 1974 premarital intercourse rose 300 per cent for white females and 50 per cent for white males.

The Alan Guttmacher Institute, a corporation dedicated to research, policy and analysis, and public education, has estimated that in the decade of the 1970s the number of teenagers that were sexually active increased by two-thirds. (*Teenage Pregnancy: The Problem That Hasn't Gone Away*, 1981). This increase was largely accounted for by an increase in sexual activity by young whites. The institute has compiled data from many sources and now estimates that of the 29 million teenagers in America, 12 million of them are sexually active. According to their data, in early adolescence, 18 per cent of the boys and 6 per cent of the girls age 13–14 are sexually active; in the 15–17 age range, approximately half of the males and one-third of the females; in the late teen years, the number of males and females who become sexually active rises sharply. By the end of the teen years, at age 20, 80 per cent of males and 70 per cent of females are sexually active.

Gallas (1980) summarized the current teenage sexuality scene by noting the following trends:

1. Vast changes toward greater liberality in attitudes toward premarital sexual activity.
2. Changes in the value systems of women toward greater independence in decision-making, giving women the sole right to decisions about sexual activity, abortions, adoption, and single parenthood.
3. Changes in social norms requiring marriage and acceptance of alternative life styles.

Gallas (1980) concluded that all these trends predict an increase in teenage premarital sexual activity and that *choice* by the teenager is the essence of these changes.

The Other Side of the Coin: Adolescents Not Sexually Active

In a permissive society adolescence is often viewed with envy by adults as a time of sexual licentiousness. This is not the case. If half of the males have had intercourse by the age of eighteen, half have not; if one third of females have similarly engaged in sexual relations, two thirds have not. Offer and Offer (1975) found that most young men in their junior year of high school disapproved of sexual relations among adolescents. Moreover, data indicate that sexual drive is not the overwhelming tidal wave that simply cannot be resisted that Hall described. One survey of college students found that 44 per cent of the men and 68 per cent of the women had yet to engage in intercourse (Miller and Simon, 1980). Of those young men and women who had chosen not to become sexually active, 64 per cent of the males and 78 per cent of the females were not unhappy with their lack of experience. Furthermore, 48 per cent of the females and 25 per cent of the males said that they rarely or never felt that they wanted to have intercourse.

One reason for sexual abstinence that young men and women gave was that they felt sexual relations among adolescents was wrong and they gave fear of pregnancy as a reason for abstinence. Beyond this, females said they abstain out of concern for parental disapproval and damage to their reputation, whereas males cited the unavailability of a willing partner.

For the older adolescent the willingness of the partner often is affected by being "in love." This is especially true for women. Among college women asked about their first sexual partner, 59 per cent reported that they had been planning to marry the partner; an additional 22 per cent said that they had been in love at the time. Among college men, 31 per cent reported having been in love, whereas 46 per cent reported *not* having been emotionally involved (Miller & Simon, 1980).

There may indeed be positive aspects to a more open attitude toward sexuality and sexual expression. Young people are attempting to integrate sex into the rest of their lives instead of holding it apart as something dirty or secret. There is no question that there is more sexual activity among adolescents; however, this activity does not appear to be radical in nature. Hunt (1974) found that the emerging sexual ethic among adolescents was that of romantic liberalism, in which sex is a physical expression of love. Although today there is an easier and more natural approach to sexual activity, recreational sex is not the predominant sexual ethic among adolescents. Hunt notes that recreational sex, such as group sex (swinging) and mate swapping occurs primarily among married couples in the thirty- to forty-year-old range. Recreational sex is devoid of emotional attachment and commitment to the partner. In general, adolescents are disdainful of such impersonal sex. The positive aspects of adolescent sexuality are heartening, but there are also negative ones: teenage pregnancy and disease.

Teenage Pregnancy

Being pregnant is one thing; being a mother is quite another. Again, we have come full circle in this book. In Chapter 3 we discussed teenage pregnancy from the standpoint of the well-being of the baby. Here we will look at teenage pregnancy from the standpoint of the young woman. When teenage girls become pregnant they must choose between seeking an abortion and carrying the child to term. The Alan Guttmacher Institute reports that there were 1,142,000 teenage pregnancies in 1978. The graph at the bottom of this page indicates how these pregnancies were terminated.

Statistics indicate that one third of all abortions are performed on teenage women. If a young woman chooses motherhood, she is faced with an additional choice as well. Provided that the father is known and he is agreeable, she must choose between marriage and rearing the child as a single parent. It is estimated that pregnancy is a factor in many teenage marriages. If the young woman chooses to rear her child as a single parent, she will face great difficulties. One half of all births to unmarried women in the U.S. are to teenage mothers. The choice she makes is often a function of her race and socioeconomic class. If she is white and middle class, she will be more likely to seek an abortion. Otherwise she may put the baby up for adoption or get married. If she is black and is from a low socioeconomic level, she is more likely to bear the child and attempt to rear it alone or to turn the rearing over to her mother.

While the birth rate is dropping in the rest of the population, it is rising among teenage women. This segment of the population produces 20 per cent of all babies born in America. The young woman who chooses, or stumbles into, early parenthood, with or without marriage, has closed the option on many life-style opportunities. Her immediate problems may be beyond her resources and capacity. Of the possible outcomes of teenage pregnancy, marriage may seem the best. However, teenage marriages are more than three times as likely to be dissolved as those undertaken by older people. Fully half of all such marriages end in divorce (Gordon, 1973).

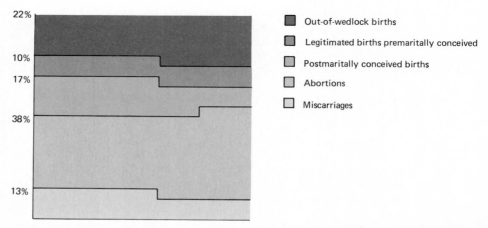

Teenage pregnancies. [Reprinted with permission from *Teenage Pregnancy: The Problem That Hasn't Gone Away* published by The Alan Guttmacher Institute, New York, 1981.]

Young girls often do not realize the changes in life style that having a child will entail. Most young mothers who drop out of school to have babies report that they want to finish high school, but only half of them do. The drop-out rate for teenage mothers is five times greater than for girls who do not have babies (Furstenberg, 1976). As a consequence of their limited education, they are less likely to find and hold employment than young women who do not have babies and are more likely to become entirely dependent on welfare. These young women seem never to get on their feet emotionally or economically.

Sexually Transmitted Diseases

With increased sexual activity comes an increase in the diseases spread through sexual contact: syphilis, gonorrhea, and herpes virus. The Public Health Service has conducted vigorous campaigns against the first two for decades. In the 1950s it was widely believed that penicillin had almost brought them under control. Recently, however, the incidence of sexually transmitted disease has risen rapidly, and some health authorities consider that we have an epidemic. This increase is the result of less protection during sexual contact and increased sexual activity. These diseases are a blow to the self-esteem of the young person, as well as a blow to his or her health. The herpes virus is especially troublesome because there is no known cure for it. The affected person risks infecting others and affecting any future children, in addition to having to bear the social stigma attached to the disease.

Real Responsibility in the Real World, or Getting It Together

Youth is a challenge: it is a time of risk, a time of individuation and separation from the familiar, a venture into the unknown. Within a very short time many aspects of responsibility are handed over to the adolescent. Young people, sensitive to this transfer, evaluate whether they and their friends have "got it together." Although the journey of growing and becoming involves many seemingly unsurmountable problems for the adolescent, it is important to recount as well the hope, the promise, and, indeed, the achievement possible in adolescence.

The virtue of youth, according to Erikson (1963a, 1963b) is fidelity, and through this faithfulness, commitment to others, to themselves, and to the larger society. Youths do not inherit a static society in which they automatically take their place. On the contrary, they must make their own place by contributing to the community. The identification processes that were developed in childhood and first applied to identifying with parents must be extended to include significant persons outside the family and significant ideas. By bringing disciplined devotion to other people and ideas, the adolescent finds importance in his or her life and feels a part of the community and of history. Without taking part in the dialogue of life through commitment, youths become alienated and despairing and life seems empty and meaningless to them. The ideas to which youth offer their loyalty and devotion are concerned with "the way things ought to be." Youths seek to become involved with experiences that reveal the essence of the era they are about to enter. They must know fully what their society's ideologies mean, for they are the beneficiaries of its traditions. They are also the practitioners and inventors of its technology. Through their ideas and commitments they will renew their era's ethical strengths, as they will discard those ideas that have outlived their usefulness. Some

These young people are teaching a group of younger children science by dissecting a frog. Adolescents need real responsibility in the real world to grow to their fullest potential. [Courtesy Greensboro Day School.]

youths will make commitments to deviant ideologies, which serve as a counterpoint and alternative to the larger society (Erikson, 1963b).

These are the potential strengths of youth in psychosocial development. We must not undermine the power of the loyalties of adolescents by offering them an identification with popular entertainers rather than with real heroes or superficial commitments to designer consumer goods rather than to important ethical ideas. We must not cut them off from identifying with their own history and rob them of a sense of historical continuity. We must offer them real experiences in the real world. We must offer them access to the world of ideas by involving them in the issues of society. We must not trivialize ideas through distortion, disinformation, and propaganda.

Our young people are the hope of the future, for they will inherit the society in which we live and recreate it in their own image. Erickson, who for decades studied children-becoming-youth and youth-becoming-adults, saw clearly the relationship between the generations and the necessary climate for optimal growth. He stated,

> *each generation of youth must find an identity consonant with its own childhood and consonant with an ideological promise in the perceptible historical process. But in youth the tables of childhood dependence begin slowly to turn; no longer is it merely for the old to teach the young the meaning of life, whether individual or collective. It is the young who, by their responses and actions, tell the old whether life as represented by the old and as presented to the young has meaning: and it is the young who carry in them the power to confirm those who confirm them and, joining the issues, to renew and to regenerate, or to reform and to rebel.* [1963b, p. 20]

We decide, in the environments that we offer, how our children and youth will grow and who they will become. It is our unavoidable responsibility.

Toward New Environments for Youth

In a publication entitled *The Transition of Youth to Adulthood* the National Commission on Youth examined the conditions of youth, analyzing the institutions serving them and the experiences available to youth in them. The commission found the institutions wanting (National Commission on Youth, 1980). The commission was composed of distinguished leaders from government, universities, labor, corporations, public schools, youth groups, and public opinion institutes. The commission did not stop with a critical appraisal of the institutions that assist youth in the transition to adulthood. They offered 27 recommendations for the creation of new environments that might better enable our young people to grow and to become the citizens our country needs. Because adolescence is a cultural invention, so, too, are the institutions that serve them. Among them are the comprehensive high school, the juvenile justice system, and labor laws aimed specifically at youth.

The Problem

In the words of the commission,*

> *The bridge of time between youth and adulthood has become a bridge too long.*
> *The transition of youth to adulthood is difficult even in the best of times. But this is the worst of times for significant numbers of American youth. Many of the traditional institutions that assist youth to adulthood are changing, crumbling, and even collapsing. The decline of the family unit is well documented. Beleaguered school systems are attacked from all sides—by students, parents, and employers—for their failure to teach marketable skills to the young. Governmental bodies on all levels remain largely unresponsive to the serious plight of youth.* [p. 9]

The commission cited the following conditions of youth:

1. Unemployment is a way of life for many of the young.
2. Some youths who have the capabilities to make a significant contribution to society are so turned off by the system that they have dropped out. They resort to such escape mechanisms as drugs and alcohol, which engender delinquency and crime, and in turn intensify their problems.
3. Another group of youths languishes in jails and juvenile detention institutions. Many of them are illiterate and are simply unprepared for the transition to adulthood. They commit violent and illegal acts to gain a measure of revenge against the system that imprisons them.
4. Self-destruction has become an option exercised by increasing numbers of the young: It is estimated that one million youth run away from home each year and suicide is now the second leading cause of death for youth between the ages of fifteen and twenty-four.

> *The problems of youth are not rooted solely in the home, the school, or the workplace; they are rooted instead in the external society, which has undermined the capacity of these institutions to operate in optimum fashion. The real secret to successful change lies in focusing our efforts on the connections between these institutions. By severing these interconnections, we have isolated the institutions from each other. But it is precisely these interconnections that count most. . . . Increased numbers of youth fall between the cracks in the institutional framework.* [p. 13]

The Commission's Solution

> *The time has come to develop a new transitional phase to assist youth to adulthood. Presently the school is the keystone of the transitional process. But societal dissatisfaction with the school's role in this process is rampant.*

* Reprinted by permission of Westview Press from *The Transition of Youth to Adulthood: A Bridge Too Long* by the National Commission on Youth, B. Frank Brown, Director. Copyright © 1980 by Charles F. Kettering Foundation.

As presently constituted, schools offer an incomplete context for the transition of youth to adulthood. Traditionally, schools have emphasized self-centered objectives, focusing on the acquisition of cognitive skills and knowledge for personal growth. Cognitive skills and knowledge are crucial to growing up, not only because of the self-discipline required but also for their central role in most jobs in the world of work. In addition, however, youth need a broader environment to learn and practice their skills.

The new transitional phase includes schooling but in a changed capacity. In this new capacity the Commission recommends that schools function as a pervasive but not an exclusive environment for youth. Schooling is simply not an island unto itself. The real world, as represented by environments in which adults operate, must be tied more intimately to the formal school setting. Young people currently operate in environments that have become impoverished in their ability to provide concrete opportunities for responsible and productive action. Schools, in conjunction with other agencies, must become action-rich institutions, providing community-based learning experiences.

Retooling of such a fundamental nature requires rethinking even the most common aspects of the way in which institutions operate. The Commission is acutely aware of the necessity to design new environments that have broader objectives than those in which the school has traditionally operated. Educators must open the schoolhouse doors to the real world, stressing relationships between their students and adults in the community. The long-standing barrier between town and gown must be overcome with all due haste. No longer should schools insulate the young from the real world.

In addition to teaching the traditional objectives of acquiring skills and knowledge, schools must also teach responsibility to others. This can only be done by providing the experience of interrelating with persons from dissimilar backgrounds and the experience of having others dependent on one's actions. In order to give youth the opportunities for interdependent activities directed toward collective goals, the Commission recommends that schools develop relationships with a host of programs and institutions that presently are not part of the formal instructional program.

The task for schools must be to break down the barriers to reality and spearhead the transition of the young into the adult world. A new national goal of educational policy must be to integrate youth into the community in functional roles that contribute materially to their maturation as adults. [pp. 15-16]

Learning

The commission directed eight recommendations toward the creation of new learning environments. The thrust of its recommendations is to enlarge the scope of experiences considered educational and to involve youth in the active life of the community.

The commission envisions an educational endeavor in which high schools become action-rich institutions with relationships to all other community institutions. In so doing, the responsibility for youth in this transition period is shared among schools, businesses, government, nursing homes, churches, and any and all institutions in the community. Second, in this utopian education, walls of the school dissolve and the classroom becomes the community as youths begin to function not as passive students, but as active contributors in the community. In living and learning in the real world, youth and adults will be represented in better proportions in all phases of business service and community living. In addition, youths would receive academic credit for such experiences. The educational arsenal should include two other types of schools: the transitional school and the optional school. The final years of secondary school should offer a transitional experience in which newly acquired competencies could be tested in internships and apprenticeships in a community-based environment. Optional schools should be established, independent of the public schools, that would serve as a safety net for those youths who find the transition schools inappropriate to their educational needs.

National Youth Service

The most radical reform suggested by the commission is the establishment of a National Youth Service.

> *The Congress of the United States should establish a National Youth Service guaranteeing all American youth the opportunity for at least one year of full-time service to their community or to the nation.*
>
> *All youth, male and female alike, between the ages of sixteen and twenty-one should be guaranteed the opportunity to participate for at least one year of full-time service in the program; all youth between the ages of fourteen and twenty-one would be eligible for part-time participation in National Youth Service programs as part of school-related cooperative programs. Part-time service would be rendered in one's own community; full-time participation would most likely entail service in distant locations. . . .*
>
> *Congress should enact legislation requiring all American citizens, both male and female, at the age of eighteen to register for the opportunity to participate in a National Youth Service program. Mandatory registration will assure that all eighteen-year-olds receive counseling and guidance in relation to National Youth Service opportunities and values.* [p. 2]

Community and national service through the National Youth Service would carry rights and obligations. The commission recommended that employers advocate at least one year of service experience as a prerequisite for employment and, conversely, youths should receive a voucher for one year of educational entitlement for each year of service experience up to a maximum of four years. Thus, every young person would be able to earn a college education through his or her contribution to the community.

Employment

Child labor laws that were designed to protect youth now contribute to their unemployment. Those laws need systematic review and revision. The commission recommended a special emphasis on employment services to study the needs and cycles of employment. Among the suggestions is that youth in apprentice jobs be allowed to receive less than the minimum wage, to make it possible for businesses to afford the expense of employing and training them.

Juvenile Justice

Juvenile justice should renew its commitment to rehabilitation by designing a wide array of remedial services to that end. A distinction should be made between serious and not so serious offenders. Youths should not be incarcerated unnecessarily. Fines, restitution, and community service should be used as sanctions for less serious offenses. ''Whenever feasible, youth offenders should render an appropriate form of service to the neighborhood or to the community as a form of restitution for criminal offenses'' (National Commission on Youth, 1980, p. 4). Emphasis should be placed on preventing crime and delinquency. Preventative measures should focus on the home, the school, the neighborhood, and the community. In addition, the classification of status offender should be eliminated.

> *The jurisdiction of the juvenile court system should be limited to those acts that if committed by an adult, would constitute a criminal offense and to dependent and neglect statutes, which allow the courts to intervene in order to protect the health and welfare of young people.* [p. 4]

Health

Health care should be built into the structure of community organizations, such as boys' clubs, so that the delivery system for health care can better serve large and diverse numbers of youth.

TV Violence

> *The viewing public should continue to pressure the television networks and their local affiliates to assume increased responsibility for decreasing the levels of crime and violence on television to which youth are exposed.* [p. 4]

Policy

The development of good institutions in a democratic society that are responsive to the needs of the people they serve, requires the thought of concerned, informed citizens, careful planning, and dedicated workers to run them. To this end, the commission recommended establishing permanent policy-making councils at the local, state, and national levels. At the local level a Youth Transitional Planning Council would be appointed by a community's mayor or chief executive. The council should consist of a cross section of interested citizens and be granted legal status

As adolescents make their way into the future the path that they follow is in our hands. [Courtesy Helen Brooks.]

and autonomy from school boards. The mission of such a council in every community would be to smooth, shorten, and enhance the transition of youth to adulthood. The council would be charged to develop policies and programs. In addition, each governor would appoint a cabinet-level special assistant for youth affairs. That person would coordinate existing youth policies and programs, design new policies and programs for youth, and articulate a coherent youth policy among states. Finally, a youth policy should be developed on the federal level that would serve all youth, and not only targeted segments as is the case at present. National policy should be long-term to enable programs and personnel to develop. Policies from federal and state levels should prescribe direction and not restrict possibilities. Implementation should encourage local efforts to apply state and federal policies in creative ways. In this way, every community would solve its problems in different ways. Periodically, such commissions would meet and give recommendations.

These possible solutions to the challenge of educating adolescents are offered for the thoughtful consideration of college students who will be working with youth. There is no possibility of maintaining the status quo. Institutions, like children, need to grow and develop. We cannot keep our schools, our churches, our homes, and our businesses from changing because we change. But we can, by thinking about what we are doing, shape our institutions into environments in which children and youth can grow and become whole human beings. The future is in our hands.

Main Points

Content of Adolescent Experience

1. Adolescent experience is marked by an internal and external quest for self and the life-choices that must be made.

2. The youth of each decade are marked by their historical period and its events.

Search for Identity

3. Adolescence is a crucial time for identity and involves three commitments: sexual orientation, ideology, and vocational choice.

4. Early adolescents form a new identity through identification with the peer group and may form strong and lasting allegiances to a movement larger than themselves or may build antisocial gangs.

5. Middle adolescents are generally comfortable with who they are and can risk rejecting identification with the peer group.

6. In late adolescence identity may be achieved, foreclosed, diffused, or in a moratorium.

Relationships: Family Relations Between Generations

7. As children advance through their adolescent years, they become more involved with peers but do not always reject parental values. Adolescents continue to rely on parents, value them as counselors, accept their influence, and become involved in family activities.

Friends

8. There is a developmental pattern in friendship: in early adolescence friendships focus on activities that can be performed together; middle adolescence is the time for the most anxiety and insecurity about friends; beyond seventeen (late adolescence), friendship becomes a relaxed, shared experience.

9. Boys and girls seek friends for different reasons and react to friends differently. Girls value intimacy and interpersonal relationships and boys value action and friends to do things with.

The Peer Group

10. Friendship patterns are arranged in larger and larger groups in a hierarchical fashion: best friends, clique, crowd, and peer group.

Popularity

11. In American high schools popularity rests on personality and good looks, plus clothes for girls and athletic ability for boys.

Delinquency

12. Delinquency is the behavior of juveniles that is in willful and deliberate violation of law and that will bring them under legal judgment if their act is brought to the attention of law enforcement officers; about 5 per cent of adolescents are actually arrested and charged with crimes.

13. Delinquency may be caused by factors within the individual (psychology) or external factors (socialization).

Mental Disorders in Adolescence

14. Two major mental disorders are especially likely to appear in adolescence: schizophrenia and depression.

15. Suicide is the leading cause of death in college students and the fourth cause of death for all adolescents.

Life-Style Choices

16. As young people reach adolescence today they are confronted with an increased variety of choices that have far-reaching consequences and affect their current and future life-style.

17. Virtually every youth will have the opportunity to "do drugs" and will have to make a choice in the matter.

18. Whether to use alcohol is another area in which the adolescent must make a choice.

19. One of the major tasks of the adolescent is establishing a sexual identity.

20. Recent surveys indicate that the incidence of teenage sexual activity is increasing.

21. There continue to be adolescents (half of them, according to some surveys) who are not sexually active but who have given thoughtful concern to the place of sexual intercourse in their lives.

22. There is an increase in teenage pregnancy, abortions, illegitimate births, and marriages because of pregnancy. Each of these creates problems that may be beyond the resources and capacity of the teenage girl.

23. With the increased sexual activity of teenagers there has been an increase in sexually transmitted diseases.

Real Responsibility in the Real World, or Getting It Together

24. Youth are the hope of the future, for they will inherit the society in which we live and recreate it in their own image.

Toward New Environments for Youth

25. The National Commission on Youth examined the conditions of youth in our society, analyzed the institutions that serve them, and found those institutions wanting. They offered 27 recommendations for the creation of new environments that might better enable our young people to grow and to become the citizens our country needs. These included the creation of new learning environments in community-based environments and of a National Youth Service for full-time service to the community or nation.

Words to Know

cohort	**schizophrenia**
delinquency	**sexuality**
depression	**suicide**
peer	

Terms to Define

identity achievement
identity diffusion
identity foreclosure
identity moratorium
peer group

Concept to Discuss

identity

PART **VI**

Research and Theory

The scientific method entails a highly structured way of asking specific questions and gathering objective data to answer those questions. Such studies may be directed at describing development or explaining behavior. Behavioral scientists hope to be able to explain exact causes of behavior and the exact effect of events; however, the ethics regarding human experimentation do not allow them to do experiments that would reveal exact information if they would harm the subjects.

Every method of scientific study has advantages and disadvantages. A method must be selected in the light of questions that are to be asked. A theory often suggests questions and, in reciprocal fashion, research verifies or refutes theory. But not all pieces of a theory can be tested by research. Theories of human development involve certain assumptions about basic human nature that are not amenable to scientific study. Scientific support for a theory can only consist of observable data, and theories often are directed to processes and mechanisms that cannot be subjected to experimental scrutiny. Theory thus sometimes weaves isolated pieces of research into a comprehensive blanket to explain broad areas of human behavior. The scientist must finally rest on his or her convictions to evaluate underlying assumptions. Students, as scientists, must rely on their conviction and a thorough understanding of theory and its supporting research to understand the complexity of human nature and behavior.

CHAPTER 18

The Scientific Study of Children

Have you ever wondered

how science helps us to understand children?

what studies that describe development really tell us?

what techniques a scientist uses to study a developmental process that may take twenty years?

if scientific studies can really identify the *cause* of development?

how to plan a scientific experiment?

if all experiments are done in a laboratory?

if a scientist can use natural situations as an experiment?

if studies on a small group of children really give us important information about a larger class of children?

if a personal world view affects how a scientist chooses and conducts research?

if scientists have limitations on the kind of research that they can perform?

Science As a Source of Knowledge

The scientific method is an important invention in the intellectual evolution of our culture. It is a powerful tool that was forged to discover new knowledge. It is a formal procedure used to ask questions about the natural world with a set of strict methods for gathering evidence to answer those questions.

The technological society in which we live is possible because we learned how to ask the right questions and to know when we had found the answers. The tools of science were first applied to understanding, predicting, and controlling the physical world. As a result we live in a world with cars, airplanes, spaceships, electricity, atomic bombs, air conditioners, radio, television, computers, and laser beams. Our society faces many problems created by this technology, but few people advocate a return to a society stripped of technological aids.

The use of the scientific method to understand, predict, and control human behavior, growth, and development is a recent application of the tool. Sir Isaac Newton (1642–1717), whose principles of physics are considered to represent the foundation of a rational scientific understanding of the natural world, published his treatise *Mathematical Principles of Natural Philosophy* in 1687. It was almost two hundred years before Charles Darwin (1809–1882) attempted to use scientific knowledge and method to explain human evolution in his book *Origin of the Species*, published in 1859. The first modern formal laboratory for the scientific study of psychology was established in Leipzig, Germany, in 1879. Since then we have increasingly attempted to apply the tools of science to understanding human behavior, creating an ever-growing body of knowledge as we did so. Methods of studying children and adults constantly improve. With improved methods increasingly difficult questions can be asked.

Child Development As a Developing Science

In the scientific study of children we are fired by the urgency of our task. Each day counts in the life of a child, for at some point negative development may become irreversible. Child development is not a speculative science. It is instead a developing field in which basic and applied research must be conducted simultaneously.

Science does not give us absolute, enduring, and final truth about the development of children, but it can give us an understanding of the developmental process based on the available evidence. Intelligent professionals can then suggest logical applications of that knowledge that are in the best interest of the development of children. When new knowledge appears, intelligent professionals may change their advice based on the new limit of our understanding. Because our field of research is rapidly changing it is important that each student of child development become skilled at interpreting research and applying basic knowledge to situations in which children are growing and developing: homes, nurseries, schools, hospitals, churches, and community organizations. A critical appraisal of new research is a crucial factor in the quest for knowledge. The scientist and his or her colleagues and serious students must know how to examine each piece of research to see whether it is in error, how more exact knowledge can be gathered, and what are the most logical implications of that knowledge.

Research and Theory: A Partnership

A scientist does not arbitrarily choose a research topic. Research may be conducted to extend existing knowledge from previous research, to replicate an early study to check its findings, or to gather evidence to support or refute a theoretical position. Research is guided by theory, but neither represents final, absolute, eternal truth. They are reciprocal tools that are used to help us understand a subject. Tomorrow, with new knowledge, we may modify our understanding.

The major purpose of studying child development is to help students build a framework within which children can be understood: how they grow and how

The partnership of theory and research.

they become men and women. You will have to complete building this body of knowledge as new information is acquired. Science is our major tool for thinking about ourselves and our world today. Had we lived in another time, in another culture, we might have different tools. We have no assurance that we are happier with our increased store of empirical data, but we have no choice. We cannot use astrology or oracles to understand our children. We must use our culture and our science.

Methods of Studying Children

Understanding children through the tools of science is quite different from understanding them as family members, friends, or neighbors. There are many ways in which children can be scientifically studied. These range from descriptive studies that attempt only to *describe* the process of normal development, to experimental laboratory studies that seek to establish a *cause* of behavior or development. There are many variations of studies between these two extremes. The method of study is largely determined by the questions the researcher seeks to answer.

Descriptive studies generally seek to describe the natural process of development, or to describe normal behavior as it occurs in ordinary settings such as families, schools, and playgrounds, with persons whom the child ordinarily interacts, such as parents, playmates, and teachers. Data for descriptive research are gathered through actual measures of children, such as height and weight, through interviews in which children and parents are asked about their behavior in certain situations, and through observations of behavior. There is often a question as to whether the techniques of observation and interview actually provide information on natural behavior, or whether the act of observing and asking questions changes the behavior under observation and the data reported in interviews. People naturally tend to modify their behavior when they know that they are being observed. Similarly, researchers have found that people tend to distort data that are reported in interviews. Parents may attempt to present their children as a little more precocious, a little less troublesome, and themselves as more patient and loving than an unbiased observer might rate them. In order to avoid these distortions researchers sometimes resort to observing children indirectly. For example, many nursery schools that are used for university demonstration schools are equipped with one-way mirrors through which students can observe the children. The logic behind this technique is that children can behave normally only if they are unaware of being observed. Researchers have developed ingenious methods for gathering information unobtrusively. For example, if a researcher wanted data on interracial attitudes in a school, he or she might observe children at lunch and tally who they chose to sit beside, rather than ask direct questions about attitudes.

Experimental studies are designed to reveal a cause-and-effect relationship between two carefully identified events called *variables*. The researcher must carefully define the variables so that they can be separated from the on-going conglomeration of natural events. For example, we assume that all behavior has a cause; the problem, of course, is to identify those conditions that caused the behavior. As children develop we know that a specific behavior may be related to age, sex, IQ, the culture of the parents (which for research purposes is classified as the socioeconomic level of the parents), as well as a number of other conditions. The logic of experimental studies is to place subjects in a laboratory setting and to gain control of all the variables that may cause or influence a specific behavior. The researcher then holds all the variables constant except the one that he or she suspects causes the behavior under study. The variable suspected of causing the behavior is called the *independent variable* and the variable that is actually under study is the *dependent variable*. The researcher has a hunch that the independent variable *causes* the dependent variable to occur. With a carefully controlled experimental study, evidence for this relationship can be gathered. Such a relationship can only be established when the researcher has full control to conduct a true experiment. With children such control often is not possible and the researcher must conduct "almost" experiments in the natural environment: that is, the researcher takes advantage of natural events to study the effect of different conditions on children. For example, those children who attend day care and those who are cared for at home can be studied and compared, as can children living in one-parent families and two-parent families, or children with a deceased parent and living parents. A researcher cannot, of course, assign children to these conditions but can carefully match them in two conditions and study them for such things as self-concept, aggressiveness, school achievement, sex-role identity, or any other dependent variable that has been hypothesized as having been caused by such independent variables.

We will now discuss the methods of studying children. We will begin with the descriptive measure of longitudinal, cross-sectional and cross-sequential research. Then we will present laboratory methods and various adaptations of this method that are suitable for studying children in natural environments.

Descriptive Studies

Our systematic knowledge of children began with the simple gathering of data to describe the changes that take place as children grow and develop. The very first studies of this type were biographies of children. One of the earliest records we have is the biography of the infant heir to the French throne, Louis XIII, as recorded by the court physician, Heroard. Louis XIII was born in 1601, and the diary was begun soon afterward (Ariès, 1962). During the next three hundred years such diaries were the only systematic data kept about child development. The interest in scientific observation of natural phenomena stimulated Charles Darwin to record his son's development, which he published as support for his theory of the evolution of the species. Darwin argued that individual development reconstructed the evolutionary path of the species.

The biography of the single child has fallen into question as a source of useful information to generalize about all children. Because each child is an individual and has, in part, a unique pattern of development, to generalize to all children from a single child is not considered scientifically valid. In spite of this drawback, one of the most important works of this century was based on the study of only three

These children are the subject of a descriptive study. The adults in the picture are recording eating behavior. The children are not asked to perform any unusual actions and the purpose of the study is to describe normal behavior. [Courtesy Helen Canaday, Preschool Programs, University of North Carolina at Greensboro.]

children by their father: Jean Piaget very carefully observed and recorded the mental development of his three children in the 1920s.

The scientific study of children began early in the twentieth century. Researchers were intent in their objective of using the tools of science, but those tools first had to be devised and tested before they could be used to study large groups of children in a systematic way. Researchers wanted to describe the normal development of the child, which could then be generalized to groups of children without actually measuring all children. In other words, these scientists wanted to be able to *predict* the growth and behavior of children. The prediction of development remains one of the major goals of the behavioral sciences.

Longitudinal Research

If a researcher is interested in documenting changes related to age, then one way to gather data is to identify some children and watch them over a period of time. This method of studying children is termed longitudinal research. If you want to find out the effect of certain childrearing practices on adult behavior using longitudinal research methods, you must wait until the children become adults. If you want to construct charts for height and weight, you would identify children to study at birth and then weigh and measure them at regular intervals of three, six, nine months, and a year. After 21 years you would have the data to construct a growth chart. Thus, a major disadvantage of longitudinal research is the time it takes to gather data. If a longitudinal research is planned for 20 years, the researcher might die or lose his or her position before the research is completed, or subjects may die, move, or be lost for other reasons. Also, if the research area is crucial to children, the researcher must wait a long time for results that could affect policy and treatment programs. For example, if we want to design programs for retarded, hyperactive, or autistic children, we must wait 20 or 30 years for the data from longitudinal research; many children will already have grown up without the benefit of the program that might result from the study. In longitudinal research the effect of individual differences is controlled because the same subjects are used over and over again.

A second disadvantage of longitudinal research is that it may be difficult to generalize data to other groups. In longitudinal research we measure the same individuals over and over and thus eliminate some variation in measurement because of individual differences. In doing so, however, there is a smaller group and, therefore, less basis to generalize about other children. If we generalize to another group of children, we must assume that the two groups of children are the same in important ways. For example, can we assume that black children are the same as white children and, therefore, use data gathered only on white children to understand black children? In a similar fashion, can we generalize data gathered on boys to understand girls? Is research conducted in one country or culture applicable to children in another? Researchers and serious students of child development must answer these questions.

Another disadvantage of longitudinal research is that it does not offer the researcher a tool to separate age-related changes from historical effects and historical changes. If changes are found it is impossible to tell if they are from age changes or other cultural changes. For example, a researcher might be conducting a longitudinal study of the educational progress. A group of children could be selected at age five (when they enter kindergarten) and followed until they graduate from high school. Suppose that a drop was found to occur in arithmetic performance at age thirteen. The researcher must offer some explanation for this statistical fact. Is this

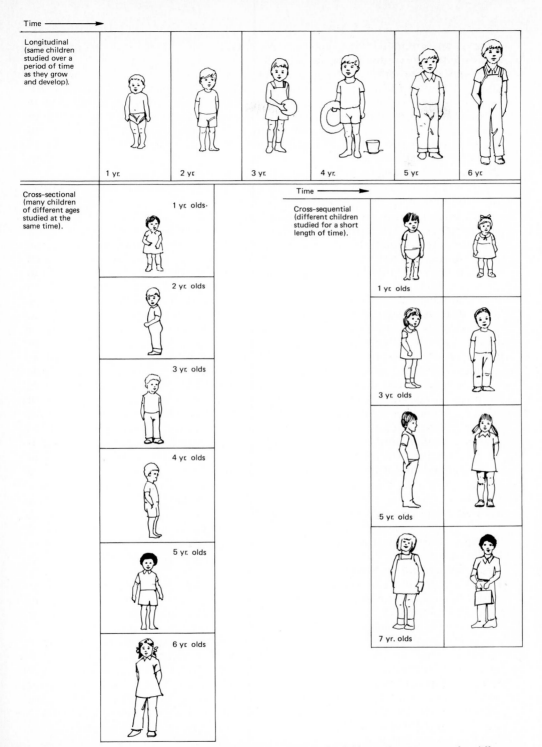

Time ⟶

Longitudinal (same children studied over a period of time as they grow and develop).

1 yr. 2 yr. 3 yr. 4 yr. 5 yr. 6 yr.

Cross-sectional (many children of different ages studied at the same time).

1 yr. olds·
2 yr. olds
3 yr. olds
4 yr. olds
5 yr. olds
6 yr. olds

Time ⟶

Cross-sequential (different children studied for a short length of time).

1 yr. olds
3 yr. olds
5 yr. olds
7 yr. olds

Longitudinal, cross-sectional, and cross-sequential research study children of various ages for different lengths of time.

drop in performance an age-related occurrence, or is it related to a particular historical event that would not be in effect for another group of children if data were gathered at another time? The researcher might so interpret the data that puberty marks a drop in arithmetic ability, or it might be that this particular study coincided with the advent of the hand-held calculator into the classroom and students stopped practicing arithmetic skills. Historical occurrences such as this are known as cohort effects. There is no way that descriptive research can identify causes that contribute to development. Only an experimetal study can do that.

Cross-Sectional Research

Cross-sectional research is a method of gathering data from a population of children using a representative sample of children at each age level. That is, a small group of children is selected from a larger group at each age level. The data the researcher needs are gathered from this *representative* cross section of age groups. If the researcher is interested in describing age-related changes in weight and height, for example, he or she would need to gather height and weight measures on children at all ages, from birth to twenty-one years of age. In a cross-sectional design, a group of children at each age interval is identified, weighed, and measured.

The advantage of a cross-sectional research design is that, in a short space of time, data can be gathered on a process that takes twenty-one years. In effect, we have compressed time. We have also used a large number of children and can more easily include children from different cultural backgrounds. An advantage of cross-sectional research is that many cultural groups can be represented in the sample. The different life experiences of children may have an effect on outcomes; these may be identifiable in cross-sectional research. A sample should represent all cultural groups for whom the resulting data will be used. The factor of different cultures in the sample may also be a disadvantage in this research design. If we are doing cross-sectional research, we must assume that age is the most important factor, and that the life experiences of children from birth to twenty-one will be about the same for children just born, as they were for the youths that are now twenty years old. This assumption may be erroneous. Another disadvantage of cross-sectional research is that each child appears only once and there may be variation in the results from individual differences rather than age-related changes. (Longitudinal designs control for individual differences.) Nevertheless, cross-sectional design is a valuable tool for gathering information on a large number of factors with a large number of children in the shortest time.

Cross-Sequential Research

Cross-sequential research design utilizes the characteristics of both cross-sectional and longitudinal research. It is an attempt to use the strength of both and to eliminate their disadvantages. A cross-sectional sample of a population is identified and then followed for a short period of time. Thus, if a researcher is interested in, for example, the growth of sex typing, groups of children might be identified representing age groups with two-year differences (for example, ages two, four, six, eight, ten, and twelve). The children then might be followed and interviewed over the period of two years. Thus, the researcher would begin with static cross-sectional research and also have the fluid changes that occur within the space of the intervening two years. This type of research can be completed within a short period of time, yet it follows individual growth and development.

Experimental Studies

A carefully controlled scientific experiment is a way of establishing a cause-and-effect relationship between two (or more) events. As previously mentioned, descriptive research can only *describe* development or behavior. With descriptive research we can describe in detail the effects of prematurity, the hyperactive child, the learning disabled child, the juvenile delinquent, and the overly aggressive child. Descriptive studies, however, can give no information on the *causes* of the condition or behavior associated with them. In order to correct such destructive developmental processes, we need to find the causes and change the causative conditions. Only experimental studies can give us information about cause of behavior. Therefore, scientists seek to conduct experimental studies that establish solid cause-and-effect relationships.

One of the cornerstones of scientific thought is that all behavior and events have a cause (or causes) that is identifiable and subject to the laws of the natural world. Because events are caused by other events, both of which are subject to the laws of nature, humans can know and control the natural environment. Such thinking was not always widespread. The Ancient Greeks, for example, believed that events (such as storms at sea and the outcome of battles) were caused by the pleasure or displeasure of the gods. If humans gained the favor of the gods, then events were favorable to them. When events were unfavorable for humans, they tried to change the course of those events by attempting to discover which god they had displeased and sought its favor. The Christian tradition in Western culture continued the belief in a supernatural control of events. For the last three hundred years or so Western thought has been dominated by the belief in rational thought and the natural cause of events. Although some people continue to believe in the intervention of a supernatural power as a cause of events, scientists, when speaking as scientists, do not. Scientists seek to find the natural cause of events. They seek causes through experiments.

In planning research that clearly establishes the cause-and-effect link, the scientist must first isolate both the condition (or conditions) suspected of being a causative agent—the independent variable—and the condition or behavior that is believed to be the effect—the dependent variable. The researcher must be able to identify two or more variations of the independent variable. For example, a researcher may suspect that physical punishment causes a child to be aggressive and express conflict in a hostile physical manner. In testing this idea through an experiment, the experimental condition, physical punishment, can be varied as (1) no physical punishment, (2) mild physical punishment, or (3) severe physical punishment. The researcher must very carefully define the independent variable and its different conditions. The dependent variable is dependent because it is caused by the independent variable, and it, too, may occur in several variations. Scientific research is a very cautious undertaking; with a carefully controlled experiment the researcher can state that independent variable A causes behavior B (the dependent variable) to occur. There are several formal steps that must be taken in designing an experiment:

1. Identify the problem.
2. Ask a question.
3. State a hypothesis.

4. Test the hypothesis.
5. Accept or reject the hypothesis.

In conducting an experiment all steps are carefully controlled by procedures and methodology. This control includes definition of the variables under study, unbiased selection of subjects, and following exact procedures in conducting the experiment. The results of an experiment are usually expressed in statistical terms, which are then analyzed using techniques that have proved valuable. The results are then interpreted.

Because we have used such physical sciences as chemistry and physics as a model for science, we think of experiments as being conducted in a laboratory. In the social sciences the laboratory may be a separate space in a research facility that is an actual laboratory, or a researcher may use the natural world as his or her laboratory. We will now look at research that is carried out in different settings and at how those settings may affect the research.

Experiments in the Laboratory

The data reported in the chapter on the visual preferences of newborns was attained through laboratory experiments. The simple statements of infants' visual preferences are summaries of many studies. A typical study might be conducted in the following way. Let us assume that a researcher is interested in knowing more about the visual preferences of newborns. Perhaps he or she ponders whether (1) infants learn to look at certain things because those things have become associated with pleasant events such as food, or (2) certain visual patterns are significant signals to which the newborn is genetically programmed to respond. This is an interesting question for armchair musing, but that will not provide an unequivocal answer. The presence or absence of an innate preference for certain visual patterns in newborns, then, is the problem that the researcher seeks to explore. Our researcher now must phrase his or her problem as a question, in such a way that it can be answered with the available tools of science. Not all questions are answerable through science. In addition, the question that our scientist asks will, by choice, be one that is consistent with his or her world view of the nature of human beings. The scientist might ask: Do newborns show a preference for certain visual forms? That question is too vague to guide an experiment. Therefore, the scientist reviews all the studies that have been done in this area and makes the next logical extension of that data. The question then might be phrased: Do newborns show a visual preference for curved forms over forms with straight lines?

This question is then rephrased in terms of a statement that is to be tested as to its truth or falseness. This statement is a hypothesis. A testable hypothesis might be: Newborns will (or will not) spend a greater amount of time looking at curved lines than at straight lines. Next the researcher must design a procedure that will test the hypothesis. This is done by systematically varying the experimental variable while holding constant all the other variables that might cause a difference in the amount of looking at the two stimuli.

The researcher must be imaginative and logical in thinking of other possible explanations; if, in a carefully designed experiment, infants look at both forms equally, then the explanation must be that infants have no innate preference for one form over the other. Some factors that might cause differences are

1. An innate preference for right or left.
2. Difference in size or brightness of the visual form.

3. The presence of a human closest to one form.
4. Peripheral light or movement closest to one form.
5. Placing the infant on a surface turned toward one form.

A good experimental design must take all these, and other, possible sources of rival explanations into consideration and control them.

The classical way in which such an experiment is conducted is to show newborns two visual forms and measure the time that each infant fixates on each form. After a large group of infants is studied, the total amount of time that all infants spent looking at both stimuli is compared. The data from such studies are in numbers. These numbers are then subjected to statistical analysis, from which the researcher can conclude whether the difference in visual fixation between the two forms is significant—that is, whether the difference had to do with the visual form or the time spent looking at the two forms was the result of random factors. This analysis allows the researcher to accept or reject the hypothesis.

The researcher will then share this new information with other scientists in the field. He or she might report the research in a professional journal that students and professionals can read or report it in a paper to be read aloud at a scientific meeting. In the final section of the report, whether written or read, the research will be interpreted in terms of its implications for understanding infants or in terms of the need for further research. The researcher might also indicate how the present research could be improved.

Experiments in the Natural Environment

Many causes of behavior that are of great interest in the field of child development cannot be tested under laboratory conditions. This is especially true of human infants. We cannot remove children from their parents and families to study their development; in fact, often it is the interaction within the context of the family that is of major interest to a researcher. Experimental control and procedures can be modified so that the natural environment becomes the laboratory. When studying subjects within the context of family situations, the researcher does not have full experimental control. Subjects cannot be randomly assigned to groups and treatment cannot be withheld and applied selectively to determine if such treatments change behavior. In such cases, researchers identify members of groups that form in the natural transactions of daily life and impose experimental design and statistical control on them. For example, we may want to identify the causes of delinquent behavior. One way to do this is to identify a group of delinquent youths, which is easily done by searching court records. Then a second group of youths could be identified, as similar to the first group as possible in age, sex, ethnic and racial membership, family composition, education and occupation of parent or parents, achievement in school, and so forth, but *without* a record of their delinquency. The two groups can then be studied and compared. Through a comparison of delinquent and nondelinquent youths we may begin to understand the factors in delinquent behavior. However, because such studies are conducted in the natural environment and experimental control is not possible, the results must be interpreted with caution. There is always the possibility that the actual cause of the behavior under study is some factor not isolated in the study. In some cases the researcher may be able to assign subjects to groups and conduct an experiment without laboratory controls. In other cases, the researcher may take advantage of a natural experiment in which the flow of events has assigned subjects to different conditions. An example of an experiment in the natural environment follows. It used strict experimental methods of random assignment—carefully matched groups that were treated differently and evaluated. This study is considered to be a classic and has been used as a model because of the careful procedures followed. It was conducted in the natural environment of women in their hospital rooms; the final data were collected in the natural situation of a well-baby clinic.

The study was designed and conducted by eight researchers (Kennell, Jerauld, Wolfe, Chesler, Kreger, McAlpine, Steffa, & Klaus, 1974). The title of the study is "Maternal behavior one year after early and extended postpartum contact." It was concerned with the effect of early contact between infant and mother. The researchers were interested in whether early contact between mothers and infants affected later maternal behavior. The study consisted of 28 women who gave birth to first children. All of the infants were full-term and healthy. The mothers were randomly assigned to an experimental or control group. The two groups were matched for age, marital status, and socioeconomic level. In addition, the infants were matched for sex and weight. In other words, the two groups were as similar in variables related to maternal behavior as was experimentally possible. The random assignment to the two groups guarded against any bias by the experimenters.

The design of the experiment called for the two groups of women to be given different amounts of contact with their new infants. The ethics of experimentation with humans dictates that an experimental condition can never be less than that provided by the normal environment, but an experimental condition can be enriching. The experimental condition was designed to provide more and earlier contact between infants and mothers than is usually provided in a hospital. The control group followed normal hospital procedures, which consisted of a brief glimpse of the baby at birth, brief contact for identification at six to eight hours after birth, and then visits of 20 to 30 minutes for feedings every four hours.

The experimental group of mothers was given their nude babies in bed for one hour in the first two hours after delivery. In addition, they were given the babies for an extra five hours on each of the next three days after birth. These mothers were the "early-contact group." The purpose of the study was to test the effect of early and extended contact with their infants on the maternal behavior of mothers. By matching the two groups, the experimenters attempted to balance within each group the variables that might affect maternal behavior. They chose one variable (early and extended contact), which they manipulated. This is the *independent* variable. The purpose of the study was to test the effect of this independent variable on maternal behavior, the *dependent* variable: that is, to test whether maternal behavior is dependent on (changed by) early and extended contact.

The researchers instituted one more control in the study. If the subjects, or those measuring the results, know the purpose of the study, they may adjust their behavior and perceptions to meet the experimenters' expectations. To guard against bias neither group of mothers was told of the existence of a different treatment group. In addition, those who made the observations in the follow-up studies did not know to which group the mothers had belonged.

Both groups of mothers were observed with their infants at one month after birth and again at one year. The context of the first observation was the infant's one-month physical examination. It was stressful for the infant. While the infant was being examined, the behaviors of the mother were observed. There was a measurable difference between the two groups. The early-contact mothers stood nearer their infants and soothed them more when they cried during the examination. The mothers were also filmed feeding their infants. Analysis of the films revealed that the early-contact mothers engaged in more eye-to-eye contact and fondling in the feeding situation. In interview, the early-contact mothers reported that they were more reluctant to leave their infants with someone else than were the mothers who did not receive early and extended contact. The mothers were observed again when the infants were one year old, during a physical examination of the infant. There was a significant difference in the percentage of time that the early-contact mothers spent assisting the physician and soothing the infants when they cried.

The researchers were interested in whether there were any long-term differences in the behaviors of these mothers as the infants grew older. When the infants were two years old, five mothers from each group were selected at random for further study. In this study the researchers were interested in the use of language with the infants. The results of the follow-up study revealed that the early-contact mothers used twice as many questions, more words per proposition, fewer content words, more adjectives, and fewer commands than did the mothers who had not received early contact with their infants. The researchers cautiously suggest that an extra 16 hours of contact in the first three days after birth appear to affect maternal behavior for as long as two years. This is a cautious conclusion because hundreds, if not thousands, of other variables and events would have intervened in the two years since the 16 hours of early contact.

Years of research and hundreds of studies have shown that seldom can development be expressed in simple linear terms. More careful research may reveal interaction with the sex and temperament of the child, the personality of the mother, the attitude of the father, perhaps racial, ethnic, and socioeconomic differences. Each of these variables needs to be untangled from the complex interaction that constitutes development. The scientific study of children is dedicated to this careful separation of interrelated variables.

Natural Experiments

The scientist often has no control over the variables suspected of affecting the development of children. The natural environment assigns children to one category or another: male or female; premature or full-term birth; low, middle, or high socioeconomic level; one- or two-parent families; normal or disordered genetics; and abusive or loving parents. Because the researcher cannot randomly assign subjects to such categories, they are selected from existing groups and the relationship between group membership (independent variable) and some other variable is then observed. The researcher makes no intervention and rather than exert control through laboratory experimentation, exerts control through statistical analysis of the data. Following is an example of a natural experiment.

This study was conducted to assess the effect of the mother's alcohol consumption during pregnancy on the newborn (Ouellette, Rosett, Rosman, & Weiner, 1977). It was conducted at Boston City Hospital, which serves a high-risk, inner-city population. Women who attended the prenatal clinic were asked to voluntarily participate in a 15-minute structured interview designed to obtain information on amount and variability of alcohol consumption. The rate of cooperation among the women was 92 per cent. On the basis of information from this interview, the women were classified as heavy, moderate, or rare drinkers. Women designated as heavy drinkers consumed an average of one and a half drinks a day, and occasion-

Table 18–1. Types of Research in Child Development and Advantages and Disadvantages of Each

Research	Advantages	Disadvantages
Descriptive Studies		
Longitudinal Same subjects measured repeatedly.	No errors due to individual differences.	Length of time required to complete. Attrition of subjects.
Cross-sectional Different subjects of different ages measured once or over short time.	Can be completed in short time.	Differences may be due to cohort differences not age. Errors due to individual differences.
Cross-sequential Different subjects measured over short time.	Short time. Both individual and cohort differences controlled.	
Experimental Studies		
Laboratory Experiments Experimental and control groups; random assignment of subjects; manipulation of independent variable.	Can establish cause-and-effect relationship. Variables can be controlled.	Subjects may not behave naturally.
Experiments in the Natural Environment Experimental and control groups; random assignment of subjects; manipulation of independent variable.	Subjects are more likely to behave naturally.	Many variables are uncontrolled that may confound results.
Natural Experiments		
Groups formed by natural selection. Experimenter has no control of assignment or manipulation of the independent variable. Results give a plausible explanation for behavior not a definite cause-and-effect relationship.	Subjects behave naturally.	Groups may be formed by an unidentified cause that is the actual independent variable (biased).

ally as many as five or six. Moderate drinkers drank more than once a month, but less than the criteria for heavy drinkers, whereas rare drinkers used alcohol less than once a month had never consumed five or six drinks on any occasion.

Interviews were conducted with 633 women. Of these, 9 per cent were classified as heavy drinkers, 39 per cent were moderate drinkers, and 52 per cent were rare drinkers. Several differences were found between the heavy drinkers and the other groups. The heavy drinkers were older, less likely to be married or living with the father of the baby, more likely to have other children, and were heavy smokers. The heavy drinkers did not report more miscarriages, abortions, or stillbirths, nor did their diet differ significantly from that of the other women.

Three hundred and twenty-two infants of these women were given detailed examinations soon after birth. These examinations included medical, neurological, and developmental aspects. The examiner did not know the drinking history of the infant's mothers, nor the details of pregnancy and delivery. (A blind procedure to guard against a biased report.) The result of the examination revealed that the offspring of heavy-drinking women were significantly more retarded in growth, as measured by length, weight, and head circumference than those of the moderate- and rare-drinking women. Seventy-one per cent of the infants of heavy drinkers had some abnormality, whereas only 36 and 35 per cent of the infants of moderate and rare drinkers, respectively, had any abnormality. The heavy drinkers had infants with twice the congenital malformations (29 per cent) as the moderate drinkers (14 per cent) and more than three time as many as the rare drinkers (8 per cent). Growth abnormalities were observed in 53 per cent of the infants of heavy drinkers, in only 18 per cent of the moderate drinkers, and 17 per cent of the rare drinkers.

The conclusion drawn from this natural experiment was the alcohol is related to malformations and retarded growth in infants when consumed in large quantities by the mother during pregnancy. In this experiment alcohol consumption was the independent variable, but the researchers were not responsible for subjecting the women to the condition. The researchers merely identified those who drank heavily, moderately, and rarely. The measure of the dependent variable was a thorough evaluation of the newborn, such as is given to many infants, especially those who are suspected of having a high probability of developmental difficulties. Thus, except for a 15-minute interview in which only information was exchanged, the researchers did not intervene in the normal course of events in the lives of either the mothers or the infants. However, by carefully identifying both the independent variable (drinking behavior) and the dependent variables (physical and neurological status of infant) and gathering data on these variables, valuable information was discovered. This is the method followed in many studies of child development. There are cautions that must be exercised in interpreting natural experiments, however, because experimental control is lacking. In this study, for example, we must look more closely at the women who drank heavily. Perhaps some third variable caused both the infants' abnormal development and the mothers' drinking behavior. We would need to find out why fewer of those women lived with a husband or father of the infant, and perhaps smoking is a rival cause for the infants' problems. Resourceful critics can think of other possible explanations. We accept the conclusions, but we also stress the need for further research to explain more fully how alcohol affects the fetus. Often the next step is conducted with animals, because human fetuses cannot be subjected to experimental manipulation. In this way one study builds on previous studies and our total knowledge grows, is modified, and is constantly re-evaluated.

Applying the Results of Experiments

One of the reasons that researchers follow these procedures and controls is to gather data that can be applied to a much larger group of infants (or children) and not merely to the individuals in the study. There are cautions, however, about generalizations. The researcher would like to be able to make statements about the larger group of children he or she has *not* studied, based on the results of the small number of children that *has* been studied. In order to do this the subjects used in the

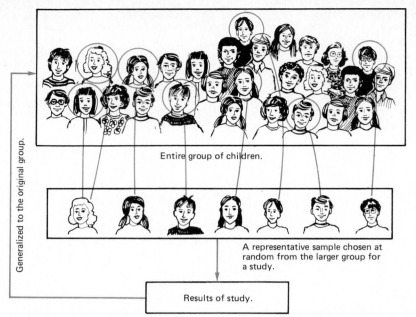

Entire group of children.

Generalized to the original group.

A representative sample chosen at random from the larger group for a study.

Results of study.

Every child cannot be studied individually. The group that is studied is a representative sample chosen at random from the larger group. Using this procedure, the results of the study can then be generalized to the entire group from which the sample was chosen.

study must be *representative* of the group about which the researcher wishes to generalize. For example, if we suspect that there is a difference in the development of boys and girls on a particular dimension, then the research subjects must consist of a comparison group of boys and a comparison group of girls. In a similar manner, we conduct research on some premature infants in order to be able to describe and predict developmental processes in all premature infants. Such data may not be applicable to full-term infants. There are many ways in which a group of subjects may differ from the larger group they represent. The researcher must guard against selecting a group that is unrepresentative or *biased*. One way to guard against bias in subject selection and to increase the chance of a representative sample is to remove the selection from the choice of the researcher.

If the subjects are chosen by random procedure, a researcher in a hospital, for example, may decide that he or she will test every third full-term healthy baby born in that hospital for three months. If the researcher needs to separate subjects by race or sex, the same procedure can be followed. Chance factors determine who is each third individual. Even with a carefully controlled experiment, generalizations about the cause of children's behavior are seldom based on a single study. If, in the entire literature of child study, we have repeated studies using different groups, different ages, and different kinds of children, all of which indicate similar results, then we can have more confidence in those results. Note that the previous sentence stated *confidence* in the results. A scientific experiment is not a foolproof method of proving truth. It is a method of gathering evidence in support of a hypothesis. Sometimes evidence erroneously supports a hypothesis and at other times fails to support a hypothesis that is actually true. Therefore, the scientist calculates the degree of confidence that can be placed in the obtained results, in statistical terms. We stated previously that the Ancient Greeks believed that events were arbitrarily caused by the will of the gods. Modern science also holds that events are arbitrarily caused, but the modern cause is random chance. Therefore, the scientist is actually trying to determine whether an event (dependent variable) can be attributed to the identified hypothetical cause (independent variable) or to random chance. Because random chance can produce the same effect as the experimental treatment, how can the scientist know whether his or her results were the result of the experimental treatment or random chance? The calculation of how often such results may have occurred by chance alone gives the degree of confidence that can be placed in results. A scientist reports results at the .05 level of confidence, if he or she calculates that the obtained results would have occurred only five times in 100 because of chance alone. When a scientist reports research at the 10 per cent level of confidence, it means that there is a 10 per cent chance that the results are due to chance alone, whereas the .01 level of confidence indicates that the chance is one in 100 that the results can be attributed to chance alone. These numbers are always reported as statistics when scientists report research in journal articles or at scientific meetings. The important thing to remember is that it is always possible in research in the social sciences that results are due to chance alone rather than to experimental manipulation. We must remember this in reporting and applying research. We can never place 100 per cent confidence in research. There is always a risk that we are wrong; we must accept the risk and proceed with our minds open to further knowledge.

Science is a powerful tool, and erroneous information can harm rather than help children. To guard against accepting information that is not applicable for certain children, studies should be subjected to critical evaluation and replication before being accepted, no matter how much the results appeal to our prior convictions, our political leanings, or our philosophy of human nature (Samelson, 1980).

World View: The Context for Studying Children

The hypothetical researcher in the sample experiment on the visual preferences of infants asked questions consistent with his or her world view, or, assumptions of the nature of humans. Those assumptions are broad and not amenable to scientific testing. The view accepted by the researcher is bounded by philosophical constraints that, in turn, determine legitimate research questions, as well as acceptable research methods (Porges, 1979).

One of the popular half-truths about science is that it is value free. That is, that all scientific research will eventually lead to the same inevitable truth. It is true that if two scientists ask the same question and use similar methods they will usually arrive at similar conclusions. Therefore, within the context of the same theory, the personal conviction of the scientist has no effect. The proposition that science is value free is half-false in that the scientist chooses the basic theoretical position within which he or she will work. In the social sciences this basic theoretical position is quite often a value position on the part of the scientist. There are a number of controversies in child development in which legitimate positions can be taken on either side. There is scientific evidence on both sides; therefore, the "truth" of the controversy cannot be ascertained from scientific evidence, contrary to the claims of the proponents of each side. Students and scientists must search their own value systems and understand the assumptions underlying their positions in assimilating evidence. Examples of controversies are the nature of IQ and abortion.

The popularization of science has led to the belief that the enterprise of "doing science" consists of a cooperative venture much like constructing a large building. Some workers lay the foundation and then carefully and consistently the building is constructed on it, floor by floor. Popular science does not envision the building of

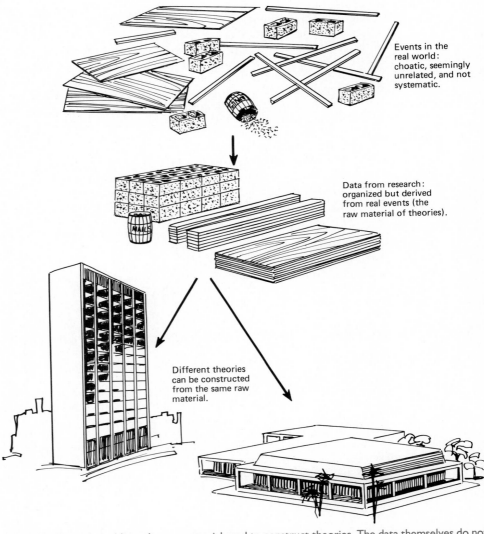

Events in the real world: choatic, seemingly unrelated, and not systematic.

Data from research: organized but derived from real events (the raw material of theories).

Different theories can be constructed from the same raw material.

Events in the real world are the raw material used to construct theories. The data themselves do not predetermine the shape and appearance of the theory. Different, and often opposing, structures (theories) can be constructed using and explaining the same events in the real world. To use an analogy, we can say that basic building materials can be used to construct two entirely different styles of architecture.

two buildings, one a windowless skyscraper and the other a one-story building, with workers vying for the available building materials. However, the actual enterprise of science more resembles the latter.

Thomas Kuhn (1970), in a book entitled *The Structure of Scientific Revolution*, presents the enterprise of science not as a smooth building process but as a process of revolution and counterrevolution. In Kuhn's view the quest for scientific knowledge results in the construction of different and irreconcilable theoretical positions. Communities of believers form around the conflicting theories and their acceptable questions and methods for answering them. Each theory is successful in explaining a part of "reality," and each can account for some of the scientific data that are accumulated through research. For a while there is a somewhat even balance between the two theories. Eventually one is able to account for more of the research data than its competing views and the balance of scientific opinion shifts to that theory, with the result that the other view loses its adherents. Thus, the enterprise of science progresses. We must keep in mind that one time the prevailing view of world geography, of intelligent and educated people, was that the earth is flat. The rash idea that it is round was ridiculed and its adherents opposed and sometimes persecuted.

In the field of human development we find two opposing world views, associated with two families of psychological theory: one sees the human being as a machine and the other as a living organism. These views are referred to as mechanistic and organismic world views, respectively.

The Mechanistic World View

The view of nature as a great machine has been the prevailing view in science since Isaac Newton (1642-1717) outlined the laws of mechanics. These laws were successfully applied to the physical and biological sciences. Early psychologists used physics (Newtonian mechanics) as a model for the scientific study of human behavior.

The machine as a model for human behavior is composed of discrete parts that operate in measurable and quantifiable ways. Psychological processes, according to the mechanistic view, operate according to immutable laws. These laws can be derived from basic principles and arranged in a hierarchy. This model sees the human, like other machines, as inherently at rest. Action is in reaction to an applied force (Overton & Reese, 1973). In the mechanistic world view, only a person's visible, objective behavior or its observable physiological processes are suitable subjects for study. Behaviors are events determined by a cause. If we can identify those causes we can then accurately predict the behavior or the events. Because we know the cause of thrust and movement in rockets and can control them, we can predict a rocket's trajectory to and from the moon and, indeed, throughout our solar system. Our scientists and technologists are able to guide (predict) the trajectory of rockets with an extremely small component of error.

Applying this model to human behavior, the reasoning of the mechanistic world view is that human behavior is as predictable as the trajectory of a rocket *provided that we can identify all the variables that are the cause of a behavior*. If we identify the causes, we can control them and thereby produce the effects we deem desirable and eliminate those we do not.

Medical science is based on the human body as a machine. The search for the cause of cancer or heart disease reflects this mechanistic model. The reasoning is that we must test various factors as the independent variables that cause the cancer or heart attack. If we can identify those causes, we can prevent cancer or cure it. The model has worked remarkably well in biology. We have not been as successful in applying this mechanistic model to behavioral science. The question is: Does behavior work the way biology does? Are the variables so many and so subtle that we can never effectively control them? The approach to solving social problems such as child abuse has been to conduct research programs that will identify the cause of the problem. The logic is that, if we can identify the variables that contribute to the incidence of child abuse, then we can change the variables and eliminate the problem.

In many cases we are frustrated in our attempt at human engineering. Both the social system and the educational system seem to resist attempts to engineer better results: achievement scores are falling, drug and alcohol abuse seem to be increasing among youth, teenage pregnancy is epidemic, and many high school graduates are functionally illiterate.

Although this mechanistic model has not given us the solution to all practical problems, it has been very productive in adding to our store of knowledge about human behavior. A member of the family of the mechanistic world view is the broad category of social-learning theory, of which behaviorism and experimental child psychology are most relevant to the study of development.

The Organismic World View

The organismic world view sees the human as a spontaneously active, organized, living system. Living organisms are inherently disposed to spontaneous action rather than to rest. The human being is seen the source and initiator of actions and not a passive reactor to external stimuli, as the mechanistic view holds. Organismic entities have parts, as do machines, but these parts cannot be adequately studied in isolation from the whole system, nor can the complete system be known from knowledge of the parts. The parts gain definition and function from their relationship to the whole, and the whole is greater than the sum of the parts. Because a functioning organism is spontaneous and dynamic, behavior cannot be fully measured and predicted. Instead, research based on the organismic view seeks to *identify* and *describe* the ways in which the parts of a living system relate and function in an integrated, dynamic way (Overton & Reese, 1973; Porges, 1979).

The organismic approach holds that organisms change in an orderly progression over time—that is, they *develop*. Development is guided by principles. The research goals of those who hold the organismic world view is to discover those principles and describe how they function in developing organisms. Some of the organismic principles follow here.

1. Development has a direction. This direction is from the simple to the complex: from the less organized to the more organized and can be described as an hierarchical arrangement.
2. Development proceeds toward an end state.
3. Development is a product of the interaction between heredity and environment.
4. The organism seeks a state of homeostasis—that is, a balance among parts. The organism can initiate internal adjustments to maintain this balance.

These principles applied to physical development are relatively clear, but it is difficult to apply them to the abstract levels of emotional and cognitive development. For example, development from the simple to the complex is easily demonstrated in prenatal development, in which the organism grows from a single cell to a human being of several billion cells. However, it is more difficult to demonstrate the increasing hierarchical complexity of social and intellectual skills. The opposite view (mechanism) recognizes that with age there is an increase in skills, but these are viewed as a horizontal elaboration, rather than as a vertical hierarchical increase in organization.

In biological terms, living organisms proceed toward nonlife, or death; but again, in considering abstract areas it is not so clear. Is intellectual development guided by an innate direction toward a certain quality of thought? Many theorists have elaborated stages of development. Underlying these stage theories is the principle that within the organism there is an innate push for development through these stages toward the highest stage of development.

The family of theories that can be grouped in the organismic world view includes the psychoanalytic approach of Sigmund Freud and Erik Erikson, the cognitive theory of Jean Piaget, Lawrence Kohlberg's theory of moral development, and the broad category of humanistic psychology expressed most eloquently by Abraham Maslow in his hierarchy of needs.

Heredity or Environment? Conflict in World Views

Proponents of the mechanistic and organismic world views have long argued over the contributions of heredity and environment in determining development and behavior. For centuries philosophers, educators, ordinary people, and scientists have debated, speculated, and experimented to answer the question of whether nature (heredity) or nurture (environment) is the more salient influence on human development. Theorists can no longer hold dogmatically to the position that either heredity *or* environment alone determines development. Developmental research points overwhelmingly to an interaction between them. Thus, the question for research is actually how the two interact to mediate development (Anastasi, 1958). The problem becomes complex because different aspects of development are affected differently by heredity and environment. These dimensions need to be identified one by one; then the question of *how* heredity and environment interact in the regulation of development must be carefully described. This requires an ingenious research design and carefully executed procedures. We will now examine heredity and environment and indicate the ways in which they interact.

Heredity

In speaking of heredity, we are referring to that clump of DNA that is at the center of each cell in the body. It is the material, half from the mother and half from the father, that contains the instructions for development. These instructions are very complex, are in effect throughout our lifetime, and are switched off and on at different times by a process that we do not yet understand. The important point is that biological inheritance is not like material inheritance. If your parents give you a legacy of money or property, you may use it or not, it is a passive factor, outside of you. Biological inheritance, on the other hand, is an active factor throughout life. Each heartbeat is guided by this genetic information; each meal is digested and absorbed using this information. When information is lacking, as in diabetes (in which sugars and starches are not converted into a usable form), the physical system is threatened. Throughout our lifetime new cells are being formed as old cells die. These cells follow the original genetic blueprint whether the organism is seven or seventy years old.

We have a fair knowledge of the regulation of physical development, defects, and disease by heredity, but we are much more vague about the genetic control of behavioral systems. Research is seeking to supply knowledge of the relationship between heredity and behavior.

Environment

Environment is also more pervasive than we sometimes think. Environment consists of all those factors that support life, as well as the physical and psychological context within which development takes place. The factors of environment are so complex that it is impractical to attempt to equate fully the two environments of two individuals. For example, we know that identical twins have the same heredity; therefore, they must have begun on an equal par yet we seldom find that twins have the same birth weight. What then, accounts for the difference in birth weight? These two individuals, with the same heredity, are subjected to subtle differences in environment from the moment of conception. It may be that one has a more favorable position in the uterus. It may be that the umbilical cord of one allows more nutrients and, thus, greater growth. One may be closer to the heartbeat of the mother and, therefore, be stimulated more by the sound. Finally, one must be born first; and the second is always in greater danger of a birth accident.

We find, in the case of twins, that one tends to be more dominant. Does one twin learn (through environment) to cry louder, and thus to cause the parent to

Table 18–2. Concordance of Heredity and Environment from Greatest to Least by Familial Relationship, Per Cent Shared Genes, and Similarity of Environment

Relation	Per Cent of Shared Genes	Environment Similarity	
		Similar	Dissimilar
Identical twins (monozygotic)			
reared together	100	extremely similar	
reared apart	100		very dissimilar
Fraternal twins (dizygotic)			
reared together	50	very similar	
reared apart	50		very dissimilar
Siblings			
reared together	50	similar	
reared apart	50		very dissimilar
Parent/child			
same household	50		dissimilar (different cohorts)
different household	50		extremely dissimilar (different cohorts)
Unrelated children			
same household	0	similar	
different household	0		very dissimilar

more quickly meet his or her needs? The factors of environment are pervasive and ever-present but must be understood, if we seek to understand human growth and development.

Interaction of Heredity and Environment

It is only at the moment of conception that we can actually separate heredity and environment. As soon as the ovum is fertilized by the sperm and begins to divide, it is dividing in time and space—that is, in an environment. Factors of this time and space, then, affect the way in which that basic genetic material is shaped and grows and what it becomes. Thus, the actual truth of development is that it is the interaction between the genetic information and time and space factors. The genetic effects themselves become part of the environment, and of course, the environment can act on the genetic material, usually in negative ways. Let us illustrate this interaction. The sex of the child is determined at conception. Early in prenatal life, that genetic assignment switches on the production by the fetus of testosterone (male hormone) or estrogen (female hormone), depending on the genetic sex assignment. The presence of those hormones becomes part of the environment in which the fetus is developing and regulates a differentiation in development.

Another factor that is extremely important is that environment does not affect each individual in the same way. We use the rather inexact terms of *predisposition* and *susceptibility* to indicate a condition in which a given individual may be more sensitive to certain environmental stimuli than another individual. The implication is that it is the genes that make an individual more susceptible. For example, let us consider the question of allergies. In allergy some condition in the environment stimulates the body to build antibodies against a substance. Certain agents, such as arsenic, cause adverse reactions to all living organisms, but in the case of allergies, it is the sensitive condition of the individual that determines whether he or she will react to the agent. This sensitivity may be the result of a previous environmental experience or a genetic inability to tolerate the substance. The point is that allergy is the result of interaction between environmental and genetic factors.

The motivation for the study of child development is to create optimum conditions for the growing and becoming of each child. Leaders in the field have expressed the view that the ultimate standard for judging research on children must be whether it is useful and relevant to social conditions (Baumrind, 1980; Mussen, 1977). To the extent that we understand the factors that regulate these developmental processes, we can provide for each child those conditions that will make possible his and her best development. We cannot, as yet, materially affect genetic endowment, but knowledge of those physical factors that limit and expand basic genetic potentialities allows us to alter those conditions. For example, although diabetes is a genetic defect, it can be controlled by diet and chemicals. We can alleviate potential damage through environmental control. In similar fashion, a child with the genetic potentiality to be an Olympic star, a creative scientist, or a talented painter needs an optimum environment for its full potential to be realized. Stern (1956) has expressed this as a rubber-band hypothesis. By it he means that the same basic genetic potential can expand or contract, according to a good or poor environment. We want to learn to engineer the best possible environments for the best expression of genetic endowment. It is clear that our speculation in this matter will not suffice. We need good scientific data. Because these factors are so intertwined, the question of how to study them is of prime importance.

Ethical Considerations in Studying Children ─────────

A psychologist trained in the scientific method wanted to investigate whether the emotion of fear was innate or learned. He found a very young child, named Albert, who spent his days in a hospital because his mother worked there. Albert, as do all babies, responded to a loud noise with a startle reflex, in which the arms are thrown out, and the body becomes rigid. The stimulus of a loud noise or sudden loss of support elicits this response. The psychologist showed Albert a white rat, to which the infant displayed no fear. He even touched the animal and seemed quite comfortable in its presence. The psychologist then clanged a hammer on a metal bar behind Albert. Albert responded to this noise with a startle reflex. For the next several days the psychologist showed Albert the rat and at the same time made a loud noise behind his head. When he heard the noise Albert cried and reacted in an upset manner. After several days, Albert cried and showed reactions of "fear" when the white rat was brought into the room even when no noise was made. The psychologist then brought a white rabbit into the room, and Albert showed the same fear reactions as to the white rat—in fact any white, furry object, including a Santa Claus mask, caused Albert to signal fear. The psychologist was quite pleased with the experiment, for he had demonstrated that the emotion of fear was a learned response to specific stimuli when paired to the innate startle response (Watson & Raynor, 1920; Watson, 1928). On the other hand, Albert's mother was quite unhappy with the treatment of her infant son and removed him from the hospital. The psychologist was J. B. Watson, the father of behaviorism, and the child was "Little Albert." Psychologists and students have since wondered if little Albert went through life afraid of white, furry objects. In all probability he did. This

Research ends do not justify the means and research must always be conducted in a way that protects children. [Courtesy Helen Canaday, Preschool Programs, University of North Carolina at Greensboro.]

experiment was performed sometime between 1917 and 1920. It could not be done now because we consider such experiments with children to be unethical. There is much information about child development and behavior that could be obtained with careful experiments done by ingenious psychologists. However, respect for the rights and welfare of children make it impossible to perform these experiments. We cannot deprive children in order to test the effects of such deprivation. Nor can we knowingly expose them to any agent that we suspect will cause physical or psychological harm. In recent decades we have become increasingly concerned about human rights. One result of this concern is a code of ethics for researchers who use human subjects. The American Psychological Association (1973) published *Ethical Principles in the Conduct of Research with Human Participants* (rev. 1977). In 1973 the Society for Research in Child Development published ethical principles specifically related to research with children. In addition, the National Commission for the Protection of Human Subjects of Biomedical and Behavioral Research has spoken for the federal government on the question of ethics when using human subjects in research (Barber, 1976).

The essence of these principles is that investigators have a dual responsibility: to science *and* to human welfare. Researchers are ethically bound to protect the dignity and welfare of participants in experiments. The document of the Society for Research in Child Development (1973) states:

> *No matter how young the child, he has rights that supercede the rights of the investigator. The investigator should measure each operation he proposes in terms of the child's rights, and before proceeding he should obtain the approval of a committee of peers.* [p. 3]

In research with children the major ethical issues concern the *right to privacy, informed consent* and, *truth in experimentation.*

Right to Privacy

One of the fundamental human rights expressed in the American system is the right to privacy. Our police cannot search our homes without a warrant, and we cannot invade others' privacy without due process. In a similar fashion, we cannot invade another person's psychological space. The right to privacy in research has several aspects. First, the results must be held in strict confidence. This is especially important in longitudinal research, in which the subjects are identified and followed. In studies in which data are gathered only once, individuals are often not identifiable in the group data.

A second aspect of the right to privacy forbids investigation in which subjects are unaware that an investigation is taking place. Many studies depend on the unawareness of the subjects; however, such studies can be damaging, especially when there is experimental manipulation, such as deceit. There is some question about an invasion of privacy when children are watched through one-way mirrors or are the subjects of studies of which neither they, nor their parents, are aware.

Informed Consent

Ethical principles from several professional organizations are in agreement: participants must be informed of the purposes and procedures of research and their participation must be voluntary and based on a clear understanding of those purposes and procedures. In studying children consent must be obtained from guardians. Consent cannot be coerced, although subjects can be paid to participate in research.

Children themselves should, whenever possible, have the freedom to participate in an experiment or to discontinue participation at any time. Special consideration must be given to research on infants and retarded or severely disturbed children. The same principle of informed consent applies to the parent or those who have the power to act in place of the parent. Consent should be obtained in writing. The underlying human value here is protection of the individual's right to free choice. In research with children we must be careful that adults who give consent act in the child's best interests and fully understand the purpose of the experiment.

Truth in Experimentation

Closely related to the principle of informed consent is the ethical principle that researchers must also be truthful about the purpose of the research. It is obvious that a subject can only give informed consent when the researcher has been truthful about the experiment's purpose and procedures. In examining certain questions it is easier for the researcher if the subjects are unaware of the actual intent of the study. For example, if a researcher wants to study truthfulness or how much resistance a group of subjects has to temptation, a true measure cannot be obtained if the subjects are told that they are going to be watched and measured for those factors. Actual behavior in speeding on a deserted road, taking a bar of candy when one cannot possibly be found out, or returning found money can only be accurately ascertained when the subject feels that he or she is alone and unwatched. To tell a subject, "Now we are going to leave some money on the floor in this room and see if you attempt to find the owner or keep it," would, of course, not be a good method to determine the honesty of subjects, even though the researcher would be adhering to the principle of truth in experimentation. These constraints do require the researcher to use creativity and invent other methods to study such questions. The reason that ethical researchers stress being truthful with subjects is that deceitful research can have harmful effects on the subjects.

Most research is conducted in a university setting or under the sponsorship of a federal agency such as the National Institutes for Mental Health. In these organizations research proposals are reviewed by a committee of scientists familiar with the field of research. The reviews have as a major concern the protection of human subjects' safety and rights. There are both institutional guidelines and professional ethics that must be met in planning and executing research. In research the ends do not justify the means; as a humane society, we must be ever mindful that while we gather knowledge we protect the children involved and apply it in a way that truly benefits their growth and development.

Main Points

Science As a Source of Knowledge

1. The scientific method uses a formalized procedure to ask and answer questions in order to understand, predict, and ultimately to control natural phenomena.

Child Development As a Developing Science

2. Child development is a developing field, and as such must both conduct basic research and apply it simultaneously. It does not provide absolute, enduring, or final truth about the development of children because it has a rapidly expanding base of knowledge.

Research and Theory: A Partnership

3. Research is guided by theory and theory weaves together isolated pieces of research.

Methods of Studying Children

4. The questions asked by the researcher determine the method used for the study.

Descriptive Studies

5. Descriptive studies seek to describe naturally occurring behavior, events, situations, and normal development.

6. Longitudinal studies examine changes by following one group of subjects over a period of time.

7. Cross-sectional research is a method in which data are gathered from representatives of a number of age levels at the same time.

8. In cross-sequential research design data are collected over time from subjects who represent different age levels.

Experimental Studies

9. Experimental studies can establish a cause-and-effect relationship between two (or more) events or conditions.

10. The causative event is known as the independent variable and the effect as the dependent variable.

11. In a laboratory setting the researcher is able to control variables suspected of causing a specific behavior so that their effect may be studied and analyzed.

12. In a natural setting the researcher may not have full experimental control but may gain some scientific control through techniques of data collection and statistical analysis.

13. Natural experiments occur in which existing groups differ on an independent variable and the effect of that difference is measured on a dependent variable, but the researcher does not assign groups or administer treatment.

14. In accepting and applying research results, the probability that the results of the research have not occurred by chance must be considered. The agreed-on acceptability of this probability is 5 in 100 and is written as .05 level of confidence.

World View: The Context for Studying Children

15. Some controversies in child development exist because questions were asked and results were found based on different assumptions about the world and human nature. Basic philosophical positions leading to these assumptions are rarely amenable to scientific testing. Researchers and students should be aware of their philosophical positions and the values they endorse.

The Mechanistic World View

16. In the mechanistic world view human beings are seen as machines that react according to immutable laws of cause-and-effect.

The Organismic View

17. In the organismic world view, human beings are seen as spontaneously active, organized living processes with structure. They are believed to change, develop, grow, and initiate activity.

Heredity or Environment?

18. The solution to the question of heredity or environment focuses on how heredity and environment interact to affect development, rather than on how much one or the other contributes.

19. Heredity and environment interact to limit or expand what is given by each.

Ethical Considerations in Studying Children

20. Ethical considerations of the rights and welfare of children make it impossible to perform many experiments that could provide answers about child development.

21. The right to privacy assures the confidentiality of data gathered in research and forbids the use of subjects for research without their knowledge.

22. Ethical principles dictate that participants in research must be informed of its purpose and procedures and that their participation must be voluntary and based on a clear understanding of the research.

23. Ethical researchers must be truthful in the information given subjects concerning the intent of the research.

Words to Know

bias	**experimental**
cross-sectional	**hypothesis**
cross-sequential	**longitudinal**
descriptive	**mechanistic**
ethical	**organismic**

Terms to Define

cause-effect relationship
dependent variable
descriptive research
independent variable
level of confidence
mechanistic world view

organismic world view
random assignment
representational sample
scientific method (experimental method)
world view

CHAPTER 19

Theories:
A Closer Look at Freud, Erikson, Piaget, Social Learning, and Humanistic Psychology

Have you ever wondered

> what Freud's theory of personality is?
>
> who has extended Freud's psychoanalytic theory and how?
>
> if there is a theory of development that covers the whole life span?
>
> how Piaget explains the development of abstract thought?
>
> what social-learning theory is?
>
> what the principles are that govern behavior?
>
> how different theories explain the same behaviors?
>
> if some needs are more important than others?
>
> what humanistic psychology is?

At this point in the development of the science of child development we do not have a comprehensive theory of how children grow and develop. Such a theory would be applicable to all facets of development. It has been the hope of the social sciences that unifying principles could be discovered that would apply across cultures, socioeconomic situations, and individual differences. This unification for the physical sciences was accomplished when Isaac Newton developed his laws of physics to describe the structure and nature of the physical world. They have proven to be applicable across many fields, have unified previously fragmented knowledge, and have made possible the technological advances of Western civilization.

We would like a theory comparable to that of growth in biology (unilinear, end-state oriented, irreversible, and qualitative). Our understanding of biology generalizes across all species and is applicable to all living organisms, both plant and animal. Principles of growth, metabolism, disease, and genetics hold across all these forms of life. In fact, Mendel's basic knowledge of heredity came through experiments on plants, yet they hold true for human heredity as well.

Theories in child development are diverse: they attempt to explain aspects of development such as cognition, personality, and moral behavior as well as discrete aspects of development such as speech, reading, and child abuse.

Because the discipline of child development is relatively young, we must be satisfied with our limited theories while we work to interpret larger and larger areas of development. In this chapter we will outline Freud and Erikson's psychoanalytic theories, Piaget's cognitive theory, and social-learning theory, including some of the proponents of this theoretical approach. Freud described *psychosexual* development and evolved a theory of personality. Erikson described *psychosocial* development and concentrated on the development of the ego and the social tasks that the individual must meet. Piaget described cognitive development in an age-graded sequence. Social-learning theory explains new forms of behavior as responses to environmental experiences. Each of these theories has been applied in the context of development in other chapters in the book. Here we will present their framework over a wide age span.

Psychoanalytic Theory: Freud

Overview

The psychoanalytic view of human behavior holds that actions are motivated by drives from within a person. Through experiences in the environment, a dynamic personality develops within each of us. Psychoanalytic theory is primarily concerned with describing the structure and dynamics of this personality. Personality is basically set in the first three years of life but continues to affect styles of behavior throughout life.

In the psychoanalytic view, personality develops as three components: the id, ego, and superego. The basic energy, and motivation, for action is instinctual. This instinctual energy, present at birth, is called id. In childhood, the ego and superego are differentiated from the original instinctual component. These three aspects of the personality are often in conflict and one of the main tasks in life is to maintain some balance (homeostasis) among them. In the psychoanalytic view, human nature is largely driven by instinctual forces, so that internal conflict is inevitable. The essence of personality is the dynamic functioning of these components. Dissecting the components will reveal little about personality. Each individual is different and the preferred method for understanding the individual is the clinical interview, which seeks to describe personal dynamics. The psychoanalytic method includes dream analysis, free association of ideas, and reexperiencing early life incidents in order to understand them. These methods of interpretation are necessary because much of behavior is controlled by unconscious wishes. The individual is often unaware of the real meaning and motivation of his or her behavior. The psychoanalytic approach has emphasized the importance of early experiences, and especially the parent-child relationship, in determining later personality development.

In this theory, the stages of development are biologically determined. That is, the *process* of development is the same for all human beings. The *content* and outcome of those developmental stages are determined by the social and psychological environment. Thus, the basic structure of development is biologically determined, whereas the final product is individualized by the environment. Development is described in age-graded stages. This theory has been productive in the construction of logical systems, but because the theory uses many *hypothetical constructs** that are not directly measurable, the research has often been questioned and interpretation has proven to be difficult. For example, the theory focuses on the importance of the quality of the love relationship between mother and infant in the first year of life. First of all, love is a very difficult dimension to measure because it is an abstract concept. Second, quantification of love is even more difficult—especially because the infant cannot relate his or her experiences in the matter and research has repeatedly found that parents' reports are often unreliable. Third, the measurement of quality (of relationship) is a much more difficult task than assessing the quantity of any behavior. Even with these difficulties, psychoanalytic theory has been, and remains, extremely useful in understanding children and the development of emotional life. Freudian theory is very complex and so we will only sketch its bare outline here, emphasizing aspects that are useful in understanding child growth and development.

Development of Personality†

Personality is a difficult term to define, but in essence it refers to an inner core of traits and/or characteristics that are consistent and stable over time. Child researchers have questioned the stability of traits over time in many different ways. Research in this area is inconclusive, but Freud was firm on the subject: the basic personality, he believed, was formed in the first few years of life within the intense relationships of the family. Certainly by the age of six the basic personality was formed. People thus must live with that structure unless they attempt to restructure their personality through the long, arduous task of psychoanalysis.

Id

The id is the source of all psychic energy. It is present at birth. Its main function is to satisfy the organism's basic biological and instinctual needs. The id represents the inner world of subjective experience and has no knowledge of objective reality. It is the repository of all instincts and is in close communication with the bodily processes and the instincts associated with them. The id derives energy from the bodily processes and the satisfaction of instincts is the driving force (motivation) behind the personality. For Freud there were two broad instincts: the life instincts (eros) and the death instincts (thanatos). Life instincts are love, growth, positive action, and, through their sublimation, cultural achievements in the arts, education, government, and culture. Death instincts are hate, hostility, destructiveness, aggressiveness, and civilization's negative tendencies: murder, torture, and war.

How do instincts motivate behavior? When all the bodily needs are satisfied, the organism is in a state of equilibrium and there is no motivation to act. When there is a deficit in bodily needs, however, tension mounts, the drive to act builds, and the organism becomes physiologically aroused. The amount of arousal determines motivation. Humans must live with this basic instinctive nature and keep it satisfied but under control.

---

* A hypothetical construct is an idea that is useful in explaining behavior or development, but for which there is no empirical proof of existence. Therefore, the researcher or theorist constructs a hypothesis (hypothetical construct) that such an entity exists.

† The following material on psychoanalytic theory has been adapted from C. S. Hall and G. Lindzey, *Theories of personality* (2nd ed.) New York: John Wiley, 1970.

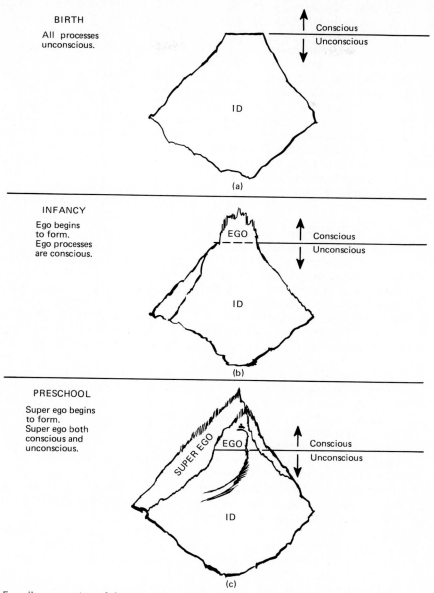

Freud's conception of the structure and development of personality. According to this theory, the basic personality structure forms in the first five years. At birth only the id (a) is present and this component is unconscious. The ego (b), the conscious component of personality, differentiates out of the id in infancy, and the third component, the superego (c), which is both conscious and unconscious, differentiates in the preschool years. These three components function in a dynamic relationship throughout life.

The id operates on the *pleasure principle*. The id asks of every experience: Is it pleasurable? If it is, the id seeks to continue it. If the experience is painful, the id seeks to avoid it. The id, however, cannot act in the objective world but can only seek to satisfy instincts through reflexes and imaging.

In considering reflex action we will trace the events in a hungry infant. Physiological hunger begins to increase tension, which mobilizes the instinctive behavior of sucking. As tension mounts, other reflexive behaviors, such as fussing and crying, are called into action. If the infant is not fed, there is soon a howling rage. One of two things might happen here. An adult may respond and feed the infant. In which case, the tension is released and equilibrium is restored. If the infant is not fed, however, the tension mounts, crying increases, and the infant may cry itself into an exhausted state. If there is repeated overwhelming tension, which the infant cannot handle, the results are dire consequences for personality development and a pervasive emotional feeling of insecurity.

A misunderstanding of the necessity of satisfying the instinctual impulses led to permissiveness in childrearing following the popularization of Freudian theory. Freud always insisted that the id must be controlled: the child must learn self-control; however, in infancy, a baby needs love (attachment) and the secure feeling that its tensions will be relieved by a loving caregiver.

The second way in which the id seeks to satisfy instinctive drives is to form a picture of an object that will satisfy the drive. The id cannot distinguish between fantasy and reality and cannot distinguish between an image *conceived* within the mind and one *perceived* through the senses from the external world. Thus, dreams, fantasies, and hallucinations are all images from the id and are attempts to satisfy instinctive drives. As tension mounts, the images become more and more insistent. Perhaps you have found yourself studying for a test and felt that you could not take time out for dinner. As you studied late into the evening the image of a hamburger and french-fries might have kept coming into your mind, so that finally you couldn't keep your mind on your studying and went out with friends to get a hamburger.

The process of the id is *not conscious*. We are not aware of the workings of instinct and reflexes. One of the great discoveries of Freud was the *unconscious mind* and its importance in determining behavior. To visualize this think of an iceberg. Only about 10 per cent of an iceberg is visible from the surface of the ocean. The other 90 per cent is unseen and unpredictable. This unseen portion constitutes a great hazard for ships in the Arctic region. The conscious mind is what is above water; but the large, unknown, and powerful portion of the mind is what is below the surface. As members of a civilized society we might be horrified at the aims and drives of the id; thus, they are often distorted, disguised, and presented in symbols. Neither imaging nor reflexive behavior alone is very effective in satisfying instinctual drives, therefore, the second system of personality comes into being: the ego.

Ego

The ego is the personality's conscious, rational system. It encompasses all that is cognitive and intellectual. The ego is called the executor of the personality. The id makes demands, but the ego must decide whether a specific object will satisfy it. While the id asks of any experience: Is it pleasurable? the ego asks: Is it real? The ego operates on the *reality principle* and finds real objects in the environment that will satisfy drives and reduce tension. The ego differentiates out of the id and begins to form in the first year of life as the infant tests the rational limits of the real world.

Do not confuse this ego with the word *egotistical.* Ego, in this sense does not mean self-centered. For that concept, Freud used the term *narcissistic.* Ego is a very positive term and is more closely related to self-concept. The ego has a very difficult position. It must constantly choose which of several actions to perform. It must meet the demands of reality, of the id, and of the third component of personality, the superego, which embodies the moral rules of society. The triumvirate of the personality is completed by the superego. Let us investigate this third component.

Superego

The superego is the last system of the personality to be differentiated and contains both the moral rules and the ideals that a society instills in a child. Although the process of personality development is innately determined, the content of the superego is dependent on the interaction with parents and other adults. It is also dependent on mental growth and language development. The superego is formed during the preschool years and substitutes internal control for external control. The superego has two components: the *conscience* and the *ego ideal.*

The conscience is moralistic and contains society's prohibitions. The function of the conscience is to control the id's instinctual impulses. It uses the internal punishment of guilt when the moral code is broken and the reward of pride when the moral code is upheld. These internal rewards and punishments are given for the acts (and their derivatives) that the parents rewarded and punished in earlier years. The major instincts that society seeks to control are sex and aggression. Let us see how this might work. Picture a group of mothers and children in the park on a sunny morning. A group of children is playing in the sandbox. A two-year-old sees a toy that another child is playing with and attempts to take the toy. Any means are acceptable to attain the toy: hitting, kicking, biting, and pushing the child down. The mother's reaction is to say, "Stop that," in a severe tone of voice; to reason with the child by saying, "We cannot simply take things that do not belong to us but we must ask if we can play with a toy"; or to punish the child in some way. Through repeated actions of this kind, the child incorporates the mother's disapproval and subsequently feels guilty when such aggressive actions are performed, even when the mother is absent. It is this way that we learn civilized rules of conduct. It is not only parents who teach the rules of conduct in society. Children learn from other adults, siblings, teachers, books, comics, movie heroes and heroines, and television.

The other aspect of the superego is the *ego ideal,* which embodies the standard by which the self and others are judged. The young woman and man who are searching for the ideal mate have a vivid picture of their ideal firmly entrenched in their superego. Romantic fantasy involves elaborating the characteristics of this ego ideal. The ego ideal is also used by people to direct their own growth and development. People who are perfectionists constantly strive to meet an impossible ideal and demand the same of others. Young children act out their fantasies by playing "mommy and daddy" and superman and other popular heroes.

Ego Defenses

Consider the following scenario as an illustration of the role of the ego in balancing the demands of the personality's three elements. Imagine that you are walking down the street and become suddenly aware that you are hungry. As you pass a small grocery store you notice that there are bushels full of beautiful apples sitting in front of it. The id gives you a big nudge to get an apple and satisfy that hunger.

The thought arises that no one is around and you could easily take one. Then the superego steps in and reminds you that there are laws against stealing, and you could get into a lot of trouble for shoplifting. So, there your ego is, caught between the conflicting demands of the amoral id and the moralistic superego.

The ego has many choices for settling this. It must effect a realistic compromise. First, the ego suggests that you buy an apple. If you find yourself without money, maybe you see a friend from whom you can borrow a little. If you cannot get the apple in a realistic, socially acceptable way, then the ego must make a choice between the two systems. If the ego decides to steal the apple, then the superego will punish you by activating guilt. For many people this guilt is so painful that the choice is not viable. The ego may decide that it cannot take that risk and then chooses to change, or distort, the id's original demand. These are called ego defenses against the instinctual pressures from the id. For example the ego might convince the id that the apple would probably have a worm in it anyway and not be worth taking (rationalization).

Some of the defenses that the ego has against these instinctual drives are repression, projection, reaction formation, fixation, regression, rationalization, and sublimation. All of these operate on the unconscious level. Their purpose is to hide the original intent of the instinctual id impulses and to convert them into more socially accepted channels.

In *repression* the wish or thought is pushed down and not allowed to come into consciousness. With repression a person may not be able to see something that is in plain sight. In *projection*, feelings or impulses that arise within the person are projected outward and assigned to someone or something in the environment. If a person feels hostility toward another, for example, instead of admitting it, he or she may say, ''That person hates me.'' *Reaction formation* occurs when a person acts out the opposite of his or her true feelings. For example, a mother may be unable to admit feelings of hostility toward her child, so she outwardly shows so much love that it becomes ''smother love.''

In understanding child development, perhaps the most important of the defense mechanisms are *fixation* and *regression*. They are tied to Freud's concept of the development of personality. In *fixation*, normal growth may be halted. The person is then stuck on a stage and cannot move on because of the anxiety that moving to the next stage engenders.

Regression, on the other hand is moving backward to a former stage of development. A child who is toilet trained may have an accident when he or she begins school. The explanation is that the situation of school is so anxiety provoking that the child regresses to a former more secure level. Many children suck their thumbs in a strange situation. Again, the explanation is that they are seeking security in behavior that was comforting (and appropriate) at an earlier stage and age. When adults throw temper tantrums, they are regressing to an immature stage of development when they did not and could not exercise control over their impulses.

Rationalization is a defense in which the well-developed powers of the intellect are used to justify an action or deny an impulse. This defense is tightly logical and argued like an experienced trial lawyer.

The defense of *sublimation* is one of the most interesting and the one that has provided the fuel and fodder for society's cultural institutions. Through sublimation the ego siphons off the instinctual energy from the demands of the id and through subtle transformations channels them into another, but related, activity. Thus, the id is somewhat satisfied and the constructive work of society is accomplished. How does this work? Let us consider the basic instinct of need for food. Suppose early in life a person develops an insatiable appetite. To satisfy this instinct continuously would result in obesity, discomfort, and probably death. The instinct may be sublimated into incorporating information into oneself and one may then "devour" books. Sports such as boxing, wrestling, and football are sublimations of the aggressive instinct. Both participants and spectators gain instinctual gratification from them. The advertising industry is based in large measure on the sublimation of the sexual instinct, so that when you smoke a certain cigarette, drive a certain car, and buy a certain designer's jeans you get some gratification of the sexual instinct by identifying the symbols with the instinct. (The id, remember, can't tell the real thing from its image.) It has been said that Leonardo da Vinci painted pictures of Madonnas in an unconscious attempt to recapture his mother, who died when he was very young. Perhaps we attain pleasure in looking at such pictures because they satisfy our very deep-seated desire for the perfect love relationship with a beautiful, idealized mother. These motivations do not diminish cultural accomplishments. On the contrary, satisfaction in life and life's productions are immeasurably enhanced by being able to reflect on such basic, enduring feelings. Art, it has been said, expresses for us what we cannot quite express for ourselves. A picture or a novel finally puts into visual form or words a feeling that we do not have the skill to express. Shakespeare is the enduring writer that he is because he touched on the truth of the human feelings, motivations, and action that transcend culture, political organization, and changing language.*

Freud found that personality development is strongly related to the psychological aspects of sexual development; therefore, his theory traces the *psychosexual* development of children.

Stages of Psychosexual Development

Freud postulated four stages of psychosexual development: three in early childhood, a period of latency in middle childhood, and a fourth stage after puberty. He emphasized that different dynamic factors are operative in each stage.

Oral Stage

The oral stage extends over the first year of life. In this stage the mouth and sucking are the major sources of pleasure to the infant. This pleasure becomes associated with the caregiver. The relationship between the infant and the primary caregiver becomes the prototype of all later love relationships. This is true for both boys and girls. Personality characteristics rooted in the oral stage are feelings of dependency, amassing possessions, and being gullible. During the first year teeth begin to erupt and oral satisfaction may be mixed with aggression. Characteristics from this stage may include biting sarcasm and argumentativeness. Obviously, language becomes associated with oral characteristics.

Anal Stage

During the second year of life the focal point for the child changes from its mouth to its bowel functions. When toilet training begins, it is the first time that the child is asked to control instinctual impulses. Personality implications rooted in this stage

---

* For students who are interested in further reading in this area, the recent field of psychohistory has investigated the personality dynamics of many famous people and explained their productions in these terms. See L. DeMause, *History of Childhood*, New York: The Psychohistory Press, 1974, and issues of *History of Childhood Quarterly: The Journal of Psychohistory*.

of development can be a retentive, constipated personality. The anal personality is a stingy, obstinate person who cannot or will not give. When toilet training becomes a contest between the will of the mother and the child, the child may expel its feces at inappropriate times. This characteristic may be identified in adults as cruelty, wanton destructiveness, and disorderliness. On the other hand, a child who is lavishly praised for the production of feces may delight in production. This becomes the source of the creative personality. Pleasure in producing and smearing feces at two may sublimate into pleasure in spreading paint or manipulating clay at twenty-five years of age. It was this theory that changed childrearing: severe toilet training at six weeks was supplanted by permissive self-training at two or three years and praise for the products. The first successful performance on the toilet has been termed a gift to the mother from the child—and what does she do with it? Flushes it down the toilet. Imagine the child's disappointment.

Phallic Stage

In the phallic stage the focus of bodily pleasure and curiosity moves to the genital organs. The phallic stage spans the years between three and six. These are the years in which there is intense interest in the appropriate behavior for boys and girls and men and women. There is also intense masturbatory activity and fantasies around such activity. These are the context within which the Oedipus and Electra complexes are raised and resolved (see Chapter 11). This stage has lasting consequences for attitudes toward the opposite sex and toward those in authority; that is, to love and power. Endless novels, plays, and philosophies deal with the human struggle with love and power.

Latency Period

With the resolution of the Oedipal complex at around six years of age, the child moves into a latency period and five or six years of relatively smooth growing up. This does not mean that the child has no problems during those years. What it does mean is that the internal psychic dynamics are relatively quiet. After the turbulent preschool years, the latency period is a quiescent time before the eruption of adolescence.

Genital Stage

The advent of puberty marks the beginning of adolescence and the genital stage in psychosexual development. Adolescence has been described in many ways, most of which indicate its disruptive nature. In normal, healthy development middle childhood is a time when the child is self-confident, positive, and optimistic about the self and the world. Adolescence breaks up this stable pattern and, even in normal development, the young man or woman entering the genital stage suffers a psychological fracturing of the inner self.

From a Freudian perspective the task in the genital period is a change from the narcissistic motivation that was characteristic of the pregenital stages to altruistic motives. This change in motivation involves a relationship with a love object, usually of the opposite sex; through this change the person becomes capable of placing the well-being of that love object before his or her own narcissistic concerns. The context within which this takes place includes all the problems of adolescence: sexual attraction, group activities, vocational planning, and preparations for marrying and raising a family. This socialization that changes the adolescent into a contributing, altruistic member of society is accomplished through identification with admired adults and displacement and sublimation of instinctual drives. Thus, the person is transformed from a pleasure-seeking narcissistic child into a reality-oriented, socialized adult. Freud emphasized that this transformation does not entail abandonment of former aspects of the oral, anal, and phallic stages, but rather fuses these elements into a new synthesis at the genital level.

One last point about stage development is in order. Although Freud first outlined development in terms of successive stages, he emphasized that there is no sharp demarcation between them. On the contrary, the transition is generally blurred and occurs in a variable time frame that reflects the child's individuality. Movement from one stage to the next, as well as growth within a stage, is often characterized by "two steps forward and one backward." A child may be able to accomplish a task one day but be unable to do so the next.

Erikson's Psychosocial Theory

Erikson reinterpreted psychoanalytic theory with an emphasis on social development and called his theory psychosocial. In addition, Erikson expanded Freud's four stages of development into eight. Freud's psychosexual stages end at adolescence and sexual maturity; Erikson postulated three additional stages in adulthood and extended development into old age. Erikson's emphasis is on the ego and the capacity of the individual to relate to society in a way that unifies inner experience and external action. Erikson remained psychoanalytic and accepted Freud's structure of personality and the oral, anal, phallic, and genital modes as important in the development of personality. Thus, his work stands not in contrast to Freud, but as an extension of psychoanalytic theory.

Overview*

Each of the eight ages in Erikson's psychosocial theory constitutes a critical step in the development of personality. Those critical steps are turning points—that is, moments of decision between progress and regression, or between integration and retardation. At each step all former developments are integrated into a new level of functioning and the scope of psychosocial (and personality strengths) widens. At each stage there is a dynamic relationship among all eight psychosocial values. Each step draws from the resolution of former stages, modifies them in some way, and foreshadows the stages to come. All eight values are present in some measure even from infancy. At successive ages each psychosocial value comes to its ascendence, meets its crisis, and finds its solution.

The use of the word crisis and the subsequent resolution of crises may create an erroneous concept. In general, a crisis situation involves a decision to be made; once a resolution is reached and the crisis is resolved, it does not recur. In psychosocial development each value in turn reaches a crisis stage and is resolved, but it is not finished forever. At each stage each value is reevaluated and reintegrated into the dynamic whole. Each situation in which a person is challenged may activate all former crises and anticipate future ones. When confronted with a particularly difficult situation a person may ask: Can I trust that person in this situation?

---

* The following material is adapted from E. H. Erikson, *Childhood and Society* (2nd ed.) (New York: W. W. Norton, 1963).

Table 19–1. Developmental Crises in Psychosocial Development

Infancy	Trust	versus (hope)	Mistrust
Early Childhood	Autonomy	versus (will)	Shame and Doubt
Play Age	Initiative	versus (purpose)	Guilt
School Age	Industry	versus (competence)	Inferiority
Adolescence	Identity	versus (fidelity)	Identity Confusion
Young Adulthood	Intimacy	versus (love)	Isolation
Maturity	Generativity	versus (care)	Self-Absorption
Old Age	Integrity	versus (wisdom)	Despair, Disgust

Can I stand alone on this issue? Should I take the initiative in proposing this new idea? Am I good enough to perform this task? Can I join this group and still be my own person? Can I share my deepest feelings with this person? Am I contributing anything worthwhile? Can I meet this difficult situation and not be overwhelmed by anxiety and fear? These questions reflect the challenge to the ego that comes from each stage. At successive stages each of these questions reaches crisis proportions, but all questions are posed in some form at each age. Even the toddler meets these questions in a rudimentary form, although at that young age he or she may not be able to phrase them as questions. Erikson states, "The personality is engaged with the hazards of existence continuously, even as the body's metabolism copes with decay" (1963a, p. 274).

Although each stage is a crisis, the resolution of each is never totally positive or negative. Each crisis is resolved with some positive aspects and some negative ones. For example, the first crisis is between trust and mistrust. In positive development the infant develops a sense of basic trust; however, it is mixed with some mistrust. The *most* adaptive personality is one with a mixture of the two. A certain amount of caution is needed in traffic, in strange situations, and in many situations where advantage may be taken of one. On the other hand, the person who is suspicious and can never trust anyone or any situation is maladapted. When the resolution of the crisis is in a favorable ratio to a positive aspect, an ego strength becomes a permanent part of the personality. Ego strengths encompass such values as hope, purpose, and wisdom. The individual uses these strengths to meet new crises, and the resolution of each crisis in turn changes in some way the ego strengths of hope, purpose, wisdom, and so forth. Similarly, a negative resolution leaves a residue of ego weaknesses in a personality. These weaknesses can be attenuated by later positive experiences because ego strengths and weaknesses are affected by solutions at each stage.

The resolution of a crisis is not a once-and-for-all event to be attained and placed, like a trophy, unchanging, on a display shelf. Which is to say, crisis resolution should not be considered an achievement like learning to read. But if not an achievement, what is the lasting effect of a developmental crisis? Erikson states that the lasting effect of crises on the personality is an all-pervading "sense of." For example, when the first crisis between trust and mistrust is positively resolved, a sense of trust becomes a component of personality that informs the actions and decisions the individual undertakes. According to Erikson, when a personality has acquired a general "sense of," (trust, for example) the person is changed in ways of experiencing, of behaving, and in unconscious inner personality structure.

1. Ways of experiencing. The person experiences a sense of well-being. This is an inner experience; it is accessible to the person through introspection but is not necessarily obvious to others.
2. Ways of behaving. The person with a "sense of" behaves in ways that we come to identify. Identification of these "senses of" comes with clinical experience, or experience with human nature. For example, we can describe the person with a "sense of trust," "a sense of autonomy," or a "sense of competence."
3. Unconscious inner states. Finally, Erikson's "sense of" pervades the unconscious inner states and is accessible through psychological tests and analysis of personality. Psychoanalysis is largely the process of understanding the dynamic relationships among these "senses of."

The sequence of the stages in Erikson's theory is invariant and age-related, making it developmental. Let us stress, however, that there are individual differences in timing and intensity in the progression of sequences. These individual variations are influenced both by individual temperament and the style of development fostered by the culture.

Finally, Erikson makes a connection between individual experience and the institutions of society. The same institutions are found in many societies, even though they differ in form among cultures. For Erikson, institutions are created to serve the basic needs of the people in a society. The source of basic needs is developmental crises. Thus, the institutions of religion, marriage, law, and so forth are created to meet needs on a societal level.

Stages of Psychosocial Development

Basic Trust Vs. Mistrust (Infancy: Birth to Eighteen Months)

The period of infancy lays the foundation of personality and of psychosocial style. In this period enduring patterns for the solution of the conflict of basic trust versus basic mistrust are established. This is the first task for the ego and is inextricably enmeshed in maternal care. The first social achievement of the infant is the willingness to let the mother out of its sight without experiencing undue anxiety or rage. In so doing the mother becomes an inner certainty as well as an outer predictability. The sense of ego *identity* rests on a continuity of the maternal experience.

This maternal care does not depend on absolute quantities of food or demonstrations of love, but on the quality of the maternal relationship. Mothers create a sense of trust in their children by a combination of sensitive response to the baby's individual needs and a sense of her own personal trustworthiness. This basic trust forms the basis in the child of a sense of identity. In later development this identity encompasses a sense of being "all right," of being oneself, and of becoming what other people trust one will become. This enduring sense of trust and identity enables the child to endure frustrations, provided that within these frustrations there is the experience of movement

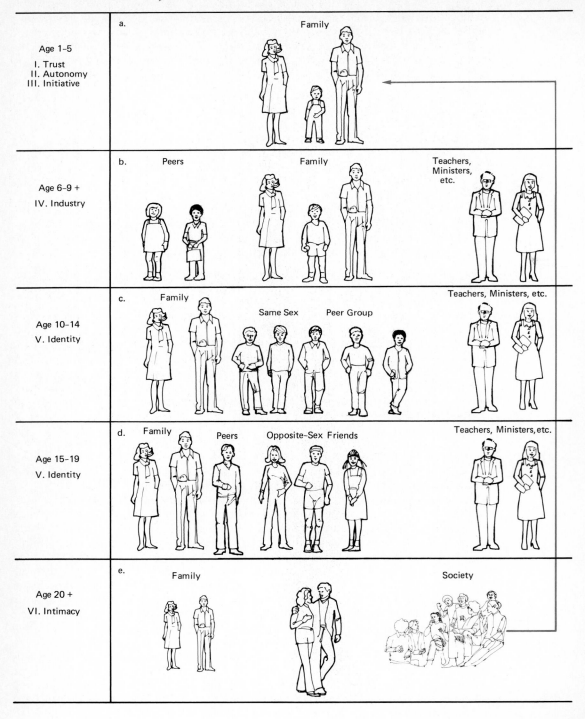

Age 1–5
I. Trust
II. Autonomy
III. Initiative

a. Family

Age 6–9 +
IV. Industry

b. Peers   Family   Teachers, Ministers, etc.

Age 10–14
V. Identity

c. Family   Same Sex   Peer Group   Teachers, Ministers, etc.

Age 15–19
V. Identity

d. Family   Peers   Opposite-Sex Friends   Teachers, Ministers, etc.

Age 20 +
VI. Intimacy

e. Family   Society

Erikson's theory of psychosocial development is psychoanalytic but stresses social relations and the development of a sense of self. This diagram illustrates the social reference groups that have most influence at successive ages. The individual begins as a dependent member of a family group, which is the social center of the child's world. In this environment the child develops trust, autonomy, and initiative (A). As the social world expands, peers and other adults are influential in developing industry (B). With the advent of puberty, the family moves to the periphery as same-sex peers increase in influence and the search for a separate identity begins (C). The identity crisis reaches a peak in the late teen years and opposite-sexed friends assume prime importance, (D). In young adulthood, the individual seeks intimacy with another person (E) and this may result in marriage, the creation of another family, and the beginning of a new cycle. The last two adult stages, generativity and ego-integrity, are not shown here, but psychosocial development continues throughout the life span and culminates in old age.

> *toward a final integration of the individual life cycle with some meaningful wider belongingness. Parents must not only have certain ways of guiding by prohibition and permission; they must also be able to represent to the child a deep, an almost somatic conviction that there is meaning to what they are doing.* [Erikson, 1963a, p. 249]

Children become neurotic, according to Erikson, because of lack of meaning in frustration. This stage introduces into psychic life a sense of inner division and universal nostalgia for a paradise lost. The sense of basic trust developed in infancy must maintain itself, throughout life, against this powerful combination of a sense of having been deprived, or having been divided, and of having been abandoned. The favorable ratio of trust over mistrust leaves the ego value of *hope* and *drive* in the personality. The institution that reflects this stage is *organized religion*.

Autonomy Vs. Shame and Doubt (Toddlers: Eighteen Months to Three Years)

In the toddler period the child develops a sense of his or her ability to control—that is, a sense of autonomy. The child at this age is subject to violent emotions. The child is threatened by the anarchy of those violent feelings. At the same time, the child is gaining the ability to control basic biological forces. In specific terms, that means gaining control over bowels and bladder. Thus, control of physical functions becomes the prototype of control of inner urges and feelings. In this stage the child assumes control of both those functions and of feelings. In psychosocial terms, the child may learn to control in a hostile destructive way or in a positive, caring, and valuing way. The role of parents and caregivers is crucial in determining how this crisis is resolved. The role of caregivers in this violent time is to maintain loving firmness and to protect the child from the anarchy of his or her own violent emotions. Caregivers should encourage the child to reach for independence and autonomy. Severe punishment and other thwarting of the child's efforts at independence may result in the child's doubting his or her ability to control situations and create shame about feelings, thoughts, and the body. A sense of autonomy develops through the gradual and guided experience of free choice. If this is denied, the child may then turn the urge to control against the self and become an obsessive personality filled with shame and doubt. The positive ratio of this crisis results in a child who has a sense of his or her own individuality and ability to control and manipulate. The lasting ego values from the positive resolution of this crisis are *self-control* and *willpower*. The counterpart of this stage of development in society is expressed in the principle of law and order.

> *The lasting need of the individual to have his will reaffirmed and delineated within an adult order of things which at the same time reaffirms and delineates the will of others has an institutional safeguard in the* principle of law and order. . . . *Thus, the*

sense of autonomy fostered in the child and modified as life progresses serves (and is served by) the preservation in economic and political life of a sense of justice. [Erikson, 1963a, p. 254]

Initiative Vs. Guilt (Preschool Age: Two to Six Years)

The sense of initiative is the quality of undertaking, planning, and attacking a task for the sake of being active and on the move; it suggests pleasure in the attack and conquest. In the period of autonomy, self-will often led to acts of defiance. The danger of this stage is a sense of guilt over the goals contemplated and the acts initiated. In this stage a split occurs in the personality and the child becomes forever divided in her- or himself. The split is between the conscience, that leads to self-observation, self-guidance, and self-punishment and that part of the personality that retains the child's goals, desires, and instincts. Through the resolution of the crisis between initiative and guilt the child develops a sense of moral responsibility and gains insight into the institutions, functions, and roles that will permit his or her later responsible participation. This is the preschool age in which exploration is done through meaningful toys and role playing. In this stage the dreams and fantasy of early childhood are more realistically attached to adult life. Social institutions offer the child of this age *ideal models* with which to replace the heroes from fairy tales and picture books. The child of this age is preoccupied with clearly understanding the functions of idealized adults and uses such handy devices as uniforms to recognize them. That is, the preschooler plays endlessly the assigned roles in order to get them straight and uses the uniforms of police, firefighter, milkman, doctor, and nurse to identify them in their societal functions. The positive ratio of initiative over shame and guilt leaves the ego values of *direction* and *purpose*.

Industry Vs. Inferiority (School Age: Six to Twelve Years)

Between the ages of six and twelve the child develops a sense of industry in which he or she adjusts to the inorganic laws of the tool world. These are the school years and in all cultures children receive some systematic instruction and gradually learn to bring a productive situation to completion and to replace the whims and wishes of play. The child's danger in this stage is in a sense of inadequacy and inferiority. If the child is not convinced of his own worth in handling the tools of his culture he may develop a sense of mediocrity or inadequacy. This is socially the most decisive stage because industry involves doing things with and beside others. In this period the child develops a sense of the culture's *technological ethos*. The lasting ego value from a positive resolution of this crisis is a sense of *method* and *competence*.

Identity Vs. Role Confusion (Adolescence: Twelve to Twenty-One Years)

A sense of ego identity emerges with puberty and the end of childhood. This stage encompasses an integration of inner feelings, past learning, and future expectations. The adolescent is a prisoner in a body undergoing revolution and is challenged by the adult tasks in the future. Caught between these two threats adolescents are preoccupied with how they appear to others. Out of this crucible they must forge an identity in the tangible form of a career choice. This identity must integrate childhood identifications from the preschool years and skills and talents developed in the school years, with opportunities offered in social roles. The danger in this period is role confusion. Threatened by the fear of not finding their own identity, youths may overidentify with popular heroes. This is a stage of falling in love. Adolescent love, according to Erikson, is not primarily a sexual matter. It is an attempt to arrive at a definition of one's own identity by projecting one's diffused ego image on another, where it is reflected and gradually clarified.

The institutional ideas that are confronted in this stage are those of *ideology* and *aristocracy*. This is an idealistic stage in which youths believe that the best people will come to rule and rule develops the best in people. The positive resolution of this crisis is the lasting ego value of *fidelity*.

The next four stages of Erikson's theory cover the adult years from approximately twenty-one to old age. Because the focus of this book is childhood, we will only briefly discuss them. Erikson has indicated the importance of development over the entire life cycle in understanding the stages of childhood.

Intimacy Vs. Isolation (Young Adulthood)

The young adult who emerges from adolescence with a firm sense of identity is able and willing to fuse that identity with that of others without the fear of losing it. In this period a person is challenged to undertake a shared relationship with the opposite sex (including close affiliations and sexual union), deep friendships, the comradeship of soldiers-in-arms, the submerging of identity in inspirational teachers, and exploring intuitive inner sources. The danger in this stage is that a person may avoid such experiences because of fear of ego loss and consequently experience a sense of isolation and self-absorption. The societal institution that embodies this stage is *marriage* and serious study. The positive resolution of this crisis results in the ego values of *affiliation* and *love*.

Generativity Vs. Stagnation (Adulthood)

Generativity is primarily a concern in establishing and guiding the next generation, but it includes a wider interpretation of productivity and creativity. Through investing psychic energy in what is being generated, ego interests and personality are expanded. The danger in this stage is regression to an obsessive need for pseudo-intimacy and a resulting sense of stagnation and personal impoverishment. Such individuals may then begin to treat themselves as though they were their own children. The principle of safeguarding and reinforcing generativity pervades all societal institutions, in that all institutions codify the *ethics* of *generative succession*. Many institutions such as religious orders and schools are concerned with the matter of their relationship to the care of the world's creatures. Recently we have begun to see people concerned with environmental protection, world hunger and world peace, all expressions of the ego value of generativity. The positive resolution of this crisis leaves the ego values of *production* and *care*.

Ego Integrity Vs. Despair (Maturity)

"Only in him who in some way has taken care of things and people and has adapted himself to the triumphs and disappointments adherent to being, the originator of others or the generator of products and ideas—only in him may gradually ripen the fruit of these seven stages" (Erikson, 1963a, p. 268). The individual who reaches the stage of ego integrity accepts his or her one and only life cycle as that which had to be. Ego integrity is a postnarcissistic love that conveys a feeling of world order and spiritual sense. In ego integrity the individual experiences unity with parents and with distant times and places. The ego value of this is *wisdom*. The lack or loss of such ego integration is signified by fear of death and despair that the time is too short to begin again and try different roads. This despair is expressed in thousands of small disgusts with life in general. Erikson ends his life cycle with the

	1	2	3	4	5	6	7	8
VIII Maturity								Ego integrity vs. despair
VII Adulthood							Generativity vs. stagnation	
VI Young Adulthood						Intimacy vs. isolation		
V Puberty and Adolescence					Identity vs. role confusion			
IV Latency				Industry vs. inferiority				
III Locomotor-Genital			Initiative vs. guilt					
II Muscular-Anal		Autonomy vs. shame, doubt						
I Oral Sensory	Basic trust vs. mistrust							

Erikson's epigenetic chart of the eight ages of man. Erikson presented his theory of psychosocial development visually, as a matrix, to illustrate the conception that ego values that are the residue of each crisis themselves become something new with each succeeding crisis. For example, if a sense of trust is developed in infancy, it becomes something new with autonomy, and evolves into a third quality with initiative. Erikson only postulated the framework, not what these values become. That is for future theorists to develop. [Reprinted from *Childhood and Society*, 2nd Edition, by Erik H. Erikson, by permission of W. W. Norton & Company, Inc. Copyright © 1963 by W. W. Norton & Company, Inc.]

observation that "healthy children will not fear life if their elders have integrity enough not to fear death" (1963a, p. 269).

Erikson's theory of personality development suggests an optimal development in which the person has met and resolved developmental crises with an enduring sense of trust, autonomy, initiative, industry, identity, intimacy, generativity, and integrity. As a result of these qualities the personality accrues the ego values of hope, will-power, purpose, competence, fidelity, love, care, and wisdom. A society created by such individuals constructs institutions that support and strengthen those qualities and values and assist the individual in his or her quest for integrity. This is in some measure an idealized view of development, yet such a developmental sequence is part of the biological heritage of all human beings.

Piaget's Cognitive Theory

Overview

According to Piaget, "intelligence is an adaptation" (1952, p. 3). Piaget was trained as a biologist and applied biological concepts to the question of intelligence. In biological adaptation the organization of physical structures enables the organism to interact with the environment in ways that increase the probability of survival. Physical structures of different species have been somehow stimulated to change so that living organisms fit the particular characteristics of the environment. For example, the same biological structure has taken different forms in the evolution of

Table 19–2.   Summary of Piaget's Periods of Cognitive Development

Period	Characteristics of the Period	Major Change of the Period
Sensori-motor (0–2 years)		Development proceeds from reflex activity to representation and sensori-motor solutions to problems.
Stage 1 (0–1 months)	Reflex activity only. No differentiation.	
Stage 2 (1–4 months)	Hand-mouth coordination. Differentiation via sucking reflex.	
Stage 3 (4–8 months)	Hand-eye coordination. Repeats unusual events.	
Stage 4 (8–12 months)	Coordination of two schemata. Object permanence attained.	
Stage 5 (12–18 months)	New means through experimentation— follows sequential displacements.	
Stage 6 (18–24 months)	Internal representation. New means through mental combinations.	
Preoperational (2–7 years)	Problems solved through representation— language development (2–4 years). Thought and language both egocentric. Cannot solve conservation problems.	Development proceeds from sensori-motor representation to pre-logical thought and solutions to problems.
Concrete Operational (7–11 years)	Reversability attained. Can solve conservation problems—logical operations developed and applied to concrete problems. Cannot solve complex verbal problems.	Development proceeds from pre-logical thought to logical solutions to concrete problems.
Formal operations (11–15 years)	Logically solves all types of problems— thinks scientifically. Solves complex verbal problems. Cognitive structures mature.	Development proceeds from logical solutions to concrete problems to logical solutions to all classes of problems.

From *Piaget's Theory of Cognitive Development*, Second edition by Barry J. Wadsworth. Copyright © 1971, 1979 by Longman Inc. Reprinted with permission of Longman Inc., New York.

different species. The structure that became arms in humans evolved into wings in birds and forelegs in four-legged animals. These adaptations were presumably evolved in response to pressures, or opportunities, in the environment.

Piaget reasoned that intelligence is only another aspect of the physical organism and therefore must function within the principles of biological adaptation. In viewing intelligence as biological adaptation, he brings two concepts of biological evolution to his understanding of the development of individual intelligence. First, the individual is continuously fitting old structures into new functions, and second, the individual develops new structures to fill old functions under changed circumstances (Baldwin, 1967). This development is firmly rooted in what already exists and is continuous with the past. One can only build on what is already present. In addition, intellectual development must be viewed in a total complex, which includes physical and emotional aspects. All of the aspects of the child and the environment are in a kind of equilibrium.

When the child walks, he is able to attain goals otherwise unattainable. At the same time, walking puts the child in a position to have goals that he would not have otherwise had. The interrelatedness of the entire pattern is illustrated by the fact that because people walk, our whole social system is set up to require walking.

Furthermore, walking and other behavior patterns are interrelated. The pattern of holding an object in the hand is modified when the child must hold it while walking, and the walking behavior changes depending upon what the child is carrying—a sack of flour, a fishing pole, or a brimful bowl of soup. [Baldwin, 1967, p. 173]

Piaget's study of the ways in which the child understands the reality of the world is known as *genetic epistemology*. In addition to having an academic background in biology, Piaget also studied philosophy. The question in philosophy that interested him was whether there is any justifiable basis for assuming that one's picture of the external world is accurate. This question has been explored for centuries by philosophers. The branch of philosophy interested in the question is called epistemology. Some of the questions that epistemology attempts to answer evolved from the following reasoning. We are all prisoners in our own perceptual world. All that we know of the external world is information that we receive from our visual, auditory, and tactical sensory modes. We can see a tree, we can touch it, and we can hear the movement of its leaves and branches. We assume that each of those modalities gives us information about the same tree in the same external world. But can we justify our assumption? Could the three modalities be bringing us information from three different external worlds? Recent thought in theoretical physics and astronomy about black holes and the possibility of universes within universes gives credence to such a question. We assume that when we turn from our tree and no longer see it that it still exists. Is there any justification for that assumption? Perhaps it disappears when we no longer see it. In addition, we assume that our reality is peopled with creatures like us and, furthermore, that they perceive the external world (worlds?) the same way we do. We assume that when we see "blue" others also see blue. Can we justify such beliefs? Children with learning problems underline the different perceptions people gain from the same sensory mode. Piaget decided to study these philosophical problems by investigating how children understand space, time, logic, and mathematics from birth. In so doing, he became the world's leading child psychologist. In discussing Piaget's theory of the development of intelligence we are concerned with the development of Western logical-scientific thought as a method of dealing with (adapting to) reality and solving problems within that reality. Cross-cultural research has failed to reveal universal principles holding across cultures. For example, children developing within an Eastern Hindu or Buddhist concept of reality may be adapting to a different one.

In Piaget's theory *intelligence consists of transforming signs and symbols* in various ways. These signs and symbols may represent pennies, glasses of water, or other *concrete* objects; *or* they may represent abstract ideas in science, logic, or other *formal* disciplines. Regardless of whether the signs and symbols represent concrete or formal objects, they refer to the culture's agreed-upon reality.

What does Piaget mean by *transforming* signs and symbols? Transformations are operations that change perceived realities in some way. For example, a child may push a doll carriage against a wall and then imagine (mentally transform) moving to the other side of the carriage to push it in the other direction. First, the operation is performed mentally and then physically. In transformations, however, some elements of reality remain unchanged. The unchanging aspects enable the object or idea to retain its essential identity, despite its changed appearances. For example, clay remains clay whether it is shaped into a ball, a snake, a dog, or a cat. Water remains water whether it is in a drinking glass, a bath tub, a lake, or an ocean. *Grasping the essential (unchanging) reality of the world while performing various operations on mental elements is the essence of Piagetian intelligence.*

The child first learns to perform operations with concrete objects and then, *and only then,* can he or she perform operations on abstract, or formal, ideas. Before the child is able to perform operations on even concrete objects, he or she must grasp the essential unchanging nature of physical reality.

Basic Unit of Intelligence: Scheme

It is fairly easy to see biological structures that adapt and through comparative anatomy to trace that adaptation. But what adapts in intellectual functioning? For Piaget the structure that changes and adapts is a mental organization he designated a *scheme* (plural, schemes). The scheme is a mental organization that guides behavior. In its simplest form it is a reliable response to a stimulus—that is, a reflex. Schemes, however, are not tied to specific reflexive stimulus-response patterns. They are flexible and mobile and can be applied to many different objects. These mental organizations (schemes) grow, develop, and become more complex.

Process of Intellectual Functioning: Functional Invariants

The way in which changes occur in schemes is the same for all people because this functioning is determined by biology. As the general process of digestion is the same for all humans, so is the general process of mental function, and this process is genetically determined. Piaget calls the elements of this process functional invariants. This means that there is no variation in how the process works from person to person. This process involves three factors:

1. The incorporation of elements into the existing mental organization *(assimilation)*.

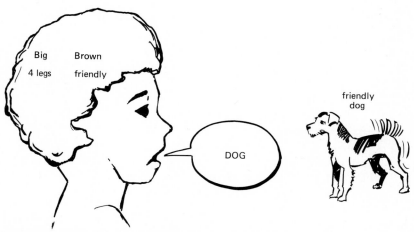

In Piaget's theory of cognitive development the basic unit is a *scheme.*

2. Changes that occur in mental organization as a result of new incorporations *(accommodation)*.

3. The balance between the two *(equilibration)*.

Assimilation

The child builds many mental structures in the process of experiencing the environment. As the child meets new experiences he or she *assimilates* them into existing schemes. If, for example, the child is riding in a car with her or his mother, in a part of the country that they have never been in before, and the child says, ''That is a tree,'' ''That is a dog,'' it is because those objects are represented by an already existing *scheme*. The child is simply assimilating them into ready-made categories. Through assimilation, the child is able to handle situations that have not been exactly encountered before. The process of assimilation is a comfortable one; it means that the child has adapted to a situation and can handle it. When the child meets new situations that are similar to those experienced in the past, the adaptive process is primarily one of assimilation.

Accommodation

When the child meets a situation that is not familiar, the process of adaptation requires some change so that the situation can be handled comfortably. The change is accommodation. Suppose our child and mother in the car drive to a roller-skating rink. If this is the child's first experience there will have to be many changes in his or her customary way of moving around in order to be able to master, or adapt to skating. At first the child will attempt to walk with the skates on. Probably she or he will fall down several times. The child *must change* (accommodate) his or her scheme. The child must change from picking up his or her feet and legs to pushing the feet alternately. This, of course, will force another accommodation in the sense of balance. Gradually the scheme will change and the skill will be mastered. Now the general physical scheme for moving through space has been *differentiated*. There are now two different schemes: walking and skating. As the child grows, this differentiation will continue, and eventually there will be riding bicycles, swimming, skateboarding, skiing, surfing, and other ways to move through space. Each of them will require accommodation on the part of the child.

Equilibration

Equilibration is a balance between assimilation and accommodation. Intellectual development proceeds through a balance of the two. If a situation is too new and strange, the child will be overwhelmed and be unable to adapt at all. On the other hand, if the situation is too much the same, the child will lose interest altogether.

Motivation

In Piaget's theory the child *seeks* new experiences, which Piaget calls aliments. This word implies an association with eating food. For Piaget the mental structures of the child seek food (for thought) just as the physical organism seeks food for nutrition. This mental food consists of new experiences and novel stimuli. Therefore, the child is *intrinsically* motivated toward mastering new skills and meeting new experiences. When a child is confronted by a new situation, a scheme is activated. If the new experience cannot be assimilated into existing schemes, a state of disequilibration results. This disequilibrium forces growth of new schemes (accom-

(A) New experiences can be assimilated into existing schemes (not always accurately).

(B) When new experiences cannot be assimilated accommodation must be made in existing schemes.

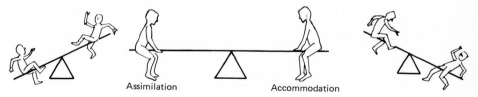

(C) Balance between assimilation and accommodation is equilibration.

Functional invariants: assimilation (A), accommodation (B), and equilibrium (C).

modation). This new growth can only be accomplished through interaction with the environment—that is, by trying to master, or understand, the new situation. Motivation is highest when a task is somewhat familiar but cannot be totally assimilated into existing structures and a new accommodation must be made. When equilibrium is reached, the task is no longer challenging and the situation can be fully assimilated. The child is, in fact, bored.

For example, consider a child at about eight months of age. This child may be unable to pick up very small objects, although large ones offer no trouble. The child is motivated to repeat the attempt to pick up small objects (such as pins on the floor or pills from a medicine chest). The gradual acquisition of the ability to pick up very small objects can be described as the process of accommodation. Once the ability has been acquired, the grasping scheme can assimilate such tiny objects (Baldwin, 1967). At this point, the task is no longer motivating to the child, because it is so easily performed.

Social-Learning Theory

Overview

At the same time that Freud was developing his theory of personality in Vienna, psychology was taking quite a different turn in America. Inspired by Pavlov's discovery that behavior could be elicited by conditioning reflexes American psychologists, under the leadership of John B. Watson and Edward L. Thorndike, directed their attention to accounting for the acquisition and retention of new forms of behavior through experience. The emphasis was on *learning* and building an objective psychology that dealt only with observable behavior. Watson emphasized that the proper concern of psychology should be *behavior*, and that it should be studied with the same objective techniques used in other natural sciences. He, thus, established the school of psychology known as behaviorism. Thorndike demonstrated the importance of reward and punishment in learning and formulated the law of effect. This law states that if the response made to a stimulus gives pleasure or satisfaction, the connection between the stimulus and the response is strengthened, and if the response made to a stimulus brings punishment, the connection between the stimulus and the response is weakened. Later behaviorists expanded the law of effect and developed *operant conditioning.* The prime principle in operant conditioning is that behavior is controlled by its consequences. Later research showed that punishment is more complicated than Thorndike postulated, but it confirmed his position on the effect of reward in increasing positive behavior. From this beginning many psychologists contributed to building an American psychology that rested on the assumption that new behaviors are the result of learning—that is—of experiences in the environment.

Psychologists began to be trained in laboratory methods; they rejected complicated theories (such as those of Freud) to explain behavior. They insisted on looking for the simplest explanation for behavior, which usually led to learning principles. The stress on the simplest answer became a tenet of social-learning advocates; it is expressed as the *law of parsimony.* This law states that, given two alternative explanations for behavior, the simplest explanation is the correct one. Many researchers and theoreticians contributed to social-learning theory, there was no one theoretical giant. The theoretical structure varies, depending on who is explaining what facet of behavior. Sometimes the structure is a blend of several different views. One group of psychologists, Robert Sears, Neal Miller, John Dollard, and

O. H. Mowrer (Baldwin, 1967), was interested in building a theory of child development that used the principles of learning and reinforcement as explanatory principles, yet used the writings of Freud to suggest hypotheses for investigation.

Social-learning theory has as a basic assumption the proposition that the human is essentially a blank slate at birth and that *all* of those aspects described as intelligence, personality, talents, and/or temperament are the result of learning in the social environment. In social-learning theory the human is viewed as essentially reactive to environmental stimuli and not the initiator of actions.

There is no core of "self" for the social-learning theorist. In general, social-learning theorists see this concept as philosophical and unscientific. Individual differences that others might label "self" or "personality" are seen as the result of different experiences in the environment, not of innate differences. Thus, there are neither instincts nor innate drives to specific behaviors. The human is essentially passive in a deterministic world. Action consists of learned behaviors that are responses to stimuli from the environment. Social-learning theorists direct their research questions to examining the relationship between environmental stimuli and human behavior.

Maturational concepts are not employed to explain the development of children in social-learning theory. Studies and observation show, however, that there is a great similarity in the development of different children. Generally, children walk, talk, and learn bowel control at about the same time; boys generally develop masculine behavior patterns and girls feminine patterns. The fact that these and similar patterns emerge in quite different children on a similar time schedule has been the crux of the furious debate as to whether such behaviors are regulated by genetically controlled maturational processes or they are the result of environmental regulation. Social-learning theory holds that these similarities in development are attributable to environmental regulation and the learning process. Two factors are responsible for the similarities in the development of dissimilar children. First, all people are subject to the same physical laws. Gravity causes things to fall and falling down hurts. In addition, fire burns, dogs bite, food satisfies hunger, and meat can be eaten when teeth grow. All people in all cultures learn from these physical realities and must adapt to them if they are to survive. The adaptive range of responses to these principles forces similarities in behavior. Second, within the same society customary patterns of childrearing assure that different children will be exposed to similar environmental influences at approximately the same age and thereby learn the same behaviors at similar ages. For example, weaning occurs at about the same time for all children in the same culture. This learning process is, of course, socialization and always involves pressure to change the behavior patterns of the child from immature behaviors to the culturally accepted adult pattern.

Social-learning theory does not systematically describe age-graded development or a sequence of stages related to age because it is not a developmental theory. Social-learning theory has taken the age-graded development and sequences described by other theories and offered an alternative explanation for the same phenomena. In doing so, many research studies have been conducted and much new knowledge has been added to our understanding of how children grow and develop and the mechanisms for the regulation of this development. In evaluating any research study it is important to identify the theoretical position of the researchers and to analyze the results and interpretation of the study in terms of this position.

Contributions from Social-Learning Theory

Behaviorism

John B. Watson developed the approach to human behavior known as behaviorism. In behaviorism, only objective, measurable behavior is suitable for scientific study. Thus, behaviorists reject the consideration of concepts such as personality traits, instincts, or any other internal cause for behavior. In the behavioristic view of human nature, each healthy newborn is essentially the same as any other. All such children have the same potential to exhibit desirable behaviors for growth and development intellectually and personally. It is the environment that determines how that potential is expressed. Watson pronounced that, given a child until it was six years old, he could make a doctor, lawyer, chief, or beggar of him (Watson, 1928). Thus, like Freud, he stressed the importance of the early years, but for quite different reasons. The implication from Freudian theory was that the child needs a warm, loving relationship with parents; Watson stated that the child should receive no outward display of affection and should be treated as a young adult—objectively and kindly, but firmly. He did not advocate hugging, kissing, and coddling children. If necessary, parents might kiss a child goodnight on the forehead, but generally, they should shake the child's hand in greeting or departing. It was the influence of Watson in the 1920s and 1930s that set the basis for the strict feeding of children on rigid schedules, early and strict toilet training, and the attitude that a child becomes spoiled if it is picked up and held when it cries.

It was Watson who conditioned Little Albert to fear white furry objects. He was using a technique developed by the Russian psychologist Pavlov, called classical conditioning. Pavlov noted that specific stimuli elicited innate responses: food elicits salivation in a dog and a loud noise elicits the startle reflex in an infant. Pavlov discovered that other stimuli could be conditioned to elicit the same response if they are paired with the original stimulus. In classical conditioning the stimulus must occur before the response and, in fact, is the stimulus for that response. Many researchers investigated aspects of conditioning after Watson, the most important of whom is B. F. Skinner.

B. F. Skinner is a student of Watsonian psychology who further refined the behaviorist approach to behavior. He is, in fact, responsible for the current definition of psychology as the science of behavior. He has devoted his career to discovering the laws that govern behavior and has published many articles and books on his research and thought. Skinner discovered that behavior was not only controlled by the stimulus that occurred before it (and thus elicited it), but also that behavior was controlled by the *consequences* that followed it. If the consequences are pleasant, the behavior increases or is maintained, whereas if the consequences are unpleasant, the behavior is suppressed. If there are no consequences the behavior simply disappears. These consequences that maintain behavior are *reinforcements*. Skinner worked out the intricate relationships between reinforcement and behavior that are called schedules of reinforcement.

In the Skinnerian view, early life history is of little importance. One may have learned behaviors or may have learned to find certain consequences reinforcing in early life, but if those behaviors are maladaptive, new behaviors can be learned with reinforcement and the maladaptive behaviors changed. To the behaviorist, development is not age graded, although there is some limitation of behavioral acquisition because of biological immaturity. In general, any behavior can be learned at any age, provided the physical apparatus is adequate. There is no concept of readiness in social-learning theory. A child of two can be taught to read as well as a child of six or seven, provided that the proper reinforcement is found and adequate biological development is present.

Behaviorists concentrate on present behaviors, reinforcing desirable ones, and suppressing or extinguishing undesirable ones. Skinner's book *Walden Two* (1948) describes a utopian society in which these principles of behavior are applied to society. In another book, *Beyond Freedom and Dignity* (Skinner, 1971), he asserts that such concepts as freedom and dignity have served the purpose of keeping humans enslaved to the ideas of freedom and dignity and to those masters who promised such empty rewards. In Skinner's view freedom is not possible because *all* behavior is controlled by events and objects in the environment. The best approach is to recognize this and to become knowledgeable about the things that actually control behavior, rather than seek elusive "freedom."

The application of Skinner's laws of behavior is known as behavior modification. The techniques developed under this theory have been applied in schools, mental institutions, hospitals, juvenile treatment centers, and in all segments of the helping professions. Techniques such as token economy, positive reinforcement, and time-out are derived from behavior modification. We will review here the principles of behavior as explicated by behaviorists.

Principles of Behavior

The first and cardinal principle of behavior established by the behaviorists is that behavior is primarily controlled by its consequences. When a behavior is followed by a consequence that is satisfying (reinforcing) that behavior will be maintained or increase. For example, in an experimental situation, if a pigeon pecks a key and receives a food pellet, key-pecking behavior will increase and continue as long as the consequence is a food pellet, or something else that is reinforcing.

The search for the principles of behavior is directed to the goal of understanding, controlling, and predicting the behavior of individuals. In the application of behavioral principles these are applied to individuals. Although the principles hold in all cases, slightly different events or objects are reinforcing for different individuals, and target behaviors differ among individuals. Similarly, research in principles of behavior is conducted on individuals rather than groups. When a behavior is changed, that individual then becomes his or her own control group. That is, the presence or absence of a behavior is compared before and after the application of treatment procedures. Behaviorists refer to learning new behavior as conditioning. Let us now examine how conditioning takes place.

Conditioning. Conditioning, quite simply, refers to the acquisition of new behaviors. Behaviorists have identified two kinds of conditioning, *respondent* and *operant*.

Respondent conditioning is most clearly seen and is most reliable in eliciting reflex behaviors. For example, a sharp tap administered to the knee (the stimulus) will reliably cause the same response (leg to jerk). Similarly, an irritant such as pepper in the nose (stimulus) will elicit a sneeze (response). When Pavlov conditioned his dog to salivate to the sound of a bell he was using respondent conditioning. He began with an *unconditioned stimulus* (meat powder) that always produced salivation in the dog (*unconditioned response*).* He then presented the meat powder

---

* According to Whaley and Malott (1971) the words *unconditioned* and *conditioned* in referring to the stimulus and/or response are misnomers; they are mistranslations from Russian to English of Pavlov's experiment. In the original the words are *unconditional* (not limited, absolute, or unqualified) and *conditional* (dependent on a condition).

(unconditioned stimulus) and the sound of a bell simultaneously to the dog. The dog salivated. In time the dog was *conditioned* (learned) to salivate at the sound of a bell. Thus, the sound of the bell became a conditioned stimulus, which elicited salivation in the dog.

In operant conditioning behavior is controlled by its consequences. When a behavior is followed by a consequence that is satisfying (reinforcing), the behavior will increase or be maintained. "Very simple," you might say. However, it isn't simple at all. Human behavior is exceedingly complex, and identifying those objects and events that are positively reinforcing is equally complex. Let us consider a situation in which a child has been told to go to bed and see what actually may happen in the situation. Perhaps the parent has finished cleaning the kitchen and is ready to relax for the remainder of the evening. The parent orders the child to bed and turns on the TV. An exciting program is on and soon both parent and child are engrossed in the story. An hour later, the parent realizes that the child has not gone to bed, and the battle ensues. To the child, the verbal command "Go to bed" actually brought a reinforcement for not going to bed.

Reinforcement is that event or object that follows a behavior and serves to reinforce it. Almost anything can serve as a reinforcer, but only if it reinforces. Some things that generally are not considered positive experiences will reinforce behavior in some people. For example, a child might continue disruptive behavior because of the negative attention that he or she receives for it. Although children generally consider scolding unpleasant, for some that attention is reinforcing. Masochists are, by definition, those who find pain reinforcing. Whatever others think of the consequence, if the individual finds it reinforcing, it will serve to increase behavior.

The strongest reinforcers are unconditioned, or primary, reinforcers. Primary reinforcers are generally those that meet biological needs such as food and a comfortable room temperature and so forth. Other sensory and social stimulation also serve as primary reinforcers for most humans. Just as unconditioned responses can be conditioned to be elicited by stimuli other than the unconditioned stimulus, so unconditioned reinforcers can be conditioned to reinforce many behaviors. Food is an unconditioned reinforcer and many different organisms maintain behaviors that are reinforced by food. When an unconditioned reinforcer (food) occurs with another event, such as verbal approval *immediately* following a behavior, that event becomes an unconditioned reinforcer for that behavior. Events or objects that are conditioned reinforcers are secondary reinforcers. Behaviors are thus chained together and whole behavioral repertoires are built. Through this intricate chaining reinforcers become far removed from their biological base and events and objects such as grades, social approval, and money become reinforcers and keep us persisting at such tasks as writing textbooks and studying for tests! To understand what reinforces a behavior is to be able to predict that behavior. To both understand and to have control of reinforcers is to have control of behavior. We need only look at totalitarian governments to see how the control of primary reinforcers such as food, clothing, shelter, and safety quickly brings control of behavior, even of entire populations.

Schedules of Reinforcement. The strength of a reinforcer is determined not only by what it is, but also by how often the behavior is reinforced. If a reinforcement is given after every response, behavior is maintained; however, there is a pause after each response, and if the reinforcer is stopped even for a short time, the behavior stops too. The most effective reinforcement schedule is a variable random schedule.

The prime example of this reinforcement schedule is the slot machine. Individuals spend hours putting quarters into these machines with no assurance that they will ever hit the jackpot. The machines are programmed to pay off on a random schedule. It may be on the first quarter, or it may be after 50, 100, or 500 quarters. Nevertheless, they effectively maintain quarter-depositing behavior. Similarly, if children are given a reward, such as chocolate candy, after each correct response, the response may fade quickly when the reinforcer is stopped.

Extinction. When the reinforcement that controls a behavior is withheld, that behavior will gradually decrease and finally disappear altogether. In other words, individuals learn behaviors to affect events in the environment. When a behavior no longer does that, it is no longer performed. Extinction is very useful for ridding children of undesirable behaviors. Parents are not aware that they reinforce many behaviors in their children. For example, when a mother responds to the cries of a young child who is in a property dispute with an older sibling, she is reinforcing crying behavior in the younger child. It is *her* behavior that is being controlled by the child. If no one is hurt, and the situation is just, the crying behavior will go away if it is not reinforced. Parents and teachers would do well to examine carefully who holds the reinforcers for whose behavior.

Punishment and Negative Reinforcement "If you don't stop that I am going to punish you," a teacher says angrily to a child who is trying to catch a fish in the fish tank. Perhaps her threat is not effective, the behavior continues, and she sends the child to the principal's office. Has she effectively changed the child's behavior? The answer is, probably not. The laws of behavior indicate that punishment is not effective in acquiring new behavior. Punishment is an effective *suppressor* of behavior, but only while the punishment is in effect. When the punishment ceases, the behavior is likely to resume. When a classroom or home is set up so that children's behavior is kept under control by punishing techniques, the techniques need to be in effect constantly to maintain order. Positive reinforcement is both more effective and easier on both adults and children.

Negative reinforcement actually refers to escape or avoidance behavior. Behavior is learned and exhibited in order to escape from another event. For example, most of us would consider nausea to the point of vomiting a very aversive event. Consider the child who, when getting ready to go to school, is suddenly gripped with an intense stomachache and vomiting. Perhaps this happens often to the child and repeated medical examinations have revealed no physical cause for the vomiting behavior. We would then look for a behavioral explanation. Vomiting becomes negatively reinforcing because this behavior removes the even more aversive threat of going to school. Thus, behavior that allows the child to escape from school becomes reinforcing, albeit negatively. Another example of negative reinforcement is the findings of several researchers that some women have a fear of success. Failure becomes negatively reinforcing because it allows them to avoid the even more anxiety-provoking situation of success.

Motivation. In everyday language we often speak of a person's being highly motivated. The implication is that he or she has an internal drive to accomplish. Behaviorists hold that motivation rests outside the person and depends on the effectiveness of the reinforcers. One condition that increases motivation is deprivation of a desired reinforcer. Food is a primary reinforcer and is highly motivating. The motivating potential of secondary reinforcers is difficult to gauge, especially when speaking of grades or teacher approval. Grades are reinforcers probably because they earn the approval of parents and peers. One of the problems that teachers face is that, for some children, grades simply do not serve as a sufficient reinforcer for acquiring the behaviors that schools attempt to establish. In such cases teachers need to look for other things that will reinforce the student. Grades are very abstract, and the presumed material reward for high grades is a nebulous job in an even more nebulous future. For the child from a disadvantaged background, in which few adults have stimulating jobs, there is simply no connection between grades in school and anything of value.

Let us stress again that, even though the principles of behavior are presented as learning theory, it is not necessary that the connection between reinforcement and the behavior be understood for the reinforcer to be effective. If a behavior is positively reinforced, it increases in frequency. In learning school material, we want the student to understand the material and the mental process involved. In social-learning theory we are referring to another whole class of behaviors. The material learned in school can, however, also be analyzed under such behavior principles as cognitive behavior, verbal behavior, test-taking responses, and any number of other approaches.

Humanistic Psychology

For many psychologists neither psychoanalytic nor social-learning theories offer an adequate explanation for the fully functioning healthy human who reaches his or her potential. Psychoanalytic theory seems based on a deficit model with the assumption that human nature is inherently destructive, held in check only by repressive measures from the individual or the culture. The pitfalls in normal development are so great that only the rare individual can hope for psychological health. The behaviorists on the other hand offer a limited view of human nature as passively learning from the environment whatever is taught with no vision or motivation to strive for a larger view. To counteract both of these views a third conception of human nature has evolved in American psychology loosely grouped under humanistic psychology.

Humanistic psychology views the individual as unique. Each person is believed to possess great potential, most of which is never used. Proponents of humanistic psychology stress conditions that would stimulate the full development of this potential. The individual is viewed as taking an active part in his or her own development, which is different both in scope and direction from any other person. Each person has value *because* of this uniqueness. The humanistic approach has many different theories, programs, and approaches to human behavior and, therefore, is difficult to categorize specifically. Humanistic psychology has been considered a "third force" in psychology (Maslow, 1968). This force incorporates some of psychoanalytic theory and some ideas from other theories but stresses the positive growth of the individual. This approach is generally optimistic about human nature but, because the theoretical hypotheses are general as opposed to observable behavior, it has not stimulated as much research as the mechanistic school. One of the reasons for a paucity of research in this area is that many humanistic psychologists consider research harmful to human growth and, in fact, rather than helping to understand human behavior, tends to distort the picture. We have found in atomic physics that the very act of observing changes the entities observed, so that research may not really tell us what happens in a natural setting. Humanistic psychologists take the same stance. They hold that when children (or adults) participate in experiments in a laboratory, the method of gathering data itself so distorts behavior that the information tells us nothing useful about human behavior. In a similar fashion they believe that an observer in a natural setting such as a home, observing the relationship between mother and child, so changes that relationship that nothing can be generalized to the behavior of mother and child at home alone. The humanistic psychologist is more interested in designing schools, programs, and strategies for the development of human potential. Development occurs when growth is perceived and only the person growing can determine whether this growth is in the "right" direction and amount. Programs for this growth have included such things as growth seminars of many descriptions, meditation, and consciousness expansion. This approach is more personal, individualistic, and philosophical than the scientific mechanistic world view and more optimistic than the psychoanalytic.

Abraham Maslow and the Hierarchy of Needs

The humanistic view is best expressed in the theory of Abraham Maslow (1908–1970). In his structure, the human is viewed as being motivated intrinsically toward satisfaction of needs. These needs are arranged in a hierarchy and the needs of one level must be met before energy is freed to pursue the satisfaction of needs at the next level. In Maslow's hierarchy of needs, the first level is concerned with basic physiological processes and ascends through self-actualization, the highest level. Maslow has proposed five levels of needs. These are physiological, safety, love and belongingness, esteem, and self-actualization. In Maslow's conception, all actions serve to fulfill intrinsic needs. Thus, the motivation for actions are internal, not external stimuli. When basic survival needs are met, then the higher needs come into being and the person searches for ways to meet and satisfy those needs. The need for self-actualization includes aesthetic and cognitive needs such as painting pictures, studying psychology, and writing a textbook for students.

The humanistic view stresses growth but is not strictly developmental, perhaps because no humanistic psychologist has attempted to explain the development of these higher needs in a systematic way. The emphasis, however, is on growth; therefore a developmental system would be compatible. We have little research or theory relating to development of talent in the visual arts, the musical or dramatic arts, or creative science for that matter. The impressionistic writing of people who have contributed significantly to our culture and experienced feelings of self-actualization give us some clues of the growth of creative personalities. Maslow drew heavily on these writings and interviews with the talented and the famous in developing his theory. This view is one that suggests many directions for both theoretical speculation and further research. The developmental patterns in creative growth could, perhaps, be outlined. We need such concepts in shaping the lives of children. The danger, it seems to your authors, is that without such a view, we might be left with detailed mechanistic techniques to train children to respond with the right answers in math, to construct grammatically correct sentences, to reproduce perfectly geometric shapes, but without access to the intrinsic motivation to self-expression that has given us the Mozarts, the Picassos, and the Einsteins. Of course, most of us, and most of the children we help to form will not be such masters. However, the humanists proclaim, each of us is capable of some measure of self-actualization, and the role of schools, homes, and other institutions of society is to provide means for the individual to actualize his or her potential.

The influence of humanistic psychology is discernible in many programs for children. Many individuals working with children state that they believe in the unique worth of each individual, that the individual must set the goals and direction for personal growth, and that the knowledge for these goals is intrinsic. Many institutions are dedicated to the "full development of the potential of each child." Without being definitively stated these ideas are probably the prevailing view of children in America today both among individuals and schools.

Main Points

Psychoanalytic Theory: Freud

1. According to Freud, the basic personality is formed in the first few years of life within the interpersonal relationships of the family.

2. The personality has three interacting components: the id, ego, and superego.

3. The main function of the id is to satisfy basic biological needs. The id operates on the pleasure principle.

4. The ego operates on the reality principle to satisfy the drives of the id and the moralistic demands of the superego.

5. The ego uses defense mechanisms to protect itself from the instinctual pressures of the id.

6. The superego contains both the moral rules and the ideals of society.

7. Freud found that personality development is related to sexual development. In sexual development different body areas become the focus of pleasure at successive ages and events related to the stimulation of those body areas affect the basic personality structure. Freud identified the psychosexual stages as the oral, anal, phallic, (latency period), and genital.

Erikson's Psychosocial Theory

8. Erikson reinterpreted psychoanalytic theory with an emphasis on social development and the adaptive capacities of the ego; he extended developmental stages into adulthood and old age.

9. The first stage of psychosocial development occurs in infancy, from birth to eighteen months of age, and is characterized by the developmental crisis of basic trust versus mistrust.

10. The second of Erikson's stages, autonomy versus shame and doubt, occurs from eighteen months to three years, is manifest in bowel and bladder control, and may result in a child who has self-control and will power or one who is obsessive.

11. The third stage of psychosocial development is initiative versus guilt and occurs from three to six years; the resolution of this crisis may develop a sense of responsibility, accomplishment, direction, and purpose or shame and guilt.

12. During the elementary school years (six through twelve years of age) the ego crisis is between developing a sense of industry, method, competence, and productivity or a sense of inferiority and inadequacy.

13. The adolescent years, twelve through twenty-one, involve meeting and resolving the conflict between establishing an integrated identity or role confusion.

14. Erikson described three adult stages: intimacy versus isolation (young adulthood); generativity versus stagnation (adulthood); and ego integrity versus despair (maturity).

Piaget's Cognitive Theory

15. Piaget termed his investigation of the child's understanding of space, time, logic, and mathematics *genetic epistemology*—i.e., knowledge through biological adaptation.

16. The biological structure that adapts is a scheme, a mental organization that guides behavior.

17. The process of intellectual functioning is biologically (genetically) determined; therefore, it is the same for all humans (functionally invariant).

18. Assimilation is the incorporation of new experiences into existing schemes; accommodation occurs when new experiences require a change in existing schemes. Equilibration is the balance between assimilation and accommodation.

19. The child is intrinsically motivated to master new skills and to seek new experiences.

Social-Learning Theory

20. John B. Watson developed behaviorism, the study of objective, measurable behavior; the theory holds that the environment determines a characteristic through reinforcement.

21. Edward L. Thorndike demonstrated the importance of reward and punishment in learning and formulated the law of effect.

22. Social-learning theory assumes that the human is a blank slate at birth and that all behavior, intelligence, personality, talents, and/or temperament are the result of learning in the social environment.

23. Skinner discovered that behaviors are controlled by their consequences, which can be examined and studied in reinforcement schedules.

24. Respondent conditioning refers to behavior that occurs in response to a stimulus; operant conditioning is behavior that is controlled by its consequences.

25. Anything that follows a behavior and strengthens or increases it is reinforcement.

26. Extinction is the disappearance of a behavior when it is no longer reinforced.

27. Punishment suppresses behavior; negative reinforcement is behavior that allows the child to escape from or avoid some other event.

28. Motivation, for behaviorists, depends on the effectiveness of the reinforcers.

Humanistic Psychology: Abraham Maslow and the Hierarchy of Needs

29. Humanistic psychology is a force between psychoanalytic theory and behaviorism that sees the human as creative and striving toward self-actualization. Maslow has expressed this intrinsic drive toward becoming as a hierarchy of needs.

Words to Know

accommodation
aggression
aliment
anal
assimilation
behaviorism
cognitive
conscience
ego
ego ideal
eros

fixation
genital
homeostasis
id
identification
latency
narcissistic
oral
phallic
preoperational
psychoanalytic

psychosexual
psychosocial
rationalization
regression
reinforcement
repression
scheme (schemes)
sublimation
superego
thanatos

Terms to Define

genetic epistemology
hierarchy of needs
hypothetical construct
instinctual gratification

pleasure principle
psychic energy
reality principle

Concepts to Discuss

humanistic psychology
instinct
psychoanalytic personality dynamics
psychosocial developmental crises
social learning

Glossary

Adam principle The principle whereby a male embryo is differentiated from the fertilized ovum by the stimulation of the hormone testosterone.

abortion The expulsion of a fetus from the uterus before it is able to support its own life processes. The expulsion may occur spontaneously (it is then termed a miscarriage) or can be induced by mechanical or chemical intervention.

accommodation Changes in mental structure that occur as the result of the incorporation of a new concept, image, or other mental material that will not fit into existing structures. One of the three invariants in the process of mental functioning, according to Piaget's theory of cognition.

achievement test A test designed to measure the knowledge or skill that a person has already acquired.

acquired adaptation The changes that a person makes in response to environmental conditions, pressures, or stimuli.

acuity Keenness of sensory perception, as vision.

aggression Hostile, injurious, or destructive behavior directed toward another person or an object.

aliment In Piaget's cognitive theory, anything that is incorporated into mental structures, especially new experiences. Piaget intended to convey that the incorporation and assimilation of perceptions by the cognitive process is analogous to the digestion of food.

ambidexterity The ability to use both hands with equal ease and skill.

amino acids The building blocks of living cells. Cells can synthesize some of these amino acids, but others must be supplied by diet. Amino acids are the chief components of proteins, either animal or vegetable.

amniotic sac A thin membrane forming a sac that encloses the fetus. It contains a fluid in which the embryo/fetus is suspended and that cushions and protects it during its development.

anal The second stage of Freud's psychosexual development, so designated because the focus of bodily pleasure and concern shifts to the anal zone as toilet training becomes paramount in physical development.

animism The belief of young children that everything has life. Characteristic of the thinking of the child in Piaget's preoperational stage of cognitive development.

anorexia nervosa A disorder of eating that is characterized by prolonged refusal to eat and is often accompanied by self-induced vomiting. It mainly affects adolescent girls.

anoxia A condition in which there is an insufficient amount of oxygen reaching the tissues of the body, often resulting in permanent damage, especially to brain and nerve cells.

anxiety A psychological state of apprehension, fear, or dread without a realistic threat of danger. This state is often accompanied by physiological signs such as sweating, tension, and increased pulse. It may also be accompanied by self-doubt as to one's ability to cope with the situation.

Apgar scale A measurement scale used for evaluating an infant's physiological functioning in the areas of pulse, breathing, muscle tone, reflex response, and color one minute and five minutes after birth.

areola The area surrounding the nipple of the breast that is lighter than the nipple yet darker than the breast. In breast development of girls at puberty this area may be raised from the surface of the breast. With further development it sinks back to the surface of the breast and only the nipple remains raised.

artificialism The belief of young children that everything is made by someone. It is the companion to animism (the belief that everything has life) in young children who are in Piaget's preoperational stage of cognitive development.

assimilation The incorporation of perceptions or other mental material into already existing mental structures. One of the three invariants in the process of mental functioning, according to Piaget's theory of cognition.

attachment The process or accomplished state in which one person has an affectional tie to another specific person, by which the two people are emotionally bound together in an affection that endures over time. Emotions are usually positive and are usually described as love.

authoritarian An attitude of parental control characterized by the attempt to shape, control, and evaluate the behavior and attitudes of their children in accordance with an absolute set of standards. Authoritarian parents tend to value obedience, respect for authority, work, tradition, and preservation of order and to discourage verbal give-and-take with their children.

authoritative An attitude of parental control characterized by the attempt to direct children by rational, issue-oriented explanations and reasons for demands and discipline. Authoritative parents encourage verbal give-and-take but use power when it is necessary.

autonomy The state of being self-governing. For the individual this indicates freedom, especially psychological independence to choose one's own goals and actions.

axillary hair Hair that grows in the armpits with the onset of puberty.

babbling The sounds that an infant makes that are clearly composed of vowels and consonants, such as *ma, ma, ma.* Infants produce these sounds in repetitive sequences and parents by selective reinforcement encourage and shape the infant's first words.

Babinski reflex A reflex that is present at birth in normal development in which the toes fan outward when the sole of the foot is stroked.

basal metabolic rate The rate at which food is converted into new tissues, energy, and waste products. This rate is highest in early infancy and immediately prior to puberty.

behavioral genetics The study of the effect of genetics on behavior.

behaviorism   A theory in psychology that holds that the proper concern of psychology is observable behavior. It opposes other theories that study hypothetical constructs such as personality, traits, or unconscious motives. Behaviorism also holds that the motivation for behavior is external stimuli rather than internal drives.

bias   A systematic error that is introduced into a scientific experiment by the preference of the experimenter for one outcome over another. Bias can enter into experiments in the selection of subjects, the assignment of subjects to groups, the presentation of the experiment to the subjects, and the interpretation of subject's responses.

bilingualism   The ability to speak two languages with equal ease.

bonding   The first stage in the process of the formation of an emotional attachment between infants and parents. Bonding begins soon after birth in the reciprocal interactions between infants and their mothers and fathers and leads to permanent attachment.

bone age   An estimate of developmental age by measuring the percentage of cartilage that has hardened into bone.

Caesarian section   A surgical technique for birth in which an incision is made in the abdomen and uterus and the baby lifted out. It is believed that Julius Caesar was born in this way; hence the name.

castration   Literally, to deprive of testes or ovaries. The term is used in psychoanalytic theory to denote the psychological deprivation of vitality or affect.

castration anxiety   The psychoanalytic term for fear that a more powerful person, originally a parent, will forcefully render one unable to undertake and execute autonomous action, that is, impotent.

cause-and-effect relationship   The rational, logical relationship between one event and another in which one event is the cause of the other. Efforts to establish such relationships have been highly successful in the physical sciences and have led to increasing control of the physical world. They are more difficult to establish in the area of human behavior because the causes of behavior are often multiple and very complex.

centered   In Piaget's theory, the characteristic tendency of the child in the preoperational stage to focus on one aspect of a problem and ignore other relevant information.

central vision   That part of vision that enables the eye to focus on an object and draw detailed information. A complement to peripheral vision in which general information is gathered. A person who has only central vision loses information and has tunnel vision.

centration   The process, in Piaget's theory, of focusing on only one aspect of a problem.

cephalocaudal development   The principle by which development proceeds from the head downward.

cerebral palsy   A disability resulting from damage to the brain that occurs before or during birth. The most common effects are lack of muscular coordination and speech disturbances.

cervix   The narrow neck of the uterus with an opening that increases in the process of birth to a size that allows the passage of the baby's head.

child abuse   The physical, sexual, and sometimes psychological mistreatment of a child by parents, teachers, or other adults responsible for the child's well-being. Abuse may involve covert actions or the withholding of necessary conditions or food, which constitutes neglect.

chromosomes   Microscopic particles that contain an individual's heredity information. Every cell of a living organism contains all the genetic information for that organism. Humans have 23 pairs of chromosomes and each chromosome contains thousands of different genetic messages, called *genes.*

class   The grouping of objects that have similar characteristics, as *boys* and *girls.*

class inclusion   The concept of a large group (class) incorporating smaller groups, e.g., the class *children* includes both the classes *girls* and *boys.* The ability to group in classes and to think in terms of class inclusion is a criterion of the transition from preoperational to operational thinking in Piaget's theory.

classification   The process of placing objects in the group or class by similarity of characteristics. Objects may be grouped by color, shape, size, and so forth. In more advanced thinking abstract concepts, such as ideas, can be classified on various dimensions.

cognition   The act or process of knowing.

cognitive   Refers to the process of knowing. The word *cognitive* requires a noun to complete a thought, as, "cognitive theory," (a theory about the process of knowing).

cohort   In behavioral research, a group of people who were born in the same time span and thus grew up in the same historical time period. An example of a cohort is the generation that was between 18 and 25 years old during the Vietnam War.

compensation   A psychological reaction by which feelings of inferiority or failure in one area are counterbalanced by feelings of achievement and superiority in another.

conception   The penetration of an ovum by a sperm; whereby the single 23 chromosomes of the ovum and sperm unite in pairs forming a full complement of heredity information for the creation of a new human being. As a result of conception, the woman in whom this conception has taken place becomes pregnant.

conceptus   The product of conception: the fertilized ovum as it develops into zygote, embryo, and fetus.

congenital   Any condition or characteristic that exists at birth, but that was acquired during development in the uterus and not through heredity.

connotation   The meaning suggested by a word or phrase beyond the explicit definition. The individual hearing the word or phrase extends its definition from his or her own experiences and emotions associated with the word. There are common connotations that a group applies to words and phrases because of common cultural experiences. For example, all Christians probably invest the word *crucifixion* with certain connotations because that was the way that Jesus died.

conscience   In psychoanalytic theory, that part of the superego that contains the rules and morals of the society, that dictates to the ego the right action required, and punishes the ego with guilt when this action is not followed or when rules are broken.

conservation   In Piaget's theory, the concept that a substance remains the same even when it is physically transformed in some way. For example, a child who can conserve perceives that the volume of a ball of clay that has been transformed into an elongated shape remains the same because nothing has been added or taken away.

conventional morality   The second stage in Kohlberg's three-stage theory of moral development in which social standards are the prevailing guide to right and wrong.

coordination of senses   The act of bringing two, or more, senses together to perform a single movement or act, as when a young infant realizes that mother's voice and her visual image belong to the same person. Later the infant coordinates these sense perceptions with hand movement and reaches for objects.

critical periods   A principle of development that states that an organism is most susceptible to environmental influences at the time of most rapid growth or development. This principle is especially evident in physical development in the early prenatal period. The developing embryo is most susceptible to organ damage by toxins at the time when those organs are developing.

cross-sectional research   A design for research in which subjects are assigned to groups according to ages and different age groups are studied for the same variable. When groups are matched for other relevant variables such as sex and family background, any differences are thus assumed to be due to age.

decoding   The process of extracting meaning from words, usually written ones. The term is used in analyzing the reading process to specify the comprehension of the words rather than a mechanical rendering of them.

deferred imitation   The imitation of a model that is not present and that was seen performing an act at some time in the past. Piaget marks the ability for deferred imitation as an important attainment in intellectual development, as the knowledge of the act must be stored in memory and retrieved at a later time.

delinquency   The behavior of a juvenile that is in willful and deliberate violation of law and that will bring him or her under legal judgment if the act is brought to the attention of law enforcement officers.

deoxyribonucleic acid (DNA)   The chemical substance that makes up genetic material. An important discovery in breaking the genetic code was the discovery of the structure of DNA, a double helix, which enables the molecule to split in half and rebuild each half, thus replicating itself.

dependent variable   A behavior or condition that is caused by (dependent on) another variable (independent variable). In experiments that establish a cause-and-effect relationship between variables, the dependent variable is the effect.

depression   A psychological state characterized by sadness, inactivity, difficulty in thinking and concentration, and feelings of dejection.

deprivational dwarfism   A condition of retarded growth caused by psychological conditions of maternal deprivation.

derived status   Status that is obtained by a relationship with an admired person, as the status that one has because of the work that one's parent or mate does.

desatellization   The process of disengagement from the psychological position of a satellite of a parent. Children begin this process around eight years of age as they begin to move toward psychological independence.

descriptive research   Research that is undertaken to describe a process of development or typical behavior at certain age levels. Descriptive research cannot identify causes of behavior.

develop   To unfold, expand, or differentiate gradually by a process of growth.

development   A process of natural growth, differentiation, or evolution that gradually takes place. The pattern of this process is set in each species.

developmental scales   An instrument used to compare the development of an individual to normal development for children of the same age. A developmental scale may indicate the average ages for the sequence of crawling and walking and an individual's progress can then be compared to this scale.

developmental tasks   Achievements that a child must accomplish in the process of growth and development. Some tasks are physical, as walking or learning sphincter control, and others are psychological, as gaining autonomy.

dialect   A variation of a language in factors such as pronunciation, grammar, and vocabulary. Dialects may be by region, as a Southern or a New England dialect; they may be characteristic of a group, as a black dialect; or they may indicate social class.

dimorphism (dimorphic)   Existing in two different forms. The presence of two sexes, male and female, is dimorphic in a species.

disinhibit   To remove previously established inhibitions. In Bandura's explanation, the relationship between viewing televised violence and aggressive behavior is that violent television models remove an inhibition to perform aggressive behavior.

dominant inheritance   A pattern of heredity by which one gene of a pair exerts control and is expressed, whereas the information in the other gene is suppressed.

early maturers   Individuals who begin the process of sexual maturation at a younger age than the norm. Precocious (early) puberty is diagnosed when this process begins before the age of eight in girls or nine and one half in boys. By the age of ten most girls have begun the process of puberty. The average girl begins the adolescent growth spurt at eleven, and menstruation by thirteen. Most boys have begun the process of puberty by age 12, the growth spurt by 13 and reach sexual maturity around fifteen.

echolalia   The repetition of what is said by others as if echoing them. Associated with pathological conditions in children, such as autism.

ectoderm   The outermost layer of cells which differentiates when the embryo first separates into three layers. The ectoderm will develop into skin, nails, hair, teeth, brain, spinal cord, and sensory organs.

ego   In Freudian theory, one of the three components of the personality. The ego consists of the rational, conscious self.

egocentric   Concern with the primary importance of one's own activities or needs that prevents taking another's point of view or the larger view of ideologies or causes.

ego-devaluation crisis   A conflict that arises between parents and child when parents begin to demand that the child control impulses. This conflict can reach crisis proportions when the child is around two years of age. The infant is allowed to indulge all of his or her impulses: eating when hungry, sleeping when tired; crying when angry. When parents demand that the older child control impulses, he or she feels devalued and fights to retain omnipotence.

ego-ideal In psychoanalytic theory, that part of the superego that contains the ideal of perfection by which the self and others are judged.

ego-maturation crisis The internal crisis that ensues when, in late childhood, the personality organization that was useful in coping with the world as a child becomes maladaptive. This crisis of maturation forces a new organization of personality, which moves the individual toward independence and responsibility for self.

ego-maturation goals Those goals that the culture sets for all members. These include being able to care for oneself physically, including earning a living; accepting the moral standards of the culture; and control of impulses by putting off their immediate satisfaction in favor of more distant goals.

ejaculation The expulsion of semen by the male during sexual orgasm.

elaborated language A spoken form of language that is formal and generally follows the rules for the written form with complete sentences, correct grammar, and little redundancy; accompanied by few gestures and little emotion.

Electra complex In psychoanalytic theory, the name applied to the feelings that young girls have of hostility and jealousy for the mother and the wish to possess the father. The name is taken from an ancient Greek story in which Electra kills her mother as revenge for the murder of her father. The Electra complex is the counterpart for girls of the Oedipus complex.

embryo The name applied to the developing human individual from the time of implantation in the uterus to the end of the eighth week after conception.

embryonic period The time from the second through the eighth week after conception, characterized by differentiation of form out of the conceptual mass, the laying down of fundamental tissues, and the formation of all organs and systems.

encoding The translation of thoughts and feelings into words, either written or spoken.

endoderm The innermost layer of cells, which differentiates when the embryo separates into three layers. The endoderm will develop into the internal organs such as the gastrointestinal tract, liver, lungs, and various glands.

epiphysis The end of a bone, especially the long bones, from which growth occurs.

eros In psychoanalytic theory, one of the two basic drives. Eros is the life drive: the propulsion within the person toward love, sexual union, and positive cultural achievements.

ethical That which conforms to accepted professional standards of conduct, as in ethical standards for conducting research.

Eve principle The law of development that states that in the absence of information to the contrary, the human embryo will develop into a female. The information that dictates the differentiation of a male is the hormone, testosterone, which the male embryo itself must supply.

executive independence The ability to undertake actions that will secure for an individual those things he or she needs for survival and satisfaction.

exosystem The community within which families and individuals are embedded, including the workplace of adults and schools, clubs, churches, and other organizations.

experimental A method of acquiring knowledge in which an operation is carried out under carefully controlled conditions to test a hypothesis or discover an unknown law or effect.

expressive language   The words and language forms that a child is actually able to produce and use.

fallopian tube   Either of a pair of tubes that are connected to the uterus and open near the ovaries. Mature ova are released from the ovaries and conducted through the fallopian tubes. Fertilization usually takes place in the fallopian tube.

fertility   The condition of being fertile, able to conceive offspring.

fetal period   The time from the end of the eighth week of gestation to birth, characterized by final perfection of form and rapid growth.

fetus   The name applied to the developing human individual from the end of the eighth week of gestation to birth.

fine motor   The small muscles of the hands and fingers that allow humans to use tools. In young children control of fine muscles is necessary to hold and use pencils, scissors, and other tools.

fixation   A psychoanalytic term that refers to being stopped or blocked at a certain psychological level and unable to move beyond that point.

gender identity   The cognitive labeling of one's gender: the assignment of male or female made by the culture. Children accept whatever assignment they are given, whether or not it is in accord with their biological gender, provided such assignment is made before approximately two and a half years of age.

gender role   The assignment of behaviors as appropriate or inappropriate according to sex. As, for example, girls and women wear dresses and boys and men do not.

genes   The smallest discrete units of heredity. Genes exist as sequences on long strands of DNA.

genetic code   The information that is coded in genes and chromosomes through the chemical structure of DNA. By duplicating this structure, the individual cells are able to "read" this information, produce the chemicals directed by the genetic code, and thus produce characteristics such as red hair, blue eyes, or Down's syndrome.

genetic defects   Deviations in genetic information that are detrimental to the individual. Errors in genetic information may result in errors in physical form (six fingers), function (mental retardation), or errors in metabolism (PKU).

genetic epistemology   The name applied to Piaget's theory of cognitive development.

genital   Having to do with the sex organs (genitalia). The fourth stage in Freud's theory of psychosexual development, in which an individual achieves satisfaction through a mutually satisfying relationship with another person involving stimulation of the genitals.

genotype   The entire genetic information that an individual carries.

germinal period   The first two weeks after conception, in which the fertilized ovum travels the length of the fallopian tube and implants in the uterus. During this time the original cell divides and the cell mass separates into the three layers: ectoderm, mesoderm, and endoderm.

gratification   The satisfaction of needs and/or drives.

gross motor   The large muscles that are used in running, jumping, riding vehicles, throwing balls, and other movements of large proportions.

growth spurt   A period of rapid physical growth that occurs in association with puberty and begins around the age of eleven in girls and thirteen in boys.

hereditary   Something that is genetically transmitted or transmittable from parent to offspring.

heredity   That which is genetically derived from one's ancestors or the transmission of qualities or characteristics from parent to offspring through genes and chromosomes.

heritability   The state of being capable of being inherited.

heterozygous   The condition in which the gene received from the father and that received from the mother differ.

holophrase   A one-word sentence that is produced by infants in their first efforts to speak.

homeostasis   A state of being physically (or psychologically) in equilibrium; as, soon after eating, the body is neither over-sated nor in a state of deprivation but in equilibrium. Living organisms seek homeostasis and drives are a motivation toward objects or events that achieve this.

homozygous   The condition in which the gene received from the father and that received from the mother for the same trait are the same, as, an individual must be homozygous for the trait of blue eyes in order to have them.

hypothesis   A tentative assumption (an educated guess) made in order to test its truthfulness by logical or experimental means. The scientific method was invented in order to test such tentative assumptions by objective experience, which is then examined by logical reasoning.

hypothetical construct   A concept or entity, the existence of which is only a hypothesis, yet which is useful for conducting experiments or building theory; as, the concept of intelligence. We have no direct evidence that such an entity exists, yet it is a useful concept: it is measured, it is evaluated, and it is assumed to influence many other things.

id   One of the three components of personality in Freudian theory. The id is the source of all instinctual drives and the seat of the unconscious.

identity   That in a person or thing that distinguishes it from all other persons or things; in a person, those elements of character or personality that are distinguishing. In Erikson's theory of psychosocial development, the adolescent years entail a crisis in each individual's search for his or her own identiy. In Piaget's cognitive theory, identity refers to the concept that physical objects remain the same (retain identity) even when they are transformed in appearance.

identity achievement   A state of self-knowledge in which an individual is pursuing self-chosen occupational and ideological goals. This state is usually preceded by a decision-making period with mental and psychological upheaval.

identity diffusion   A state of confusion and indecision about occupational and ideological directions, usually preceded by a decision-making period but without clear conclusions.

identity foreclosures A state of commitment to occupational and ideological positions that were made for the individual by parents.

identity moratorium The decision-making period about occupational or ideological issues, the outcome of which is uncertain.

identification A psychological mechanism by which a child incorporates the personality, values, and actions of a parent into his or her own personality: they become the same. In psychoanalytic theory this is accomplished by introjection of the parents' personality. In social-learning theory, it is accomplished by modeling and imitation and the desire of the child to be like the parent.

imaginary audience The belief and feeling in early adolescence that every action and detail of appearance is being observed and judged by others.

imprinting The process by which newly hatched ducks and geese become attached to a maternal object. The stimulus for this attachment is the visual perception of a large moving object, which may be a person, a cardboard box, the mother goose, or any other object. Imprinting takes place soon after hatching and is evidence for a critical period for attachment between mother and offspring.

impulse In psychoanalytic theory, a drive toward gratification that originates in the unconscious (id).

impulse control The conscious and willful control of aggressive and destructive drives. In psychoanalytic theory it is the role of the ego to satisfy impulses through means that are rational and socially acceptable, or to deflect these impulses into more acceptable pursuits.

independent variable In experiments, the variable that is hypothesized to be the cause of an effect; can be manipulated by the experimenter to test the effect of this manipulation.

individuation The psychological separation of child from parents. There are three periods of individuation: at the end of infancy, at the end of the preschool years, and in adolescence.

inhibition A psychological mechanism that forbids or restricts the spontaneous expression of impulses or actions.

innate Inherent in an individual; present from conception.

instinct Behavior patterns or aptitudes that are inherited rather than learned from experience but that may be released by environmental stimuli. Instinct in lower animals is easily identified, as when birds of the same species build identical nests; however, the role of heredity in human behavior is debatable. Freud postulated two classes of instincts that were operative and often in conflict in humans: the life instincts (eros) and the death instincts (thanatos). Social learning theorists postulate no instincts.

instinctual gratification The satisfaction of drives that are below the conscious level.

intelligence A quality of the conscious mind that enables a person to learn quickly and easily, to reason logically, to solve problems, and to cope with new situations. As psychologists study intelligence, they are unable to arrive at a definition that all theories agree upon. Perhaps the definition that most would agree upon is that intelligence is the ability to learn, that is, scholastic aptitude.

intelligence quotient (IQ) A score obtained on an intelligence test that is reported in numbers. Most IQ tests measure an individual's aptitude for learning in school. The average IQ in the general population is 100.

intelligence test A test designed to measure intelligence.

interactionism The theory that development proceeds through a complex interaction of heredity and environment.

intervention The act of interfering in the natural course of development. Programs such as Head Start and others designed to compensate for presumed deficits of a group of people intervene in the patterns of child-rearing that the parents and community have evolved in an attempt to better equip the children to function in the technological society.

introjection The psychological process by which a child incorporates the personality of a parent into his or her own. Identification with a parent is the result of introjection.

irreversibility In Piaget's theory, a quality of thinking characteristic of the preoperational child in which processes cannot be mentally reversed; as for example, when a child sees a sphere of clay rolled into an elongated shape and is unable to mentally reverse this process and imagine the clay as it was previously—a sphere.

karyotype An actual photograph of chromosomes in which they are arranged in pairs according to size.

Lamaze method A techique of education for childbirth in which the woman is taught exercises and breathing techniques to be used in childbirth.

Language acquisition device An innate structure for learning language that renders the child receptive to vocabulary, grammar, and inflection; however, the content, the specific language, is learned.

late maturers Individuals who begin the process of sexual maturation at a later age than the norm.

latency In Freud's theory of psychosexual development, a period (not a stage) between the phallic stage of early childhood and the genital stage of adolescence in which psychological conflict is quiescent.

lateralization The process by which specific areas of the brain assume control of specific functions. In early development many areas of the brain serve multiple purposes. If the brain is damaged in a young organism before lateralization another area of the brain may take over the function.

locomotion The act of moving from one place to another.

longitudinal research A design for research in which the same subjects are studied repeatedly over a long period of time to determine changes that occur with increasing age.

macrosystem The larger culture, including the nation and system of beliefs, in which local communities, families, and individuals are embedded.

maternal deprivation A loss of the mother figure or inadequate mothering by one who is present, with negative effects on the child's emotional, intellectual, social, and sometimes physical development.

maturation The process of growth in which time is the most important factor because development is seen as an unfolding process of forms and qualities that are inherent in the organism, as, the way a bud unfolds into a flower.

mechanistic world-view The philosophical conviction that nature is essentially a great machine that operates by laws in a predictable pattern. In this mechanical universe all events have identifiable causes that are knowable and controllable.

menarche The beginning of menstruation.

menstruation The breakdown of the lining of the uterus that results in a discharge of blood and tissue in monthly cycles; occurs in women who have reached sexual maturity.

mental operations Piaget's term for the transformations that are performed on mental representations.

mesoderm The middle layer of cells that differentiates when the embryo separates into three layers. The mesoderm will develop into the circulatory and excretory systems, the skeleton, and the muscles attached to it.

microsystem The smallest social system to which an individual belongs: the family or those living in the same household and interacting daily.

miscarriage The name applied to a spontaneous abortion.

morality The principles, rules, or reasoning by which behavior is judged as right or wrong.

Moro reflex A reflex, present in the newborn, in which the infant flings the arms wide, arches the back and slowly brings the arms together in response to a sudden loud noise or loss of support.

motor development The development of movement and muscular skill and coordination. "Motor" refers to motion.

narcissism Preoccupation with one's own body or concerns. In psychoanalytic theory the term applied to a person who is unable to go beyond self-concerns and form relationships with others.

natural childbirth A name erroneously applied to educated childbirth. "Natural" childbirth implies that behavior is unlearned, as natural digestion, whereas all programs for training in childbirth entail learning new techniques and behaviors to use during labor and delivery.

negativism The tendency to oppose whatever is suggested by someone else. Often a characteristic of children between eighteen months and three years as they discover their own independence.

neonatal period The period immediately after birth, extending through the first month.

neonate An infant that has been recently born; the infant in the first month after birth.

nonverbal Conveyed through means other than words, such as gestures, facial expressions, or general bodily movements.

norm A statistical term that refers to a standard to which an individual is compared. For example, the height of an individual child can be compared to data compiled from a national sample to determine how the child ranks in comparison to all children in the United States.

nutrition The total process of obtaining and utilizing the food necessary to promote growth and maintain repairs in the body.

obesity The condition of having excessive fat content in the body.

object permanence Piaget's term for the mental concept that an object continues to exist even when no longer perceived by the senses.

Oedipus complex Freud's term for the feelings that children have of hostility and jealousy for the parent of the same sex and desire to possess the parent of the opposite sex; named for the Greek myth in which Oedipus kills his father and marries his mother.

omnipotent The quality or state of being all-powerful. The infant, because all wishes and impulses are satisfied, feels himself or herself to be omnipotent.

oral The first stage in Freud's theory of psychosexual development, so designated because in the first year of life the focus of bodily pleasure and concern is the mouth; and the world, including the mother, is experienced by incorporation through the mouth.

ordinal Arranged by rank, as *first, second, third,* and so forth.

organismic world-view The philosophical conviction that the best model for studying human behavior is the living organism, which is spontaneously active, is organized, and changes in an orderly progression over time.

ossification The process in which cartilage is replaced with bone; used as an estimate of developmental age.

ovum (*plural* ova) The name applied to the human egg that is matured in the ovary of the female and released. A released ovum is swept into the fallopian tube and may be fertilized there by a sperm from the male to begin the development of a new individual.

ovulation The process whereby a mature ovum (egg) is released from the ovary.

papilla The anatomical name for the nipple of the breast.

penis The anatomical name that refers to part of the external sexual organs of the male; the other part being the testes.

penis envy A psychoanalytic term for the feelings of inadequacy and castration that girls might experience on the discovery that they do not possess a penis.

peer In the study of children, a child who is the same age as the subject.

peer group The term that designates the entire group of children or adolescents of similar age; most often applied to adolescents, in referring to the historical cohort of teenagers or to the total sum of cultural or behavioral influences from the adolescent same-age group.

perception The act of receiving information through the senses, or the result of such a reception, such as a visual image.

peripheral That which is located away from a central position. In vision, refers to images that are outside the central focus, but nevertheless supply information used to direct focus to objects moving into view.

permissive An attitude of parental management characterized by few controls. Permissive parents tend to accept a child's impulses, desires, and actions, place few demands on the child for mature behavior, and give in to the child's demands.

personal fable The myth that young adolescents construct about themselves, which includes dreams for accomplishment and the belief in their own immortality and ability to accomplish great feats in the world.

personality   A psychological term that refers to the total of internal traits, characteristics, and consistent attitudes that identify the individual as unique. In psychoanalytic theory, the personality is a dynamic relationship among three components: the id, the ego, and the superego. Social-learning theorists and behaviorists view personality as a "mentalistic" fiction and not a useful concept.

phallic   The third stage in Freud's theory of psychosexual development, so named because the focus of bodily gratification is centered on the manipulation of the genitals themselves. This stage extends from the approximate ages of three to six years; during this time the Oedipus complex is the major psychological dynamic.

phenotype   The genetic characteristics that are expressed in an individual.

phonemes   The smallest discrete units of sound that comprise speech.

phylogenetic   Being a characteristic or trait acquired in the course of the development of the species and present in all members of the species, as speech.

Piagetian   Having to do with Piaget and his theory of cognitive development.

placenta   A small disc-shaped organ that unites the fetus to the maternal uterus. The placenta is attached to the uterine wall by many small root-like capillaries and to the fetus by the umbilical cord. All nutrients and waste products are exchanged between mother and fetus through the placental system.

placental barrier   The screening offered by the placenta that prevents certain molecules from passing from the system of the mother into the fetus. The placental barrier is not as effective as it was once believed; it is now known that most drugs and many disease organisms can cross this barrier.

pleasure principle   In psychoanalytic theory, the principle whereby the organism seeks to prolong pleasure and seeks the gratification of impulses. The id is governed by the pleasure principle.

polygene and single gene control   The determination of whether a trait under genetic control is determined by a single gene, or by the combination of many different genes.

postconventional morality   The third and highest in Kohlberg's stages of moral development, in which moral reasoning is based on universal principles. Universal principles are deemed higher than the conventional rules of society and therefore take precedence over society's conventions.

preadolescent   A child between the ages of nine and twelve and generally in the beginning stages of puberty.

preconcept   The first ideas that the child develops about the world, often wrong, and usually based on the assumptions that everything is alive and was made by someone. As these erroneous preconcepts are modified and changed they develop into true concepts.

preconserver   A child who has not yet attained the concept that a substance remains the same even when the physical appearance is transformed in some way. When this concept is attained, the child is said to be able to *conserve;* in Piaget's theory, this is a necessary attainment for logical thought and for the performance of consistent mental operations.

preconventional morality   The first stage in Kohlberg's three stages of moral development. At this stage of moral reasoning, the welfare of the individual is paramount and morality is a question of mutual back-scratching.

prehension   The act of grasping with the hands.

premature An event that occurs before the appointed time, as a premature birth, when an infant is born before the full gestation period has elapsed.

prenatal Before birth. The period between conception and birth, and events and conditions relating to this period.

preoperational The second of four stages in Piaget's theory of cognitive development. This stage covers the ages between two and six or seven and is characterized by barriers to logical thought such as egocentrism, centering on only one aspect of a problem, the inability to reverse thought, the inability to take into account the process of transformation from one state to another, and reasoning that if two things occur together one caused the other.

primary circular reaction A typical behavior of infants in which the infant performs an action which produces an effect which causes the action to be repeated in a circular manner. For example, from the reflex of sucking the infant spontaneously puts a thumb into his or her mouth. The sensation of sucking the thumb is pleasurable, both in the mouth and on the thumb, which tends to cause the act of thumbsucking to be repeated. Primary circular reactions are generally centered on the infant's own body.

primary status Status that the individual gains by his or her own actions.

process of labor The process by which a fetus is expelled from the uterus, which begins with contractions of the uterus and ends after the birth of the baby with the expulsion of the placenta and membranes from the uterus.

prosocial behaviors Positive social behaviors such as cooperation, sharing, and caring. Prosocial behaviors have been studied as the other side of the effect of television. Research has shown rather conclusively that violent television can cause aggressive behavior. Thus researchers asked the logical question, "Could socially positive television cause prosocial behavior?"

psychic energy A term in psychoanalytic theory that refers to energy freed from the id (unconscious) for the use of the ego (conscious). Such energy from the id can be sublimated into cultural activities such as art productions, sports, and even war. In fact, all cultural achievements come into being using energy diverted from the unconscious id.

psychoanalytic A term referring to the psychological theory developed by Sigmund Freud known as psychoanalysis.

psychoanalytic personality dynamics The theory that personality functions through a dynamic (ever-changing) relationship among the three components of the personality: the unconscious source of instinctual behavior (id); the rational, conscious mind (ego); and the internalized morals and standards of the culture (superego). These three may often be in conflict but must be kept in some kind of dynamic equilibrium for healthy functioning.

psychoprophylaxis The technical name that refers to the Lamaze method of childbirth education (**prophylaxis:** the prevention of; **psycho:** by psychological means). Therefore the word means "the prevention, by psychological means, (of fear and pain in childbirth)".

psychosexual The dynamic relationship between sexual development and psychological processes; Freud's term for the development that he outlined describing this progressive interaction.

psychosocial The dynamic relationship between social development and psychological processes. Erikson's term for the development described in his theory.

psychosocial crisis   In Erikson's theory, the crisis between a positive and a negative outcome that is evident in each of the eight stages in his theory of development from infancy through old age.

pubertal   Having to do with puberty.

puberty   The period of development in which boys and girls become sexually mature. Puberty is a process rather than an event, although in primitive societies the change of status from child to adult is marked with a ceremony of a "rite of passage." In modern societies first menstruation is sometimes considered the event of puberty.

pubescent   Refers to boys and girls who are in the process of arriving or who have recently arrived at puberty.

random assignment   A technique used to prevent bias in the selection of subjects in experiments, in which selection and assignment to groups is made according to chance.

rationalization   In psychoanalytic theory, a mechanism of the ego that defends against the impulses of the id, or the superego, by converting them into rational tightly constructed arguments.

reality principle   In psychoanalytic theory, the principle of rational logic that governs the ego. The ego is the only component of the personality that is rational.

receptive language   The language that is understood, even though the person may not be able to produce and use the same language. Receptive language is always greater than expressive language, or that at the person's command.

recessive inheritance   A pattern of heredity in which information is needed from both genes in a pair in order to be expressed, as blue eyes require a gene from each pair.

reflex   An involuntary behavior that occurs in response to a specific stimulus, as a leg-jerk in response to a sharp tap on the knee.

regression   Movement from a higher to a lower level of organization or development.

reinforcer   Anything that increases the likelihood that a given response will occur again. A key principle in behaviorism is that behavior is maintained by its consequences, that is, by whatever has reinforced that behavior. Usual reinforcers for children are candy, food, a smile, and (in school) grades.

representative sample   In research, the selection of a group of subjects for a study that represents the entire group to which the researcher wishes to generalize the results. A representative sample of children from the United States would need to include children from all 50 states, rural and urban children, and children in the same ethnic and economic proportion as the general population.

representational thought   In Piaget's theory, the ability to form mental images of objects or events and to solve simple problems by mentally manipulating these images. This ability is reached around two years of age.

repression   In psychoanalytic theory, the unconscious forcing of material that is anxiety-provoking or in some way threatening into the unconscious so that it is lost to the conscious mind. For example, many traumatic events of childhood are repressed into the unconscious and as a result details, and sometimes the entire event, cannot be recalled.

resatellization The psychological identification that adolescents make with the peer group; resembles in some ways the satellizing identification that was formed earlier with parents, especially in merging their egos into the consciousness of the group.

restricted language A spoken form of language that is informal, ungrammatical, repetitive, redundant, and highly charged emotionally. The message is conveyed more emphatically in its non-verbal accompaniments than in its words and is an inefficient method of conveying precise information.

reversibility Piaget's term for the ability to reason backward and forward and up and down hierarchies.

rooming-in A practice of keeping the newborn infant in the same room with the mother.

satellization The process whereby the child who is intrinsically valued by parents invests his or her own ego in that of the parent and temporarily gives up pursuit of his or her own striving for status and independence. The result of this satellization is identification with the parent and the incorporation of the mores and rules of the culture.

scheme (*plural* schemes) The basic unit of mental organization in Piaget's theory. In its simplest form, a scheme is a reflex that is present at birth. Schemes are mental structures that change, adapt, generalize and through which the individual gradually constructs a mental representation of the world. Schemes are flexible and mobile; as, the scheme "round" can be applied to many different objects in many different situations.

schizophrenia A mental disorder characterized by loss of ability to function appropriately in the world of reality. Persons with this disorder do not act or think coherently and logically, have difficulty establishing and maintaining interpersonal relationships, often lose control of impulses and express inappropriate ideas and emotions.

scientific method (experimental method) A formalized method of gaining knowledge through objective observation. The method entails the clear statement of a hypothesis, then testing the truth of this hypothesis by observation of events in the real world.

screening tests Tests that quickly identify children that are in need of special treatment. The most common type of screening test is for general development. These tests do not identify the cause of problems, but they identify children with developmental delays who can then be studied further to determine the cause of the delay.

secondary Of a second order of appearance or importance, as a secondary infection, or of a higher level of organization, as a secondary school.

secondary circular reaction The second level of interaction of infants with objects. At this level, the infant accidentally performs a behavior that causes a *new* effect in the environment. For example, the infant might kick or strike a toy hanging above the crib. The infant then repeats the behavior in order to see the effect and the effect elicits the behavior in a repetitive manner.

secondary sex characteristics Physical characteristics that are associated with male and female and that develop at puberty, such as breasts and widened hips in girls, facial hair and enlarged muscles in boys, and distribution of body hair in the pubic area and armpits in both.

secular trend   The systematic tendency of boys and girls to reach puberty at an ever younger age and to attain a greater height at maturity that has become evident through an analysis of statistics collected over the last century.

self   That collection of self-perceptions, attitudes, motives and values that constitute the essential core of a person's identity.

self-concept   Those rational thoughts and unconscious feelings of what one holds oneself to be.

sensorimotor   The first of Piaget's four stages of cognitive development, which extends from birth to approximately age two. In this stage the infant handles the world through the immediate interaction of sensory perception and motor action without the intervening function of mental representation.

sensorimotor intelligence   The use of motor skills and sensory perception to explore and manipulate the environment. Sensorimotor intelligence is slow and is the mode of the infant before acquiring the ability to form mental representations.

sensory perception   The registration of information in the brain from sense organs. The most important source of sensory information for humans is vision, followed by hearing. Touch, taste, and smell are less important but nevertheless useful sources of information.

seriation   The arrangement of objects or ideas in a sequence on some logical basis such as largest to smallest, most important to least important, or most to least and so forth.

sex-linked inheritance   A pattern of inheritance that involves genes that are carried on the 23rd chromosome, which also determines sex. The 23rd chromosome (Y) of the male contains very few genes while the X of the female contains many genes and sex-linked inheritance is most often carried on this 23rd chromosome of the female (X). Thus, sex-linked inheritance is usually carried by the female and evident only in males.

sex-typing   The assignment of objects or behaviors as appropriate to male or female.

sign   Something that represents an object but that has no resemblance to the object, as, a word used as a name to specify a thing.

social learning   The name applied to a theory of development that postulates that all behavior and psychological development is the result of experiences in the social and physical environment.

socialization   The process whereby the rules, customs, attitudes, mores, and other details of the culture are learned. The pressures of socialization are unremitting and continuous. They act not only on children, but through socialization parents learn to parent, and the elderly learn to be old as the culture requires.

sperm   The male sex cell. Sexually mature males produce millions of sperm each day. These cells are very small and essentially contain only the single 23 chromosomes attached to a long whip-like tail. Millions of sperm are deposited in the vagina during intercourse, but only one can penetrate and fertilize an egg.

startle reflex   The name sometimes applied to the Moro reflex. (*see* Moro reflex)

states of consciousness   A continuum of awareness and receptivity to environmental stimuli that extends from deep sleep to rapt attention. Brazelton has identified six states of consciousness in the newborn.

stimulus   An event or condition that elicits a physiological or behavioral response.

standardized test   A test that has been administered to a representative sample of people for whom the test is designed; the scores of this sample are available in statistical tables of norms that can be used to compare the score of any individual taking the test at a later time.

strategic interactions   Interpersonal encounters that have as their aim the acquisition, concealment, or revelation of information through indirect means. Elkind has identified early adolescence as the time that skill in such interactions is acquired. These entail strategies for situations involving friends, the opposite sex, and forbidden acts.

sublimation   The diversion of energy from an original source to a higher purpose. In psychoanalytic theory, the diversion of the expression of a primitive impulse or desire into a form more socially or culturally acceptable. For example, the game of football may be a sublimation of the more primitive impulse toward combat and aggression.

superego   In Freudian theory, one of the three components of personality. The superego is the repository of the moral rules of the culture (conscience) and the standards of perfection for self and others (ego ideal).

symbol   A representation of a real object that bears some resemblance to the actual object. A drawing or three-dimensional representation of an object is a symbol of that object. In symbolic play children use objects as symbols of other objects and in imitation they may use sounds and movements as symbols of people and animals.

symbolic play   Play of children in which one object represents another, as, a cardboard box may be an airplane or a stuffed animal may be a child.

syntax   That part of grammar that concerns the way in which words, phrases, and sentences are put together.

telegraphic sentences   Two-word sentences consisting of a noun or a pronoun and a verb; characteristic of children in the second year.

temperament   A consistent pattern of response to stimuli that is characteristic of an individual. From birth infants can be differentiated by their placid, emotionally charged, or in-between response to stimuli.

tertiary circular reaction   Piaget's designation of the interaction of infants and objects, in which the infant invents new ways of handling objects and actively experiments in order to find these new methods. Once the new ways are discovered, the child repeats them in a circular manner, but with slight variations each time.

testes   The anatomical name that refers to the external sexual organs of the male in which sperm are produced.

testosterone   A hormone, produced in the testes, that is responsible for inducing and maintaining male secondary sex characteristics and for the prenatal differentiation of a male from the conceptus.

thanatos   In psychoanalytic theory, one of the two basic drives. Thanatos is the death drive: the propulsion within the person toward aggression, destruction of property and others, and self-destruction.

toxemia   A condition in which toxic substances collect in the blood, especially during pregnancy; poses a threat to the fetus as well as the mother.

transductive   A type of reasoning characteristic of children in the preoperational stage of cognitive development, in which cause and effect are inferred because the events occur close in time or have some physical characteristic in common. For example, the child who notes that Italians eat spaghetti and asks if he will become Italian by eating spaghetti is reasoning transductively.

transitional A period between stages of development in which a child may exhibit some of the characteristics of both stages. In addition, the behavior of a transitional child is unstable and may exhibit the behavior of the higher stage one day and regress to the lower stage another day.

uterus The female sexual organ in which the fertilized egg is implanted and which contains the developing embryo and fetus until birth.

volitional independence An independence of will: the ability to conceive desires and set goals. Infants can formulate and express desires and needs, that is, they have volitional independence, but are not able to perform the actions needed to reach these goals or satisfy these needs.

world-view The assumptions, largely philosophical, that a person believes to be true about the world and human nature. Such assumptions are generally not amenable to scientific testing and are a matter of conviction rather than scientific proof.

zygote The fertilized ovum in the first two weeks after conception, that is, in the period from conception to implantation in the uterus.

References

Ainsworth, M. D. S. The development of infant-mother attachment. In B. Caldwell & H. Ricciuti (Eds.), *Review of Child Development Research* (Vol. 3). Chicago: University of Chicago Press, 1973.

Ainsworth, M. D. S. Infant-mother attachment. *American Psychologist,* 1979, *34,* 932–937.

Ainsworth, M. D. S., & Bell, S. M. Attachment, exploration, and separation: Illustrated by the behavior of one-year-olds in a strange situation. *Child Development,* 1970, *41,* 49–67.

Als, H. *The human newborn and his mother: An ethological study of their interaction.* Ann Arbor, Mich.: Dissertation Abstracts, 1975.

Als, H., Tronick, E., Lester, B. M., & Brazelton, T. B. Specific neonatal measures: The Brazelton Neonatal Behavior Assessment Scale. In J. D. Osofsky (Ed.), *Handbook of infant development.* New York: John Wiley & Sons, Inc., 1979.

American Psychological Association. *Ethical principles in the conduct of research with human participants.* Washington, D. C.: American Psychological Association, 1973.

American Psychological Association. Revised ethical standards of psychologists. *APA Monitor,* March 1977, 22–23.

Ames, B. N. Identifying environmental chemicals causing mutations and cancer. *Science,* 1979, *204,* 587–593.

Anastasi, A. Heredity, environment and the question "How." *Psychological Review,* 1958, *65,* 197–208.

Anastasi, A. *Psychological testing* (4th ed.). New York: Macmillan Publishing Co., Inc., 1976.

Apgar V. & Beck, J. *Is my baby all right?* New York: Trident Press, 1973.

Ariès, P. *Centuries of childhood: A social history of family life.* New York: Vintage Books, 1962.

Arieti, S. *Interpretation of schizophrenia* (2nd ed.). New York: Basic Books, Inc., Publishers, 1974.

Ausubel, D. P., Sullivan, E. V., & Ives, S. W. *Theory and problems of child development* (3rd ed.). New York: Grune & Stratton, Inc., 1980.

Axline, V. M. *Dibs: In search of self; personality development in play therapy.* Boston: Houghton Mifflin Company, 1965.

Baldwin, A. L. *Theories of child development.* New York: John Wiley & Sons, Inc., 1967.

Bandura, A. *Principles of behavior modification.* New York: Holt, Rinehart and Winston, 1969.

Bannister, D., & Agnew, J. The child's construing of self. In J. K. Cole & A. W. Landfield (Eds.), *Nebraska Symposium on Motivation.* Lincoln: University of Nebraska Press, 1976.

Barber, B. The ethics of experimentation with human subjects. *Scientific American*, 1976, *234*, 25–31.

Barnet, A. B., & Goodwin, R. S. Averaged evoked electroencephalographic responses to clicks in the human newborn. *Electroencephalography and Clinical Neurophysiology*, 1965, *18*, 441–450.

Barth, R. *Open education and the American school.* New York: Schocken Books, Inc., 1972.

Bates, E. On the evolution and development of symbols. In E. Bates, *The emergence of symbols: Cognition and communication in infancy.* New York: Academic Press, Inc., 1979.

Bates, E., Benigni, L., Bretherton, I., Camaioni, L., & Volterra, V. Cognition and communication from nine to thirteen months: Correlational findings. In E. Bates, *The emergence of symbols: cognition and communication in infancy.* New York: Academic Press, Inc., 1979.

Baumrind, D. Child care practices anteceding three patterns of preschool behavior. *Genetic Psychology Monographs*, 1967, *75*, 43–88.

Baumrind, D. Current patterns of parental authority. *Developmental Psychology Monograph*, 1971, *4*, 1–103.

Baumrind, D. The development of instrumental competence through socialization. In A. D. Pick (Ed.), *Minnesota Symposium on Child Psychology* (Vol. 7). Minneapolis: University of Minnesota Press, 1973.

Baumrind, D. *Socialization determinants of personal agency.* Unpublished paper presented to the Society for Research in Child Development, New Orleans, La., March, 1977.

Baumrind, D. New directions in socialization research. *American Psychologist*, 1980, *35*, 639–652.

Baumrind, D., & Black, A. E. Socialization practices associated with dimensions of competence in preschool boys and girls. *Child Development*, 1967, *38*, 291–327.

Bayley, N. The development of motor abilities during the first three years. *Monographs of the Society for Research in Child Development*, 1935, *1* (Serial no.1).

Bayley, N. *Bayley Scales of Infant Development.* New York: Psychological Corporation, 1969.

Bayley, N., & Schaefer, E. S. Maternal behavior and personality development: Data from the Berkeley Growth Study. In G. R. Medinnus (Ed.), *Readings in the psychology of parent-child relations.* New York: John Wiley & Sons, Inc., 1967.

Becker, W. C. Consequences of different kinds of parental discipline. In M. L. Hoffman & L. W. Hoffman (Eds.), *Review of child development research* (Vol. 1). New York: Russell Sage Foundation, 1964.

Beilin, H. Learning and operational convergence in logical thought development. *Journal of Experimental Child Psychology*, 1965, *2*, 317–339.

Belsky, J. Child maltreatment: An ecological integration. *American Psychologist*, 1980, *35*, 320–335.

Bennetts, A. B., & Lubic, R. W. The free-standing birth centre. *The Lancet*, 1982, *Nov.*, 378–380.

Berezin, N. *The gentle birth book: A practical guide to Leboyer family-centered delivery.* New York: Simon & Schuster, 1980.

Berg, W. K., & Berg, K. M. Psychophysiological development in infancy: State, sensory function, and attention. In J. D. Osofsky (Ed.), *Handbook of infant development.* New York: John Wiley & Sons, Inc., 1979.

Berger, K. S. *The developing person.* New York: Worth Publishers, Inc., 1980.

Bergling, K. *The development of hypothetico-deductive thinking in children: A cross-cultural study of the validity of Piaget's model of the development of logical thinking.* International Association for the Evaluation of Educational Achievement, Monograph Studies, No. 3. New York: John Wiley & Sons, Inc., 1974.

Bergman, T., Haith, M. M., and Mann, L. *Development of eye contact and facial scanning in infants.* Unpublished paper presented to the Society for Research in Child Development, Minneapolis, Minn., March, 1971.

Berko, J. The child's learning of English morphology. *Word,* 1958, *14,* 150–177.

Bernstein, B. *A sociolinguistic approach to socialization: Perspectives on a theme.* Chicago: Markham, 1970.

Bertenthal, B. I., & Fischer, K. W. Development of self-recognition in the infant. *Developmental Psychology,* 1978, *14,* 44–50.

Bettleheim, B. *Uses of enchantment: The meaning and importance of fairy tales.* New York: Random House, Inc., 1976.

Biller, H. B. Father absence and the personality development of the male child. *Developmental Psychology,* 1970, *2,* 181–201.

Blank, M., & Solomon, F. A tutorial language program to develop abstract thinking in socially disadvantaged preschool children. *Child Development,* 1968, *39,* 379–390.

Blank, M., & Solomon, F. How shall the disadvantaged be taught? *Child Development,* 1969, *40,* 47–61.

Bloom, B. S. *Stability and change in human characteristics.* New York: John Wiley and Sons, Inc., 1964.

Bloom, L. *One word at a time.* The Hague: Mouton, 1973.

Bond, E. K. Perception of form by the human infant. *Psychological Bulletin,* 1972, *77,* 225–245.

Botvin, G. J., & Murray, F. B. The efficacy of peer modeling and social conflict in the acquisition of conservation. *Child Development,* 1975, *46,* 796–799.

Bowerman, C. E., & Kinch, J. W. Changes in family and peer orientation of children between the fourth and tenth grades. *Social Forces,* 1959, *37,* 206–211.

Bowlby, J. *Maternal care and mental health.* Geneva: World Health Organization, 1951.

Bowlby, J. The nature of the child's tie to his mother. *International Journal of Psychoanalysis,* 1958, *39,* 350–373.

Bowlby, J. Grief and mourning in infancy and early childhood. *Psychoanalytic Study of the Child.* 1960, *15,* 9–52. (a)

Bowlby, J. Separation anxiety. *International Journal of Psychoanalysis,* 1960, *41,* 69–113. (b)

Bowlby, J. Childhood mourning and its implications for psychiatry. *American Journal of Psychiatry,* 1961, *118,* 481–498.

Bowlby, J. *Attachment.* New York: Basic Books, Inc., Publishers, 1969.

Bowlby, J. *Separation.* New York: Basic Books, Inc., Publishers, 1973.

Bradley, R. H., Caldwell, B. M., & Elardo, R. Home environments and cognitive development in the first 2 years: A cross-lagged panel analysis. *Developmental Psychology,* 1979, *15,* 246–250.

Bradley, R. H., & Caldwell, B. M. The relation of infant's home environments to mental test performance at fifty-four months: A follow-up study. *Child Development,* 1976, *47,* 1172–1174.

Braine, M. The ontogeny of English phrase structure: The first phase. *Language,* 1963, *39,* 1–13.

Brainerd, C. J. Learning research and Piagetian theory. In L. S. Siegel & C. J. Brainerd

(Eds.), *Alternatives to Piaget: Critical essays on the theory.* New York: Academic Press, Inc., 1977.

Brazelton, T. B. Psychophysiologic reactions to the neonate, I: The value of observation of the neonate. *The Journal of Pediatrics,* 1961, *58,* 508–512.

Brazelton, T. B. Effect of prenatal drugs on the behavior of the neonate. *American Journal of Psychiatry,* 1970, *126,* 1261–1266.

Brazelton, T. B. *Neonatal Behavioral Assessment Scale.* Clinics in Developmental Medicine (No. 50). Philadelphia: Spastics International Medical Publications, J. B. Lippincott Company, 1973.

Brazelton, T. B. *Toddlers and parents: A declaration of independence.* New York: Dell Publishing Company, 1974.

Brazelton, T. B. Early parent-infant reciprocity. In V. C. Vaughn, III, & T. B. Brazelton (Eds.), *The family—can it be saved?* Chicago: Year Book Medical Publishers, Inc., 1976.

Brazelton, T. B. *On becoming a family: The growth of attachment.* New York: Delacorte Press, 1981.

Brazelton, T. B., Koslowski, B., & Main, M. The origins of reciprocity: The early mother-infant interaction. In M. Lewis and L. A. Rosenblum (Eds.), *The effect of the infant on its caregiver.* New York: John Wiley & Sons, Inc., 1974.

Brazelton, T. B., & Robey, J. S. Observations of neonatal behavior. *Journal of the American Academy of Child Psychiatry,* 1965, *4,* 613–625.

Breger, L. *From instinct to identity: The development of personality.* Englewood Cliffs, N.J.: Prentice-Hall, Inc., 1974.

Bretherton, I., Bates, E., Benigni, L., Camaioni, L., & Volterra, V. Relationships between cognition, communication, and quality of attachment. In E. Bates, *The emergence of symbols: Cognition and communication in infancy.* New York: Academic Press, Inc., 1979.

Bridges, K. Emotional development in early infancy. *Child Development,* 1932, *3,* 324–341.

Brittain, C. V. Adolescent choices and parent-peer cross pressures. *American Sociological Review,* 1963, *28,* 385–391.

Brittain, C. V. A comparison of rural and urban adolescence with respect to peer versus parent compliance. *Adolescence,* 1969, *13,* 59–68.

Bronfenbrenner, U. Toward an experimental ecology of human development. *American Psychologist,* 1977, *32,* 513–531.

Bronfenbrenner, U. Contexts of child rearing. *American Psychologist,* 1979, *34,* 844–850. (a)

Bronfenbrenner, U. *The ecology of human development: Experiments by nature and design.* Cambridge, Mass.: Harvard University Press, 1979. (b)

Bronfenbrenner, U., Belsky, J., & Steinberg, L. *Daycare in context: An ecological perspective on research and public policy.* Washington, D. C.: Department of Health, Education, and Welfare, 1976.

Brown, R. *A first language: The early stages.* Cambridge, Mass.: Harvard University Press, 1973.

Burgess, R. Child abuse: A behavioral analysis. In B. Lakey & A. Kazdin (Eds.), *Advances in child clinical psychology.* New York: Plenum Publishing Corporation, 1978.

Burgess, R., & Conger, R. Family interaction in abusive, neglectful and normal families. *Child Development,* 1978, *49,* 1163–1173.

Bushell, D. The behavior analysis classroom. In B. Spodek (Ed.), *Early childhood education.* Englewood Cliffs, N.J.: Prentice-Hall, Inc., 1973.

Cantor, P. Personality characteristics found among youthful female suicide attempters. *Journal of Abnormal Psychology, 1976, 85, 324–329.*

Carey, S. The child as word learner. In M. Halle, J. Bresman, & G. A. Miller (Eds.), *Linguistic theory and psychological reality.* Cambridge, Mass.: The MIT Press, 1977.

Cavior, N. and Dokecki, P. R. Physical attractiveness, perceived attitude similarity, and academic achievement as contributors to interpersonal attraction among adolescents. *Developmental Psychology, 1973, 40, 27–34.*

Chase, H. P. The epidemiology of malnutrition in the United States. In C. A. Canosa (Ed.), *Nutrition, growth and development, modern problems in paediatrics. 1975, 14, 1.*

Chauncey, H., and Dobbin, J. E. Testing has a history. In C. I. Chase and H. G. Ludlow (Eds.), *Readings in educational and psychological measurement.* Boston: Houghton Mifflin Company, 1966.

Chilman, C. S. *Adolescent sexuality in a changing American society: Social and psychological perspectives.* (DHEW Publication No. 79-1426, NIH). Washington, D.C.: U.S. Government Printing Office, 1978.

Chukovsky, K. *From two to five.* M. Morton (Ed. and trans.). San Francisco: University of California, 1963.

Cicirelli, V., Evans, J., & Schiller, J. *The impact of Head Start. An evaluation of the effects of Head Start on children's cognitive and affective development.* Report to the U.S. Office of Economic Opportunity by Westinghouse Learning Corporation and Ohio University. Washington, D.C.: U.S. Government Printing Office, 1969.

Clark, E. V. From gesture to word: On the natural history of deixis in language acquisition. In J. S. Bruner & A. Garton (Eds.), *Human growth and development.* Oxford: Clarendon Press, 1978.

Clarke-Stewart, A. *Child care in the family: A review of research and some propositions for policy.* New York: Academic Press, Inc., 1977.

Cohen, L. B., DeLoache, J. S., & Strauss, M. S. Infant visual perception. In J. D. Osofsky (Ed.), *Handbook of infant development.* New York: John Wiley & Sons, Inc., 1979.

Coleman, J. C. The adolescent sub-culture and academic achievement, *American Journal of Sociology, 1960, 65, 337–347.*

Coleman, J. C. *The adolescent society.* New York: The Free Press, 1961.

Coleman, J. C. *Equality of educational opportunity.* Washington, D.C.: U.S. Department of Health, Education, and Welfare, 1966.

Coleman, J. C. *Relationships in adolescence.* Boston: Routledge and Kegan, 1974.

Coleman, J. C. Friendship and the peer group in adolescence. In J. Adelson (Ed.), *Handbook of adolescent psychology.* New York: John Wiley & Sons, Inc., 1980.

Coleman, J. C., George, R., & Holt, G. Adolescents and their parents: A study of attitudes. *Journal of Genetic Psychology, 1977, 130, 239–245.*

Comstock, G. A. *Television violence: Where the surgeon general's study leads.* Santa Monica, Calif.: The Rand Corporation, #P-4831, 1972.

Comstock, G. A. *Effects of television on children: What is the evidence?* Santa Monica, Calif.: The Rand Corporation, #P-5412, 1975. (a)

Comstock, G. A. *Television and the young: Setting the stage for a research agenda.* Santa Monica, Calif.: The Rand Corporation, #P-5550, 1975. (b)

Comstock, G. A. *Research and the constructive aspects of television in children's lives: A forecast.* Santa Monica, Calif.: The Rand Corporation, #P-5622, 1976.

Comstock, G. A., & Lindsey, G. *Television and human behavior: The research horizon, future and present.* Santa Monica, Calif.: The Rand Corporation, #R-1748,-CF, 1975.

Conel, J. L. *The postnatal development of the human cerebral cortex: The cortex of the three-month infant* (Vol. 3). Cambridge, Mass.: Harvard University Press, 1947.

Conel, J. L. *The postnatal development of the human cerebral cortex: The cortex of the six-month infant* (Vol. 4). Cambridge, Mass.: Harvard University Press, 1951.

Conel, J. L. *The postnatal development of the human cerebral cortex: The cortex of the twenty-four-month infant* (Vol. 6). Cambridge, Mass.: Harvard University Press, 1959.

Connell, D. B. *Individual differences in attachment: An investigation into stability, implications, and relationships to the structure of early language development.* Unpublished doctoral dissertation, Syracuse University, Syracuse, N.Y., 1976.

Conway, E., and Brackbill, Y. Delivery medication and infant outcome: An empirical study. In W. A. Bowes, Jr., Y. Brackbill, E. Conway, and A. Steinschneider, The effects of obstetrical medication on fetus and infant. *Monographs of the Society for Research in Child Development,* 1970, *35* (Serial no. 137), 24–34.

Corbin, C. *A textbook of motor development.* Dubuque, Iowa: William C. Brown Company, Publishers, 1973.

Cowan, P. A. *Piaget with feeling.* New York: Holt, Rinehart and Winston, 1978.

Cowles, M. Four views of learning and development. *Educational Leadership,* 1971, *28,* 790–795.

Cratty, B. J. *Perceptual and motor development in infants and children.* New York: Macmillan Publishing Co., Inc., 1970.

Darwin, C. *Origin of the species by means of natural selection; or The preservation of favored races in the struggle for life.* New York: D. Appleton and Company, 1896. (Originally published 1859.)

Damon, W. *The social world of the child.* San Francisco: Jossey-Bass, 1977.

Dayton, G., Jones, M., Aiu, P., Rawson, R., Steele, B., & Rose, M. Developmental study of coordinated eye movements in the human infant: I. Visual acuity in the newborn human. *Archives of Opthalmology,* 1964, *71,* 865–870.

de Lissovoy, V. Toward the definition of "abuse provoking child." *Child Abuse and Neglect,* 1979, *3,* 341–350.

DeMause, L. *History of childhood.* New York: The Psychohistory Press, 1974.

Desmond, M. M., Rudolph, A. J., & Phitaksphraiwan, P. The transitional care nursery: A mechanism of a preventative medicine. *Pediatric Clinics of North America,* 1966, *13,* 651–668.

Douvan, E., & Adelson, J. *The adolescent experience.* New York: John Wiley & Sons, Inc., 1966.

Duke-Elder, S., & Cook, C. *Systems of Ophthalmology* (Vol. III). St. Louis, Mo.: The C. V. Mosby Company, 1963.

Dunn, L., & Smith, J. *Peabody language development kits, level 2.* Circle Pines, Minn.: American Guidance Service, Inc., 1966.

Dunphy, D. C. The social structure of urban adolescent peer groups. *Sociometry,* 1963, *26,* 230–246.

Eichorn, D. H. Physical development: Current foci of research. In J. D. Osofsky (Ed.), *Handbook of infant development.* New York: John Wiley & Sons, Inc., 1979.

Eisenberg, R. B. *Auditory competence in early life.* Baltimore: University Park, 1976.

Elkind, D. Strategic interactions in early adolescence. In J. Adelson (Ed.), *Handbook of adolescent psychology.* New York: John Wiley & Sons, Inc., 1980.

Elkind, D., & Bowen, R. Imaginary audience behavior in children and adolescents. *Developmental Psychology,* 1979, *15,* 38–44.

Elkind, D., & Weiner, I. B. *Development of the child.* New York: John Wiley & Sons, Inc., 1978.

Elmer, E., & Gregg, G. Developmental characteristics of abused children. *Pediatrics,* 1967, *40,* 596–602.

Emmerich, W., Goldman, K. S., Kirsh, B., & Sharabany, R. *Development of gender constancy in economically disadvantaged children.* Report of the Educational Testing Service. Princeton, N.J.: Educational Testing Service, 1976.

Erikson, E. H. *Childhood and society* (2nd ed.). New York: W. W. Norton & Company, Inc., 1963. (a)

Erikson, E. H. (Ed.). *Youth: Change and challenge.* New York: Basic Books, Inc., Publishers, 1963. (b)

Erikson, E. H. *Studies of play.* New York: Arno Press, 1975.

Erikson, E. H. *Toys and reasons: Stages in the ritualization of experience.* New York: W. W. Norton & Company, Inc., 1977.

Ervin-Tripp, S. An overview of grammatical development. In D. Slobin (Ed.), *The ontogenesis of grammar.* New York: Academic Press, Inc., 1971.

Escalona, S. The use of infant tests for predictive purposes. *Bulletin of the Menninger Clinic,* 1950, *14,* 117–118.

Espenschade, A. Motor development. In W. R. Johnson (Ed.), *Science and medicine of exercise and sports.* New York: Harper & Row, Publishers, 1960.

Evans, E.D. *Contemporary influences in early childhood education* (2nd ed.). New York: Holt, Rinehart and Winston, 1975.

Fantz, R. L. The origin of form perception. *Scientific American,* May, 1961, 66–72.

Fantz, R. L., & Miranda, S. B. Newborn infant attention to form of contour. *Child Development,* 1975, *46,* 224–228.

Fantz, R. L., Ordy, J. M., & Udelf, M. S. Maturation of pattern vision in infants during the first six months. *Journal of Comparative and Physiological Psychology,* 1962, *55,* 907–917.

Ferreira, J. Emotional factors in prenatal environment: A review. *Journal of Nervous and Mental Disease,* 1965, *141,* 108–118.

Flavell, J. H. *Cognitive development.* Englewood Cliffs, N.J.: Prentice-Hall, Inc., 1977.

Flavell, J. H., Botkin, P., Fry, C., Wright, J., & Jarvis, P. *The development of role-taking and communication skills in children.* New York: John Wiley & Sons, Inc., 1968.

Fontana, V. *The maltreated child.* Springfield, Ill.: Charles C. Thomas, Publisher, 1971.

Frankenburg, W. K., & Dodds, J. B. The Denver developmental screening test. *Journal of Pediatrics,* 1967, *71,* 181–191.

Frasier, S. D., & Rallison, M. L. Growth retardation and emotional deprivation: Relative resistance to treatment with human growth hormone. *Journal of Pediatrics,* 1972, *80,* 603.

Friedrich, L. K., & Stein, A. H. Aggressive and prosocial television programs and the natural behavior of preschool children. *Monographs of the Society for Research in Child Development,* 1973, *38.* (Serial no. 115)

Friedrich, L. K., & Stein, A. H. Prosocial television and young children: The effects of verbal labeling and role playing on learning and behavior. *Child Development,* 1975, *46,* 27–38.

Friedrich, W., & Boriskin, J. The role of the child in abuse: A review of the literature. *American Journal of Orthopsychiatry,* 1976, *46,* 580–590.

Furstenberg, F. F., Jr. *Unplanned parenthood: The social consequences of teenage childbearing.* New York: The Free Press, 1976.

Gallas, H. B. Introduction. *Journal of Social Issues,* 1980, *36,* 1–6.

Gallup, G. Self-recognition in primates. A comparative approach to the bidirectional properties of consciousness. *American Psychologist,* 1977, *32,* 329–338.

Garbarino, J. The price of privacy: An analysis of the social dynamics of child abuse. *Child Welfare,* 1977, *56,* 565–575.

Gardner, R. A., & Gardner, B. T. Teaching sign language to a chimpanzee. *Science,* 1969, *165,* 664–672.

Garn, S. Growth and development. In E. Ginsberg (Ed.), *The nation's children.* New York: Columbia University Press, 1966.

Garvey, C. *Play.* Cambridge, Mass.: Harvard University Press, 1977.

Gelles, R. Child abuse as psychopathology: A sociological critique and reformation. *American Journal of Orthopsychiatry,* 1973, *43,* 611–621.

Gelles, R. The social construction of child abuse. *American Journal of Orthopsychiatry,* 1975, *45,* 363–371.

Gelles, R. Demythologizing child abuse. *Family Coordinator,* 1976, *25,* 135–141.

Gelman, R. Conservation acquisition: A problem of learning to attend to relevant attributes. *Journal of Experimental Child Psychology,* 1969, *7,* 167–187.

George, C., & Main, M. Social interactions of young abused children: Approach, avoidance and aggression. *Child Development,* 1979, *50,* 306–318.

Gesell, A., & Amatruda, C. S. *Developmental diagnosis* (2nd ed.). New York: Hoeber-Harper, 1947.

Gibson, E. J. *Principles of perceptual learning and development.* New York: Appleton-Century-Crofts, 1969.

Gil, D. G. *Violence against children.* Cambridge, Mass.: Harvard University Press, 1970.

Gil, D. G. Violence against children. *Journal of Marriage and the Family,* 1971, *33,* 639–648.

Gilligan, C. *In a different voice.* Cambridge, Mass.: Harvard University Press, 1982.

Goffman, E. *Strategic interaction.* Philadelphia: University of Pennsylvania Press, 1969.

Gold, M. *Delinquent behavior in an American city.* Belmont, Calif.: Brooks/Cole, 1970.

Gold, M., & Petronio, R. J. Delinquent behavior in adolescence. In J. Adelson (Ed.), *Handbook of adolescent psychology.* New York: John Wiley & Sons, Inc., 1980.

Goldfarb, W. Effects of early institutional care on adolescent personality. *Journal of Experimental Education,* 1943, *12,* 106–129.

Gordon, S. *The sexual adolescent.* Belmont, Calif.: Wadsworth Publishing Co., Inc., 1973.

Goren, C. *Form perception, innate form preferences and visually-mediated head turning in human newborns.* Paper presented to the Society for Research in Child Development, Denver, Colo., March 1975.

Govatos, L. A. Relationships and age differences in growth measures and motor skills. *Child Development,* 1959, *30,* 333–340.

Gray, J. A., Lean, J., & Keynes, A. Infant androgen treatment and adult open-field behavior: Direct effects and effects of injections to siblings. *Physiology and Behavior,* 1969, *4,* 177–181.

Green, A. A Psychodynamic approach to the study and treatment of child abusing parents. *Journal of Child Psychiatry,* 1976, *15,* 414.

Greenberg, M., & Morris, N. Engrossment: The newborn's impact upon the father. *American Journal of Orthopsychiatry,* 1974, *44,* 520–531.

Greenblatt, B. *Responsibility for child care.* San Francisco: Jossey–Bass, 1977.

Greenfield, P. M. On culture and conservation. In J. S. Bruner, R. Oliver, & P. M. Greenfield (Eds.), *Studies in cognitive growth.* New York: John Wiley & Sons, Inc., 1966.

Grotberg, E. *Review of research: 1965–1969.* Washington, D.C.: Project Head Start, U.S. Office of Economic Opportunity, 1969.

Gruen, G. E. Experiences affecting the development of number conservation in children. *Child Development,* 1965, *36,* 963–979.

Gunnar, M., & Donahu, M. Sex differences in social responsiveness between six months and twelve months. *Child Development,* 1980, *51,* 262–265.

Guttmacher, A. *Pregnancy, birth, and family planning.* New York: New American Library, 1973.

Haith, M. M. *Organization of visual behavior at birth.* Paper presented at a symposium on perception in infancy at the Twenty-first International Congress of Psychology Meetings, Paris, July 1976.

Hall, C. S., & Lindzey, G. *Theories of personality* (2nd ed.). New York: John Wiley & Sons, Inc., 1970.

Hall, E. A conversation with Jean Piaget and Barbel Inhelder. *Psychology Today,* 1970, *3,* 25–32; 54–56.

Hall, G. S. *Adolescence: Its psychology and its relations to physiology, anthropology, sociology, sex, crime, religion, and education.* New York: Appleton, 1904.

Hallowell, I. The child, the savage, and human experience. In A. Skolnick (Ed.), *Rethinking childhood: Perspectives on development and society.* Boston: Little Brown and Company, 1976.

Hanson, J. W., Jones, K. L., & Smith, D. W. Fetal alcohol syndrome. *Journal of American Medical Associaton,* 1978, *235,* 1548.

Harlow, H. F. Love in infant monkeys. *Scientific American,* 1959, *200,* 68–74.

Harlow, H. F. The development of affectional patterns in infant monkeys. In B. M. Foss (Ed.) *Determinants of infant behaviour.* London: Methuen & Co., Ltd., 1961.

Harlow, H. F. Early social deprivation and later behavior in the monkey. In L. Stone, H. Smith, & L. Murphy (Eds.), *The competent infant.* New York: Basic Books, Inc., Publishers, 1973.

Harlow, H. F., & Harlow, M. K. Learning to love. *American Scientist,* 1966, *54,* 244–272.

Harlow, H. F., & Harlow, M. K. Social deprivation in monkeys. In *The nature and nurture of behavior: Readings from Scientific American.* San Francisco: W. H. Freeman and Company, Publishers, 1973.

Harlow, H. F., & Suomi, S. J. Social recovery by isolation-reared monkeys. *Proceedings of the National Academy of Science,* 1971, *68,* 1534–1538.

Harrington, M. *The other America: Poverty in the United States.* New York: Macmillan Publishing Co., Inc., 1964.

Harris, W. H., & Levey, S. (Eds.). *The new columbia encyclopedia.* New York: Columbia University Press, 1975.

Harris, P., & MacFarlane, A. The growth of the effective visual field from birth to seven weeks. *Journal of Experimental Child Psychology,* 1974, *18,* 340–348.

Hartup, W. W., & Moore, S. G. Avoidance of inappropriate sex-typing by young children. *Journal of Consulting Psychology,* 1963, *27,* 467–473.

Heinonen, O. P., Slone, D., & Shapiro, S. *Birth defects and drugs in pregnancy.* Littleton, Mass.: Publishing Sciences Group, 1976.

Herbst, A. L., Kurman, R. J., Scully, R. E., & Poskanzer, D. D. Clear-cell adenocarcinoma of the genital tract in young females. *New England Journal of Medicine,* 1972, *287,* 1259–1264.

Hetherington, E. M. Divorce: A child's perspective, *American Psychologist,* 1979, *34,* 851–858.

Hetherington, E. M., Cox, M., & Cox, R. Divorced fathers. *The Family Coordinator,* 1976, *25,* 417–28.

Hetherington, E. M., Cox, M., & Cox, R. Beyond father absence: Conceptualization of the effects of divorce. In E. M. Hetherington & R. D. Parke (Eds.), *Contemporary readings in child psychology.* New York: McGraw-Hill Book Company, 1977.

Hetherington, E. M., Cox, M. & Cox, R. Stress and coping in divorce: A focus on women. In J. E. Gullahorn (Ed.) *Psychology and women: In transition.* Washington, D.C.: V. H. Winston & Sons, 1979.

Hetherington, E. M., & Parke, R. D. *Child psychology: A contemporary viewpoint.* New York: McGraw Hill Book Company, 1975.

Higham, E. Variations in adolescent psychohormonal development. In J. Adelson (Ed.), *Handbook of adolescent psychology.* New York: John Wiley & Sons, Inc., 1980.

Hill, R. Drugs ingested by pregnant women. *Pharmacology Therapeutics,* 1973, *14,* 654–659.

Hoffman, L. W., & Nye, F. I. *Working mothers.* San Francisco: Jossey-Bass, 1974.

Hoffman, L. W. Changes in family roles, socialization and sex differences. *American Psychologist,* 1977, *32,* 644–658.

Horney, K. *New ways in psychoanalysis.* New York: W. W. Norton & Company, Inc., 1939.

Hoyenga, K. B., & Hoyenga, K. T. *The question of sex differences.* Boston: Little, Brown and Company, 1979.

Hughes, M., Wetzel, R., & Henderson, R. *The Tucson early education model.* Tucson: University of Arizona, 1969.

Hunt, J. McV. *Intelligence and experience.* New York: The Ronald Press Company, 1961.

Hunt, J. McV. The utility of ordinal scales inspired by Piaget's observations. *Merrill-Palmer Quarterly,* 1976, *22,* 31–45.

Hunt, M. *Sexual behavior in the 1970's.* Chicago: Playboy Press, 1974.

Hurley, S. *Developmental Nutrition.* Englewood Cliffs, N.J.: Prentice-Hall, Inc., 1980.

Hutt, C., & Ounsted, C. The biological significance of gaze aversion with particular reference to the syndrome of infantile autism. *Behavior Science,* 1966, *11,* 346–356.

Inhelder, B., & Piaget, J. *The growth of logical thinking from childhood to adolescence.* New York: Basic Books, Inc., Publishers, 1958.

Inhelder, B., & Sinclair, H. Learning cognitive structures. In P. H. Mussen, J. Langer, & M. Covington (Eds.), *Trends and issues in developmental psychology.* New York: Holt, Rinehart and Winston, 1969.

Inhelder, B., Sinclair, H. & Bovet, M. *Thinking and the development of cognition.* Cambridge, Mass.: Harvard University Press, 1974.

Jacobs, J. *Adolescent suicide.* New York: John Wiley & Sons, Inc., 1971.

Jensen, A. R. *Genetics and education.* New York: Harper & Row, Publishers, 1972.

Jessor, S., & Jessor, R. Transition from virginity to nonvirginity among youth: A social-psychological study over time. *Developmental Psychology,* 1975, *11,* 473–484.

Johnson, H. R., Myhre, S. A., Ruvalcaba, R. H. A., Thuline, H. C., & Kelley, V. C. Effects of testosterone on body image and behavior in Kleinfelter's syndrome: A pilot study. *Developmental Medicine and Child Neurology,* 1970, *12,* 19–23.

Josselson, R. Ego development in adolescence. In J. Adelson (Ed.), *Handbook of adolescent psychology.* New York: John Wiley & Sons, Inc., 1980.

Kagan, J. *Personality development.* New York: Harcourt Brace Jovanovich, Inc., 1971.

Kagan, J., Kearsley, R. B., & Zelazo, P. R. *Infancy: Its place in human development.* Cambridge, Mass.: Harvard University Press, 1978.

Kagan, J., Sontag, L. W., Baker, C. T., & Nelson, V. L. Personality and IQ change. *Journal of Abnormal and Social Psychology,* 1958, *56,* 261–266.

Kallman, F. J., & Jarvik, L. F. Individual differences in constitution and genetic background. In J. E. Birren (Ed.), *Handbook of aging and the individual.* Chicago: University of Chicago Press, 1959.

Kangas, J. & Bradway, K. Intelligence at middle-age: A thirty-eight year follow-up. *Developmental Psychology,* 1971, *5,* 333–337.

Kantner, J. F., & Zelnik, M. Sexual experience of young unmarried women in the United States. *Family Planning Perspectives,* 1972, *4,* 9–18.

Kayler, C. T. *The language use and language development of blind and sighted preschool children.* Unpublished doctoral dissertation. University of North Carolina at Greensboro, 1983.

Keating, D. P. Thinking processes in adolescence. In J. Adelson (Ed.), *Handbook of adolescent psychology.* New York: John Wiley & Sons, Inc., 1980.

Kempe, C. A practical approach to the protection of the abused child and rehabilitation of the abusing parent. *Pediatrics,* 1973, *51,* 804.

Kennell, J., Jerauld, R., Wolfe, H. Chesler, D., Kreger, N., McAlpine, W., Steffa, M., & Klaus, M. Maternal behavior one year after early and extended post-partum contact. *Developmental Medicine & Child Neurology,* 1974, *16,* 172–179.

Kennell, J. H., Voos, D. K., & Klaus, M. H. Parent-infant bonding. In J. D. Osofsky (Ed.), *Handbook of infant development.* New York: John Wiley & Sons, Inc., 1979.

Keogh, J. F. Motor performance in elementary school children. *Monographs.* Los Angeles: University of California, Physical Education, 1965.

Kessen, W., Salapatek, P., & Haith, M. The visual response of the human newborn to linear contour. *Journal of Experimental Child Psychology,* 1972, *13,* 9–20.

King, W. L., & Seegmiller, B. Performance of fourteen- to twenty-two-month-old black, firstborn male infants on two tests of cognitive development: The Bayley Scales and the Infant Psychological Development Scale. *Developmental Psychology,* 1973, *8,* 317–326.

Kinsey, A. C., Pomeroy, W. B., & Martin, C. E. *Sexual behavior in the human male.* Philadelphia: W. B. Saunders Company, 1948.

Kinsey, A. C., Pomeroy, W.B., Martin, C. W., & Gebhard, P. H. *Sexual behavior in the human female.* Philadelphia: W. B. Saunders Company, 1953.

Klaus, M. H., & Kennell, J. H. *Maternal-infant bonding: The impact of early separation or loss on family development.* St. Louis, Mo.: The C. V. Mosby Company, 1977.

Klaus, M. H., & Fanaroff, A. A. *Care of the high-risk neonate* (2nd ed.). Philadelphia: W. B. Saunders Company, 1979.

Klein, M., & Stern, L. Low birth weight and the battered child syndrome. *American Journal of Diseases of Childhood,* 1971, *122,* 15–18.

Kohlberg, L. Development of children's orientation towards a moral order (Part I). Sequence in the development of moral thought. *Vita Humana,* 1963, *6,* 11–36.

Kohlberg, L. Development of moral character and moral ideology. In M. L. Hoffman & L. W. Hoffman (Eds.), *Review of child development research* (Vol. 1). New York: Russell Sage Foundation, 1964.

Kohlberg, L. A cognitive developmental analysis of children's sex-role concepts and attitudes. In E. Maccoby (Ed.), *The development of sex differences.* Stanford, Calif.: Stanford University Press, 1966.

Kohlberg, L. Early education: A cognitive-developmental view. *Child Development,* 1968, *39,* 1013–1062.

Kohlberg, L. Stage and sequence: The cognitive-developmental approach to socialization. In D. A. Goslin (Ed.), *Handbook of socialization theory and research.* Chicago: Rand McNally & Company, 1969.

Kohlberg, L. The future of liberalism as the dominant ideology of the west. In R. W. Wilson & G. J. Schochet (Eds.), *Moral Development and Politics.* New York: Praeger Publishers, Inc., 1980.

Kormondy, E. J. *Introduction to genetics: A program for self-instruction.* New York: McGraw-Hill Book Company, 1964.

Kotelchuck, M. The infant's relationship to the father: Experimental evidence. In M. E. Lamb (Ed.), *The role of the father in child development.* New York: John Wiley & Sons, Inc., 1976.

Kreisman, D. Social interaction and intimacy in preschizophrenic adolescence. In J. Zubin & A. M. Freedman (Eds.), *The psychopathology of adolescence.* New York: Grune & Stratton, Inc., 1970.

Kuhlen, R. G., & Lee, B. J. Personality characteristics and social acceptability in adolescence. *Journal of Educational Psychology,* 1943, *34,* 321–340.

Kuhn, T. *The structure of scientific revolutions* (2nd ed.) Chicago: University of Chicago Press, 1970.

Lamb, M. E. The development of mother-infant and father-infant attachments in the second year of life. *Developmental Psychology,* 1977, 13, 639–649. (a)

Lamb, M. E. Father-infant and mother-infant interaction in the first year of life. *Child Development,* 1977, *48,* 167–181. (b)

Larson, L. E. The influence of parents and peers during adolescence: The situation hypothesis revisited. *Journal of Marriage and the Family,* 1972, *34,* 67–74.

Lavatelli, C. *Piaget's theory applied to an early childhood curriculum.* Boston: American Science and Engineering, 1970.

Lazar, I. & Darlington, R. B. *Lasting effects after preschool.* Washington, D.C.: U.S. Government Printing Office, 1978. DHEW Publication No. 79-30178.

Leakey, R. *Origins.* New York: E. P. Dutton & Co., Inc., 1977.

Leboyer, F. *Birth without violence.* New York: Alfred A. Knopf, Inc., 1975.

Lesser, G. S., & Kandel, D. B. Parental and peer influences on educational plans of adolescence. *American Sociological Review,* 1969, *34,* 213–223.

Levin, S. R., Petros, T. V., & Petrella, F. W. *Preschoolers' discrimination of television programming and commercials.* Paper presented to the Society for Research in Child Development, San Francisco, March 1979.

Lewis, M., & Brooks, J. Self, other and fear: Infants' reactions to people. In M. Lewis & L. A. Rosenblum (Eds.), *The origins of fear.* New York: John Wiley & Sons, Inc., 1974.

Lewis, T. L., & Maurer, D. *Newborns' central vision: Whole or hole?* Paper presented at the meeting of the Society for research in Child Development, New Orleans, La., March 1977.

Liebert, R. M., Neale, J. M. & Davidson, E. S. *The early window: Effects of television on children and youth.* New York: Pergamon Press, Inc., 1973.

Liss, M. B., & Reinhardt, L. C. *Behavioral and attitudinal responses to prosocial programs.* Paper presented to the Society for Research in Child Development, San Francisco, March 1979.

Lorenz, K. Comparative study of behavior. In C. H. Schiller (Ed.), *Instinctive behavior.* New York: International Universities Press, 1957.

Lowe, M. Trends in the development of representational play in infants from one to three years: An observational study. *Journal of Child Psychology,* 1975, *16,* 33–48.

Lowery, G. H. *Growth and development of children* (7th ed.). Chicago: Year Book Medical Publishers, 1978.

Lubic, R. W. The Maternity Center Association's childbearing center. *Journal of Reproductive Medicine,* 1977, *19,* 5.

Lubic, R. W. The impact of technology on health care—The childbearing center: A case for technology's appropriate use. *Journal of Nurse-Midwifery,* 1979, *24,* 6–10.

Lubic, R. W. Evaluation of an out-of-hospital maternity center for low-risk patients. In Aiken, L. H. (Ed.), *Health policy and nursing practice.* New York: McGraw-Hill Book Company, 1980.

Lyle, J. Television in daily life: Patterns of use (overuse). In E. A. Rubinstein, G. A. Comstock, & J. P. Murray (Eds.), *Television and social behavior* (Vol. 4). *Television in day-to-day life: Patterns of use.* Washington, D.C.: Government Printing office, 1972.

Maccoby, E. E. Social development: *Psychological growth and the parent-child relationship.* New York: Harcourt Brace Jovanovich, 1980.

Maccoby, E. E., and Jacklin, C. N. *The psychology of sex differences.* Stanford, Calif.: Stanford University Press, 1974.

Maccoby, E. E., & Masters, J. C. Attachment and dependency. In P. H. Mussen (Ed.), *Carmichael's manual of child psychology.* New York: John Wiley & Sons, Inc., 1970.

MacFarlane, A., Harris, P., & Barnes, I. Central and peripheral vision in early infancy. *Journal of Experimental Child Psychology,* 1976, *21,* 532–538.

Mander, J. *Four arguments for the elimination of television.* New York: William Morrow & Co., Inc., 1978.

Mann, I. *The development of the human eye.* London: British Medical Association, 1964.

March of Dimes. *Genetic counseling.* White Plains, N.Y.: March of Dimes Birth Defects Foundation, 1980.

March of Dimes. *Genetic defects: Tragedy and hope.* White Plains, New York: National Foundation/March of Dimes, 1979.

March of Dimes. *Birth defects: Tragedy and hope.* White Plains, N.Y.: National Foundation/March of Dimes, 1981.

March of Dimes. *Facts.* White Plains, N.Y.: March of Dimes Birth Defects Foundation, 1983.

Marcia, J. E. Identity in adolescence. In J. Adelson (Ed.), *Handbook of adolescent psychology.* New York: John Wiley & Sons, Inc., 1980.

Martin, B. Parent-child relations. In F. D. Horowitz (Ed.), *Review of child development research* (Vol. 4). Chicago: University of Chicago Press, 1975.

Martin, J. A. A longitudinal study of the consequences of early mother-infant interaction: A microanalytic approach. *Monographs of the Society for Research in Child Development,* 1981, *(46),* no. 3.

Marvin, R. S. An ecological-cognitive model for the attenuation of mother-child attachment behavior. In T. Alloway, P. Pliner, & L. Krames (Eds.), *Attachment behavior.* New York: Plenum Publishing Corporation, 1977.

Maslow, A. H. *Toward a psychology of being* (2nd ed.). New York: Van Nostrand Reinhold Company, 1968.

Maslow, A. H. *Toward a psychology of being* (2nd ed.). New York: Van Nostrand Reinhold Company, 1968.

Maurer, D., & Salapatek, P. Developmental changes in the scanning of faces by young infants. *Child Development,* 1976, *47,* 523–527.

McCarthy, D. Language development in children. In L. Carmichael (Ed.), *Manual of child psychology* (2nd ed.). New York: John Wiley & Sons, Inc., 1954.

McGlothlin, W. H. Drug use and abuse. *Annual Review of Psychology,* 1975, *26,* 45–64.

McLuhan, M. Understanding media: *The extensions of man.* New York: McGraw-Hill Book Company, 1964.

McNeill, D., & McNeill, N. B. What does a child mean when he says "No"? In E. M. Zale (Ed.), *Language and language behavior.* New York: Appleton-Century Crofts, 1968.

Meehl, L. E., & Peterson, G. H. Spontaneous peer psychotherapy in a day care setting: A case report. *American Journal of Orthopsychiatry,* 1981, *51,* 346–350.

Menyuk, P. Alteration of rules in children's grammar. *Journal of Verbal Learning and Verbal Behavior,* 1964, *3,* 480–488.

Meredith, H. V. Body size of contemporary groups of eight-year-old children studied in different parts of the world. *Monographs of the Society for Research in Child Development,* 1969, *34* (Serial no. 1).

Mermelstein, E., & Shulman, L. S. Lack of formal schooling and the acquisition of conservation. *Child Development,* 1967, *38,* 39–52.

Miller, P. Y., & Simon, W. The development of sexuality in adolescence. In J. Adelson (Ed.), *Handbook of adolescent psychology.* New York: John Wiley & Sons, Inc., 1980.

Milunsky, A. *Know your genes.* Boston: Houghton Mifflin Company, 1977.

Minton, C., Kagan, J., & Levine, J. A. Maternal control and obedience in the two-year-old. *Child Development,* 1971, *42,* 1873–1894.

Money, J. Ablatiopenis: Normal male infant sex-reassigned as a girl. *Archives of Sexual Behavior,* 1975, *4,* 65–72.

Money, J. *Love and love sickness: The science of sex, gender difference, and pair-bonding.* Baltimore: The Johns Hopkins University Press, 1980.

Money, J., Ehrhardt, A., & Masica, D. N. Fetal feminization induced by androgen insensitivity in the testicular feminizing syndrome: Effect on marriage and maternalism. *Johns Hopkins Medical Journal,* 1968, *123,* 105–114.

Money, J., Hampson, J. G., & Hampson, J. L. Imprinting and the establishment of gender role. *AMA Archives of Neurology and Psychiatry,* 1957, *77,* 333–336.

Money, J., & Pollitt, E. Cytogenetic and psychosexual ambiguity: Kleinfelters' Syndrome and transvestism compared. *Archives of General Psychiatry.* 1964, *11,* 589–595.

Moore, K., & Meltzoff, A. *Neonate imitation: A test of existence and mechanism.* Paper presented to the Society for Research in Child Development, Denver, Colo., March, 1975.

Moore, N., Evertson, C., & Brophy, J. Solitary play: Some functional reconsiderations. *Developmental Psychology,* 1974, *10,* 830–836.

Morris, J. *Conundrum.* New York: Harcourt Brace Jovanovich, Inc., 1974.

Mueller, E., & Vandell, D. Infant-infant interaction. In J. D. Osofsky (Ed.), *Handbook of infant development.* New York: John Wiley & Sons, Inc., 1979.

Mueller, E., & Lucas, T. A developmental analysis of peer interaction among toddlers. In M. Lewis and L. A. Rosenblum (Eds.), *Friendship and peer relations.* New York: John Wiley & Sons, Inc., 1975.

Munsinger, H. *Fundamentals of child development* (2nd ed.). New York: Holt, Rinehart and Winston, 1975.

Murray, F. B. Acquisition of conservation through social interaction. *Developmental Psychology*, 1972, *6*, 1–6.

Mussen, P. Choices, regrets, and lousy models (with reference to prosocial development). Presidential address to the Division of Developmental Psychology, presented to the American Psychological Association, San Francisco, August 1977.

National Center for Health Statistics, *Vital and Health Statistics,* 1970, Series II, No. 104. Health Services and Mental Health Administration. Washington, D.C.: U.S. Government Printing Office.

National Center for Health Statistics, *Vital and Health Statistics,* 1973, Series II, No. 124. Health Services and Mental Health Administration. Washington, D.C.: U.S. Government Printing Office.

National Center for Health Statistics, *Monthly Vital Statistics Report,* 1976, *25,* Supplement (HRA).

National Center for Health Statistics. *Monthly Vital Statistics Reports,* 1977, *25.*

National Commission on Youth. *The transition of youth to adulthood: A bridge too long.* Boulder, Colo.: Westview Press, 1980.

Neimark, E. D. Intellectual development during adolescence. In F. D. Horowitz (Ed.), *Review of child development research* (Vol. 4). Chicago: University of Chicago Press, 1975.

Nelson, K. *Lexical acquisition.* Paper presented to the Society for Research in Child Development, New Orleans, La., April 1977.

Nilsson, L., Furuhjelm, M., Ingelman-Sundberg, A., & Wirsen, C. *A child is born.* New York: Delacorte Press/Seymour Lawrence, 1977.

Novak, M. A., & Harlow, H. F. Social recovery of monkeys isolated for the first year of life: 1. Rehabilitation and therapy. *Developmental Psychology,* 1975, *11,* 453–465.

Offer, D., & Offer, J. *From teenage to young manhood: A psychological study.* New York: Basic Books, Inc., Publishers, 1975.

Opie, I., & Opie, P. *The lore and language of schoolchildren.* Oxford: Clarendon Press, 1959.

Osofsky, J. D., & Connors, K. Mother-infant interaction: An integrative view of a complex system. In J. D. Osofsky (Ed.), *Handbook of infant development.* New York: John Wiley & Sons, Inc., 1979.

Osterriech, P. A. Adolescence: Some psychological aspects. In G. Caplan & S. Lebovici (Eds.), *Adolescence: Psychosocial perspectives.* New York: Basic Books, Inc., Publishers, 1969.

Ouellette, E. M., Rosett, H. L., Rosman, N. P., & Weiner, L. Adverse effects on offspring of maternal alcohol abuse during pregnancy. *New England Journal of Medicine,* 1977, *297,* 528–530.

Overton, W. F. & Reese, H. W. Models of development: Methodological implications. In J. R. Nesselroade and H. W. Reese (Eds.). *Life-span developmental psychology: Methodological issues.* New York: Academic Press, 1973.

Parke, R. D. Perspectives on father-infant interaction. In J. D. Osofsky (Ed.), *Handbook of infant development.* New York: John Wiley & Sons, Inc., 1979.

Parke, R. D., & O'Leary, S. E. Father-mother-infant interaction in the newborn period: Some findings, some observations and some unresolved issues. In K. Riegel and J. Measham (Eds.), *The developing individual in a changing world,* Vol. II: *Social and environmental issues.* The Hague: Mouton, 1976.

Parke, R. D., O'Leary, S. E., & West, S. Mother-father-newborn interaction: Effects of maternal medication, labor and sex of infant. *Proceedings of the American Psychological Association,* 1972, *7,* 85–86.

Parke, R. D., & Sawin, D. B. The father's role in infancy: A re-evaluation. *The Family Coordinator*, 1976, *25*, 365–371.

Parke, R. D., & Sawin, D. B. *The family in early infancy: Social interactional and attitudinal analyses.* Paper presented to the Society for Research in Child Development, New Orleans, La., March 1977.

Parten, M. B. Social participation among pre-school children. *Journal of Abnormal and Social Psychology*, 1932, *27*, 243–269.

Parten, M. B. Social play among pre-school children. *Journal of Abnormal and Social Psychology*, 1933, *28*, 136–147.

Peiper, A. *Cerebral function in infancy and childhood.* New York: Consultants Bureau, 1963.

Penderson, F. A. & Robson, K. S. Father participation in infancy. *American Journal of Orthospsychiatry*, 1969, *39*, 466–472.

Petersen, A. C. Physical androgyny and cognitive functioning in adolescence. *Developmental Psychology*, 1976, *12*, 524–533.

Petersen, A. C., & Taylor, B. The biological approach to adolescence: Biological change and psychological adaptation. In J. Adelson (Ed.), *Handbook of adolescent psychology.* New York: John Wiley & Sons, Inc., 1980.

Phoenix, C. H. Prenatal testosterone in the nonhuman primate and its consequences for behavior. In R. C. Friedman, R. M. Richart, & R. L. Vandeweile (Eds.), *Sex differences in behavior.* New York: John Wiley & Sons, Inc., 1974.

Piaget, J. *The child's conception of the world.* J. Tomlinson & A. Tomlinson (Trans.). London; Routledge & K. Paul, 1964. (Originally published 1926)

Piaget, J. *The moral judgment of the child.* New York: The Free Press, 1948. (Originally published 1932)

Piaget, J. *The origin of intelligence in children.* New York: International Universities Press, 1952.

Piaget, J. *Play, dreams and imitation in childhood.* New York: W. W. Norton & Company, Inc., 1962.

Piaget, J., & Inhelder, B. *The child's conception of space.* F. J. Langdon and J. L. Lanzer (Trans.). London: Routledge and Paul, 1963.

Pines, M. The civilizing of Genie. *Psychology Today*, 1981, *15*, 28–34.

Plato. *Dialogues on love and friendship.* B. Jowett (Trans.). New York: The Heritage Press, 1968.

Ponder, C. *Pray and grow rich.* Englewood Cliffs, N.J.: Prentice-Hall, Inc., 1968. (Reward Press).

Porges, S. W. Developmental designs for infancy research. In *Handbook of infant development*, J. D. Osofsky, (Ed.). New York: John Wiley & Sons, 1979.

Provence, S., & Lipton, R. *Children in institutions.* New York: International Universities Press, 1962.

Pulaski, M. A. S. *Understanding Piaget: An introduction to children's cognitive development.* New York: Harper & Row, Publishers, 1971.

Radin, N. The role of the father in cognitive, academic, and intellectual development. In M. E. Lamb (Ed.), *The role of the father in child development.* New York: John Wiley & Sons, Inc., 1976.

Reed, D. M., & Stanley, F. J. (Eds.). *The epidemiology of prematurity.* Baltimore: Urban & Schwarzenberg, 1977.

Rementeria, J. L. (Ed.). *Drug use in pregnancy and neonatal effects.* St. Louis, Mo.: The C. V. Mosby Company, 1977.

Resnick, L. *Designs of an early learning curriculum.* Pittsburgh, Pa.: University of Pittsburgh Learning, Research, and Development Center, 1967.

Rest, J. R. *Development in judging moral issues.* Minneapolis, Minn.: University of Minnesota Press, 1979.

Rheingold, H. L., & Bayley, N. The later effects of an experimental modification of mothering. *Child Development,* 1959, *30,* 363–72.

Risley, T. *Juniper Gardens nursery school project.* Lawrence: University of Kansas Department of Human Development, 1969.

Robertson, J., & Bowlby, J. Responses of young children to separation from their mother. II. Observations of the sequences of response of children aged 16 to 24 months during the course of separation. *Courrier du Centre International de l'Enfance,* 1952, *2,* 131–142.

Rohn, R., Sarles, R., Kenny, T., Reynolds, B., & Heald, F. Adolescents who attempt suicide. *Journal of Pediatrics,* 1977, *90,* 636–638.

Rosenblatt, D. *Learning how to mean: The development of representation in play and language.* Paper presented at the conference on the Biology of Play, Farnham, England, June 1975.

Ross, J. B., & MacLaughlin, M. M. (Eds.). *A portable medieval reader.* New York: The Viking Press, Inc., 1949.

Rubin, K. H. (Ed.). *Children's play: New directions for child development.* San Francisco: Jossey-Bass, 1980.

Rubin, R. Attainment of the maternal role: I processes. *Nursing Research.* 1967, *16,* 237–246. (a)

Rubin, R. Attainment of the maternal role: II models and referrants. *Nursing Research,* 1967, *16,* 342–346. (b)

Rugh, R., & Shettles, L. B. *From conception to birth: The drama of life's beginnings.* New York: Harper & Row, Publishers, 1971.

Rumbaugh, D. M. (Ed.). *Language learning by a chimpanzee: The Lana project.* New York: Academic Press, Inc., 1977.

Rutter, M. Sex differences in children's responses to family stress. In E. J. Anthony and C. Koupernik (Eds.), *The child in his family.* New York: John Wiley & Sons, Inc., 1970.

Samelson, F. J. B. Watson's little Albert, Cyril Burt's twins, and the need for a critical science. *American Psychologist,* 1980, *35,* 619–625.

Saxon, L., & Rapola, J. *Congenital defects.* New York: Holt, Rinehart and Winston, 1969.

Schaefer, E. S. A circumplex model for maternal behavior. *Journal of Abnormal and Social Psychology,* 1959, *59,* 226–235.

Schaffer, H., & Emerson, P. Patterns of response to physical contact in early human development. *Journal of Child Psychology and Psychiatry,* 1964, *5,* 1–13.

Schaffer, H. R., & Emerson, P. E. The development of social attachments in infancy. *Monographs of the Society for Research in Child Development,* 1964, *29,* (Serial no. 3).

Schardein, J. L. *Drugs as teratogens.* Cleveland: CRC Press, 1976.

Sears, R. R. *Survey of objective studies of psychoanalytic concepts.* New York: Social Science Research Council, 1943.

Sears, R. R., Rau, L., & Alpert, R. *Identification and child rearing.* Stanford: Stanford University Press, 1965.

Seiden, R. H. *Suicide among youth.* U.S. Department of Health, Education and Welfare, Public Health Service Publication No. 1971. Washington, D.C. U.S. Government Printing Office, 1969.

Seward, J. P., & Seward, G. H. *Sex differences: Mental and temperamental.* Lexington, Mass.: D. C. Heath & Company, 1980.

Sherman, L. An ecological study of group glee in small groups of preschool children. *Child Development,* 1975, *46,* 53–61.

Shinn, M. Father absence and children's cognitive development. *Psychological Bulletin,* 1978, *85,* 295–324.

Sinclair-deSwart, H. Developmental psycholinguists. In D. Elkind & J. H. Flavell (Eds.), *Studies in cognitive development.* New York: Oxford University Press, 1969.

Skinner, B. F. *Walden* Two. New York: Macmillan Publishing Co., Inc., 1948.

Skinner, B. F. *Beyond freedom and dignity.* New York: Alfred A. Knopf, Inc., 1971.

Slaby, R. G., & Frey, K. S. Development of gender constancy and selective attention to same-sex models. *Child Development.* 1975, *46,* 849–856.

Smith, D. W. Alcohol effects on the fetus, *In Drug and chemical risks to the fetus and newborn,* R. H. Schwarz & S. J. Yaffe, (Eds.). New York: Alan R. Liss, Inc., 1980.

Smith, M. E. *An investigation of the development of the sentence and the extent of vocabulary in young children.* University of Iowa Studies in Child Welfare, 1926, *3,* no. 5.

Smith, P., & Connolly, K. Patterns of play and social interaction in preschool children. In N. Blurton-Jones (Ed.), *Ethological studies of child behavior.* Cambridge: Cambridge University Press, 1972.

Smith, P. K., & Daglish, L. Sex differences in parent and infant behavior in the home. *Child Development,* 1977, *48,* 1250–1254.

Society for Research in Child Development. Ethical standards for research with children. *SRCD* Newsletter, 1973 (Winter), 3–4.

Spearman, C. "General intelligence" objectively determined and measured. *American Journal of Psychology,* 1904, *15,* 201–293.

Spearmen, C. E. *The abilities of man: Their nature and measurement.* New York: Macmillan Publishing Co., Inc., 1927.

Spinetta, J., & Rigler, D. The child-abusing parent: A psychological review. *Psychological Bulletin,* 1972, *77,* 296–304.

Spitz, R. A., & Wolf, K. M. The smiling response: A contribution to the ontogenesis of social relations. *Genetic Psychology Monographs,* 1946, *34,* 57–125.

Sroufe, L. A. The coherence of individual development: Early care, attachment and subsequent developmental issues. *American Psychologist,* 1979, *34,* 834–841. (a)

Sroufe, L. A. Socioemotional development. In J. D. Osofsky (Ed.), *Handbook of infant development.* New York: John Wiley & Sons, Inc., 1979. (b)

Starr, R. H., Jr. Child abuse. *American Psychologist,* 1979, *34,* 872–878.

Stein, A. H., & Friedrich, L. K. Impact of television on children and youth. In E. M. Hetherington (Ed.), *Review of child development research* (Vol. V). Chicago: University of Chicago Press, 1975.

Steinmetz, S. The use of force for resolving family conflict: The training ground for abuse. *Family Coordinator,* 1977, *26,* 19–26.

Steinmetz, S., & Strauss, M. (Eds.). *Violence in the family.* New York: Dodd, Mead & Company, 1974.

Stent, G. A., & Calender, R. *Molecular genetics: An introductory narrative* (2nd ed.). San Fráncisco: W. H. Freeman and Company, Publishers, 1978.

Stern, C. Hereditary factors affecting adoption. In *A study of adoption practices* (Vol. 2). New York: Child Welfare League of America, 1956.

Stern, D. *The first relationship: Mother and infant.* Cambridge, Mass.: Harvard University Press, 1977.

Surgeon General's Scientific Advisory Committee on Television and Social Behavior. *Television and growing up: The impact of televised violence.* Report to the Surgeon General, United States Public Health Service. Washington D.C.: Government Printing Office, 1972.

Symonds, P. M. *The psychology of parent-child relationships.* New York: Appleton-Century-Crofts, 1939.

Tanner, J. M. Earlier maturation in man. *Scientific American,* 1968, *218,* 21–27.

Tanner, J. M. Physical growth. In P. H. Mussen (Ed.), *Carmichael's manual of child psychology* (3rd ed., Vol. I). New York: John Wiley & Sons, Inc., 1970.

Tanner, J. M. Sequences, tempo, and individual variation in growth and development of boys and girls aged twelve to sixteen. In J. Kagan & R. Coles (Eds.), *12 to 16: Early adolescence.* New York: W. W. Norton & Company, Inc., 1972.

Tanner, J. M. Sequence and tempo in the somatic changes in puberty. In M. M. Grumbach, G. D. Grave, and F. E. Mayer (Eds.), *Control of the onset of puberty.* New York: John Wiley & Sons, Inc., 1974.

Teenage pregnancy: The problem that hasn't gone away. New York: The Alan Guttmacher Institute, 1981.

Teicher, J. D. The alienated, older male adolescent. *American Journal of Psychotherapy,* 1972, *26,* 401–407.

Telfer, M. A., Baker, D., Clark, G. R., & Richardson, C. E. Incidence of gross chromosomal errors among tall, criminal American males. *Science,* 1968, *159,* 1249–1250.

Terman, L. *Measurement of intelligence.* Boston: Houghton Mifflin Company, 1916.

Thissen, D., Bock, R. D., Wainer, H., & Roche, A. F. Individual growth in stature: A comparison of four growth studies in the USA. *Annals of Human Biology,* 1976, *3,* 529–542.

Thomas, R. M. *Comparing theories of child development.* Belmont, Calif.: Wadsworth Publishing Co., Inc., 1979.

Thompson, S. K. Gender labels and early sex-role development. *Child Development,* 1975, *46,* 339–347.

Thornburg, H. D. (Ed.) *Preadolescent development.* Tucson: University of Arizona Press, 1974.

Thurstone, L. L., & Thurstone, T. G. Factorial studies of intelligence. *Psychometrics Monographs,* 1941, No. 2.

Uzgiris, F. D., & Hunt, J. McV. *Assessment in infancy: Ordinal scales of psychological development.* Urbana: University of Illinois Press, 1975.

Vandenberg, B. Play and development from an ethological perspective. *American Psychologist,* 1978, *33,* 724–738.

Vandenberg, B. Play, problem-solving, and creativity. In K. H. Rubin (Ed.), *Children's play,* San Francisco: Jossey-Bass, 1980.

VanderMaelen, A. L., Strauss, M. E., and Starr, R. H., Jr. Influence of obstetric medication on auditory habituation in the newborn. *Developmental Psychology,* 1975, *11,* 711–714.

Vener, A. M., & Stewart, C. S. Adolescent sexual behavior in middle America revisited: 1970–1973. *Journal of Marriage and the Family,* 1974, *36,* 728–735.

Wachs, T. D. Utilization of a Piagetian approach in the investigation of early experience effects: A research strategy and some illustrative data. *Merrill-Palmer Quarterly,* 1976, *22,* 11–30.

Walder, R. The psychoanalytic theory of play. In D. Muller-Schwarze (Ed.), *Evolution of play behavior.* Stroudsburg, Pa.: Dowden, Hutchinson, & Ross, 1978.

Warren, W. A study of adolescent psychiatric inpatients and the outcome six or more years later: II The follow-up study. *Journal of Child Psychology and Psychiatry,* 1965, *6,* 141–160.

Watson, J. B. *Psychological care of infant and child.* New York: W. W. Norton & Company, Inc., 1928.

Watson, J. B., & Morgan, J. J. B. Emotional reactions and psychological experimentation. *American Journal of Psychology,* 1917, *28,* 163–174.

Watson, J. B., & Rayner, R. Conditioned emotional reactions. *Journal of Experimental Psychology,* 1920, *3,* 1–14.

Watson, J. D. *The double helix: A personal account of the discovery of the structure of DNA.* G. S. Stent (Ed.). New York: W. W. Norton & Company, Inc., 1980.

Watt, N. F. Patterns of childhood social development in adult schizophrenics. *Archives of General Psychiatry,* 1978, *35,* 160–165.

Watt, N. F., & Lubensky, A. W. Childhood roots of schizophrenia. *Journal of Consulting and Clinical Psychology,* 1976, *44,* 363–375.

Wechsler, D. Intelligence defined and undefined. *American Psychologist,* 1975, *30,* 135–159.

Weiner, I. B. Depression in adolescence. In F. F. Flach & S. C. Draghi (Eds.), *The nature and treatment of depression.* New York: John Wiley & Sons, Inc., 1975.

Weiner, I. B. Psychopathology in adolescence. In J. Adelson, (Ed.), *Handbook of adolescent psychology.* New York: John Wiley & Sons, Inc., 1980.

Weir, R. *Language in the crib.* The Hague: Mouton, 1972.

Whaley, D. L., & Malott, R. W. *Elementary principles of behavior.* New York: Appleton-Century-Crofts, 1971.

White, B. L. *Human infants.* Englewood Cliffs, N.J.: Prentice-Hall, Inc., 1971.

White, B. L. *The first three years of life.* Englewood Cliffs, N.J.: Prentice-Hall, Inc., 1975.

White, B. L., Kaban, B. S., Marmor, J., & Shapiro, B. *Pre-school project: Child rearing practices and the development of competence.* Final Report Grant No. CG-9909 A/2. Washington, D.C.: Office of Economic Opportunity Head Start Division, September, 1972.

White, B. L., Kaban, B. S., & Attanucci, J. Competence and experience. In I. C. Uzgiris & F. Weizmann (Eds.), *The structuring of experience.* New York: Plenum Publishing Corporation, 1977.

White, S. Children in perspective. *American Psychologist,* 1979, *34,* 812–814.

Wilson, C. *New pathways in psychology; Maslow and the post-Freudian revolution.* New York: Taplinger Publishing Co., Inc., 1972.

Winn, M. *The Plug in drug: Television and the family.* New York: The Viking Press, Inc., 1974.

Witter, F. & King, T. M. Cigarettes and pregnancy. In *Drug and chemical risks to the fetus and newborn,* R. H. Schwarz & S. J. Yaffe (Eds.). New York: Alan R. Liss, Inc., 1980.

Wolff, P. H. Observations on newborn infants. *Psychosomatic Medicine,* 1959, *21,* 110–118.

Wolff, P.H. The causes, controls and organization of behavior in the neonate. *Psychological Issues,* 1966, *5,* 1–105.

Wolff, P. H. Mother-infant relations at birth. In J. G. Howels (Ed.), *Modern perspectives in international child psychiatry.* New York: Bruner/Mazel, 1971.

Wolkind, S., & Rutter, M. Children who have been "in care"—an epidemiological study. *Journal of Child Psychology and Psychiatry,* 1973, *14,* 97–105.

Wood, R. Sex differences in mathematics attainment at GCE ordinary level. *Educational Studies,* 1976, *2,* 141–160.

Yakovlev, P., & Lecours, A. The myelogenetic cycles of regional maturation of the brain. In A. Minkowski (Ed.), *Regional development of the brain in early life.* Oxford: Blockwell, 1967.

Yalisove, D. The effect of riddle structure on children's comprehension of riddles. *Developmental Psychology,* 1978, *14,* 173–180.

Yang, R. K. Early infant assessment: An overview. In J. Osofsky (Ed.), *A handbook of infant development.* New York: John Wiley & Sons, Inc., 1979.

Yarrow, L. J. Historical perspectives and future directions in infant development. In J. D. Osofsky (Ed.), *Handbook of infant development.* New York: John Wiley & Sons, Inc., 1979.

Zelnik, M., and Kantner, J. F. Sexual and contraceptive experience of young unmarried women in the United States, 1976 and 1971. *Family Planning Perspectives,* 1977, *9,* 55–71.

Zelnik, M., & Kantner, J. F. First pregnancies to women aged 15–19: 1976 and 1971. *Family Planning Perspectives,* 1978, *10,* 11–20. (a)

Zelnik, M., & Kantner, J. F. Contraceptive patterns and premarital pregnancy among women aged 15–19 in 1976. *Family Planning Perspectives,* 1978, *10,* 135–142. (b)

Zetterstrom, B. The clinical electroretinogram. IV. The electroretinogram in children during the first year of life. *Acta Opthalmologica,* 1951, *29,* 295–304.

Zetterstrom, B. Flicker electroretinography in newborn infants. *Acta Opthalmogica,* 1955, *33,* 157–166.

Zigler, E. Child care in the seventies. *Inequality in Education,* 1972, *13,* 17–28.

Zigler, E. Controlling child abuse in America: An effort doomed to failure. In R. Bourne & E. Newberger (Eds.), *Critical perspectives on child abuse.* Lexington, Mass.: D.C. Heath & Company, 1978.

Zigler, E., & Trickett, P. K. IQ, social competence, and evaluation of early childhood intervention programs. *American Psychologist,* 1978, *33,* 789–798.

Zimbardo, P. G., & Ruch, F. L. *Psychology and Life* (9th ed.). Glenview, Ill.: Scott, Foresman and Company, 1976.

Zimmerman, B. J., & Lanaro, P. Acquiring and retaining conservation of length through modeling cues and reversibility cues. *Merrill-Palmer Quarterly,* 1974, *20,* 145–161.

Name Index

Subject Index